A+ GUIDE TO PC HARDWARE MAINTENANCE AND REPAIR

Michael W. Graves

THOMSON

DELMAR LEARNING

Australia • Canada • Mexico • Singapore • Spain • United Kingdom • United States

THOMSON

DELMAR LEARNING

A+ Guide to PC Hardware Maintenance and Repair

by Michael W. Graves

Vice President, Technology and Trades SBU:
Alar Elken

Editorial Director:
Sandy Clark

Senior Acquistions Editor:
Stephen Helba

Senior Channel Manager:
Dennis Williams

Senior Development Editor:
Michelle Ruelos Cannistraci

Marketing Director:
Dave Garza

Marketing Coordinator:
Casey Bruno

Production Director:
Mary Ellen Black

Production Manager:
Larry Main

Senior Project Editor:
Christopher Chien

Art/Design Coordinator:
Francis Hogan

Senior Editorial Assistant:
Dawn Daugherty

Library of Congress Card Number: 2004110548

A+ Guide to PC Hardware Maintenance and Repair /
Michael W. Graves

ISBN: 1-4018-52300

NOTICE TO THE READER

TABLE OF CONTENTS

APPENDICES

PREFACE

In this day and age, there aren't a lot of jobs that one can achieve without a college education that pay a living wage. One key exception to that rule of thumb is the job of computer repair technician or help desk technician. Many people find either one of these jobs attractive not only for the pay, but because it's actually a fun job!

There are a lot of other reasons for wanting to work with computers as well. It's also one of the fastest-growing career fields in America and the rest of the world. But for those of us who believe that variety is the spice of life, the sheer diversity of responsibilities and people that you work with is every bit as rewarding as the money.

Whatever your reasons for wanting a book of this nature may be, there is a lot in this book that will benefit virtually every level of reader. The concept of this book is to provide a textbook for PC hardware classes. The simplified writing style makes it ideal for the beginning student with little or no background in hardware, whereas the depth of content provides the reader with detailed information about how different components work. The structure and organization of the book also makes it a perfect candidate for the "five-day boot camp" environment.

ORGANIZATION

In explaining PC hardware in this book, the author has taken what he calls a component-level approach. In the same way that computers are assembled using components, this book has been structured around the discussion of components. Hardware is divided into system-level components and user-level components. System-level components are those which make up the foundation of the computer itself. These types of components include memory, CPUs, and storage devices. User-level components include those devices with which the end user has intimate contact. These would include input devices, printers, networking, and Internet access.

The first three chapters of this book act as an introduction to the basics of PC hardware. In these hundred or so pages, prior PC hardware knowledge is not required. These chapters lead the reader through the basics of what constitutes a computer. In addition, an explanation of how computers talk in ones and zeros is covered, as well as an introduction to some basic system architecture.

The second part of the book covers core components. In Chapters Four through Eight, the reader is treated to detailed discussions about motherboards, BIOS, CPUs, and memory. These discussions cover not only the function of these components, but their history as well. Upgrading and troubleshooting techniques top off each component.

Chapters Nine through Fourteen cover the moving of data through the system and different forms of data storage. I/O busses are covered in detail. After this, different chapters cover removable storage, hard disk storage and management, and the SCSI interface.

Chapters Fifteen through Twenty-one discuss the user side of computing. These chapters cover graphics, networking, printing, and the Internet. Chapter Twenty-two provides a brief description of how operating systems interface with the hardware.

FEATURES

As you browse through the pages of *The A+ Guide to PC Hardware Maintenance and Repair*, a few key qualities should pop out at you right away. The organization of the chapters is such that the reader learns how data moves through the PC from creation to output. The author's light-handed approach to presenting the information makes the material easier to read and much easier to learn. There are hundreds of high-quality illustrations that supplement the text and dozens of tables that organize information into an easy-to-understand format. Advice on troubleshooting is supplemented by the field experiences of the author himself.

The text includes the following features:

1. A+ Objectives mapped to the textbook are placed in the Introduction.
2. Each chapter begins with identifying the **Objectives** to be covered for the A+ Core Hardware Exam.
3. PC is full of acronyms and technical terms that you need to understand, so each chapter integrates **Buzz Words, Tricky Terminology**, and **Acronym Alert** to introduce and reinforce key terminology.
4. **Exam Notes** for the student are given throughout the text providing helpful hints in preparing for the A+ Exam.
5. A **Chapter Summary** provides a quick refresher and reviews key points from the text.

6. Each chapter concludes with two sets of questions, called **Brain Drain** and **64K$ Questions**. The first set is a series of challenging, essay-oriented questions, and the second set is a series of multiple-choice, true/false, and short answer review questions.

7. A comprehensive **Glossary** and **Answers to Odd-Numbered Questions** are placed at the end of the book.

8. A **CD** placed in the back of the book includes **sample video clips** from the *Mastering the A+ Exam DVD Series* and **additional practice test questions.**

SUPPLEMENTS

Lab Manual. The lab manual includes a set of 15 lab experiments ranging from installing IDE devices to setting up a peer-to-peer network.
ISBN: 1401852319

Instructor's CD. Textbook solutions and practice test questions are available on this CD-ROM.
ISBN: 1401852327

A+ DVD Series: Mastering the A+ Exam. This comprehensive, five-part DVD series of 20 videos has been designed to assist viewers in preparing for the 2003 A+ Exam.
ISBN: 1401858880

ACKNOWLEDGMENTS

The Author and Thomson Delmar Learning would like to thank the following reviewers:

Shaikh Ali, City College, Fort Lauderdale, FL
Russ Davis, Pittsburgh Technical Institute, Midland, PA
Raj Desai, Southeast Missouri State, Cape Girardeau, MO
Billy Graham, Northwest Technical Institute, Springdale, AR
Kyle Muldrow, DeVry University, Long Beach, CAS
David Patzarian, Albany Vo-Tech Center, Albany, NY
Roger Peterson, Northland Community and Technical College, Thief River Falls, MN
Jack Williams, Remington College, Tampa, FL

INTRODUCTION

WHO IS COMPTIA, AND WHY SHOULD I GET CERTIFIED?

Just what is certification? Look at it this way. Everywhere you go in life, you constantly have to prove yourself. You may be one of those people who can take apart a computer and put it back together with your eyes closed and one hand tied behind your back. When you're done, your old 486 outperforms your neighbor's brand new Athlon 1300. The only problem is, when you enter the job market, not many employers are willing to listen to your success stories. All they want to know is how much paper you carry. In other words, are you certified?

Virtually every professional field has some sort of certification program in place. Every state has building codes that require a certified electrician to install wiring in new houses or to make wiring changes during a remodel. Likewise, furnace installers, carpenters, heavy equipment operators, and even beauticians all require certificates. State and local authorities won't let them pick up their tools until they show their paper.

As of yet, I know of no states that *require* certification from computer professionals. As technical as computers are, one would not think that could be the case. Therefore, just anybody can hang out a shingle and call himself or herself a pro. Employers, on the other hand, expect a bit more. The computer industry has many, many certification programs—probably more than any other singular career field. Fortunately, for you, however, there is only one certification dealing with your expertise in matters of hardware that anybody pays any attention to. And that is CompTIA's A+ Certification.

CompTIA stands for the *Computing Technology Industry Association.* CompTIA is an organization of companies and professional consultants who get together and agree on various standards for the industry to follow in a valiant effort to keep things consistent. The A+ Certification exam is one of the things that they administer. A group of hardware specialists from various areas of the industry provide input on the materials that should be covered on the exam, review and approve the questions. Then they make sure that what you are tested on adequately demonstrates that you have sufficient knowledge to successfully pursue a career as a hardware technician. Once you are awarded your certificate, you have all the proof you need to show a potential employer that you are fit for the job.

The Exams

To receive your certification, you must pass two separate exams. It does not matter in what order you take them, but it is important that you finish them both within ninety days of each other. Today's exams are in linear format. Once a candidate has been processed and validated by the examiner, a bank of questions averaging eighty questions is downloaded to a computer. The number of questions a candidate sees in any given objective is based on the formula seen in the lists below.

The two tests consist of what are called the "Core Hardware Exam" and the "Operating Systems Technologies Exam." The core exam tests your knowledge of how the hardware in a computer actually works. While not targeted specifically as an exam prep book, everything you need to pass the core exam can be found in these pages. To pass this exam you need to be able to troubleshoot situations, interpret problems, and know how the parts of your computer work together to make the whole thing functional.

The Operating Systems Exam deals with Windows 9x, NT, and Windows 2000, with some emphasis on Unix and Linux as well. That subject matter is covered in another book in this series.

CompTIA has a massive database of questions that it draws from in the administration of these exams. When your examiner schedules an exam for you, he or she will make a request through CompTIA's authorized Exam Provider (currently Sylvan Prometric). The questions for your particular exam will then be assembled and transmitted over the Internet. You could take the exam a hundred times and not see the same question twice. However, there is a standardized approach to assure that the core material is covered on each exam.

Earlier I mentioned that each exam is broken down into knowledge categories. CompTIA has a formula it follows for setting the proportions of questions on any given exam. The proportions it uses for assembling the questions on the Core Exam are listed here.

Core Exam:
- 35% = Installation and configuration and upgrading
- 21% = Diagnosing and troubleshooting
- 5% = Preventative maintenance
- 11% = Motherboards, processors, and memory
- 9% = Printers
- 19% = Basic networking

The second test that you are required to take covers your proficiency in operating systems. In this respect, you will need to know some basic fundamentals of DOS and the personal Windows applications, including WIN95, WIN98, and WINME. You'll need to be able to navigate Windows NT 4.0 and Windows 2000, and CompTIA expects you to have a fundamental understanding of Unix and Linux. On the latter two systems, only a brief overview is covered. Here is a pretty good idea of how CompTIA breaks down the questions you'll be asked from its database.

Operating Systems Exam

- 28% = OS fundamentals
- 31% = Installation, configuration, and upgrading
- 25% = Diagnosing and troubleshooting
- 16% = Networks

Questions you might expect to see would include things of this nature:
Memory mapping is controlled by:

1. The memory mapping module
2. The CPU
3. The 8087 chip
4. The memory control chip

Which is **not** a common memory package?

1. SIPP
2. DIMM
3. DIPP
4. RISC
5. SIMM

You also might be presented with a scenario from which you will be asked specific questions. The following is an example.

A technician is charged with the task of installing memory on a batch of older 486DX computers at a client's site. Upon opening the case, she detects that the motherboard is equipped with eight 30-pin memory sockets. She knows from her work order that all the PCs are equipped with 4MB each. She was provided with a supply of 4MB 70ns SIMMs. Upon examining the SIMMs already installed she finds that they are all 80ns.

Because of the difference in speed she knows she cannot use the 4MB SIMMs.

1. True
2. False

She knows that the four sockets the 1MB SIMMs came out of are:

1. Bank 0
2. Bank 1
3. Bank 2
4. She can only tell what bank they're in by referring to the motherboard manual.

Taking the exam need not be a stressful ordeal. Proper preparation so you feel comfortable with the material, a good night's sleep the night before, and a relaxed attitude can help matters immeasurably. Another key is to avoid second-guessing yourself. When the day arrives, show up at the testing center early so you can relax for a few minutes before diving right in. Remember this: even if you fail your first attempt, it will give you a good idea of where you need to strengthen your knowledge.

THE EXAM OBJECTIVES

As I mentioned earlier, The CompTIA A+ Core Hardware Exam, which is the subject of this book, is broken down into six different domains of knowledge, and the exam is structured around those domains. This format allows for a more structured approach to preparing for the exam. Table I.1 lists the various domains and their relative importance to the exam.

Table I.1 The Objective Domains

Domain	Percentage of Exam
1.0 Installation, Configuration, and Upgrading	35%
2.0 Diagnosing and Troubleshooting	21%
3.0 Preventative Maintenance	5%
4.0 Motherboard/Processors/Memory	11%
5.0 Printers	9%
6.0 Basic Networking	19%
Total	100%

The CompTIA A+ Core is broken down into six domains.

The individual domains are further broken down into specific objectives that you must demonstrate that you have achieved in preparing for the exam. The next few pages discuss each domain.

DOMAIN 1: INSTALLATION, CONFIGURATION, AND UPGRADING

IDENTIFY THE NAMES, PURPOSE, AND CHARACTERISTICS OF SYSTEM MODULES. RECOGNIZE THESE MODULES BY SIGHT OR DEFINITION.

Examples of concepts and modules are:

Motherboards (Chapter 1, Chapter 2, and Chapter 5)

Firmware (Chapter 5, Chapter 9, and Chapter 15)

Power supplies (Chapter 2 and Chapter 3)

Processors/CPUs (Chapter 2, Chapter 6, and Chapter 7)

Memory (Chapter 2, Chapter 8, and Chapter 15)

Storage devices (Chapter 2, Chapter 11, and Chapter 12)

Display devices (Chapter 2, Chapter 15, and Lab Manual)

Adapter cards (Chapter 2, Chapter 9, Chapter 14, Chapter 15, Chapter 16, Chapter 18, and Lab Manual)

Ports (Chapter 2, Chapter 4, Chapter 5, Chapter 9, and Lab Manual)

Cases (Chapter 2, Chapter 4, and Lab Manual)

Riser cards (Chapter 2 and Chapter 5)

1.2 IDENTIFY BASIC PROCEDURES FOR ADDING AND REMOVING FIELD-REPLACEABLE MODULES FOR DESKTOP SYSTEMS. GIVEN A REPLACEMENT SCENARIO, CHOOSE THE APPROPRIATE SEQUENCES.

Desktop components:

Motherboard (Chapter 2 and Chapter 5)

Storage devices

    FDDs (Chapter 11 and Lab Manual)

    HDDs (Chapter 13 and Lab Manual)

    CD/CD-RW (Chapter 16 and Lab Manual)

    DVD/DVD-RW (Chapter 16)

    Tape drives (Chapter 11)

    Removable storage (Chapter 11 and Lab Manual)

Power supplies

    AC adapters (Chapter 3)

    AT/ATX (Chapter 3 and Chapter 5)

Cooling systems
  Fans (Chapter 7)
  Heat sinks (Chapter 7)
  Liquid cooling (Chapter 7)
Processors/CPUs (Chapter 7 and Lab Manual)
Memory (Chapter 8 and Lab Manual)
Display devices (Chapter 15)
Input devices
  Keyboards (Chapter 10)
  Mouse/Pointer devices (Chapter 10)
  Touch screens (Chapter 10 and Chapter 15)
Adapters
  Network Interface Cards (Chapter 18 and Lab Manual)
  Sound cards (Chapter 16 and Lab Manual)
  Video cards (Chapter 15)
  Modems (Chapter 19 and Lab Manual)
  SCSI (Chapter 14 and Lab Manual)
  IEEE 1394/FireWire (Chapter 14)
  USB (Chapter 9)
  Wireless (Chapter 18)

1.3 IDENTIFY BASIC PROCEDURES FOR ADDING AND REMOVING FIELD-REPLACEABLE MODULES FOR PORTABLE SYSTEMS. GIVEN A REPLACEMENT SCENARIO, CHOOSE THE APPROPRIATE SEQUENCES.

Portable components:

Storage devices
  FDDs (Chapter 20)
  HDDs (Chapter 13 and Chapter 20)
  CD/CD-RW (Chapter 20)
  DVD/DVD-RW (Chapter 20)
  Removable storage (Chapter 20)
Power sources
  AC adapter (Chapter 20)
  DC adapter (Chapter 20)
  Battery (Chapter 20)

Memory (Chapter 8 and Chapter 20)

Input devices

Keyboard (Chapter 20)

Mouse/Pointer devices (Chapter 10 and Chapter 20)

Touch screen (Chapter 10 and Chapter 20)

PCMCIA/Mini PCI Adapters (Chapter 9 and Chapter 20)

Network Interface Card (Chapter 18)

Modem (Chapter 19 and Chapter 20)

SCSI (Chapter 14)

IEEE 1394/FireWire (Chapter 14)

USB (Chapter 9 and Chapter 20)

Storage (memory and hard drives) (Chapter 8, Chapter 13, and Chapter 20)

Docking stations/Port replicators (Chapter 20)

LCD panels (Chapter 15 and Chapter 20)

Wireless

Adapters/Controllers (Chapter 18)

Antennae (Chapter 18)

1.4 IDENTIFY TYPICAL IRQs, DMAs, AND I/O ADDRESSES AND PROCEDURES FOR ALTERING THESE SETTINGS WHEN INSTALLING AND CONFIGURING DEVICES. CHOOSE THE APPROPRIATE INSTALLATION OR CONFIGURATION STEPS IN A GIVEN SCENARIO.

Content may include the following:

Legacy devices (e.g., ISA sound cards) (Chapter 5 and Chapter 16)

Specialized devices (e.g., CAD/CAM) (Chapter 2 and Chapter 9)

Internal modems (Chapter 2, Chapter 19, and Lab Manual)

Floppy drive controllers (Chapter 2, Chapter 5, and Chapter 9)

Hard drive controllers (Chapter 2, Chapter 5, and Chapter 13)

Multimedia devices (Chapter 2, Chapter 5, and Chapter 16)

NICs (Chapter 18)

I/O ports

Serial (Chapter 9 and Lab Manual)

Parallel (Chapter 9 and Lab Manual)

USB (Chapter 9 and Lab Manual)

IEEE 1394/FireWire (Chapter 14 and Lab Manual)

Infrared (Chapter 18)

1.5 IDENTIFY THE NAMES, PURPOSES, AND PERFORMANCE CHARACTERISTICS OF STANDARDIZED/COMMON PERIPHERAL PORTS, ASSOCIATED CABLING, AND CONNECTORS. RECOGNIZE PORTS, CABLING, AND CONNECTORS BY SIGHT.

Content may include the following:

Port types
    Serial (Chapter 9 and Lab Manual)
    Parallel (Chapter 9 and Lab Manual)
    USB (Chapter 9 and Lab Manual)
    IEEE 1394/FireWire (Chapter 14 and Lab Manual)
    Infrared (Chapter 18)
Cable types
    Serial (Straight through versus null modem) (Chapter 2 and Chapter 9)
    Parallel (Chapter 2 and Chapter 17)
    USB (Chapter 9)
Connector types
    Serial
            DB-9 (Chapter 2 and Chapter 9)
            DB-25 (Chapter 2 and Chapter 9)
            RJ-11 (Chapter 2 and Chapter 18)
            RJ-45 (Chapter 2 and Chapter 18)
    Parallel
            DB-25 (Chapter 2 and Chapter 17)
            Centronics (Lab Manual)
    PS2/MINI-DIN (Chapter 2 and Chapter 9)
    USB (Chapter 2 and Chapter 9)
    IEEE 1394 (Chapter 2 and Chapter 14)

1.6 IDENTIFY PROPER PROCEDURES FOR INSTALLING AND CONFIGURING COMMON IDE DEVICES. CHOOSE THE APPROPRIATE INSTALLATION OR CONFIGURATION SEQUENCES IN GIVEN SCENARIOS. RECOGNIZE THE ASSOCIATED CABLES.

Content may include the following:

IDE interface types
    EIDE (Chapter 13)
    ATA/ATAPI (Chapter 13)

Serial ATA (Chapter 13)

PIO (Chapter 13)

RAID (0, 1, and 5) (Chapter 14)

Master/Slave/Cable select (Chapter 13)

Devices per channel (Chapter 5 and Chapter 13)

Primary/Secondary (Chapter 5 and Chapter 13)

Cable orientation/Requirements (Chapter 2 and Chapter 13)

1.7 IDENTIFY PROPER PROCEDURES FOR INSTALLING AND CONFIGURING COMMON SCSI DEVICES. CHOOSE THE APPROPRIATE INSTALLATION OR CONFIGURATION SEQUENCES IN GIVEN SCENARIOS. RECOGNIZE THE ASSOCIATED CABLES.

Content may include the following:

SCSI interface types

Narrow (Chapter 14)

Fast (Chapter 14)

Wide (Chapter 14)

Ultra-wide (Chapter 14)

LVD (Chapter 14)

HVD (Chapter 14)

Internal versus External (Chapter 14)

SCSI IDs

Jumper block/DIP switch settings (binary equivalents) (Chapter 14)

Resolving ID conflicts (Chapter 14)

RAID (0, 1, and 5) (Chapter 14)

Cabling

Length (Chapter 14)

Type (Chapter 14)

Termination requirements (Active, Passive, Auto) (Chapter 14)

1.8 IDENTIFY PROPER PROCEDURES FOR INSTALLING AND CONFIGURING COMMON PERIPHERAL DEVICES. CHOOSE THE APPROPRIATE INSTALLATION OR CONFIGURATION SEQUENCES IN GIVEN SCENARIOS.

Content may include the following:

Modems and transceivers (Dial-up, Cable, DSL, ISDN) (Chapter 19 and Lab Manual)

External storage (Chapter 11, Chapter 13, and Chapter 16)

Digital cameras (Chapter 9)

PDAs (Chapter 20)

Wireless access points (Chapter 19)

Infrared devices (Chapter 19)

Printers (Chapter 17)

UPS (Uninterruptible Power Supply) and suppressors (Chapter 3)

Monitors (Chapter 15)

1.9 IDENTIFY PROCEDURES TO OPTIMIZE PC OPERATIONS IN SPECIFIC SITUATIONS. PREDICT THE EFFECTS OF SPECIFIC PROCEDURES UNDER GIVEN SCENARIOS.

Topics may include:

Cooling systems
   Liquid (Chapter 7)
   Air (Chapter 7)
   Heat sink (Chapter 7)
   Thermal compound (Chapter 7)
Disk subsystem enhancements
   Hard drives (Chapter 13)
   Controller cards (RAID, ATA-100, etc.) (Chapter 13 and Chapter 14)
   Cables (Chapter 2)
NICs (Chapter 18)
Specialized video cards (Chapter 15)
Memory (Chapter 8)
Additional processors (Chapter 6)

1.10 DETERMINE THE ISSUES THAT MUST BE CONSIDERED WHEN UPGRADING A PC. IN A GIVEN SCENARIO, DETERMINE WHEN AND HOW TO UPGRADE SYSTEM COMPONENTS.

Issues may include:

Drivers for legacy devices (Chapter 9 and Lab Manual)

Bus types and characteristics (Chapter 9, Chapter 14, and Chapter 15)

Cache in relationship to motherboards (Chapter 5 and Chapter 8)

Memory capacity and characteristics (Chapter 5)

Processor speed and compatibility (Chapter 6)

Hard drive capacity and characteristics (Chapter 13)

System/firmware limitations (Chapter 5 and Chapter 21)

Power supply output capacity (Chapter 3)

Components may include the following:
Motherboards (Chapter 5 and Chapter 19)

Memory (Chapter 8 and Chapter 19)

Hard drives (Chapter 12 and Chapter 19)

CPUs (Chapter 6 and Chapter 19)

BIOS (Chapter 5)

Adapter cards (Chapter 9)

Laptop power sources

  Lithium ion (Chapter 19)

  NiMH (Chapter 19)

  Fuel cell (Chapter 19)

PCMCIA Type I, II, III cards (Chapter 19)

DOMAIN 2: DIAGNOSING AND TROUBLESHOOTING

2.1 RECOGNIZE COMMON PROBLEMS ASSOCIATED WITH EACH MODULE AND THEIR SYMPTOMS, AND IDENTIFY STEPS TO ISOLATE AND TROUBLESHOOT THE PROBLEMS. GIVEN A PROBLEM SITUATION, INTERPRET THE SYMPTOMS AND INFER THE MOST LIKELY CAUSE.

Content may include the following:

I/O ports and cables

  Serial (Chapter 9 and Chapter 21)

  Parallel (Chapter 9 and Chapter 21)

  USB (Chapter 9 and Chapter 21)

  IEEE 1394/FireWire (Chapter 14 and Chapter 21)

  Infrared (Chapter 18 and Chapter 21)

  SCSI (Chapter 14 and Chapter 21)

Motherboards

  CMOS/BIOS settings (Chapter 5, Chapter 13, Chapter 16, and Chapter 21)

  POST audible/visual error codes (Chapter 5, Chapter 21, and Appendix C)

Peripherals (Chapter 5 and Chapter 21)

  Computer cases

    Power supplies (Chapter 3 and Chapter 21)

Slot covers (Chapter 4)

Front cover alignment (Chapter 5)

Storage devices and cables

FDDs (Chapter 2, Chapter 5, Chapter 11, and Chapter 21)

HDDs (Chapter 13 and Chapter 21)

CD/CD-RW (Chapter 16 and Chapter 21)

DVD/DVD-RW (Chapter 16 and Chapter 21)

Tape drives (Chapter 11 and Chapter 21)

Removable storage (Chapter 11 and Chapter 21)

Cooling systems (Chapter 13 and Chapter 21)

Fans (Chapter 4, Chapter 7, and Chapter 21)

Heat sinks (Chapter 7 and Chapter 21)

Liquid cooling (Chapter 7)

Temperature sensors (Chapter 7)

Processors/CPUs (Chapter 7 and Chapter 21)

Memory (Chapter 8 and Chapter 21)

Display devices (Chapter 15 and Chapter 21)

Input devices

Keyboards (Chapter 10 and Chapter 21)

Mouse/Pointer devices (Chapter 10 and Chapter 21)

Touch screens (Chapter 5, Chapter 10, and Chapter 21)

Adapters

Network Interface Cards (NIC) (Chapter 18 and Chapter 21)

Sound cards (Chapter 16 and Chapter 21)

Video cards (Chapter 15 and Chapter 21)

Modems (Chapter 19 and Chapter 21)

SCSI (Chapter 14 and Chapter 21)

IEEE 1394/FireWire (Chapter 14 and Chapter 21)

USB (Chapter 10 and Chapter 21)

Portable Systems

PCMCIA (Chapter 10 and Chapter 21)

Batteries (Chapter 20 and Chapter 21)

Docking stations/Port replicators (Chapter 20 and Chapter 21)

Portable unique storage (Chapter 20 and Chapter 21)

2.2 IDENTIFY BASIC TROUBLESHOOTING PROCEDURES AND TOOLS, AND HOW TO ELICIT PROBLEM SYMPTOMS FROM CUSTOMERS. JUSTIFY ASKING PARTICULAR QUESTIONS IN A GIVEN SCENARIO.

Content may include the following:

Troubleshooting/Isolation/Problem determination procedures (Chapter 21)

Determining whether a hardware or software problem (Chapter 21)

Gathering information from user (Chapter 21)

Customer environment (Chapter 21)

Symptoms/Error codes (Chapter 21 and Appendix D)

Situation when the problem occurred (Chapter 21)

DOMAIN 3: PC PREVENTATIVE MAINTENANCE, SAFETY, AND ENVIRONMENTAL ISSUES

3.1 IDENTIFY THE VARIOUS TYPES OF PREVENTATIVE MAINTENANCE MEASURES, PRODUCTS, AND PROCEDURES AND WHEN AND HOW TO USE THEM.

Content may include the following:

Liquid cleaning compounds (Chapter 17)

Types of materials to clean contacts and connections (Chapter 17)

Nonstatic vacuums (chassis, power supplies, fans) (Chapter 2 and Chapter 3)

Cleaning monitors (Chapter 15)

Cleaning removable media devices (Chapter 10)

Ventilation, dust, and moisture control on the PC hardware interior (Chapter 4)

Hard disk maintenance (Defragging, ScanDisk, CHKDSK) (Chapter 13 and Chapter 21)

Verifying UPS (Uninterruptible Power Supply) and suppressors (Chapter 3 and Chapter 21)

3.2 IDENTIFY VARIOUS SAFETY MEASURES AND PROCEDURES, AND WHEN/HOW TO USE THEM.

Content may include the following:

ESD (electrostatic discharge) precautions and procedures

What ESD can do, how it may be apparent or hidden (Chapter 3 and Chapter 21)

Common ESD protection devices (Chapter 3)

Situations that could present a danger or hazard (Chapter 3, Chapter 5, and Chapter 17)

Potential hazards and proper safety procedures relating to:

High-voltage equipment (Chapter 3, Chapter 5, and Chapter 17)
Power supplies (Chapter 3 and Chapter 17)
CRTs (Chapter 5 and Chapter 17)

3.3 IDENTIFY ENVIRONMENTAL PROTECTION MEASURES AND PROCEDURES, AND WHEN/HOW TO USE THEM.

Content may include the following:

Special disposal procedures that comply with environmental guidelines.
Batteries (Lab Manual)
CRTs (Lab Manual)
Chemical solvents and cans (Lab Manual)
MSDS (Lab Manual)

DOMAIN 4: MOTHERBOARDS/PROCESSORS/MEMORY

4.1 DISTINGUISH BETWEEN THE POPULAR CPU CHIPS IN TERMS OF THEIR BASIC CHARACTERISTICS.

Content may include the following:

Popular CPU chips (Pentium class compatible) (Chapter 7)
Voltage (Chapter 5 and Chapter 6)
Speeds (actual vs. advertised) (Chapter 5)
Cache level I, II, III (Chapter 5, Chapter 6, Chapter 7, and Chapter 8)
Sockets/Slots (Chapter 2, Chapter 5, Chapter 6, and Chapter 8)
VRM(s) (Chapter 5)

4.2 IDENTIFY THE TYPES OF RAM (RANDOM ACCESS MEMORY), THEIR FORM FACTORS AND OPERATIONAL CHARACTERISTICS. DETERMINE BANKING AND SPEED REQUIREMENTS UNDER GIVEN SCENARIOS.

Content may include the following:

Types
EDO RAM (Extended Data Output RAM) (Chapter 8)
DRAM (Dynamic Random Access Memory) (Chapter 8)

SRAM (Static RAM) (Chapter 8)

VRAM (Video RAM) (Chapter 15)

SDRAM (Synchronous Dynamic RAM) (Chapter 8 and Chapter 15)

DDR (Double Data Rate) (Chapter 8 and Chapter 15)

RAMBUS (Chapter 8)

Form factors (including pin count)

SIMM (Single In-line Memory Module) (Chapter 8)

DIMM (Dual In-line Memory Module) (Chapter 8)

SODIMM (Small outline DIMM) (Chapter 8 and Chapter 20)

MicroDIMM (Chapter 8)

RIMM (Chapter 8)

Operational characteristics

Memory chips (8-bit, 16-bit, and 32-bit) (Chapter 8)

Parity chips versus nonparity chips (Chapter 8)

ECC versus non-ECC (Chapter 8)

Single-sided versus double-sided (Chapter 8)

4.3 IDENTIFY THE MOST POPULAR TYPES OF MOTHERBOARDS, THEIR COMPONENTS, AND THEIR ARCHITECTURE (BUS STRUCTURES).

Content may include the following:

Types of motherboards

AT (Chapter 2 and Chapter 5)

ATX (Chapter 2 and Chapter 5)

Communication ports

Serial (Chapter 2 and Chapter 5)

USB (Chapter 2 and Chapter 5)

Parallel (Chapter 2 and Chapter 5)

IEEE 1394/FireWire (Chapter 2 and Chapter 5)

Infrared (Chapter 2 and Chapter 5)

Memory

SIMM (Chapter 2, Chapter 5, and Chapter 8)

DIMM (Chapter 2, Chapter 5, and Chapter 8)

RIMM (Chapter 2, Chapter 5, and Chapter 8)

SODIMM (Chapter 2, Chapter 5, and Chapter 20)

MicroDIMM (Chapter 2 and Chapter 5)

Processor sockets

Slot 1 (Chapter 2, Chapter 5, and Chapter 6)

Slot 2 (Chapter 2, Chapter 5, and Chapter 6)

Slot A (Chapter 2, Chapter 5, and Chapter 6)

Socket A (Chapter 2, Chapter 5, and Chapter 6)

Socket 7 (Chapter 2, Chapter 5, and Chapter 6)

Socket 8 (Chapter 2, Chapter 5, and Chapter 6)

Socket 423 (Chapter 2, Chapter 5, and Chapter 6)

Socket 478 (Chapter 2, Chapter 5, and Chapter 6)

Socket 370 (Chapter 2, Chapter 5, and Chapter 6)

External cache memory (Level 2) (Chapter 5 and Chapter 6)

Bus Architecture

ISA (Chapter 2 and Chapter 9)

PCI (Chapter 2 and Chapter 9)

PCI 32-bit (Chapter 2 and Chapter 9)

PCI 64-bit (Chapter 2 and Chapter 9)

AGP

2X (Chapter 2, Chapter 9, and Chapter 15)

4X (Chapter 2, Chapter 9, and Chapter 15)

8X (Pro) (Chapter 2, Chapter 9, and Chapter 15)

USB (Chapter 2 and Chapter 9)

AMR (audio modem riser) slots (Chapter 2 and Chapter 5)

CNR (communication network riser) slots (Chapter 2 and Chapter 5)

Basic compatibility guidelines

IDE (ATA, ATAPI, ULTRA-DMA, EIDE) (Chapter 13)

SCSI (Narrow, Wide, Fast, Ultra, HVD, LVD) (Chapter 12)

Chipsets (Chapter 5 and Appendix D)

4.4 IDENTIFY THE PURPOSE OF CMOS (COMPLEMENTARY METAL-OXIDE SEMICONDUCTOR) MEMORY, WHAT IT CONTAINS, AND HOW AND WHEN TO CHANGE ITS PARAMETERS. GIVEN A SCENARIO INVOLVING CMOS, CHOOSE THE APPROPRIATE COURSE OF ACTION.

CMOS Settings: (Chapter 5, Chapter 19, and Chapter 21)

Default settings (Chapter 5 and Chapter 19)

CPU settings (Chapter 5)

Printer parallel port (Uni., bidirectional, disable/enable, ECP, EPP) (Chapter 5 and Chapter 19)

COM/Serial port (Memory address, interrupt request, disable) (Chapter 5)

Floppy drive (Enable/disable drive or boot, speed, density) (Chapter 5)

Hard drive (Size and drive type) (Chapter 5)

Memory (Speed, parity, nonparity) (Chapter 5)

Boot sequence (Chapter 5)

Date/Time (Chapter 5)

Passwords (Chapter 5)

Plug 'n Play BIOS (Chapter 5)

Disabling onboard devices (Chapter 5)

Disabling virus protection (Chapter 5)

Power management (Chapter 5)

Infrared (Chapter 5)

DOMAIN 5: PRINTERS

5.1 IDENTIFY PRINTER TECHNOLOGIES, INTERFACES, AND OPTIONS/UPGRADES.

Technologies include:

Laser (Chapter 17)

Dot Matrix (Chapter 17)

Ink Dispersion (Inkjet)

    Solid ink (Chapter 17)

    Thermal (Chapter 17)

    Dye sublimation (Chapter 17)

Interfaces include:
Parallel (Chapter 9 and Chapter 17)

Network (Chapter 19)

USB (Chapter 17)

Infrared (Chapter 19)

Serial (Chapter 17)

IEEE 1394/FireWire (Chapter 14)

Wireless (Chapter 19)

Options/Upgrades include:
Memory (Chapter 17)

Hard drives (Chapter 17)

NICs (Chapter 17)

Trays and feeders (Chapter 17)

Finishers (e.g., stapling, etc.) (Chapter 17)

Scanners/fax/copier (Chapter 17)

5.2 Recognize common printer problems and techniques used to resolve them.

Content may include the following:

Printer drivers (Chapter 17)

Firmware updates (Chapter 17)

Paper feed and output (Chapter 17)

Calibrations (Chapter 17)

Printing test pages (Chapter 17)

Errors (printed or displayed) (Chapter 17)

Memory (Chapter 17)

Configuration (Chapter 17)

Network connections (Chapter 18)

Connections (Chapter 17)

Paper jams (Chapter 17)

Print quality (Chapter 17)

Safety precautions (Chapter 17)

Preventative maintenance (Chapter 17)

Consumables (Chapter 17)

Environment (Chapter 17)

Domain 6: Basic Networking

6.1 Identify the common types of network cables, their characteristics and connectors.

Cable types include:

Coaxial

    RG-6 (Chapter 18)

    RG-8 (Chapter 18)

    RG-58 (Chapter 18)

    RG-59 (Chapter 18)

Plenum/PVC
UTP
    CAT3 (Chapter 18)
    CAT5/e (Chapter 18 and Lab Manual)
    CAT6 (Chapter 18)
STP (Chapter 18)
Fiber
    Single mode (Chapter 18)
    Multimode (Chapter 18)
Connector types include:
BNC (Chapter 18 and Lab Manual)
RJ-45 (Chapter 2, Chapter 18, and Lab Manual)
AUI (Chapter 2, Chapter 16, Chapter 18, and Lab Manual)
ST/SC (Chapter 18)
IDC/UDC (Chapter 18)

6.2 IDENTIFY BASIC NETWORKING CONCEPTS INCLUDING HOW A NETWORK WORKS.

Concepts include:

Installing and configuring network cards (Chapter 18 and Lab Manual)
Addressing (Chapter 18 and Lab Manual)
Bandwidth (Chapter 18)
Status indicators (Chapter 18 and Lab Manual)
Protocols
    TCP/IP (Chapter 18)
    IPX/SPX (NWLINK) (Chapter 18)
    AppleTalk (Chapter 18)
    NETBEUI/NETBIOS (Chapter 18)
Full-duplex/Half-duplex (Chapter 19)
Cabling—Twisted pair, Coaxial, Fiber optic, RS-232 (Chapter 18)
Networking models
    Peer-to-peer (Chapter 18)
    Client/server (Chapter 18)
Infrared (Chapter 18)
Wireless (Chapter 18)

6.3 Identify common technologies available for establishing Internet connectivity and their characteristics.

Technologies include:
LAN (Chapter 18)

DSL (Chapter 19)

Cable (Chapter 19)

ISDN (Chapter 19)

Dial-up (Chapter 19)

Satellite (Chapter 18)

Wireless (Chapter 18)

Characteristic include:
Definition (Chapter 18)

Speed (Chapter 18)

Connections (Chapter 18)

CHAPTER 1

PC BASICS

Before I get started in on discussions of the individual components, there are a few basic concepts I'd like to go over. In addition, a few concise definitions are going to be necessary for those just beginning in the field of computer hardware. This chapter is targeted at the beginning student.

A+ EXAM OBJECTIVES

CompTIA exam objectives introduced in this chapter include the following:

1.1 Identify the names, purpose, and characteristics of system modules.

1.5 Identify the names, purposes, and performance characteristics of standardized/common peripheral ports, associated cabling, and their connectors. Recognize ports, cabling, and connectors by sight.

4.1 Distinguish between the popular CPU chips in terms of their basic characteristics.

4.2 Identify the types of RAM (Random Access Memory), form factors, and operational characteristics. Determine banking and speed requirements under given scenarios.

4.3 Identify the most popular types of motherboards, their components, and their architecture. (Bus structures)

THE RAW BASICS

First thing I ought to do is get one thing out of the way right off the bat. Just what is a computer? The first thing a complete beginner might think is that it is the thing that looks like a TV sitting on top of the desk. Somebody that's one step beyond the beginner stage might point to the box on the floor that everything plugs into and identify that as a computer. They'd be a little closer to correct. However, the definition of a computer is far more basic than all that. A *computer* is simply this:

It is a device that performs three basic functions.

■ It accepts input of data.

Table 1.1   The Standard Computer Model

Central Processing Unit (CPU)	Sometimes called the "brain" of the computer. I'll be arguing that point later in this book.
Random Access Memory (RAM)	Used for temporary storage of data.
Input/Output (I/O)	Conduit through which data is exchanged between CPU and outside.
Storage	Long-term storage of data for when computer is turned off.

The standard computer model defines the minimum components required to make up a computer system.

- It processes that input according to a specific set of instructions (either through the execution of requests or the manipulation of data).
- It provides output of processed data.

With that in mind, it's relatively easy to construct a standard computer model. While these components in no way comprise everything that makes up a computer, without them, you wouldn't have a computer. **Table 1.1** outlines the essential components that constitute the basic recipe for a barebones computer system.

Each of the aforementioned components of the computer model (illustrated in **Figure 1.1**)

Buzz Words

Computer: Any device that can accept the input of user data, process that data according to a specific set of instructions, and then provide the results of that processing in the form of output to the end user.

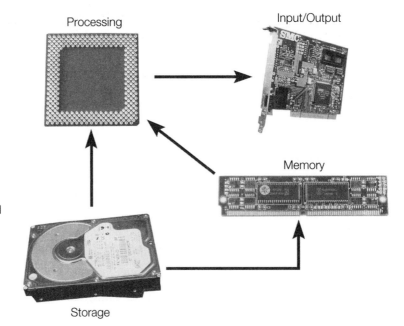

Figure 1.1   The standard computer model at a minimum calls for central processing, memory for short-term storage, some form of long-term storage, and an input/output path for data.

will be covered in great detail in the general body of this book. However, I would like to start with an overview of what's going on inside the system before I tackle system components in detail. With this model in mind, take a look at the three basic functions of the computer, as laid out in the "definition" of a computer.

> **BUZZ WORDS** ——————
>
> **Input:** Any data that is intended and/ or ready to be sent to the CPU for processing.

> **EXAM NOTE:** Make sure you can explain the Standard Computer Model, as defined by CompTIA.

INPUT

Input is defined as any form of information that is ready for entry into the system. Without data, the system has nothing to do. Information can enter the system in the form of raw data or as instructions. This data is presented to the system by way of any one of a variety of devices. Some common input devices are listed in **Table 1.2**.

Input devices come in either internal or external incarnations. Some of them are cards that you install; others sit on your desk waiting for your attention. Some devices, such as a modem, are available as either an internal or an external device. Be able to recognize various input devices. And be aware that many devices can have split personalities, functioning as both an input device and an output device. The hard drive in **Figure 1.2** is an example of just such a device.

Figure 1.2   You don't often think of a hard drive as providing either input or output. But in reality, as a mass storage mechanism, it functions as both at the same time.

Table 1.2   Standard Input Devices

Floppy diskette	Hard drive	Joystick
Keyboard	Modem	Mouse
CD-ROM	Scanner	Touchpad
Touchscreen	Trackball	Voice
Digital camera	Network	Proprietary device

A collection of common devices used to input data.

Processing

Processing occurs whenever data or instructions are executed, manipulated, updated, or in any way altered. Simply through-putting data from an input device, such as a keyboard, to an output device, such as a monitor, constitutes processing. It would be an easier job to understand computers if the CPU (**Figure 1.3**) was the only device in the system that was involved in processing data. Unfortunately, data is getting massaged, manipulated, recalculated, and crunched practically the entire time it is in the computer. Every device I'll look at throughout this book has its own little collection of integrated circuits (ICs) that have certain functions to perform. An IC is an electronic chip onto which specific instruction sets have been "burned." These instructions tell the device what to do with all those signals that are traveling through it.

Figure 1.3 A typical microprocessor. As powerful as it is, it only does a fraction of the total processing that goes on in a computer system.

Output

If users are going to be able to take advantage of the results of the actions of processing, those results must somehow be exported from the computer to the world in which people actually live. It doesn't do a whole lot of good if the CPU simply lets the information it created float to digital heaven when it needs to make room for more data. *Output* can be printed, transmitted, displayed, stored, or played back. There are literally hundreds of devices on the market that collect the output of your computer and put it into some useable form. **Table 1.3** shows just a small number of output devices on the market today.

Buzz Words

Processing: Any manipulation of data that can occur between the time the data has been input into the computer and the time that it is provided as output. Processing can consist of calculations performed on the data, replication of that data to alternative locations, and the comparison of one data set to another. Not all processing is done by the CPU.

Output: Data that is being transmitted by one device to another once that data has been processed.

Table 1.3 Typical Output Devices

Floppy diskette	Hard disk drive	Modem
Monitor	Network	Printer
Sound	Tape	Tactile

Some of the output devices found on a typical system.

> **EXAM NOTE:** There is likely to be a list of devices for you to identify as to whether they are input devices or output devices. Some will be both. Examine the question carefully.

HOW YOUR COMPUTER EATS DATA:
ONE BYTE AT A TIME

Of course, data doesn't just magically move from your fingertips or from the lens of that fancy digital camera you just bought. The various components of your system, as well as the peripheral devices you choose to employ, must provide data in a form that the CPU can understand. And contrary to what manufacturers would have you believe, CPUs are basically stupid. They are nothing more than a very complex collection of transistors crammed into a tiny package. They know ON and they know OFF. In written form, this is expressed as 0 or 1. On its most basic level, all computer data can be broken down into a series of 0s and 1s. This is *binary*. The counting method used by humans is *decimal*, a Base10 system consisting of the characters 0 through 9.

> **BUZZ WORDS** ─────
>
> **Binary:** A Base2 counting system that consists of the two characters 0 and 1.
>
> **Decimal:** A Base10 counting system that consists of ten characters, 0 through 9.

Binary is based on the principles of George Boole, who in 1854 developed an entire branch of algebra based on "true/false," "yes/no," and "on/off." This fit the concept of the transistor perfectly. Numerically, you could consider OFF to be the equivalent of zero, while ON could equal one. Therefore, machine language is a stream of zeros and ones. To translate this language of zeros and ones, programmers have various languages for writing programs. Fortunately, as a hardware technician, there are only a few basic concepts of binary you need to understand. There are also some basic terms.

- *Bit:* a single zero or one
- *Byte:* any combination of eight zeros or ones
- *Nibble:* Four bits
- *Word:* Two to four bytes
- *Page:* One to twenty kilobytes
- *Kilobyte:* Two to the tenth power bytes, or 1024 bytes
- *Megabyte:* Two to the twentieth power bytes, or 1,048,576 bytes

The most basic unit of data is the bit. A single bit is represented as either 0 or 1. As you will see later on, a single bit can be significant.

> **EXAM NOTE:** Know intimately the vocabulary of binary, and be able to perform a simple binary-to-decimal or decimal-to-binary conversion.

As defined in the previous list, a byte consists of eight individual bits, or eight different switches that can be turned on or off. A byte is treated by the system as a single entity and allows programmers to create values greater than 0 or 1. The number of values a byte can represent can be determined by taking the number of positions the switch can occupy (2) and multiplying it by the number of switches (8). $2 \times 2 \times 2 \times 2 \times 2 \times 2 \times 2 \times 2$ (or two to the eighth power) = 256. Therefore, from an 8-bit byte, 256 different combinations can be achieved. Counting in binary can be interesting, too. It looks like this: 0, 1, 10, 11, 100, 101, 111, 1000, 1001, 1010, 1011, 1100, and so forth. This isn't just theoretical material I'm discussing here. Later in the book, when I discuss configuring addresses to network interface cards, certain types of addresses consist of four 8-bit binary values, literally connected by dots. To configure the IP address, you type in the decimal alliteration.

The order of bits in a byte is significant as well. Programmers refer to this order by way of *least significant bit* and *most significant bit.* The most significant bit of a single byte has a mathematical value of 256, whereas the least significant bit has a value of zero. **Figure 1.4** illustrates the value of each position. It's actually easy to calculate the mathematical value of a byte. Everywhere there is a one in the position, multiply the relative value of that position by one. Everywhere there is a zero, you have a value of zero. Now add the numbers up.

Therefore, while having to deal with numbers like 1010 1101 might seem a little intimidating at first, it needn't be overwhelming. All you really have to do is start from the right, and everywhere the bit is set to 1, add the relative value for that position. So, as **Figure 1.5** illustrates, the decimal value for 1010 1101 would actually be 173. To achieve numbers higher than 256, you simply use more bytes.

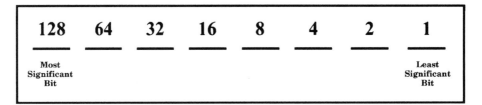

128	64	32	16	8	4	2	1

Most Significant Bit

Least Significant Bit

Figure 1.4   Relative values of bits in a byte

Actual Bit Values

1	0	1	0	1	1	0	1
128	64	32	16	8	4	2	1

Relative Value in Bytes
Multiply the actual bit value by its relative value. Add the totals.

$(1 \times 128) + (0 \times 64) + (1 \times 32) + (0 \times 16) + (1 \times 8) + (1 \times 4) + (0 \times 2) + (1 \times 1) = 173$

Figure 1.5   Calculating the relative value of a byte

HEXADECIMAL

Dealing with binary by itself can be a little cumbersome. If you had eight bytes of data you wanted to communicate to another technician, you might finding yourself writing something along the lines of 0110 1111, 1100 0000, 0001 1010, 1110 0000, 1011 0001, 0000 0001, 1001 0001, 1111 0000.

Needless to say, there must to be a better way. That way is called *hexadecimal*. Hexadecimal is a way of counting in Base16.

EXAM NOTE: You can almost count on having some hexadecimal thrown your way on the exam. Be comfortable with the basics of hex.

A byte consists of eight bits. If you divide a byte into two nibbles, there will be two four-bit chunks to deal with. Hexadecimal provides a single character that represents each possible combination of four bits. Two raised to the fourth is sixteen, so a character set based on Base16 must have a total of sixteen symbols. The numerical symbols 0-9 cover the first ten, and the remainder is represented as the alphabetic symbols A-F. Therefore, in Base16 you count 0, 1, 2, 3, 4, 5, 6, 7, 8, 9, A, B, C, D, E, and F.

There are several different places where the computer provides information in hex, so having a good understanding of the concept is important. **Table 1.4** translates numerical values into hex.

DIGITAL CODE FORMATS

All this would be wonderful as long as all you ever had to deal with was numbers. However, people don't communicate exclusively with numbers. They also use letters and punctuation marks. This collection of letters, numbers, punctuation marks, and other symbols that humans use in order to read is known as a *character set*. People also don't communicate in binary. While it's not difficult to translate the value of a byte, it is obvious that communicating in binary is cumbersome.

In order to translate the stream of zeros and ones into something humans could understand, a common data format had to be developed that all computers could work with. 0010 1000 couldn't mean one thing for one computer and another for someone else's system. Way back in the earliest days of computers a basic character set was developed to transliterate binary into a written language. As computer technology has advanced, so has the need for a more complex character set.

ASCII   The American Standard Code for Information Interchange (ASCII), was the first set of characters that translated binary into something mere mortals could understand. However, ASCII wasn't exclusively a character set. The eight bits of the byte were used to generate 256

Table 1.4   The Hexadecimal Chart

Dec	Hex	Dec	Hex	Dec	Hex	Dec	Hex	Dec	Hex	Dec	Hex	Dec	Hex	Dec	Hex
0	0	32	20	64	40	96	60	128	80	160	a0	192	c0	224	e0
1	1	33	21	65	41	97	61	129	81	161	a1	193	c1	225	e1
2	2	34	22	66	42	98	62	130	82	162	a2	194	c2	226	e2
3	3	35	23	67	43	99	63	131	83	163	a3	195	c3	227	e3
4	4	36	24	68	44	100	64	132	84	164	a4	196	c4	228	e4
5	5	37	25	69	45	101	65	133	85	165	a5	197	c5	229	e5
6	6	38	26	70	46	102	66	134	86	166	a6	198	c6	230	e6
7	7	39	27	71	47	103	67	135	87	167	a7	199	c7	231	e7
8	8	40	28	72	48	104	68	136	88	168	a8	200	c8	232	e8
9	9	41	29	73	49	105	69	137	89	169	a9	201	c9	233	e9
10	a	42	2a	74	4a	106	6a	138	8a	170	aa	202	ca	234	ea
11	b	43	2b	75	4b	107	6b	139	8b	171	ab	203	cb	235	eb
12	c	44	2c	76	4c	108	6c	140	8c	172	ac	204	cc	236	ec
13	d	45	2d	77	4d	109	6d	141	8d	173	ad	205	cd	237	ed
14	e	46	2e	78	4e	110	6e	142	8e	174	ae	206	ce	238	ee
15	f	47	2f	79	4f	111	6f	143	8f	175	af	207	cf	239	ef
16	10	48	30	80	50	112	70	144	90	176	b0	208	d0	240	f0
17	11	49	31	81	51	113	71	145	91	177	b1	209	d1	241	f1
18	12	50	32	82	52	114	72	146	92	178	b2	210	d2	242	f2
19	13	51	33	83	53	115	73	147	93	179	b3	211	d3	243	f3
20	14	52	34	84	54	116	74	148	94	180	b4	212	d4	244	f4
21	15	53	35	85	55	117	75	149	95	181	b5	213	d5	245	f5
22	16	54	36	86	56	118	76	150	96	182	b6	214	d6	246	f6
23	17	55	37	87	57	119	77	151	97	183	b7	215	d7	247	f7
24	18	56	38	88	58	120	78	152	98	184	b8	216	d8	248	f8
25	19	57	39	89	59	121	79	153	99	185	b9	217	d9	249	f9
26	1a	58	3a	90	5a	122	7a	154	9a	186	ba	218	da	250	fa
27	1b	59	3b	91	5b	123	7b	155	9b	187	bb	219	db	251	fb
28	1c	60	3c	92	5c	124	7c	156	9c	188	bc	220	dc	252	fc
29	1d	61	3d	93	5d	125	7d	157	9d	189	bd	221	dd	253	fd
30	1e	62	3e	94	5e	126	7e	158	9e	190	be	222	de	254	fe
31	1f	63	3f	95	5f	127	7f	159	9f	191	bf	223	df	255	ff

Hexadecimal Conversion Table. Note that all leading 0's are dropped.

values. As I've emphasized before, a combination of eight zeros and ones constitutes a single character. In the original ASCII, that one set of characters had to deal with both the human interface and also be used to send commands to graphics devices, such as printers. In the original ASCII, there were actually only 128 printable characters. The remainder of the set was used as commands. You can check out both sets of characters in the ASCII Character Set tables in Appendix C.

Without going into a lot of programming detail, in ASCII the same byte can represent a number or it can represent a character or it can represent a command. This is dictated by programmers and the language or program they are working in. The decimal value of each character is used to express the text in numeric code. For example, the capital A is the decimal character 65, or binary 0100 0001.

Extended ASCII   Extended ASCII eliminated the need for putting control characters into the character set. All available 256 characters became printable symbols. This allowed for more characters than the standard alphabet in upper- and lowercase, numbers, and punctuation. Popular symbols could now be included, such as the trademark symbol. The makers of font sets put Extended ASCII to use when they want to create specialty symbols.

ISO Latin-1   ISO Latin-1 is a set of printing characters that specify European characters and symbols in addition to the 128 printing characters of ASCII. Because of the international nature of the Internet, this has been adopted as the character set of choice for some Web sites and Web browsers. See the ISO Latin Character Set table in Appendix C for a complete listing.

ANSI   The ANSI character set is the one used in Windows 3.x and Windows 9x versions. This is a 256-character set that uses the 128 printing characters of ASCII as the base and then adds another set of printing characters similar to that of ISO Latin-1. However, Microsoft extended this set somewhat, so it is not one hundred percent compatible with ISO Latin-1.

UNI Code   UNI increased character depth to 16 bits, allowing for a much greater number of characters. These additional characters were mapped out to include the character sets from all the major languages of the world, allowing for the first multilingual character set. This is the character set used by Windows NT and Windows 2000 as well as Unix. Most of the Web servers that provide international support these days provide support for UNI code.

DATA COMMUNICATIONS

Knowing what makes up bits and bytes and why character sets are necessary is very important. But the computer needs to be able to move that data around. The data that a computer system processes has to come from somewhere. In fact, data frequently has to be brought in from remote sources before you can use it. While there are many different methods of packaging data for transmission across a network, or even just from a disk drive to a hard drive, there are really only two ways of sending it over a wire. Those two ways are parallel communication and serial communication.

PARALLEL COMMUNICATION

While it may not seem like it at first glance, *parallel communication* is the simplest, most basic, and most primitive communication used by computer systems today. It is also the slowest.

With parallel communications, a byte is broken down into its individual bits and each bit travels over a different wire. For this to work, the timing and synchronization between devices must be extremely precise. All eight of the bits that are part of a single byte must arrive at their destination at the same time. Otherwise the bits from different bytes may get scrambled together.

Parallel communications is used internally on the majority of motherboard components. It's also still a popular form of hooking up printers. And even though it isn't called parallel when your hard drives do it, they do, in fact, for the most part, communicate in parallel.

SERIAL COMMUNICATIONS

When a computer connection makes use of *serial communications,* it is basically lining all the bits in a row and then sending them over the wire, one right after the other. It may sound like parallel communications would be faster, because the data is moving over eight separate wires, and not just one. It doesn't work that way, however.

Serial communications can be either synchronous or asynchronous. *Synchronous communication* is the fastest form of serial hookup. Large amounts of data are collected into chunks called packets and sent out that way; therefore, a lot of data moves on a single transfer. A header, which consists of additional control data, is added to the front of the packet, and a trailer, which contains error correction information, is added to the end. These headers and trailers tell the receiving device where one packet ends and the next begins. Synchronous communications are used by modems, network controllers, and some forms of hard drive controller.

Asynchronous communication bundles together the individual bits of a single byte and moves data

BUZZ WORDS ────────────

Serial communications: The act of transferring data a single bit at a time over a single connection.

Parallel communications: The act of transferring an entire byte of data on a single cycle, using eight separate conductors.

Synchronous communication: A form of serial communication that transmits large amounts of data at once in packets.

Asynchronous communication: A form of serial communication that transmits data a byte at a time over a single conductor.

Starting delimiter: A single bit at the beginning of a data byte being transmitted asynchronously that marks the beginning of the byte.

Ending delimiter: A single bit at the end of a byte of data being transmitted asynchronously that marks the end of a byte.

Parity: A form of error detection used by serial communications and some forms of memory to detect the presence of a single-bit error.

over the wire a single byte at a time. To separate the bytes, a *starting delimiter* and an *ending delimiter* are added to each of the eight bits. A form of error correction called *parity* may or may not be added, depending on how a particular device is configured. Parity is discussed in detail in Chapter Eight, Searching Your Memory.

PC SYSTEM ARCHITECTURE

Computers are very complex, very complicated devices. Face it. You're looking at a device that is capable of performing as many as several million instructions per second (IPS). The CPU may be performing several billion IPS. Since the CPU is working faster than the rest of the system, it relies on the components on the motherboard to keep it fed with data.

The motherboard acts as the base plane for the entire system. It is on this surface that all electronic impulses travel between input devices and CPU and then to output devices. A motherboard consists of several layers (usually four), not just one. If you look closely at a motherboard, you'll see fine paths of copper covering both the front and back surface in nice little geometric patters (**Figure 1.6** shows the back surface, so that the motherboard components won't be distracting). These are called traces. Traces aren't just on the front and back surfaces. If you were to peel back the layers, you'd also find them in between the layers.

These traces provide the path that data takes to move from Point A to Point B. The path itself is called the bus. The term bus can get a little confusing because it's used in so many different ways. To keep things simple, just remember that it is the path data takes. Computers are considered to have five primary busses. The traces are the physical incarnation of those

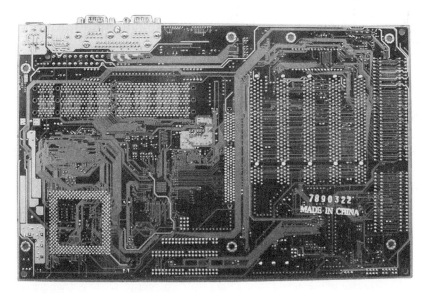

Figure 1.6 The system busses can be seen in all of those tiny copper paths you see on a motherboard.

busses. They carry the data, or in the case of the power bus, raw electricity, from its source to its destination. The motherboard is like a big city. There are lots of places where data can live and other places where it must go to work. Just like in a real city, different busses move data in different ways, to different places.

THE FIVE BUSSES

The five primary busses of the computer system consist of the CPU Bus, the Address Bus, the Local Bus, the I/O Bus, and the Power Bus. Each one of these has a specific role to fulfill and a good understanding of what each one does is critical to understanding the basics of computer hardware. Be aware, however, that throughout the course of your career, and throughout this book, you'll see many other busses discussed. Try not to let that confuse you. There are more than just the five primary ones listed here. Don't let the theory get you down, though. These busses are actually simpler than they appear at first.

CPU Bus

This is the information path between the CPU and other primary controller chips in the system. As you'll learn as you move through this book, different chips perform different functions. By itself, the CPU can't talk to the keyboard. It has no idea what the signals coming from that device mean. Located among the chips you see planted here and there along the surface of the motherboard is one that holds a program that does nothing but translate keyboard signals into pure binary code that the CPU can digest. All the chips that perform functions of this nature are located along the CPU Bus. These are the devices that can communicate directly with the CPU, at the CPU's speed.

ADDRESS BUS

Data that is stored either in memory or on a device must be available for the CPU to access. Otherwise how would the system work properly? Since the motherboard is like a big city, all the places where data lives, as well as the places where it must go, need to have addresses, so everything can find each other. When a device is installed, the operating system will assign an I/O address. When data is stored in memory, it is given an address that identifies exactly where on the memory chip the data is physically located. These addresses are generally listed as hexadecimal numbers.

The Address Bus is a bus directly from the CPU to the rest of the system that keeps track of everybody's location. Using the analogy of the Motherboard City, this is more like the Post Office than part of the transportation system.

LOCAL BUS

Like every other big city in the world, some data is in a bigger hurry to get where it's going than other data. If a peripheral or component is designed to make use of the Local Bus, then data can move from that component to its destination (which can either be the chipset of the motherboard or L2 cache) at the same speed as the CPU itself. Data moves along this bus, not only at a higher speed, but also in a more direct route. Consider this to be the Express from the suburbs to downtown.

I/O BUS

The problem with computer users is that they don't live in Motherboard City. They live outside of town. Therefore, there has to be a bus system that moves data from the computer's town to your location and vice versa. This would be the I/O Bus, or Input/Output, as it were.

POWER BUS

Here's where the analogy of the bus routes breaks down. Few busses are designed to carry nothing but raw electricity. But that's what the Power Bus does. Every component in the system needs electricity to run. This includes the CPU, RAM chips, logic chips—everything! Without electricity, you have no computer. So this is more like the power company than it is a bus line. But you get the idea.

CHAPTER SUMMARY

This chapter may have been on the basic side for the more advanced readers. But then, that is why the chapter is titled "PC Basics." There is no way that anyone can call him- or herself a professional hardware technician if the information in this chapter isn't as firmly imbedded as name, age, and social security number.

Don't make the mistake of assuming that because you've been working on computers for a while that you will know all the material that is contained here. If you're planning on pursuing the A+ Core Exam, there are some details specific to CompTIA here.

BRAIN DRAIN

1. List and explain each of the basic functions that define a computer.

2. Given an IP address of 192.168.0.115, convert that address to its decimal form.

3. You have a hexadecimal address of 02FE:CCC0. Convert that address to binary.

4. Describe in as much detail as you can the differences between ASCII and UNI Code.

5. Describe the five primary systems busses and their functions.

THE 64K$ QUESTIONS

1. Which of the following is not a basic function of a computer?

   a. Provide user data for input

   b. Accept the input of user data

   c. Provide output of processed user data

   d. Process user data

2. An IC is:
   a. Instruction Code
   b. Internal Circuit
   c. Informational Control
   d. Integrated Circuit

3. A byte that consists of the bits 0111 0010 has a decimal value of:
   a. 256
   b. 114
   c. 122
   d. 124

4. The hexadecimal value 03FF:26FF looks like _____ in binary.
   a. 0000 0010 1111 1111:0010 0110 1111 1111
   b. 0000 0011 1111 1111:0010 0110 1111 1111
   c. 0000 0110 1111 1111:0010 0110 1111 1111
   d. 0000 0010 1111 1111:0010 0100 1111 1111

5. Which character set included control codes as part of the basic set?
   a. ASCII
   b. Extended ASCII
   c. ANSI
   d. UNI Code

6. How many possible combinations can be made of a 16-bit binary value?
   a. 1024
   b. 16,384
   c. 65,536
   d. 1,048.576

7. Which of the primary system busses provides direct communications between the CPU and the chipset?
   a. The CPU Bus
   b. The Local Bus
   c. The I/O Bus
   d. The Address Bus

8. Which of the primary system busses provides direct communications between an installed device and the chipset?
   a. The CPU Bus
   b. The Local Bus
   c. The I/O Bus
   d. The Address Bus

9. Which of the primary system busses is responsible for locating data in the system?
   a. The CPU Bus
   b. The Local Bus
   c. The I/O Bus
   d. The Address Bus

10. Which primary system bus provides electrical power to the various components in the system?
   a. The CPU Bus
   b. The Power Bus
   c. The I/O Bus
   d. The Address Bus

Tricky Terminology

Asynchronous communication: A form of serial communication that transmits data a byte at a time over a single conductor.

Binary: A Base2 counting system that consists of the two characters 0 and 1.

Bit: A single zero or one, resulting in a single transition between off and on.

Byte: Any combination of eight zeros or ones.

Character set: The code used to generate printable symbols that human users can understand.

Computer: Any device that can accept the input of user data, process that data according to a specific set of instructions, and then provide the results of that processing in the form of output to the end user.

Decimal: A Base10 counting system that consists of ten characters, 0 through 9.

Ending delimiter: A single bit at the end of a byte of data being transmitted asynchronously that marks the end of a byte.

Hexadecimal: A counting system that uses Base16 as it root. As such, this system requires a total of sixteen different characters to represent base values.

Input: Any data that is intended and/or ready to be sent to the CPU for processing.

Nibble: Any combination of four zeros or ones.

Output: Data that is being transmitted by one device to another once that data has been processed.

Page: The amount of data that can be moved on a single memory read/write cycle; usually between 1 to 20KB.

Parallel communications: The act of transferring an entire byte of data on a single cycle, using eight separate conductors.

Parity: A form of error detection used by serial communications and some forms of memory to detect the presence of a single-bit error.

Processing: Any manipulation of data that can occur between the time the data has been inputted into the computer and the time that is provided as output. Processing can consist of calculations performed on the data, replication of that data to alternative locations, and the comparison of one data set to another. Not all processing is done by the CPU.

Serial communications: The act of transferring data a single bit at a time over a single connection.

Starting delimiter: A single bit at the beginning of a data byte being transmitted asynchronously that marks the beginning of the byte.

Synchronous communication: A form of serial communication that transmits large amounts of data at once in packets.

Word: The amount of data that can move across the CPU's external data bus in one clock cycle; usually between two and four bytes.

ACRONYM ALERT

ANSI: American National Standards Institute. This term refers to an organization charged with establishing standards for several different industries, including the computer industry. It also refers to an early character set developed by that organization.

ASCII: American Standard Code for Information Interchange. An early character set used by computers.

CPU: Central Processing Unit. The primary microprocessor used by a computer in order to perform calculations or otherwise manipulate data.

I/O: Input/Output. The process of sending or receiving data between devices.

IC: Integrated Circuit. A single microchip onto which the code necessary to provide several different functions has been burned.

IPS: Instructions per Second. An early measurement of CPU performance that was based solely on how many times in one second the device could execute commands.

RAM: Random Access Memory. A device used for short-term storage of data or instructions that are or will soon be required by the CPU in order for it to do its job.

CHAPTER 2

THE BASIC COMPONENTS

Key to your success as a computer technician is going to be your ability to properly identify the primary components of the average computer system using the correct terminology. Communication is one of the biggest problems a technician faces when trying to troubleshoot a problem over the telephone. True knowledge will come with time. You'll pick up a lot of it in this book, but the buzz words sometimes seem to change by the hour. This chapter will deal with identifying the different ports, sockets, chips, wires, cables, and various bells and whistles that were used to build your system.

A+ EXAM OBJECTIVES

CompTIA exam objectives that will be either introduced or covered include the following:

1.1 Identify the names, purpose, and characteristics of system modules. Recognize these modules by sight or definition.

1.5 Identify the names, purposes, and performance characteristics of standardized/common peripheral ports, associated cabling, and their connectors. Recognize ports, cabling, and connectors by sight.

3.2 Identify various safety measures and procedures, and when/how to use them.

3.3 Identify environmental protection measures and procedures, and when/how to use them.

4.1 Distinguish among the popular CPU chips in terms of their basic characteristics.

4.2 Identify the types of RAM (Random Access Memory), form factors, and operational characteristics. Determine banking and speed requirements under given scenarios.

4.3 Identify the most popular types of motherboards, their components, and their architecture (bus structures).

5.1 Identify printer technologies, interfaces, and options/upgrades.

INTERNAL COMPONENTS

You have to open the case in order to see most of the critical components that make a computer system work. These are the internal components. If you have a computer at your side that you can dig into as you work through this chapter, you will get a lot more out of it. If not, make use of the illustrations provided as best you can. Unfortunately, while it may be true that one picture is worth a thousand words, there's no substitute for the real thing. These days, it's pretty easy to locate used computers at extremely low prices. Many colleges have surplus outlets where they unload older technology. Online auction houses are another good source. Having a system that you don't mind poking around in as you read this book can only help, even if it happens to be older technology.

CAUTION: Before poking around inside a computer that actually *works*, make sure you provide the system with some sort of protection against *electrostatic discharge.* This is ordinary static electricity. A spark you can't even feel has the potential to destroy the delicate circuitry contained in a computer chip. Either use an antistatic wrist strap specifically designed for this purpose, or frequently ground yourself onto a large piece of metal you know goes to ground, such as a radiator for your furnace.

THE MOTHERBOARD

The average person looking inside of a computer case for the first time might not consider this to be the logical place to start at all. For many people it won't even be the first thing they notice. It's buried under all those wires and hidden behind the drives. With all those cards sticking out of it, you can barely see anything on the board itself. At least, that's the way it is on many computers. However, because the system board is the core to the whole system, it is indeed the place to start. As you can see from the one illustrated in **Figure 2.1**, it is a very complex device. Fortunately, it isn't all that hard to figure out.

Figure 2.1 While motherboards may differ from brand to brand, most will look pretty similar to this.

FORM FACTOR

There are two different form factors (the way it's built) that you will see in motherboards. I'll get into a more detailed discussion of form factors in Chapter Four, Computer Enclosures. For now, suffice it to say that in this day and age, the most common form factor is some variation on ATX (Advanced Technology Extended). Some older ones will fall under the designation AT (Advanced Technology).

> **BUZZ WORDS** ————————
>
> **Form factor:** A preconfigured size, orientation, and design layout for a particular component used in order to assure compatibility among manufacturers.

EXAM NOTE: Make sure you know the difference between form factors before you take the exam. In Chapter Four, Computer Enclosures, we will revisit the form factor and how it relates to computer cases.

The original AT board itself measured 12″ × 13″ and provided fairly uniform layout of expansion cards, location of memory chips, and so forth. Another form of AT-style motherboard is the more common "Baby" AT. This board measures 8.5″ × 13″, keeping the proper orientation of expansion slots, plugs, and things like that. About the only externally accessible port on an AT-style motherboard is the keyboard port. Ports such as serial and parallel ports in AT-style systems were installed using expansion cards, so they weren't directly accessible on the system board.

The majority of computers built in recent years have been based on one of several variations on the ATX theme. ATX differs from AT in several important respects. First, the board is oriented differently. Key components on the board are rotated approximately ninety degrees off the original AT design specifications. The intent of this was to reduce the overlap of key motherboard components with other major system components, such as power supplies and drives.

ATX boards also incorporate quite a few more of the peripheral components onto the motherboard. Constructed into the board itself you will find the parallel port, serial ports, keyboard and mouse port, and connections for the Universal Serial Bus. On many boards you

---

NONSTANDARD FORM FACTORS

In the course of performing upgrades on existing systems, you are likely to run into a number of proprietary designs. Not all manufacturers have consistently used the "standard" form factors in every line of computers they've produced. Older LBX systems were famous for being unique to the system they housed. Finding replacement motherboards for these systems is not always possible. Also note that a common source of failure in these systems is in the *riser card*. LBX systems do not have their expansion slots on the motherboard, but rather have a proprietary slot into which a single card fits, rising above the system board. Hence the name, riser card. While some manufacturers maintain a supply of replacement parts longer than others, even if you find the parts, they are likely to be more expensive than can be justified for repairing a system of that vintage.

may also find video, sound, and network cards and even modems built into the system board itself. As this book unfolds, I'll be discussing the advantages and disadvantages of using onboard peripherals.

Power Connectors

Another major difference between AT and ATX is in the connection between the system board and the power supply. AT-style computers have two plugs coming off the power supply that provide juice to the system board, frequently called the P8 and the P9 (see **Figure 2.2**). It is relatively easy to plug these in backward from how they're designed, and the results can be disastrous. The ATX form factor incorporates a single 20-pin connector that is notched and only plugs in one way.

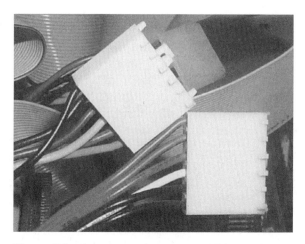

Figure 2.2   Incorrect placement of P8 and P9!!!
When working with AT-style motherboards, it is critical that the P8 and P9 power plugs go in correctly. Plugging them in with the color sequence in the order illustrated here will fry the board!

A more subtle advantage ATX power supplies provide over their AT counterparts is that of more advanced power management. "Soft" power-down of the system can be controlled more efficiently by the operating system.

> **Exam Note:** The next several pages are going to introduce you to features of the motherboard. Even if you think you know this like the back of your hand, go over the material at least once for review. A popular feature of the Core Exam is to give you a very rough illustration of a motherboard with numbered arrows pointing at key components. Your task is to identify those components. This one exercise can be worth several points.

The Expansion Bus

Early in the development of computers, engineers realized that people were going to want to add new toys. Therefore, they designed in a way of expanding the machines. If you examine the rear half of the computer you will see different slots for mounting adapter cards onto the board. These are the slots that make up a large portion of the *expansion bus*. In fact, they're called expansion slots.

The astute reader may think back to Chapter One, PC Basics, when I spoke of the five primary busses, and won't recall that I ever mentioned the expansion bus. That's because, while every computer has an expansion bus, the expansion bus is

> **Buzz Words**
>
> **Expansion Bus:** A circuit on a motherboard that allows accessory devices to be added to the system. The expansion bus straddles several of the primary system busses.

not a primary bus. In fact, it straddles several of the primary busses. That will be covered in greater detail in Chapter Nine, Examining the Expansion Bus.

The number of expansion slots on a system can range from as few as one to as many as eight (or even more on some full-sized AT boards). On many boards, you'll see some longer ones out toward the edge. On most boards these slots are either black or very dark gray. If you look closely, they actually appear to be two different connectors, back to back. (In fact, they are. More on that in Chapter Nine, Examining the Expansion Bus). There is a front slot with sixty-two connectors, backed up by another, shorter one with thirty-six connectors. These are your ISA slots. ISA

Figure 2.3   Here is a typical expansion bus using PCI and ISA slots.

stands for Industry Standard Architecture, and was developed by IBM years ago. Not all boards have these. If your board or computer system says anywhere on it "PC-2000 Compliant," it will not have these expansion slots.

There will also be anywhere from one to who knows how many shorter slots. These are nearly always white in color. These are your PCI slots. PCI stands for Peripheral Components Interconnect, and is the slot of choice for virtually every device made today, except the video card. If your board (and anything less than a couple of years old will have one, unless the motherboard sports onboard video) has a shorter slot that is seated a bit farther back from the edge than the rest of the slots, this is the AGP slot, or the Advanced Graphics Port. The motherboard illustrated in **Figure 2.3** offers the user the choice of ISA or PCI slots.

Collectively, these slots constitute the Expansion Bus. This little collection of connections is of sufficient importance that Chapter Nine is dedicated exclusively to a detailed discussion of the expansion bus.

MEMORY SOCKETS

Typically, computer manufacturers currently make use of one of two types of *Dual Inline Memory Modules* (DIMM). The first of these sockets to come along had 168 pins and clips on either side that lever the chip out of the socket when the need arises. Motherboards vary in how many of these are present. I've seen a few that only have a single socket. Providing only two sockets is relatively common, but this provides only a minimal upgrade capability. The majority of boards provide three or four sockets.

Figure 2.4 DIMM and SIMM sockets can exist on the same board. Check with your manual before you attempt using them both at the same time.

The second style of DIMM that is becoming more common, and now outpacing 168-pin production, is the 184-pin socket required by *double data rate* (DDR) memory. These sockets are larger than the earlier style socket and are keyed differently. Therefore, the memory modules are not interchangeable. There are, however, motherboards that are equipped with both 168-pin and 184-pin sockets.

DIMM sockets aren't all you will see, however. Several manufacturers still make boards that support older-style Single Inline Memory Modules (SIMM). These boards will have two different types of memory sockets, like the one shown in **Figure 2.4** (really old ones can get more complicated, and I'll cover them in more detail in Chapter Eight, Searching Your Memory). If this is the situation for you, there will be anywhere from two to four 72-pin connectors with a ridge directly in the middle of the socket for the SIMMs. These sockets will have small spring clips on each end for holding the SIMM in place.

CPU Sockets

First and foremost among the things you need to be able to identify and recognize on a motherboard is the Central Processing Unit (CPU). The CPU is an important consideration in your form factor. CPUs come in four different flavors as of this writing. There are two different competing versions of Slot CPUs and several versions of socket CPUs as well. The sockets are recognized by the hundreds of holes for the CPU pins, while the slots look like overgrown memory slots.

Other, more proprietary sockets you might bump into would include the Socket 8 on older Pentium PRO-based computer systems. Also, AMD uses a Socket A for its Duron line of CPUs as well as some of the Thunderbirds. These are 453-pin ZIFs. Proposed sockets as of this writing (which may well be out by the time you read this) include the Socket 423 by Intel. This is a 423-pin socket designed to support its Tehama, Tulloch, and Willomette chips, when (and if) they're ever released. Other proposed chips by Intel will require the Socket 603. Containing 603 pins, as the name suggests, this is likely to be the socket of choice for the socket-based CPUs with speeds exceeding a gigahertz.

The Chipset

A critical component of your system board is the *chipset*. Throughout the course of this book, I will be referring back to these very critical chips. Several different companies manufacture excellent chipsets, and as this book unfolds, I will make a case that the chipset, in conjunction with the CPU, makes up the "brains" of your computer, not the CPU alone. The chipset illustrated in **Figure 2.5** is one of those made by ETEQ which supports a number of onboard peripherals.

The chips that constitute the chipset are sophisticated microprocessors that are preprogrammed to handle the hardware functions of your computer. It is your

Figure 2.5   The chipset is easily distinguished by the brand name emblazoned on the chips.

chipset that will determine what speed front-side bus your computer supports. What's a front-side bus, you ask? That's a very good question, and I'll go into it in more detail in Chapter Six, Understanding CPUs. For now suffice it to say that the term describes how quickly data moves back and forth between the CPU and motherboard components.

The chipset also determines, to a very great extent, what hardware your computer is capable of supporting. For example, Rambus memory is extremely fast, but operates in a fashion completely foreign to most chipsets. You must have a chipset specifically designed to support it.

You can identify the components of the chipset more easily than most of the other chips on the board (except the CPU, of course), because the name brand will be emblazoned on each of the chips that are part of it. These brands include ALI, Intel, Opti, SiS, and VIA, among others.

BUZZ WORDS

Chipset: Two (possibly three on some older boards) ICs that provide hardware support and control all system speeds on a motherboard.

BIOS

Another chip you need to be able to recognize on sight is the BIOS chip. This stands for *Basic Input Output Services*, and along with the chipset, determines your computer's capabilities. Generally, this will be a chip that has either a foil or paper label pasted onto it with a brand name and a copyright date. This is one of the few components on your system board that you might be called on to replace, so knowing what it looks like is useful. Major BIOS manufacturers include AMI, Award, and Phoenix. The one in **Figure 2.6** is quite obviously made by Award.

Like the chipset, the BIOS will determine your computer's overall capabilities. Unlike the chipset, though, if something new comes along, most modern motherboards make it possible to replace an older version of BIOS with a newer version, thereby upgrading your system. This process is called *flashing* the BIOS.

Figure 2.6   The BIOS used to be easily recognizable. It was the one with the foil label. Modern BIOS chips aren't always so easy to identify.

ONBOARD CONNECTORS

Now let's move on to the common connectors that exist on your motherboard. Nearly all boards produced today include several different connectors where ribbon cables of varying widths can be attached. While each connector performs its own function, some commonality exists among them. For example, if you look closely at a ribbon cable, you'll see that one edge is colored, usually red or pink (**Figure 2.7**). The colored wire is the "number one" conductor.

Each of the connectors on your motherboard has an associated "number one" connector. This is always labeled in some manner. It just isn't always easy to figure out how it's labeled. Sometimes, the manufacturer will have the number "1" printed on the board next to the socket. Another equally common and easier-to-read, method is to put a white dot or triangle next to number one. One other way is to have a rectangle with one corner filled in with white. That corner indicates conductor number one. However they do it, one thing remains common. Once you've properly mounted one cable, the rest will line up in the same manner.

Figure 2.7   Ribbon cables always have one wire over which the insulating material is given a different color, usually pink or red. This denotes the number one conductor on the cable.

> **EXAM NOTE:** Get to know the various connectors very well. As with the motherboard illustration I mentioned earlier, examinees are frequently given a block of illustrations with numbered arrows and asked to identify the connector to which the arrow points.

Two of those sockets will be 40-pin connectors. These are your *Integrated Drive Electronics* (IDE) ports (**Figure 2.8**). Don't fall into the habit of calling them the IDE controllers. IDE devices, by their nature, have their own controller embedded in the device itself. The connector on the system board where you connect the ribbon cable is simply a port. There will be a Primary IDE and a Secondary IDE port. Some motherboards actually ship with four of these ports. On some versions of BIOS, putting the boot drive on the primary port is necessary, because many boards require that the bootable IDE device be the master device on the primary port. Many newer BIOS versions allow you to set virtually any device as the primary boot device. I'll discuss that in more detail in Chapter Twelve, Hard Disk Drive Structure and Geometry.

The 34-pin socket that looks very similar to the IDE ports is the floppy drive connector. There will only be one of these. Some sockets that exist on AT-style boards, but not ATX, include a 25-pin connector for your parallel port and two 9-pin connectors for the serial ports. ATX-style boards will have these ports built directly onto the back edge of the board for direct connection. Older AT boards shipped with something called a "dongle" that consisted of the appropriate ribbon cable snaking up to a backplane (one of those little metal tabs that fits into the slots in back of the computer case).

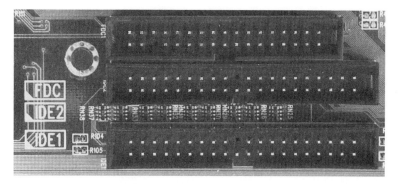

Figure 2.8   In this illustration, you can see the 40-pin connector for IDE and the 32-pin connector for the floppy drive controller side by side. On this board, they are clearly labeled. That is not always the case. Note that on each of the connectors, there is a "missing" pin. This is a null cable and not used.

Figure 2.9   This illustration shows the basic assortment of I/O connectors on the back of an ATX motherboard. Depending on brand and model of motherboard, there may be others as well. Use this illustration in the following discussions of the different connectors.

BACKPLANE CONNECTORS

I can cover the AT really quickly, because, with a few exceptions, it will have only a single externally accessible port directly embedded on the board. That will be a round 5-pin plug, about three-eighths of an inch across. That would be the AT-style keyboard connector, and the plug itself is called a DIN connector.

The I/O backplane on ATX boards (**Figure 2.9**), on the other hand, can have a plethora of connections. There will be two mini-DIN connectors, one for the keyboard and one for the mouse. These are not always as clearly labeled as one might like either. Convention places the keyboard connector closest to the edge of the case and the mouse connector toward the inside.

In addition, there will be the two 9-pin male DB connectors I discussed earlier, which are the serial ports. You might want to do yourself a favor from the start and not get into the habit of calling those ports the COM ports, as is so common. COM ports are predesignated IRQs and IO addresses. Serial ports are places to plug cables. This will be discussed in greater detail in Chapter Nine. On older PCs you may also see a 25-pin male connector. This is also a serial port. Even though it has twenty-five pins, only nine of them actually carry a signal.

The parallel port is the longer 25-pin female DB connector. It is the one with two rows of pin sockets. Also on the ATX board will be two small connectors that look like a couple of little slits, rather than plugs. These are the places to plug Universal Serial Bus (USB) devices. Few, if any, AT-class boards have the USB ports directly on the board. They generally hook up by way of a dongle that you usually have to purchase separately.

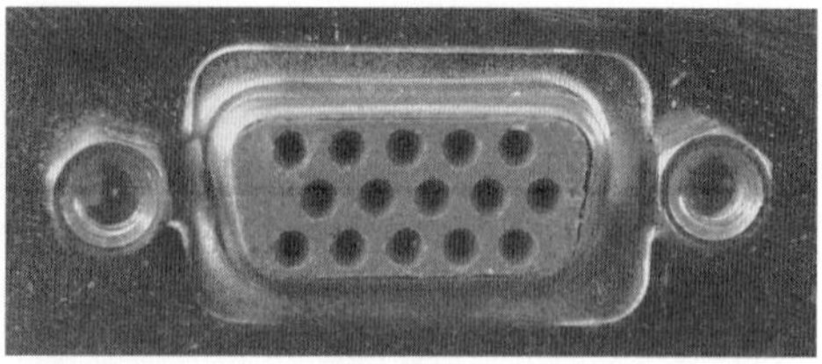

Figure 2.10 The 15-pin VGA connector is the only connector on the back of your motherboard with three rows of pins.

Those are the external peripherals that you generally will see on all ATX boards. Many boards, however, will also ship with other embedded peripherals, as well. For example, it is very common to see onboard video adapters. If so, the board will have a 15-pin female DB (**Figure 2.10**) with three rows of pins instead of the two rows we've been seeing. This is to hook up VGA (Video Graphics Array) monitors.

It's also not unusual to see onboard sound. The illustration in **Figure 2.11** is actually from a sound card, but the connectors will be the same either way. Sound cards or boards that have onboard sound will have the one-eighth-inch miniplugs for line in, microphone, and speaker out. You might also have a fourth one for line out. There is also usually a 15-pin female DB connector. This is easily differentiated by the VGA in that it is significantly longer and has only two rows of pins.

Other devices that have been known to be coupled with ATX boards include modems and network adapters. Boards that have both can cause minor confusion for the beginner because the RJ-45 connector and the two RJ-11 connectors of the modem are similar. The RJ-11s, however are the smaller ones with only four connectors. The big one with 8 connectors is the RJ-45 (**Figure 2.12**).

Figure 2.11 The outputs for sound are the same, whether they're onboard or on a separate sound card.

Figure 2.12 RJ-45 connectors look just like telephone jacks, only bigger. They feature eight connectors, but on most network interfaces only four are "live."

EXPANSION CARDS

Identifying the different boards that go into machines might take a little practice, but for the most part the ones you see will be the expansion card equivalents of some of the devices I discussed above. In addition, many proprietary devices are available only as expansion cards. The majority of cards you'll see these days will consist of PCI and AGP, with a few examples of ISA cards still running around. Chapter Nine will deal with the individual busses in great detail. For now, I'll stick to the physical characteristics.

RECOGNIZING THE BUS

All expansion cards you see today are going to fall under one of three categories. They will be ISA, PCI, or AGP. ISA is becoming more uncommon with each passing day. Later on in the book, when I discuss the expansion bus in detail, I'll cover some other types that are now obsolete. But for now, I'll only consider the ones you'll actually use in your lifetime.

PCI: Devices designed for the PCI bus, similar to the one shown in **Figure 2.13**, are easy enough to distinguish from most cards. They have an edge connector on the bottom that starts $1^3/4''$ from the backplane. The actual conductor tabs are small; twenty-two per inch to be exact. There will be a notch, $1/8''$ wide, whose center is $2^1/2''$ from where the edge connector starts, or $4^1/4''$ from the backplane. Looking from the top down, the backplane offsets to the left of the printed circuit card.

ISA: To the beginner, 8-bit ISA cards can be difficult to distinguish from PCI, but it won't take long before you can tell them apart. Compare the ISA card in **Figure 2.14** to the PCI card in Figure 2.13 and you'll see why. The edge card connector starts only $1''$ back from the backplane. The conductor tabs are quite a bit larger, allowing only ten per inch. They're nearly twice as deep as the tabs on PCI cards as well. The 16-bit ISA is a lot easier to distinguish. It has the same edge card as the 8-bit ISA, and behind that is an extension that is $1^5/8''$ long. This extension is separated by a notch that is $1/4''$ wide.

Figure 2.13   A typical PCI card.

Figure 2.14   A typical ISA card (16-bit).

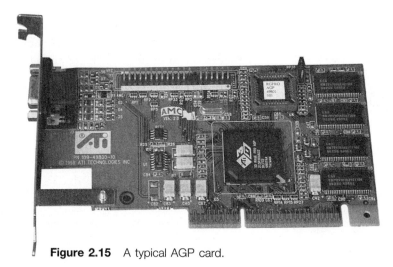

Figure 2.15   A typical AGP card.

AGP: AGP is used only for video cards like the one in **Figure 2.15**. An AGP card is easily differentiated from all other devices. The edge card sits $2^{1}/2''$ from the backplane. This makes the slot on the motherboard easy to distinguish as well. It sits farther back from the other slots on the board. The edge card is $2^{9}/16''$ wide, divided by a $^{1}/8''$ notch about a third of the way back.

TYPES OF EXPANSION CARDS

The cards you have to deal with when repairing, upgrading, or building computers may look pretty confusing at first. Fortunately for the beginner, there are relatively few types that are used on a day-to-day basis.

VGA Cards Video Graphics Array (VGA) cards are primarily available in PCI (increasingly rare) and AGP (the most common). In the event that you absolutely had to have an ISA video card, you could have a problem finding one. It has been several years since ISA video cards were produced on a regular basis. VGA cards have the same 15-pin connector shown in Figure 2.10. This is the most distinguishing mark. Some more advanced cards will also have a coaxial connector, just like the ones on your VCR, and possibly a round plug for SVHS output. I'll go over some of these different connectors in Chapter Fifteen, Your Computer and Graphics, and provide more detailed discussion as to their function.

You will also see a lot more chips on video cards than many other connectors. As with motherboards, video cards will have their own chipset. The chipset for a video card is easily recognized by the brand name etched on the chips. Typical chipsets include ATI, Cirrus Logic, S3, and several others. Also unique to the video card is a 24-pin accessory plug.

Sound Cards As far as the number of chips, sound cards can be the most sparsely populated of all. Many inexpensive cards have only two or three chips on board. The connectors are what make the sound card easy to identify. On the backplane there will be either three or four ¹/₈″ audio connectors like the one shown in **Figure 2.16**. These are simply holes in the back of the card. Another plug on the back of sound cards is a 15-pin female connector with only two rows of pins. This is typically a game port and/or MIDI (Musical Instrument Device Interface) connector.

The sound card is one of the devices most commonly built into the ATX motherboards. If this is the case, then those connectors will be a part of the motherboard and will line up to specific openings in the computer case.

Figure 2.16 A typical sound card.

Modems The modulator-demodulator, more commonly known as simply the modem, is also easy to identify. The modem is the device that converts serial data to parallel and digital signals to analog signals so that they can be sent out over a telephone wire. There are two standard four-conductor RJ-11 telephone ports on the back. These are easily seen in **Figure 2.17**. One of the ports is for the line input. The modem has to be able to dial out and bring data in. The second is for plugging a real telephone in. Most people only have one telephone jack available in the room where they keep their computers, and they don't want to sacrifice voice services for data.

Modems are another device that commonly show up on "all-in-one" motherboards. As with the sound card, you will get all of the same connections. They'll simply have a spot on the backplane of the motherboard. It is also increasingly common for a motherboard to support a modem riser. A motherboard that supports this function will have a short 46-pin slot for the riser, which may be sold separately.

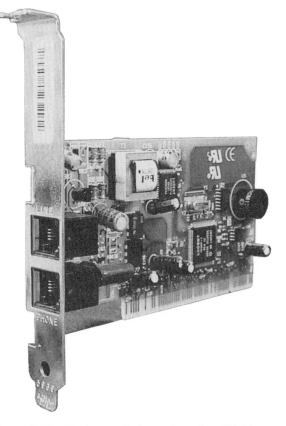

Figure 2.17 Modems will always have two RJ-11 sockets. One is to hook up to the incoming line, and the other is for your telephone.

Network Cards The network card in **Figure 2.18** is superficially similar to a modem, but not close enough to cause much confusion. The network card has a connector called the RJ-45 that resembles a telephone connector. The RJ-45 is an eight-conductor terminal that is physically larger than the RJ-11.

Older network cards might make use of something called the Bayonet Neil-Conselman (BNC) connector. This looks a little like a coaxial connector, like the one on your VCR. They differ in one major respect. The connector locks on with a twist, whereas coaxial cable has a screw-on connector. Also seen on older cards is a 15-pin Attachment Unit Interface (AUI) connector. This is a connector that can cause some confusion. It makes use of precisely the same DB-15 connector that the sound card uses for the MIDI port. There is absolutely no visible difference. When you're attempting to hook up a computer by touch, this is an easy one to mess up. Fortunately, confusing the two will do no permanent harm. The device hooked up simply won't work.

SCSI Adapters The Small Computer Systems Interface (SCSI) was invented with the purpose of hooking seemingly unlike devices together on a single chain of devices. Without prematurely worrying about precisely what SCSI means or how it works, for now lets stick to a description of what it looks like. Chapter Fourteen, The Many Faces of SCSI, has a detailed overview of the technology involved.

A SCSI adapter will usually have a 50-pin high-density connector on the back for hooking up external peripherals. Inside, depending on the type of adapter it is, it will have either one or two connectors for ribbon cables. Nearly all will have a 50-pin cable. More recent ones will also be equipped with a 68-pin or 80-pin high-density connector. These internal connectors are commonly located toward the back of the card, facing upward. Some designs have the connector facing into the computer from the back edge. Once a card is in-

Figure 2.18 While the port on a network card is similar to that of a modem, it is physically larger, with eight conductors instead of four, and there is only one place to plug a cable into.

stalled, it can be very difficult to attach a cable to an adapter of the latter design.

SCSI cards have their own BIOS chips as well. These can be identified by brand and will generally be imprinted with the version number. Some SCSI cards provide sockets for adding memory chips. The purpose of this will be discussed in Chapter Fourteen.

Specialty Cards These are rather difficult to describe, because there is a plethora of them out there, and they're all different. A few devices ship with their own hardware controller cards. Certain DVD players are examples of this. Other cards, like video accelerators, can be purchased separately and interface with an existing video card. That is the reason for the accessory plug on the video card that I mentioned earlier in this chapter.

Specialty cards can be difficult to identify if somebody simply places one in your hand and says, "What's this?" I'm including them here only as a warning that there will be some cards you'll encounter that do not lend themselves to ready identification unless you happen to either already be familiar with them from experience, or have some documentation available that describes them. Usually, there will be some form of model number etched onto the circuit board. You can use this number as a search string and look up what kind of card it is on the Internet.

THE POWER SUPPLY

That silver-colored box you see in **Figure 2.19** is usually located up toward the top of the case and to the back, or perhaps to one side in desktop designs. This is the power supply. It's what brings the juice out of the wall socket and into the computer to power everything that goes on inside. Coming out of the box will be a number of cords with two or maybe three different terminations, depending on the power supply. There is a separate section in this book on power supplies; therefore, I will discuss the finer details when the time comes. For now, I'll stick to making sure you can identify the plugs as the power plugs, the Molex, and the mini.

Figure 2.19   This ubiquitous silver box is the power plant of your computer system. Don't take it lightly.

Power supplies are made specific to their form factor. There are AT and ATX power supplies, and the two are not interchangeable. The ATX power supply will only have a single 20-pin power connector that hooks to the motherboard, usually labeled P1 (although this can vary from manufacturer to manufacturer). The AT power supply will have two 6-pin plugs for bringing power to the motherboard. These are usually labeled P8 and P9, but like the ATX connector, labeling can vary among manufacturers. It is critical that the power plugs from an AT power supply are properly oriented or you'll fry the board. The easy way to tell is that the black conductors should always be on the inside once the plugs are in place.

CAUTION: A couple of times throughout the book, I have either already mentioned, or will mention, that if you work on a computer system while it's plugged in, static electricity can drain either from the system or from your body, through the chassis and out to the ground. For the most part, this is safe enough. There is never more than 12V of low-amperage current flowing through the system even if you forget to power it off (won't do the system much good if you drop a metal part on the motherboard while it's powered up, though!)

DO NOT EVEN THINK of working on a power supply while it is plugged in. The amount of current moving across some of the circuitry is potentially lethal. If you're wearing a wrist strap, it can be worse. Most people wear the strap on their left hand, and that would direct the current right through the heart.

The plugs that bring power to internal peripherals are the Molex and the miniplug. The Molex is the larger of the two and can be recognized by the fact that two of the corners have been beveled to prevent the plug from going in backward. It has four conductors, two black and two colored. The miniswitch also has four conductors, but is substantially smaller. This plug has grooves on one side and a ridge on the other. This is the plug that powers your floppy disk drive. Some power supplies also provide a micro-miniplug for CPU fans. This is the one with only two conductors, one black and one red.

THE BOX ITSELF

Far too many people underestimate the importance of the case itself. This is one component that is frequently purchased on the basis of aesthetics rather than function. While having a pretty case is certainly important, there are other, more important factors to consider. Having a box that doesn't cut your hands to shreds every time you poke around inside is a nice feature also.

In most cases, when you select a computer case, by default you have now selected your power supply. Therefore, that is something that you need to factor into the equation. Does the case you're considering have sufficient power for your needs? Some manufacturers, on the other hand, allow you to purchase their case *sans* power supply and then select the one you need from a generous list of those available. This is a more expensive approach, but in general, not only do you have the opportunity to decide how much power you need, but the cases themselves are of better quality.

THE DRIVE BAYS

Computer cases feature both internal and external drive bays. Both are equally important. The number of drive bays that you as a user can access without opening the case varies considerably from box to box. The Micro-ATX cases so popular with the makers of those so-called Internet machines may have as few as two, while a Super Server case might have eighteen or more. As you might imagine, a Micro-ATX isn't all that good if you need to build a computer with half a dozen different drives. The following list describes the most common varieties of enclosure and how they can be recognized.

- *Minidesktop:* ~65W power supply, two 5.25″ plus one 3.5″ external drive bays and one 3.5″ internal drive bay
- *Full desktop:* 200–250W power supply, two 5.25″ plus two 3.5″ external drive bays and two 3.5″ internal drive bays
- *Minitower:* ~65W power supply, two 5.25″ plus one 3.5″ external drive bays and one 3.5″ internal drive bay
- *Midtower:* 200–250W power supply, two 5.25″ plus two 3.5″ external drive bays and two 3.5″ internal drive bays
- *Full tower:* 250–300W power supply, four to six 5.25″ plus two 3.5″ external drive bays and three to five 3.5″ internal drive bays
- *Server case:* 300–600W power supply, 10-24 5.25″ plus two 3.5″ external drive bays; rarely any internal drive bays, as it is assumed that hot-swappable devices will be employed

THE BACKPLANE

The back of the computer is the section that requires the most discussion. This is where everything hooks up. The older AT-style cases differ somewhat from the ATX cases of today, as I pointed out earlier in this chapter. The onboard peripherals I discussed when describing ATX motherboards will protrude through openings in the back of the case. While you had the motherboard in your lap it was pretty easy to pick out the VGA connector from the serial port. Now that you're leaning over the back of the box looking at everything upside down it isn't so easy, is it?

The computer in **Figure 2.20** is pretty typical for today's systems. Get to know the connectors back here so well you can identify them by touch. It makes life a whole lot easier when you're working on computers for a living. Many a time I've had to disconnect and then reconnect a computer while lying on the client's floor, all because the cables for external peripherals snaked through channels in the office furniture and/or the network cable extended about six inches from the wall. Since the cables won't stretch out to you, you have to go to the cables.

Figure 2.20 The back of your computer is where everything hooks up. Get to know it well. This particular computer is different than many in that it has two network cards.

CHAPTER SUMMARY

The purpose of this chapter is to introduce the novice to the physical components that make up a system. How these components work will be discussed in various chapters later in the book. However, being able to physically pick up a device and identify it is a basic skill that you must develop. Going back to something I said earlier, it's a very good idea for someone training to work inside of computers to get his or her hands on one or more older machines just for puttering around with. An exercise I strongly recommend is to completely dismantle a computer down to the barest essentials, then wait a day or two. After you've had plenty of time to forget what went where, go back and put it back together. But you might want to take some notes during the teardown process as to what wires went where.

BRAIN DRAIN

1. List as many onboard components as you can that will be found on both AT-style and ATX-style motherboards.

2. Now come up with as many externally accessible connectors as you can that would be found on an ATX board, but not typically on an AT board.

3. Put together a list of as many expansion devices as you can think of that would require a slot on the expansion bus.

4. From what you have learned in this chapter, what are several considerations to think about when selecting a new motherboard?

5. This task should be accomplished with a partner. Place a fully assembled computer on the table in front of you. Without looking at the back and using the sense of touch only, reach around to the back of the computer and identify as many connectors as you can.

THE 64K$ QUESTIONS

1. A key precautionary measure to take before working inside a computer system is to:
   a. Protect the carpet against dust and debris that may fall out.
   b. Protect yourself against severe electrical shock.
   c. Protect vital components from ESD.
   d. Protect the CPU from EMI.

2. Two key differences between an ATX-style motherboard and an AT-style motherboard are: (select two)

   a. Physical size of CPU sockets.
   b. The number of memory slots installed.
   c. The number of externally accessible connectors protruding from the rear.
   d. The orientation of onboard connectors and memory slots relative to the backplane.

3. On an AT-style power supply the correct orientation of the P8 and P9 connectors is:
   a. Black wires to the inside, colored wires to the outside.
   b. Black wires to the outside, colored wires to the inside.
   c. The clip holder on the P8 faces the front of the computer, while that of the P9 faces the back.
   d. It doesn't matter.

4. Modern motherboards can be adapted to new technology because they incorporate _____.
   a. Replaceable chipsets
   b. Bootblock
   c. Flash BIOS
   d. ZIP BIOS

5. A DIMM socket is equipped with _____ pin connectors.
   a. 133
   b. 168
   c. 186
   d. 184

6. The two components common to all contemporary motherboards that determine the hardware and speed capabilities of a computer are: (pick two)
   a. The CPU

b. The BIOS

c. The memory

d. The chipset

7. A 40-pin connector is the hookup for
    _____.

    a. The parallel port

    b. The floppy disk drive

    c. Serial ports

    d. The IDE port

8. A 25-pin male connector with two
    rows of male pins is _____.

    a. A serial port

    b. A VGA port

    c. A parallel port

    d. An external SCSI port

9. A 25-pin male connector with two
    rows of female pins is _____.

    a. A serial port

    b. A VGA port

    c. A parallel port

    d. An external SCSI port

10. A 15-pin female connector with three
    rows of pin sockets is _____.

    a. A serial port

    b. A VGA port

    c. A parallel port

    d. An external SCSI port

TRICKY TERMINOLOGY

Chipset: Two (possibly three on some
older boards) ICs that provide hardware support and control all system
speeds on a motherboard.

Form factor: A preconfigured size, orientation, and design layout for a particular
component used in order to assure
compatibility among manufacturers.

Expansion bus: A circuit on a motherboard
that allows accessory devices to be
added to the system. The expansion
bus straddles several of the primary
system busses.

ACRONYM ALERT

AGP: Advanced Graphics Port. A high-
speed bus designed exclusively for
graphics.

AT: Advanced Technology. A form factor
promoted by IBM in the early days of
personal computing.

ATX: Advanced Technology Extended. An
improvement of the older AT form
factor that provided greater accessibility
to components and far more efficiency
in the use of space.

AUI: Attachment Unit Interface. A 15-pin
female connector used by some early
network cards and sound cards.

BIOS: Basic Input Output System. Basic
instruction, usually (but not always)
loaded onto a Read Only Memory
chip that leads the system through the
process of startup and provides instructions as to how to communicate with
different forms of hardware.

BNC: Bayonet Neil-Conselman. A barrel-
shaped connector named after the two
engineers involved in the design.

CPU: Central Processing Unit. The
primary microprocessor on a modern
computer that is responsible for
executing programs and processing user
data.

DIMM: Dual Inline Memory Module. A
168- or 184-pin memory module that
allows the connection on either side
of the base to perform disparate
functions.

IDE: Integrated Drive Electronics. A method of managing hard drives and other devices that takes the controller circuitry off the motherboard or separate controller card and places it on the device itself.

ISA: Industry Standards Architecture. An 8- or 16-bit expansion bus designed by IBM.

PCI: Peripheral Components Interconnect. A 32- or 64-bit expansion bus designed by Intel.

SCSI: Small Computer Systems Interface. An interface that allows several different types of device to hook up to the same controller circuit.

SIMM: Single Inline Memory Module. A 30- or 72-pin memory module on which two opposing pins on the base perform the same function.

USB: Universal Serial Bus. A moderate speed bus that allows 127 devices to share a single chain and a 12Mb/s bandwidth.

VGA: Video Graphics Array. The most commonly used video display in use today.

CHAPTER 3

BASIC ELECTRICITY AND THE POWER SUPPLY

A fundamental knowledge of electricity is important if you expect to have any hope of understanding how computers work. Computers run off of electricity just like your body runs off food. Having a basic comprehension about what it is that powers your computer will accomplish two things. Hopefully, it will keep you from getting killed or seriously injured. Second, knowing how electricity works is essential in understanding how electronic signals can be used to convey information.

A+ EXAM OBJECTIVES

CompTIA exam objectives covered in this chapter include the following:

   1.1   Identify the names, purpose, and characteristics of system modules. Recognize these modules by sight or definition. (Power Supply)

   1.2   Identify basic procedures for adding and removing field-replaceable modules for desktop systems. Given a replacement scenario, choose the appropriate sequences. (Power Supply)

   2.1   Recognize common problems associated with each module and their symptoms, and identify steps to isolate and troubleshoot the problems. Given a problem situation, interpret the symptoms and infer the most likely cause. (Power Supply)

   3.3   Identify environmental protection measures and procedures, and when/how to use them.

THE BASICS OF ELECTRICITY

Electrical circuits have a number of measurable identifying characteristics. Knowing what they are, what impact they have on everything around you, and how to accurately measure them is a key ingredient to success in any field that even touches on electricity. There are three fundamental characteristics I'm going to look at in this chapter. Those are voltage, current, and resistance.

Voltage

Voltage is probably the most confusing term in electricity. Common household circuits are either 110-120V or 220V. I say 110-120, because the current we all receive from the power company is hardly pure and rarely 100 percent consistent. This is considered the acceptable range. 220V is generally reserved for the heavy-duty appliances in your house. If you have an electrical water heater, chances are extremely good it's 220V. Your computer, television, VCR, and such will invariably be 110-120V.

Voltage refers to a differential charge between two objects. So when you set up a 110V circuit, the difference between the charge in your television circuit and that of the power box is basically 110V. The technical term for this is electromotive force. This is how much electrical "pressure" you have. You measure air pressure in pounds per square inch; you measure electrical pressure in volts.

There is a common misconception that just because a circuit carries high voltage, it is dangerous. Most of the time they are. It isn't, however, the voltage that makes them dangerous. People get zapped by charges in excess of 50,000 volts on a regular basis and only jump a bit. You see, that's about how much voltage is in one of those sparks that jumps from your fingers to a brass doorknob after you walk across new carpet. But there isn't much current in that little spark.

Current

It's the *current* that will kill you. Current is measured in amperes, or more commonly, amps. It describes the flow of electrons through the medium. And it's the number of unwanted electrons in your body that makes an electrical shock uncomfortable. The static spark I described in the previous section was carried over an extremely low current.

One amp is a pretty hefty amount of current. The technical definition of one amp is equal to the transfer of one coulomb of charge per second. A coulomb is a fixed quantity of electrons—specifically, 6.26×10^{18} electrons. When that many electrons try to fit into your body all at once (especially considering your nervous system uses the transfer of electrons in order to function), there's generally a reaction.

> **Exam Note:** Make sure you can define each one of these different measurements. You aren't likely to see them all, but you can count on seeing at least one of them. The question is, which one?

Resistance

Those electrons don't just jump across the ether of nothingness, however. They have to move from one atom to the next, on down the line, until they can't move any more. Not all substances are as willing to give up the electrons they've got just so a few decillion homeless electrons can crowd their way in. When electricity, which is nothing more than an expression for the flow of electrons, encounters a substance of this nature it encounters *resistance*. A substance with a great deal of electrical resistance, such as rubber, is an *insulator*. A substance that freely contributes to the flow of electrons is a *conductor*. Most metals are good conductors.

Technically speaking, there is no such thing as a perfect conductor (although I know a few musicians who would say they've met conductors who *think* they are perfect...). Every substance known to science exhibits resistance to greater or lesser degrees. The physical number of electrons that comes out of the end of a 100-foot length of copper wire won't be the same as the number that tried to go in. A few billion filled in some areas that didn't have enough electrons to begin with (this creates something called ionization), a few billion more were sent back from whence they came.

> **BUZZ WORDS**
>
> **Resistance:** The tendency for a substance to block the flow of electrons.
>
> **Insulator:** Any substance that tends to resist the flow of electricity.
>
> **Conductor:** Any substance that encourages the flow of electricity. Also the man at the podium that waves a white stick in front of the musicians.

Likewise, there is no such thing as the perfect insulator. Even rubber allows some juice to pass. Therefore, you should not assume that, just because an electrical wire has a thick layer of insulation over it, it is safe to pick it up off your yard while standing in a mud puddle. That may well be a mistake from which you are unable to learn anything.

The measure of resistance is in a unit called an ohm (Ω). As you might imagine, voltage, current, and resistance have relationships that are meticulously intertwined. They all interact with each other, and each has an effect on the other. Ohm's Law is rather neatly described by the following three formulae.

V = IR states that Voltage is a function of Current (in amperes) multiplied by Resistance (in Ohms).

R = V/I tells us that Resistance, on the other hand, is arrived at by dividing Voltage by Current.

I = V/R is the converse of the above. In this equation, Current is derived by dividing Voltage by Resistance.

EXAM NOTE: As with the terms of measurements, you should know the three formulae listed about.

AC/DC

When it comes to electrical current, it can be either *alternating current* (AC) or *direct current* (DC). In an AC circuit, the flow of current changes direction a specific number of times each second. The number of times each second that the current changes direction is measured in hertz. When you turn on your DVD player so you can soothe your battered nerves with a couple hours of the *Matrix*, that device is plugged into a 110-120V, 60Hz AC circuit. 60Hz is pretty standard.

An AC outlet (**Figure 3.1**) in a modern building will consist of three sockets. The smaller of slotted openings is the hot lead. This is the current coming into your building from the power company. The larger slit is the return. As its name implies, this is the conductor that returns current to the power company. The rounded socket is the ground. In the event of a short circuit, the ground wire will carry unwanted current to a copper spike pounded into the ground outside the building. Under normal circumstances, there should be no measurable current on this wire.

Direct current flows in one direction only. Therefore, a DC circuit will have to deal with issues of *polarity*. The current has to flow from the positive end of the circuit to the negative side. This will be measured with little symbols. A plus sign ($\oplus$) tells you you're dealing with the positive electrode while the minus (–) indicates negative.

A computer system relies on DC current for its power. It is the job of the power supply to convert the AC current coming out of the wall socket to DC. Therefore, in truth, power supply is actually an inaccurate name for this component. It's actually a power converter. It steps the 110-120V AC current from your outlet down to 5V and 12V DC current. And there's a very good reason it has to do that.

One of the things that will repeatedly be emphasized in later chapters is just how transient the information in a computer system really is. If current is lost for as few as 7.5ns, all information stored in memory is lost as well. If AC is changing directions sixty times per second, there's a whole lot more time during the transition than 7.5ns that a RAM chip is going to be without power. You'll be losing data more than sixty times per second. Current that is delivered to computer circuits must not only be constant; it must be stable. DC is the only type of current that will work.

SPIKES AND SAGS

Just what do I mean by the current being stable? If you think back to when you went into the computer store to buy your system, the salesperson

Figure 3.1 An AC outlet consists of the hot, the return, and the ground.

BUZZ WORDS

Alternating current: An electrical current that reverses the direction of current flow many times each second.

Direct current: An electrical current that exhibits a steady directional flow from a source of relative positive voltage to a target of relative negative voltage.

Polarity: The characteristic of an electrical circuit to have one point of relative positive charge (or pole) and another point of relative negative charge (or pole).

Spike: A sudden transient increase in voltage.

Sag: A sudden transient decrease in voltage.

probably tried to convince you to purchase a surge suppressor as well. Hopefully, he or she was successful. Household current is far from pure. If it were, you would be able to say, "I have 112V coming into my house." Not 110-120. That variation would not exist. Fact of the matter is, 110-120 is only the "average" acceptable range.

A *sag* in current is when voltage takes a significant drop. This can happen as a result of many things, and in fact happens thousands of times each day. Your refrigerator goes on, voltage drops for a second or so until it stabilizes. Somebody turns on the vacuum cleaner and voltage drops.

Spikes occur when, for whatever reason, voltage suddenly increases. Lightening hitting a power line a few blocks away can cause intense voltage spikes. The refrigerator that caused that sag a few minutes ago has cooled down to the preset temperature and the thermostat tells it that it's time to shut off. For a few thousandths of a second, voltage spikes.

That's just what's going on inside your own house. There are hundreds or even thousands of houses on the grid from which you draw your power. It would be impossible for the electric company to provide pure voltage. The things you can blame them for (to a certain extent, anyway) are brownouts and blackouts. A *brownout* is a sag in voltage that lasts for more than a second or so. A *blackout* is when you lose power all together. Another outside influence that can affect the purity of electrical current is radio frequency interference (RFI), also known as electromagnetic interference (EMI). This will be discussed in greater detail in the next section.

There are a number of hardware devices on the market to protect your computer from this malfeasance. Some handle the little variations while others handle the big ones. *Surge suppressors* (**Figure 3.2**) handle the minor spikes that occur on a regular basis. They work by clamping voltage to a certain level. If a spike hits, a device called a metal oxide varistor (MOV) absorbs the differential and sends it to ground. The better ones handle bigger spikes and more of them. Each time the MOV takes a hit, a little more of its life span is used up. It's like the character in the computer games that people play. Every hit takes away some of its health points. When all the health points have been used up, the surge suppressor is no longer a surge suppressor. It's now an outlet strip that provides no protection. Get the best you can afford.

Line conditioners clean up a couple of other forms of current pollution. They deal with the sags and filter out RFI from the incoming current. In most

BUZZ WORDS

Brownout: A drop in voltage that lasts a noticeable period of time.

Blackout: A complete loss of power to an entire area.

Surge suppressor: A device that is able to filter out voltage surges and prevent them from reaching the devices plugged into their outlets.

Line conditioner: A device that is able to filter out transient noise, such as EMI, from the current.

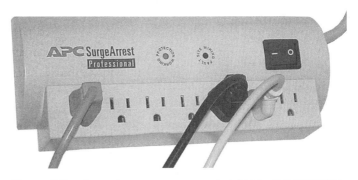

Figure 3.2 A good surge suppressor can keep your computer system alive and well even after a number of electrical spikes have come its way.

cases a good surge suppressor also has a line conditioner built in, so it is taking on both tasks.

Standby power supplies and *uninterruptible power supplies* take care of the brownouts and blackouts. They perform similar functions, just in slightly different ways. The SPS kicks in only when power is disrupted. Any other time, the computer draws its power directly from the wall. The UPS, on the other hand, provides current to the computer 100 percent of the time.

With the UPS (**Figure 3.3**), electricity comes in from the wall and passes through a rectifier circuit. A *rectifier circuit* converts the power from AC to DC. This DC current charges the batteries in the UPS. The batteries feed power to a circuit called an *inverter*, which turns it back to AC again. This AC current powers the computer. It has to revert to AC because that is the current the power supply requires. The power that feeds the computer is now filtered power. All sags and spikes have been filtered out and there is no residual EMI or RFI.

It sounds from this description like the UPS would be the only way to go, and that the SPS should have been provided a mercy death by now. In critical installations, however, this is not the case. They'll have both. The SPS is an off-line generator powered by gasoline or kerosene. It can be in another section of the building and provide current for the entire building for extended periods of time.

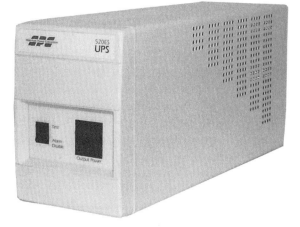

Figure 3.3 A UPS is a valuable asset for any computer, but it is essential that critical servers be equipped with one.

RFI, EMI, AND ESD

In a perfect world, electricity would be electricity, radio would be radio, and light would be light. Unfortunately, the planet earth is a miniscule speck in a universe governed by its own set of rules. Energy of all forms has a tendency to interact. Go into any physics lab and it'll have a poster of the electromagnetic spectrum hanging on the wall somewhere. One version I've seen overlaps all light waves, and magnetic, electronic, and radio frequencies onto a single chart.

I mentioned earlier that power lines could pick up radio waves the same way an antenna does. If the energy it picks up is strong enough, it will have an effect on all of your electrical appliances. For example, if you happen to live very near a transmission station for your local talk radio, you might have a hard time getting decent TV reception. Wavy lines creep all over the screen, and if it's really bad, the audio portion breaks up a bit. This is the result of Radio Frequency Interference (RFI).

RFI has some pretty nasty effects on computers and networks. If it creeps past the power supply and into the computer, it can cause some pretty oddball problems. Potentially it can cause cells within memory chips to alter their charge. This could result in corrupted data. This explains a tendency for computers in or near radio stations to lock up with far greater frequency than normal. Unshielded network cable can pick it up and start sending corrupted packets all over the place. This slows down network traffic dramatically, because all of those bad packets have to be resent.

If, for any reason, you suspect RFI to be a problem that you have to deal with, about the only solution is to invest in shielded cables. For RFI coming in off the AC, there are inline filters you can purchase at most electrical supply houses that are similar to a surge suppressor, except that they filter RFI instead of surges.

Electromagnetic Interference (EMI) is actually the same thing as RFI, except that the frequencies do not necessarily fall in the range used to transmit radio and television signals. Air-conditioning compressors generate huge amounts of EMI. Many older appliances throw out quite a bit of EMI, and your computer itself is a heavy contributor. In corporate America, a big source of EMI are the ballasts that power fluorescent lights in office buildings. When running network cable, it is essential for cable that runs through the *plenum* (that's the area between your ceiling and the floor upstairs) to be properly shielded.

In Chapter Two, The Basic Components, I introduced the concept of electrostatic discharge (ESD). It's one of the biggest thorns a technician has to deal with, because it's everywhere. You create it simply by passing through your environment. It is easy to assume that lightning storms are the biggest source of ESD, but that assumption is wrong. People are the biggest source. Every time you reposition yourself in that nice comfy fabric chair, every time you scoot your feet across the carpet, and every time you comb your hair, you generate enough static electricity to kill every chip in your computer twice over. That's why it is critical that you take steps to protect the equipment on which you work from ESD.

There are several steps you can take. If you're setting up a shop, do it right from the start. There are specially designed floor mats that drain static away, as well as bench mats. Invest in both. It's money well spent. Also, pick up a good antistatic wrist strap. These wrap around your wrist and clip to any piece of metal that goes to ground. Don't waste your money on one of those cheap plastic ones. They don't do a very good job and can be uncomfortable enough that you wind up not using them anyway.

CAUTION: When you're working on an open computer system, it is generally safe to keep the power supply plugged into the wall while you work. This keeps the system grounded and you can clip your wrist strap onto the metal chassis of the enclosure. There is very little current even when the system is turned on, and voltages are less than 12V. However, if there is any cause to work with the power supply, you should ground yourself to something other than the computer. Power supplies can deliver a shock of up to 15 amps at 110-120V. This is potentially fatal, although it generally stops at delivering a nasty shock. However, most people work with the wrist strap on their left hand. This would direct the current through the heart, greatly enhancing the chances that an electrical shock could be fatal. Also, never work on laser printers or monitors while they are plugged in. Unless you have received specific training, monitors should be left completely alone.

ELECTRICAL PARTS

This is a technical world we live in. There are a number of different electrical parts that any hardware technician must be able to recognize. There are not, however, very many in a computer (if any at all) that you would be wise to attempt to fix or replace.

Capacitors (**Figure 3.4**) are electrical storage devices that act as a sort of warehouse for electricity. Incoming electrical current charges the capacitor the way a battery charger revitalizes a rechargeable battery. The capacitor then provides current to the downstream circuit as it's needed. Capacitors also act as filters for electrical current. They are valuable components in your PC and show up all over the motherboard, and are a huge part of the reason the power supply works as well as it does. Capacitors are measured in *farads* (*f*) and *microfarads* (m*f*).

Figure 3.4 In a way, capacitors act as storage batteries for an electrical circuit.

Coils, such as the one shown in **Figure 3.5**, are another form of electrical filter. Instead of filtering out noise, spikes, and sags the way a capacitor does, it filters out AC. DC current passes through a coil with virtually no interruption. AC, on the other hand, has a really hard time getting through it. Therefore, one or more coils will generally protect any component that shows ill effect in the presence of AC current (such as a RAM stick). Coils can also be used to filter out specific frequencies below a certain range.

Diodes are very small devices that exhibit a very useful characteristic. They freely permit the flow of electrons in one direction, but act as a resistor when it tries to go the opposite way. The one-way streets found in so many downtown locations are traffic rectifiers. It isn't impossible for a car to go the

BUZZ WORDS

Capacitor: An electrical component that stores electrical current and provides it to the circuit as needed.

Farad: The major measurement of a capacitor's ability to store energy.

Microfarad: The minor measurement of a capacitor's ability to store energy.

Coil: An electrical component consisting of tightly wound wire that is used to filter out AC current and low frequency signals.

wrong way. Happens all the time. But travel is certainly restricted for the vehicle going the wrong way. Diodes are one-way streets for electrons.

Fuses really aren't used as much in computers as they used to be. Most power supplies may still have them installed. They are used to make sure that current flow in a circuit doesn't exceed a certain point. The filament consists of a conductive material that will vaporize above a certain point. Therefore, if you have a circuit protected by a 5A fuse, and something happens that causes 10A of electricity to flow, the conductor inside the fuse will vaporize and current flow will stop. If you can't see the filament inside a fuse, you can always test it with a multi-meter to see if it's good. A good fuse will generally register as 0.0000 ohms if you set the meter to impedance and put it in the range closest to the value of your fuse. It'll register infinite resistance if the fuse is blown.

Resistors are devices that resist the flow of electricity. That makes the name conveniently easy to remember. They are measured in ohms. Since they're so tiny, the manufacturers couldn't really expect to be able to print their value on the side. Therefore a color-coding scheme was adopted by the industry. The manufacturer paints little colored stripes around the outside of the tube, and as long as you've memorized the code, you can use the colored stripes to calculate the value of any given resistor. The code consists of four stripes. The first two are "significant" digits. The third stripe represents a multiplier, while the fourth indicates tolerance. In more simple terms, the first two are real numbers, 0 through 9. The third will represent a value, starting with 1 and going up in multiples of 10. 1, 10, 100, 1000, etc. Tolerance values (or the fourth stripe) will only be red, gold, or silver. You

BUZZ WORDS

Diode: An electrical component that freely permits the flow of electrons in one direction, but resists electron flow in the opposite direction.

Fuse: An electrical component that consists of a filament that vaporizes when more than a certain amount of current tries to pass.

Resistor: An electrical component that restricts the flow of current by a precisely measured amount.

Figure 3.5 Coils are useful for filtering out spurious AC as well as low frequency noise.

need to be able to determine that it's a 10,000,000 ohm, +/– 5% resistor just by looking at four colors. One of the CompTIA exam objectives is to be able to calculate the value of a resistor using color codes. **Table 3.1** outlines the industry standard color-coding scheme for resistors.

THE POWER SUPPLY

As I said before, the power supply is somewhat inappropriately named. It doesn't supply power to the computer. The power company does that. The power supply draws AC current from the wall and then converts it to something the computer can make use of—nice, clean DC current.

Table 3.1   Industry Standard Color Coding for Resistors

Color	Number	Multiplier	Tolerance Value
Black	0	1	Not Used
Brown	1	10	Not Used
Red	2	100	+/- 2%
Orange	3	1,000	Not Used
Yellow	4	10,000	Not Used
Green	5	100,000	Not Used
Blue	6	1,000,000	Not Used
Violet	7	10,000,000	Not Used
Gray	8	100,000,000	Not Used
White	9	Not Used as Multiplier	Not Used
Gold	Not Relevant	Not Used as Multiplier	+/− 5%
Silver	Not Relevant	Not Used as Multiplier	+/− 10%

Converting AC to DC

As I've already pointed out, the primary difference between AC current and DC current is that AC changes direction sixty times every second. This occasionally leads the beginner into believing that AC current does not exhibit polarity. Quite to the contrary, it is every bit as polarized as DC current. It's just that polarity is changing sixty times per second, along with current flow.

The fundamental job of a computer's power supply is to take that AC current and make it DC. There are three basic stages to that conversion that I am going to take a look at.

The first is the rectifier circuit. I covered what a rectifier circuit does earlier in the chapter. It consists of a series of diodes wired in series with one another. As I said earlier, a diode freely allows the flow of current in one direction, but resists flow in the opposite direction. If you pump AC current through enough diodes, backflow of current will cease to exist. Therefore, AC current is piped into the rectifier circuit with current flowing in both directions, trading sides sixty times a second. It comes out the other end going in only one direction.

Unfortunately, it's still pulsing at sixty cycles. This is because you've only filtered out electricity traveling in the reverse direction. There's what amounts to a "hole" in the current where it used to flow the other direction. Now you have a flow of electrons that is 120V for a few nanoseconds and 0V for a few nanoseconds. CPUs and RAM aren't going to like that any more that they would AC.

So the next step is to dump the electricity into capacitors. Since capacitors act somewhat like a storage battery, the incoming current charges the capacitor, and then the device releases

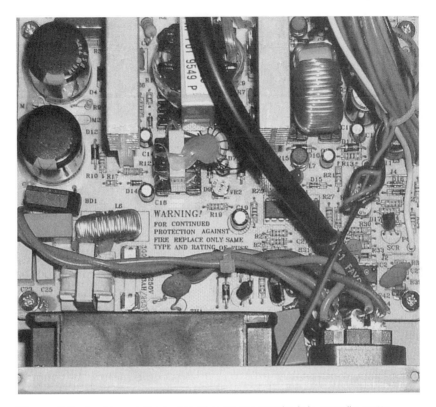

Figure 3.6 Looking at the inside of a power supply, it is actually pretty easy to see the basic components of the unit. The large cylinders are the capacitors, and the circles of coiled wire are the coils. The rectifier circuit is the only part that is not easily seen in this illustration.

current in a relatively steady flow out the other end of the circuit. **Figure 3.6** shows you what the inside of a power supply looks like.

At this point in time, you have predominantly DC current. However, even now, not all reverse flow has been completely eliminated. To filter out any residual AC current that may still exist, the current now flows through a series of coils. The nature of coils is to filter AC current, so what comes out of the power supply is now relatively clean.

AT, ATX, AND SFX POWER SUPPLIES

Currently there are only two basic types of power supplies for computer systems on the market that you'll have to deal with. Those are the older-style AT power supplies and the more recent ATX. In Chapter Two I touched on the basic differences between the two. Here, I'll go into a little more detail.

AT POWER SUPPLIES

All power supplies used in modern PCs evolved from the original PC-XT. The primary change between the XT and AT was in form factor. The PC-AT was modified in many respects for easier accessibility to internal parts. The power supply was reduced in size and redesigned to accommodate the newer case.

The first AT power supplies were 5.9″ high × 5.9″ wide × 8.35″ deep. They ranged in power from a low of about 85W to as high as 800W, with most of them being in the 200W–250W range. When the "baby-AT" form factor became popular, a power supply to fit that case became very popular. Those were 5.9″ × 5.9″ × 6.5″ in size.

The AT power supply delivers +12V, −12V, +5V, and −5V current. +/−12V isn't used for much of anything these days. Some devices made in the early days of PCs required this current, but about the only voltage used in AT-style computers now is the +5V current. The ISA bus calls for −5V to be routed through the slots, so that particular voltage is required for ISA cards. All other devices will operate off of +5V.

On the majority of AT power supplies you will only find two types of connector for powering components coming off the power supply. These will each have four conductors leading to the plug. In addition to those, there will be two power plugs for the motherboard. Generally, these are labeled P8 and P9, although a few manufacturers have deviated from that standard.

The larger of the component feeds, the one with two of the corners beveled, is called the *Molex*, after the manufacturer that developed it. These are the plugs you will use for hard drives, CD-ROMs, and other devices you install in your machine that draw their power from the power supply. **Figure 3.7** illustrates the voltages your multimeter should read were you to take a reading from the Molex. If that voltage varies by more than 10 percent, it is time to consider buying a new power supply.

There will also be a smaller plug called a *miniconnector* (sometimes there are two). The voltages of the conductors are the same as with the Molex. These smaller plugs power the floppy drives.

Coming off the power supply are two other connectors with six conductors each. These are the P8 and P9 mentioned earlier. Once again, keep in mind that some manufacturers have used their own numbering system. These plug into the power connector on the motherboard, and on AT-style

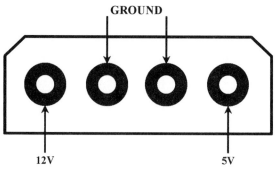

Figure 3.7   Current carried by the connectors of a Molex plug.

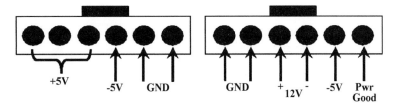

Figure 3.8 Voltage levels of conductors on the motherboard power supply cables of an AT power supply.

systems it is critical that these be plugged in correctly. The conductors carrying voltage will be brightly colored, usually shades of red, yellow, and orange. The ground cables will be black. The black ground cables must go on the inside as the connectors line up in the socket. Reversing power and ground will destroy the motherboard. **Figure 3.8** outlines the voltages coming from each conductor.

AT-style power supplies are hard-switched. By that, I mean that the on-off button on your computer case is directly coupled to the power supply. When you switch the computer on or off, you are directly interfacing with the power supply. There are three different methods that manufacturers use to provide an interface for the user. Some have a rocker switch installed directly on the power supply. It is located on the back facing of the power supply and the user turns the system on and off by reaching to the back of the machine.

This is not the most convenient approach in the world to take, and most manufacturers have moved the switch to the front of the case. On the majority of these, there is a pigtail that comes off the power supply with the switch attached to the end. This reaches around to the front of the case and couples to a button. Others keep the switch on the case and have a plastic extension arm that reaches from the button to the power supply. You see these on desktops for the most part. That particular design isn't terribly efficient to begin with and is very difficult to configure into a tower model. If you ever find yourself in the position of having to replace an AT power supply, make sure you know which type of switch you need. Otherwise, you'll be making another trip back to the store.

ATX AND SFX

Electrically, these two form factors are very similar. The primary difference is in size. The ATX is for full-size towers, midtowers, and desktops, while the SFX was designed for the micro-ATX cases. SFX cases are physically smaller and generally use power supplies that deliver lower wattages.

ATX power supplies differ from AT in several respects. A significant change is that the ATX power supply supports soft switching. By this, I mean that the power switch from your case connects to the motherboard where logic circuitry handles power functions. When you turn your ATX machine off, one of two things will happen, depending on how the BIOS is configured.

If soft power is selected in the CMOS (See Chapter Five, Motherboards, BIOS, and the Chipset), the machine will not turn off simply by your pressing the button. This prevents an inadvertent switch-off in the middle of an application. In order to turn the power supply completely off, you must hold the power button in for several seconds before the power supply will switch off.

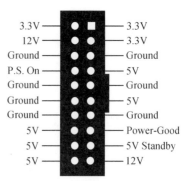

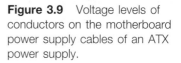

Operating systems such as Windows 9x and later take advantage of this soft power switching. When you select Shut Down from the Start menu, and then select Shut Down, your computer appears to turn off. What you really did was put it to sleep. A minimal supply of current keeps the CPU, RAM and BIOS operational.

Power management settings, both in the BIOS and in the operating system, also make use of soft power logic to control the shutdown functions of various components. Different time settings can be selected for different components, like the monitor or the hard drive, and when that amount of time has

Figure 3.9   Voltage levels of conductors on the motherboard power supply cables of an ATX power supply.

elapsed, the device turns off. However, the CPU and RAM stay active and your program will be right where you left it when you come back and reactivate your machine (usually, anyway).

Another big difference is in how the power supply hooks up to the motherboard. ATX and SFX power supplies have added +3.3V to the voltage options, and also require additional circuitry to support the soft power options. When Intel designed the ATX power supply, it also wanted to eliminate the human-error factor of feeding power to the motherboard. It replaced the P8 and P9 with a single 20-pin connector (**Figure 3.9**), which is keyed in such a fashion that it can only plug in one way.

TROUBLESHOOTING POWER SUPPLIES

Depending on how exacting you want to be, troubleshooting power supplies can either be the most difficult part of your job, or the easiest. Power supplies are like people in one respect. When they die, it's either a sudden death, or a long, drawn-out ordeal. Unfortunately, with power supplies, if it's the latter type of death, it can be a real pain to diagnose.

Many of the books I've read tell you to test a power supply by checking output voltage with a multimeter. If the voltage is plus or minus 10 percent of rated voltage, the power supply is good. I'm going out on a limb and arguing with that technique. If a power supply constantly provides output that deviates that far from the norm, it's safe to assume the power supply is dead.

The problem I see with the plus or minus 10 percent theory is that if the power supply is already that far gone, your machine is already not working and it's pretty easy to see that the power supply is the culprit. For the other 299 machines, it won't be that easy. Power supplies usually die slowly.

When this happens, output voltage will be fine 99.99999 percent of the time, and then for a few milliseconds deliver either a massive spike or a big sag. Either deviation is equally harmful. A severe spike can damage ICs on the motherboard or even drives that are plugged into it. A sag can cause memory to lose its charge, resulting in all of your RAM dumping its contents. This can result in program crashes or blue screens.

Generally if you have a machine that's been working great up until recently, and is now starting to hang a lot—or if the machine has suddenly started blue-screening on you in Windows, these may be symptoms of a failing power supply.

Blue screens are a lot more informative than many people imagine. Every time it happens, the screen provides a memory address at which the "exception" occurred, along with which CPU register was in use at the time. Any time a machine is starting to blue-screen a lot, start recording those addresses. It makes a great troubleshooting tool. I will bring this up again a couple of times in this book.

A failing power supply will generally deliver random addresses. CPU registers will rarely be the same, although since there are a lot fewer of those than there are memory addresses, you're bound to see some duplication. If it's never the same program running when the system fails, and never the same addresses, that is a strong indication of a power supply problem.

On AT power supplies, another indication of a failing power supply appears when turning the machine on for the first time in a day. If the machine routinely hangs during the POST process, but then after you turn it off and back on again, it boots fine, that's a symptom of a failing power supply. What is happening is that the capacitors in the power supply aren't charging fast enough, and a critical component in the system isn't powering up in time for POST. On the second attempt, there is more juice in the capacitors and the machine boots fine.

In theory, this isn't supposed to happen. One of the leads on the connectors powering the motherboard is the power good (PG) circuit. When the power supply is up and running, it sends a signal down the PG wire telling the motherboard that it is now okay to start the boot process. A failing power supply may start sending a PG signal before the power supply capacitors are fully charged.

The problem with failing power supplies is that they mimic the problems of other components, such as failing RAM or a bad CPU. All too often, a technician replaces the RAM, then the CPU, and then the motherboard, only to find out it was the power supply all along. I've made it a habit of keeping an AT and an ATX power supply on hand and trying that first any time my diagnostics software can't pinpoint an exact reason for the system to be malfunctioning. Pop in a new power supply and try it for a few hours. See if the problem goes away.

CHAPTER SUMMARY

The computer hardware technician doesn't need to store an encyclopedia of knowledge about electricity in his or her head. However, there are three good reasons for having a good understanding of how electricity works. First off, you need that knowledge to pass the A+ Exam. Second, that knowledge can help you troubleshoot problems that occur with computer systems. And finally—although there are some people who might consider this to be the primary reason—understanding electricity can keep you alive.

Power supplies were discussed in this chapter because they are the component that provides electrical current to all the devices in your computer. They can be very entertaining to try and troubleshoot and all but impossible to fix when they break. So if they do, just toss the old one and install a new one.

Brain Drain

1. Discuss the three primary measurements of electricity covered in this chapter and how they relate to one another.

2. Open a computer and find the following devices on the motherboard: a capacitor, a resistor, and a coil.

3. Discuss why those three components would be needed by a motherboard.

4. Jot down the color pattern you find on one of the resistors and use the chart found earlier in this chapter to calculate its value.

5. Talk about why a power supply can be such a problem to troubleshoot when it fails slowly.

The 64K$ Questions

1. Which of the following devices is used to reduce the amount of amperage on a circuit?
   a. A capacitor
   b. A diode
   c. A resistor
   d. An MOV

2. Which two of the following are critical components in converting AC current to DC current?
   a. A capacitor
   b. A resistor
   c. An MOV
   d. A coil

3. Which of the following devices would be measured in microfarads?
   a. A capacitor
   b. A resistor

   c. An MOV
   d. A coil

4. Which of the following components would be measured in ohms?
   a. A capacitor
   b. A resistor
   c. An MOV
   d. A coil

5. What device will keep an individual computer running for a few minutes after a total power failure?
   a. A surge suppressor
   b. A line conditioner
   c. A standby power supply
   d. An uninterrupted power supply

6. Which of the following devices can keep an entire room operational during a total power failure?
   a. A surge suppressor
   b. A line conditioner
   c. A standby power supply
   d. An uninterrupted power supply

7. Power is provided to the motherboard from an AT power supply by way of _____.
   a. A single 20-pin connector
   b. A pair of 8-pin connectors
   c. A pair of 6-pin connectors
   d. A single 24-pin connector

8. One feature supported by ATX power supplies that was not supported by AT power supplies was _____.
   a. The power good signal
   b. Soft-switching
   c. Built-in surge suppression
   d. Self-diagnostics circuitry

9. Which of the following could be signs of a failing power supply?

    a. Reported memory errors

    b. Intermittent "blue screens of death"

    c. Intermittent and unexpected reboots

    d. All of the above

10. It is critical that you wear your wrist strap at all times when working on a power supply.

    a. True

    b. False

Tricky Terminology

Alternating current: An electrical current that reverses the direction of current flow many times each second.

Blackout: A complete loss of power to an entire area.

Brownout: A drop in voltages that lasts a noticeable period of time.

Capacitor: An electrical component that stores electrical current and provides it to the circuit as needed.

Coil: An electrical component consisting of tightly wound wire that is used to filter out AC current and low-frequency signals.

Conductor: Any substance that encourages the flow of electricity. Also the man at the podium that waves a white stick in front of the musicians.

Current: The number of electrons that flow through a circuit in a fixed amount of time.

Diode: An electrical component that freely permits the flow of electrons in one direction, but resists electron flow in the opposite direction.

Direct current: An electrical current that exhibits a steady directional flow from a source of relative positive voltage to a target of relative negative voltage.

Farad: The major measurement of a capacitor's ability to store energy.

Fuse: An electrical component that consists of a filament that vaporizes when more than a certain amount of current tries to pass.

Insulator: Any substance that tends to resist the flow of electricity.

Inverter: A device or circuit that converts DC current to AC current.

Line conditioner: A device that is able to filter out transient noise, such as EMI, from the current.

Microfarad: The minor measurement of a capacitor's ability to store energy.

Miniconnector: A smaller four-pin connector coming off a power supply that delivers current to devices such as floppy disk drives.

Molex: The larger four-pin connector coming off a power supply that delivers current to devices such as CD-ROM drives or hard drives. Technically speaking, it is the name of the company that invented the plug.

Plenum: An architectural term referring to the space between the ceiling of one floor in a building and the floor of the one above it.

Polarity: The characteristic of an electrical circuit to have one point of relative positive charge (or pole) and another point of relative negative charge (or pole).

Rectifier circuit: A specialized series of components that converts AC current to DC current.

Resistance: The tendency for a substance to block the flow of electrons.

Resistor: An electrical component that restricts the flow of current by a precisely measured amount.

Sag: A sudden transient decrease in voltage.

Spike: A sudden transient increase in voltage.

Standby power supply: A device that uses a generator to provide electrical current to a room or building in the event of a total power failure.

Surge suppressor: A device that is able to filter out voltage surges and prevent them from reaching the devices plugged into its outlets.

Uninterruptible power supply: A device that uses batteries to provide electrical current to another device in the event of a total power failure.

Voltage: The difference in charge between two objects or surfaces. This is sometimes referred to as electrical pressure.

ACRONYM ALERT

AC: Alternating Current. Current that reverses direction many times in a second.

DC: Direct Current. A unidirectional current that flows from the positive side of the circuit to the negative side.

MOV: Metal Oxide Varistor. An electrical component that can absorb abrupt spikes in current.

SPS: Standby Power Supply. A device that uses a generator to continue to provide power to an entire room or building after a total loss of electricity.

UPS: Uninterruptible Power Supply. A device that uses a bank of batteries to continue to provide current to the devices plugged in when there has been a total loss of electricity.

CHAPTER 4

COMPUTER ENCLOSURES

Okay, you've made the decision. You're going to build your own computer from the ground up. You've put together a list of components and you're ready to go shopping. The biggest problem you face is budget. You want to build the ultimate power station, but your pocketbook has other ideas. All too often, the first component that designers look to in order to shave a few bucks off the bottom line is the enclosure.

For a low-end machine that will never do much more that format a few letters to Mom and spend a couple of hours a day browsing the Internet, an inexpensive case might just be the solution. Conversely, a system being designed with the idea of future expansion in mind will suffer greatly from an inferior case. As this chapter unfolds, I'm going to make the case (sick pun intended) that the enclosure (**Figure 4.1**) should really be the first component you decide upon when designing a system.

The enclosure truly needs to follow the concept of "form follows function." Computer cases perform several functions. First and foremost, they house the components that make up your system. But their job doesn't end there. They also do all of the following:

- Act as the interface between the system and peripherals
- House the power supply that keeps your system fed with energy
- Direct the flow of fresh air over internal components
- Provide user access to all internal components
- Provide adequate space for future expansion
- Reflect the designer's aesthetic taste

That's a load of responsibility to place on the component you are most likely to try and skimp on, isn't it? A good understanding of how computer enclosures are designed can go a long

Figure 4.1 The computer enclosure isn't just another pretty face. This important component has several key functions to perform.

way in helping you make an informed decision. There is really only one stated CompTIA exam objective that is touched on in this chapter. Despite that, there are a few issues I'll point out as the chapter unfolds.

A+ Exam Objectives

There is only one CompTIA exam objective introduced in this chapter:

   1.1   Identify the names, purpose, and characteristics of system modules. Recognize these modules by sight or definition.

Form Factor

Form factor is a term that defines the physical layout of a specific component. Form factor is not the exclusive domain of the enclosure. The motherboard and computer enclosure must share the same form factor or they won't work together. Aspects of form factor that the motherboard and enclosure must agree upon include:

- Physical size and logical orientation of motherboard within the enclosure
- Physical and electrical design of the interface between the power supply and the motherboard
- Interface between the power switch and system board (or power supply, in the case of older designs)
- Size and shape of the circuit board used to manufacture the motherboard
- Positioning of screw holes used to position the motherboard (and other components)
- Positioning of externally accessible motherboard components to the enclosure's backplane

There are some aspects of form factor that are the exclusive domain of the enclosure. These features do not affect the choice of motherboard used, beyond the parameters listed above. These include whether the case is a desktop or tower model and which of several relative sizes the case happens to be. The various case sizes and configurations were covered in Chapter Two, The Basic Components.

In the early years of personal computing, there was little or no agreement on any of these issues. Shortly after the release of the IBM PC in 1981, the market was flooded with PC clones from a variety of manufacturers. While there were similarities among the different brands, they weren't similar enough that one manufacturer's motherboard could be used in another's case. Starting with the release of the PC-AT, IBM published standards for other manufacturers to follow, and the AT form factor was born, the first standardized form factor to be adopted by a large number of different manufacturers. Since then, there have been a large number of form factors over the years. Some were more readily accepted by the industry than others. The majority of issues directly related to form factor are more commonly associated with motherboard design than with cases. Therefore a detailed discussion of the different form factors will be reserved for Chapter Five, Motherboards, BIOS, and the Chipset. For now, I will simply list some of the more common form factors, along with a brief description.

- *PC/XT:* Very little consistency or compatibility among manufacturers. Cases large, heavy, and bulky.
- *AT/Baby AT:* IBM defined strict standards for orientation of components of the motherboard, as well as placement for mounting screws. AT defined a 12″ width for the board. Length varied, but averaged around 13″. Baby AT boards were reduced to an 8.5″ width, allowing for smaller cases. Power switches connect directly to the power supply and power to the motherboard is routed through a pair of 6-connector plugs. The only externally accessible port on most AT-style boards is a full-sized 6-pin DIN (short for Deutsches Institut fur Normung) keyboard connector.
- *ATX/Mini ATX:* Overall size varies from manufacturer to manufacturer, but placement of screws is consistent. Motherboards are rotated 90º in relationship to I/O slots. The power switch connects to the motherboard rather than the power supply, and power management is a function of the motherboard. Electricity is fed to the motherboard through a keyed 20-pin connector. A variety of ports are externally accessible, including built-in serial and parallel ports, onboard sound, and, in many cases, onboard video.
- *LPX/Mini LPX:* LPX is an acronym for Low-Profile Extended. In order to reduce space, expansion slots are taken off the motherboard. Instead, a single slot exists on the motherboard onto which a riser card is installed. This riser card holds the expansion slots and cards are installed parallel to the motherboard. As with ATX, a variety of common ports are built onto the board and are externally accessible. Power switching and feed to the motherboard were frequently proprietary designs, and there was little compatibility among manufacturers.
- *NLX/Mini NLX:* This is short for New Low-Profile Extended. This form factor is an evolution of LPX. Intel has attempted to standardize a form factor based on the concept of the riser.
- *ITX:* If it's an acronym, VIA, the company that developed the form factor, isn't telling us what it means. It's a computer in a shoebox. All system components fit into a very small enclosure. Most system components, including sound, video, modems, NIC, the CPU, and many others, are soldered right onto the system board

EXAM NOTE: While CompTIA includes form factor as an objective covered in the Motherboard domain, it should be clear by now that form factor is not exclusive to motherboards. There are questions in the database that relate to the form factor of enclosures as well.

STRUCTURE OF THE ENCLOSURE

While the structure of a computer case can vary widely among manufacturers and among form factors, there are certain necessary commonalities. For the purposes of this discussion, I'll be looking at a typical ATX midtower enclosure.

THE FRAME

The key to making a cheap computer case is making a cheap *frame* (**Figure 4.2**). By using thinner-gauge substrate material and streamlining the manufacturing process, manufacturers can shave quite a few dollars off the bottom line. What kind of impact does this have on the final product? Nothing is lost in terms of overall system performance. Therefore, cheap cases make for improved cost/performance ratios. These shortcuts lead to other types of problems later on down the road, however.

There are two metals commonly used to manufacture computer cases these days. For years, steel has been the material of choice. In recent years there has been a surge in the popularity of cases made of aluminum. Both materials have their advantages and their disadvantages.

Plain old steel is substantially less expensive than aluminum. It is also easier to shape, drill, and cut. One quality of steel that should be carefully considered in some situations is that it is far more efficient than aluminum in blocking EMI (see Chapter Three, Basic Electricity and the Power Supply). On the downside, steel cases are heavier and, well, face it, they're just plain ugly! Steel cases are generally resplendent in fancy plastic faceplates and paint jobs that completely conceal the frame itself. In general, the sheet metal used in manufacturing steel cases is measured in thickness. The term used is *gauge*. When measuring gauge, smaller numbers mean thicker steel. For example, 14-gauge is thicker than 18-gauge.

Now, a nice brushed aluminum enclosure needs no cosmetic embellishments. Elegant—almost stately—appearance is combined with lighter weight for an appeal that's hard to resist. Add to that the fact that aluminum dissipates heat much more efficiently than steel, and it becomes

Figure 4.2   With the varnish and plastic veneer stripped away, the enclosure frame is a one-piece metal bracket for holding the rest of the system together.

a natural material for today's multi-gigahertz systems equipped with tons of peripherals. The downside is primarily cost. Aluminum is much more expensive than steel. To offset some of this cost differential, many manufacturers create shortcuts in their manufacturing process.

CASE COVERS

The actual covers that allow access to the interior of a computer enclosure, such as the one in **Figure 4.3**, tend to draw as much attention as any other feature. There are good reasons for that. They're like the front door to your house. A beautifully designed entrance with elegance in both form and function draws positive comments. If someone trips over a jutting transom and breaks an arm, the comments tend to run to the contrary.

Different styles of enclosures require different approaches to opening them. Manufacturers frequently like to camouflage cover screws or access latches. They think that somehow these relatively important components of a computer case detract from the design, and they go to great lengths to hide them.

I was once working on a rack-mount server that completely baffled me. There were no apparent screws to hold the cover on anywhere to be seen. On the surface of the top cover was a series of wide V shapes that appeared to be pointing to the back panel of the system. After puzzling over this enclosure for far more time than it deserved, I brought in a couple of my coworkers to see if they had serviced this particular model. It was brand new and they hadn't seen it yet either. Neither one of them had any better luck than I had.

We finally swallowed our pride and called tech support for that particular manufacturer. We were directed to two panels on the front of the case. They had to be pried off with a flat-blade screwdriver. When removed, they revealed two screws. Once these screws were removed, the top panel slid forward. The V shapes on the top panel meant nothing. They were only there for aesthetic reasons. (And to confuse technicians!) Once the panel was removed, taped to the inside of the top panel were instructions on how to open the case!

Fortunately, most enclosures will follow one of the following standardized designs. Some of them require the correct screwdriver for the job while others are "tool-free."

The U-shaped (**Figure 4.4**) design can be found in both desktop and tower models. It consists of a single cover for the top

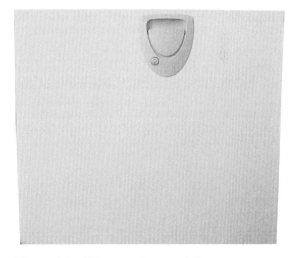

Figure 4.3 This cover from an Antec case illustrates beautiful execution of both form and function. A single latch holds it in place. Opening the case is simply a matter of lifting up on the handle, but the hinged mechanism makes sure the fit is smooth and secure.

and both sides. On either the front or the back of the cover will be a lip that wraps around the frame. Designers frequently incorporate some form of tongue-in-groove mechanism to assure that the cover securely fits over the frame. If you don't get these properly aligned, the cover will not fit over the frame. Generally, if the case screws fit onto the back of the case, they will be in plain sight. Front-mounted covers hide the screws behind the faceplate, so it must be removed prior to removing the cover.

Some of the more proprietary designs (especially the older LPX and some current NLX cases) rely on a complex tongue-in-groove fit with only a single screw holding the cover in place. Then the manufacturer hides the screw. Once again, if the screw is on the back, it will usually be in plain sight. Front-mounted screws might be behind a removable faceplate, but don't count on it. If there doesn't appear to be any logical method of removing the faceplate, start looking for small panels on the front cover.

The majority of current enclosures utilize side panels as covers. Some provide access only to the top surface of the system board. This is generally adequate as long as drive bays are removable (more on that later). Others have both left and right side panels.

Figure 4.4 The U-shaped cover is gradually giving way to single access panels. Still, there are a number of manufacturers that use this design for both desktop and tower models.

A NOTE ON SELECTING ENCLOSURES

Several enclosure manufacturers have lately been cashing in on the newest fad that entails putting a computer into a "custom" case. Of course, since their cookie cutters are stamping out several hundred copies of each so-called custom enclosure each day, it doesn't really seem right to call them custom, does it? Before shelling out two to three times as much for one of these computer cases as you would for a more conventional design, there are a couple of things to consider. Cost is obviously one of them. If your pocketbook is deep enough that you can afford to spend that much money just for cosmetics, that won't be an issue. One thing that is definitely an issue, however, is the ability of some of these cases to block EMI. Many of them include little windows so you can peek in and see the lovely components that make up the computer. They even include colorful cables, lighted fans, and case lights to add to the effect. These windows don't just let light pass. They are also a gateway for EMI. Your computer becomes a source of EMI that can affect other computers in the area as well as other electronic components such as television sets and radios. The lights themselves emit a certain amount of EMI, although probably not enough to affect the system, but they also add more heat to the inside of the enclosure that must be dissipated.

These panels will either be affixed with screws or by one of several tool-free designs. Some manufacturers use thumbscrews that, as long as they aren't tightened down too aggressively, can be removed without a screwdriver. With other designs, you never know from model to model whether you need a flathead screwdriver, a Torx, or a Phillips.

The more pleasant enclosures to work with are the tool-free designs. A single latch, or in some U-shaped designs, a latch on either side, holds the cover in place. Release the latch and lift the cover off.

TEMPERATURE CONTROL

Today's high-performance components generate much more heat than did the computers of yesteryear. In the old days, a single fan in the power supply and some strategically located ventilation holes were all that was needed to keep a computer running cool. These days computers need much more. The enclosure used for **Figure 4.5** comes standard with two case fans and has room to install two more.

The power supply fan continues to be a key component in temperature regulation. But it needs a lot of help. Nearly all CPUs these days must be equipped with an appropriate heat sink/fan combination. The more recent releases of chipsets have started running so hot that they are coming equipped with heat sinks as well. High-end video cards also now need heat sinks and fans to keep them running cool.

All that heat has to go somewhere. A decent case will come with at least one auxiliary case fan to supplement the power supply fan. The case fan blows cool air in and the power supply fan evacuates hot air. Some models of enclosure allow up to six fans, or even more, to be added as options.

Two other features of case design that were not simply added to make the case prettier are the ventilation holes (**Figure 4.6**) and the backplane fillers (**Figure 4.7**). The ventilation holes generally are designed to work with the case fan to provide more efficient heat dissipation than the power supply fan alone can provide. Backplane fillers make sure air follows the path the designers intended it to follow. When you remove an expansion card from your computer, make sure you install a filler to cover the empty slot opening. Otherwise air

Figure 4.5 Modern enclosures generally provide at least one case fan to supplement the fan in the power supply. This particular case ships with two fans installed and has room for two more.

Figure 4.6 Ventilation holes are not simply there to add aesthetic appeal. This is where cool air can get sucked into the interior of the case. This example, shown with the front panel removed, shows how these holes can serve double duty. I don't know if the detail will survive reproduction, but in the original image, you can see that the PC speaker projects its sound through these same holes.

from the case fan may simply exit through the backplane without ever passing over critical components, such as CPUs and chipsets. This defeats the purpose of having the extra case fan to begin with.

DRIVE BAYS

Every enclosure sold comes with a certain number of spaces designed for the installation of additional devices (usually disk drives of some sort). These are the *drive bays*. Drive bays come in two forms: accessible and hidden. Another set of terms frequently used is internal and external drive bays. They also come in two sizes: $3^1/2''$ and $5^1/4''$. With most modern enclosures it is safe to say that all $5^1/4''$ drive bays are externally accessible. There will generally be at least one $3^1/2''$ bay that is accessible as well as one or more $3^1/2''$ drive bays that are hidden.

The $5^1/4''$ drive bays found in conventional computer cases are referred to as *half-height* drive bays. A half-height bay is 1.62″ in height. $3^1/2''$ drive bays are nearly always 1″ high. **Figure 4.8** clearly shows the difference in size. The term half-height is a throwback to the early years of computing technology when a hard disk drive was 8″ wide × $3^1/2''$ high.

Figure 4.7 The function of the backplane filler is to keep dust out and to regulate airflow within the enclosure. If for any reason you remove an expansion card, make sure that you insert a new filler.

BUZZ WORDS

Drive bay: A metal frame within a computer enclosure (that may or may not be removable) that supports disk drives.

Full–height bay: A term that describes a disk drive that is $3^1/2''$ from top to bottom.

Half–height bay: A term that describes a disk drive that is 1.62″ from top to bottom.

Figure 4.8   Here is a half-height drive seen side by side with a 1″ high drive. There are still some tape drives on the market that are full-height. These drives take up two of your 5¼″ bays.

Sometimes you might run into a situation where all available 3½″ accessible drive bays are filled and you have just acquired a new device that needs to be installed. Don't panic. There are step-down adapters that securely fit 3½″ drives into 5¼″ bays. Some device manufacturers are even kind enough to provide one with the new drive. If not, they're generally available for around five dollars at most computer stores. Another thing to look for is removable hard drive bays. Fixed bays, such as the ones seen in **Figure 4.9**, make it very difficult to swap and/or install new drives.

Some server models incorporate hot-swappable drive bays. A *hot-swappable* bay will be an externally accessible 5¼″ drive bay that is specially designed to allow a disk drive to be removed while the computer continues to run. The drives themselves must be mounted in a hot-swap frame to accommodate the enclosure's drive bay. This type of drive bay can add considerable cost to the case. But for a server designed to run 24/7 they are an essential addition.

Drive rails are frequently incorporated into the drive cage structure as a replacement for screws to hold drives in place. Drive rails are available in two different incarnations. There are those whose rail guides simply snap into place on the sides of the drive and those that need to be screwed on. Once the rail guides are in place, you simply line the guides up to the rails and slide the drive in until it snaps into place.

I say "simply," but this is an area where the concept of fit really comes into play. If alignment

> **BUZZ WORDS** ————
>
> **Hot swap:** The ability to replace or remove a device from a computer system without having to shut the system down.
>
> **Drive rails:** Devices that attach to the side of a disk drive that allow the user to install or subsequently remove it without needing any tools.

between the rails and the guides is even the tiniest fraction of an inch off, properly mounting the drive becomes a chore. This is rarely a problem with the major manufacturers, but can become an issue when price is the overall design parameter.

Figure 4.9 The number of drive bays in this enclosure allows for a great deal of expansion. However, the fact that all drive bays are fixed, increases the complexity and difficulty of mounting a new device.

Navigating the Front Panel

The front of most enclosures will be adorned with buttons and lights. Some manufacturers prefer to keep it simple, like the one in **Figure 4.10**, while others seem to be competing with your neighbors for the annual Christmas display award.

There will generally be two switches on the front of your case. Some older enclosures feature a third. The two main ones are Power and Reset. Power, as its name implies, provides the means for turning your computer on and off. Reset provides the means for restarting your computer when it locks up.

The third button occasionally seen on older computers is the Turbo button. This may well be the most inappropriately named component in computer history. On those computers where it performs any function at all, its function is to slow the speed of the CPU down to 8MHz. Some earlier software, especially games, was designed with a specific CPU in mind. A faster machine made your game run too fast. Once you pressed Start, before you could even react, your car, or your spaceship, or whatever, had already crashed at the other end of the course. So the Turbo button was really a brake pedal. These days, algorithms within the software automatically detect system speed and make the appropriate adjustments. This button has disappeared from most machines.

Figure 4.10 The front panel of most enclosures is designed with simplicity in mind.

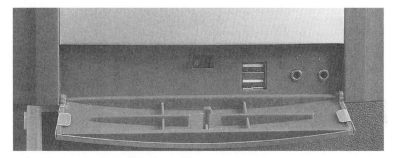

Figure 4.11 This particular enclosure sports sound ports and USB ports accessible from the front, but hidden by a flip-down door when not in use.

At a minimum, your enclosure will have two LEDs on the front of the case. One is the power indicator and the other is the hard drive activity light. Properly hooked up, the power indicator provides a steady glow whenever power is applied to the machine. The hard drive activity light flickers whenever the hard disk is active. Wiring them backward does no harm. Simply tell people you have a very erratic power source coming into your house and that your hard drive is always active.

It is becoming more and more common to see other amenities moved to the front of the case for the sake of convenience. In the example shown in **Figure 4.11**, sound and USB ports are accessible from the front.

Another feature found on some, but not all, enclosures is a key lock. When enabled, a key lock allows you to secure your system from casual unauthorized access. When somebody tries to power up a system that is locked, this condition is detected during the boot process and the system won't boot. Before you get lulled into a false sense of security, however, you should be aware that disabling the key lock is simply a matter of unplugging one pair of wires from the motherboard.

The Back Panel

The back panel of a computer is less familiar to many users simply because, well, it's on the back! Whoever looks there except computer technicians? Most of what you see on the back is actually not related directly to the enclosure. The power supply will have one or possibly two switches, and any expansion cards that have external ports can be accessed here. These will be discussed in the appropriate chapters in this book. Before those accessories are added, the back of the case will be very similar to what you see in **Figure 4.12**.

The things that I'll be examining that are related to the enclosure are mostly structural. Different form factors will have different features.

On older PC/XT- and AT-style enclosures, there were punch-outs for DB9 and DB25 connectors. These allowed the more conscientious manufacturer to properly mount the serial and parallel ports on the back panel in a location that was easier for the end user to access. Most manufacturers simply used multi-IO cards, so these punch-outs were rarely used.

ATX, LPX, and NLX motherboards sport all of these peripherals, and usually several others, as integrated features of the circuit board. These protrude through a single rectangular opening on the back of the enclosure. To control airflow, these ports line up to an I/O template that fills this opening.

Expansion cards installed on the motherboard need a slot that allows access to any ports they sport. Along the backplane are a number of removable covers, one for each expansion slot. In order to install an expansion card, you remove the backplane cover for the appropriate slot, mount the card, and screw the backplane of the expansion card into place.

Figure 4.12 Once a computer has been assembled, the back panel can be a fairly complex forest of ports. Before assembly, it's a featureless plane.

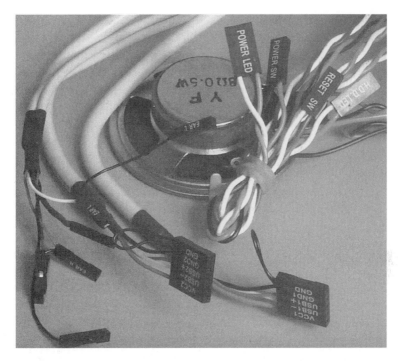

Figure 4.13 The wiring harness of many enclosures can make you think you're trying to manage a pot of boiled spaghetti. Most enclosure manufacturers are kind enough to label each lead. Unfortunately, not all motherboard manufacturers show the same courtesy.

In the old days, these backplane covers were nicely machined and shaped strips of metal that screwed into place when there was no expansion card installed. A recent development in the industry that I find distressing is an increasing propensity to cover unused slots with metal punch-outs. When it comes time to install a new device, the technician must knock out the cover for the chosen slot. Should it become necessary to uninstall that device, the old cover cannot be reused.

THE WIRING HARNESS

Earlier in the chapter, while discussing the front panel, I provided a tour of the various switches and LEDs adorning the front of the computer. For those to properly function, there must be some way of interfacing these devices with the system. That imposing cluster of wires dangling from the inside of the front panel (**Figure 4.13**) is that way.

Usually, the leads to each wire are clearly labeled as to what device they hook up to. At least it is clear as long as you understand the abbreviations that most manufacturers use. The most commonly seen leads include:

- PWR – Power
- RST – Reset
- SPK – Speaker
- TRB – Turbo (when present)
- HDD – Hard drive LED

On the motherboard, there will be wiring pins associated with each of these wires. Usually, these jumpers are labeled with similar abbreviations, so it's pretty easy to tell what wire goes where. Unfortunately, there are manufacturers to this day that give the motherboard informative labels such as J-11, J-12, J-13, and so on and so forth. When you stumble across one of these boards, have the manual ready.

CHAPTER SUMMARY

Hopefully, by now you understand that the computer enclosure is not just another pretty face. It not only has to provide a secure and safe environment for your system components, it has other tasks to perform as well. It must block spurious EMI, provide a path for cool air from the outside to follow across heated components, and provide safe and convenient access to the inside.

When shopping for a new enclosure, you'll find that enclosures range in price from under $20 to well into four digits. There are many reasons for this disparity in price. These include the type and gauge of materials used in the manufacturing process, the size of the enclosure, the number of drives, and the type of drive bays used.

Another key component housed in the enclosure that frequently ships already installed is the power supply. This was discussed in detail in Chapter Three, Basic Electricity and the Power Supply, and I did not feel it was necessary to repeat that material. The point I'm making here is that, if the overall cost of your enclosure includes a power supply, you need to ask a critical question. Is it possible to get the quality of enclosure that is required along with the quality of power supply needed for the price that the manufacturer is asking? Can a $20 case, with a 300W power supply, really be of sufficient quality?

I suppose that all goes back to a key question you should always ask before building your own computer. What is the computer going to be used for? For the Internet surfer who fires up a word processor once every six months, whether he or she needs to or not, very likely the answer will be yes. That person is unlikely to be going in and out of the case a lot, adding drives and experimenting with new toys several times a month. But for a server or a more powerful and/or complex workstation, such as a gaming box or an audio/video workstation, you'll probably want to invest a bit more into this very critical component.

BRAIN DRAIN

1. Discuss why the computer enclosure might be the first decision a designer makes when putting together a new model of computer.

2. What are the critical functions that a computer enclosure must successfully perform?

3. What are the pros and cons of using aluminum versus steel in designing a computer case?

4. Discuss some of the pitfalls of selecting an inferior enclosure.

5. List as many individual components that make up the enclosure as you can think of.

THE 64K$ QUESTIONS

1. Which of the following is a low-profile form factor?
    a. AT
    b. ATX
    c. LBX
    d. Desktop

2. LBX cases differ from ATX cases primarily in that ____.
    a. They use a different connector for motherboard power.
    b. LBX cases use a unique power supply.
    c. LBX cases were only available in desktop designs.
    d. LBX was designed around the concept of a riser that supported all the expansion cards.

3. An advantage of aluminum over steel in enclosure construction is _____. (Choose all that apply.)
    a. Light weight
    b. Blocks EMI better
    c. Easier to machine
    d. Dissipates heat better

4. 24-gauge steel is 33 percent thicker than 18-gauge steel.
    a. True
    b. False

5. Failing to replace the backplane filler after removing an expansion card is not a good idea, because _____.
    a. It disrupts air flow inside the case.
    b. It releases more EMI.
    c. It allows dust to get inside the computer case more easily.
    d. All of the above.

6. Internal (hidden) drive bays are almost always _____.
    a. $5^1/4''$ half-height bays.
    b. $3^1/2''$ half-height bays.
    c. $1''$ half-height bays.
    d. $3^1/2''$ 1-inch height bays.

7. Hot-swappable drives are designed to fit into a ____ bay.
    a. $5^1/4''$ half-height
    b. $3^1/2''$ half-height
    c. $1''$ half-height
    d. $3^1/2''$ 1-inch height

8. Which of the following are buttons that can be found on the front of an older AT-style case? (Choose all that apply.)

a. Power

b. Voltage Select

c. Reset

d. Turbo

9. Which of the following is not likely to be a part of a typical wiring harness found in an enclosure?

a. PWR

b. RLL

c. RST

d. HDD

10. Which of the following is a good feature of an enclosure?

a. Stamped metal structure

b. Removable drive cages

c. 28-gauge steel frame

d. tongue-in-groove covers

TRICKY TERMINOLOGY

Drive bay: A metal frame within a computer enclosure (which may or may not be removable) that supports disk drives.

Drive rails: Devices that attach to the side of a disk drive that allow the user to install or subsequently remove it without needing any tools.

Form factor: Preset design specifications regarding size, orientation of components, and screw positions that allow different manufacturers' motherboards to fit into other manufacturers' enclosures.

Frame: The metal skeleton that provides the primary support for a computer enclosure.

Full-height bay: A term that describes a disk drive that is $3^1/2''$ from top to bottom.

Gauge: A measurement of the thickness of a substance such as sheet metal or wire. Larger numbers indicate smaller sizes.

Half-height bay: A term that describes a disk drive that is 1.62″ from top to bottom.

Hot swap: The ability to replace or remove a device from a computer system without having to shut the system down.

ACRONYM ALERT

LPX: Low-Profile Extended. A form factor designed to take up a minimum of desktop real estate that puts the expansion slots onto a single riser card that supports the cards parallel to the motherboard. Most LPX designs were proprietary.

NLX: New Low-Profile Extended. An industry-supported form factor that took the concept of the riser card, but established strict standards for development.

CHAPTER 5

MOTHERBOARDS, BIOS, AND THE CHIPSET

The motherboard may well be the most complex device in the entire computer system. Since it controls everything that goes on in the computer, that shouldn't be much of a surprise. Just how complex is it? Take a look at the circuit board itself. It looks like a single thick layer of fiberglass. In reality, a motherboard consists of four to eight layers of substrate. Each of these layers acts as a surface upon which the engineers can apply traces.

Traces are those copper paths that cover the front and the back of the motherboard in pretty geometric patterns. Now examine all the chips, slots, switches, jumpers, sockets, capacitors, resistors, and so on and so forth. All of those have to be interconnected to the components with which they interact. That is the function of those traces. The reality of the situation is that there are far too many traces on a motherboard to apply to a single layer. Therefore, the traces you see on the front and back of a four-layer motherboard constitute approximately half of the total number of traces present on the motherboard. The remainder are applied between the layers.

In Chapter One, PC Basics, I talked about the five primary busses of the computer system. These traces are the physical implementation of those busses on the motherboard. The job of the motherboard is to integrate these five disparate functions into one. Each component of the motherboard is directly soldered to the appropriate traces, at whatever layer they reside, and connected to one (or more) of the five busses. Motherboard manufacturers have some very sophisticated manufacturing processes that they use to make the solder connections. All of the devices that are connected to the computer, either through ports on the back of the PC or through the various connectors on the motherboard, link either directly or indirectly to the motherboard in some fashion. If they didn't, they wouldn't be able to communicate with the rest of the computer.

BUZZ WORDS

Trace: The fine copper path seen on printed circuit boards that acts as a conductor for a signal.

A+ EXAM OBJECTIVES

There's going to be a lot of material covered on the exam in this chapter, and if you're perusing the objectives lists too superficially, some of them might not strike you as being related to this chapter. In this chapter, I will either introduce or discuss in detail the following objectives:

1.1 Identify the names, purpose, and characteristics of system modules. Recognize these modules by sight or definition.

1.2 Identify basic procedures for adding and removing field-replaceable modules for desktop systems. Given a replacement scenario, choose the appropriate sequences (System Board).

1.5 Identify the names, purposes, and performance characteristics of standardized/common peripheral ports, associated cabling, and their connectors. Recognize ports, cabling, and connectors by sight.

1.10 Determine the issues that must be considered when upgrading a PC. In a given scenario, determine when and how to upgrade system components.

2.2 Identify basic troubleshooting procedures and tools, and how to elicit problem symptoms from customers. Justify asking particular questions in a given scenario.

4.3 Identify the most popular types of motherboards, their components and architecture (bus structures and power supplies).

4.4 Identify the purpose of CMOS (Complementary Metal-Oxide Semiconductor) memory, what it contains, and how and when to change its parameters.

AN OVERVIEW OF THE MOTHERBOARD

Take a look at the motherboard shown in **Figure 5.1**. As you can see, this is a complicated device. A computer technician must be able to identify the key components on the board just

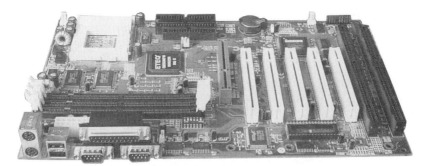

Figure 5.1 This motherboard is based on the ATX form factor. One of the ways you can tell is that most of the I/O ports are soldered directly onto the board.

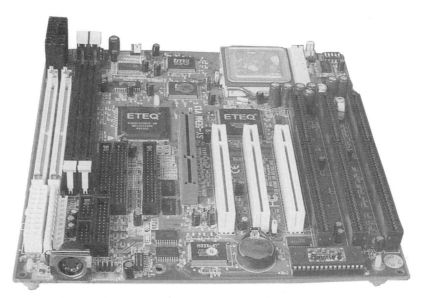

Figure 5.2 The AT-style motherboard differs from the ATX in several aspects. The feature most easily recognized is that the only peripheral directly attached is the keyboard connector.

by sight. In this section, I'll give you the grand tour. The remainder of the chapter will cover some of these components in greater detail.

Throughout this chapter, I'll be pointing out differences between two different styles of motherboard—the AT and the ATX. Later in the chapter, I will provide a complete discussion of the differences between them, but to make sure you're on the right track visually, I suggest that you examine the board in **Figure 5.2** carefully and pick out the differences as the chapter progresses.

CPU SOCKETS AND SLOTS

The CPU socket or slot dictates the type of CPU that the motherboard supports. Obvious factors, such as the number of pins, represent some of the physical differences, but there are also aspects of the CPU socket that must be considered, such as whether it supports variable voltage configurations.

There are basically two forms of CPU form factor. The most common is the *socket*. Sockets are designed to accommodate the CPUs that have hundreds of pins protruding from their base. There have been a large variety of different sockets developed over the years to accommodate different families of CPUs. **Figure 5.3** illustrates a Socket 7. The Socket 7 is just one of several variations on the zero insertion force (ZIF) socket. Sockets over the years have been released as pin grid array (PGA) and staggered pin grid array (SPGA). Other terms you will see include low insertion force (LIF) and very low insertion force (VLIF). These are merely variations on the ZIF.

Figure 5.4 is the *slot* into which a Single Edge Contact Cartridge (SECC), or slot-mounted CPU would be mounted. Slot-mounted CPUs are built around an edge card design and mount accordingly. While the SECC is falling out of favor, there are still a lot of computers in the field today that use this form factor.

Exam Note: While it is highly unlikely the A+ exam will go into extensive detail about processor sockets and slots, you are expected to be able to identify each type. This may be done with an accompanying diagram of a motherboard.

As I will cover in greater detail in Chapter Seven, The Evolution and Development of the CPU, different brands of CPUs, and even different models by the

Figure 5.3 The ZIF socket is one of the most common CPU sockets in use today, although there are a wide variety of forms it will take.

Figure 5.4 CPU slots are easily recognized by the large number of pins and sockets that need to be properly aligned. There are generally two large retaining clips that need to be installed before the CPU can be mounted. In this illustration, those clips are in place.

same manufacturer, use different voltages and run at different speeds. Some sockets are designed to work with an onboard voltage identifier, voltage regulator module (VID VRM), while some earlier styles of socket were either fixed voltage or made use of DIP switches or jumpers to allow the user to manually set voltage. **Table 4.1** is a detailed list of different sockets and slots that have been released since the days of the 486 microprocessor.

Memory Slots

The three memory slots visible in **Figure 5.5** are 168-pin Dual Inline Memory Module (DIMM) slots. Chapter Eight, Searching Your Memory, has a detailed discussion on different memory packages that have been used over the years. As of now, the popular favorite is the DIMM. Another form that is appearing on a vast number of newer motherboards is the 184-

Table 5.1   CPU Sockets and Slots, Past, Present, and Future

Socket/slot	# Pins	Voltage	Multiplier variations	CPUs supported
486 Socket	168	5v	1.0x, 2.0x, 3.0x	80486DX, 80486DX2, 80486DX4
Socket 1	169	5v	1.0x, 2.0x,3.0x	80486DX, 80486DX2, 80486DX4, 80486SX
Socket 2	238	5v	1.0x, 2.0x, 3.0x	80486DX, 80486DX2, 80486DX4, 80486SX
Socket 3	237 ZIF	3.3v 5v	1.0x, 2.0x, 3.0x	80486DX, 80486DX2, 80486DX4, 80486SX
Socket 4	273 ZIF	5v	none	Pentium
Socket 5	296 ZIF	STD VR VRE	1.5x, 2.0x	Pentium
Socket 6	235 ZIF	3.3v	2.0x, 3.0x	80486DX4
Socket 7	321 ZIF	Split STD VR VRE VRT	1.5x, 1.75x, 2.0x 2.33x, 2.5x, 2.66x 3.0x, 3.33x, 3.5x 4.0x, 4.5x, 5.0x 5.5x, 6.0x	Pentium, K5, K6, 6x86
Socket 8	387 ZIF	VID VRM (2.1v~3.5v)	2.0x, 2.5x, 3.0x 4.5x, 5.0x, 5.5x 6.0x, 6.5x, 7.0x 7.5x, 8.0x	Pentium Pro
Socket 370	370 ZIF	VID VRM (1.3v~2.1v)	4.5x, 5.0x, 5.5x 6.0x, 6.5x, 7.0x 7.5x, 8.0x	Celeron, Pentium III
Socket 423	423 ZIF	VID VRM	13.0x, 14.0x, 15.0x, 16.0x, 17.0x, 18.0x, 19.0x, 20.0x	Intel P4 Willamette, Northwood, and Celeron Willamette
Socket 478	478 ZIF	VID VRM	15.0x, 16.0x, 17.0x, 18.0x, 19.0x, 20.0x, 22.0x, 24.0x, 25.0x, 26.0x	Intel P4 Willamette, Northwood, Prescott, and Celeron Willamette and Northwood
Socket 603/604	603/602 ZIF	VID VRM	14.0x, 15.0x, 17.0x, 18.0x, 20.0x, 22.0x	Intel Foster, Prestonia, Nocona, Gallatin
Socket 754	754 ZIF	VID VRM	4x, 5x, 6x, 7x	Athlon Clawhammer, San Diego
Socket 940	940 ZIF	VID VRM	Not Available	Opteron, Sledgehammer
PAC418	418 VLIF	VID VRM	5.5x. 6.0x	Intel Merced
PAC611	611 VLIF	VID VRM	4.5X, 5.0X	Intel McKinley, Madison, Deerfield, Montecito, Shavano
Socket A	462	VID VRM (1.3v~2.05v)	6.0x, 6.5x, 7.0x, 7.5x, 8.0x	Athlon, Duron
Slot A	242	VID VRM (1.3v~2.05v)	5.0x, 5.5x, 6.0x, 6.5x , 7.0x, 7.5x, 8.0x	Athlon
Slot 1	242	VID VRM (1.3v~3.3v)	3.5x, 4.0x, 4.5x, 5.0x, 5.5x, 6.0x, 6.5x	Celeron, Pentium Pro, Pentium II, Pentium III
Slot 2	330	VID VRM (1.3v~3.3v)	4.0x, 4.5x, 5.0x, 5.5x, 6.0x	Xeon

An overview of different CPU sockets and slots

pin DIMM. That slot is used for a more recent form of memory called Dual Data Rate (DDR) memory. Once again, for a detailed description, refer to Chapter Eight.

Even though it's been a while since new systems have shipped with them, there are still a number of machines

Figure 5.5   168-pin DIMM slots are still seeing a lot of action these days, but they are rapidly giving way to the newer 184-pin variety.

on desktops that use the Single Inline Memory Module (SIMM). As of this writing, replacement boards can still be found that make use of SIMMs.

> **EXAM NOTE:** It is not uncommon for an examinee to be presented with a very crude diagram of a motherboard with arrows pointing to specific devices. The candidate is then asked to identify what motherboard components each arrow points to. It wouldn't be a bad idea to have a motherboard available for examination while you read this chapter.

IDE PORTS

Most motherboards typically have two ports designed for hooking up Integrated Drive Electronics (IDE) devices (**Figure 5.6**). IDE devices come in a variety of forms. Hard drives, CD and CD-RW drives, DVD drives, and tape drives can all be acquired in IDE form. Some newer boards sport four IDE ports. There can be compatibility and configuration issues that arise when trying to make all four ports work, so the majority of manufacturers keep it simple. They only give you two. Chapter Twelve, Hard Disk Drive Structure and Geometry, will cover this matter in detail.

As I mentioned in Chapter Two, these are not controllers. They are merely an interface. As the term Integrated Drive Electronics implies, on an IDE device, the electronics that control the device are imbedded into the device itself. Every IDE drive has its own controller built right in.

THE FLOPPY DRIVE CONTROLLER

Unlike the IDE port, the 34-pin floppy disk connector (it's the smaller of the three ports illustrated in Figure 5.6) is actually the interface to a controller circuit. So far,

Figure 5.6   Zooming in on the IDE ports of an ATX motherboard, you can see that the IDE ports are directly adjacent to the floppy disk connector.

all PC motherboards on the market still support the floppy disk drive. Apple has dropped this device from most of the computers in its Macintosh line. While there has been talk of the PC market following suit, so far the floppy is still alive and well.

THE CHIPSET

Finding the *chipset* on a motherboard usually isn't too difficult. **Figure 5.7** makes that readily apparent. Recent boards make it even easier because the newer chipsets

Figure 5.7   The motherboard's chipset has more to do with how well the computer functions than the CPU does.

require protection from thermal overload. Like the CPU, they will be fitted with at least a heat sink, and some manufacturers make cooling fans designed for the chipset. One of the chips is very likely to be labeled with its maximum speed, or it may be covered with a heat sink. You may recall that I mentioned in Chapter Two that the microprocessor has two speeds: its internal processing speed and its front-side bus. The maximum speed of the chipset is the maximum speed at which you can set the front-side bus.

> **BUZZ WORDS**
>
> **Chipset:** A matched set of two (three on some of the older systems) ICs that control critical system functions, including bus speeds, memory types and capacity, and the type of hardware supported by a motherboard.

Modern chipsets consist of two chips, as you can see here. Later in this chapter I'll examine each of the chips and see what its functions are. However, the fact that one of these chips is equipped with its own heat sink tells you one thing. Of the two, it runs at the highest speed.

THE AMR, THE CNR, AND ACR

A slot that has recently begun to appear on inexpensive system boards is the audio-modem riser (AMR). AMR is a specification developed by Intel for packaging the audio functions required by modems together with a chip called a *codec* that converts data back and forth from analog to digital. These are combined on a small board that plugs directly into a computer's motherboard. The term riser refers to the fact that it rises above the motherboard instead of being an embedded circuit. This design means that it doesn't have to be part of the motherboard itself. It can be provided as an optional accessory and not add to the cost of the motherboard when the circuit is not required.

It isn't just modems that benefit from this technology. With AMR design, the slot can now be used for other purposes. The AMR card can also provide the foundation for higher-quality audio solutions such as 3D positional audio and better MIDI music production.

Two key issues that arise with AMR is that if an AMR is installed, it utilizes motherboard resources instead of providing its own. System performance can be degraded by up to 25 percent. Another factor that degrades performance is the amount of noise that an AMR device can generate. Also, the AMR slot reduces the number of available PCI slots by one.

Buzz Words

Codec: A coined term derived from two other terms, coder and decoder. A Codec is an IC that has been programmed to convert data from one form to another. An example of this would be a chip that takes analog signals and converts them to digital, and vice versa.

To counter these complaints, Intel released the Communications and Networking Riser (CNR) standard. CNR was designed to incorporate not just audio and modem functions, but could work as a network interface as well. It did not consume a PCI slot. Instead, it "shares" a PCI slot. The system designer can choose to either use the CNR slot or the adjacent PCI slot, but not both. CNR is not backwardly compatible with AMR.

The Audio-Communications Riser (ACR) specifications were developed by a coalition of manufacturers whose members include 3COM, AMD, VIA Technologies, and Lucent Technologies. Like CNR, it defines a form factor and interfaces for a variety of communications and audio subsystem designs. Building on the concept of AMR, ACR expands the riser card definition beyond the limitation of audio and modem to include networking technologies, including broadband capability. But just as with AMR, both CNR and ACR use quite a bit of system resources, and will slow the machine down significantly.

FORM FACTOR

In Chapter Two, The Basic Components, and again in Chapter Four, Computer Enclosures, I introduced the concept and the importance of form factor. Here, I will explore the different form factors as they relate to motherboards and go into a little more detail.

The most common form factor in use today is the ATX, although technicians still run into a number of computers out there that are using the older AT style. Two other styles that you see pop up from time to time are a couple of low-profile form factors known as NLX and WTX. The ones you'll really love are the LPX-based machines, because each individual design is proprietary. Still, there are enough machines out there sitting on people's desktops using LPX that a discussion of the form factor is in order. There are significant differences among these different formats that you'll need to understand.

THE ORIGINAL AT

First off, let it be said that the AT form factor was far from being the first to be used by early computers. IBM's first release was the Personal Computer (PC). Early PC motherboards were large ungainly things that often required huge cases. There were hundreds of chips spread across the surface and making any changes whatsoever required major surgery. The few companies that did spring up to mimic the IBM PC generally came up with their own designs for both case and motherboard. By the time the PC XT was released, there were a lot more companies making IBM-compatible clones. Despite this, there wasn't anything that could really be called a standard. As a result, it would be difficult to come up with anything anyone would agree on as the "PC" or "XT" form factor.

With the release of the IBM PC-AT, IBM made significant improvements to the layout of both the motherboard and the case. The layout used by IBM was embraced by the industry as a new "standard." For many years, virtually every PC manufactured used the AT form factor.

Physically the motherboard didn't shrink that much, if any. However, by changing the location and orientation of the power supply inside the case, the motherboard could be redesigned to allow easier access to the individual components. The original AT form factor was 12″ wide × 13.8″ deep. The "Baby AT" was reduced to 8.5″ × 13″, but kept the orientation and positioning of components the same. Both AT and Baby AT were marketed side by side. Large server cases benefited from the larger size of the AT, allowing for easier access to components.

Most early AT systems did not have onboard serial or parallel connectors, nor did they offer onboard connectors for hard drives. A device called the I/O controller provided all these functions. This controller occupied a single ISA (later moved to PCI) slot. Toward the end of the effective life of the AT design, these functions migrated to the motherboard, but they still did not provide the interconnects for external access. A cable with these connectors, called a dongle, hooked up the motherboard. It snaked around to the backplane of the case, where there was an appropriately shaped opening for the port.

On most AT boards, the only connector that will be accessible from the outside is a full-sized 5-pin DIN connector coming off the back of the board, as you can see in **Figure 5.8.**

Processor and SIMM slots were located on the front of the motherboard for easier access. Unfortunately, this had the adverse affect of interfering with the expansion slots. Full-length cards either had to be installed in slots away from processor or memory, or the card itself must be designed in such a way to fit over them without interfering with the heat sink/fan or the memory chips.

ATX

ATX motherboards integrate many more connectors directly to the board. The keyboard, mouse, serial ports, and parallel ports will almost always be soldered directly to the motherboard. These are called

Figure 5.8 An AT-style motherboard is easily recognized by the fact that the only part of it exposed to the outside world is the 5-pin DIN connector that the keyboard plugs into.

integrated or embedded ports or controllers (see **Figure 5.9**). Most ATX systems today will also have either two or four Universal Serial Bus (USB) ports, and some may include game connectors for sound and joystick devices.

Figure 5.9   The backplane of the ATX motherboard supports a number of I/O ports. Make sure you don't try to cram one of these into an AT-style case. They don't fit very well.

The ATX form factor emerged in 1995, a product of Intel design. This form factor made several changes, both physically and electrically. Intel incorporated these changes with the goal of reducing overall system size without interfering with access to critical components. ATX was the initial design to take advantage of newer power management technologies. On the physical side ATX made the following changes:

■ Orientation of the board was rotated 90º, relative to the AT. Lengthwise, the board extended from the front of the case to the back. The AT design went from right to left. As a result, the drive cages on the case don't block as many key components.

■ Standard I/O connectors such as serial, parallel, USB, keyboard, and mouse ports were integrated into the structure of the motherboard. These ports slide through openings specifically designed into the case. Two mini-DIN connectors (PS/2) provide the interface for keyboard and mouse.

■ Processor sockets and memory slots were moved from the front to the back. In addition, they were relocated to the right side close to the power supply. Full-length expansion cards can now be used in virtually any slot.

■ The old AT had been designed around CPUs that didn't run that hot. They worked by pushing hot air out of the machine. New CPUs needed more efficient thermal control. The fans were turned around and moved cool air from outside into the machine. Fans were relocated to stream air over critical components.

■ ATX supports additional peripherals, including network interface cards, video, sound, and even modems by soldering those components directly onto the system board.

The ATX form factor also made several modifications on the electrical side. Some of these changes were made to improve efficiency and safety. Others were made to support advancements in power management techniques. Electrical changes include the following:

■ Power connectors from the power supply to the motherboard were changed from two 12-pin plugs to a single 20-pin plug. The 20-pin plug can only plug in one way, preventing a user from inadvertently putting it in backward, which could destroy a motherboard.

- The power supply can deliver 3.3V power to the motherboard, reducing the amount of circuitry required to step 5V down to 3.3V (or lower).
- Soft-power support. Instead of the power switch being purely on or off, a "sleep" mode is provided.

ATX motherboards come in full-sized ATX and micro-ATX to accommodate different cases. It is important to make sure that the case and motherboard are compatible. Full-sized ATX boards will not fit in micro-ATX cases. With the exception of the very few cases designed to accept both styles, no ATX board can be used in an AT-style case. An ATX motherboard also requires the use of an ATX power supply.

LOW-PROFILE FORM FACTORS

There has always been a demand for computers that fit into tiny spaces. Not everybody needs a gargantuan device that holds hundreds of toys. Schools and corporations, and sometimes regular people like you and me, frequently want something simple and small that can be tucked out of the way. Manufacturers came up with a couple of approaches to this over the years.

The problem with many of the earliest low-profile designs was that they had a tendency to be proprietary. Manufacturers had boards built to their specifications and most were not interchangeable. If you fry one of these boards, you go back to the original manufacturer and pay its price.

LPX Several companies have tried to make their mark on the industry by introducing their own form factors. LPX boards were one of the designs aimed at low-profile systems that almost made it. The design was aimed at very slim cases; pancake computers, if you will. Unfortunately, the companies that adopted it usually made their own modifications. As a result, there was little, if any, standardization among case manufacturers. Technicians pretty much hated them because human hands weren't made to go inside those things. Especially if that human was an adult. Changing anything at all required removing something that was in the way. There were designs that required removing the power supply in order to add or replace memory. And removing the power supply was no easy trick.

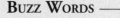

BUZZ WORDS

Riser: A specialized expansion card that supports other expansion devices such as PCI or ISA cards horizontally, parallel to the motherboard, in order to save space.

Like the NLX that I will discuss next, LPX computers put expansion slots onto a specialized card called a riser. The *riser* supported the expansion cards horizontally, parallel to the motherboard. Installing or replacing a device could be a lot of fun.

Despite these shortcomings, some computer manufacturers continue to have cases and motherboards that are made to their specifications that would fall under this category. If called upon to service one of these units, be prepared to pay large sums of money for replacement motherboards and risers.

NLX In 1996, a standardized version of a low-profile design was released called NLX (New Low-profile Extension). The idea was to set universally acceptable standards so that boards and cases would be more interchangeable. For the most part, the industry has preferred to use micro-ATX for its smaller designs, and NLX hasn't really received the acceptance the designers would have liked.

Like the LPX design, these boards have no expansion slots directly on the board. Instead, there is a riser card that plugs into a dedicated, and usually proprietary, slot on the motherboard. Generally, this design only provides for two or three slots. The design does, however, allow for a very slim case. Because so few cards fit into a low-profile system, there are usually more ports and controllers integrated onto the motherboard than you would typically see on a Baby-AT or ATX system. The majority of low-profile boards integrate, at the very minimum, sound and video. Many include a network interface and/or a modem as well.

EBX and ITX Short for Embedded Board Expandable, the EBX form factor was designed for highly compact computers that need to fit into very small spaces. This design came out of a collaboration between Motorola and Ampro. Motherboards designed around the EBX specifications have virtually everything embedded into the motherboard. Audio, video, telecommunications, and networking are all part of the motherboard. Expansion slots are stacking slots, as in the NLX form factor, and can be either PCI or ISA. Everything fits onto a 5.75″ × 8″ board.

EBX hasn't seen a lot of success on the market as of this writing, whereas ITX is starting to become quite popular. ITX may or may not be an acronym for something, but if it is, VIA Technologies, the company that developed the form factor, isn't telling us what it means. Unconfirmed articles have defined it as meaning Integrated Technology Extended. In most respects, ITX is identical to EBX in design philosophy. Cram everything you can onto the board.

All functions, including video, audio, telecom (including broadband), networking, and even SCSI are integrated onto a board that is 215mm × 191mm (that's 8.46″ × 7.52″, if you want to compare it to the other boards I've discussed) in size. The CPU is soldered on some boards, so you select your motherboard based on the CPU you want as well as the features you desire. Other boards, including models offered by VIA, use a Socket 370, so other CPUs that fit in that socket can be used.

WTX The purpose of the Workstation Technology Extended (WTX) form factor is to expand the capabilities of system design beyond those that the standard ATX form factor provides. WTX motherboards provide for longer expansion cards, as well as more of them. A new technology introduced by WTX is the flex slot. A flex slot is a standard PCI slot that happens to allow an expansion card to be twice as thick. This will allow for the development of devices that require larger chips, cooling systems, or perhaps the ability to use standard memory on an expansion card.

Flex cards could also be multifunction device, with multiple ports embedded into the backplane. Such cards would allow for significant expansion without tying up as many precious resources.

WTX specifications provide for motherboards up to 14″ × 16.5″. As you might imagine, this board will not fit in standard cases. Therefore, in addition to providing for motherboard specifications, the WTX advisory committee also defined case and power supply specifications. Because WTX is designed to support more devices, and more robust devices, the board is designed for a somewhat larger power supply. WTX specifies two different power supplies for this standard. The "nominal" power supply is a mere 350W unit with only one fan installed. The second power supply defined is a dual-fan 850W job designed to power major workstations. The power supplies mount on a swing-out panel situated on the side of the case for easy access.

BIOS

A critical component of the motherboard is the Read Only Memory-Basic Input Output Services (ROM BIOS). On most machines, this chip is easily recognized by the fact that it is labeled with the manufacturer's name, the BIOS version, and a copyright date. All of this is important information if you ever find yourself having to break down and call technical support for help.

So what does the BIOS do? A few things, actually. A key function is supplying device support for the CPU. By itself, the CPU is actually pretty stupid. As sophisticated as it is, there are only so many commands it is capable of handling. Most devices have a completely different set of commands that control them. The BIOS contains a collection of very small programs, permanently stored on a read only memory (ROM) chip, which the CPU has been programmed to access on startup. These programs interpret the data coming from other devices and convert it into the commands the CPU can use.

There are also three programs on the BIOS chip that are critical to the functioning of the computer. These are the power on, self-test (POST), the CMOS setup, and the bootstrap loader. Without these programs, you would not be able to start your computer.

THE ADDRESS BUS AND BIOS

Needless to say, the CPU has to be able to find the information stored on the BIOS when it needs it. It does so the same way it addresses any other information in the computer. That is through the address bus. In the chapter on RAM, I'm going to discuss the address bus in much greater detail. So for now, suffice it to say that, in the old days of computers, the maximum amount of memory the 8088 CPU could address was 1MB (1,048,576 bytes). A chunk of that memory was set aside for use by hardware. In the early days of computers when IBM and Microsoft worked together on the first business-class PC, engineers allocated 384K for video memory and hardware. That left 640K of *conventional memory*. These days, the first 640K of memory in any computer system is still called the conventional memory. But in those days, the conventional memory was the only place where programs could run. The way memory was allocated at that time can be seen in

Figure 5.10. Many early XTs actually had a total of 512K on the system board and let the BIOS fend for itself. These computers read the BIOS instructions directly off the chip.

Regardless of how the PC chooses to access the BIOS during normal operation, the CPU requires its services in order to start the computer. Therefore, it was necessary to standardize the address for the POST program and preprogram the CPU to search for that address as the initial command when it is first turned on.

For the most part, BIOS is stored on a Read Only Memory (ROM) chip. Over the years the form of this chip has changed quite a bit. The first ROM chips had to be manufactured at the factory with the code already burned onto the chip. A later version, called the Programmable ROM (PROM), allowed the chip to be programmed in the field as long as the technician had a programming device called a PROM burner available. Once programmed, the PROM chips assumed their permanent form. One form of PROM that was popular for a long while was the Erasable Pro-

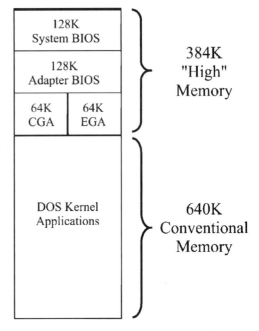

Figure 5.10   The first megabyte of physical memory was originally mapped out to specific functions.

grammable ROM (EPROM), which could be erased and then reprogrammed. These were easily recognized because of the foil label that covered a small glass window on the chip. Ultraviolet light was used to erase the data. This was supplanted by the Electronically Erasable Programmable ROM (EEPROM), which could be erased using the PROM burner. Today's computers almost all ship with Flash ROM. Flash ROM can be reprogrammed by the end user using a program that runs from a floppy diskette.

The Programs of ROMBIOS

I mentioned earlier that there are three critical programs that run from BIOS. These are programs that, if they can't be run from BIOS, can't be run at all, because they're the ones you need when the computer is not fully functional yet. Here is a look at those programs and what they do.

Power On, Self Test

POST is the program the CPU first accesses on startup. When the user first applies power to the motherboard, a special wire in the CPU acts as an on/off switch. The CPU is programmed to jump to the address FFFF:FFF0h and run the code it finds there. This is the first line of POST. This program does a diagnostic on the computer and checks to see that everything is in working order. POST signals each device it is programmed to control and waits for a reply. Any device that fails to reply causes POST to generate an error message. Error messages occur either as a series of beeps or, if the video infrastructure has already tested out, a numerical or text message that appears on the screen. Having the chart of beep codes available will assist in diagnosing any problem. The speaker test is performed by sending a signal to it. Therefore on every POST, you will hear a single beep. Any subsequent beeps you hear after that first one can be considered a bad sign. A detailed list of commonly used beep codes can be found in Appendix D.

Once video has been tested and determined to be functional, subsequent errors may or may not be issued in numeric error codes on old computers. Newer computers actually provide a full text message describing the problem, such as "Keyboard not found. Press any Key to Continue." However, there are still plenty of machines out there using numeric codes. Once again, having a chart of these readily available is a good idea for any service bench. Such a chart appears in Appendix D along with the beep codes.

CMOS SETUP

Some of the instruction sets loaded into BIOS are fixed. They never change. These would include information concerning the location and type of chipset installed or other support chips that may be present. Serial and parallel ports are controlled by BIOS as well. Their location never changes, although you might change their IRQ or their I/O address. Chapter Nine, Examining the Expansion Bus, will cover that in more detail.

There are other things in the computer that might require changes throughout the life of the system. Details concerning the amount of memory installed or the size and number of hard drives installed will change with the user's needs. That's where the *CMOS Setup* comes into play.

CMOS stands for Complimentary Metal-Oxide Semiconductor. That actually refers to the kind of chip used to store the information. CMOS chips resemble conventional memory in some ways and ROM in others. You can write information to the chip whenever you want without having to completely change all of the information stored within. Also, unlike the BIOS chip, the CMOS requires a constant supply of electrical current. On the motherboard is a battery that provides the current when the machine is turned off. Without this battery, the information you write to the chip would be lost when you shut your computer down. This is what is referred to as *volatile* information. Most, if not all, motherboards also have a capacitance circuit in line with the battery. These little capacitors can provide anywhere from several seconds to a couple of minutes worth of current to the CMOS while you're changing the battery. The idea is to keep your CMOS settings from being erased while you change a battery.

Going into the BIOS setup for the first time can be a little intimidating for a beginner. In order to get there, the manufacturer will have provided a specific keystroke combination, which varies from one manufacturer to the next. So watch the splash

BUZZ WORDS ————————

CMOS setup: One of the programs loaded on the BIOS chip. This particular program allows user-defined parameters relating to BIOS settings to be configured.

Volatile: Unstable or changeable. Requires constant power in order to continue to exist.

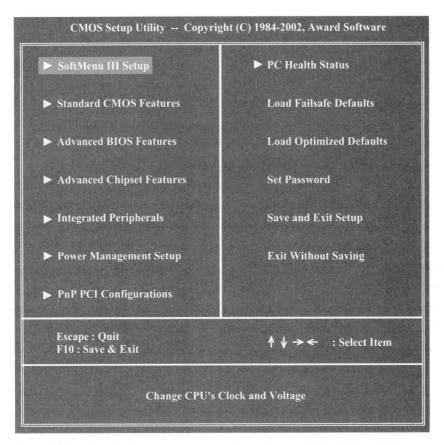

Figure 5.11 Here is the opening screen for an Award BIOS. Refer to this illustration while trying to navigate Table 5.2.

screen that comes up as the system boots, or check the documentation to find out which key(s) to press.

I've tried to make it a little easier by including a list of the common settings on an Award BIOS. Other brands include AMI and Phoenix. They will have similar settings, but may be located in different menu trees.

To make it easier while trying to browse through the BIOS settings, it might be useful to have a computer in front of you and try to see the individual settings for themselves. While the different screens will vary from brand to brand, most of these settings will appear (with minor variations) in practically every system BIOS Setup. If you can't use an actual computer, make extensive use of **Figure 5.11**.

BOOTSTRAP LOADER

The third critical program that your BIOS runs is the *bootstrap loader*. Without this small but rather important routine, your computer wouldn't be able to get past POST. Bootstrap loader

Table 5.2

Standard CMOS Setup

Setting	Options	Description
Date	Page Up/Page Down	Changes system date
Time	Page Up/Page Down	Changes system time
Hard Disks/Type	Auto/User/None	Settings for IDE HDD
Hard Disks/Mode	Normal/LBA/Large/Auto	HDD translation method
Drive A	Various settings	Enables/disables floppy A
Drive B	Various settings	Enables/disables floppy B
Video	EGA/VGA, CGA-40, CGA-80, Mono	Establishes type of video used
Halt On	Various options	Stops POST on selected errors

BIOS Features Setup

Setting	Options	Description
Boot Virus Detection	Enabled/Disabled	Warns of any attempt to write to the boot sector
CPU Level 1 Cache	Enabled/Disabled	Enables read/write operations to L1 cache built into CPU
CPU Level 2 Cache	Enabled/Disabled	Enables read/write operations to L2 cache built into CPU
CPU Level 2 Cache ECC Check	Enabled/Disabled	Turns on/off ECC mode
Quick Power On Self Test	Enabled/Disabled	Full Test/Tests only selected system components on cold boot
HDD Sequence	IDE/SCSI	Where to look for MBR
Boot Sequence	Options vary	Determines the order of devices in which POST looks for the MBR
Boot Up Floppy Seek	Enabled/Disabled	Tests floppy drive to see if it has forty or eighty tracks
Floppy Disk Access Control	R/W, Read Only	Security access for floppy drive
HDD Block Mode Sectors	Options vary	

Table 5.2 (Continued)

BIOS Features Setup

Setting	Options	Description
HDD S.M.A.R.T Capability	Enabled/Disabled	IDE SMART capable?
PS2 Mouse Function Control	Enabled/Auto	Looks to PS2 for mouse
OS2 Onboard Memory	Enabled/Disabled	Use OS2 memory mapping
PCI/VGA Palette Snoop	Disabled/Enabled	Allows video adapters to directly access RAM looking for video information
Video ROM/BIOS Shadowing	Enabled/Disabled	Allows copying of BIOS routines to upper memory for enhanced performance
C8000-DFFFF Shadowing	Enabled/Disabled	Allows copying of Supplemental BIOS to specific addresses (multiple entries)
Boot Up NumLock Status	On/Off	Determines whether number lock on keyboard is on or off after system boots
Typomatic Rate Setting	Disabled/Enabled	Disabled turns off Typomatic Rate and Typomatic Delay
Typomatic Rate	Options vary	Sets speed at which characters repeat when a key on the keyboard is held down.
Typomatic Delay	Options vary	Sets time that elapses before keys begin to repeat when a key on the keyboard is held down.
Security Option	System/Setup	Determines where security is controlled

Chipset Features Setup

Setting	Options	Description
EDO Autoconfiguration	Enabled/Disabled	Allows chipset to control EDO timing functions
EDO Read Burst Timing	Options vary	Sets number of clock cycles for Burst Mode read operations
EDO Write Burst Timing	Options vary	Sets number of clock cycles for Burst Mode write operations
EDO RAS Precharge	3T, 4T	Sets number of clock cycles for RAS Precharge

	Options	Description
EDO RAS/CAS Delay	2T, 3T	Sets number of clock cycles for RAS/CAS Delay
SDRAM Configuration	Options vary	Sets clock speed of SDRAM
SDRAM RAS Precharge	Auto, 3T, 4T	Sets number of clock cycles for RAS Precharge
SDRAM RAS/CAS Delay	Auto, 3T, 2T	Sets number of clock cycles for RAS/CAS Delay
SDRAM Banks Close Policy	Arbitration, Page-Miss	
Graphics Aperture Size	Options vary	
Video Memory Cache Mode	UC, USWC	Determines how Video Memory addresses cache
PCI 2.1 Support	Enabled/Disabled	Disabled setting drops system back to PCI Version 1.0
Memory Hole at 15M-16M	Enabled/Disabled	Enables/disables use of these memory addresses
Onboard FDC Controller	Enabled/Disabled	Allows you to disable the floppy disk drive
Onboard Floppy Swap A/B	Enabled/Disabled	Switches drives A and B
Onboard Serial Port 1	Various settings/Disabled	Allows reconfiguring or disabling Serial Port 1
Onboard Serial Port 2	Various settings/Disabled	Allows reconfiguring or disabling Serial Port 2
Onboard Parallel Port	Various settings/Disabled	Allows reconfiguring or disabling Parallel Port
Parallel Port Mode	Normal, ECC, ECC/ECP	Sets up parallel communications
ECP DMA Select	Options vary	Sets DMA channel used by ECP Parallel mode
UART2 Use Infrared	Enabled/Disabled	Sets infrared port to UART2
Onboard PCI/IDE Enable	Both, Primary, Secondary, Disabled	Enables/disables IDE ports
IDE DMA Mode	Auto/Disable	Disables, autoselects Direct Memory Access
IDE 0/1 – Master/Slave	Options vary	Sets PIO mode and DMA channel for specific device

Power Management Setup

Setting	Options	Description
Power Management	User Defined, Disabled, Min, Max	Determines PM method
Video Off Option	Suspend → Off, Always On	Determines how the monitor is managed

Table 5.2 (Concluded)

Power Management Setup

Setting	Options	Description
Video Off Method	Options vary	Determines method by which monitor is shut down
HDD Power Down	Options vary	How long before hard drive shuts down
Suspend Mode	Options vary	How long before hard drive goes into suspended mode
PWR Button	Soft-off, Suspend, No Function	Determines how the power button affects power supply
Power Up on Modem ACT	Enabled/Disabled	Modem wakes machine?
AC Power Loss Restart	Enabled/Disabled	Automatically restarts machine when AC power is restored
Wake on LAN	Enabled/Disabled	NIC wakes machine?

PNP and PCI Setup

Setting	Options	Description
PNP OS Installed?	Yes/No	Is the operating system PnP compliant?
Slot 1-? IRQ (several entries)	Auto, various settings	Manually assign an IRQ to a specific slot or let PnP handle allocations?
PCI Latency Timer	Various settings	Number of clock cycles for PCI latency
IRQ 3-15 Used by ISA (several entries)	Yes/No	Is this IRQ assigned to a legacy ISA device?
Force Update ESCD	Enabled/Disabled	Forces reallocation of resources on POST
LOAD BIOS DEFAULTS?	Reloads factory Settings. No internal settings.	
SUPERVISOR PASSWORD	Allows entry of supervisor password	
USER PASSWORD	Allows entry of user password	
IDE HDD AUTODETECT	Automatically detects and configures devices on primary and secondary IDE ports	

scans all of the drives that you configured as possible boot devices in the setup program looking for something called the Master Boot Record (MBR). I will talk more about the MBR in Chapter Twelve, Hard Disk Drive Structure and Geometry. For now, suffice it to say that the MBR is 512 to 1024 bytes of some of the most important data on your computer. There is information stored there that is prerequisite for making the machine work.

Older machines can only look to hard disk drives or floppy drives for an MBR. That is not the case in most current machines. Bootstrap loaders are now smart enough to consider CD-ROMs, Zip drives, and many other storage devices as capable of containing a viable MBR.

BUZZ WORDS

Bootstrap loader: A program that resides on the BIOS chip that is responsible for locating and initializing the Master Boot Record.

Boot block: A feature present on most modern system boards that allows the system to boot to a minimal configuration, including floppy drive support, in the event that the BIOS is corrupted or destroyed by a virus.

It is possible for you to have multiple devices in your computer containing an MBR. In this case, how would the computer know which one to boot to? That's where the CMOS setup comes into play. In the BIOS Features setup section, there is a setting for Boot Sequence. Here, you will tell the computer in what order you want it to look for an MBR. Once it finds one, it stops looking.

TROUBLESHOOTING BIOS

BIOS is fixed, read only memory. It is very difficult to accidentally lose it. CMOS settings, on the other hand, can be lost in several ways. As far as the BIOS is concerned, exposure to high levels of magnetic energy, an electrical surge, or a spark of static electricity from your finger can either destroy it completely or simply damage bits and pieces of code stored on the chip. If it is destroyed completely, POST won't even run. Unfortunately, it is far more common for the BIOS to be damaged than it is to be destroyed. In this case, the machine may or may not make it past POST. If it makes it past POST, the machine performs erratically. Another thing that can destroy the BIOS code is peeling the foil label off to see what's underneath. If your BIOS chip happens to have a foil label, it isn't there just for looks. It covers a window to the chip itself. Exposure of UV radiation to that cell will erase the data on the chip.

Some newer motherboards have a new feature known as *boot block* that allows you to boot the machine in the event of failed BIOS. If the corruption isn't too serious, sometimes boot block can either fix it on the fly or in some cases bypass the problem component. In most cases, boot block works by booting the machine to a bootable floppy diskette that contains a flash utility and a copy of the BIOS data file. This allows you to restore the BIOS.

As I said before, the CMOS is volatile information. If power to the chip is discontinued for a significant amount of time, the information on it is lost. It is essential that this information be made nonvolatile. This is done through an onboard battery. When you turn off a computer, the battery on the motherboard keeps it and the real time clock (RTC) alive. If the battery goes dead, so does the CMOS. Other ways of losing the CMOS include electrostatic discharge, surges or dips in power from a faulty power supply, and physical impact or a short circuit caused by dropping something across its leads while the computer is powered up. Simply removing an expansion card while the computer is running has been known to kill the CMOS.

Normally, in all of the aforementioned circumstances, the CMOS can be restored. On a heavily configured and/or altered machine this can be time consuming. Running a utility such as CMOSSAVE.EXE is a good idea if you administer a lot of computers.

Changing the battery on most motherboards is a relatively simple thing. Modern motherboards use a coin-style battery. Simply flip the old one out with your fingernail and pop the new one in, oriented in the same direction for correct polarity. Some modern machines also have an RTC/battery chip, however, and these can be a bit more problematic. On older machines, you frequently have rechargeable batteries that are soldered onto the motherboard. Consider these motherboards disposable unless you're a really good practitioner of the soldering arts.

CHIPSETS

On the earliest computers, every function on the motherboard required a separate chip. There was a chip for managing IRQs, one for managing DMA channels (managing resources will be covered in detail in Chapter Nine, Examining the Expansion Bus), and one for every other function you can think of. The more functions you added the more chips you needed. The more chips you added, the more complex addressing became. And production costs increased accordingly. It was a vicious cycle. As technology advanced, and as production levels rapidly increased, it was quickly becoming apparent that there had to be a better way. The chipset is that better way. It interacts with all hardware on the system, dictates the abilities and limitations of a system, determines system bus speeds, and handles all addressing functions for the CPU.

COMPONENTS OF THE CHIPSET

Traditionally, modern chipsets are a two-chip set, the northbridge and the southbridge, although Intel's more recent designs are departing from that tradition. There is also a third chip that is integrated with many chipset designs called the Super I/O chip. Since this chip is not designed along with the other two, and frequently motherboard manufacturers get the Super I/O chip from different manufacturers, it is not technically considered part of the chipset. However, since its functions are so similar, I have chosen to include it in this section.

Choice of the chipset directly impacts the performance of the machine. All system functions are either directly or indirectly controlled by the chipset. These functions include, but are not limited to the following:

- Advanced device support
- Amount of memory supported
- Types of memory supported
- Bus Speed
- Type and number of expansion busses supported
- Number of processors

- Processor speeds supported
- Processor voltage
- Power management

NORTHBRIDGE

The faster of the two chips in the chipset is the System Controller Chip. This is the one frequently known as the *northbridge.* It handles the high-speed components of the system. It is the northbridge that directly connects the CPU's front-side bus (See Chapter Six, Understanding CPUs) to RAM, the AGP port, and other high-speed peripherals. It also sets the pace for the FSB. You just bought yourself a new 3.1GHz CPU? Congratulations, but if the chipset on your motherboard only supports up to 2GHz it isn't going to do you a whole lot of good. And if your CPU is designed with a 133MHz FSB and you put it on a board that only supports 100MHz, then 100MHz is what the CPU's data bus will run at. In many cases, incorrect setting will prevent the machine from booting properly.

> ## BUZZ WORDS
>
> **Northbridge:** The faster of the ICs in the chipset that is responsible for managing RAM, cache, and AGP functions.
>
> **Southbridge:** The slower of the ICs that make up the chipset. The South Bridge manages serial and parallel communications, USB, and most of the expansion slots.

The northbridge also decides how much RAM you're going to be able to use in your machine. Theoretically, all Pentium-based systems should be able to address up to 4GB of RAM. Pentium IIs and higher should be able to address 64GB. The sad truth is that no chipset ever manufactured has taken advantage of more than a fraction of that capability. Current motherboards are designed to support anywhere from as little as 384MB to 2GB on boards designed for desktop machines. Those designed for servers are more generous, and there are models available that support up to 16GB.

The Memory Controller Chip (MCC) is a key function absorbed by the chipset. The original MCC did the actual job of mapping data to memory, as well as directing the functions that dictated refresh cycles and timing of RAS and CAS (see Chapter Eight, Searching Your Memory). This is now handled by the northbridge component of the chipset. This also determines the kinds of memory you can use on any given system.

SOUTHBRIDGE

The Peripheral Bus Controller, also known as the *southbridge,* takes care of communication between the CPU and the slower components of the system. The southbridge takes care of things like the ISA bus, IDE ports, USB ports, and any other devices not specifically handled by the Super I/O chip. All expansion bus platforms prior to PCI are under the control of this chip as well.

SUPER I/O CHIP

This is the chip that, technically speaking, is not part of the chipset. As I said earlier, in many cases, the super I/O doesn't even come from the same manufacturer as the chipset. What makes this possible is that the super I/O controls the I/O functions that are typically found in all motherboards. These would include the floppy drive controllers, serial ports, parallel ports, IDE ports, and so on. Some super I/O chips also provide keyboard controller functions and the real time clock.

BEYOND THE BRIDGES

It is Intel's stated goal to eliminate everything on the system that slows it down. That includes the ISA bus. With the release of the 820 chipset, Intel began doing just that. They are starting to move away from the traditional northbridge/southbridge

BUZZ WORDS

Memory controller hub: The IC in the newer Intel chipsets that manages RAM and AGP bus.

Enhanced I/O controller hub: The IC in the newer Intel chipset that manages all function other than memory and AGP.

design. The 820 is similar to the old design only in that they both make use of two separate chips. However, they handle system resources in a completely different manner. In place of the northbridge component is a device called the *memory controller hub*. As its name infers, this device controls all system memory. It also has the responsibility for managing the AGP bus. The second chip, the *Enhanced I/O Controller Hub* handles all other functions.

Intel has made this a modular design. Engineers who design motherboards can make a simple system based on the chipset's bare essentials. However, more advanced systems can be designed with some of the optional components available. If the manufacturer wants to build a board that supports 64-bit 66MHz PCI slots, the optional P64H PCI controller hub can be implemented. Manufacturers who wish to add an additional memory channel can make use of the 862803AA memory repeater hub. This design philosophy was carried over into the 850 chipset for the Pentium 4 and most likely represents the future of Intel chipsets.

Other manufacturers aren't quite so eager to see an early funeral for ISA or any of the other slower busses. People still use it. And as long as people still use it, manufacturers can continue to make money off of the technology. Therefore, manufacturers such as VIA continue to crank out traditional chipsets.

MOTHERBOARD REPLACEMENT

One thing every technician is eventually going to have to do is replace a motherboard. A heavy surge, lightening striking the electric pole outside the customer's house, any number of things can kill a motherboard. Even plugging the P8 and P9 cables in with the black wires on the outside. As a computer technician, changing the motherboard needs to become second nature to you.

At first it might look a little intimidating. A novice looking inside the case sees nothing but a tangle of cables and cards sticking out of the board. On top of that, the power supply and all those drives are in the way. You're going to have to take the whole computer apart just to replace the motherboard!!!

In many situations, that's the case. Then again, sometimes it's not quite so complicated. Taking a systematic approach will make it a lot easier. A little practice doesn't hurt.

Step 1:   Know what kind of case you're working with. ATX motherboards do not go in AT cases. It doesn't matter how big a hammer you use. They line up in the case in different manners, and they use different types of power supplies. If you are replacing an AT-style motherboard, then you need to find an AT-style motherboard with which to replace it. And vice versa. Size is no longer an issue. For years, cases have been designed to take varying sizes of boards.

Step 2:   Make sure the motherboard comes with the manual!!! Every motherboard has anywhere from a few to a multitude of jumpers and/or DIP switches and wiring connectors. There's no such thing as a universal standard. If you don't have the manual for the motherboard you're working on and try to get by with a "similar" model, it'll be like trying to make chicken teriyaki from a chili recipe. If you don't have hard copy of the manual, then before you start removing the old board carefully note where every single cable was plugged in. Later on, while the two boards are out on the bench, make sure all jumpers and/or DIP switches are configured identically from the old board to the new.

Step 3:   First, remove all cards from the expansion slots. Set them aside (preferably in static-free bags) and then remove all cables. IDE, floppy, serial, and parallel cables (if present) are all ribbon cables and you should be able to readily identify them by sight. Remove the CPU fan from the CPU and the wires connecting LEDs, the PC speaker, CD-ROM audio, and others. If you don't have the manual, make careful note of where these wires plug in! Frequently, the wires coming out of the case are clearly labeled "HD LED," "TURBO," "SPKR," and "RESET." All too often, however, the motherboard is labeled J12, J13, J14, and J27, or something like that.

Step 4:   Once you have everything removed from the motherboard, remove the screws that hold it on. There are usually three to five of them. If the power supply is in the way, you're better off removing it. They're not that hard to pull and replace. Drop the new board in place, put the screws in to hold it in and reverse the procedures of removing the board. The one thing to remember here is that, on AT-style computers, it is essential that you get the P8 and P9 plugs properly aligned.

Before you put the case back together, double-check all the cables to make sure they are connected, and connected properly. Then check again. Once you're reasonably confident that everything is hooked up right, fire the machine up while it's still open. That way you can put the floppy cable back on correctly and reconnect that Molex that fell off the hard drive when you weren't looking. If the machine boots fine, then wrap it up.

One potential problem you might encounter after a motherboard replacement is related to the operating system. If the board you replaced was not an identical duplicate, OSs that support Plug 'n Play will detect that the device list has changed. It will reinstall all system device drivers. Most of the time, this is simply an inconvenience. It requires that the system reboot as many as three times before the procedure is complete. Once in a great while, you may encounter a situation where the OS must be reinstalled. Unless there is critical data and/or settings on the machine that prevent you from doing this, I would recommend that you do this anyway.

Chapter Summary

If you've gotten this far, you now realize the importance of the motherboard to the computer system. It is the very heart of the system. All system busses pass through the motherboard and all critical functions are under its control.

In Chapter One, PC Basics, I told you that I would make a case for the CPU not truly being the brains of the computer. I made the first installment of my case in this chapter when I pointed out how many vital system functions were under the control of the chipset and not the CPU. I'll continue making my case in the next two chapters, when I discuss CPUs.

Troubleshooting motherboard issues is one of those things that take up a great deal of the lives of most computer hardware technicians. Understanding the different errors reported by the board and being able to identify them need to be second nature to the tech.

Brain Drain

1. Discuss as many differences between an AT-style motherboard and an ATX-style motherboard as you can think of.

2. List at least five features of a motherboard that will be common to all motherboards, regardless of form factor.

3. Give an overview of the functions of the system BIOS.

4. List as many functions of the chipset as you can.

5. Discuss why there needs to be a separate expansion bus.

The 64K$ Questions

1. A typical motherboard consists of _____ layers of substrate.
    a. One
    b. Two
    c. Four
    d. Six

2. Which of the following is not an example of a pin-mounted CPU socket?
    a. PGA
    b. SECC
    c. SPGA
    d. ZIF

3. How many IDE controllers typically reside on an ATX-style motherboard?
    a. Two
    b. Four
    c. One
    d. Zero

4. Which of the following form factors make use of a riser? (Choose all that apply.)
    a. AT
    b. NLX
    c. ATX
    d. LPX

5. POST is a function of _____.
    a. The CPU
    b. The chipset
    c. The BIOS
    d. RAM

6. Which BIOS program locates and initializes the Master Boot Record?
    a. POST
    b. Setup
    c. Startup
    d. Bootstrap loader

7. CMOS stands for _____.
   a. Common Motherboard Operational Settings
   b. Common Master Operating System
   c. Complimentary Metal-Oxide Semiconductor
   d. Creative Metaphors for Our Supervisor

8. AGP is typically under the control of _____. (Choose all that apply.)
   a. The southbridge chip
   b. The northbridge chip
   c. The memory controller hub
   d. The Super I/O controller

9. The Plug 'n Play Recognition Scan is a part of _____.
   a. Loading the OS
   b. POST
   c. Bootstrap loader
   d. Device installation

10. All computer systems, past and present, load BIOS instructions on a ROM chip.
    a. True
    b. False

TRICKY TERMINOLOGY

Boot block: A feature present on most modern system boards that allows the system to boot to a minimal configuration, including floppy drive support, in the event that the BIOS is corrupted or destroyed by a virus.

Bootstrap loader: A program that resides on the BIOS chip that is responsible for locating and initializing the Master Boot Record.

Chipset: A matched set of two (three on some of the older systems) ICs that control critical system functions, including bus speeds, memory types and capacity, and the type of hardware supported by a motherboard.

CMOS setup: One of the programs loaded on the BIOS chip. This particular program allows user-defined parameters relating to BIOS settings to be configured.

Codec: A coined term derived from two other terms, coder and decoder. A codec is an IC that has been programmed to convert data from one form to another. An example of this would be a chip that takes analog signals and converts them to digital, and vice versa.

Conventional memory: The first 640K of any computer system. In the old days of DOS, the only place where programs could run was in conventional memory.

Enhanced I/O controller hub: The IC in the newer Intel chipsets that manages all function other than memory and AGP.

Memory controller hub: The IC in the newer Intel chipsets that manages RAM and AGP bus.

Northbridge: The faster of the ICs in the chipset that is responsible for managing RAM, cache, and AGP functions.

Riser: A specialized expansion card that supports other expansion devices such as PCI or ISA cards horizontally, parallel to the motherboard, in order to save space.

Slot: A mounting assembly designed to support edge card-mounted devices.

Socket: A mounting assembly designed to support pin-mounted devices.

Southbridge: The slower of the ICs that make up the chipset. The southbridge manages serial and parallel communications, USB, and most of the expansion slots.

Trace: The fine copper path seen on printed circuit boards that acts as a conductor for a signal.

Volatile: Unstable or changeable. Requires constant power in order to continue to exist.

ACRONYM ALERT

ACR: Audio Communications Riser. A specialized card that takes the concept of the AMR and adds networking functionality as well.

AMR: Audio Modem Riser. A specialized card found on certain motherboards that supports either a modem, a sound card, or a device that combines both functions.

CMOS: Complimentary Metal-Oxide Semiconductor. The type of chip that houses the user-configurable parameters needed by BIOS.

CNR: Communications Network Riser. A specialized card that takes the concept of the AMR and adds networking functionality as well.

DDR: Dual Data Rate. A form of memory that is capable of executing two transfers of data on each clock cycle.

EBX: Embedded Board Expandable. One of several form factors whose objective was to keep the system as small as possible.

EEPROM: Electronically Erasable Programmable Read Only Memory. A more modern implementation of an IC that can be wiped clean and rewritten if necessary.

EPROM: Erasable Programmable Read Only Memory. An IC that can be wiped clean and rewritten if necessary.

LPX: Low-Profile Extended. One of several form factors whose objective was to keep the system as small as possible.

MBR: Master Boot Record. The first one or two sectors of a bootable medium that contains information about the file system, the partition tables, and a pointer to the OS.

MCC: Memory Controller Chip or Memory Controller Circuit. The chip or circuitry on the chipset that manages memory mapping and refresh functions.

NLX: New Low-profile Extended. One of several form factors whose objective was to keep the system as small as possible.

PGA: Pin Grid Array. A pin-mounted CPU on which the pins are arranged in perfectly symmetrical patterns of squares.

POST: Power On, Self Test. A program run from the BIOS chip that initializes system hardware and handles the Plug 'n Play scans.

PROM: Programmable Read Only Memory. An IC that can be programmed once.

ROM BIOS: Read Only Memory-Basic Input Output Services. A chip on the motherboard that contains all the necessary code for jumpstarting a computer from a dead off condition to the point where the OS can take over.

RTC: Real Time Clock. The chip that keeps actual time, as humans keep track of it, on the systems.

SECC: Single Edge Contact Cartridge. A type of CPU package that makes use of an edge card connector and mounts in a slot.

SPGA: Staggered Pin Grid Array. A pin-mounted CPU on which the pins are arranged in offsetting rows of pins that results in a pattern of diagonal rows.

UV: Ultraviolet. Wavelengths of light beyond the upper range of the visible light spectrum.

VID-VRM: Voltage Identifier, Voltage Regulator Module. A device that automatically locks on to the correct voltage of the installed chip and configures the device accordingly.

WTX: Workstation Technology Extended. One of several form factors whose objective was to keep the system as small as possible.

CHAPTER 6

UNDERSTANDING CPUs

In this chapter, I will discuss what many refer to as the "brain" of the computer. However, as I pointed out in the previous chapter, the central processing unit (CPU) really does not deserve to claim that title exclusively. In reality, it is nothing more than an overgrown calculator. It basically shuffles 0s and 1s at an incredibly high rate of speed. It is a device that has evolved over the years, and each generation has assumed new responsibilities. So in a sense, it is creeping in on the title of main brain.

Even in its infancy, the CPU was a complicated device. Those that power today's computers transcend complexity and border on the world of magic. Because of the amount of information centering around the CPU, I have chosen to break it up into two separate chapters. In this chapter I will examine the structure and function of the CPU as well as some of the technologies that improve performance. In Chapter Seven, I will discuss the chronology and evolution of the microprocessor.

A+ EXAM OBJECTIVES

CompTIA exam objectives covered in the chapter include the following:

1.1 Identify the names, purpose, and characteristics of system modules. Recognize these modules by sight or definition. (CPU)

1.9 Identify procedures to optimize PC operations in specific situations. Predict the effects of specific procedures under given scenarios.

1.10 Determine the issues that must be considered when upgrading a PC. In a given scenario, determine when and how to upgrade system components.

TRANSISTORS, BINARY, AND LOGIC GATES

The only language the computer speaks is binary. Binary is a simplified computer language consisting of 0s and 1s. Therefore, the commands native to the CPU can be no larger than its internal data bus (I'll be taking this up in detail in a few moments). The programs that you run consist of extremely detailed sets of instructions that consist of several words. If you recall from Chapter One, PC Basics, a word generally consists of the amount of data the CPU can swallow in one gulp. These instructions tell the CPU what to do every step of the way in order to achieve a specific objective. Even a single step left out of the flow of logic will cause the program to either malfunction or to stop functioning altogether. On a machine level, all these commands are really doing is telling the computer which of the CPU's wires to light up, and which to leave dormant. Turning little devices called *transistors* on and off does all of this. These combinations of on and off cascade through the computer, creating a series of logic gates.

A *logic gate* is nothing more than two or more transistors working together. The relative position of these transistors (on or off) determines how the next pair of transistors in the circuit will be switched.

A transistor is a semiconductor that acts as a switch, existing in either an on position, or an off position. A *semiconductor* is any substance that conducts electricity well enough to be considered a conductor, and resists electrical flow well enough to be considered an insulator. In other words, it's a

BUZZ WORDS

Transistor: A microscopic on/off switch that uses the electrical characteristics of a semiconductor to reverse positions.

Logic gate: Two or more transistors whose position will direct the positioning of the next bank of transistors downstream.

Semiconductor: A substance that exhibits the characteristics of both a conductor and a resistor, depending on the amount of voltage passing through.

Threshold voltage: The amount of electrical differential required to move a semiconductor from a state of resistance to a state of conductance.

Register: A bank of transistors grouped together to perform a specific function.

substance with an identity crisis. But that property makes it an ideal substance for the manufacture of transistors. Any electrical current that reaches a certain strength is allowed to flow. This is the semiconductor's *threshold voltage*. Any current less than threshold voltage is blocked. Therefore, current either flows or it doesn't, depending on how much current there is. The transistor is either on or off. Inside the CPU, transistors are grouped together as registers. A *register* is one of a series of transistor banks that will provide a pathway for the processing of data.

The binary language can be credited to work originally done by George Boole in the mid-1800s. His paper, "An Investigation Into the Laws of Thought, on Which Are Founded the Mathematical Theories of Logic and Probabilities," was published in 1852, a culmination of several years' worth of work. In this paper, he defined a new form of algebra based exclusively upon the numbers 0 and 1. These ideas would be the basis of binary as it is used by computers today. I discussed binary in Chapter One, PC Basics, and provided some key terms.

THE MICROCOMPONENTS OF THE CPU

Examine a CPU closely, and consider this. That little device that nestles easily into the palm of your hand can perform anywhere from several hundred million to a few billion transactions per second. What is even more impressive is that the actual microprocessor is only a fraction of what you're holding. The ceramic device in your hand includes the circuit board and wires necessary to interconnect the chip to the rest of the system. The chip itself is a trifle larger than your thumbnail. That tiny piece of silicon has been subdivided into several smaller sections called subcomponents. Each one of those subcomponents has a specific job to do. Understanding how a CPU works is a lot easier if you understand the purpose of each of the internal devices. As you read through the next few sections, keep referring back to the diagram in **Figure 6.1**.

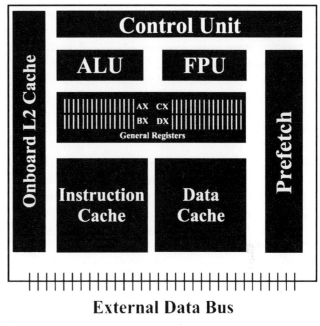

The various subcomponents of the CPU along with their basic functions include the following:

Figure 6.1   The CPU is subdivided into several sub-components, each of which has a specific task to perform.

- *The Control Unit:* The component that directs the activities of all other components in the CPU
- *The Prefetch:* The component that locates and retrieves data as the CPU requires it
- *External Data Bus:* The wires that bring data into the CPU from the outside world
- *The Instruction Cache and the Data Cache:* Storage areas for instructions that have been brought in the by the prefetch, but not yet used by the CPU
- *The Arithmetic Logic Unit:* Performs basic math functions
- *The Floating Point Unit:* Performs advanced math functions
- *Registers:* A storage point for data and/or instructions that are in current use by the CPU

Also shown in the figure is the Onboard L2 Cache; it is often included on the die of CPUs these days, but it is not part of the primary CPU circuitry. I'll discuss this later in the chapter.

THE EXTERNAL DATA BUS

I have no intention of going over each and every component of the CPU in this book. It is not an engineering text, and the average hardware technician does not need that information either in real life or on the exam. I do feel that a discussion of the *external data bus* (EDB) is in order, though.

If the data required by the CPU is located outside of the CPU, there must be some way to move that data from wherever it's stored to the internal registers of the CPU. The EDB is the front door that moves information in and out of the CPU. It is a part of the CPU that, despite the huge advances in technology over the past few decades, has seen little change.

To keep the explanation simple, I'm going to refer back to the first microprocessor used by IBM in the IBM PC. This particular CPU had an 8-bit EDB. Modern CPUs have far more than eight bits, but I'll get into that a little later. The EDB consists of a series of switches that can be either on or off. These switches are turned on and off at regular intervals, called the clock cycle. Eight switches permits 256 combinations of on/off that can be understood by the CPU on any given clock cycle.

The EDB actually exists in two different places on the CPU. One term used frequently is the *front-side bus* (FSB). The FSB is the path that data takes from the chipset and/or memory to get to the CPU. The *back-side bus* (BSB) is the channel that data located in Level One cache takes. Level One is a fancy name for the instruction and data caches discussed earlier. In the early days of CPUs, the speed of the FSB and BSB were the same. This is no longer the case.

In the early days of computing, the first CPU used by IBM possessed a 4.77MHz EDB. It had no Level One cache, so there was only an FSB. This CPU could examine the switches of the EDB 4,770,000 times per second, interpret the on/off pattern as a byte of data, and move it onto the internal registers. On today's CPUs, the FSB begins at 100MHz and has reached 466MHz on some of the new Athlons and 533MHz on the Pentium 4. Intel describes in its literature CPUs that will exceed a 1GHz FSB, perhaps by the time this book has come

to print. The BSB can function at the same speed of the FSB on some CPUs and much higher speeds on others. I will examine this in more detail a bit later.

Now, how does the CPU use the EDB to move data onto the CPU? That's actually pretty simple. Remember that there is a pin on the CPU that represents each individual data bit (**Figure 6.2**). Current on a pin during any given clock cycle represents a 1, while a lack of current is interpreted as a 0. On both the internal and external sides

> **BUZZ WORDS**
>
> **External data bus:** The wires that move data from outside the CPU to the internal registers of the CPU.
>
> **Front-side bus:** A portion of the EDB. It is the path that data takes from outside locations to make its way into the CPU.
>
> **Back-side bus:** A portion of the EDB. It is the path that data takes as it moves from cache loaded on the CPU's die into the CPU's registers.

Figure 6.2 The external data bus is nothing more than a series of wires. They are but a few of the pins you see protruding from the base of a CPU. The presence or absence of current on any given wire during a specific clock cycle is interpreted as data.

of the bus are microswitches that control the state of the wire. As you might imagine, for this to work properly, on any given clock cycle, both switches must be set to the same position.

THE CLOCK

Technically speaking, the clock is not part of the CPU. However, understanding what is going on inside of the CPU is difficult without knowing what the clock does and how its role affects every-

> **BUZZ WORDS**
>
> **Clock cycle:** A timing signal generated by an electrical current that synchronizes data movement throughout the system. As an electrical current, a clock cycle resembles a sine wave with a rising half of the signal and a falling half.

thing else. There has to be some sort of mechanism that tells the CPU when to check for incoming data. This mechanism is the CPU clock. This is also the derivation of the term *clock cycle*. The clock ticks, and the CPU turns to the telegraphs, takes note of which switches are on, which are off, and promptly takes action. What makes the clock tick is electrical current. On earlier computers, the clock consisted of nothing more than a crystal. When hit with current, it vibrated. The nice thing about nature is that, while on the outside it looks like pure chaos, on a molecular level, things are pretty predictable. The crystal used in the early PC vibrated 4,770,000 times per second when excited by electricity. That was its clock cycle. The CPU requires a minimum of two clock cycles to act on any given command.

The clock cycles are measured in Hertz (Hz). 1Hz is equal to 1 clock cycle. 1 million clock cycles = 1MHz. 1 billion clock cycles = 1GHz. Early CPUs, up until the 80486 DX-2 series, had external data busses that operated at the same speed as the CPU. A 33MHz chip was a 33MHz chip inside and out. With the advent of "clock doubling" technology, manufacturers started making CPUs that could execute instructions internally faster than they were able to communicate with the rest of the computer. The first example of this was the Intel DX2 25/50. The external bus ran at 25MHz, but inside the CPU processed data at twice that speed.

Modern computers run on 100MHz, 133MHz, 200MHz, 266MHz, and 400MHz external data busses. Yet the chips themselves run much faster than that. Therefore, your 1.3GHz CPU is capable of processing instructions internally at 1.3 billion clock cycles per second. The FSB, however, is limited to its own speed. For example, the Athlon Thunderbird has an FSB of 266MHz. So, while the CPU is executing commands or moving data 1.3 billion times each second, the external data bus puts data on the telegraph wire, or retrieves processed data from it, only 266 million times per second. That means that, for every tick of the clock that the CPU is being fed data or instructions, it has another five ticks to act upon it while the prefetch locates more data.

THE CPU AND MEMORY

Because programs do consist of so many lines of code, it is necessary to have some fast method of feeding the instructions to the CPU. Even the 8088 could execute instructions at a rate of 4.77 million per second. You can't type them in that fast. In the early days of computing, holes were punched in cards and these were fed to the computer. Early card readers were capable of several thousand cards per second, or less than one tenth of one percent of the speed of the slowest CPU ever used on a PC. Magnetic tape was fast enough to feed data to these earlier CPUs, but a program needed to be able to jump from one section of code to another. IF/THEN statements were a good example of that. If the user or the program returned a YES, one section of the program would be executed; if a NO was returned, a completely different section of code was run. Magnetic tape could not be accessed in this way very efficiently. Even if it could, the life span of the machine would be very short. So random access memory was invented.

ACCESSING RAM

Random Access Memory (RAM) is not only extremely fast, but any line of code stored within it can be accessed at any time. By itself, the CPU is incapable of addressing RAM directly. The MCC that I discussed in Chapter Five, Motherboards, BIOS, and the Chipset, keeps track of the data stored in RAM. The MCC treats RAM like a giant spreadsheet with a column for each bit the CPU can access per clock cycle and as many rows as there are bytes of RAM. A 1MB 8088 would have eight columns and 1,048,576 rows. (This is, of course, a very simplified logical explanation of how information is stored in RAM. For more detail, refer to Chapter Eight, Searching Your Memory.) The CPU could scan up and down this spreadsheet as though it were a menu and grab the byte it needed.

The Address Bus

In order to find whatever byte is needed, the CPU needs a roadmap to all that memory. Well, this is more work than the registers in the CPU were designed to handle. In the original IBM PC, a separate chip, called the Memory Control Chip, assumed this responsibility. As I said earlier, current PCs count on the chipset for this task. The MCC is the master of the RAM spreadsheet. To communicate with the MCC, the CPU's prefetch circuit uses its address bus. The address bus is a collection of wires that allows the CPU to tell the MCC exactly which line of code in the RAM spreadsheet, or which byte in RAM, it currently needs. The 8088 CPU was developed with twenty wires on the address bus. Subsequent CPUs increased this number, but for now, let's stick with the twenty of the 8088. While technology has changed the amount of memory that can be addressed, the method by which it does its job is fundamentally the same.

With twenty wires available, that was a collection of twenty switches that could be either on or off, or twenty switches that were either open or closed. The number of possible combinations of on/off or open/closed that is offered by twenty wires is 2^{20}. Use your scientific calculator, and you'll see that 2^{20} will always total 1,048,576. That is the total number of bytes that the 8088 can address. This became the infamous *megabyte*. Therefore, any

> **BUZZ WORDS**
>
> **Address bus:** A bank of wires running throughout the system and into the CPU that identifies specific locations. The total addressable space is calculated as 2x, where x represents the total number of wires in the bus.

time you hear the term megabyte in reference to memory, it does not refer to 1 million bytes. It refers to 1,048,576 bytes. (This can get little confusing because to hard drive manufacturers, a megabyte is an even million bytes. More on that in Chapter Twelve, Hard Disk Drive Structure and Geometry.) If we should carry that out a little further, we see that sixteen megabytes is 16 × 1,048,576, or 16,777,216 bytes. 128MB is 128 × 1,048,576, or 134,217,728 bytes.

The combination of ON/OFF that the CPU lights up on any given clock cycle on the Address Bus tells the MCC which of the 1,048,576 rows of the RAM spreadsheet from which to extract the byte of data it seeks.

Which pattern goes to which line of RAM? That's pretty easy. The operating system controls how memory is used. It tells the CPU where everything is loaded. The "cells" in our imaginary spreadsheet are numbered from 0000 0000 0000 0000 0000 to 1111 1111 1111 1111 1111. Remember, in binary, you don't count 0, 1, 2, 3, etc. You count 0, 1, 10, 11, 100, 101, etc. To see the 20-bit address space of the 8088, simply keep counting like that until you get to 1111 1111 1111 1111 1111. Take your time. I'll wait. So it doesn't matter how many bytes of information are stored in the 1,048,576 available rows. The CPU only requires twenty wires to find what it needs. Remember, however, that later CPUs increased the size of the address bus in subsequent generations of CPUs, so they use a few more wires.

CACHE

One thing that has remained constant throughout the history of computing has been that the CPU is faster than the rest of the system. RAM can be a bottleneck, but mass storage is much worse. In the event that the CPU has to go out to the hard drive for data, there can be several hundred, or even several thousand, clock cycles in which the CPU sits idle waiting for data. Designers sidestepped this issue by adding very fast SRAM memory (see Chapter Eight, Searching Your Memory) to the motherboard as an area to store data that the CPU will probably need next. Code is accessed sequentially, and generally, so is data. With this in mind, as the system accesses the piece of data or code actually requested by the CPU, it will also retrieve the next few lines and store it in cache until the CPU requests it. Programmers developed several algorithms for predicting what data or code will be needed next. Now, the prefetch unit has an additional place to look for data before it hits the RAM or hard drive.

Starting with the 80486, CPU designers started putting small amounts of cache onboard the CPU itself. Data can be retrieved from there even quicker. The two areas of cache that are found on CPUs are Level One (L1) and Level Two (L2). Some motherboard designers have gone so far as to provide Level Three (L3) cache. Early CPUs didn't have L2 cache. However, engineers discovered that, working in conjunction with L1, L2 cache provided such a substantial

Table 6.1 CPU Onboard Cache Comparison

CPU	L1	L2	L3
Intel or AMD 80486DX and DX2	8K	N/A	N/A
Intel or AMD 80486DX4	16K	N/A	N/A
Intel Pentium	16K	N/A	N/A
Intel Pentium Pro	16K	256K, 512K, or 1M	N/A
Intel Pentium MMX	32K	N/A	N/A
Intel Pentium II and III	32K	256K	N/A
Intel Celeron	32K	0K, 32K, 128K or 256K	N/A
Intel Itanium	32K	96K	2MB or 4MB
Intel Itanium II	32K	256K	1.5MB or 3MB
Intel P4 Xeon	8K*	256K	N/A
Intel Pentium III CopperMine	32K	256K, 512K	
Intel Pentium 4	*	12K data + 8K ETC*	256K
AMD K5	16K Instruction, 8K Data	N/A	N/A
AMD K6 and K6-2	64K	N/A	N/A
AMD K6-3	64K	256K	N/A
AMD K7 Athlon	128K	512K	N/A
AMD Duron	128K	64K	N/A
AMD Athlon Thunderbird	128K	256K	N/A
AMD Athlon XP	128K	256 or 512K	N/A
AMD Athlon XP-MP	128K	256K	N/A

Different models of CPU have different amounts of cache loaded onboard. Many include L2 cache.

*The Pentium 4 and the P4 Xeon replace conventional L1 cache with something they call Execution Trace Cache. Because of its low latency of only two clock cycles, engineers dropped the cache size down to accommodate this change.

boost in performance that the major CPU manufactures began putting L2 on the CPU as well. Because the amounts of L1 and L2 cache vary among the manufacturers, and indeed among models by the same manufacturer, this is a factor that should be carefully considered when selecting CPUs.

The effect of L2 cache should not be underestimated. A couple of years back I performed some tests to see how much gain I actually got from adding cache to the system. I started with a motherboard that shipped with 0K L2 cache, but that allowed the user to add cache using 256K, 512K, or 1MB COAST (Chip on a Stick) modules. The basic system was a Pentium 166 CPU with 32MB of RAM. I chose such an old architecture because this was the only way I could keep the CPU constant and make sure that any differences I obtained were a result of differences in cache.

I made the measurements using Winstone. Performance with 0K of L2 cache was acceptable for a CPU of that vintage, but nothing to write home to Mom about. Adding a 256K module increased performance by a full 42 percent. Going from 256K to 512K boosted it by another 22 percent. Yet bumping it to 1MB provided only negligible gains. Admittedly, this was not a scientific process, and these results should not be construed as anything conclusive. CPU speed, the chipset used, and the amount of physical RAM installed in a machine will all have an impact on these results. However, I do feel that the results give a realistic view of the impact cache can have on performance.

CPU FORM FACTOR

In Chapter One, I talked about how motherboards and cases came in specific form factors in order to assure that one manufacturer's product worked with another's. As with these devices, CPUs come in different form factors as well. Traditionally, CPUs have been available in either PGA (Pin Grid Array) or SPGA (Staggered Pin Grid Array). Other terms you might see tossed around on occasion are IPGA (Interstitial Pin Grid Array) and FC-PGA (Flip-Chip PGA). These are simply variations on SPGA. The only difference between PGA and SPGA is that PGA utilized perfectly arranged pins, laid out in a square grid as shown in **Figure 6.3**.

SPGA "staggered" the rows of pins across the chip. This allowed for tighter placement of pins, nearly doubling the number of pins that could be fit onto the same size package. This became necessary with the Pentium CPU because of the number of pins needed to support its wider busses and its advanced features. **Figure 6.4** shows the base of an SPGA chip very clearly.

Figure 6.3 The PGA package has a perfect grid of pins extruding from the base of the chip.

Figure 6.4 SPGA chips cram more pins onto the base of the chip by alternating the rows. Not only can the pins be placed closer together, but the rows can also be tightened up.

Intel introduced a new form factor with the release of the Pentium II called the SECC (discussed in Chapter Five, shown here in **Figure 6.5**, top). This CPU was mounted on an edge card connector, not at all dissimilar to an expansion card. Intel felt that this design would provide for better cooling. Its more recent CPU design has gone back to the PGA form factor in one it calls PPGA, or Plastic Pin Grid Array. Essentially, it is an SPGA chip using a plastic housing instead of a ceramic one.

Naturally, the form factor of the CPU must match that of the motherboard. Specifically, the CPU must fit the appropriate socket. A complete discussion of CPU sockets can be found in Chapter Five, Motherboards, BIOS, and the Chipset.

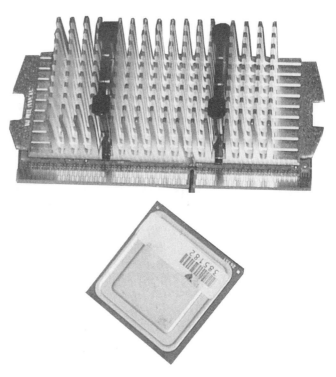

Figure 6.5 When you see them side by side like this, it's pretty hard not to be able to tell the difference between a Slot One CPU and a Socket 7 CPU.

Caution: Just because a motherboard says that it's for a Pentium 4, or supports a Celeron processor, is no clear-cut indication that it supports specific models. For example, there were two different versions of the FC-PGA 370 socket used by the Celeron processor, and more recent Celerons fit on a 478-pin socket. Pentium 4s have been manufactured for both 423-pin sockets and 478-pin sockets. Make sure your processor and motherboard match before confirming an order.

ADVANCED CPU CAPABILITIES

When the microprocessor first hit the scenes, it was amazing enough that it could do what it did. Here was a device that not only could add, subtract, multiply, and divide several million operations per second, but you could actually give it orders and it would follow them! The thought that a CPU could see into the future, and to a certain extent, read your mind (or at least the programmer's mind) was inconceivable. Yet, to a very great extent, many modern chips do just that. The best of CPU advances come about when the manufacturers teach them new tricks.

PROTECTED MODE

The first CPUs to come out could work only in Real Mode. What this means is that data could only be accessed across a 20-bit address bus, which was derived from joining two 16-bit registers. The end result of that was that programs operating in real mode could only "see" a total of 1MB of total memory space, and could only access data in chunks that were a maximum of 64K (a limit imposed by the 16-bit

registers used). In order to allow programs to use the full capacity of larger address busses, operating systems had to be modified as well as the electronics. Older programs written to access the 20-bit address bus had to work differently than the newer ones that could move into the extended space offered by a larger bus. And the CPU had to process the data accordingly.

Protected mode makes use of additional registers by allowing applications and operating systems to make use of the extended space without allowing legacy programs that can only operate in real mode to blow up the rest of the system. An older DOS program that needs to run in real mode gets its own address space that is protected from all other applications.

The real protection, however, occurs because a misbehaving application won't necessarily bring down the rest of the system. If it crashes, other applications, each running in their own protected space, continue blithely along neither knowing, nor caring, that some poor legacy app just bit the bullet.

FLOATING POINT OPERATIONS

I've already made mention of the FPU and described what it does. However, many chips optimize performance simply in redefining how this particular portion of the CPU does its job. In the 80486, simply the fact that a separate Math Coprocessor was no longer required (the circuitry was part of the CPU) was a huge advantage. It simplified the design of motherboards and shaved a few dollars off the average price of systems that required this function.

Some newer models of CPUs improve performance by reducing the number of clock cycles required to perform an FPU operation. Enhanced instruction sets provide most of this performance increase. Another method used by manufacturers is to increase the amount of circuitry dedicated to the FPU. Most modern CPUs provide multiple FPUs so that several operations can be going on at once.

In terms of overall system performance this has a minimal impact on the system. Unless you happen to be running very complicated programs requiring complex mathematical operations, changes in FPU design have only nominal affect.

INSTRUCTION PIPELINING

Another limitation of the first CPUs was that once an instruction or set of instructions was submitted to the CPU for processing, everything else in the computer sat back and waited until it was finished before submitting any more requests. Complex instructions could take many clock cycles to pass through the various stages of the CPU before the results finally made their way out the external data bus.

Instruction pipelining, generally just called pipelining, moves the next instruction onto the external data bus while the one before it is still going through its processes. Therefore, during any given clock cycle, multiple instructions can be in varying stages of completion, while others are waiting in the instruction cache for their turn at bat.

You could compare this to two different methods of emptying an aquarium. In the days before pipelining, you had to empty the fish tank with a cup. You'd fill the cup, move it over to the sink and dump the water, then go back and fill it again. You'd have to repeat this process until the tank was empty. Pipelining allowed you to put several siphon hoses into the tank, hang the other end of each one of them into the sink and start the instructions flowing through.

The impact of pipelining can depend heavily on a couple of factors. The first of these is in how linear the code being processed happens to be. If one instruction follows the other in precise order, or if the correct instructions happen to reside in L1 cache as the prefetch is lining up commands, then it works very well. As soon as the cycle is broken and the CPU has to go out looking for commands or data to process, the effect is lost. You've thrown off its groove.

> **BUZZ WORDS** ────────────
>
> **Instruction pipelining:** The ability of certain CPUs to be loading the next set of instructions or data at the same time they process the current set.
>
> **Superscalar architecture:** A microprocessor design that provides multiple pathways for data to take as it is being processed. This allows several lines of code to be processed simultaneously.

SUPERSCALAR ARCHITECTURE

Superscalar architecture was introduced to the world of CPUs with the fifth generation of microprocessors (more on the processor generations later in this chapter). This technology opens up more than just one path for instructions to follow through the processor. While there is still only a single external data bus bringing data into the CPU, once it's inside, there are two different layers of circuitry to process the data. Multiple lines of code can be processed simultaneously. In a way, it is similar to having a second CPU on board. There are some limitations, however. The second execution unit can't handle the full load of commands. Also, programs have to be written specifically to take advantage of this architecture as well. Otherwise, all that fancy new circuitry goes ignored.

To understand how this benefits most applications, consider the following scenario. If you've ever tried to get into the parking lot at the State Fair, you've seen an example of the effect this can have on the speed of throughput. When you first arrive, only a single lane is open, and the cars move through very slowly. Then somebody starts showing signs of intelligence and opens a second gate. The parking lot now fills twice as fast. This scenario is doubly accurate because the prefetch even allows instructions to slip in from the back of the line and scoot in ahead of those that have been waiting a while. A good fair attendant won't do that.

BRANCH PREDICTION

Writing computer programs is an art. I've always had the greatest respect for good programmers. They have to anticipate every possible event and accommodate that event in the code. However, code is written in blocks. And sometimes the block of code that needs to be run will be determined by the outcome of what's going on inside the CPU.

The purpose of adding cache memory to a computer system was to try to minimize the amount of time required for the CPU to find the instructions or data it needs. The more often the prefetch finds what it needs in cache, the faster the system runs overall. Of course, programs frequently run into forks in the road, situations where if the user answers "YES" to a query, it runs one routine, and conversely, a "NO" will require loading a different section of code. When this happens, the CPU will stall because the prefetch has no idea which direction to go for code. Or it can gamble by picking a direction and going there. Some programmers chose the latter method, because there was at least a fifty-fifty chance of the CPU finding what it needed in cache.

Unfortunately, the fifty-fifty-ninety rule usually applied. This rule states that if there is a fifty-fifty chance of making the correct choice, there's a ninety percent chance you'll choose wrong. *Branch prediction* allows the prefetch to bring in several lines of code from either branch, so whichever way the CPU winds up heading, there are commands there for it to process.

SPECULATIVE EXECUTION

Speculative execution takes branch prediction to the next level. The CPU takes a wild guess about which way the code is going and preprocesses the first few lines of code. When it guesses right, it's got a head start in running the subroutine. If it's wrong, it simply dumps the registers and starts over, using the data provided by the prefetch. No harm, no foul. That isn't any slower than it would have been had it not even tried. When it's right, a trip to the hard drive is avoided. As I will discuss in Chapter Twelve, Hard Disk Drive Structure and Geometry, this shaves hundreds, or even thousands of clock cycles off of the total processing time.

OUT-OF-ORDER EXECUTION

Computers being what they are, it is pretty easy to assume that data always arrives at the CPU in precisely the order in which it is needed. Instructions always arrive in the right sequence and data is always there when you need it. Right?

And your spouse is always ready when you are, and you're never late for work either. Right?

The fact of the matter is, data is not always there when the processor needs it and the more complex programs become, the more the CPU starts seeing sets of instructions it is going to eventually need before it gets the ones it needs now. In the old days, the CPU just waited. If you were lucky, instructions waited in cache until the CPU was ready, and would be there when the processor was ready for them. The control unit would then make sure that those instructions ran in the correct order. More often, too many clock cycles would elapse and the instructions would be flushed from cache.

Modern CPUs employ a process knows as out-of-order execution to keep busy and minimize dead time. A CPU can run certain types of instructions in advance and store the results in the data cache. Then when the data or instructions it was waiting for arrive, it processes those instructions.

Buzz Words

Hyperthreading: The ability of certain CPUs to execute multiple lines of code at the same time.

Streaming SIMD: The ability of certain CPUs to execute an instruction only once, but apply that instruction to several sets of data.

HYPERTHREADING

One of the limitations of all the technologies discussed above is that they assume that only one line of code, or thread, as it is called, will be running on the CPU at any instant in time. In today's world of multitasking operating systems and multitasking users, this is rarely the case. *Hyperthreading* allows the CPU to process two (or more) threads of code simultaneously. In the past, multiple threads could be processed, but they did so by "time-sharing" the CPU.

STREAMING SIMD EXTENSIONS

SIMD is an acronym for Single Instruction, Multiple Data. A processor frequently has a single instruction that will be executed on multiple data sets. Prior to the incorporation of *streaming SIMD extensions* (SSE), in order to do this the CPU would have to process the instruction separately for each data set to be run. SSE allows the CPU to process the instructions once and simply apply them to each data set in turn. This can reduce processing time by several clock cycles per data set.

CPU COOLING

When computers first came out, there was no need to take any special measures in order to keep the CPU running cool. At 4.77MHz, the fan in the power supply kept the air moving inside the case well enough. These days, thermal issues take the forefront. CPUs running at several gigahertz, combined with chipsets running several hundred megahertz and video cards that run at several hundred megahertz create a major problem. The CPU, without some form of cooling mechanism, can actually heat up enough to fry your eggs for you in the morning. The problem is that it's hard to keep the computer running when that happens.

CONVECTIVE COOLING

Starting with the 80486, it became necessary to add some form of device that would dissipate the heat from the CPU and expel it from the enclosure. The earliest CPU heat sinks, such as the one seen in **Figure 6.6**, simply consisted of metal fins. Heat from the CPU was moved into the fins and a cooling fan in the case sucked the warm air out of the enclosure. This process of moving heat from one metal object to another is called convection.

When the Pentium was first released, it was quite obvious that a simple passive heat sink would not be sufficient. Those babies cranked out some temperature! Innovative designers came up with various designs of heat sink that incorporated a fan built right in. This allowed the heat sink/fan combination to suck the heat out of the CPU and actively blow it away. Enclosure fans evacuated the hot air from inside the case.

LIQUID COOLING

These days, it is possible to install liquid cooling systems into computers. These elaborate systems work exactly like the radiator in an automobile. A small pump moves liquid through tubes that run in direct contact with the CPU. The cooled liquid in the tubes draws the heat away the chip and carries it to fins that are located near the outside of the case. The fins draw the heat from the liquid and a fan blows across the fins keeping them cool. The cooled liquid circulates back to the CPU to pick up more heat.

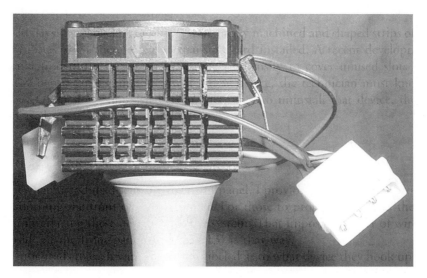

Figure 6.6   A simple CPU heat sink.

Liquid cooling has a couple of advantages over convective cooling. For one thing, it's much more efficient. Components on liquid-cooled systems run far more coolly than do those of convective systems. An advantage that often gets overlooked is the fact that since the fans don't have to spin nearly as fast in a liquid-cooled system as they do in convective systems, the system also runs more quietly.

CHAPTER SUMMARY

Okay, I've now completed my case that the CPU cannot stand alone as being the "brains" of the computer. Still, as you saw, it is a very complicated device and a technological marvel. And each year they get faster and more complex.

As a device, the CPU predates the PC by several years, having served in devices such as pocket calculators and mainframes. It is important that you have a good understanding of the history and evolution of microprocessors as they developed, and it won't hurt to have a good understanding of how they work.

BRAIN DRAIN

1. Describe how a semiconductor works, and explain why it is such a useful material in making CPUs.

2. List the key subcomponents of a CPU and briefly describe their function.

3. Explain why the 8088 CPU was only capable of recognizing 1MB of memory.

4. Just what do engineers mean by "protected mode" and why is it important today?

5. Describe in as much detail as you can how the system moves data into the CPU after you press a certain key on your keyboard.

THE 64K$ QUESTIONS

1. The binary language is an offshoot of the work of _____.

   a. George Boole

   b. Frederick Hoffner

   c. Ted Hoff

   d. Al Shugart

2. When the microprocessor is processing a thread of code and realizes it need additional data, the _____ instructs the _____ to locate that data.

   a. Prefetch, External data bus

   b. Prefetch, Control unit

   c. Control unit, Prefetch

   d. Control unit, Data cache

3. The address bus of the 8088 was _____ bits wide.

   a. 8

   b. 16

   c. 20

   d. 32

4. A microprocessor is running a line of code and comes to a place where either one of two different subroutines will be run next, depending on whether the user selects "Yes" or "No." What technology allows the

CPU to load a few lines of each subroutine even before the user makes a selection?

a. Protected mode

b. Instruction pipelining

c. Branch prediction

d. Speculative execution

5. In the example used in Question 4, what technology would allow the CPU to actually process those lines of code before the user made a selection, discarding any data generated by the wrong subroutine?

a. Protected mode

b. Instruction pipelining

c. Branch prediction

d. Speculative execution

6. The first CPU used in an IBM PC ran at _____ MHz.

a. 2.77

b. 4.77

c. 8

d. 12

7. It is not possible for a CPU to have more than one FPU.

a. True

b. False

8. Why is the 64K block of data so important to CPU operations?

a. Because all registers are only 16 bits wide.

b. It is a throwback to the days of 16-bit CPUs.

c. Because the Pentium CPU is limited to a 64-bit external data bus.

d. It is a throwback to the pre-PC days when microprocessors only had a 16-bit address bus.

9. The following is a collection of very useful circuits that appear on all modern CPUs, but was not a part of the original 8088.

a. Decode unit

b. Instruction cache

c. Control unit

d. L2 cache

10. Superscalar architecture is a technology that allows _____.

a. Multiple lines of code to be processed simultaneously.

b. Multiple processors to be installed on a single die.

c. Multiple processors to be installed on a single system board.

d. Merged audio/video streams to be processed as a single stream of code.

TRICKY TERMINOLOGY

Address bus: A bank of wires running throughout the system and into the CPU that specifies specific locations. The total addressable space is calculated as 2x, where x represents the total number of wires in the bus.

Arithmetic logic unit: A subcomponent of a microprocessor responsible for executing simple mathematical calculations, such as add, subtract, multiply, and divide. It cannot perform floating point calculations.

Back-side bus: A portion of the EDB. It is the path that data takes as it moves from cache loaded on the CPU's die into the CPU's registers.

Branch prediction: The ability of certain CPUs to be able to predict a situation where either one of two separate subroutines may be run, depending on the results of processing code not yet completed. A CPU capable of branch prediction will load a few lines of code from each subroutine.

Clock cycle: A timing signal generated by an electrical current that synchronizes data movement throughout the system. As an electrical current, a clock cycle resembles a sine wave with a rising half of the signal and a falling half.

Data cache: A set of registers used for storing data loaded by the prefetch until such time as the CPU is ready to use it.

Decode unit: The subcomponent of a microprocessor that takes complex instructions and breaks them down into a series of simpler instructions that the CPU is able to understand.

External data bus: The wires that move data from outside the CPU to the internal registers of the CPU.

Floating point unit: A subcomponent of a microprocessor that is responsible for more complex mathematical calculations.

Front-side bus: A portion of the EDB. It is the path that data takes from outside locations to make its way into the CPU.

Hyperthreading: The ability of certain CPUs to execute multiple lines of code at the same time.

Instruction cache: A set of registers used for storing instruction code loaded by the prefetch until such time as the CPU is ready to use it.

Instruction pipelining: The ability of certain CPUs to be loading the next set of instructions or data at the same time they process the current set.

Linewidth: The actual thickness of traces used within the CPU.

Logic gate: Two or more transistors whose position will direct the positioning of the next bank of transistors downstream.

Megabyte: Depending on whether you are calculating a value in binary or decimal, a megabyte is either 1 million bytes (decimal) or 1,048,576 bytes (binary). A binary megabyte is used in virtually every circumstance except when calculating hard drive capacity. Hard drive manufacturers typically define capacity in decimal values.

Prefetch: The subcomponent of a microprocessor that is responsible for retrieving data and moving it into the CPU.

Protected mode: A function of a CPU that prevents two separate programs from seeing each other's code or from attempting to use overlapping memory addresses. Should either event occur, the CPU would lock up.

Register: A bank of transistors grouped together to perform a specific function.

Semiconductor: A substance that exhibits the characteristics of both a conductor and a resistor, depending on the amount of voltage passing through.

Speculative execution: When two different subroutines have been loaded by branch prediction, speculative execution will actually process the lines of each branch loaded.

Streaming SIMD: The ability of certain CPUs to execute an instruction only once, but apply that instruction to several sets of data.

Threshold voltage: The amount of electrical differential required to move a semiconductor from a state of resistance to a state of conductance.

Transistor: A microscopic on/off switch that uses the electrical characteristics of a semiconductor to reverse positions.

ACRONYM ALERT

ALU: Arithmetic Logic Unit. The subcomponent of a CPU that handles rudimentary mathematical functions.

BSB: Back-Side Bus. The portion of the EDB that moves data back and forth between onboard cache and the CPU.

CPU: Central Processing Unit. The primary microprocessor that executes program code and processes user data in a computer system.

EDB: External Data Bus. The path that data uses to move from the CPU to an outside circuit, or vice versa.

FC-PGA: Flip Chip Pin Grid Array. A CPU socket designed for easy CPU installation or replacement used in modern machines.

FPU: Floating Point Unit. The subcomponent of the CPU that handles more advanced mathematical functions.

FSB: Front-Side Bus. The portion of the EDB that moves data in and out of the CPU from external locations.

Hz: Hertz. A measurement for frequency, or the number of times during any given timing cycle that the measured event occurs.

L1: Level 1. A small amount of extremely fast memory used to store data or instructions that the CPU expects it will need within a few clock cycles, or that it uses frequently.

L2: Level 2. A secondary level of slower cache memory. This is usually a larger amount of memory than the L1 and is the second place the CPU looks for needed instructions or data.

L3: Level 3. A third layer of cache supported only by a select few CPUs.

MB: Megabyte. In binary, this would be 1,048,576 bytes. In decimal, it would be 1 million bytes.

SIMD: Single Instruction, Multiple Data. A process by which a CPU can execute an instruction once, but apply that instruction to several sets of data simultaneously.

SSE: Streaming SIMD Extensions. The set of instructions that supports the execution of a single instruction on several sets of data at once.

CHAPTER 7

THE EVOLUTION AND DEVELOPMENT OF THE CPU

Now that you have a grasp of how the CPU works and some of the things going on underneath the hood, let's take a look at a detailed timeline of CPU evolution. This may not seem like such critical information at the outset, but two things make it important. First of all, knowing what CPU powers a particular computer will tell you whether or not it can run certain OSs or applications. Second, you need it to pass the A+ Core exam.

A+ EXAM OBJECTIVES

Some of the material covered in this chapter includes the following:

   1.1   Identify the names, purpose, and characteristics of system modules. Recognize these modules by sight or definition (CPU).

   1.2   Identify basic procedures for adding and removing field-replaceable modules for desktop systems. Given a replacement scenario, choose the appropriate sequences.

   1.10 Determine the issues that must be considered when upgrading a PC. In a given scenario, determine when and how to upgrade system components.

   4.1   Distinguish among the popular CPU chips in terms of their basic characteristics.

THE EVOLUTION OF THE CPU

Of all the components in a computer system, none gets more publicity than the CPU when it comes time for a new release. It seems that everyone is waiting on the sidelines in anticipation of each new generation of CPU. Some new releases are based on speed alone, while every once in a while an actual new technology emerges. Examples of technology improvements would

Table 7.1 A Timeline of Intel CPUs

CPU	Year Intro	Clock Speeds (MHz)	Ext. Bus	Int. Bus	RAM	Transistors
8086	1978	4.77, 8, 10	16-bit	16-bit	1MB	29,000
8088	1979	4.77, 8	8-bit	16-bit	1MB	29,000
80286	1982	6, 8, 10, 12	16-bit	16-bit	16MB	134,000
80386	1985	20, 25, 33	32-bit	32-bit	4GB	275,000
80386SX	1988	16, 20, 25, 33	16-bit	32-bit	16MB	275,000
80486DX	1989	25, 33, 50	32-bit	32-bit	4GB	1.2M
80486SX	1991	16, 20, 25, 33	32-bit	32-bit	4GB	900,000
80486DX2	1992	25/50, 33/66	32-bit	32-bit	4GB	1.2M
80486DX4	1994	25/75, 33/100	32-bit	32-bit	4GB	1.2M
Pentium	1994	60,66	64-bit	32-bit	4GB	3.1M
Pentium MMX	1997	166, 200, 233, 266	64-bit	32-bit	4GB	3.1M
Pentium PRO	1995	150, 166, 180, 200	64-bit	32-bit	64GB	5.5M
Pentium II	1997	233-450MHz	64-bit	32-bit	64GB	7.5M
Pentium III	1999	450MHz to 1.4GHz	64-bit	32-bit	64GB	28M
Pentium 4	2000	1GHz and up	64-bit	32-bit	64GB	42M

Evolution of Intel CPUs

include an FSB, new instruction sets moved onboard, or a new process added to chip functions. Also, from time to time, CPU manufacturers encode certain instructions into the CPU. As a result, when the prefetch goes looking for those instructions, it finds them waiting in the parlor, ready to serve.

For the first several years of PC evolution, it was Intel putting the vast majority of CPUs into PC-compatible computers (**Table 7.1**). However, a number of other chip manufacturers, including Advanced Micro Devices (AMD), Texas Instruments, Cyrix, and others, entered the fray with competing clones. Since there is not room in this book to discuss every chip ever made, I'll limit my discussions to the primary CPU families from the major manufacturers.

AMD entered the fray early with a competing line of CPUs, even though it would be several years before it would begin to give Intel any serious competition. For many years, its CPUs were identical to those of Intel. Then, after a well-publicized lawsuit between Intel and AMD, AMD began developing significant new technologies of its own (**Table 7.2**).

EXAM NOTE: Before going in to take the exam, make sure you know order in which the different models of CPU came out. Also be able to describe key differences among models, such as bus speed and width.

Table 7.2 A Timeline of AMD CPUs

CPU	Year Intro	Clock Speeds (MHz)	Ext. Bus	Int. Bus	RAM	Transistors
AM5x86[1]	1995	133	32-bit	32-bit	4GB	1.6M
K5	1996	75, 90, 120, 133, 166	64-bit	32-bit	4GB	4.3M
K6	1997	166, 200, 233, 266, 300	64-bit	32-bit	4GB	8.8M
K6-2	1998	266, 300, 333, 350, 366, 380, 400, 450, 475, 500, 533, 550	64-bit	32-bit	64GB	9.3M
K6-3	1998	400, 450, 500, 550	64-bit	32-bit	64GB	N/A
Athlon	1999	500, 550, 600, 650, 700, 750, 800	64-bit	32-bit	64GB	22M[2]
Duron	2000	600MHz to 1.3GHz3	64-bit	32-bit	64GB	25M
Thunderbird	2000	700MHz to 1.3GHz	64-bit	32-bit	37M	
Athlon XP	2001	1.7GHz to 3GHz[3]	54-bit	32-bit	64GB	37.5M

Evolution of AMD CPUs

[1] The 5x86 was not AMD's first CPU. However, all prior CPUs were manufactured using technology acquired under a cross-licensing agreement with Intel, and are therefore identical to equivalent Intel CPUs.
[2] Transistor count does not include L2 cache.
[3] CPU in current production as of this writing. Speeds are likely to exceed these before their life cycle ends.

PROCESSOR GENERATIONS

Over the years, as CPUs have evolved, there have been relatively few drastic breakthroughs in technology. Manufacturers will produce lengthy runs of various models of CPU based on the technology of the day. When a new breakthrough occurs, a new generation is launched. Thus begat the generations of the modern CPU.

FIRST-GENERATION PROCESSORS

The first Intel CPU used by IBM in its Personal Computer was the 8088. An optional math coprocessor, the Intel 8087, was available for motherboards that supported these chips. The 8088 was actually a revision of an existing chip, the 8086. The 8086 had a 16-bit external data bus (EDB), a 16-bit internal data bus (IDB), and a 16-bit address bus. IBM wanted to make use of the 8-bit devices already on the market, so the 16-bit EDB was a problem. It also wanted to address more than the 64K of RAM that a 16-bit address bus accommodates.

It approached Intel, who agreed to produce a modification of the 8086 that it called the 8088. This chip had an 8-bit EDB, 16-bit internal registers, and a 20-bit address bus. The

Table 7.3 First-Generation Processors

Chip	Date Released	Ext. Bus	Voltage	Die Size	MIPS
8088-4.77	1979	8-bit	5V	3 μ	.3
8088-8	1980	8-bit	5V	3 μ	.4
NEC V20	1984	8-bit	5V	Unknown	Unknown
80186-8/16	1982	8/16 hybrid	5V	3 μ	N/A

First-generation CPUs

20-bit address bus was achieved by combining two 16-bit registers onto a 20-bit register. A 16-bit register can basically address 64K of memory. By using two 16-bit registers, programmers could slice programs and data into 64K chunks. This also allowed for backward compatibility to earlier systems.

Intel was to see the start of competition with this first "IBM-compatible" release. Within months, American Micro Devices, Inc. (AMD) had come out with its own 8088, and NEC released a chip called the V20. Of the three major manufacturers, NEC's was probably the best performer and showed up on a number of clones.

SECOND-GENERATION PROCESSORS

This level of CPU is really only populated by a single family of chips. That is the 80286 along with its various clones. The biggest improvements in this chip line were the address bus and the ability to work in protected mode. The address bus was extended to 24-bit, allowing up to 16MB addressable physical memory.

I discussed protected mode in detail in Chapter Six. But to review, protected mode allowed the CPU to run multiple programs in "time slices," first focusing on one program for a few lines of code, and then allowing another program access to the CPU. In addition to time-sharing the CPU, individual programs could be given their own slice of the memory pie. Each program running on the PC had its own memory address, which was "protected" from invasion by other programs, hence the name.

Protected mode, of course, required an operating system that supported it. Windows did not yet exist as we know it, and MS-DOS had no built-in provision for either protected mode or managing memory beyond 1MB. During the life of the 286, a version of UNIX, a version of OS2, and one of Novel Netware was written to work in this mode. They allowed you to work in protected mode. However, in order to return to working in real mode, you had to reboot the machine.

The real can of worms that the 286 opened up was all that extra memory. It was invisible to MS-DOS, which was the operating system of choice for well over 80 percent of the computers being manufactured. In order to take advantage of it, certain third party companies wrote extensions to DOS that accommodated the extra addressable memory in other ways.

Table 7.4 Second-Generation Processors

Chip	Date Released	Ext. Bus	Voltage	Die Size	MIPS
80286-6	1982	16-bit	5V	1.5 μ	.9
80286-10	1982	16-bit	5V	1.5 μ	1.5
80286-12	1983	16-bit	5V	1.5 μ	2.66
80286-16	1983	16-bit	5V	1.5 μ	N/A
80286-20[1]	1990	16-bit	5V	N/A	N/A

Second-generation CPUs

[1] Clones of the 80286 series of CPUs were manufactured by AMD, Harris, and Siemens. There are no notable differences among the brands. Intel never manufactured the 80286-20. Harris and Siemens produced these after Intel had discontinued the line for use in PCs.

Expanded memory allowed data to be stored in available memory above 1MB. This required loading the EMM device driver in lower memory (taking up a big chunk of conventional memory needed by DOS programs). Out of necessity, the program ran in conventional memory. Data could be stored in expanded memory. Data from expanded memory was fed to the program in 64K chunks.

For this to work, you needed, first of all, the expanded memory installed on your computer. Then you needed to install a program designed specifically to manage expanded memory. Finally, you could run programs that had been written specifically to address expanded memory.

BUZZ WORDS

Expanded memory: Memory beyond the first megabyte of RAM that can be used for storing data. Expanded memory could not be used for executing programs.

Virtual memory: A slice of hard drive space that is reserved for the OS for temporary storage of data needed by dormant programs that is treated as if it were system memory.

THIRD-GENERATION PROCESSORS

Intel's 80386 represents this generation of microprocessors. These CPUs incorporated the first true 32-bit registers. Internal, address, and external busses were all 32-bit. This allowed for up to 4GB of addressable physical RAM and an unthinkable 64TB of addressable virtual memory. Virtual memory was an entirely new concept introduced by the 386. In addition, an advanced instruction set known as the x86 instruction set was introduced into the CPU. These core instructions continue to be the basis for Intel-based CPUs to this very day. An often-overlooked attribute of the 80386 is its ability to pipeline instructions.

The 32-bit registers allowed for twice as much data to be processed in a single clock cycle. More importantly, they allowed for commands to be 32 bits wide. Instructions could be more complex and the operating systems were subsequently more powerful. When more work can be done in a single clock cycle, everything speeds up.

EXAM NOTE: The 80386 microprocessor represented a major breakthrough in personal computing. As a result, it is not at all uncommon to see questions specific to this processor on the exam.

Virtual memory is a way of convincing the programs running on the computer that there is more memory installed than there really is. It reserves a portion of hard disk space for a *swap file*. This file takes program data, user data, and so on, and loads it onto the hard drive in the same way it would have been loaded into RAM, had there been sufficient physical memory to support it. The operating system reports this swap file as memory to the applications. The release of Windows 3.0 and all subsequent versions made full use of this technology.

Another advanced operating mode that the 386 offered was called *virtual real mode* (sometimes called Virtual 8086). In this mode, "bubbles" of 1MB memory spaces are created in which separate DOS programs could run. An operating system, such as Windows, that supported virtual real mode could load all the necessary device drivers and core program files into one of these address spaces and convince DOS programs that this memory constitutes the entire machine. As a result, the DOS program thinks it's the only program running and more than one DOS program at a time could be running.

A performance enhancement that began with the 386 and that is now a part of all CPUs is the process of pipelining instructions. As one set of instructions is being executed, the CPU is already in the process of lining up the next set to send through the "pipeline." This process not only enhanced the performance of the then-present lines of chips, it also opened the door to the dual-speed CPUs of today that have faster internal processing speeds than their external data bus.

The only problem with the 80386 was that, since it utilized a 32-bit external data bus, the CPU required newly designed 32-bit motherboards. There were several manufacturers that weren't tooled up to build these boards, but there were millions of 16-bit motherboards being built. In order to increase the acceptance of the 386 family, the 80386SX was released with a 16-bit external data bus. It was basically a crippled 386. It had all the advanced functions of the 386, however, and was therefore able to run Windows.

The 386SL was the first line of CPUs to be developed for the lower voltages required for laptop computers. There had been a number of 286 laptops, but they required about three hours of charging for every half hour of use. By running at 3.3V instead of 5V, the life of the portable computer's battery was greatly enhanced. Other brands, including AMD and Cyrix, released lower-voltage CPUs.

BUZZ WORDS

Swap file: The file on the hard disk that stores the data reserved in virtual memory.

Virtual real mode: A technique of creating separate address spaces and time slicing the CPU time so that legacy applications think they're the only programs running on the machine, even though there may be several running at once.

Table 7.5 Third-Generation Processors

Chip	Date Released	Ext. Bus	Voltage	Die Size	MIPS
80386DX-16	1985	32-bit	5V	1.5 μ	5-6
80386DX-20	1987	32-bit	5V	1.5 μ	6-7
80386DX-25	1988	32-bit	5V	1.5 μ	8.5
80386DX-33	1989	32-bit	5V	1.5 μ	11.4
80386DX-40[1]	1989	32-bit	5V	1.5 μ	
80386SX-16	1988	16-bit	5V	1.5 μ	2.5
80386SX-20	1989	16-bit	5V	1.5 μ	2.5
80386SX-25	1988	16-bit	5V	1.5 μ	2.7
80386SX-33	1992	16-bit	5V	1.5 μ	2.9
80386SL-20[2]	1990	16-bit	3.3V	1 μ	4.2
80386SL-25	1991	16-bit	3.3V	1 μ	5.3

Comparison of 80386 microprocessors. While these numbers are based on Intel CPUs, it should be noted that equivalent CPUs were also manufactured by AMD and Cyrix.

[1] The 80386DX-40 was never manufactured by Intel. This was a product that was put out by both AMD and Cyrix.
[2] Other variations on the SL CPU included the SLC and the SLX. These chips were manufactured by AMD, Cyrix, IBM, and Intel.

FOURTH-GENERATION PROCESSORS

The 80486DX was basically an evolution of the 386. None of the registers or busses was altered. The real advances were in other forms. The biggest real advance of the CPU was an advanced instruction set. The most commonly used instructions were permanently loaded into the CPU and instantly available when those instructions were called upon. This prevented the CPU from having to load and unload those instructions from memory each time they were called upon.

One of the key limitations of CPUs prior to the 80486 is that the only arithmetic functions they could perform were basic addition, subtraction, multiplication, and division. Also, they could only handle full-integer mathematics. Anything more advanced required programmers to break the formulae down to their basic steps. The other option was to install the MathCo specific to the CPU. The 486DX was the first CPU to have a coprocessor built right in.

Another improvement of the 486 was to add 8K of L1 cache right on the CPU. It could also make use of L2 cache installed on the motherboard. In order to make the L2 cache faster, a special form of memory called *static RAM* (SRAM) was used. SRAM was designed differently than DRAM and did not require frequent refreshes.

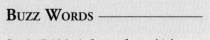

BUZZ WORDS

Static RAM: A form of very high-speed memory that is frequently used for cache.

There are actually two varieties of cache. Write-through cache sends data directly out of the CPU to RAM, whether the MCC is ready or not. If not, the CPU simply sets up a wait state. In other words, the data waits in line for a seat on the external data bus. Write-back cache will store the data in L2 cache until a clock cycle comes along that can transmit it back to RAM.

The 486 had the capability of talking to the local bus at either 25 or 33MHz, depending on the CPU. ISA devices were still limited to 8.33MHz for backward compatibility, but VESA Local Bus and the Peripheral Components Interconnect (PCI) both came out during the 486 reign. I'll be discussing these busses in detail in Chapter Nine, Examining the Expansion Bus. VESA stands for Video Electronic Standards Association, which was the organization that defined the 32-bit VESA standard popular in 486s. PCI allowed for even faster bus speeds. Both tapped into the local bus to allow components to operate at the external bus speed of the CPU in order to overcome the 8.33MHz limitation of ISA.

> **NOTE:** Just changing the speed of a CPU is no guarantee of a noticeable performance gain. A rule of thumb is that to achieve a barely perceivable gain in performance, you must double CPU speed. On the other hand, new technologies, such as on-chip instruction sets that relate to the type of work you do or a faster front-side bus, can provide substantial gains.

Under earlier technology, the maximum speed of the CPU was limited to that of the external data bus. That was before Intel developed a technology called clock doubling that allowed the CPU to operate at twice the EDB speed. This allowed for a 66MHz microprocessor. These CPUs were called DX2s. Then came the DX4. DX-4 CPUs processed data internally at a speed three times that of the EDB. Therefore, the 25MHz 486 DX-4 ran internally at 75MHz, and the 33MHz DX-4 ran at 100MHz. (Note that the actual speed of the CPU was 33.32MHz.)

The 486SX was released as an "economy" 486. The official version of how this chip was different than other 486s was that it lacked a math coprocessor. This was purely marketing hype. Intel never bothered to retool for a different CPU. It simply disabled the math coprocessor. Therefore, a product that actually had to go through an extra manufacturing step was sold at a lower price simply to appease the public.

FIFTH-GENERATION PROCESSORS

Now for a quick history lesson. Throughout the reign of the 386s and 486s Intel kept a pretty tight grip on the market. It had the marketing clout, it had the engineering clout, and it had the best research and development. What it lacked was sufficient production capabilities to keep up with increasing demand for its chips. To pick up the slack, Intel signed into a cross-licensing agreement with Advanced Micro Devices, Inc. (AMD). Intel would provide the R&D, cross-license the patents to AMD, and the two companies would outsource chips to each other.

This worked out pretty well for both companies for a while. It was an almost-perfect symbiotic relationship. Unfortunately, somewhere along the line, relations between the two companies began to deteriorate. Intel had opened two new production facilities and no longer needed the services of AMD. There followed a rather unpleasant legal battle, with decisions being reversed and then restored and then being reversed again as the case was passed from one

Table 7.6 Fourth-Generation Processors

Chip	Date Released	Ext.Bus	Voltage	Die Size	iCOMP (version)	MIPS
80486DX-25	1989	32-bit	5V	1 μ	122 (1.0)	20
80486DX-33	1990	32-bit	5V	1 μ	166 (1.0)	27
80486DX-50	1991	32-bit	5V	1 μ	249 (1.0)	41
80486DX2-50	1992	32-bit	5V	.8 μ	231 (1.0)	41
80486DX2-66	1992	32-bit	5V	.8 μ	297 (1.0)	54
80486DX4-75	1992	32-bit	5V	.6 μ	319 (1.0)	53
80486DX4-100	1992	32-bit	5V	.6 μ	435 (1.0)	70.7
80486SX-16[1]	1991	32-bit	5V	1 μ	63 (1.0)	13
80486SX-20[2]	1991	32-bit	5V	1 μ	78 (1.0)	16.5
80486SX-25[2]	1991	32-bit	5V	.8 μ	100 (1.0)	20
80486SX-33[2]	1992	32-bit	5V	.8 μ	136 (1.0)	27
Blue Lightening-75[3]	1993	32-bit	5V	.8 μ	?	?

Comparison of 80486 microprocessors. AMD, Cyrix, and IBM also made competing chips.

[1] SX chips differed from DX models primarily in the fact that the onboard math coprocessor was disabled.
[2] An SL version of these chips was available in a low-power version for notebook computers.
[3] The Blue Lightening was manufactured only by IBM and could not be purchased separately. Intel's licensing agreement with IBM stated that the chip could be sold only on a board.

judge to another. While, theoretically, Intel won, it ended in a decision not entirely favorable to Intel. It was decided that the cross-licensing agreements did indeed allow AMD to continue to produce CPUs based on technology that had been licensed to it. Unfortunately for AMD, this only included technology up to the 80386. In another related case, the courts determined that the terms 80486, 80386, and so forth, had come to be generic terms for a type of CPU, in that Intel, AMD, and Cyrix had produced chips using this nomenclature without challenge from Intel. Therefore, Intel could not copyright the trade name 80486.

Of course, Intel hadn't been sitting back on its heels doing nothing the whole time the courts were deciding the outcome of the lawsuit. The 80586 was already behind the curtains, waiting for its debut. Intel had been procrastinating release of the CPU until it knew what impact the ruling may have on its intellectual property rights. The resultant release, the Pentium, was so named because it was a trademark that could be copyrighted. In addition, a few engineering tweaks used technology that had not been cross-licensed to AMD.

THE P5

The first Pentiums to be released were 5V chips. There were two speeds of the P5 made available, the 60MHz and the 66MHz. In actuality, the original design called for all P5s to be

66MHz. Unfortunately, manufacturing yields were resulting in a lot of chips that just couldn't run at 66MHz without overheating. They could, however, run at 60MHz. They were labeled as 60MHz and shipped out.

This CPU was redesigned to have a 64-bit EDB. This was passed through to two internal 32-bit data busses. Therefore, internally, data could be processed only in 32-bit chunks, but two chunks could be sent along two different pipelines in a single clock cycle. This process is known as superscalar architecture. Operating systems were only using 32-bit code; many still contained large amounts of 16-bit code. Therefore, this new architecture was a more efficient method for processing data as long as it was 32-bit code. Intel named these pipelines the U pipeline and the V pipeline. Neither available literature nor Intel's representative was able to tell me why.

Changes made to the Pentium make it quite a bit faster than the fourth-generation processors aside from raw speed and bus width. The speed of the EDB was increased as well. The fastest EDB on any 486-class CPU was 33MHz. For the Pentiums, this was increased to 60MHz for the P5-60 and 66MHz for the remainder of the fifth-generation CPUs. Another technological improvement was an ability to perform branch predictive processing. This is the same branch prediction I discussed in Chapter Six, Understanding CPUs.

The L1 cache was divided into two sections. 8K of L1 cache was set aside specifically for instructions, while another 8K was there for data. Each cache section was specifically designed for the unique requirements of each function.

The P5s were not without their problems. A 5V chip running at this speed ran very hot. They all had to be cooled very efficiently or they would fry. The most infamous defect was a design flaw in the FPU. Certain patterns resulted in mathematical calculations that were off. At first, Intel tried to play the issue down, but as more and more demonstrations of the error emerged, it finally acknowledged it as an issue.

The P-54C and P-55

The P5 endured a very short life and was quickly replaced by 3.3V versions, often referred to as the P-54Cs. As the P-54C went through its life span it eventually reached a speed of 200MHz. Starting with the 200MHz, Intel began incorporating a technology it named MMX. The MMX eventually reached a top speed of 266MHz. Unlike the 486 with internal clock doublers, the Pentium made use of circuitry on the motherboard to set the internal clock speed. The 66MHz EDB on most motherboards allowed for 100MHz (1.5x), 133MHz (2x), 166MHz (2.5x), 200MHz (3x), 233MHz (3.5x), and 266MHz (4x). On earlier Pentium-class computers, this multiplier circuit was something that had to be set. If you set the multiplier too slow, the CPU would simply run at the speed you assigned it. For example, if you purchased a 233MHz CPU and set the multiplier at 3x, it would simply run at 200MHz. Likewise, if you purchased, the 200 and set it at 3.5x, it would run at 233MHz. This was a technique called overclocking. This practice had an inherent risk of overheating the CPU and has been blamed for data processing errors as well.

Buzz Words

Overclocking: A technique of forcing a CPU or system bus to run faster than its rated speed in order to extract maximum performance.

MMX technology was developed in answer to increasing demand for improved multimedia performance. Chips incorporating MMX are known as P-55s. It incorporated four new registers and fifty-seven internally programmed commands that greatly enhanced multimedia technology. When a program called for one of these instructions, the CPU didn't have to go out onto the address bus looking for it. It was right there at home, where it belonged. MMX also extended the i386 instruction set to allow multiple bytes of data or instructions to be stored in a single set of registers. All manipulations performed on the set simultaneously affected all instructions or data stored within. This further enhanced performance.

BUZZ WORDS

P-rating: Short for performance rating, this was a labeling method that, instead of designating a CPU by its clock speed, labeled it as the Intel CPU that it could be compared to, even though the actual clock speed and bus speed of the non-Intel chip were both lower.

While MMX was not exclusive to multimedia, software had to be written to take advantage of it. The person who spent his or her entire existence poring over text documents or pounding numbers into a spreadsheet saw little or no performance gain. Also, Intel's design called for the MMX decoder and the FPU to share the same sets of registers. As a result, processing routines that require the simultaneous usage of the MMX unit and the FPU exhibited extreme slowdown.

Cyrix also released some product lines that it claimed (and others confirmed) were faster than Intel's offerings at the same clock speed. It shared with the AMD K5 the ability to reorder instructions prior to executing them. Unique to the Cyrix CPU was a feature known as speculative processing. This was when the CPU executed an instruction it thought was going to be required even before the programming code confirmed it. Some of the features that were common with the Intel processor were improved upon. For example, Cyrix's branch predictive processing was capable of multiple branches, not just a single branch. Cyrix chose to design in seven integer execution stages, compared to Intel's five stages.

As a result of these enhancements, Cyrix's 6x86, while only clocking out at 133MHz, could keep up with, and in some circumstances outperform, an Intel Pentium 166. As a result, it joined with AMD to begin using something it called *P-ratings* for its CPUs. P-ratings do not represent true clock speeds. This can make setting the multiplier on older motherboards that are still set manually a little problematic. You would definitely want to have a copy of the manual for the motherboard before attempting to configure one of these non-Intel CPUs.

EXAM NOTE: The subject of P-ratings is no longer of concern to the modern technician. CompTIA, however, still expects candidates to be able to define the concept.

Other companies quickly stepped up to the table with their "586" offerings. They weren't allowed to call them "Pentium" or even "Pentium-class." The word Pentium is a registered trademark, and Intel is righteously (and rightfully) protecting its intellectual property. AMD's first offering, the K5, was not warmly embraced by the technical community. Many complained of significant compatibility issues, claiming frequent lockups in Microsoft Windows. Others praised its virtues and called it the "Intel-killer."

Table 7.7 Intel Fifth-Generation CPUs

Chip	Date Released	Ext.Bus	Voltage	Die Size	iCOMP (version)	MIPS
Pentium 60	1993	64-bit	5V	.8 µ	510 (1.0)	100
Pentium 66	1993	64-bit	5V	.8 µ	567 (1.0)	112
Pentium 75	1994	64-bit	3.3V	.6 µ	67 (2.0)	127.5
Pentium 90	1994	64-bit	3.3V	.6 µ	81	149.8
Pentium 100	1994	64-bit	3.3V	.6 µ	90	166.3
Pentium 120	1995	64-bit	3.3V	.35 µ	100	203
Pentium 133	1995	64-bit	3.3V	.35 µ	111	218.9
Pentium 150	1996	64-bit	3.3V	.35 µ	114	N/A
Pentium 166	1996	64-bit	3.3V	.35 µ	127	N/A
Pentium 200	1996	64-bit	3.3V	.35 µ	142	N/A
Pentium 150MMX	1997	64-bit	3.3V	.35 µ	~118	N/A
Pentium 166MMX	1997	64-bit	2.8V	.35 µ	160	N/A
Pentium 200MMX	1997	64-bit	2.8V	.35 µ	182	N/A
Pentium 233MMX	1997	64-bit	2.8V	.35 µ	203	N/A

Fifth-generation CPUs from Intel

Table 7.8 AMD Fifth-Generation CPUs

Chip	Date Released	Clock Speed	Bus Speed	Multiplier	Norton SI Rating[1]	Die Size
K5-PR75	1995	75MHz	50MHz	1.5x	286	.35 µ
K5-PR90	1995	90MHz	60MHz	1.5x	359	.35 µ
K5-PR100	1996	100MHz	66MHz	1.5x	390	.35 µ
K5-PR120	1996	90MHz	60MHz	1.5x	380	.35 µ
K5-PR133	1996	100MHz	66MHz	1.5x	407	.35 µ
K5-PR150	1996	116.5MHz	60MHz	1.75x	435	.35 µ
K5-PR166	1997	116.5MHz	66MHz	1.75x	470	.35 µ
K5-PR200	Never released	133MHz	N/A	1.5x	N/A	.35 µ

Fifth-generation CPUs from AMD

[1] AMD never adopted the Intel iCOMP Rating system, and chose to compare their CPUs on the basis of Norton SI standards.

In many respects, the K5 was superior to the Pentium on a technological level. It was closer akin to a Reduced Instruction Set Computing (RISC) processor than it was to the old i386 code. It used a front-end decoder to make it i386 compatible (which may well have been the source of many of the issues reported). It also possessed the ability to process instructions outside of the order in which they were delivered. Overall, it could be argued that it was a better processor (on paper, anyway). Unfortunately, whether earned or not, it carried with it a bit of a bad reputation.

SIXTH-GENERATION PROCESSORS

The CPUs that fall under the category of Sixth Generation is quite a mixed bag. They emerged at a time when technological developments had picked up their pace rather dramatically. As a result, there are a number of different microprocessors from different companies with radically different designs and specifications. The diversity of processors that exist in this category leads to a little confusion and some disagreement as to where a couple of the processors should really fall. Where possible, I've let the manufacturer dictate.

THE PENTIUM PRO

Intel marked the introduction of its P6 with the Pentium PRO 150. This was the first of Intel's CPUs that was designed specifically to run pure 32-bit operating systems. Therefore, users running Windows NT 4.0 or pure 32-bit UNIX enjoyed noticeably faster performance. It employed a process of superpipelining. This increased the number of execution steps the CPU could process on an instruction set to a total of fourteen. L1 cache was divided into two independently addressable areas. There were separate instruction and data caches of 8K each.

This was the first chip into which Intel placed L2 cache directly onto the die. Depending on model, 256K, 512K, or 1MB of L2 cache was available. Placement of L2 cache directly onto the CPU increased performance rather dramatically. Onboard L2 cache also made the CPU the perfect candidate for servers or workstations designed for multiprocessor capability. As each processor maintained its own cache, they weren't competing for whatever cache may be available on the motherboard.

The address bus was bumped from 32-bit to 36-bit, increasing addressable memory to 64GB. This was another feature that made it the perfect choice for servers in its day.

INTEL PENTIUM II AND PENTIUM III PROCESSORS

With these CPUs, Intel combined the technology of the Pentium PRO and MMX. One of the key complaints of the Pentium PRO was that, since it was designed exclusively to handle 32-bit code, it had a tendency to bog down when forced to run OSs such as Windows 95 or Windows 98 that contained a mixture of 32-bit and 16-bit code. Through the use of *segment register caches*, 16-bit and 32-bit code could be run independently through the pipelines. Like the Pentium PRO, the II and III incorporate 512K L2 cache onboard. One significant change

Table 7.9   Pentium Pro

Chip	Date Released	Ext. Bus	Voltage	Die Size	iCOMP (version)
Pentium PRO 150	1995	32-bit	3.3V	.6/.35 μ^1	N/A
Pentium PRO 166	1995	32-bit	3.3V	.6/.35 μ^1	N/A
Pentium PRO 180	1995	32-bit	3.3V	.6/.35 μ^1	197
Pentium PRO 200	1995	32-bit	3.3V	.6/.35 μ^1	220

Pentium PRO Processors

Pentium PRO processors were available in versions with either 256KB or 512KB of L2 onboard the CPU.
[1] Die size was .6 for 256KB modules and .35 for 512KB

here, however, was that the onboard L2 cache was designed onto an independent back-side bus that ran at one-half the clock speed of the processor itself. Still, this is somewhat of an improvement over L2 cache on the motherboard, which can only be addressed at the speed of the front-side bus. The amount of L1 cache was doubled as well. Each of the L1 registers was increased to 16K, for a total of 32K L1 cache. All of the MMX commands and registers were incorporated onto the CPU as well.

> **BUZZ WORDS** —————
>
> **Segment register cache:** Separate cache locations maintained by Pentium II (and later) for keeping 16-bit code running separately from 32-bit code.

Differences between the Pentium II and III were primarily feature-oriented. The Pentium III added extensions to the instruction set that permitted the CPU to execute 3D graphics functions more efficiently. (The impact of this improvement might have been slightly hampered by the fact that AMD had been shipping CPUs with that feature for nearly a year already.) One controversial feature that Intel added to the chip was an electronic serial number (ESN).

The ESN was a number, unique to each CPU that was manufactured, that would identify that particular chip. This ESN could be used for many different purposes, some good, some not so good. On the positive side, a network administrator could use it to manage networks more efficiently with systems management software designed to take advantage of ESNs. However, it also could be used to track Internet usage and to gather information about users' activities while on the Internet. Consumer advocacy groups protested this potential invasion of privacy, and just prior to shipping, Intel reversed its philosophy and shipped the chip with the ESN disabled by default. As it currently stands, in order to make use of the ESN, network administrators have to run a control utility that allows them to enable or disable the ESN.

The first generation of Pentium II and some models of the Pentium III CPU brought with them a significant design change as well. Intel incorporated the chip onto an SECC. This proprietary design was intended to keep all other manufacturers from designing anything directly like it. Later releases would revert back to a conventional socketed CPU using variations on the Socket 370.

Table 7.10   Pentium II Processors

Chip	Date Released	Ext. Bus	Voltage (Core/IO)	Die Size	L2 Cache Speed	iCOMP (version)	Cacheable RAM
PII-233	1997	66MHz	2.8/3.3	.35 μ	116MHz	267 (2.0)	512MB
PII-266	1997	66MHz	2.8/3.3	.35 μ	133MHz	303 (2.0)	512MB
PII-300K	1997	66MHz	2.8/3.3	.35 μ	150MHz	332 (2.0)	512MB
PII-300D	1997	66MHz	2.0/3.3	.35 μ	150MHz	860 (3.0)	4GB
PII-333	1998	66MHz	2.0/3.3	.25 μ	166MHz	366 (2.0) 940 (3.0)[1]	4GB
PII-350	1998	100MHz	2.0/3.3	.25 μ	175MHz	1000 (3.0)	4GB
PII-400	1998	100MHz	2.0/3.3	.25 μ	200MHz	1130 (2.0)	4GB
PII-450	1998	100MHz	2.0/3.3	.25 μ	225MHz	1240 (3.0)	4GB

Pentium II CPU comparisons

[1] The Pentium II-350 was the one microprocessor for which I could locate accurate results for both iCOMP 2.0 and iCOMP 3.0 ratings. The drastically different numbers indicate the disparity in results, demonstrating why it is impossible to make accurate comparisons using different versions of the rating method.

AMD K6, K6/2, AND K6/3 PROCESSORS

AMD's excursion into the sixth generation included three different versions of the K6. I've decided to lump them all together as a group, because the technical differences were minimal. With these processors, the P-rating system was abandoned. The CPUs are rated at their actual clock speeds. AMD incorporated a full 64K in L1 cache onto these chips, 32K data and 32K instruction. To further enhance performance, a total of four instruction decoders keep data flowing through the pipelines. And, since it was adding extra components to the processor, AMD decided it might be a good idea if there was more than a single arithmetic logic unit (ALU). Six integer execution units were added. All AMD K6 series CPUs fall into the Socket Seven form factor.

The K6 series improved performance slightly over the equivalent Pentium II CPUs by Intel when running certain types of applications. However, the Pentium II instruction set seemed to give it a slight advantage when running 32-bit code. The K6/2 series added a dedicated set of forty-five instructions for handling 3D rendering of graphics that it called 3DNOW! This was a feature that enthralled the gaming crowd, and the AMD chip took its first steps into becoming a serious competitor for Intel.

Prior to the release of the K6/3, the AMD chips had taken the approach of putting the L2 cache onto the motherboard. This put the choice of how much L2 cache to use onto the motherboard manufacturer's lap. A typical Socket Super 7 board to support the AMD K6 would have anywhere from 512K to as much as 2MB of L2 cache.

The K6/3 put 256K of L2 cache onto the chip die. Still, it could be used on the majority of motherboards that supported the K5/6 CPU (though many required a BIOS upgrade) and would use the motherboard cache as a third level, or L3 cache. As a result, it was possible to have a system with up to 2.3MB of total cache.

Table 7.11 AMD K6, K6/2, and K6/3 Processors

Chip	Date Released	EDB Speed	Voltage (core/IO)	Die Size
K6-166 through 233	1997	66MHz	2.9/3.3	.35 μ
K6-233L through 300	1997	66MHz	2.2/3.3	.25 μ
K6/2-266	1998	66MHz	2.2/3.3	.25 μ
K6/2-300 Model 8	1998	100MHz	2.2/3.3	.25 μ
K6/2-300 Model 8 CXT	1998	100MHz or 66MHz	2.2/3.3	.25 μ
K6/2-333 Model 8	1998	95MHz	2.2/3.3	.25 μ
K6/2-333 Model 8 CXT	1998	95MHz or 66MHz	2.2/3.3	.25 μ
K6/2-350 Model 8 or CXT	1998	100MHz	2.2/3.3	.25 μ
K6/2-366	1998	66MHz	2.2/3.3	.25 μ
K6/2-380	1998	95MHz	2.2/3.3	.25 μ
K6/2-400	1998	100MHz	2.2/3.3	.25 μ
K6/2-450	1999	100MHz	2.2/3.3	.25 μ
K6/2-475	1999	95MHz	2.2/3.3	.25 μ
K6/2-500	1999	100MHz	2.2/3.3	.25 μ
K6/2-533	1999	97MHz	2.2/3.3	.25 μ
K6/2-550	2000	100MHz	2.2/3.3	.25 μ
K6/3-400	1999	100MHz	2.4/3.3	.25 μ
K6/3-450	1999	100MHz	2.4/3.3	.25 μ

AMD K6 sixth-generation microprocessors

The K6/2 series was available in the K6/2+ for notebook computers in speeds of 450, 475, 500, 533, and 550MHz. These differed from the standard K6/2s primarily in that they used a .18 circuit width.

SEVENTH-GENERATION PROCESSORS

It was with the Seventh-Generation processors that AMD managed to take the lead in microprocessor technology away from Intel, if but for a short while. It was first with its K7, or Athlon, processors. AMD initially followed Intel's lead in that the first few releases shipped in a Slot A form factor that was cosmetically identical to Intel's Slot 1. This was its first foray into a cartridge design (although it would later revert to producing the CPUs in a newer Socket A form factor).

AMD ATHLON AND DURON

The first Athlons to be released, the Model 1, were based on .25-micron technology. This began to be a bit of a problem as AMD started pushing the envelope of speed for transistors that size, and it made the move to .18-micron manufacturing with the Model 2.

The Thunderbird series of Athlon CPUs is its flagship line of processors. It was the first to break the gigahertz barrier and the first to hit the market with a commercially available CPU using copper instead of aluminum for the interconnects between the layers of the chip.

The Athlon chips can credit much of their superior performance not to the high processing speed but rather to a 200MHz FSB. This is a full 50 percent faster than equivalent Intel products (except for the Pentium 4, which I will get to next). More recently, supported by its own AMD 760 chipset, it has achieved a 266MHz FSB. Processors using this technology are available in 1GHz and up.

The new Athlon bus is divided into three channels. Controlling the bus is the universal processor request channel and a universal snoop channel. Data moves back and forth across the bus on a 72-bit bidirectional data channel. The data channel provides 32 bits of bandwidth in each direction plus an additional 8 bits for error-correction code.

Realizing there was a market for higher-end, low-priced chips, it came out with a line of CPUs it labeled the Duron. Following Intel's lead (when it made the Celeron), it is a scaled-down version of the Athlon. It maintains the clock speeds, but drops back to a lower 64K of on-chip L2 cache. Still, with its 128K of L1, evenly divided between instruction and data registers, performance manages to maintain very high levels.

THE PENTIUM 4

Half the fun of working in the computer industry is watching companies such as AMD and Intel play leapfrog with each other. The spirit of competition, in my opinion, is more prevalent in this industry than anywhere else in the world. Intel proves that with its Pentium 4.

The first release of the CPU was based on Intel's new 400MHz FSB and supported only by the i850 Willamette chipset. The only memory supported by this chipset is Rambus memory. This turned out to be a bit shortsighted on Intel's part, in so much as the perceived superiority of the first generation of Rambus memory was overrated. (Subsequent generations are markedly superior, but that will be discussed in Chapter Eight, Searching Your Memory.)

Subsequent chipsets were designed that could either use conventional PC-133 memory or, more recently, double data rate (DDR) memory. (These two different technologies will also be discussed in greater detail in Chapter Eight.) They also provide a 533MHz FSB.

The first P4s to hit the streets were based on the same .18-micron technology used by Pentium III CPUs. However, in 2001 the Northwood became Intel's first copper-based chip using .13-micron technology. Subsequent CPUs have followed suit.

One note on the actual FSB speeds of the Pentium 4 is this. These CPUs use something called *quad-pumped* technology. The actual clock speeds of the bus are 100MHz × 4 on the chips with a 400MHz rating and 133MHz × 4 on the 533MHz chips. What quad-pumping does is to move data four times on every clock cycle.

BUZZ WORDS ——————

Quad-pumped: A technique of moving four bits of data over each wire on each clock cycle of the front-side bus.

CHAPTER SUMMARY

In Chapter Six, I discussed in detail how CPUs were manufactured and what makes them tick. This chapter goes into more detail on the development of CPUs over the years and the evolution of all the bells and whistles you've come to expect. If your purpose in reading this book is to pass CompTIA's Core Exam, then there is actually more exam material in this chapter than there was in Chapter Six.

Here I covered the generations of microprocessors and the different bus speeds and widths used by each subsequent generation. As the CPUs get more advanced, knowing the different technologies employed that I discussed in Chapter Six is essential in understanding the differences among generations discussed in Chapter Seven. I just figured that two twenty-page chapters were going to be easier on the reader than a single forty-page chapter.

BRAIN DRAIN

1. Briefly describe the processor generations and how they differ in speed and bus width.

2. Discuss as many differences as you can between the 386 and the 486 CPUs.

3. Discuss why raw processor speed has far less impact on system performance than other factors, such as the amount of L1 cache or the amount of system memory installed.

4. Why did Intel suddenly stop using numerical designations for its CPUs?

5. The fifth-generation CPUs showed a rather remarkable diversity of characteristics. Discuss some of the Generation 5 CPUs and how they differed from each other.

THE 64K$ QUESTIONS

1. Which of the following saw no change in the migration from the 8086 to the 80286?

   a. The address bus

   b. The IDB

   c. The EDB

   d. The ALU

2. The 80286 CPU was capable of addressing _____ of RAM.

   a. 1MB

   b. 4MB

   c. 16MB

   d. 64MB

3. Which CPU was the first to support protected mode?

   a. 8088

   b. 8086

   c. 80286

   d. 80386

4. Two changes IBM wanted to make on the 8086 microprocessor before it used it in its computers was _____.

   a. The width of the address bus

   b. Core speed

   c. Voltage

   d. The width of the external data bus

5. The 80286 microprocessor has a
   _____-bit address bus.

   a. 16

   b. 20

   c. 24

   d. 32

6. The 80386 microprocessor has a
   _____-bit EDB.

   a. 16

   b. 20

   c. 24

   d. 32

7. The address bus of the 80486 was
   twice that of the 80386.

   a. True

   b. False

8. The 80486SX differed from the
   80486DX in that the SX had
   _____.

   a. A wider EDB

   b. A larger address bus

   c. It lacked an FPU

   d. It had to be soldered onto the
       board

9. The AMD series of 80386 CPUs
   suffered several compatibility issues
   when using Microsoft operating
   systems.

   a. True

   b. False

10. The Pentium 4 CPU sports either a
    _____ FSB or a _____ FSB.

    a. 400, 533

    b. 100, 133

    c. 266, 333

    d. 100 x 4, 133 x 4

TRICKY TERMINOLOGY

Benchmarking: A method of measuring the base performance of a device or system before any load is placed on it.

Expanded memory: Memory beyond the first megabyte of RAM that can be used for storing data. Expanded memory could not be used for executing programs.

Extended memory: Memory beyond the first megabyte of RAM that can be used for data storage and the execution of program code.

i386 instruction set: The basic CPU-level instructions embedded in the 80386 microprocessor. These instructions went on to become the core instructions for subsequent generations of Intel-compatible microprocessors.

Overclocking: A technique of forcing a CPU or system bus to run faster than its rated speed in order to extract maximum performance.

P-rating: short for performance rating, this was a labeling method that, instead of designating a CPU by its clock speed, labeled it as the Intel CPU that it could be compared to, even though the actual clock speed and bus speed were both lower.

Quad-pumped: A technique of moving four bits of data over each wire on each clock cycle of the front-side bus.

Segment register cache: Separate cache locations maintained by Pentium II (and later) for keeping 16-bit code running separately from 32-bit code.

Swap file: The file on the hard disk that stores the data reserved in virtual memory.

Virtual memory: A slice of hard drive space that is reserved for the OS for temporary storage of data needed by dormant programs that is treated as if it were system memory.

Virtual real mode: A technique of creating separate address spaces and time slicing the CPU time so that legacy applications think they're the only programs running on the machine, even though there may be several running at once.

Acronym Alert

DDR: Double Data Rate. A technology that allows two bits of data to move over each wire on every clock cycle.

ESN: Electronic Serial Number. On Pentium III CPUs (and later) this is a number embedded by Intel at the factory that identifies that specific CPU.

iComp: Intel Comparative Microprocessor Index. A benchmarking method developed by Intel.

MMX: Multi-Media Extensions. A set of instructions targeted specifically at multi-media.

SRAM: Static RAM. A form of very high-speed memory typically used for cache.

CHAPTER 8

SEARCHING YOUR MEMORY

One of the smallest components that you'll find in a computer system is actually one of the most complex. For some people, understanding how memory works can be more difficult even than understanding the workings of the CPU. Yet a computer's memory (**Figure 8.1**) is among the simplest upgrades to perform, and that upgrade can have a more noticeable impact on overall system performance than even changing the speed of the CPU. In Chapter Six, Understanding CPUs, I introduced the concept as well as the importance of RAM.

RAM isn't the only kind of memory your computer uses, however. Computers use all kinds of different memory. I talked about how the CPU uses cache memory in Chapter Four. Video cards have anywhere from a few megabytes to 256MB (or even more) of memory. Many of the accessories you plug into the expansion slots have memory of their own. The list goes on and on.

Without memory, a computer is incapable of doing anything. If the RAM modules are missing, POST will return an error and the system will not boot. And even if it could boot, it

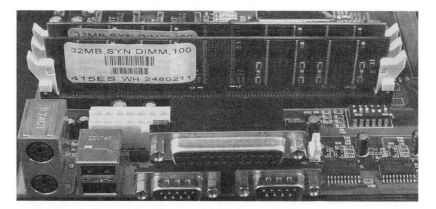

Figure 8.1 Your RAM is the central access point from which the CPU accesses all programs and data. Not too long ago, the 64MB shown here would have been sufficient for most anything. With today's OSs and applications it's a bare minimum!

wouldn't be able to accomplish anything. Until a file is loaded into memory, the CPU cannot access it. While the performance of conventional memory has improved dramatically over the past few years, it still isn't as fast as a CPU. Therefore, it can act as a bottleneck for system performance. To at least partially overcome this, today's CPUs contain anywhere from 8KB to as much as 128KB of L1 cache. Nearly all contain varying amounts of L2 cache as well. Some CPUs even provide support for L3 cache. In addition, cache memory is installed on hard drives, SCSI adapters, and even some sound cards. Somehow, the system needs to be able to keep track of all that memory, and precisely what is stored where.

A+ EXAM OBJECTIVES

CompTIA exam objectives that will be introduced or covered in this chapter include:

1.1 Identify the names, purpose, and characteristics of system modules. Recognize these modules by sight or definition. (Memory)

1.2 Identify basic procedures for adding and removing field-replaceable modules for desktop systems. Given a replacement scenario, choose the appropriate sequences. (Memory)

1.3 Identify basic procedures for adding and removing field-replaceable modules for portable systems. Given a replacement scenario, choose the appropriate sequences. (Memory)

1.9 Identify procedures to optimize PC operations in specific situations. Predict the effects of specific procedures under given scenarios.

1.10 Determine the issues that must be considered when upgrading a PC. In a given scenario, determine when and how to upgrade system components.

2.1 Recognize common problems associated with each module and their symptoms, and identify steps to isolate and troubleshoot the problems. Given a problem situation, interpret the symptoms and infer the most likely cause.

4.2 Identify the types of RAM (Random Access Memory), form factors, and operational characteristics. Determine banking and speed requirements under given scenarios.

4.3 Identify the most popular types of motherboards, their components, and their architecture (bus structures).

HOW MEMORY WORKS

Memory, until recent years, was actually a passive device, surrendering itself to the manipulations of the chipset. In the first generations of personal computers, memory was managed by a chip called the memory controller chip (MCC). Once the MCC was absorbed by the chipset, this became a function of the northbridge, or more recently the memory controller hub. Therefore, as you're reading these next few pages, keep in the back of your mind that until I tell you otherwise, the chipset, and not the memory chip itself, will actually perform most of the active functions I'll discuss. The circuit itself is now known as the memory control circuit, and therefore is still simply the MCC.

DYNAMIC RAM

If you were to look at an actual memory chip under a microscope, you would see what looks like a grid etched into the chip. You might even compare that grid to the cells you see in a spreadsheet, complete with rows and columns. And that is exactly how the MCC treats it. The cells that make up this grid consist of microscopic transistors, each one of which is coupled with an associated microcapacitor (**Figure 8.2**). When fully charged, one of these capacitors acts to open the associated transistor. This is interpreted as a one in binary. A discharged cell fails to open the transistor and is interpreted as a zero.

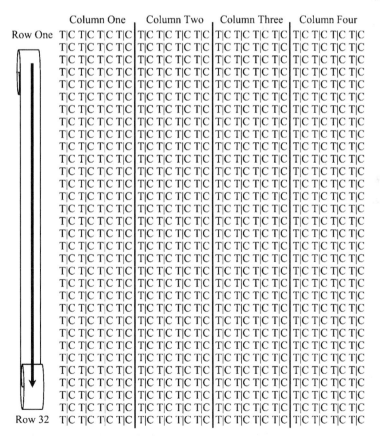

Figure 8.2   A typical memory chip is comprised of a vast number of individual cells consisting of a transistor (T) coupled with a capacitor (C). The cells are laid out in rows and columns, just like a spreadsheet.

The pattern of rows and columns is what the MCC uses for addressing purposes. How many rows there are available to the chip determines how many bits "deep" a particular chip is. Columns aren't as easily counted under a microscope because design engineers frequently embed more than a single bit into a column. An example of an early DRAM chip was designated 4 × 4. It had four columns of cells with 1,048,576 cells in each column. Into each cell was incorporated four bits. The refresh rate then determines how many columns the array has. A typical 256MB module is manufactured with either 32 × 16 or 32 × 64 chips.

The chips themselves are designed with their refresh requirements in mind. *Refresh* is a necessary process that standard DRAM must go through. All those little capacitors that activate the transistors are constantly leaking out their charge. Unless something is done to correct this, all the ones will turn into zeros. In order to prevent this from happening, an additional circuit was added to periodically recharge those little capacitors. That is what is meant by refresh.

Of course, if a cell is supposed to represent a zero you don't want to add a charge to it. This would corrupt data just as surely as losing an existing charge. Therefore, the first phase of the refresh cycle consists of determining the relative charge of a particular cell. Essentially, if the cell is less than half charged the MCC assumes it to contain a zero. That cell is not recharged. Any cells containing charges greater than half will receive a fresh charge.

Refresh rate is specified as to how many thousands of columns are affected by a single refresh cycle. Early RAM refreshed 1000 columns in a sweep, and the refresh rate was designated 1K. Subsequent generations of RAM have included 2K, 4K, 8K, and 16K. *Capacity* of a chip is therefore determined by three factors. The formula is as follows: Capacity = bit width × columns × rows. This is how manufacturers determine chip density.

In order for a computer to properly address memory, the chipset and the RAM must be marching to the same drum. Synchronizing the chipset and RAM is achieved by properly setting the timing of the memory. On the most basic level, that of the DRAM chip itself, there are two fixed parameters that constitute timing. These two measurements are Row Access Strobe (RAS), and Column Access Strobe (CAS). As you now know, memory access on the chip level is controlled in a spreadsheet-like manner. When the CPU first initializes a request for data, it will initialize a RAS cycle in order to locate the particular row that holds the information it's looking for. Once RAS has found the row, the MCC will order a CAS cycle. First, CAS has to lock onto the row address. Once it finds that, it moves across the rows until it finds out what column holds the first bit of data it is looking for.

One of the bottlenecks in RAM has always been something called the *RAS to CAS delay*. This is an interval of between two and four clock cycles (on earlier forms of RAM) between the completion of the RAS cycle and when CAS can next initiate its cycle. Another term you'll see for this delay is *CAS latency*. Memory that is advertised as CL2 has a CAS latency of two clock

BUZZ WORDS

Refresh: The process of recharging the capacitors that link to the transistors of each memory cell on a chip.

Refresh rate: The number of columns of memory cells per cycle that the MCC will recharge.

Capacity: The total number of bits a memory chip holds.

cycles. Reducing the RAS/CAS delay can have a significant effect on memory performance.

The key to understanding memory access is this. Even though the CPU can only access data 32 bits or 64 bits at a time, it is accessing that data from cache whenever possible. Since the CPU can absorb more than a single byte, memory delivers information in double words, or dwords. Since that data doesn't move directly across the CPU bus, but is rather stored in cache, on any single read operation more than one dword at a time will be retrieved. A single memory I/O operation might deliver anywhere from two to eight dwords on a single cycle. Anything the CPU can't use immediately will be stored in cache. By nature, data is most often read sequentially. The next time the prefetch goes out looking for data, the CPU is likely to find what it needs in cache.

STATIC RAM

Static RAM (SRAM) is built differently than DRAM. SRAM is a whole lot faster than DRAM, but requires much more space. It ends up eating up more of the motherboard's precious real estate. Specifically, a 512KB SRAM is approximately the same size, if not slightly larger than a 32MB × 8 SDRAM (256MB). Therefore, in order to fit 256MB of SRAM into a computer, you're going to need a really big motherboard.

One of the things that makes SRAM so much faster is that it uses only transistors. There are no capacitors in its circuitry. On the plus side, this eliminates the necessity for a refresh cycle. Electricity moves at its own rate through the chip, and the individual transistors act like on/off switches to direct the flow. However, between four to six transistors are needed for each bit of data an SRAM chip can store. A single transistor can't affect a bit by itself. The end result is that a whole lot more electricity is used to operate the transistors. The side effect of this is that the chip runs a lot hotter.

SRAM is also substantially more expensive than DRAM. That 512K chip that was the size of a 256MB chip also costs about four times as much. If a manufacturer were to design a computer that used only SRAM in its design, the cost of the computer would be prohibitive. Therefore, a primary use for SRAM is the L2 or L3 cache on those motherboards that support secondary cache.

DRAM TIMING AND MEMORY TYPES

The evolution of memory has occurred predominantly through improvements in, or in some cases elimination of, timing cycles. Improvements in die-making technology have certainly helped, but overall, the basic design of RAM hasn't changed a whole lot. You still have DRAM made from transistors coupled with capacitors, and SRAM, which is only capacitors.

Some more recent types of DRAM have made some significant advances in how they address certain timing issues, however.

DRAM and Fast Page Mode

The first generation of PCs used a form of memory called fast page mode. While primitive by today's standards, it was a step up from the conventional dynamic random access memory (DRAM) used prior to that. The steps for retrieving data from the first memory chips were cumbersome and slow. Every time the CPU made a request for data, the MCC would initiate a RAS in order to find the appropriate row. Then it would hand off the search to the CAS, which would then locate the required data. The chip would then hand over one bit of data. The other chips in the bank would hand over their bits, and the CPU had a byte to chew. On computers that ran at 4.77MHz, this didn't create much of a bottleneck. Just having a computer delighted most people. They had yet to cultivate the demand for raw speed. However, as CPUs began to run faster, the number of clock cycles wasted waiting for data from memory increased accordingly. The first major improvement in DRAM to come along was Fast Page Mode (FPM).

FPM found data in memory exactly the same way that the original DRAM found it. However, engineers made a change in the way it transferred that data. Working on the assumption that data is retrieved sequentially, they designed the chip so that, once the first bit of data was found, a new RAS cycle was not required for data that resided in the same row as the previous memory I/O operation. Since that RAS/CAS delay that I discussed earlier is one of the biggest bottlenecks in the system, eliminating a few of those made memory less of a bottleneck. Once data was located, the memory controller could move more than a bit at a time across the bus. The idea was that if the data was coming off the chip in streams, the CPU could process it accordingly.

FPM memory was used on computer systems from the days of the 80286 until well into the days the 80486. Many chipsets designed for Pentium machines supported FPM, although by that time few manufacturers chose to shoot themselves in the foot by actually using it. It has been released as DIPPs, 30-pin SIMMs, and 72-pin SIMMs. Other technologies came along to supplant FPM prior to the release of DIMMs; therefore, it is not found in that package. FPM is still alive and well, however. Some computerized circuits that require small amounts of memory where speed is not a critical issue will use a few FPMs.

EDO

FPM was king of the hill until 1994, when a new breed of memory took center stage. Extended Data Out (EDO) is actually pretty similar to FPM in many ways. What gave it a slight advantage was that there was no delay between read operations. As with FPM, if the next few bytes of data the CPU needs are located in the same row as the previous block, the RAS operation is eliminated. However, EDO also either reduces or eliminates the cycle required by CAS in order to lock on to the row address provided by RAS. RAS is still having to do its job.

It's just that the chipset can order a new RAS cycle while the data is still being read from the previous search. Therefore, by the time the MCC has finished the transfer of data from one read operation, RAS and CAS have already lined up data for the next.

EDO, like FPM, was available in both parity and nonparity modules. This is something I've had to teach some of the sales reps of otherwise excellent memory suppliers. It is true that EDO in parity form was extremely rare (and priced accordingly), however, it has been manufactured in the past. If you do happen to stumble across a box built with parity EDO, don't bother trying to upgrade with the same stuff. Before you waste a lot of time on a long, drawn-out search, consider this. First off, there will be no performance gain. Differences between parity and nonparity, regardless of what kind of memory it may be, have nothing to do with how well a system performs. Second, if you do accidentally stumble across some, and the company that has it knows what it has, it's likely to charge you through the nose. Save yourself the time and effort, and just install nonparity.

EDO hit the streets somewhat toward the end of the 80486 cycle. Therefore, pretty much any Pentium-based machine will support it. There are a few exceptions to this, so if in doubt, check the chart on chipsets provided in Appendix D. You can also find 80486-based machines that use it. The reason this becomes an issue is that, unless the module has been labeled, it is virtually impossible to tell the difference between FPM and EDO simply by looking at it. Mixing the two on the same machine is a recipe for disaster.

SDRAM

Up until now, none of the improvements I've discussed required changing the basic architecture of the DRAM chip itself. With the release of Synchronous Dynamic Random Access Memory (SDRAM), users began to see improvements in the circuitry of the module. I've repeatedly emphasized that a basic bottleneck in the system is the number of clock cycles that the CPU sits idle if it fails to find information that it needs in cache and has no other code to process. Additional clock cycles are wasted because the CPU has to use some of them in order to issue requests to the MCC.

With the development of SDRAM, designers moved a significant portion of the MCC circuitry onto the memory module itself. In effect, this means that the CPU can now access RAM directly. More importantly, data stored in RAM is available to the CPU on every single clock cycle. This provided a substantial gain in performance, but also required a chipset designed to address the memory. You would need to own a machine equipped with Intel's 440EX, VIA's VP, an OPTi Viper, an SIS 5171, or any of these companies' later chipsets to do this. Otherwise, SDRAM was actually treated in much the same way as EDO.

Even on advanced chipsets, there is little or no performance gain any time the CPU is accessing data a word at a time. EDO could find data in as few as four clock cycles on some of the newest releases, with the data being moved to the cache in bursts requiring two clock cycles each after that. SDRAM actually requires between five and seven clock cycles to set up a single read. After that, it sends more data on each burst, and sends a burst on each clock cycle. As a result, single word access is actually slower but burst mode is much faster. Since data moves in large chunks a vast majority of the time, SDRAM was the preferred memory for several years.

A newer type of SDRAM, called Virtual Channel Memory (VCM), has recently hit the market and reduces this latency to two clock cycles. Therefore, it's faster in every respect. It will be covered later, in its own section.

Since SDRAM operates in synchronization with the CPU's front-side bus, you need to make sure your memory equals the CPU bus speed. If the CPU has an external data bus of 133MHz, it will not be possible to use 66MHz memory. There is generally no problem using the faster memory on machines with slower busses. However, it is not a good idea to mix speeds on the same machine. The computer will probably boot up fine. On many motherboards, there won't be any problems at all. On some, however, mixing speeds leads to substantial increases in the number of "blue screens of death" and "fatal exceptions" in Windows. Save yourself some headaches. Just don't do it to start with.

RDRAM

Rambus DRAM (RDRAM), developed by Rambus Technologies, takes a completely different approach to the storage and retrieval of data. Intel believed in this technology so much that it invested heavily in co-developing products with Rambus. It also provided engineering support for developing the bus and chipsets to support the memory. RDRAM operates on its own direct bus to the CPU. The first generation of Rambus worked on a 400MHz operating frequency. The more recent releases feature up to 1.06GHz.

A big change is in how RDRAM moves data across that bus. Conventional memory can either transmit or receive data only on the rising end of the clock cycle. RDRAM can do so on both the rising and falling edge (see **Figure 8.3**). In effect, this doubles throughput without increasing speed.

It's also moving data in 16-bit chunks, rather than the 64-bit bandwidth of SDRAM (and other forms I'll discuss later). Since the CPU possesses a 64-bit FSB, something has to piece that 16-bit data back together into 64-bit slices. That is the job of the chipset. Intel learned the hard way that making a board that supports both SDRAM and RDRAM probably wasn't going to be feasible.

On the 820 chipset, Intel added a circuit it called the Memory Translator Hub (MTH) to handle the data path conversions. Some boards with this chipset shipped with both 168-pin DIMM sockets and 184-pin RIMM sockets. The theory was that the user could choose which memory to use. It worked fine with RDRAM. It quickly became apparent that there was a problem using SDRAM. Any form of electronic noise, whether it came from inside the computer system or got picked up from external sources, caused severe memory errors. People reported a wide range of problems. The most common were system hangs for no apparent reason, and intermittent and unexpected system reboots. Many people reported data corruption.

Once the problem became obvious, Intel initiated a voluntary recall. Customers were given several options as far as replacing their boards. In all, between 900,000 and 1 million boards based in the i820 chipset were affected.

Intel's 840 chipset uses an SDRAM Memory Repeater Hub (MRH-S) instead of an MTH. It is a far superior alternative and does not suffer from the problems described above. It does, however, have the limitation of supporting only RDRAM.

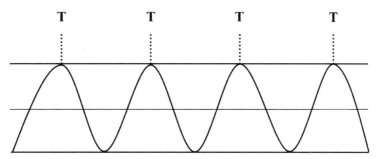

Until recent years, most memory, including EDO and SDRAM, could only move data on the rising wave of the carrier signal.

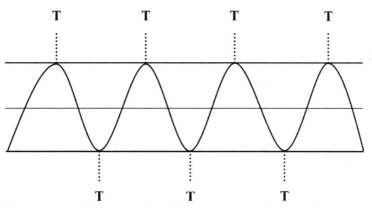

Recent memory technologies allow data to be moved on both the rising wave and the falling wave, effectively doubling throughput.

Figure 8.3   While conventional memory can only move bits of information on the rising edge of the cycle, many of the advanced memory types make use of both the rising and falling edge.

The first generations of Rambus memory met with a great deal of skepticism. Benchmark tests by several different organizations routinely reported performance gains, but they were minimal, ranging from as little as five percent to around fifteen percent. Nobody reported anywhere near the performance boost Rambus claimed. Since these earlier versions cost up to two times more than more conventional types, the cost/performance ratio made Rambus a questionable choice.

All that changed with the release of the Pentium 4, with its quad-pumped FSB. This CPU was designed to take advantage of the Rambus technology. More efficient production methods and greater acceptance of Rambus memory resulted in price drops that brought it in line with the cost of other technologies. The new 1.06GHz Rambus memory matches well with the 533MHz bus of the most recent Pentium 4 CPUs. Of all different forms of memory tested, 1.06GHz RDRAM provided the fastest benchmarks.

DDRAM

The biggest obstacle RDRAM faced in the non-Intel world was that there is a royalty assessed by Rambus on every stick of RDRAM used and on every RIMM socket installed on a motherboard. Ours is an industry that does not like paying royalties if it can avoid it.

Working with VIA Technologies (the chipset people), AMD invented its own technology that addresses the issue of memory bottleneck without the problems it insists are presented by RDRAM. Double Data Rate SDRAM (DDR or DDRAM) takes the best of RDRAM and melds it with the best of SDRAM. From RDRAM, it borrows the ability to move data across the bus on both the rising and the falling edge of the clock cycle. It doesn't claim the 1.06GHz speed of RDRAM, but on the other hand, it works in the 64-bit increments of SDRAM. Therefore, it doesn't need any fancy circuitry to reconstruct the data path. Not only does this reduce the complexity of the circuitry, but it also doesn't require retooling for manufacturers who want to make the chips. The same machines that manufacture SDRAM DIMMs can also put out DDRAM DIMMs.

DDRAM has a slightly different method of labeling its modules based on overall memory bandwidth. DDRAM is marketed as PC1600 through PC3700. PC1600 DDRAM has a maximum theoretical burst rate of 1,600MB/s and PC3700 boasts a throughput of 3,700MB/s. Each of these different types of DDRAM is rated to run a different bus speed as well. Another note is that since data moves twice on each clock cycle, DDRAM speeds are generally twice as fast as the actual clock speed. **Table 8.1** lists currently available forms of DDRAM with their appropriate bus speeds and bandwidths.

Table 8.1 A Comparison of Different DDRAM Types

JEDEC Name	Bus Speed	Burst Bandwidth
PC1600	200MHz	1.6GB/s
PC2100	266MHz	2.1GB/s
PC2700	333MHz	2.7GB/s
PC3200	400MHz	3.2GB/s
PC3500	433MHz	3.5GB/s
PC3700	466MHz	3.7GB/s

When shopping for DDRAM, make sure you purchase the correct type.

Note that the bus speeds of DDRAM are double the actual clock speed of the system bus for which they are designed. That is because this is how the manufacturers describe them in their literature.

DDRAM is getting support from a number of manufacturers at this point in time. At least half a dozen have thrown their support behind DDRAM, including Hitachi and Hyundai, two of the world's largest DRAM fabricators. It remains to be seen which of the two, RDRAM or DDRAM, will pick up the lion's share of the market.

VC SDRAM

One bottleneck that none of the previous technologies has addressed has to do with how the CPU must manage the multitasking of several programs at once while working with memory that can read only a single string of data at a time. I as a user might be working on my computer

BUZZ WORDS ————————

Channel: A dedicated path for data to take that prevents other data from competing for time on the bus.

hardware book and playing some boogie-blues MP3s at the same time. My email client is open in the background, checking my ISP for more comments from my editor every fifteen minutes. Meanwhile, the playoff game between the Patriots and the Dolphins is playing in a window in the lower corner of the screen. The CPU has no problem with this at all, although *I* was a bit put out by the Patriots going for it on fourth and fifteen. My system does, however, spend a lot more time waiting for data than it needs to, because the memory can only be retrieving data for one program at a time. Virtual Channel SDRAM (VC SDRAM) is the first step in solving that problem.

One of the improvements of VC SDRAM is in requiring fewer clock cycles to set up a memory read operation. Its key claim to fame, however, is that it can establish up to sixteen different address lines, or *channels*, and store the instructions and/or data for each specific program in a separate channel. The memory module can then stream data from all of those locations at once. Therefore, VC SDRAM can be feeding the CPU data for any given application on any given clock cycle. Obviously, VC SDRAM requires a chipset that supports these advanced functions, and the memory is more expensive.

THE PACKAGING OF MEMORY

In the years that the PC has been on the market, probably no single component has gone through more changes in its physical packaging than the memory module. It started out as single chips that populated the motherboard like high-priced spiders, and over the years has evolved into the sophisticated modules in use today. Thanks to an organization called the *Joint Electron Device Engineering Council* (JEDEC), this evolution has been reasonably orderly. Manufacturers who design a new memory package submit it to JEDEC for approval.

> **EXAM NOTE:** For the exam, be able to describe each and every one of the memory packages described in this section. Even the venerable old DIPP has its occasional day in the sun on the exam.

Changes in packaging have predominantly kept up with the evolution of the CPU. Each generation of microprocessor was taking a bigger byte out of memory, so to speak, and was doing so at faster and faster clock rates. Therefore, in addition to improvements in memory design, which will be discussed later in this chapter, improvements also had to be made in the way memory was assembled. For the technophiles among you, the pinouts for many of these modules can be found in Appendix C.

WHO THE HECK IS JEDEC?

Long before the personal computer was released on the public, electronics manufacturers recognized a need to standardize the packaging of certain electronic components. This became particularly critical with computers. Imagine the confusion, if every manufacturer of computers came up with its own design for memory chips. In 1960 an organization was created solely for the purpose of maintaining standards for the manufacture of semiconductor devices in general. This group, the Joint Electron Device Engineering Council (JEDEC) was handed the additional responsibility of overseeing memory packaging in 1970. For nearly three decades, if a memory manufacturer had a better idea for a design, that design had to undergo the scrutiny of JEDEC. Will it continue to hold the power it has enjoyed in the past? We can only hope that **somebody** maintains control.

DUAL INLINE PIN PACKAGE

In the earliest days of computers, memory was installed a single chip at a time, using a module called a Dual Inline Pin Package (DIPP). Individual memory chips were encased in a ceramic enclosure with pins extruding from the base. These days, DIPPs are not used in conventional PC designs, although computerized circuits requiring small amounts of memory occasionally make use of them. Many BIOS manufacturers still use the DIPP to package their product. **Figure 8.4** is an example of BIOS on a DIPP.

Early PCs used CPUs with an 8-bit data bus. Each of these chips could only generate a single bit of data per clock cycle. Therefore, to give the CPU the eight bits it required, eight chips worked in unison. This was called a bank.

Most computers actually required a ninth chip because earlier computers made use of an error-checking mechanism known as parity. Parity required an additional bit of data. Eight of the chips generated a byte of data to put onto the address bus, with the ninth being the parity bit.

Figure 8.4 This Award BIOS chip is a good example of a DIPP chip.

Increasing memory requirements were creating design problems for the engineers. Motherboards have to be made to a preordained size. There are only so many chip sockets that can fit into this space, and many of them are reserved for system-critical chips. As a result, memory expansion cards became popular. These were cards you fit into a slot on your expansion bus that were filled with as much memory as they could hold (or, as was more often the case, as you could afford). The downside to this was that you only have so many expansion slots as well. More importantly, when you put memory on an expansion card, you were now clocking that memory at the speed of the bus onto which it was installed and not the speed of the rest of the RAM on the system. As a result, computer manufacturers stopped using the DIPP shortly after release of the 80286 microprocessor.

SIPP

The Single Inline Pin Package (SIPP) was the first attempt at combining multiple DRAM chips into a single module. It was a disaster. The designers that came up with this design soldered an entire bank of chips onto a single circuit board that had one row of pins extruding from the bottom edge. This design accomplished its goal, in that it took up substantially less space on a motherboard than an entire row of DIPPs. Still, it didn't receive the acclaim its inventors would have liked. Planting one of these things into its socket was actually more difficult than mounting DIPPs, and they were easier to damage. The only real advantage was that you had fewer of them to break.

SIMM

Single Inline Memory Modules (SIMM) very quickly replaced SIPPs. SIMMs resemble tiny little expansion cards. DRAM chips are soldered onto small edge card connectors. The interface of the card is lined with the termination pads for the traces that interconnect the chips. The first SIMMs had thirty of these connectors and were referred to as 30-pin SIMMs, despite the fact that the concept of true pins had thankfully been abandoned. To this day, memory modules continue to be designated by the number of their "pins."

The 30-pin SIMM worked fine with the 286 and 386 computers of the day. It provided an 8-bit data path, which, while not ideal for the 80386, was sufficient for the 80286. Shortly after the release of the 80386, the 72-pin SIMM (**Figure 8.5**) was put on the market to accommodate the 32-bit EDB of that CPU. This module provided a 32-bit data path as well. Oddly enough, there were relatively few 386 motherboards with 72-pin sockets. The 72-pin SIMM hit the market about the same time that the 80486 microprocessor was released. Still, it would be a couple of years before the 30-pin SIMM was phased out. As a result, there were a number of 486-based motherboards that supported 30-pin memory.

Over the years, several different kinds of memory have been distributed as SIMM modules. You'll find FPM, EDO, and ECC. Therefore, make sure you don't make the mistake of confusing the memory package with the memory type. Earlier in the chapter, when I discussed the different types of memory, I pointed out several compatibility issues that can arise.

Unfortunately, manufacturers rarely labeled their products as to what type of memory they were. You might see a label with a part number, but that was about it. You would have to cross-reference that number in the manufacturer's catalog to find out what you had. As far

Figure 8.5 For several years, the SIMM was the memory module of choice for most motherboard manufacturers. This 72-pin SIMM replaced earlier 30-pin versions shortly after the release of Intel's 80386 microprocessor.

as just looking at a stick of RAM and being able to tell what it is? Forget it. EDO looks, feels, smells and tastes just like FPM. Unfortunately, it doesn't work the same.

There are some factors that are consistent with packaging regardless of the type of chip that was soldered onto the SIMM. For example, all 30-pin SIMMs are 8-bit memory. All 72-pin SIMMs are 32-bit memory. It doesn't matter whether it is a 72-pin FPM or a 72-pin EDO module, it is still a 32-bit piece of memory. What this means is that on any given read cycle, a 30-pin SIMM will transfer 8 bits of data, while a 72-pin SIMM will move 32 bits. Remember this. You're going to need to know it when I move on to talking about memory banking.

Physically, the circuit board that a 30-pin SIMM is built onto is about 3.5″ long and slightly less than an inch high. 30-pin SIMMs were available in 256K, 512K, 1MB, 4MB, and 16MB modules. It is unfortunate that very few motherboard chipsets supported the 16MB module. 30-pin SIMMS were notched slightly differently on one vertical edge than on the other. Unfortunately, not all SIMM sockets were made equally, and it was actually pretty easy to mount a 30-pin SIMM onto a motherboard backward. It wouldn't work that way.

Each pin in the SIMM is responsible for a separate function. For those of you with a driving need to know, those functions are defined in Appendix C.

72-pin SIMM modules were keyed with a notch in the middle and one cut into one vertical edge. They are there to prevent you from inserting the stick backward. The center notch fits over a ridge built into the SIMM socket located on the motherboard. The module installs into the socket by lining up the notch with the ridge, tilting the stick about fifteen degrees forward, and then levering it up to a vertical position. Spring clips located on either end of the socket snap into place, holding the module securely in the socket.

A 72-pin SIMM is about 4.25″ long, but they tend to vary in height. This can become an issue if a SIMM socket is positioned under a nonmovable part. Also, 72-pin SIMMs come in single-sided and double-sided modules. In other words, the DRAM chips themselves were mounted either on just one side or on both sides. Some motherboards did not support double-sided SIMMs. In many cases, the sockets were positioned so close together, the double-sided chips just didn't fit into the space they had available. In addition, there were certain versions of BIOS that had difficulty recognizing double-sided SIMMs.

As with the 30-pin SIMMs, each pin has a separate function. The same pinouts are used whether the chip is parity or nonparity; manufacturers simply don't hook up the connections used for parity if the SIMM does not generate parity. The relative pinouts for the SIMM are detailed in Appendix C.

DUAL INLINE MEMORY MODULES

Time marches on and so did CPUs. The Pentium provided the CPU with a 64-bit path to the outside world, so now two SIMMs were needed to fill a bank. The Dual Inline Memory Module (DIMM) was designed to overcome that issue. Designers improved more than just the data path while they were at it. Certain functions of the MCC were transferred over to the memory chip itself. To accommodate the extra bit width and the new functions, a few more electrical connections were required. Currently, DIMMs are manufactured in a 168-pin (**Figure 8.6**) and a 184-pin form factor. The 184-pin DIMM is used for DDR.

Figure 8.6 A 168-pin DIMM.

Those pins are symmetrically aligned along either side of the base of the module. This isn't that much different than how the 30-pin or 72-pin SIMMs were designed. What makes the DIMM different is that the terminators on each side of the module are able to perform different functions. On the SIMM, any two connectors opposite of each other had to be wired for the same function.

EXAM NOTE: Be able to describe the physical and electronic differences between the DIMM and the SIMM.

The module also mounts into its socket differently. Unlike the spring clips that held the SIMM in place, a DIMM snaps down into its socket and is secured by levers. There are two notches cut into the base of the card, not just one. These notches perform two different functions. First, they prevent you from mounting the DIMM in the socket backward. Second, since there were 5V and 3.3V DIMMs, the position of the second notch varies according to the voltage. It keeps you from mounting a 5V chip into a 3.3V board, and vice versa.

Just like with the SIMM, different kinds of memory ship on DIMMs. You can get EDO, ECC, SDRAM, DDRAM, and VC SDRAM on a DIMM. And once again, getting these to work together is an exercise in futility. Fortunately, with DIMMs, it is more common for manufacturers to actually label their product so that you know what it is you're getting when you buy it.

RAMBUS INLINE MEMORY MODULE

A little earlier, I introduced the memory that was developed by Rambus, with a little help from Intel. When Rambus first published the specs on its new memory and revealed the details of its involvement with Intel, the company's stock skyrocketed. It was an overnight success.

It was an overnight success that took eight years to materialize. The company started corporate life making memory for video games. But the PC world didn't care about that type of memory. RDRAM was the memory that interested it.

RDRAM doesn't ship on a standard module. The module that supports it is known as the Rambus Inline Memory Module (RIMM) as seen in **Figure 8.7**. It is a 184-pin module with two notches located toward the center of edge card. A single Rambus channel can support only two RIMMs. To prevent this from being a limiting factor, Intel's i840 and i850 chipsets offer an optional 862803AA Memory Repeater Hub that allows a motherboard designer to pop in another pair of slots.

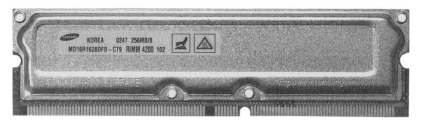

Figure 8.7 A 184-pin Rambus module. (Photo Courtesy of Rambus, Inc.)

One thing you need to keep in mind is that on motherboards that use RDRAM, all RIMM sockets must be filled. If you plan on using a single bank you need to fill the empty socket with a *continuity module*. Many motherboards that use RIMMs ship with one or more of these as a standard accessory. However, if your board doesn't, or if you lose it, it is something you'll need to purchase. The system will not boot with only a single RIMM installed.

SMALL OUTLINE DIMM

Not too long after the DIMM became popular, memory designers released a smaller version of the chip specifically for notebook computers. The DIMM was just a trifle large for installing into the small form factor these computers use. This module is called the Small Outline Dual Inline Memory Module (SO-DIMM), as seen in **Figure 8.8**. These devices not only come in a much smaller package, but they also consume less power than a standard DIMM.

The first SO-DIMMs to ship were 72-pin modules that provided a 32-bit data path. These were eventually phased out in favor of a 144-pin, 64-bit SO-DIMM. They snap into a socket

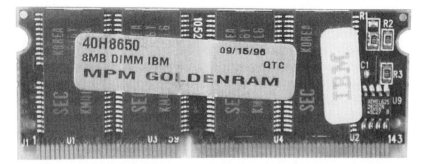

Figure 8.8 The 144-pin SO-DIMM is a type of memory frequently used in notebook computers and on some types of video card.

(**Figure 8.9**) specially designed to endure the jarring and bumping to which notebook computers are constantly exposed without being knocked out.

There are different variations on the types of memory installed on SO-DIMMs. Depending on what kind of memory it is, there are minor variations on the functions of the individual connections.

Figure 8.10 provides a visual overview of the way that memory packages developed alongside CPUs.

Figure 8.9 The SO-DIMM socket is a bit different than the other sockets discussed so far. It is designed to hold the memory module flat against the circuit board.

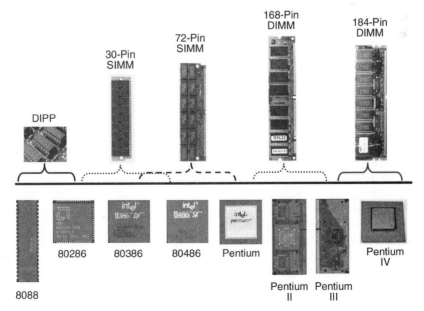

Figure 8.10 A comparison of a timeline of CPU development to the development of memory packages

Module Sizes and Banks of Memory

I've taught computer hardware courses on both a college level and a professional level, and one subject that seems to provide a whole lot more stress than it really should is *memory banking*. Understanding the concept shouldn't be that difficult. The real problem exists with individual chipsets that have their own special needs.

The math is simple. If you have a CPU with a 32-bit bus, then you need 32 bits worth of memory. And by that, I don't mean quantity, but rather bit width. How big of a piece of data can move across the memory bus? If you have a 64-bit bus, then you need memory that is 64 bits wide. **Table 8.2** shows you how wide the external data bus of several popular CPUs happens to be. Unless there is a full bank of memory for the CPU to access, the computer will not boot. A bank must contain enough chips to equal the external data bus of the CPU in use.

> **Buzz Words**
>
> **Memory bank:** The total number of memory modules required to assure that the bit width of available memory matches the bit width of the CPU in use.

> **Exam Note:** The concept of memory banking doesn't affect us as much now as it did in the past. Still, there are plenty of older machines out there that people want supported for which it can be an issue. It's also a concept that's emphasized on the exam.

Earlier in the chapter, I pointed out that the different memory packages have their own unique bit widths (see **Table 8.3**). That CPU I was talking about that had the 32-bit external data bus needs a 32-bit path to memory or the computer won't even try to finish the boot process. Anything with a 64-bit bus needs two 72-pin SIMMs to complete a bank, whereas a single 168-pin DIMM does the job all by itself. It's easy. Take the bus width of the CPU, divide it by the bus width of the memory you're using, and that's how many modules you need to fill a bank.

Table 8.2 Evolution of the External Data Bus

CPU	External Data Bus
80286	16-bit
80386DX	32-bit
80386SX	16-bit
80486 (all)	32-bit
Pentium (all)	64-bit
AMD K5	64-bit
AMD K6	64-bit
AMD Athalon	64-bit

Each generation of CPU, up to and including the Pentium, increased the width of the EDB. It is essential that the bank of memory be the same bit width.

If only that's all there was to banking. There's always something that has to crop up to make life a little more difficult. So let me discuss a few basic rules.

■ *Never put sticks of a different size into the same bank.* If you need two SIMMs to fill a bank, then you need two SIMMs that are exactly the same size. You cannot put one 32MB SIMM and one 64MB SIMM into the same bank. It just won't work.

■ *Never put two different speeds in the same bank.* If one SIMM is 60ns, then the other must be 60ns. You can usually get away with having different speeds of memory in different banks, although some boards get finicky as to which bank you should put the faster memory into. On the other hand, mixing speeds, even between banks, has been known to result in increased memory errors. You're better off avoiding it if you can.

Table 8.3 Evolution of the Memory Data Bus

Memory Package	Bit Width
DIPP	1-bit
30-pin SIMM	8-bit
72-pin SIMM	32-bit
168-pin DIMM	64-bit
184-pin RAMBUS	64-bit

As with the generations of CPU, each different memory package incorporates a specific bit width.

■ *Never mix different types of memory.* I've said that over and over again, but it's worth repeating. On any machine, mixing types of memory is a very bad idea. In most cases, it will not work at all. Put SDRAM and EDO into the same computer, and you'll get those awful beeps telling you there is bad or missing memory, and the boot process halts. Those are the easy ones to diagnose. The hard ones to figure out are when the computer boots fine and all appears to be well on the Windows of the world. But as you work, one of two things begins to happen. Either you start getting lots and lots of blue screens and memory-related errors, or your data starts going corrupt on you. Neither situation is fun.

Now, here are some situations that, while they're not hard and fast rules, are good bits of knowledge to possess. Following a few simple guidelines will save you hours of headaches.

■ *Larger memory should go in the first bank.* On some older computers, that's not just a good idea, it's a rule. On many 486 and earlier Pentium computers, if the smaller memory modules were located in the first bank, the following banks wouldn't even be recognized.

■ *Try not to mix brands of memory in the same bank.* Generally, this doesn't cause problems. However, minor differences in capacitance values can theoretically lead to data corruption.

■ *Avoid mixing memory with tin leads with gold-plated sockets, and vice versa.* On some machines this doesn't cause any problems with data, but interfacing the two metals will lead to faster corrosion of the tin component. On some motherboards, it simply doesn't work. The memory won't be recognized.

Another issue you should be careful of is mixing SIMMs and DIMMs. It isn't that the two packages aren't interchangeable. They frequently are. It's knowing what kind of memory each stick is equipped with that matters. The most common memory type shipping on the DIMM happens to be SDRAM. As far as I've been able to ascertain, SDRAM never shipped on 72-pin SIMMs.

Therefore, if you open a box and find the computer is using SIMMs, it's a safe bet the memory is not SDRAM. If it is a Pentium-class machine, it's probably a safe bet that you've got EDO. EDO and SDRAM doesn't mix. Therefore, you have two choices. Either you can sacrifice the EDO and upgrade to SDRAM, or you can go out looking for EDO on a DIMM. That is possible to find.

The thing to consider is this. If the computer has a chipset that supports SDRAM, performance will be significantly faster if you go that direction. Also, pricing might become an issue. Because EDO is now only being manufactured in small quantities, it is a bit pricier than SDRAM. You'll probably find that the EDO will set you back three to four times as much as SDRAM in terms of cost per megabyte. It's probably cheaper to swap it out.

Error Correction Methods

On your personal computers running typical desktop applications, the importance of error correction isn't quite as critical as it used to be. It used to be a major problem. When I talked about how memory worked, I pointed out that a DRAM chip basically consists of a collection of microscopic capacitors linked to transistors. Whether any given capacitor is charged or discharged determines whether it is read as a one or as a zero in binary. Should a capacitor lose too much of its charge between refresh cycles, the MCC will not recharge that cell on the next cycle. What was once a one is now a zero.

When you consider how many hundreds of billions of zeros and ones zip through your computer every second, it may not seem important if you drop an occasional bit here and there. And in many situations, it isn't. A picture you download off the web might have tens of thousands, hundreds of thousands, or even millions of bits that define the individual pixels that make up the image. Even if you were to lose more than one bit on the same pixel, color definition would not be seriously affected.

On the other hand, you're going to be a trifle upset if that lottery check for $1,000,000 you just won shows up in the mail made out for $0,000,000. Dropping a bit in an executable can make the program hang or even go so far as rendering the system unstable. Therefore, it doesn't matter how rare memory errors may be. You can't take a chance on one occurring in a critical situation. Errors must be detected, and if possible, corrected.

Over the years, two methods have evolved to prevent memory errors from resulting in disaster. The one users suffered with for several years was called parity. This was a simple error checking mechanism. It let you know something had screwed up. It just didn't do anything to fix the problem. Error Correction Code (ECC), as its name implies, not only detects the error, but also is able to dynamically correct it.

Parity Versus Nonparity

Memory wasn't always as reliable as it is today. Nor was the MCC as effective in doing its job. Therefore, it was not at all uncommon for bits to be dropped on a regular basis. *Parity* was developed as a mechanism to prevent these dropped bits from resulting in corrupted data.

The way it works is pretty simple and a bit crude, and, in many cases, the cure was worse than the disease. The memory bank had to include eight bits for data, and those bits would make up a collection of zeros and ones. Engineers added an additional bit for parity for each full byte of information generated. Now there are nine bits for each byte. Standard PCs used

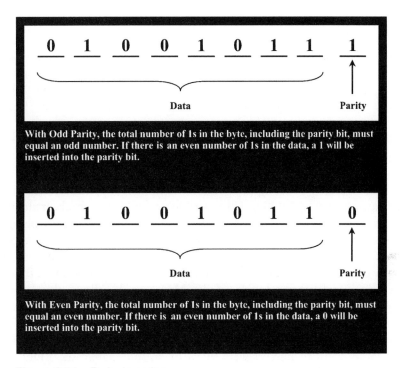

Figure 8.11 Parity in action.

a method known as odd parity. If you count up the number of ones in each byte, including the parity bit, you will have either an even number of ones or an odd number of ones.

Parity checking can be either even or odd. Any time odd-parity checking finds an even number of ones the parity bit gets set for one. If an odd number is found, the bit gets set for zero. When the CPU receives the byte and does its own count, including the parity bit, it should always find an odd number of ones. Even parity should always create an even number of ones (**Figure 8.11**). Either way, if the CPU is presented with an incorrect number, counting the parity bit, it generates a signal called a nonmaskable interrupt (NMI), which brings the system screeching to a halt with one of several equally dismaying messages on the screen.

There are two things wrong with this picture. First of all, it isn't out of the question for the memory chip to drop two ones in the same byte. In this event, even though the data was twice as corrupted, parity checking can't detect this, and lets it pass. The other problem is that when an error is detected, the method of dealing with it is a bit abrupt. The parity circuit knows one of the bits is wrong; it just doesn't know which one. The designers of this scheme figured that killing the computer, a situation of which you would immediately be aware, was better than killing the data, something you might not discover until it was way too late.

> **EXAM NOTE:** It is essential that you be able to describe how parity works and the effect of a memory parity error on the computer system.

Even in the bad old days of computing, not all computers supported parity checking. Those that did had settings in the CMOS to either enable or disable the check. It should be obvious that the memory itself had to be parity memory. On the old XTs and their clones, there needed to be nine sockets in each bank. You're not likely to stumble across many of those these days.

On most 30-pin and 72-pin SIMMs, you can usually determine whether the chip is parity or nonparity by counting the number of individual DRAM chips installed on the SIMM. Three or nine chips (six or eighteen on double-sided SIMMs) would tell you that it is a parity chip. Two or eight chips (four or sixteen on double-sided) is a sure sign that you have nonparity memory. Unfortunately, none of this tells you whether the chip uses FPM or EDO.

The type of memory wasn't actually any different between parity and nonparity SIMMs. The actual memory chips themselves were FPM, or, in some rare cases, EDO. Some SIMMs used higher density memory for the data chips along with a "nibble chip" for parity. Others used *faux parity,* which was a fancy way of saying fake parity. These chips didn't use a real memory chip for parity and returned a zero, regardless of the contents of the chip. In other words, they did nothing positive. All they accomplished was to provide cheaper memory to use on computers that required parity checking.

The fact that the DRAM used was identical whether parity was built in or not was something that could be used to a technician's benefit. If a computer that provides for optional parity checking needs to have the memory upgraded, and you can't find anything but nonparity memory, you can install the nonparity memory into a separate bank and then go into the CMOS Setup and disable parity checking. In most cases the computer will work fine. Don't try to mix parity and nonparity memory in the same bank, however. I doubt you'll like the results. The machine won't boot.

ERROR CORRECTION CODE

Error Correction Code (ECC) expands upon the concept of parity, taking it to the next level. It only works with 72-pin and 168-pin modules. You can purchase special ECC memory or, on some older computers, standard parity SIMMs can be configured to use ECC. The way it works is that a 72-pin SIMM will deliver four full bytes of data, along with half of a byte of parity information. A 168-pin ECC module moves eight bytes of data and a full byte of parity. The bits of information that would have once been parity bits are grouped together as an ECC cluster.

The chipset runs an algorithm on the entire block of information being handled by the chip and stores the results of that calculation in the ECC cluster. In the event that a bit is dropped, when that algorithm is run once again on the receiving end, the equation will come up with a different answer. Instead of crashing the computer, that group of four or eight bytes is simply sent once again. The user never knows anything happened.

> **NOTE:** Even in this day and age, it is possible for multiple bits of data to be lost from the same cluster of information. If this happens, the system will react in the same way parity checking did when it encountered an error. The CPU generates an NMI and the system shuts down. These days, however, memory errors occur at a rate of less than one per every several million reads. Multiple drops are incredibly rare. If you have a system configured to use ECC and it is repeatedly generating NMIs, you've got problems other than simple memory errors on your hands. You might want to check and see if a "less-than-ept" integrator took a system that shipped with ECC and upgraded it with either EDO or SDRAM. This would result in a system that was performing ECC checks on non-ECC memory, and you would therefore see a lot of mistakes.

For ECC to work, the system BIOS must support ECC, and the CMOS settings must be configured properly. Some systems require that you make two adjustments. There will most likely be a place where you turn on parity checking, and another where you tell the system to use ECC mode. On systems that have both of these settings, both must be configured. Most computers don't make you jump through as many hoops. You simply enable ECC, and the system works fine.

TROUBLESHOOTING MEMORY

When memory begins to fail, trying to figure out what is wrong can literally drive you nuts. Understanding how memory works and being able to figure out the problems it may cause are two different issues altogether. A big problem is that a number of symptoms that sick computers exhibit can indicate issues with memory, CPUs, or motherboards. Also, memory problems are frequently intermittent. Which basically means they'll never show their face in the presence of a technician. Do yourself a favor and develop a systematic approach to all troubleshooting. With memory, you can start with the fact that there are three basic guises in which memory errors generally appear.

MEMORY NOT DETECTED

One of the first diagnostics run by the POST program is a memory test. Failure to detect memory during POST can happen in two different ways. Each failure has a different impact on the boot process. If the system finds no memory at all, the speaker will emit a series of beeps and the boot process will halt. The other situation is when the system finishes the boot process successfully, but reports an amount of memory you know to be incorrect.

If the machine is unable to boot, analyze the situation a step at a time. Is this the first time a new computer has ever been turned on? If so, first check and see if the manufacturer installed any memory. Don't laugh! It's rare, but it happens.

If there are memory chips installed, make sure they are properly seated. If they're not, don't automatically call the company and start screaming. SIMM and DIMM modules alike sometimes come loose due to the rigors of ground shipping. Simply reseat the memory and try again. If the memory is securely seated and still not working, it is possible that you have a bad module.

What if you're trying to diagnose an older machine that's been around a while? The first thing to do is to try and figure out what, if anything, changed since the last time the computer worked properly. Was service recently done on the computer? Maybe the memory got knocked loose. It can happen.

Perhaps you just completed a memory upgrade, and things aren't working as planned. If the machine was working fine before attempting the upgrade, there are a couple of things to look at. Once again, is all the memory seated properly in the sockets? Mounting memory into sockets is not always as easy as the makers of boards would have you believe, especially if they used lower-grade sockets. Run your fingers along the top edge of the modules. If there is more than one, then the edges should be perfectly parallel. If one seems to be either tipping or sinking, it isn't seated. Try again. If any of the conductors fail to make contact, the memory won't be recognized.

Once it has been confirmed that the memory is properly seated, verify that the right kind of memory is being used. At the risk of sounding like a broken record, it is very rare that two different types of memory will work together in the same computer. If SDRAM is installed in a machine alongside of EDO, you're going to have problems.

Okay, the memory's all seated properly and you know they're all the same. If you have any empty sockets, check the numbering of the sockets. Memory sockets need to be filled from Bank 0 (or 1, depending on how the sockets are numbered) on up. On some computers, if the initial bank is empty, the system won't see the memory that is installed. The computer will not boot.

If it's not a new computer, and you haven't performed any upgrades, you now ask, "What changed since the last time it worked?" Were any other components either added or replaced? As I mentioned before, it is possible for a stick of memory to get dislodged from its socket any time you're poking around inside the case.

Sometimes, however, the computer boots up just fine, but only a fraction of the memory is available to the user. On some computers, this is not an error. Motherboards with video adapters built right on frequently grab a portion of system RAM to be used as video memory. This memory is reserved by the CMOS and is neither seen nor tested during POST. Only the memory left over after video RAM has been allocated will be reported. This doesn't qualify as a memory error. The system is doing its job correctly.

If a lack of memory is causing programs to not run, or making them run too slowly, go into the CMOS and allocate a smaller amount of memory for video. Some boards allow as much as 64MB (or more) of system memory to be used for video. On a computer that only has 64MB to start with, assigning 32MB for video probably isn't the wisest choice.

Once you've determined that the problem is really a problem, reread the first half of this section. Everything I wrote about concerning a computer that fails to boot due to memory errors also applies to computers that report memory incorrectly. However, there's another problem that might occur after an upgrade. If the first bank is recognized, the machine might recognize only that memory and continue the boot process. Memory installed in other sockets might go ignored. Therefore, check all the memory installed for poor seating or incorrect memory type.

It's easy to get spoiled by working only on computers that use nothing but DIMMs. One stick is always one bank. That's not the case with earlier Pentium-class machines that use

SIMMs. You need two to fill a bank. If you try to get away with using just one, the machine will not boot at all. Also, trying to mix two sizes of memory in the same bank will halt the machine on boot up. In many cases, using two different speeds of memory in a bank will cause a boot failure. That's if you're lucky. Other times, the boot process is successful, but you end up with excessive numbers of memory errors while running applications.

MEMORY ERRORS IN APPLICATIONS

Much of the process of troubleshooting memory starts when the applications or operating system starts reporting errors. Some of these are the result of situations I discussed above. Others are the result of how the application manages the memory it has available. Most of these errors can be resolved by restarting the system.

Some messages that suggest hardware failure overstate their case. Parity errors would suggest a bad memory module, yet frequently those errors are software related. The same holds true of General Protection Faults (GPF). I have seen so-called parity errors show up on machines using nonparity EDO.

"Out of Memory" errors don't always mean that you're actually out of memory. In Windows, that can simply mean that a particular application has used up the resources available to it. Another frequently seen message is "Stack Overflow." For the most part, these are errors generated by the OS, not the hardware. As such, I don't want to go into a whole lot of detail as to what a stack overflow is or why it is bad. Any good book on operating systems can explain that. However, applications installed by the user can generate some of these same errors. Even the best-designed application suffers from amnesia from time to time.

However, if the frequency of these error messages seems to be increasing, that's a good indication of hardware failure, either pending or imminent. Some good information hangs out in those error messages you've been roundly cursing. For example, in Windows, a *fatal exception* error will report a memory address and a CPU register address where Windows thinks the fault occurred. Fatal exceptions occur when the CPU is asked to do the impossible, such as divide by zero, or when it is faced with an NMI it can't resolve. The address reported is usually right. If you've got a machine that is starting to come up with a lot of these messages, start keeping a log of those addresses. They're not as useless as they might look.

If the memory address is the same time and again, the next step is to find out what occupies that address. This isn't as impossible as it may sound. If the system is running Windows, click on Start, go up to Settings, and select Control Panel. Down toward the bottom you'll find an icon labeled System. One of the folders here is Device Manager. There are two selections here that can help you find what memory addresses are in use by the system. All the I/O addresses in use are listed here. The address in the error message is in hexadecimal. Compare it to the ranges of addresses listed in Device Manager and see if the address reported by the error falls within any of these ranges. If so, you have found the piece of hardware causing the failure.

BUZZ WORDS ────────────

Fatal exception: Any event that stops the CPU completely. These can include programming errors, such as a request to divide any number by zero, or a hardware event that returns a nonmaskable interrupt.

Another section is Memory. Some files, such as device drivers, load to the same address each time the system starts. Once again, you're reading in hex. Does your address show up here? If so, find out what that file relates to (if you can). If it is a device driver, reload the driver. If it is a system file, try getting a new copy of that file and copying over the one in your system. If the address does not appear, or the errors seem to occur randomly, it might be time to replace a memory module.

If you're got more than one memory module installed in your system, figuring out which one to replace can be a lot of fun. You can do it through trial and error. Replace one and see if the problem goes away. If not, move on to the next one and try again. If you're a practicing professional, you'll probably want something a little more sophisticated. Applications such as *CheckIt Professional Edition* by Touchstone Software or Ultra-X's *Professional Diagnostics* include a utility for running diagnostics on the memory and locating the problem for you.

Memory errors don't always occur in main system memory. In the very first part of this chapter, I mentioned that add-on cards frequently are equipped with their own memory. Many of these devices use standard SIMM or DIMM modules. If that memory should fail, it will generate error messages just like the main system memory will. The best way to determine if this is the source of your problem is to start logging those errors all over again and try to determine if a particular piece of hardware is being accessed every time the error occurs.

Regardless of where the memory is located, memory does fail. The biggest reason any IC fails is electrostatic discharge. In Chapter Three, Basic Electricity and the Power Supply, I discussed the damage ESD can cause. If a chip had to be handled at any time, for any reason, a spark might have killed it. Just remember, for you to even feel a spark of static electricity, that spark needs to be between 10,000 and 20,000 volts. Less than 2,000 volts can kill an IC. You can kill a memory chip or CPU and never even know it. If you actually feel a spark move from you to the chip, you can assume its dead, even if it appears to work on the outset.

Electrical surges in power can also damage memory. Too much current can destroy any circuit. And in fact the memory can quite simply be getting old. You'd think that something with no moving parts would be immune to that. However, every substance in the world contains minute traces of radioactive elements called isotopes. When a single molecule of an isotope decays, it will emit a burst of energy sufficient to destroy one or more of the individual memory cells in a RAM chip. This is going on every day of the chip's life. You don't miss one or two cells from a row or column in a single DRAM. But it's like your brain cells. When enough are gone, you can't remember if it's doing any harm or not. Unfortunately, it is.

I mentioned at the outset of this section that memory errors frequently mimicked those created by other devices. Every once in a while, the memory tests fine (you had it tested in a professional DIMM checker), applications errors are ruled out (you had Microsoft tech support on the phone for hours), and the errors are still occurring on a regular basis. It is now time for you to look at something besides memory for the source of the problem.

The CPU itself is a good source of memory-related issues. After all, it is the device that initiates virtually all memory I/O operations. Try to keep at least one or two current CPUs hanging around that you know to be good. Use a CPU you trust for a while and see if that makes the errors go away. If they do, the problem is solved.

If not, it's possible that the motherboard itself could be at fault. By now, it should be pretty clear that the chipset is arbitrating memory operations. If the chipset starts to fail, it can generate all kinds of eerie problems. Memory problems are high on the list. A bad chipset can almost make you think the computer is haunted.

A problem that can drive you completely insane, and that you can never truly isolate, is when another chip, completely unrelated to memory, begins to fail. Dying ICs can spill a lot of electronic noise out onto the circuit. This can be interpreted as random data, and can result in memory read errors.

In cases such as I've just described, a failing chipset or other IC, the only solution is to replace the system board. On most system boards, a failing CPU can be replaced.

CHAPTER SUMMARY

I realize this was a long chapter. And there was a lot of vital information in it. Some of the most important things that I hope you take away from this chapter are some of the things you're least likely to be tested on when you take the exam. One of those subjects I feel is important is how RAM actually works. A good understanding of the workings of a memory chip help immensely when trying to troubleshoot problems.

Some of the things that I covered in this chapter can almost be put down as historical artifacts. Memory banks are an example of this. It has been several years since any new systems have been released that require an intimate knowledge in this regard. On the other hand, if you're trying to fix an older machine, that knowledge will serve you in good stead.

Troubleshooting memory can be one of the most challenging issues you will face. A good diagnostics utility is in order here. There are some out there that can save you hours of trial and effort troubleshooting. And remember to log those error messages!

BRAIN DRAIN

1. In as much detail as you can recall, describe a typical memory I/O operation, from beginning to end.

2. You have an old 486-based machine that the customer insists on keeping in operation, despite your advice to the contrary. The customer has acquired four new 16MB SIMMs. They look like they should fit, but you can't seem to get the system to recognize them. What are some of the issues that could cause this problem?

3. What were some key differences that made SDRAM so much faster than EDO?

4. Describe how parity worked as a memory error checking mechanism, and why it was a less than desirable option.

5. Describe how ECC differs from parity and what makes it a superior error checking mechanism.

THE 64K$ QUESTIONS

1. Memory I/O operations are controlled by _____.
   a. The CPU
   b. The operating system
   c. The MCC
   d. BIOS

2. The process of adding a fresh charge to the memory cells in DRAM is called _____.

   a. Precharge

   b. Refresh rate

   c. Flush

   d. Refresh

3. A SIMM differs from a DIMM in its design in that _____.

   a. All SIMMs are faster than DIMMs

   b. The terminating tabs on either side of the base of a DIMM can be assigned a separate function

   c. The DIMM moves some of the MCC circuitry from the chipset to the DIMM

   d. Physical size is the only difference.

4. SO-DIMM is an acronym for _____.

   a. Stand-Off Dual Inline Memory Module

   b. Switched Output Dual Inline Memory Module

   c. Small Outline Dual Inline Memory Module

   d. None of the above

5. A typical DRAM cell consists of a transistor paired with _____.

   a. Other transistors

   b. A diode

   c. A microscopic resistor

   d. A microscopic capacitor

6. Refresh rate is measured in _____.

   a. Milliseconds

   b. Nanoseconds

   c. How many thousands of columns refreshed per cycle

   d. Megahertz

7. Once the MCC has determined that the data being sought actually resides in RAM and resolves the address, the next thing to happen is a _____.

   a. Prerefresh

   b. CAS

   c. RAS

   d. RAS/CAS delay

8. SRAM differs from DRAM in that it consists of a transistor coupled with _____.

   a. Other transistors

   b. A diode

   c. A microscopic resistor

   d. A microscopic capacitor

9. DDRAM is so named because it _____.

   a. Operates at twice the clock speed of the FSB

   b. Operates at twice the clock speed of conventional SDRAM

   c. Moves two bits of data for each clock cycle

   d. Only requires two clock cycles to set up an I/O operation

10. Which of the following memory types move parts of the MCC circuitry onto the die of the memory module?

    a. FPM

    b. EDO

    c. SDRAM

    d. RDRAM

TRICKY TERMINOLOGY

Capacity: The total number of bits a memory chip holds.

CAS latency: The delay that occurs between RAS and CAS. Also known as RAS/CAS delay.

Channel: A dedicated path for data to take that prevents other data from competing for time on the bus.

Continuity module: A null memory module that fills the empty banks on a system using Rambus memory.

Fatal exception: Any event that stops the CPU completely. These can include programming errors, such as a request to divide any number by zero, or a hardware event that returns a non-maskable interrupt.

Faux parity: A null chip that fools a system into thinking parity memory was installed, when in fact, it was not.

Latency: The delay that occurs from the time the CPU makes a request for data and the time that information can be accessed from the device holding the data. All devices, including memory and hard drives, exhibit latency.

Memory bank: The total number of memory modules required to assure that the bit width of available memory matches the bit width of the CPU in use.

Parity: An error checking mechanism that simply counted the number of 1s in a byte of data. A ninth bit is available on a parity chip for the parity bit. With odd-parity checking, if an even number of 1s is found in the byte, a 1 is placed in the parity bit to keep the number of 1s odd. With even parity, a 0 would be placed in that position to keep the number of 1s even.

RAS/CAS delay: The delay that occurs between RAS and CAS. Also known as CAS latency.

Refresh rate: The number of columns of memory cells per cycle that the MCC will recharge.

Refresh: The process of recharging the capacitors that link to the transistors of each memory cell on a chip.

ACRONYM ALERT

CAS: Column Access Strobe. A circuit that is part of the MCC, responsible for locking onto the first column in a memory module in which the target data is located.

DDRAM: Double Data-rate RAM. A form of memory that moves two bits of data for each clock cycle.

DRAM: Dynamic Random Access Memory

Dword: Double Word

ECC: Error Correction Code. An error correction method that stored a mathematical image of data being moved on a nibble chip and could correct single-bit errors as they were detected.

EDO: Extended Data Out. A form of memory that replaced FPM and that allowed the RAS/CAS operations for the next I/O operation to be performed at the same time as data from the previous operation is being moved out of the chip.

FPM: Fast Page Mode. An early form of memory that eliminated the RAS cycle from any read operation retrieving data from the same row as the previous operation.

GPF: General Protection Fault. A failure of an application (and possibly the CPU) that results from one program invading another program's address space.

JEDEC: Joint Electron Device Engineering Council. An organization that oversees standards for many of the electronic devices in use, including memory modules.

MRH-S: SDRAM Memory Repeater Hub. A chip in newer Intel chipsets used to arbitrate memory requests between multiple banks of memory.

MTH: Memory Translator Hub. A chip in newer Intel chipsets that replaces the northbridge chip used by contemporary chipsets.

NMI: Nonmaskable Interrupt. Similar to the IRQs used by devices, an NMI is an interrupt to the CPU indicating that immediate action is required. If the CPU cannot resolve the issue, the NMI will cause the CPU to lock up.

RAS: Row Access Strobe. A circuit that is part of the MCC responsible for locking onto the first row in a memory

module in which the target data is located.

RDRAM: Rambus Dynamic Random Access Memory. A specialized form of memory manufactured by Rambus, Inc.

SDRAM: Synchronous Dynamic Random Access Memory

SIPP: Single Inline Pin Package. An earlier memory module that put eight or nine DRAM chips on a single IC and mounted into the system board by way of a single row of pins protruding from the base.

SO-DIMM: Small Outline Dual Inline Memory Module. A compact form of memory used primarily in notebook computers, but also seen in some video cards.

VC-SDRAM: Virtual Channel SDRAM. A newer form of memory that gives each operational application its own address space and path to move data back and forth, so that they don't compete for bandwidth.

CHAPTER 9

EXAMINING THE EXPANSION BUS

A function of the computer system most often visited by technicians is unfortunately also an area that is all too frequently the least understood. That is the expansion bus (see **Figure 9.1**). A vast percentage of upgrades and/or replacements involve devices that reside on this all-important bus.

In Chapter One, PC Basics, I discussed the five primary busses of the computer system. Those were the CPU bus, the address bus, the I/O bus, the local bus and the power bus. Not once did I mention the expansion bus. Why? Because the expansion bus straddles several of the primary busses. Without the services of each of the primary busses, the expansion bus ceases to exist. Without the expansion bus, you lose the important ability of being able to add new devices to a computer once it leaves the factory.

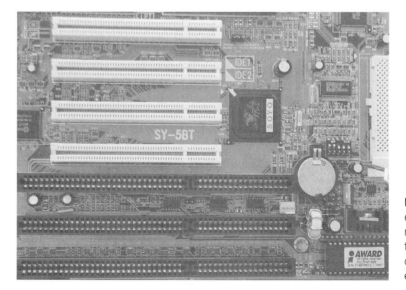

Figure 9.1 The expansion bus on a modern motherboard typically allows for different types of expansion cards.

A+ EXAM OBJECTIVES

There's quite a bit in this chapter that you can expect to see on the A+ Core exam. Among the objectives introduced or covered in this chapter are the following:

1.1 Identify the names, purpose, and characteristics of system modules. Recognize these modules by sight or definition.

1.2 Identify basic procedures for adding and removing field-replaceable modules for desktop systems. Given a replacement scenario, choose the appropriate sequences.

1.4 Identify typical IRQs, DMAs, and I/O addresses, and procedures for altering these settings when installing and configuring devices. Choose the appropriate installation or configuration steps in a given scenario.

1.5 Identify the names, purposes, and performance characteristics of standardized/common peripheral ports, associated cabling, and their connectors. Recognize ports, cabling, and connectors by sight.

2.1 Recognize common problems associated with each module and their symptoms, and identify steps to isolate and troubleshoot the problems. Given a problem situation, interpret the symptoms and infer the most likely cause.

4.3 Identify the most popular types of motherboards, their components, and their architecture (bus structures).

WHY DO YOU HAVE AN EXPANSION BUS?

The very nature of a personal computer is that it is personal. No manufacturer can possibly come up with a design that will perfectly suit every user. Most people wouldn't buy a computer without sound. Others prefer to live without it. Many people live on the Internet. To them, a modem is a standard feature. Yet for a networked office system this may not only be unnecessary, it might be a security risk. The expansion bus allows the user to customize his or her computer to fill specific needs.

The expansion bus is not unique to PC-compatible computers. Macintosh computers and mainframes all sport an expansion bus. Even computers made prior to the release of the IBM PC were equipped with a form of expansion bus. One earlier bus that enjoyed some popularity was the S100. Computers equipped with this bus used a series of 100-pin connectors through which edge cards could be inserted into the system.

IBM wasn't strictly looking to launch a product line when it came out with the PC. It was trying to launch an industry. There were already a number of computing systems on the market aimed at the end user by several manufacturers and confusion reigned. The devices that were designed for an Altair were no good for you if you later decided to move over to a Commodore 64.

IBM realized that a stable market was a healthy market and invested a lot of time and money into engineering a "standard" that it hoped other companies would follow. The folks at IBM had several issues to address. First off, they knew that CPUs would not remain the same speed forever. The first CPUs used in the IBM PC operated at 4.77MHz. Within two years, other processors hit the streets that operated at 8MHz, 10MHz, and 12MHz. Therefore, devices couldn't be designed to communicate on the CPU bus. Imagine being a modem manufacturer and having to change your product line every time CPU speeds bumped up another notch. To address this problem, IBM put the expansion bus on its own clock crystal and ran it at a speed independent of that of the CPU.

Another issue designers faced was how to incorporate existing technology into their designs so that existing manufacturers of expansion cards would not rebel. After all, these companies had invested huge sums of money tooling up their plants to make edge card circuit boards. They weren't likely to start all over simply because IBM told them they should. IBM borrowed heavily from existing technology in designing its bus. A primary source of inspiration was the Multibus designed by Intel in 1974.

When IBM launched its first line of personal computers, it also released the specifications for its expansion bus to the rest of the industry at no charge. This display of generosity was not completely altruistic in nature. It had precisely the effect that IBM wanted. Its design became the industry standard.

THE FUNCTIONS OF THE EXPANSION BUS

Because the expansion bus is not directly linked to the CPU, it needs to be able to fulfill the needs of both the device that plugs into it and the CPU. And it needs to make sure that those needs don't conflict. First off, it has to be able to properly utilize system resources, which would include interrupt requests (IRQ), input/output (I/O) addresses, and direct memory access (DMA) channels. It also needs to be able to synchronize the transfer of data across the bus. To do that, it needs to be able to interface with the address bus and the I/O bus. **Figure 9.2** illustrates the way that the expansion bus depends on four of the five primary busses on the system. Since it works at a different speed than the CPU, timing issues need to be resolved and the flow of data must be synchronized. To do all this, it needs power. So let me break down the job description of the expansion bus, task by task.

DEALING WITH SYSTEM RESOURCES

Interfacing a device with the computer system is no easy task. The fact that installing new devices in a computer system has become so simple is a tribute to the engineers who design the expansion busses you use. Devices built onto the system board are configured by the manufacturer, via the BIOS, to deal with issues such as addressing memory and communicating with the CPU.

Newly installed devices must be configured before they will correctly interface with the system. In the old days, configuration was done manually. For the most part, modern devices

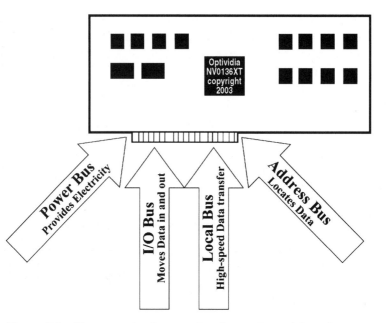

Figure 9.2 The expansion bus requires the services of the primary system busses in order to function.

do a lot of this work for you by way of Plug 'n Play (PnP). However, since PnP is known to occasionally have its ups and downs, it is necessary to have an understanding of system resources in order to deal with issues that do arise. Things that generally need to be configured include IRQs, DMA channels, and I/O addresses. A conflict in any one of these between two devices will result in one or both of the devices not working.

INTERRUPT REQUEST LINES

The interrupt request line (IRQ) is the element of configuration that is most frequently adjusted by the user. The nature of the microprocessor prevents any device from being able to initiate communication between itself and the CPU. Only the CPU can do that. Therefore, if a device needs to transmit data, it needs a way to get the processor's attention. When visitors come to your door, they get your attention by ringing the doorbell. When a device wants to attract the attention of the CPU, it makes use of its own doorbell—the IRQ.

EXAM NOTE: Be prepared to explain the concepts of IRQs, I/O addresses, and DMA channels, and not simply parrot off what device uses what resource.

The IRQ consists of a wire that connects from the expansion card (or onboard device) to the motherboard. When the device needs to notify the CPU that it needs to transmit data, it sends an electrical signal along that path. In other words, it rings the doorbell. Now, if every device on the system rang the same doorbell, the CPU would have no way of knowing which device needed attention. So each device is assigned its own doorbell. When a particular wire lights up, the CPU knows exactly which device is trying to get its attention.

The original IBM PC used a chip called the 8259 to manage IRQs. This chip directed traffic for eight different IRQs, numbered 0 through 7. This was a bit of a problem, because system devices required most of them (see **Figure 9.3**). Users found that they had an extremely limited number of options for adding new devices. They clamored for more.

When the AT was released, an additional 8259 was added to the system. Since the CPU only wants to deal with a single IRQ controller, these two chips were *cascaded* together. The chips are wired from the first 8259 through what had originally been IRQ2, into IRQ9 of the second 8259. The result is that there are two chips controlling eight IRQs each, and there are fifteen usable IRQs. Because IRQ2 and IRQ9 are physically on the same wire, they provide a single interrupt. Systems using the cascaded 8259s by necessity had to reallocate system IRQs. **Figure 9.4** shows the conventional IRQ allocations of a modern computer system. Even though the 8259 chips have been absorbed by the chipset in today's motherboards, the IRQ allocations haven't changed.

Conventional wisdom is that two devices cannot share the same IRQ. That would, in theory anyway, result in the system locking up. This is, in fact, not the case. It is quite possible to have multiple devices on a single IRQ, as long as only one device is ever active at a time. You will see an example of that process at work later in this chapter when I discuss the concept of COM ports.

However, for the most part, when dealing with expansion cards, it is a good idea to follow the conventional wisdom. The first ISA cards all used a method called *edge-triggered* interrupt sensing. The card has a specific connector on its interface that generated its interrupt requests. The system could

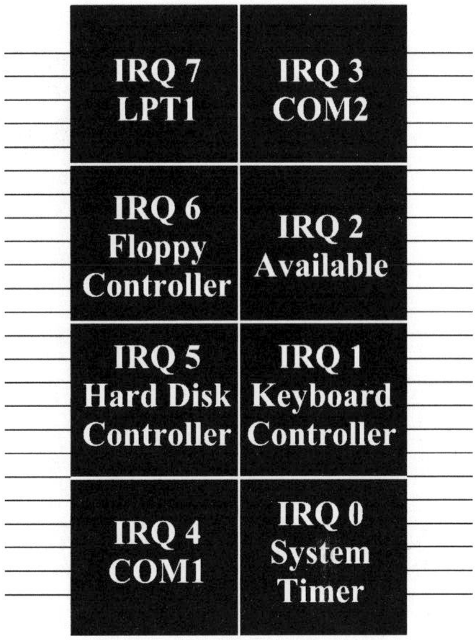

Figure 9.3   The first IBM PC possessed a mere eight IRQs for the entire system. A whopping total of one of those was available.

BUZZ WORDS

Cascade: A process by which multiple circuits are linked together in such a way that they appear to the system as a single device.

Edge triggered: Any response that elicited and/or was controlled by a direct electrical signal coming from a pin or wire on a device. The voltage is applied, and the device depends on the interrupt controller to "remember" that it sent the signal.

Level triggered: A response that is arbitrated by a control circuit and/or device driver that allows the same device to make use of one of several interrupt channels. The level-triggered interrupt raises the voltage on the appropriate wire and holds it until the expected response is received.

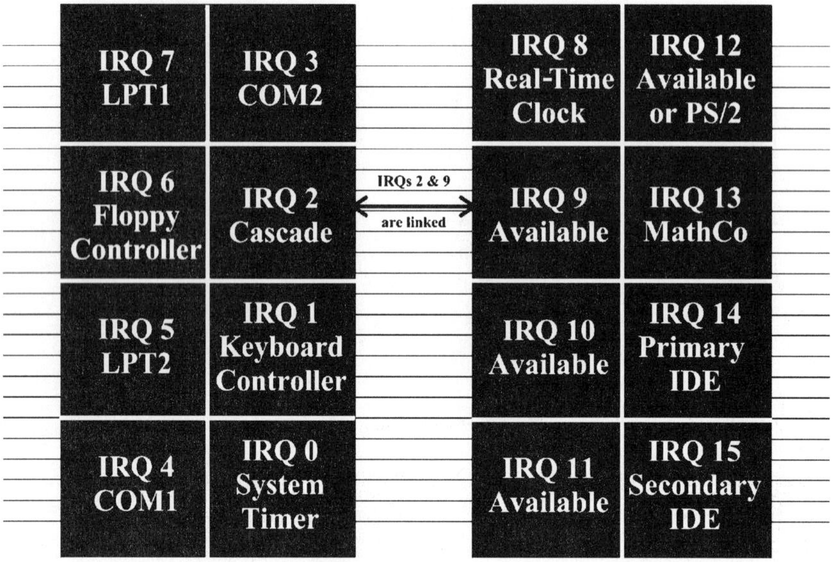

IRQ 7 **LPT1**	**IRQ 3** **COM2**	**IRQ 8** **Real-Time** **Clock**	**IRQ 12** **Available** **or PS/2**
IRQ 6 **Floppy** **Controller**	**IRQ 2** **Cascade**	**IRQ 9** **Available**	**IRQ 13** **MathCo**
IRQ 5 **LPT2**	**IRQ 1** **Keyboard** **Controller**	**IRQ 10** **Available**	**IRQ 14** **Primary** **IDE**
IRQ 4 **COM1**	**IRQ 0** **System** **Timer**	**IRQ 11** **Available**	**IRQ 15** **Secondary** **IDE**

IRQs 2 & 9 are linked

Figure 9.4 A second 8259 didn't quite double the number of IRQs. IRQs 2 and 9 are linked in a cascade, leaving a total of fifteen physical IRQs.

tell what device a signal was coming from by way of its IRQ. It couldn't, however, determine which physical slot in which a card was installed. Therefore, the only way to avoid confusion was to make sure that no two cards shared the same IRQ, even if they weren't active on the bus at the same time.

PCI devices incorporate *level-triggered interrupts*. The device is designed to operate at any one of several different IRQs, which can either be assigned by the BIOS, or through a setup program. A chip on the device manages four different interrupt channels. Once the IRQ is assigned, when the device needs to communicate, it simply raises the voltage on the appropriate connector.

Another concept that you should be aware of is that IRQs are numbered in order of priority. If two devices both signal the CPU at exactly the same moment, the device with the higher priority will have precedence. Therefore, critical system devices are given the highest priority. Also take note that the order of priorities does not directly map to the IRQ number. **Figure 9.5** shows the fifteen physical IRQs and their relative priorities.

INPUT OUTPUT ADDRESSES

Input output addresses (I/O addresses) can get a little confusing to the beginner. They look, feel, smell, and taste just like a memory address, because that is exactly what they are. In order to communicate with a particular piece of hardware, the system creates a little drop box in memory at a specific location. This address correlates to the address in memory of the first instruction of a device driver or BIOS instruction. In order to keep track of what device is using what

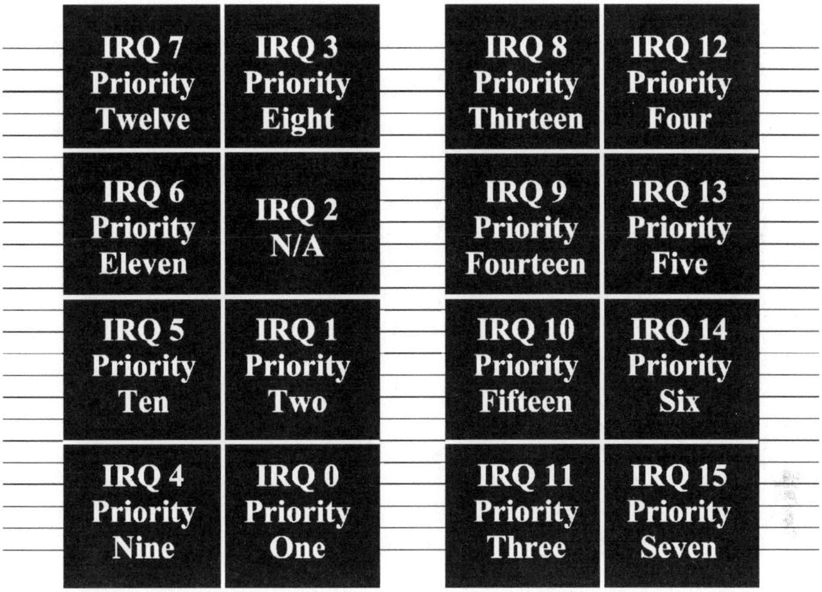

IRQ 7 Priority Twelve	IRQ 3 Priority Eight		IRQ 8 Priority Thirteen	IRQ 12 Priority Four
IRQ 6 Priority Eleven	IRQ 2 N/A		IRQ 9 Priority Fourteen	IRQ 13 Priority Five
IRQ 5 Priority Ten	IRQ 1 Priority Two		IRQ 10 Priority Fifteen	IRQ 14 Priority Six
IRQ 4 Priority Nine	IRQ 0 Priority One		IRQ 11 Priority Three	IRQ 15 Priority Seven

Figure 9.5   The physical IRQs and their relative priorities

address, an I/O address table is maintained by the CPU. When a device needs to communicate with the CPU, it first lights up its IRQ channel. When the CPU is ready to interface with that device, it looks up the IRQ in the address table and then knows where to go looking for the device driver or BIOS instruction that manages the device.

The number of available I/O addresses is limited. They consist of one or more 8-bit ports. There are 256 of these 8-bit ports, or 65,536 available 16-bit ports. Any two contiguous 8-bit ports can be combined to form a single 16-bit port, and any four contiguous 8-bit ports can be combined to form a single 32-bit port. Many of these ports are assigned by IBM for specific functions, and others have been claimed by other companies to support their devices.

EXAM NOTE: For the exam and in the real world, understand that while it may be possible for peripherals to share an IRQ, attempting to share an I/O address is sure to result in a conflict.

Most devices possess more than one I/O address. Depending on the needs of a particular piece of hardware, it may receive an I/O address range of anywhere from an address a single byte wide to one as much as 32 bytes wide. In general, I/O addresses are not something that a technician assigns manually. However, for many devices, it is possible to change the I/O address of a particular device, either through a CMOS setting or from the OS. This sometimes becomes necessary when two devices compete for the same address range. A couple examples of this would be a system that was equipped with a second parallel port and a certain brand of network interface card. The default I/O addresses of these devices frequently overlap. **Table 9.1** lists a few of the most common I/O addresses.

Table 9.1 Common I/O Address Assignments

I/O Address Range	Device
000-00Fh	DMA controller, channels 0 to 3
010-01Fh	(System use)
020-023h	Interrupt controller #1 (020-021h)
024-02Fh	(System use)
030-03Fh	(System use)
040-043h	System timer
044-04Fh	(System use)
050-05Fh	(System use)
060-063h	Keyboard & PS/2 mouse (060h), speaker (061h)
064-067h	Keyboard & PS/2 mouse (064h)
068-06Fh	Free to use
070-073h	Real-time clock/CMOS, (Non-maskable Interrupt - 070-071h)
074-07Fh	(System use)
080-083h	DMA page register 0-2
084h	DMA page register 3
089-08Bh	DMA page register 4-6
08Fh	DMA page register 7
090-09Fh	(System use)
0A0-0A3h	Interrupt controller #2
0A4-0BFh	(System use)
0C0-0CFh	DMA controller, channels 4-7 (0C0-0DFh, bytes 1-16)
0D0-0DFh	DMA controller, channels 4-7 (0C0-0DFh, bytes 17-32)
0E0-0EFh	(System use)
0F0-0FFh	Floating point unit (FPU/NPU/Math coprocessor)
100-12Fh	(System use)
130-15Fh	Commonly used for SCSI controllers
160-167h	Free to use
168-16Fh	Quaternary IDE controller, master drive
170-077h	Secondary IDE controller, master drive
178-1E7h	Free to use
1E8-1EFh	Tertiary IDE controller, master drive
1F0-1F7h	Primary IDE controller, master drive

(Continued)

Table 9.1   *(Continued)*

I/O Address Range	Device
1F8-1FFh	Free to use
200-207h	Joystick controller
208-20Bh	Free to use
20B-20Fh	(System use)
210-21Fh	Free to use
220-22Fh	Sound card
230-23Fh	Some SCSI adapters
240-24Fh	Some sound cards, some SCSI adapters, some NE2000 network cards
250-25Fh	Some NE2000 network cards
260-26Fh	Some NE2000 network cards, some non-NE2000 network cards, some sound cards
270-273h	(System use)
274-278H	Plug and Play system devices
279-27Fh	LPT2
280-28Fh	Some sound cards, some NE2000 network cards
290-29Fh	Some NE2000 network cards
2C0-2E7h	Free to use
2E8-2EFh	COM port 4
2F0-2F7h	Free to use
2F8-2FFh	COM port 2
300-301h	MIDI port
300-30Fh	Some NE2000 network cards
310-31Fh	Some NE2000 network cards
320-323h	Some non-NE2000 network cards
320-32Fh	Some NE2000 network cards
320-327h	PC-XT hard disk controller
330-333h	MIDI port
330-33Fh	Some NE2000 network cards, some SCSI controllers
340-34Fh	Some SCSI controllers
350-35Fh	Some NE2000 network cards, some SCSI controllers
360-363h	Some tape backup controller cards
360-36Fh	Some NE2000 network cards

(Continued)

Table 9.1 *(Concluded)*

I/O Address Range	Device
370-373h	Some tape backup controller cards
370-37Fh	Some NE2000 network cards
378-37Fh	LPT1 (or LPT2 on monochrome systems)
380-387h	Free to use
388-38Bh	FM synthesizer
38C-3AFh	Free to use
3B0-3BBh	VGA or monochrome video
3BC-3BFh	LPT1 on monochrome systems
3C0-3CFh	VGA or CGA video
3D3-3DFh	VGA or EGO video
3E0-3E3h	Some tape backup controllers
3E8-3Efh	COM port 3
3EC-3Efh	Tertiary IDE controller
3F0-3F7h	Floppy disk controller
3F8-3FFh	COM port 1
3f6-3F7h	Primary IDE

Common I/O address assignments

Note: While it may appear on this table that some devices overlap in their I/O address range, in fact, this is not possible. These indicate devices that may potentially occupy the range. If one device already possesses an address within the range, no other device may share it.

Direct Memory Access Channels

Some devices don't need a lot of help from the CPU just to transfer data between themselves and RAM. Forcing the CPU to arbitrate every byte that moves between them would be a waste of CPU time and bog the system down. Those devices should be able to learn to move data directly to memory without CPU intervention. Devices that can make use of a direct memory access (DMA) channel are able to perform this feat. An example of this is a floppy drive transfer, or a .wav file playing over your sound card.

As was the case with IRQs, originally DMA channels were under the control of a specific chip. Early computers used an 8237 chip to handle DMA functions. One of these chips was able to direct traffic for four channels. When IBM doubled the number of IRQ controllers in the PC-AT, it also doubled the number of 8237 chips. As with the 8259, the two chips were linked through two of the channels: DMA0 and DMA4. Therefore, these two DMA numbers constitute the same channel. The 8237s joined the 8259s in being swallowed by the chipset.

There is 8-bit DMA access and 16-bit DMA access. DMA channels are also directly linked to the ISA bus, and therefore can run only at the 8MHz speed of the ISA bus. Therefore, DMA is used only on devices that require relatively slow throughput. Such devices would include floppy disk drives and some sound cards. Also, if you elect to configure your parallel port to Extended Capabilities Port (ECP) mode when configuring your parallel port, you will need to select a DMA channel.

To configure an 8-bit device on a DMA channel, you need to use either one of channels DMA1 or DMA3. DMA0 and DMA2 can't be used because they are reserved by the system. DMA0 is allocated to the memory refresh circuit, while DMA2 is tied to the floppy disk drive. 16-bit devices need to be configured on DMA5, DMA6, or DMA7. DMA4 can't be used because it's the cascaded channel. **Table 9.2** summarizes DMA channel usage in a more visual way.

COM AND LPT PORTS

One thing I want to emphasize right off the bat is that COM ports and serial ports are not the same things. Nor are LPT and parallel ports the same. Serial and parallel ports are physical places into which you plug cables. COM and LPT ports are preconfigured combinations of IRQ and I/O addresses.

When IBM was first writing the book on the personal computer, it decided that serial devices would be easier to configure if the user had a fixed I/O and IRQ to use. Likewise, printers would be easier to deal with if you just put them on LPT1 rather than having to fight with individual parameters. The engineers defined two COM ports and two LPT ports.

> **EXAM NOTE:** Know the resource settings for all the COM and LPT ports backward and forward. You may be asked to identify them directly. Or worse yet, you may be given a detailed configuration that includes the use of COM ports and be expected to know what resources are still available for allocation.

Early on, IBM realized that two COM ports weren't enough. There were just too many devices that worked off of a serial port. Rather than tie up an additional two IRQs, the designers at IBM made a tactical decision. How often would somebody be trying to access two different

Table 9.2 Common DMA Channel Usage

DMA Channel	Usage
8-bit Channels	
DMA0	Memory Refresh
DMA1	Available
DMA2	Floppy Disk Drive
DMA3	Available
16-bit Channels	
DMA4	Cascade
DMA5	Available
DMA6	Available
DMA7	Available

Available and assigned DMA channels

BUZZ WORDS

COM port: A predefined combination of an IRQ and an I/O address configured for communications devices.

LPT port: A predefined combination of an IRQ and an I/O address configured for line printers.

external devices at the same time? (Keep in mind, this was in the days of DOS, when a computer couldn't climb stairs and chew gum at the same time.) Therefore, when they added COM ports 3 and 4 to the mix, they used the same IRQs as COM ports 1 and 2. They simply gave the ports different I/O addresses so the CPU would know it was talking to a different device. However, if the user did hit both devices simultaneously, the system would freeze. A classic example of this was putting the modem on COM3 and a serial mouse on COM1. The system works great as long as you don't try to use the modem and the mouse at the same time. Then, both devices hit IRQ4 at the same time and the system freezes.

Table 9.3   COM and LPT Port Assignments

Port Name	IRQ	I/O
COM1	4	3F8h
COM2	3	2F8h
COM3	4	3E8h
COM4	3	2E8h
LPT1	7	378h
LPT2	5	278h

The standard COM and LPT ports, as defined by IBM

Another example is putting a parallel scanner in line with your printer on the same parallel port. One parallel port will have one LPT port. This won't matter as long as you scan when you scan and you print when you print. If you try to scan when you print, you'll have a problem. **Table 9.3** lists the COM and LPT ports as defined by IBM.

SERIAL AND PARALLEL PORTS

Two interfaces frequently overlooked by novices as being part of the expansion bus are the serial and parallel ports. Yet these ports are commonly used to interface with external devices. Many of the toys you go out and buy today hook up to one of these ports.

SERIAL PORTS

The initial IBM PC shipped with two serial ports. At the time, that was considered sufficient. However, in the years before USB and FireWire (see the section immediately following this one), those were the only places to put devices such as external modems. Some printers also hooked up to the serial port as well. On most PCs of that era, the serial and parallel ports were on an expansion card called the I/O card. Once IBM had defined an additional two COM ports, it was relatively easy for the user to add additional ports.

On most of the earlier computers, the two serial ports consisted of a single DB-9 and a single DB-25. The DB-9 connector on a computer consists of a 9-pin male connector about a half an inch long by a quarter of an inch high. The matching cable would be a nine-socket female connector. **Figure 9.6** shows a close-up of a DB-9 connector.

Figure 9.6   A DB-9 connector

The DB-25 serial ports (**Figure 9.7**) used on older machines differed from their 9-pin counterparts only in cosmetics. The DB-25 doesn't use any more conductors than the DB-9. The remaining pins are null. Serial ports, whether DB-9 or DB-25, sometimes get referred to as RS-232 ports, after the standards that described the port.

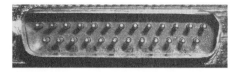

Figure 9.7   The 25-pin serial port actually doesn't use any more pins than the 9-pin port. It just uses bigger plugs.

Most current computers have a single DB-9. A few models still sport a pair of DB-9s. It is pretty rare to stumble across DB-25 ports on recent machines. This particular interface has become a historical artifact.

PARALLEL PORTS

Parallel ports are also DB-25 connectors. This shouldn't, however, cause any confusion with the 25-pin serial ports that may exist on the same machine. Serial ports are always male plugs on the back of the computer; the parallel port is female. Unlike the 25-pin serial port, parallel ports make use of nearly all of the conductors available. They have to transmit eight bits of data on each cycle, and on the more modern parallel modes, need to send and receive. In Chapter Seventeen, Printing Technologies: Getting it All on Paper, I will go over the various parallel port modes and how they have differed over the years.

THE UNIVERSAL SERIAL BUS

While not the most recent of the technologies to emerge, the Universal Serial Bus (USB) still enjoys immense popularity. The USB interface is 100 percent Plug 'n Play, and devices are hot-swappable. This means that the user can add and remove USB devices on the fly without having to shut the computer down. It also only loads drivers for those devices that are attached. It is theoretically possible to string together up to 127 devices in a single chain and still only tie up one IRQ.

The first commercial release of USB, Version 1.0, provided a shared bandwidth of 12Mb/s. With one device hooked up, that device enjoyed the entire 12Mb/s to itself. A second device added to the bus dropped the respective speed of each by half. A third device caused the bandwidth to be shared three ways, and so on and so forth. A USB 1.0 cable run could be as long as 100′.

USB 2.0 added a new device class called high-speed and upped total bandwidth to 480Mb/s. This added speed takes its toll in terms of cable length. A USB 2.0 cable can only be as long as 15′. USB 2.0 is completely backwardly compatible to 1.0. Therefore all manufacturers are currently shipping nothing but Version 2.0 product.

BUZZ WORDS ——————

USB hub: A device that manages the I/O for two or more USB device chains.

USB host: Any computer or other device equipped with USB-compatible BIOS, firmware, and controller.

USB device: Any component designed to be operated on the USB.

USB requires three different components to be active in order to work. Those are the host, the hub, and the device. The *host* would be any computer equipped with a USB-compatible BIOS, chipset, and controller. This would be practically any computer built since about 1998. The *hub* is the actual USB port where the cable connects. On the back of the computer, the USB hub would be the one or two USB ports provided by the manufacturer. A hub located on the computer itself is the root hub. Most electronics stores also provide devices that allow additional connections. These are external hubs. The *device* completes the chain. Devices, in USB terminology, are also known as the function.

Exam Note: Make sure you know the number of devices that can be managed by USB and the maximum throughput of both USB 1.0 and USB 2.0.

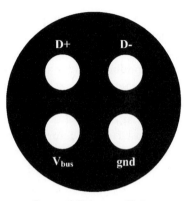

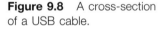

D+ and D– carry Data.
V_{bus} and gnd provide power.

Figure 9.8   A cross-section of a USB cable.

A USB cable (**Figure 9.8**) consists of two pairs of 28-gauge wire. One pair transfers data between the device and the computer. The second pair provides power to the devices in either low-power or high-power mode. In low-power mode, it will provide up to 100mA of electricity to the device. High-power mode can provide up to 500mA. If a device requires more current than either mode provides, it must provide its own power supply. These are self-powered devices. Printers and scanners need a place to be plugged in. Anything that can operate on 500mA or less is bus-powered and won't need an outlet. Keyboards and modems fall into that category.

The nice thing about many USB devices is that they are able to double as an external hub. I am currently using a CTX USB monitor. On the back is an external hub built into the monitor that has an additional four plugs. I can plug my USB keyboard into the monitor and not have to worry about stringing the cable around the back of the desk and all the way to the computer.

FireWire   *FireWire* was originally the brainchild of Apple Computer Corporation, released in 1986. The Institute of Electrical and Electronic Engineers (IEEE) assumed development of the technology and formalized the standards as IEEE-1394 in 1995. Technically, FireWire is a form of the Small Computer Systems Interface (SCSI), which will be discussed in Chapter Fourteen, The Many Faces of SCSI. However, because it competes directly with USB as an I/O bus, I've decided to include a discussion of FireWire in this chapter.

Long a popular favorite on Macintosh Computers, it is rapidly picking up interest in the PC world as well. FireWire is everything you could want in a bus. It is auto-configuring. A new device introduced to the bus sends out its information and the FireWire protocols load all the appropriate drivers. Once the device is shut down, drivers can be shelled out of memory. Like USB, FireWire

Buzz Words ————

FireWire: A high-speed serial SCSI connection originally developed by Apple Computer Corporation that is capable of 400Mb/s throughput.

is hot-pluggable. Devices can be put in or taken out at will, without shutting the system down. FireWire requires no termination or device ID configuration.

A standard FireWire cable consists of six conductors (**Figure 9.9**). There are two sets of 28-gauge twisted-pair wire for data transmission, plus two 22-gauge wires for carrying current. IEEE-1394 specifications call for FireWire cable to be capable of carrying up to 40V at 1.5A. However, relatively few devices actually make use of the power lines. This cable can be up to 14′ long.

Current standards support up to 400Mb/s data transfer and up to sixty-three devices on a chain. Proposed standards increase throughput to 800Mb/s. The real beauty of FireWire is that it is platform independent. In fact, it is device independent. It works on Macs as well as PCs and

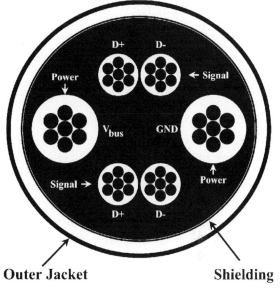

Outer Jacket   **Shielding**

Figure 9.9   Cross-section of a FireWire cable

could easily be ported to mainframes. Two FireWire-enabled devices could be linked directly together, without even requiring an intervening computer to handle data transfer. This makes it an ideal interface for digital consumer electronic devices, including audio-visual equipment.

At this point in time, FireWire practically owns the Apple market. While it's gaining headway in the PC world, it still hasn't overcome the perceived advantages of the Universal Serial Bus, and USB 2.0 is actually faster. **Table 9.4** compares both versions of USB to FireWire.

FireWire does require that both the system BIOS and the OS support IEEE-1394. All Microsoft operating systems released from Windows 98, 2nd Edition and later support FireWire. Microsoft does have supplemental files posted on its Web site for enabling Windows 98. Previous operating systems will not support it. Various Linux support sites, including most companies that provide Linux distribution packages, have patches that will enable FireWire in Linux as well.

Table 9.4   A Comparison of USB to FireWire

Specification	USB 1.0	USB 2.0	FireWire
Data transfer rate	12Mb/s	480Mb/s	400Mb/s
Cable length	100′	15′	14′
Number of devices on a chain	127	127	63

Both versions of USB and FireWire support hot-swapping devices and are capable of powering peripherals by way of their respective connectors.

The Data Bus: Moving Data across the Bus

The primary reason for having an expansion bus is to be able to add new devices to a system. Your new computer didn't arrive with all the toys you wanted. So you went down to the computer store and bought that high-end sound card you just couldn't live without. Now you can play back all the fancy sounds your game can generate, but until you get those sounds moved from RAM to the sound card, none of that information is going to do you a whole lot of good.

In a perfect world, the devices would all operate at the same speed as the processor and would have data busses exactly the same width. You've already seen why that isn't possible. CPUs just don't stay the same from one generation to the next. As new generations of CPUs have been released, new expansion busses are also developed. Many computers (in fact most of them) have at least two separate types of expansion bus. Some even have three. Later in this chapter, I will provide a detailed description of each of the busses. To help you get through this section, **Table 9.5** outlines the various busses that have appeared over the years and ties them together with the release of CPUs.

Exam Note: Make sure you know the order in which the different expansion busses evolved, along with details such as bit width and maximum bus speeds.

Table 9.5 The Evolution of the Expansion Bus

BUS	Year Released	Bus Width	Maximum Speed	Address Space	Available Memory	Bandwidth	CPU Release
PC1	1981	8-bit	4.77MHz	8-bit	1MB	7.9MB/s	8088
ISA	1984	16-bit	8MHz	20-bit	16MB	15.9MB/s	80286
MCA	1987	32-bit	10MHz	20-bit	16MB	~38.6MB/s	80386
EISA	1988	32-bit	8MHz	32-bit	4GB	31.8MB/s	80386
PC Card	1990	16-bit	8MHz	24-bit	64MB	~15.8MB/s	80386
VLB	1991	32-bit	33MHz	32-bit	4GB	127.2MB/s	80486
PCI 1.0	1992	32-bit	33MHz	32-bit	4GB	127.2MB/s	80486
PCI 2.1	1995	32- or 64-bit	66MHz	32-bit	4GB	~510MB/s	Pentium
AGP 1.0	1996	32-bit	66MHz	32-bit	4GB	254MB/s	Pentium
AGP 2.0	1998	32-bit	66MHz	32-bit	4GB	~533MB/s	Pentium
PCI-X 1.0	2000	64-bit	133MHz	64-bit	N/A	~1.2GB/s	Pentium II
PCI-X 2.0	2002	64-bit	<533MHz	64-bit	N/A	~4.3GB/s	Pentium 4

Each new release of a PCI bus is not only faster, but can also have increased bit-width and more efficient transfer of data in each clock cycle.

So how does the CPU deal with 16-bit chunks of data coming off the ISA bus, and not choke on the 64-bit data that the PCI-X devices are delivering? For one thing, if the bus is not of equal size to the CPU, delivery of data must occur over multiple bus cycles. For example, if you have a CPU that has a 133MHz front-side bus (see Chapter Six, Understanding CPUs), and is moving data from a conventional PCI device, the bottleneck created is two-fold. First off, the CPU has a 64-bit external data bus; the PCI has 32-bit. This means that it will require two cycles of the PCI bus to move enough data to fill the CPU's bus for just one of its cycles. Second, the CPU cycle is 133MHz while the PCI bus is 33MHz. That means each cycle for the CPU represents 7.5 nanoseconds (ns), while a cycle for PCI is a hair over 30ns. Therefore, it's taking 60ns, or eight CPU clock cycles, for each chunk of data moved from the bus to the CPU.

In order to arbitrate this transfer, a special circuit is required. As you may have already guessed, this is another function of the chipset in most cases. In the case of the older ISA bus, the southbridge chip (see Chapter Five, Motherboards, BIOS, and the Chipset) is in control. Faster busses, such as AGP, will link to the northbridge chip. As I shall explain later in this chapter, PCI can be arbitrated by either the northbridge or the southbridge.

THE MEMORY BUS: ADDRESSING RAM

When I discussed the CPU in Chapter Six, I pointed out that one of the limitations of a CPU is how much memory it can "see." This is a limitation imposed by its address bus. Expansion cards interconnect to the expansion bus and address memory in a similar manner. However, with many bus devices, greater limitations are imposed.

The ISA bus is enabled with a 24-bit address bus. Therefore, even if the CPU has a 32-bit address bus, the device installed in the slot can't see as much memory as the CPU can. It will be limited to the lower 16MB of RAM. Devices attached to the ISA bus, by default, have to locate their memory buffers in this area. DMA access can occur only with data located in the lower 16MB, which means that when the data is located elsewhere, the device driver needs to relocate the information. This adds to the many reasons why ISA is not a suitable bus for most devices communicating with modern CPUs.

TIMING ISSUES

As I discussed earlier, one of the key reasons for having a separate expansion bus is so that there doesn't have to be a new device made every time CPU speeds move up. Therefore, the expansion bus will most likely be running at a rate different that that of the CPU. On the original IBM PC, that wasn't a problem. The expansion bus and the CPU ran at the same speed. Once they started to move apart, the issue had to be faced.

While the system clock paces the CPU, the expansion bus has its own signal, generated by a bus clock. For a successful transfer of data to occur, that data has to be paced to arrive on the CPU bus at intervals in which the CPU can receive it. Early computers made use of *synchronous timing*. CPUs were developed at speeds that were either a multiple or a submultiple of the clock speed. For example, the 12MHz 80286 was 1.5× that of the 8MHz bus. Data was easily buffered. *Asynchronous timing* works by letting the bus move data however it sees fit, and then delivering that data at a rate optimal to the CPU. This does require more complex circuitry and a buffer area for the data to be held, but it also allows for better efficiency in data transfer. Most modern CPUs are designed to operate either synchronously or asynchronously. The chipset controls timing.

COMMUNICATING ACROSS BUSSES

Timing, data access, and data transfer are all complicated enough issues when there is only a single bus on the system. However, most computers have different types of expansion bus available. The computer I'm working on right now has two ISA slots, five PCI slots, and an AGP slot. Each one of those operates at a different speed, transfers data in different sized chunks, and has to handle timing issues in different manners. As a result, the system needs some way of refereeing among the different busses for them to be able to communicate among themselves.

This becomes particularly problematic when the busses don't even interface with the same part of the chipset. For example, the AGP bus doesn't see the southbridge chip at all. ISA doesn't communicate with the northbridge chip. Yet both have to coexist with each other, and neither operates at the speed of the CPU. To solve this problem, designers incorporated *bridges* into the circuitry. These bridges act as translators between busses.

Another place where bridges become necessary is across PCI busses. By design, as I'll discuss a little later in this chapter, a PCI bus is limited to only four slots. It can use even less than that if there are PCI devices incorporated onto the board. Yet we all know that motherboards come with more than four PCI slots. As I just said, the one I'm working on has five. This is possible because of something called the PCI to PCI Bridge (PPB). In theory, a designer could incorporate as many as 256 different PPBs onto a motherboard, supporting over a thousand slots. That would be one big motherboard!

THE EVOLUTION OF THE EXPANSION BUS

By now, it should be clear that as the CPU became faster and more complicated, the expansion bus had to be redesigned to keep up. When IBM first designed the PC bus in the postpartum days of the personal computer, it took a major step forward by making the bus available to one and all. This provided a certain degree of compatibility, which was precisely what IBM had in mind. With a few notable exceptions, this compatibility has been the mainstay of the computer industry. In fact, the task of maintaining those standards has fallen under the strict control of IEEE. Table 9.5, earlier in this chapter, provides an overview of the different busses. Here, I will

Figure 9.10 Compared to modern computers, a system based on the old XT design was a very simple thing.

take you on a more detailed bus tour. For those of you interested in specific pinouts of some of the busses discussed here, refer to Appendix C.

THE PC BUS

The bus shown in **Figure 9.10** is often called 8-bit ISA. This isn't technically correct, because the ISA standards that I will discuss next wouldn't be defined for a couple of more years. IBM called it the PC bus or sometimes the XT bus. Once the PC-AT was released in 1984, IBM referred to the 16-bit bus as the AT bus. However, those were trademarked names, so the term ISA, for Industry Standard Architecture, was coined. Nothing would officially become labeled ISA until 1987 when IEEE would formalize the standards. Writers who have fallen into the 8-bit ISA trap can be forgiven, because it was from this bus that the ISA standards were drawn. Nothing in the physical structure magically changed simply because IEEE had given it its blessing. The difference is purely semantic (and in most cases, purely bureaucratic).

The original PC bus consisted of a 7.66MHz 8-bit slot designed to accommodate the external data bus of the Intel 8088 CPU. The speed of the bus would be bumped to 8.33MHz the following year. The slot was a 62-pin edge card connector. It supported only the 20-bit address bus of the 8088. The PC bus only addresses a total of eight IRQs. Since computers of this era only made use of a single DMA controller chip, the 8-bit slot only had four conductors dedicated to DMA channels. The PC bus had a relatively long life span, despite the fact that the PC-AT rendered it virtually obsolete a year later. For the most part, most ISA devices of the day continued to be made in 8-bit versions. 8-bit "ISA" slots would continue to appear in machines all the way into the era of computers based on the 80486 CPU.

INDUSTRY STANDARD ARCHITECTURE

When IEEE released the official standards for the ISA bus in 1987, it took the design, as implemented by IBM, and strictly defined it. It was at this point in time that the industry had an "official" ISA bus. In a publication released as IEEE Draft Standard P996, the committee strictly defined signal and timing specifications that all companies had to follow. It also defined the specifications for the 16-bit extensions (see **Figure 9.11**).

The 8-bit incarnation of the bus remained as described in the section on the PC bus. The 16-bit version was extracted directly from IBM's schematics for the AT bus. The only real differences were in the strict definitions of electrical signals, something IBM had not been as informative about. For reasons of backward compatibility, the 8.33MHz speed was retained.

The 16-bit bus had to address issues other than simply a wider data path. The AT had also incorporated a second 8259 chip, enabling seven additional IRQs, and a second 8237 chip, adding three more DMA channels. Also, because of the newer CPU used in the PC-AT, the 80286 had a 24-bit address bus, and the 16-bit ISA was modified to enable it to use the extended address space as well.

In order to make sure that this new bus didn't make all those 8-bit devices that had been manufactured over the previous years obsolete, the added pins required for the changes were implemented in an extension to the original 8-bit design. This consisted of a 36-pin connector added onto the back of the 62-pin 8-bit slot. This extension is separated by a null space known as the *key*. The end result is that an 8-bit device will occupy only the front section of the slot and the system will recognize it as an 8-bit device. The 16-bit card fills the whole slot.

Figure 9.11   IBM kept the 16-bit ISA slot compatible with the 8-bit PC slot by adding the additional wires onto an extension hung off the end of the old PC slot.

The 16-bit ISA became the de facto standard for many years and continues to appear on motherboards manufactured today. It was only recently that Intel and Microsoft banded together to end the days of the ISA reign. According to their PC2002 standards, motherboards will no longer support ISA. Judging by the number of systems still appearing with ISA in 2003, I would have to assume that many manufacturers are finding other uses for the papers written by these two companies on the subject. However, as hard as the bus is to kill, there is good logic in what Intel and Microsoft are trying to do.

The ISA bus never made it past the 8.33MHz level. The newer chipsets by Intel no longer have a southbridge component, and therefore cannot support anything that slow. Other manufacturers will eventually have to follow suit. Also, the 24-bit address space is still an inherent limitation of the bus, as I discussed in the section on addressing. Therefore, I think it's safe to say that the days of ISA are dwindling rapidly.

MICRO CHANNEL ARCHITECTURE

When Intel released its 80386 microprocessor, the ISA bus first started becoming a bottleneck. On this CPU, Intel increased both the external data bus and the memory address bus to 32 bits.

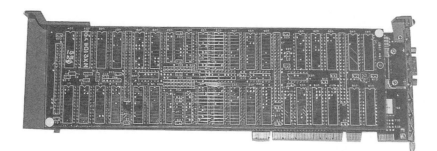

Figure 9.12 Micro Channel devices have a unique interface that won't fit into any other slot.

At this same time, VGA video adapters were taking the world by storm and replacing all previous video standards (see Chapter Fifteen, Your Computer and Graphics). These devices seriously challenged the ISA bus in its throughput requirements, even with standard MS-DOS applications. Microsoft's nearly simultaneous release of Windows 3.0 exacerbated that problem greatly with its graphical interface. An MCA video card, like the one in **Figure 9.12**, could significantly improve performance.

It wasn't just graphics that were seeing the bottleneck either. Network operating systems were demonstrating that a group of PCs attached to a server could be a more attractive option than simple dumb terminals getting all their data from a mainframe. Network cards would also benefit from a faster, wider bus. Basically, the world was clamoring for something that could more easily keep up with the 386.

IBM came to the table first in 1987 with its Micro Channel Architecture (MCA). MCA was an elegant design. In many respects it established the minimum standards that subsequent bus designs would later emulate. One of the changes IBM was to make was to increase bus speed from 8.33MHz to 10MHz (it would later release a 20MHz version in a belated attempt to fend off the challenge of EISA), and to double the data path from 16 bits to 32 bits.

The most user-friendly change IBM made was that an MCA device was software-configurable. With every Micro Channel device IBM included a configuration diskette that made installation of the device nearly idiot-proof. On this disk was a program called the Programmable Option Select. When the user ran this program, it scanned the system to determine what resources might be available. Any MCA device already installed on the system simply reported its own resources. The program would scan existing config.sys and autoexec.bat files (key configuration files for the older MS-DOS and Windows 3.xx operating systems) for information on legacy devices.

Another aspect in which Micro Channel was far superior to ISA was in its handling of IRQs. When IBM first designed the PC bus, it had been the intent all along that IRQs be shared when possible. Unfortunately IBM never provided any defined standards by which this could be done. Since the devices being manufactured all used edge-triggered signaling, it was difficult (although not impossible) to implement IRQ sharing. Manufacturers of ISA devices simply didn't bother to try. That was where the rule "one device, one IRQ" came from. MCA design specifications required that MCA devices negotiate use of the data path. This prevented the IRQ line from being used simultaneously and allowed IRQs to be successfully shared.

Micro Channel pioneered a technology still in use called *bus mastering*. By adding a circuit known as the *Central Arbitration Point*, the CPU could be relieved of the duties of managing the expansion bus. A bus master was any device that was able to take control of the bus. Obviously, the CPU was the primary bus master. Also, any MCA device could be designed as a bus master. Two bus-mastering devices could transfer data directly back and forth between themselves without needing the CPU to act as a referee.

You would think that, with all these technological advancements, the computer world would have beaten a path to IBM's door. As it turned out, this wasn't the case. IBM had not been overly ec-

static with the way the rest of the industry had profited from ISA. Many of these companies had actually surpassed IBM in total sales of personal computers. IBM decided not to make this technology publicly available, instead charging royalties for its use. This was an industry that had gotten spoiled by the concept of something for nothing. They flocked away from MCA in droves. Scant few companies outside of IBM ever integrated this technology onto their motherboards, and the number of card manufacturers that anted up wasn't that much greater. It turned out to be a short-lived architecture as far as the PC world was concerned. It enjoyed a long life, however, as the bus of choice for many of IBM's mini-mainframe computers.

ENHANCED ISA

The failure of MCA didn't mean the industry wasn't interested in a faster bus. It only meant that they weren't willing to pay for it. There was still a driving need for a technology more advanced than that offered by ISA. Compaq Computer Corporation along with eight other companies cooperated in a joint effort to design a new industry standard that could be used without having to pay royalties. In 1988, they released the Enhanced Industry Standard Architecture (EISA) standards.

With the aid of a little reverse engineering, they managed to assemble a collection of technologies not patented by IBM. Their design incorporated many of the best features of MCA, yet managed to keep it backward compatible with ISA. EISA was a 32-bit bus operating at 8.33MHz. Like MCA, it could be configured through software.

Despite being the same speed as ISA, the designers achieve performance gains over and above simply doubling the data path. By drastically reducing the number of clock cycles involved in the average transaction, EISA devices were able to boast throughput by up to an additional 50 percent.

The biggest feat that the "gang of nine" managed was that they maintained backward compatibility with ISA. IBM didn't even attempt this with MCA. This compatibility was achieved by converting the slot into a two-story condo, as opposed to the single-floor apartment that ISA represented. There were two layers of connectors, one on top of the other. The top layer was identical to a 16-bit ISA slot and directly replicated the functions. The bottom layer of conductors could only be engaged by an EISA device. With this design, a user was able to use either a 16-bit ISA device or a 32-bit EISA device.

VESA LOCAL BUS

MCA and EISA were both significant improvements over ISA. However, neither one of them was particularly adept at handling graphics loads. Companies that made video cards realized that if anybody was going to address their particular needs, it was going to have to be them. An organization of these manufacturers, the Video Electronics Standards Association (VESA), got together and created the first bus that actually tapped into the computer's local bus and communicated directly with the CPU at the speed of its external data bus. It called its brainchild VESA Local Bus (VLB).

By tapping the local bus, video card manufacturers could add a processor to the video card and offload some of the processing load to the device itself. This design obviously favored video cards, but could also allow for advanced I/O controllers as well. High-end VESA Local Bus video cards had ROM chips that contained many of the elements of the Windows interface, and could pop them onto the screen without having to go through the process of drawing them anew each time. Examples of these elements would include scroll bars, buttons, icons, and other items of that nature.

VLB slots were designed as an extension of the 16-bit ISA slot. The cards themselves made use of only the 8-bit portion. The pinout of the front half of the card was identical to an 8-bit card in every respect. This portion of the slot handles I/O functions and power requirements. Directly behind this ISA slot was an extension which tapped into the local bus. This is where 32-bit data transfers and the advanced functions of VLB were controlled.

VESA advertised its new bus as being capable of bus mastering. In reality, it was somewhat limited in this respect. Timing issues prohibited more than three devices on a system, and, in fact, the majority came equipped with only one or two.

PERIPHERAL COMPONENTS INTERCONNECT

Intel had a slight advantage when it was designing the Peripheral Components Interconnect (PCI) bus. It had been busy at work for some time designing the CPU it was to support. Not too long after its release, Intel turned over further development of the design to an organization called the PCI Special Interest Group (PCI-SIG).

The first PCI design was based on a 33MHz, 32-bit bus. In other words, it wasn't a whole lot different from VLB in terms of speed. It directly supported the 80486 CPU. Later revisions of PCI standards, however, included definitions for a 64-bit slot and bus speeds of 66MHz. PCI 2.1 will be discussed in greater detail later in this section. The slots shown in **Figure 9.13** are typical of the 32-bit devices that flood the market.

One of the advantages Intel enjoyed was that it had designed the Plug 'n Play standards as well. By default, PCI is a Plug 'n Play device. This means that part of its core design is the ability to be software-configured. Each PCI card manufactured is equipped with a ROM chip that reports to the BIOS its *class code* and its *extended capability ID* (ECI). The class code tells the BIOS precisely what kind of device it is. The ECI reports any additional features it supports beyond the minimal standards.

The PCI bus has its own method for dealing with IRQs as well. PCI devices address IRQs through four interrupt channels, INTA#, INTB#, INTC#, and INTD#. Despite this, there are a few PCI devices that only address a single IRQ. Under PCI-SIG specifications, these devices must operate on INTA#. The other channels allow manufacturers to cascade multiple devices onto a single circuit board and dole out interrupts accordingly.

A limitation of the PCI bus shows up in how it handles electrical loads. A single PCI bus is only able to handle ten loads. As for what constitutes a load—any single-chip PCI device, either onboard or in a slot, adds one load. Any PCI card with a connector adds two loads. The end result is that there is a limitation of four PCI slots on a single circuit. Each slot will require two loads, and the interconnecting circuitry will add additional loads.

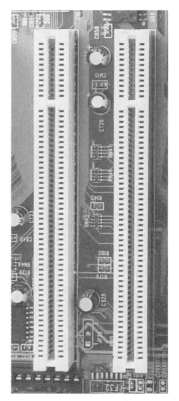

Figure 9.13 The PCI slots are the shorter (usually white) slots that make up the majority of slots on your system.

> **BUZZ WORDS**
>
> **Class code:** Information programmed onto a PCI device that tells the BIOS precisely what it is.
>
> **Extended capability ID:** Information programmed onto a PCI device that defines any enhanced features beyond the basic features of its device class that it may support.

Of course, you know that systems support more than four PCI slots. In the section Communicating Across Busses I touched on this issue. Designers install a PPB between each of the PCI busses they want on the system. Properly designed and implemented, this circuit connects two PCI busses together, treating one of the busses as primary, the other as secondary. As I mentioned, it is mathematically possible to cascade up to 256 of these busses. Unfortunately, the bandwidth and higher speed of the 64-bit 66MHz PCI bus described by the PCI 2.1 standards does not allow cascading multiple busses. In fact, a 66MHz, 64-bit bus is limited to a maximum of two slots per board.

Any PCI device is capable of bus mastering. Whether or not that capability is exploited is entirely up to the designer. Bus mastering is actually a very simple concept to understand. The CPU is only required to initiate the session between two devices. Once the "handshaking" has been completed, the devices can transfer their data directly between themselves. They don't need further help from any of the other system busses, including the CPU bus and the address bus, in the process. The way this works is that one device acts as an *initiator*. This is generally the device that acts as the data source. It is also the device that will assume the role of master during the data transfer. The other device becomes the *target*, or the slave. It is up to the master device to determine the type of data transfer that is to occur. Will it be a memory read/write operation, an I/O read/write operation, or some other type of signal transfer?

Once the process has been initiated, the transfer of data happens in two stages. The first stage is the *address phase*. This is where the master device tells the target device what kind of transfer is about to occur. Once the target device acknowledges the transfer, the data will move from master to target in one or more *data phases*. The beauty of having two bus mastering devices is that all of the data will be transferred in a single data phase in one big chunk. This is known as *burst mode*. Read or write operations to memory or I/O operations to any non-bus-mastering device may require several data phases.

> **BUZZ WORDS**
>
> **Initiator:** The device in a bus-mastering chain that is to act as the source of the data being transferred.
>
> **Target:** Any device that is to be the intended recipient of data.
>
> **Address phase:** The portion of an I/O operation that identifies the type of transaction that is about to occur.
>
> **Data phase:** The portion of an I/O operation that performs the actual transfer of data from device to device.
>
> **Burst mode:** The ability of a device to transfer a large chunk of data in a single data phase.

Sometimes one device is intrinsically capable of higher speeds than another is. If the data is streaming into the target device faster than it is capable of handling, it can initiate a wait state at any time. It tells the master to chill out a bit and give it time to swallow some of the data it already has before it has to take another byte.

PCI 2.1 added several capabilities to the PCI bus. I've already mentioned that this version supports 64-bit 66MHz devices. Now, the 64-bit isn't a problem. The first PCI slots were designed to support up to 64-bit data paths. It's just that most manufacturers didn't always take advantage of this data path. You can tell if your system supports 33MHz 64-bit devices. The slot is longer. Intel borrowed from the ISA book in designing the slots. The 32-bit slots consist of two segments, divided by a key. The front section will consist of forty-nine pairs of conductors (although they're so small, it's hard to count them). Behind that section will be a smaller collection of eleven pairs. This is a relatively short slot. The 64-bit slot adds another key, followed by thirty-two pairs of conductors. It's a bigger slot.

> **EXAM NOTE:** Be prepared to differentiate between PCI 1.0 and PCI 2.1. Later in the chapter, I'll be discussing PCI-X in detail as well. Since this technology is new to the exam, you might want to make sure you understand that as well.

Implementing the 66MHz speed, on the other hand, can be a problem. Putting a 33MHz device into a 66MHz slot will illustrate the problem far more eloquently than I ever could. That fragrance of frying circuitry will explain everything. To prevent this, the 66MHz slot is keyed differently. The slot contains the same number of conductors as the 64-bit 33MHz slot, except that the order is different. The 11-pair section goes up front, followed by a key. Behind this is the 49-pair conductor followed by its key. After this is the 32-pair section. The location of the keys prevents you from inserting a 33MHz device into a 66MHz slot or vice versa.

The extra speed also provides bandwidth issues. A 66MHz PCI bus can support only two devices per bus, not four as I discussed earlier. A system that provides 66MHz PCI support will have two slots isolated in their own bank, separate from the rest of the PCI slots.

Devices that take advantage of the greater bandwidth would include things like gigabit Ethernet adapters and the newer high-speed SCSI interfaces. Chapter Fourteen, The Many Faces of SCSI, will take a closer look at a device known as a RAID controller that is a perfect candidate for the interface.

Accelerated Graphics Port

For the last several years, the bus of choice for graphics adapters has been the Accelerated Graphics Port (AGP). AGP is a dedicated 66MHz port (**Figure 9.14**), designed specifically for graphics adapters. That in and of itself greatly increases performance over the 33MHz PCI bus. On the basis of speed alone, you wouldn't expect much improvement over a 66MHz PCI card. However, Intel wove in some technological enhancements when it drew up the specifications in 1996.

Figure 9.14 The AGP slot sits a bit farther back from the other slots on the motherboard.

> **Exam Note:** Know that regardless of whether an AGP bus is 2x, 4x, or 8x, it always operates at a clock speed of 66MHz.

AGP texturing is one of these enhancements. In order to speed up the rendering of images on the screen, programmers usually separate images into a minimum of two components. The basic outline of the image, called the vector, is stored as one data source, while the textures are managed independently. The video card is only equipped with so much memory, so textures can be stored in system memory. However, to access this data, the AGP card has to know where to find it. The AGP protocol uses the PIPE# command to access system memory directly for the complex operation of texture mapping.

The only method by which previous video cards could retrieve textures was through a technology called local texturing. Under this method, the card had to move the information from the computer's memory to local memory on the graphics adapter before the textures could be processed. AGP provides the graphics card with two methods of directly accessing texture maps in system memory: pipelining and sideband addressing. Pipelining is the same technology I introduced in Chapter Six, Understanding CPUs. In addition to pipelining, AGP enhances performance through *sideband addressing*. This allows the device to concurrently receive and request data during a single bus or memory access. Earlier technologies, such as PCI, would make one request and could not make another until the data it requested had been transferred.

Another way in which AGP cards dramatically speed up throughput is the way in which they utilize the bus signal. All devices on the system bus, regardless of which technology is being used, must keep time with the clock that controls them. Conventional devices, including PCI, can execute an instruction set or retrieve data in synch with the rising end of the clock cycle (see **Figure 9.15**). PCI was a little more efficient in using the clock cycle in that it places the timing signals on the falling edge, but still could only move data in the rising edge. AGP-2x is capable of reading or writing data on both the rising edge and the falling edge. AGP-4x is actually able to either execute instructions or transfer data on each of the cycle's edges. New standards recently introduced by Intel include AGP-8x and 8x PRO. **Table 9.6** covers the different speeds of AGP and compares them to PCI.

A key limitation of AGP is that you can only have a single AGP device per computer. That is why if you purchase a motherboard with AGP graphics built into

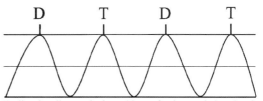

Earlier signaling methods could transfer data or timing signals on the rising crest of the wave.

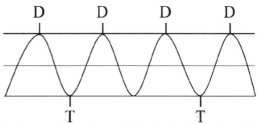

PCI improved on earlier methods in that timing signals could move on the falling end, and each transfer didn't require a separate timing signal.

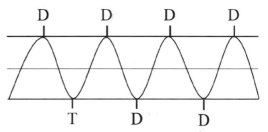

AGP took the next logical step and allowed either data or timing to move on both the rising and falling end, and one timing signal could manage a large burst of data. 2x, 4x, and 8x AGP simply moves multiple bits on each wave.

Figure 9.15 Improvements in bus signaling were not based exclusively on speed. Efficiency in timing and use of the bandwidth played a vital role.

the board most of them have no separate AGP slot. Those that have both onboard AGP graphics and an AGP slot allow only the use of one or the other; you can't use both. Also, if you're designing a high-speed graphics workstation and want dual video capability, you can't do it the easy way and just add two video cards, if you want the cards to be identical. And for the sake of your sanity, you **do** want the cards to be identical. Some of your top-of-the-line graphics adapters have dual monitor capability built right in. This feature will assure that the graphics speed of both monitors is identical.

> **EXAM NOTE:** Know that there can be only one AGP device active on a computer at any given time. If a computer is equipped with an AGP slot as well as onboard AGP graphics, you can use either one or the other, but not both.

Table 9.6   Comparison of AGP vs. PCI in Graphics Adapters

AGP	PCI
Single access/clock cycle	Multiple accesses/clock cycle
Pipelined requests	Nonpipelined requests
Address/data demultiplexed	Address/data multiplexed
533Mbps peak in 32-bit	133Mbps peak in 32-bit
Single target, single master	Multitarget, multimaster
Comparison of AGP-2x and PCI data transfer	

The most recent of AGP Standards is AGP-PRO. This might get a little confusing at first, but don't assume a video card is faster just because is carries the "PRO" label. It probably will be, because there is no point in putting slower chips on a Pro card. But the Pro designation refers to the slot's ability to handle power, and not to its relative speed.

The faster the video cards become, the hotter their processors run. Also, the type of memory used on high-end video cards tends to run hotter as well. When you start piling on more and more memory, power consumption and heat dissipation both become major issues. The original AGP slot was designed to deliver a maximum of 25W of power to the device. AGP-PRO adds additional connectors to the slot to access more power. An AGP-PRO50 is capable of calling on the power supply for 50W, while AGP-PRO110 can demand 110W.

Alas, you never get something for nothing. If you change a 25W lightbulb immediately after it pops, you might comment on how warm it is. Try that with a 110W bulb and you'll burn your fingers. Video cards are no different. When they burn more electricity, they run hotter. Therefore, AGP-PRO cards require supplementary cooling that standard cards don't. An AGP-PRO50 only needs a decent-sized heat sink to keep it cool. However, that heat sink is sufficiently large that you'll lose the PCI slot directly next to it in order to make room for it. AGP-PRO110 cards consume even more space. They need a heat sink and a cooling fan, and TWO PCI slots must be left open.

PCI-X

The developers of PCI have responded to the challenge of AGP with PCI Extended (PCI-X). The first release of PCI-X, Version 1.0, was a 64-bit 133MHz bus that was designed to be backwardly compatible with standard PCI cards. PCI-X, Version 2.0 now provides effective bandwidths of 266MHz and 533MHz as well. The latter speeds are running at an actual clock speed of 133MHz. Their effective bandwidth is derived from the fact that on each clock cycle the devices can move two and four bits of data, respectively.

All PCI-X slots and PCI-X devices are backwardly compatible with 64-bit PCI 2.1 slots and devices. That means that a conventional PCI device has no problem plugging into a PCI-X 533 slot, and a PCI-X 533 device works comfortably (albeit much more slowly) in a 33MHz PCI slot.

This is because PCI-X supports something called *speed mismatch compatibility*. Both slots and devices are designed to be able to clock down to the speed of its partner. The faster of the two simply throttles down to the speed of the slower device. This occurs transparently and seamlessly with no active intervention or configuration required by the user or technician installing the device.

> **BUZZ WORDS**
>
> **Speed mismatch compatibility:** A technology that allows two devices on the same bus to operate at different speeds and still successfully communicate with one another.

There are some limitations that motherboard manufacturers need to observe. If a device is installed on the system that runs at 133MHz, it is the only device that will run on the PCI-X bus. Two 100MHz devices could be installed, and up to four 66MHz devices. However, multiple PCI-X busses can be linked by way of PPBs.

Look at it as if a single PCI-X bus is a four-gallon bucket. You can only put four gallons in it, and each of the PCI-X devices represents an amount of liquid. A 66MHz device puts a gallon of data onto the bus, so the bus doesn't fill up until there are four devices installed. A 100MHz device has two gallons of data, so two of them fill the bucket. The 133MHz is four gallons of data all by itself. Add one and you're done.

Since PCI-X does support bridging of multiple PCI-X busses with a PPB, you can stack up several of these slots across multiple busses and provide support for several 133MHz devices. The user doesn't have to know that the 133MHz slot is on a bus all by itself and that the two 100MHz slots occupy a separate bus. Since the slots are color-coded, the end user or technician knows in which slot a particular device should go for maximum performance. But again, since all slots and devices are interchangeable, the only thing that will happen if a device is put in the wrong slot is that it might suffer a performance loss, or that a high-speed slot is being wasted on a slower device.

Even if all you ever use are 66MHz devices, you should still see a significant performance increase. At its maximum speed of 133MHz, PCI-X 133 has a total bandwidth of around 1.2GB/s. Standard PCI limits throughput to 133MB/s, while 66MHz PCI approaches 512MB/s. A system that employs a gigabit Ethernet card, a PCI video card, and one or two other devices is seriously pushing the envelope of PCI. PCI-X will expand that envelope rather significantly.

THE DIFFERENT BUSSES IN REVIEW

One of the primary advances that has occurred with each subsequent generation of expansion bus has been an increase in speed. In fact, that increase has been practically exponential. **Figure 9.16** gives an overview of the relative speeds of the different busses I have discussed in this chapter.

That speed has come about in part because of increases in clock speed. As I pointed out earlier, the speed of the first PC bus was only 7.66MHz, and not all devices took advantage of the maximum speed. Now there are busses that operate at clock speeds of 133MHz.

Raw clock speed is actually a relatively small part of the overall speed equation. Increased efficiency in the use of available bandwidth has contributed greatly. Reducing the amount of

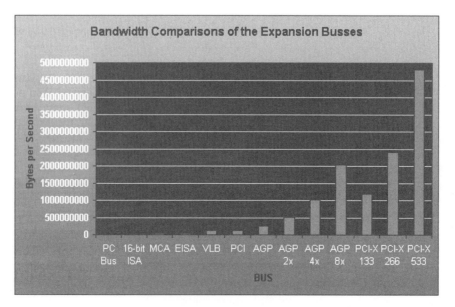

Figure 9.16 The speeds of the different expansion busses have increased at a nearly exponential rate since the PC was first developed. Notice that ISA and the PC bus speeds can't even be seen in this chart!

control data needed by each transfer means more user data is being transferred on each I/O cycle. And increasing the number of bits than can move on each clock cycle makes an even greater contribution to efficiency. **Table 9.7** summarizes the clock speed and actual data transfer rates of the various busses.

Table 9.7 An Overview of the Expansion Busses

BUS	Width (bits)	Bus Speed	Bus Bandwidth
8-bit ISA	8	7.66MHz/8.33MHz	7.9MB/s
16-bit ISA	16	8.33MHz	15.9MB/s
EISA	32	8.33MHz	31.8MB/s
MCA	32	10MHz	38.2MB/s
VLB	32	33MHz	127.2MB/s
PCI	32	33MHz	127.2MB/s
64-bit PCI 2.1	64	66MHz	508.6MB/s
AGP	32	66MHz	254.3MB/s
AGP (x2 mode)	32	66×2MHz	508.6MB/s
AGP (x4 mode)	32	66×4MHz	1017.3MB/s

Bus speed and bit width both contribute to the overall data rate of the expansion bus.

TROUBLESHOOTING THE EXPANSION BUS

Your future as a computer professional may well hinge on how well you diagnose and fix problems related to the expansion bus. For certain, you'll have your share of other problems. You'll find, however, that failures in the core system are far less frequent than those encountered when adding or changing peripheral devices.

The original intent of Plug 'n Play was to eliminate any problems that might occur in this respect. In Chapter Five, Motherboards, BIOS, and the Chipset, I went over the PnP process in some detail, and I pointed out some ways of troubleshooting the process.

Most problems are a result of resource conflicts. IRQ conflicts are increasingly rare as PnP has become more efficient. Still, they occasionally raise their little heads. I/O address problems also appear occasionally, but PnP is able to handle I/O addressing far more efficiently than it does IRQs. This isn't a function of PnP so much as it is the way I/O addresses are mapped. The final conflict you might encounter relates to use of DMA channels.

There are several symptoms that might point to a resource conflict. And unfortunately, not all of them result in the device failing to work. Two devices arguing with each other can cause many computer malfunctions that don't appear to have anything to do with the expansion bus. Some of these symptoms include the following:

- System hangs or locks up
- An erratic mouse pointer, or one that intermittently freezes
- Sound cards generating spurious noise
- Errors and crashes of applications for no apparent reason
- Your printer starts spewing out garbage
- Error messages such as "device not responding"

The key to most of these symptoms is that they will occur sporadically. Some are easier to detect than others are. An older computer that still uses a serial mouse might freeze every time the modem starts to dial. This is an obvious conflict between those two devices. And in fact, since a mouse requires a COM port the same way a modem does, it is a fairly common problem.

For some of the others, you might need to do a little detective work. The first question you might ask is, "What changed?" Take the example of the printer suddenly spewing out junk. If you decided to move from EPP or Bidirectional mode (see Chapter Seventeen, Printing Technologies: Getting it All on Paper) to ECP, ECP claimed a DMA channel. If that happens to be the same DMA your sound card was using, you'll get some interesting aftereffects. If the sound card is active, for example, if you're playing MP3s while you work, and you send a job to the printer, your system will most likely lock up like a stone. Both devices tried to actively use the channel at the same time. Even if the sound card isn't active, it can cause problems such as described above.

If you're getting system crashes, you need to ascertain if something new was added to the system. Sometimes sound cards and network cards don't like each other. This might be one of those cases where I/O addressing is actually the culprit. While the majority of sound cards default to I/O 220h for their address, there are other addresses that are frequently used. Several of these supplemental addresses fall within the range of addresses frequented by certain types of network cards. You might need to do some manual tweaking to resolve this issue. A good place to start is in Device Manager if you're running Windows. This little applet not only detects that the conflict exists, but offers suggestions for its resolution.

IRQ conflicts generally prevent one of the devices from being recognized. The card that gets the IRQ first is there and most likely works fine. The other device simply isn't seen. Windows users can once again use Device Manager for detection and resolution. The application is not always as successful here, though. If a new device has been added and can only use an IRQ owned by another device, it will be necessary to force one of them to change IRQs. This might be as easy as simply having the devices switch slots. As I pointed out earlier, PCI slots are prioritized, and PCI devices have only a fixed number of resources they can use. If one card is more limited than another, give it priority. Let it take its IRQ first, and the other card will simply have to pick another. **Table 9.8** provides a listing of the most common devices you'll have to contend with and the resources they most commonly use.

What happens if you start to run out of IRQs? Is there a way around this? The answer to that is a definite maybe! Look back in the section on COM ports. Two serial devices can be put on the same IRQ, with a different I/O address, as long as the two devices are never active on the bus at the same time.

The PCI bus is far more forgiving in this respect. Since PCI devices are able to share, sometimes PnP will tie two of them together onto a single IRQ by way of the IRQ Holder for PCI Steering. This is a virtual device that owns the IRQ and time-shares it with the devices it manages. If both devices try to hit the IRQ at the same time, IRQ Holder arbitrates the access.

CHAPTER SUMMARY

So now you understand why the expansion bus is so important. Without it, you can't add new toys. And who wants a computer that won't let you add new toys?

I showed you in this chapter just how the system makes use of four of the five primary busses to create an expansion bus. And I introduced the all-important concepts of IRQs, I/O addresses, and DMA channels. Many books choose to discuss these issues along with the motherboards, because they're considered to be motherboard resources. I chose to include the discussion in the same chapter as the components for which you as a technician will be dealing with them.

The CompTIA exam puts heavy emphasis on the history and development of the different busses over the years. That includes the ones which were short-lived, such as EISA, MCA, and VLB. Be ready to identify the characteristics of each.

Finally, I provided the basic information you need for trying to troubleshoot issues surrounding the expansion bus. This is an area where a technician spends a lot of his or her time. Be very familiar with the problems that might arise and be ready to deal with them.

Table 9.8 Commonly Used IRQ and I/O Combinations

Device	IRQ	I/O Range	DMA
		System Devices	
System timer	0	040-04Fh	N/A
IRQ cascade	2	0A0-0AFh	N/A
Real-time clock	8	070-071h	N/A
Math coprocessor	13	0F0-0FFh	N/A
		Parallel Ports	
LPT1	7	378-37Fh	1 or 3 (ECP)
LPT2	5	278h	1 or 3 (ECP)
		Serial Ports	
COM1	4	3F8-3FFh	N/A
COM2	3	2F8-2FFh	N/A
COM3	4	3E8-3FFh	N/A
COM4	3	2E8-2EFh	N/A
		Video	
VGA	11 or 12	3B0-3BBh	N/A
EGA	9	3C0 to 3CFh	N/A
		Sound	
Sound card	5 (or any available)	220-22Fh, 240-24Fh, 280-28Fh, 330-33Fh, 388-28Bh	1,3,4,6 or 7
Voice modem	May use multiple IRQs		
		Input Devices	
Keyboard	1	060-064h	N/A
PS2 mouse	12	060-064h	N/A
Joystick	N/A	200-207h	N/A
		Disk Drives	
Floppy	6	3F0-3F7h	2
IDE primary	14	1F0-0F7h AND 3F6-3F7h	N/A
IDE secondary	15	170-177h AND 376-377h	N/A
IDE tertiary	11 or 12	1E8-1Efh AND 3EE-3EFh	N/A
IDE quaternary	10 or 11	168-16Fh AND 36E-36Fh	N/A
SCSI host	May use any	130-14Fh, 140-05Fh, 220-23Fh, 330-34Fh, 340-35Fh	1, 3 or 5

Here's a list of the most common devices you'll have to contend with, and the resources they most commonly use.

Brain Drain

1. Discuss how IRQs, I/O addresses, and DMA channels are critical to configuring a device on the expansion bus, and list some of the problems you might encounter.

2. A computer system has been configured as follows: The system board has two serial ports (both active), a parallel port, and a USB hub that has been made active. There is a VGA card on IRQ 9, a network card on IRQ 11, and a sound card that is taking both IRQ 10 for normal usage and IRQ 5 for legacy applications. Both IDE channels are active and have devices hanging off of them. Assuming that IRQ steering is not being used, what IRQs remain available?

3. What is the purpose of an I/O address?

4. You have two PCI devices installed in a machine. Either one will work by itself, but when you install Device A into PCI slot 1 and Device B into PCI slot 2, Device B won't work. When you swap slots, there is no problem. Explain what is going on here.

5. List the different expansion busses used by computer systems over the years in the order that they appeared.

The 64K$ Questions

1. An I/O address is _____.
   a. An electrical channel that notifies the CPU (or allows the CPU to notify a device) that there is data ready to be moved
   b. A buffer area used by DMA to make sure data moves smoothly
   c. A direct transfer of data from a device to memory
   d. A specific memory location that the CPU uses to locate data from a specific device

2. A DMA channel is _____.
   a. An electrical channel that notifies the CPU (or allows the CPU to notify a device) that there is data ready to be moved
   b. A buffer area used by DMA to make sure data moves smoothly
   c. A direct transfer of data from a device to memory
   d. A specific memory location that the CPU uses to locate data from a specific device

3. An IRQ is _____.
   a. An electrical channel that notifies the CPU (or allows the CPU to notify a device) that there is data ready to be moved
   b. A buffer area used by DMA to make sure data moves smoothly
   c. A direct transfer of data from a device to memory
   d. A specific memory location that the CPU uses to locate data from a specific device

4. A computer system has been configured as follows. The system board has two serial ports (both active), a parallel port, and a USB hub that has been made active. There is a VGA card on IRQ 9, a network card on IRQ 11, and a sound card that is taking both IRQ 10 for normal usage and IRQ 5 for legacy applications. Both IDE channels are active and have devices hanging off of them.

You try to install a PCI modem and the system will not recognize it. What is the most likely culprit?

a. A conflicting DMA channel

b. A conflicting IRQ

c. A conflicting I/O address

d. A faulty modem

5. Which of the following busses were backwardly compatible with ISA? (Choose all that apply.)

a. PCI

b. VLB

c. EISA

d. MCA

6. Which of the following busses was developed specifically by the video industry to address the issues of moving large amounts of graphics data?

a. PCI

b. VLB

c. EISA

d. MCA

7. At what speed does an AGP 8x video card run?

a. 33MHz

b. 66MHz

c. 133MHz

d. 533MHz

8. A circuit that interconnects two unlike busses is called _____.

a. A PCB

b. A bridge

c. A PPB

d. A Bryston Circuit

9. When two devices on two different busses that operate at completely different speeds need to communicate, the process that allows this is _____.

a. Data arbitration

b. Speed mismatch compatibility

c. Buffering

d. Flow control

10. You have a motherboard that has onboard AGP graphics as well as an AGP 8x compatible slot. A video card occupies that slot and is working perfectly. You decide you want to set up a dual-monitor system and plug the second monitor into the onboard connector. It doesn't work, so you go into the CMOS and enable onboard support. Now your original monitor doesn't work. Why?

a. An IRQ conflict exists between the onboard video and the graphics adapter.

b. Both display adapters require the same I/O address ranges.

c. You can only have one AGP device on a system at once.

d. There shouldn't be a problem. They should both work.

TRICKY TERMINOLOGY

Asynchronous timing: A device on a bus can deliver its data at any speed it sees fit to a reserved area of memory called a buffer. Data is then fed to the CPU at a rate optimal to the CPU.

Bridge: A specialized circuit that moves data between two disparate devices or busses in a such a manner that both devices become compatible.

Burst mode: The ability of a device to transfer a large chunk of data in a single data phase.

Bus mastering: A technology that allows two compatible devices to exchange data directly without requiring arbitration or processing of that data by the CPU.

Cascade: A process by which multiple circuits are linked together in such a way that they appear to the system as a single device.

Central Arbitration Point: A circuit that offloads the responsibility for refereeing and processing the transfer of data between two bus-mastering devices.

COM port: A predefined combination of an IRQ and an I/O address configured for communications devices.

Data phase: The portion of an I/O operation that performs the actual transfer of data from device to device.

Edge triggered: Any response that elicited and/or is controlled by a direct electrical signal coming from a pin or wire on a device. The voltage is applied and the device depends on the interrupt controller to "remember" that it sent the signal.

FireWire: A high-speed serial SCSI connection originally developed by Apple Computer Corporation that is capable of 400Mb/s throughput.

Initiator: The device in a bus-mastering chain that is to act as the source of the data being transferred.

Key: A null space on an edge card connector or memory module that is used for properly aligning the device into its slot.

Level triggered: A response that is arbitrated by a control circuit and/or device driver that allows the same device to make use of one of several interrupt channels. The level-triggered interrupt raises the voltage on the appropriate wire and holds it until the expected response is received.

LPT port: A predefined combination of an IRQ and an I/O address configured for line printers.

Sideband addressing: The ability of a device to send and receive data in a single memory access.

Speed mismatch compatibility: A technology that allows two devices on the same bus to operate at different speeds and still successfully communicate with one another.

Synchronous timing: Bus speeds are a submultiple of the CPU's clock speed, and data is delivered at a steady rate based on that speed.

Target: Any device that is to be the intended recipient of data.

USB device: Any component designed to be operated on the USB.

USB host: Any computer or other device equipped with USB-compatible BIOS, firmware, and controller.

USB hub: A device that manages the I/O for two or more USB device chains.

Acronym Alert

ECI: Extended Capabilities ID. Information programmed onto a PCI card that defines any enhanced functions that device can perform beyond the basic functions defined by its device class.

EISA: Enhanced ISA. A 32-bit 8.33MHz bus released by a coalition of manufacturers led by Compaq. VLB was designed to be backwardly compatible with ISA.

MCA: Micro Channel Architecture. A proprietary 32-bit 12MHz bus released by IBM shortly after Intel's release of the 80386 CPU.

PCI-X: PCI Extended. A recently released 133MHz version of the PCI bus.

PPB: PCI to PCI Bridge. The circuitry that arbitrates data transfer between two different PCI busses on the same system.

VESA: Video Electronics Standards Association. The organization charged with maintaining standards surrounding graphics adapters and monitors.

VLB: VESA Local Bus. A 32-bit 33MHz bus designed by VESA to address issues surrounding the transfer of large amounts of graphics data. VLB was designed to be backwardly compatible with ISA.

CHAPTER 10

INPUT DEVICES

Okay. You now have a good idea about how data is processed, stored, and shuffled around in the system. Now I'll discuss how that data gets into the machine to begin with. The applications you run don't come on preprogrammed chips soldered onto the motherboard (although Tandy Corporation did that successfully when it shipped its 2000TL computer with DeskMate software installed on a PROM). You need disk drives that can read data from external sources before that data will appear on a hard disk drive. A large percentage of data processed by the computer has to come from the user. (This book certainly didn't come preprogrammed on a chip!) For that to happen there needs to be a way for the user to communicate with the computer. This chapter deals with the various devices designed for the purpose of getting information from the outside world moved into the digital world of the computer.

The problem I see with a chapter of this nature is that the variety of input devices is so vast; it would be impossible to cover them all in a single chapter. Since the primary focus of this book is on PC systems, I will cover only the basic input devices common to all systems.

A+ EXAM OBJECTIVES

Candidates for the A+ Core Exam will find the following topics introduced or covered in this chapter:

1.2 Identify basic procedures for adding and removing field-replaceable modules for desktop systems. Given a replacement scenario, choose the appropriate sequences.

1.5 Identify the names, purposes, and performance characteristics of standardized/common peripheral ports, associated cabling, and their connectors. Recognize ports, cabling, and connectors by sight.

1.8 Identify proper procedures for installing and configuring common peripheral devices. Choose the appropriate installation or configuration sequences in given scenarios.

2.1 Recognize common problems associated with each module and their symptoms, and identify steps to isolate and troubleshoot the problems. Given a problem situation, interpret the symptoms and infer the most likely cause.

3.1 Identify the various types of preventive maintenance measures, products, and procedures, and when and how to use them.

The Keyboard

The computer industry has probably seen more changes, new technology, and new products emerge than any other. Yet, as the old adage goes, the more things change, the more they stay the same. The primary device through which we enter data on a daily basis is still the humble, but ever so productive, keyboard (**Figure 10.1**). All the

Figure 10.1 Without the venerable old keyboard sitting at my desk, typing this manuscript would be a completely different job altogether.

data that goes into your spreadsheets; all the emails you send to friends, family, and coworkers; and this very manuscript are all accomplished though the simple technology of the keyboard.

One thing I won't discuss in this chapter is how to fix a keyboard. They're far too inexpensive to justify paying a technician for his or her time. I will go over some basic maintenance issues, but my primary goal is to show you how they work.

How the Keyboard Does Its Job

Just looking at the outside of the thing, you expect the keyboard to be a complicated device. Some are, some aren't. It all depends on how well made the model in question actually is. We all know how to use a keyboard. You press a key and a letter appears. It's that simple, right?

Well, not really. If you press the <Shift> key while holding down the letter, it goes from being a lowercase letter to an uppercase. So how does it know to do that? Also, those buttons that you seen running across the top of the keyboard with the letter F followed by a number don't type anything at all. Those are the function keys and they actually run programs for you. And, depending on what you're running as software, the <Ctrl> key, pressed in conjunction with one or more other keys will activate functions within that program. For example, when I press <Ctrl>+B, the text goes from normal to bold-faced. <Ctrl>+I makes it italics. So as you see, there is more going on inside the keyboard than simply typing letters.

Keycaps and Keyswitches

The button you push to activate a particular key is called the *keycap*. This is what most people simply call the key. The keycap on modern keyboards is removable, just like the A shown in **Figure 10.2**, allowing you to replace a worn-out keycap. In most cases, they simply pop off with a little prying by a flat-head screwdriver. Most of them are equally easy to get back on. However, that isn't always the case. The <Space> key can be particularly difficult. It requires getting the springs and clips properly aligned, then holding them in place and simultaneously snapping the keycap into position. On some keyboards, <Shift> and <Enter> are equally entertaining.

Figure 10.2 Even the lowly keycap is governed by pre-defined industry standards to make sure that keyboards have a uniform feel from one brand to the other.

You wouldn't think of a keyboard as necessarily being under the control of any particular standard. On the other hand, think how difficult typing would be if, every time you moved from one computer to the next, the amount of space between keys changed or the rows were separated by different distances. If you've ever moved from a "standard" keyboard to one of those ergonomic models, you know that there is a period of adjustment before typing seems natural.

Aside from the function keys, there are four rows to a standard Qwerty keyboard. From the bottom up, you have the Z row, the A row, the Q row, and the Number Row. With the exception of the distance between the A-row and the Q-row, these rows are .375″ apart. The A and Q rows are separated by a space of .188″. Spacing between keys is .75″ from center to center.

What about the "feel" of a keyboard? Anyone who works on multiple computers knows that there is no "standard" feel. Some are soft and mushy and other have a crisp click when you press down on them. This is where the human factor comes in. I like a keyboard that clicks when I press down on it. Makes me feel like I'm really typing. Other people like the quieter approach. How a keyboard feels is a function of two different things. First is how far the keycap travels in order to make contact, and second is the type of keyswitch used.

Keycap travel can range anywhere from a tenth of an inch to as much as .20″. Unless there's a decent amount of travel, the keyboard has a very stiff feel. Too much travel and you feel like your fingers are treading water. What you get accustomed to is what will be better for you. Most touch typists find they work faster on keyboards with a longer throw.

The kind of *keyswitch* you use will determine if your keyboard is clicky or mushy. The keycap snaps into place over the keyswitch. Depending on the model of keyboard, the keyswitch is a component that is either impossible to replace or simply so difficult as to be practically impossible. On some particularly inexpensive models, there are no switches. There is simply a pad of rubber nipples, called a membrane, that provide the keypad resistance (**Figure 10.3**). When you press down on the keycap, it makes contact with a circuit grid laid out on a piece of plastic (**Figure 10.4**). These wouldn't be that difficult to repair if the replacement parts didn't cost nearly as much as a new keyboard! Better keyboards have individual switches. These can be replaced, but the cost of the parts plus labor time doesn't really make it worthwhile.

When designing a keyboard, manufacturers take a number of factors into consideration. Some are user-oriented while others are business decisions.

- *Cost:* How much is the anticipated resale price of the keyboard. This will affect the type of switching mechanism used in the construction. If the keyboard is to be a minimally priced Original Equipment Manufacturer's (OEM) model, there's not going to be a lot of money poured into fancy switches. These are the keyboards that generally use membrane switching. A nicely designed tactile switch can cost $.05 to $.15 per switch.

On a 104-key device, this adds up pretty quickly. Factor in the cost of assembling such a board, and you have a pricey keyboard for most OEMs.

Figure 10.3   The little rubber "bubbles" keep the keycaps away from the circuit board until the user presses down on one.

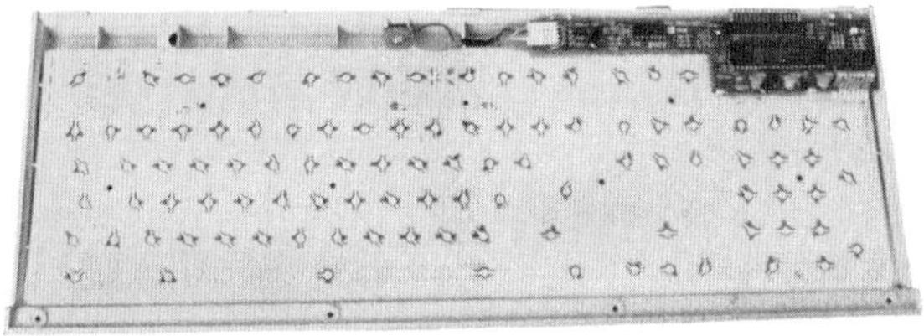

- *Durability:* How long can you expect your keyboard to last? End users are going to answer this question differently than computer manufacturers. For most OEMs, the answer to this question is another question. How long is the warranty, and is the keyboard going to be covered under that warranty? Read the fine print of many computer warranties and you find out that it isn't. If the keyboard has to last for a while, then higher-quality keyswitches must be used.

Figure 10.4   When the user does press down on a keycap, it will come into contact with the appropriate circuit on the grid beneath.

- *Feel:* This is a combination of two different factors, as I mentioned. Travel and tactile feedback are strong contributors to how a keyboard feels to the typist. Neither of these factors necessarily impacts cost. One company that manufactures high-quality keyswitches, Alps, Inc., makes all levels of switch in both tactile-click and soft designs.

Keyswitches have one task to do. They complete a circuit, sending a signal to the controller that a particular key has been depressed. These switches come in several forms. The older style keyboards all used mechanical contact switches. You'll generally know if you have one of these. The keycap is not removable. Or if it is, it is so difficult to remove that replacing it might be even more so. These switches perform the actual completion of the circuit internally. When you press down, you're activating the switch. A spring returns the switch to the open position when you release it.

The next type of switch is the Foam and Foil Switch. This is the first of two variations I'll discuss on keyboards using membrane circuits. The keypad presses down on a plunger. Beneath the keys, a foam pad with a foil surface on the bottom is placed over the circuit pad. The circuit for any given key consists of two copper contacts. When the key is depressed, it forces the foil into contact with the copper conductors and the circuit is completed. A spring pushes the plunger back into position. The foam acts as a shock absorber and return mechanism for the foil. These are your generally cheap keyboards which have a very soft and spongy feel.

A better variation on this theme is the Rubber Dome Switch shown in Figure 10.3. These still make use of a membrane over which the copper circuitry is embedded. A plunger presses a button down onto the copper contacts (Figure 10.4) and the circuit is completed. Rubber dome switches use a sheet of rubber into which a dome-shaped elevation has been formed. This rubber dome forces the key back into place when it is released. These are the most prevalent OEM keyboards on the market today, as they have a much nicer feel than the older foam and foil units. They provide a semblance of tactile feedback, as well as a higher resilience to pressure. People actually feel like they're typing.

INTERNAL CIRCUITS

Now that you know how the signal gets generated, I'll take a look at how the computer knows it's getting the word "elevator" and not the <Shift>. If you're daring enough to take your keyboard apart and peek inside, you'll see a small circuit board with some chips on it. Before you do this, however, I feel morally and legally obligated to tell you that some keyboards were designed to be disposable. Taking them apart will be easy enough. But they don't go back together when you're done, and you'll have that excuse you were looking for to go out and buy a newer and nicer unit. The ones with screws can usually be disassembled and put back together. If they snap apart, I wouldn't count on it. Either way, be careful.

Now, back to that circuit board. Your keyboard will have one, with two or three main chips soldered onto the board along with some other minor components, as shown in **Figure 10.5**. One of these chips is a microprocessor. It does the keyboard's "thinking." On older keyboards, this was frequently an Intel 8048 or a Motorola 6805. There will also be a ROM chip that holds the program that translates the keyboard's signals. New keyboards use an IC that has an integrated CPU and ROM. Examples of this chip would include the 8049 and the 8255. Programmable keyboards, the kind that let you make a single key run an entire series of keystrokes, will also have an EEPROM (see Chapter Five, Motherboards, BIOS, and the Chipset) built in for holding those instructions. The 8255 is an example of a CPU/EEPROM. There is also a 16-byte buffer for streaming data in a controlled manner.

This board does require electricity to perform, as do those little LEDs that tell you the status of NUM Lock, CAPS Lock, and Scroll Lock. Therefore, one of the functions of the keyboard is to get electricity from somewhere. Power is supplied through the cable from the computer's power supply. On most keyboards, this is a 5V current.

To know what specific key has been pressed, the keys on the keyboard are laid out in a series of rows and columns called the *key matrix*. Each key holds a position related to a row and column. When a key is depressed, the keyswitch in that position closes a circuit, sending a signal

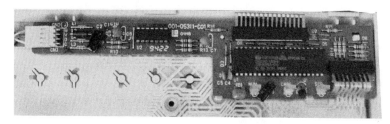

Figure 10.5 This small circuit board with only a couple of chips does all the work of translating the user's keystrokes into electrical signals the computer can use.

to the circuit board inside the keyboard. Each key sends two separate signals. The first, called the *make code*, is sent the instant the keyswitch closes the circuit. The second signal, the *break code*, occurs when the key is released. It is because of these two signals that you can make your software repeat letters just by holding a key in place. It is also why one key can be held down while another is depressed. If only a single signal was generated, neither of those features would be possible. The one signal would be sent, and that would be that.

Every key has a unique make/break code. This is true even between two keys with the same name.

For example the right <Shift> and the left <Shift> generate their own specific codes. So do the right <Ctrl> and the left <Ctrl>, or the right and left <Alt>. This is why some games can use the left <Alt> key for firing a weapon and the right for another game function.

When you press a key, the position of the key that was pressed is denoted by its position in the matrix. Once that position is established the program that resides in ROM generates the make/break code for that key. The 8048 (or later) chip then translates that code into digital signals that the computer can use. The translated signal travels along the keyboard cable to the computer.

THE KEYBOARD CABLE

The cable (**Figure 10.6**) consists of four conductors that are actually used. One of these is the 5V signal previously mentioned, while a second comprises the ground. One of the other wires provides the keyboard data signal, and the fourth carries the keyboard clock signal.

Keyboards send data across the wire in serial form. They also use asynchronous communication. What more do you need? You're not sending data across the wire very fast at all. The buffer makes sure it goes in the right order. Therefore only a single conductor is needed for carrying data. The keyboard clock makes sure the keyboard stays in synch with the rest of the system. Clock signals travel over a separate wire. Then, to provide power, two other cables provide power and ground.

The purpose of the clock signal is to properly synchronize the data coming in

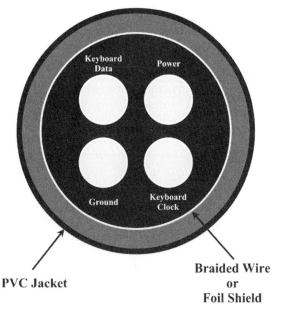

Figure 10.6 The keyboard cable is very simple. Only four wires are needed, while a layer of shielding material deflects interference.

from the keyboard with the rest of the system functions. That isn't as easy as it sounds. A very fast typist can type approximately eighty words per minute. That is barely over 5KB of data. Add the make/break codes, and that person can push about 16K of data over the keyboard wires every minute. If you recall, the bus speed of most modern motherboards is a minimum of 100MHz. The job of the clock is to see that the data from the keyboard gets there in a timely manner without slowing the rest of the computer down.

THE KEYBOARD CONTROLLER

On the receiving end, the computer has a special circuit just for interfacing with the keyboard. Not surprisingly, this circuit is called the keyboard controller. On older computers, this was the 8042 keyboard controller chip. This chip was a mini-microprocessor that had a 2KB ROM and about 128 bytes of RAM to act as a buffer. More recent computers use an 8255, which is reprogrammable, and on some motherboards, the task is handled by the chipset.

The keyboard controller receives the signals sent by the 8048 chip and translates scan codes into data the CPU can use. It also has the responsibility for generating the interrupt over IRQ1 to let the CPU know there's data coming in. In addition, periodically the system checks the status of the keyboard. The keyboard controller maintains I/O port 64h for the purpose of status checks.

KEYBOARD MAINTENANCE AND REPAIR

As I said before, for the most part, you're not going to fix a broken keyboard. But as we all know, nobody's ever written a rule that didn't have exceptions. And there are some simple maintenance routines that can delay the inevitable day of replacement. I'll start with some basic maintenance.

First rule of thumb: no matter how much you like coffee, your keyboard doesn't like it at all. It is not a good idea to have drinks near your keyboard (he sanctimoniously typed as he took a sip from his coffee). Since we all break that rule on a regular basis, spills are going to happen. Oddly enough, it's the cheapest keyboards that survive liquid exposure the best. When this happens, shut down immediately and shake out as much of the liquid as you possibly can. Better keyboards are inside of a clamshell-style case held together by screws. If the affected keyboard is of this type, open it up and use some cotton swabs to clean out as much of the rest as you can. Now's as good a time as any to clean out the dust, potato chip crumbs, and other debris that has accumulated since you first set up the machine. A can of compressed air can be used, but it's probably better if you can get your hands on a miniature vacuum cleaner.

Worn keycaps are fairly easy to replace as long as you're not dealing with an older board with mechanical contact switches. A small flat-head screwdriver is a good tool for prying them off the keyswitch. It might be worth replacing a worn or broken key on a particularly expensive keyboard or one that happens to have a feel to it that you've not found elsewhere.

While it is rare for a keyboard cable to fail before the keyboard dies of either junk poisoning or plain old wear and tear, it does happen. Once again, it would have to be a particularly special keyboard to justify the effort, but the cable can be replaced if you are reasonably adept with a soldering gun. Pop open the keyboard and follow the cable to where the leads are soldered on. Desolder the old leads and solder on the new. Be careful not to allow the solder joints to overlap.

If you're wondering where to find a replacement keyboard cable, there are two ways to go about it. Most electronics parts warehouses will sell a replacement for a moderate cost. However, practically any place that repairs computers would sell you a broken keyboard a whole lot cheaper. They might even give you one just to save them the trouble of discarding it. The chances of the problem with that keyboard also being the cable are pretty slim.

THE MOUSE

The second most common input device is the mouse. Douglas Englebart invented this innocuous little device when he worked at the Stanford Research Institute. Initial reaction to Mr. Englebart's invention could best be described as skeptical. Apple Computer Corporation incorporated the device into the graphical interface of its OS, and then PC users began to ask why they couldn't have a toy like that. These days you probably take the mouse for granted until it starts to give you trouble. Only then do you really notice it that much. Mice come in two different forms—mechanical and optical. In each of those forms you can also get standard and cordless versions. This section will deal with how these devices work and how to configure and troubleshoot them.

THE MECHANICAL MOUSE

When you use a mouse, you move the device across a surface, usually a mouse pad, and the arrow on the screen follows the direction of your movements. It seems simple enough until you realize what all is going on to make that seemingly simple procedure work right.

First of all, the mouse has to be able to detect your motions. If you look at the base of your mouse (assuming you use a mechanical mouse), you will see a small rubber ball protruding from a window on the base of the device, just like in **Figure 10.7**. This ball rolls along the surface of your mouse pad.

Now open the retaining plate that holds the ball in place. It's probably past time to clean your mouse anyway. I know it sure was for this one! Peek inside and you should see three rollers, just like the ones you see in **Figure 10.8**. One is located directly toward the front or back of the mouse and one is located on one side or the other. A third roller is positioned at 45 degrees.

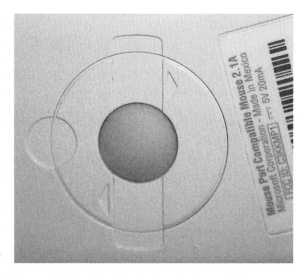

Figure 10.7 That little ball on the bottom of your mouse is what tells the cursor on your screen where to go.

Figure 10.8   As the ball moves across the surface of your mouse pad, these three rollers keep track of the direction that you're moving the mouse.

Figure 10.9   The LED shown at the base of the image shines a light through the teeth on the end of the wheel. A photosensitive receptor turns the flickering light into electronic pulses.

As the ball rolls along the surface, it moves these rollers. Direction and angle of movement directly affect the speed at which the rollers rotate. As they rotate, they move a wheel attached to one end of the roller. That wheel has a bunch of teeth cut into it. An LED shines a light past the wheel. On the other side of the wheel, a photosensitive receptor picks up the light from the LED (see **Figure 10.9**). When one of the teeth is in the way, no light hits the receptor. The space between the teeth lets the light through. As a result, the wheel generates a flickering light. In turn, that flickering light causes the receptor to generate a series of electronic pulses, which are sent to the computer. The mouse driver installed in the computer keeps track of the number of pulses generated by each roller and uses the information to move the cursor across the screen.

So let's break this down into the individual parts needed to make a mouse work. Along with that, I'll discuss how they perform their function.

- The ball rolls along the desktop, changing direction of rotation every time you change the direction in which you're moving the mouse. The ball is in contact with...

- The rollers, which change the speed at which they rotate based on the direction that the mouse is moving. If you are moving the mouse straight up, with no right/left motion whatsoever, then the side roller and diagonal roller aren't moving at all, while the up/down roller is moving at whatever speed you happen to be moving the mouse. If there is very slight right/left motion, then the other two sensors will be moving at their own speed. Each roller is attached to its own...

- Shaft, which turns a small wheel. Here is where two different technologies diverge. A few mice use a magnetic sensor, but by far the majority use an LED (as in Figure 10.9).

The LED shines its light onto an optical sensor. The wheel has thirty-six small slits cut into it. As it rotates between the path of the LED and the sensor, the light is alternately shielded and allowed to pass. In effect, the motion of the wheel is creating what appears to the sensor to be a pulsating light. The speed at which the light pulsates is determined by the speed at which the wheel is turning. These signals are transmitted to the...

- Logic chip, which translates the pulses of light into binary data, which is sent to the mouse driver. The mouse driver uses that data to position the cursor.

This is the method by which a large majority of mechanical mice work. These are known as *optomechanical mice.* There are a few out there that use a magnetic sensor on the wheel in place of an optical sensor. Aside from this difference, the function is the same.

THE OPTICAL MOUSE

The optical mouse differs significantly from its mechanical counterpart in that it has no ball. Instead of this physical interface, an optical mouse uses a pair of LEDs, a pair of optical sensors, and a mouse pad that has a distinct pattern. The LEDs shine down on the mouse pad and reflect back to photoreceptors on the base of the device. As you move the device across the pad, the reflections of light coming back from the mouse pad provide the light pulses that the mouse drivers use for tracking.

> **BUZZ WORDS** ⸻
>
> **Optomechanical mouse:** A mouse that uses perforated wheels passing in front of an LED to generate pulses of light that are used to track movement along the X and Y axis.

This is good in that there are no moving parts to get dirty or to break. This is bad in that I can't use my Queen Amidala mouse pad.

SENDING DATA

In terms of the number of conductors needed, the mouse is virtually identical to the keyboard in its requirements. There needs to be a +5V carrier, a ground, a data cable, and a clock cable. They all perform exactly the same function as their counterparts on the keyboard. It doesn't matter whether you have an older serial mouse or a PS2. Only four conductors are being used. The data that is actually sent, however, differs significantly.

The keyboard has hundreds of different signals it must send. There are only two or three buttons on most mice. Manufacturers are now tripping over each other to add new buttons and functions to confuse the user even more, but generally you're either clicking a button once or double-clicking it. There aren't a whole lot of options here. So what happens when you click a button on a mouse is that three bytes of data get sent. The first byte of data carries eight bits indicating the status of the mouse. These bits carry information as shown in **Table 10.1**.

The next two bytes provide values that indicate the total movement along the X and Y-axes, respectively. They include information that indicates precisely how many pulses were detected in each

Table 10.1 Status Byte of Mouse Signal

Bit Number	Indicates
Bit 0	Left button state. 1 = ON, 2 = OFF
Bit 1	Right button state. 1 = ON, 2 = OFF
Bit 2	0
Bit 3	1
Bit 4	X coordinate = Positive or X coordinate = Negative
Bit 5	Y coordinate = Positive or Y coordinate = Negative
Bit 6	X Overflow indicates excessive movement along the X-axis
Bit 7	Y Overflow indicates excessive movement along the Y-axis

For each click of a mouse, the first byte returns information concerning the status of the mouse.

direction since the last data was sent. Programmers do the rest of the magic, which is why different operating systems and different applications respond to the mouse in their own unique ways.

TRACKBALLS

A trackball is basically a stationary mouse. It performs the same function as a mouse while staying in one place. Many people do not like the repetitive motion involved in using a mouse. In fact, it has caused medical problems with many people. Also, a mouse is rarely where you need it when you need it there. The mouse will be at the top of the mouse pad, but the cursor will be at the bottom of the screen. You're always having to make adjustments.

The trackball is an upside-down mouse. It performs in the same manner, except that the ball is positioned at the top of the device and you move it with your thumb and/or fingers. Manufacturers seem unable to agree on how you should move the ball, so when shopping for one of these toys, try them all until you find one that feels right to you.

MOUSE MAINTENANCE

In terms of physical maintenance, cleaning is about the only thing that you can do to help your mouse. The balls pick up small particles of dust and lint, potato chip crumbs, and other debris as they move along the surface of your mouse pad. This sticks to the rollers and once enough junk accumulates, the rollers and ball won't be in synch with each other. As a result, you get erratic movement of the cursor as it moves across the screen. The fix here is simple. Clean it. Remove the ball and you'll see debris buildup on the rollers.

Many of the problems people report that are mouse-related have to do with the mouse setting in their operating system. You can adjust the sensitivity of your mouse. If it is not set sensitively enough for your taste, the mouse will require excessive movement across the pad in order to get the cursor where you want it. Conversely, if you use your mouse to make extremely minute corrections, then you might need to increase sensitivity.

Game Controllers

As you probably already realize, most of us do not own computers. We own $2000 decks of cards and $4000 home video arcades. Playing games can frequently introduce input requirements that the more mundane functions, such as word processing, don't present. As a result, there is a booming business in producing specialized input devices whose exclusive domain is that of making games easier and more enjoyable.

Some people are perfectly happy committing mayhem on aliens using a keyboard and mouse combination. But armchair jet pilots and virtual racecar drivers like something with a little more control, and that gives them a greater sense of reality. For those folks, there are joysticks, game paddles, steering wheels, and other assorted gaming controls to make computer fun more realistic. One company even has a nicely upholstered tactile feedback interactive recliner for the avid gamer. My wife was supposed to get me one of those for Christmas, but I guess she forgot.

Joysticks, Game Paddles, and Steering Wheels

Since these all work functionally the same way, I'll group them together in a single discussion and simply refer to joysticks. The joystick has a rather unique feature that endears it to many technicians. It requires no IRQ. The system polls the device to determine when and if there is data to be moved across the bus. Physically, the joystick consists of a handle onto which buttons have been installed. That handle is seated into a base and connects to the computer by way of a 15-pin D-shell connector (**Figure 10.10**).

A pair of devices called variable resistors generates the data sent to the computer by the joystick. These consist of a strip of insulating material that varies in thickness across its length; the thicker the material is, the greater the resistance. In joysticks, these variable resistors cover a range from slightly less than one ohm to a value in excess of 100,000 ohms. One variable resistor changes values as you move along the X-coordinate, the other keeps track of the Y-coordinate. The joystick driver translates resistance values into screen coordinates. The button or buttons are simple switches. When you press down on one, it merely closes a circuit. The game you're playing determines what effect closing the circuit has.

A greater sense of realism is attained when the joystick in use is capable of tactile feedback. Tactile feedback controllers are equipped with small motors that make use of data provided by the game in play to vibrate, kick back or forward in the hand, or provide resistance to the user when he or she tries to move the joystick. This technology moves a step forward with data gloves. These are devices that users wear on their hands. Position and flexure of the hand provides input to the computer. Games and other programs that support this little toy interact far more directly with the user.

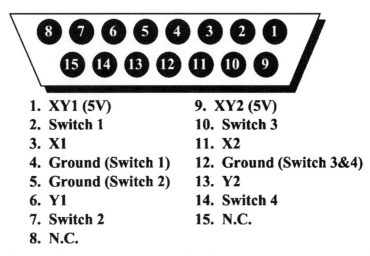

1. **XY1 (5V)**
2. **Switch 1**
3. **X1**
4. **Ground (Switch 1)**
5. **Ground (Switch 2)**
6. **Y1**
7. **Switch 2**
8. **N.C.**
9. **XY2 (5V)**
10. **Switch 3**
11. **X2**
12. **Ground (Switch 3&4)**
13. **Y2**
14. **Switch 4**
15. **N.C.**

Figure 10.10   Pinouts for 15-pin joystick connector

DIGITAL CAMERAS

Of all technology products used by consumers today, digital cameras have probably enjoyed the most significant widespread growth. While plummeting prices certainly haven't hurt this growth, perceived need has probably had a greater effect. While scanners make it relatively easy to convert a paper print into a digital file, it's still a cumbersome process. On top of that, you have the expense of film and developing, and you have to find the time to drop it off to get it developed.

A digital camera eliminates all of these inconveniences. A 16MB memory chip allows the equivalent of a whole roll of film, even in high-resolution mode. When you get home, you upload the images you want to the computer, erase the camera's memory and start all over! Not only that, but while you're taking pictures, you can preview what you've got. If a shot doesn't come out the way you'd like, delete it and do another one. Each of the photos in this book was made with a digital camera.

A lens captures an actual scene and directs light waves to a chip called the charge coupled device (CCD). The resolution of a camera is dictated by the number of sensors built into the CCD and is measured in dots per inch. The camera I own is kind of middle-of-the-road. It was relatively inexpensive, but is still a good performer. It has a maximum resolution of 2048 × 1536. Advertising slicks refer to it as a 3.2-megapixel camera. More recent cameras have exceeded the 10-megapixel range, and in the world of professional photography resolutions go far beyond these listed. I have the choice of saving files in JPEG, Tagged Image File Format (TIFF), or in a proprietary native format.

One of the biggest differences among models of digital cameras lies in how they react to color. Computers allow for extremely accurate color management. Unfortunately, the camera is not a computer. It grabs the shot based on certain settings that the user can change and others that the user can't. One of the things the user has no control over is the CCD that the manufacturer uses in the camera. These devices must be calibrated to something called "white balance" for them to accurately portray color. Typical white balance settings include "Daylight," "Fluorescent," and "Tungsten." Some may also include "9300K." This is in deference to a Macintosh default color setting. What all this boils down to is a lot simpler than the last few lines make it sound. Some cameras record colors "warm" and other record them "cool." Warm color reflects a tendency for the overall image balance to be biased toward yellow and red, while cool refers to a slightly

Buzz Words

White balance: A measurement of how pure the reproduction of white is accomplished in an image.

Cool: A shift in the color of an image toward the blue side.

Warm: A shift in the color of an image toward the red side.

bluish shift. Which you prefer will dictate your choice in a camera. And keep in mind that this is also something that is easily correctable by most photo-editing packages.

The biggest complaint that consumers had about digital cameras was that the image did not resemble that of one taken with a conventional film camera. Film tends to render colors more naturally and does not contain the digital noise so many digital cameras are notorious for producing. Recently, some manufacturers of digital cameras have taken to substituting a CMOS (see Chapter Five, Motherboards, BIOS, and the Chipset) for the CCD.

A CMOS chip more closely approximates the size of a standard 35mm negative or transparency, whereas a CCD is rarely much larger than the nail on your left pinky. As a result, if you're simply comparing cameras on the basis of raw resolution, you might mistakenly assume that a CMOS-based camera is inferior. In fact, a CMOS imaging chip that is only rated at 3.2 megapixels is capable of rendering an image that many professional photographers acknowledge is better than what they can achieve with conventional film.

Probably the biggest choice you'll have to make is how your camera interfaces with the computer. You have to get those images from the camera to the computer somehow. Might as well make it as easy as possible. In this respect, manufacturers have been incredibly creative. The cameras themselves can directly link to the computer by way of either a serial cable or a USB cable. As you will recall from the section on data busses, USB is going to be a lot faster. There are also devices that let the user plug the actual memory card from the camera into a reader that can be installed into the computer, just like a floppy disk drive or other externally accessible drive. The data can then be read directly off the chip. These are available in both internal and external models. Finally, printer manufacturers have included a memory card reader as a feature of some of their models of color printers. Plug the memory cartridge directly into the printer and send the image straight from memory to page. Of course, this precludes any ability to alter the image.

Throughout this discussion, I have made constant mention of photo-editing packages. For the professional, this choice will have as much, if not more, impact than the choice of hardware. Most cameras, scanners, and printers come bundled with some rudimentary software that will allow limited editing. For many people that's about all they'll ever need. The imaging professional, however, needs professional tools. You'll find the capabilities of almost any piece of imaging hardware greatly enhanced by a collection of software tools that are up to the task at hand.

VIDEO CAPTURE

Once the process of capturing still images was mastered, the next logical step was to digitize motion pictures. However, a computer is not, by default, equipped with a device for generating live video. And even if it was, who would want to carry a computer around with them just to film his or her child's softball game? A more logical step at the beginning was to import the images created by existing devices. For this to happen, there needed to be an interface between the device and the computer, and then the appropriate software to convert the images into digital form.

Like everything else in this industry, at first video capture devices were very expensive and could be problematic to install and configure. Most were add-on cards that worked alongside the existing video card. What they did was allow the user to hook up any video camera, video tape recorder, or television tuner to the computer and "film" the output into a digital file. Modern technology has allowed single cards to perform all of the user's video functions, including capture.

To do this properly, there are several considerations that must be taken into account. Not only do you have to have the necessary hardware to do the actual capture, but also the rest of your system has to keep up. Graphic images require a lot more horsepower than processing text files. Assume that as you filmed the softball game mentioned earlier, you ended up with a sixteen-minute clip you wanted to preserve. You select a file format developed by the Motion-picture Joint Photographic Experts Group (MJPEG). The conversion of this clip is going to result in a file that is approximately 1.2GB in size. Therefore adequate free hard disk space is a critical factor. But just processing that image puts a lot of stress on the system. The conversion is extremely processor intensive and memory intensive. Anyone who plans on doing a lot of video capture will want a very powerful system with as much memory as he or she can afford. Most software designed for processing streaming video supports multiple processor systems. Having multiple processors will provide a dramatic improvement in performance.

The type of file system you select will determine two things—throughput requirements and storage requirements. MJPEG file compression has by far the least compression capability of any of the motion picture formats. It requires that your graphics subsystem be capable of pretty high performance, and you'd best have some heavy-duty storage space available. However, it allows for frame-by-frame editing, claims smoother bit streaming, and allows real-time compression/decompression. A file format developed by the Motion Picture Experts Group (MPEG), called MPEG II, allows for far greater file compression, but limits the user's ability to manipulate the data. What most professionals will do is create the file in MJPEG, perform their digital wonders, then convert the file to MPEG II for the rest of the world to enjoy. While each manufacturer of video cards handles the file formats in a slightly different way, for the most part, MJPEG and MPEG II can be considered standards. **Table 10.2** compares some of the conventional video compression formats in terms of file size and bandwidth needed for transmission.

Table 10.2 Bitstream and Storage Requirements for Streaming Video

File Format (by brand)	Bitstream (Kb/s)	Storage needed for 1 hr.	Video that will fit CDR
Low Resolution			
Matrox MJPEG (HQ)	1425	4.9GB	8 minutes
Matrox MJPEG (LQ)	715	2.5GB	16 minutes
Elsa MJPEG	822	2.8GB	14 minutes
ATI MPEG II	420	1.4GB	28 minutes
3D/fx MPEG II	305	1.0GB	39 minutes
High Resolution			
Matrox MJPEG (HQ)	2734	9.4GB	4 minutes
Matrox MJPEG (LQ)	1585	5.4GB	8 minutes
Elsa MJPEG	1606	5.5GB	7 minutes
ATI MPEG II	550	1.9GB	22 minutes
3D/fx MPEG II	NOT POSSIBLE		

Different file formats offer varying degrees of compression. As a result, storage and data transmission requirements can vary as well.

TOUCHSCREEN MONITORS

We've all seen them work. You order your hamburger, fries, and a large drink and the attendant simply touches the picture of the burger and a price pops up. She touches the picture of fries and another price pops up. Then she touches the large cup of soda on the screen and that price shows up on the register. Then, she touches "TOTAL" and tells you how much it's all going to cost you. The computer tells her how much change to give you so she doesn't even have to think about that. She counts out your change and then the guy bagging your order still manages to get it wrong. But that's not the computer's fault now, is it?

Touchscreen monitors are no doubt miracles of modern technology. But just how do they work? There are actually three ways of making touchscreen monitors. They all involve putting a special coating over the surface of a standard cathode-ray tube and then wiring it through the controller circuitry. Finally, a software driver interprets the position of where the touch occurred and processes the commands. These methods include an analog-resistive surface, a capacitive surface, and a surface acoustive wave surface.

- *The Analog-Resistive Monitor:* The touchscreen panel is coated with a conductive surface below the glass surface of the monitor. Contact with the screen causes an electrical charge to be sent to the controller circuitry. Monitors that use this form of technology don't care what touches them. The person using it can use bare fingers, or can wear gloves. Sometimes, the monitor is equipped with a special stylus that the user presses against the screen. The beauty of this technology is that it doesn't really matter how big or small somebody's finger is. The monitor calculates the center point of the area being touched and generates the signal accordingly.

- *The Capacitive Monitor:* These monitors use a super-thin conductive coating on the outside surface that is transparent to the naked eye. At all four corners of the screen, a circuit applies a uniform voltage. When somebody touches a finger to the screen, it draws voltage from all four corners in direct proportion to the distance at which the touch occurs. The closer to the corner, the more current its drawn. Based on how much current is drawn from each of the four corners, the touchscreen controller is able to calculate the exact position that the touch occurred. The controller communicates this information to the application, which in turn executes the appropriate commands. The only shortcoming to this technology, if you could call it that, is that only the tip of a finger or a conductive object works here. If someone is wearing gloves, the fabric insulates the screen from the touch and it doesn't work.

- *The Surface Acoustive Wave Monitor:* To make this technology work, electrical signals are converted into ultrasonic sound waves. The glass surface of the monitor is linked to two piezoelectric transducers, one for the X-axis and one for the Y-axis. By touching the monitor, you absorb some of those waves. When that happens, the controller circuitry calculates where the disruption of the signal occurred. Based on a mathematical calculation, considering the X and Y axes, the position of the disruption is determined. Any object that doesn't damage the screen can be used for touching.

Regardless of the technology employed, the touchscreen monitor works by determining precisely where somebody or something touched the surface of the cathode-ray tube (CRT). Once it does this, the device driver sends the coordinates of where the touch occurred. The software takes that information and uses it to call a specific set of instructions or input a predefined set of data. Properly programmed, this approach limits the amount of information that actually has to be provided by the operator. Any time you do that, you limit the number of errors of which we humans are capable.

Unfortunately nobody has managed to migrate this technology over to the guy bagging the order.

CHAPTER SUMMARY

The last fifteen pages or so covered a number of different ways by which the user can import data from the outside world into the digital realm of the computer. I discussed everything from the basic keyboard to more evolved technologies, such as digital cameras and touchscreen monitors.

One thing I should point out here is that the devices covered in this chapter do not represent an all-encompassing list. Many other devices that will be covered in other chapters are also input devices. Modems, network cards, and sound cards are examples of other specialized devices that provide input.

Brain Drain

1. Briefly describe how pressing the W key on a keyboard generates data and moves it to the CPU for processing.

2. How does an optical mouse differ from a mechanical mouse?

3. Briefly describe how a mouse does its job.

4. What are the three different types of touchscreen monitor, and how do they differ from one another?

5. Describe a method by which computerization will assure that the person bagging your order does not give you onion rings instead of fries.

The 64K$ Questions

1. When you press down on a key, data is generated by two signals. These are the _____ and the _____. (Select two.)
   a. Timing
   b. Break
   c. DMA
   d. Make

2. Another channel that the keyboard will activate is the _____.
   a. DMA
   b. IRQ
   c. DSP
   d. Timer

3. The type of mouse that uses a perforated wheel that spins in front of an LED is called a _____ mouse.
   a. Optical
   b. Mechanical

   c. Photoresisive
   d. Optomechanical

4. The one device that can be installed on a computer system that does NOT use an IRQ is_____.
   a. A video card
   b. The mouse
   c. A joystick
   d. A NIC

5. A CCD is a _____.
   a. Color coupling device
   b. Capacitive charge developer
   c. Central computing device
   d. Charge coupled device

6. CCDs are used by _____.
   a. Scanners
   b. Digital cameras
   c. Touchscreen monitors
   d. Display drivers

7. The file format frequently used by video editors is _____.
   a. MPEG-III
   b. JPEG
   c. TIFF
   d. MJPEG

8. The characteristic of a digital camera that has the most impact on color accuracy is _____.
   a. The lens
   b. The file format chosen
   c. Light balance
   d. White balance

9. Which of the following is not a form of touchscreen monitor?
   a. Resistive interpolative monitor
   b. The analog-resistive monitor

c.   The capacitive monitor

d.   The surface acoustive wave monitor

10.   Which touchscreen technology does not allow the use of a gloved hand?

a.   Resistive interpolative monitor

b.   The analog-resistive monitor

c.   The capacitive monitor

d.   The surface acoustive wave monitor

TRICKY TERMINOLOGY

Break code: A signal generated by a keyswitch when the key is released.

Cool: A shift in the color of an image toward the blue side.

Digital noise: Unwanted color artifacts introduced into a digitized image during capture and/or by imaging software during the processing of that image.

Key matrix: The specific geometric layout of the keyswitches on a keyboard.

Keycap travel: The actual distance a user must press a key on a keyboard in order to produce results.

Keycap: The plastic button the user presses down when typing on a keyboard.

Keyswitch: The electromechanical connection that informs the keyboard controller circuitry that a key has been pressed.

Make code: A signal generated by a keyswitch when the key is first pressed down.

Optomechanical mouse: A mouse that uses perforated wheels passing in front of an LED to generate pulses of light that are used to track movement along the X and Y axis.

Warm: A shift in the color of an image toward the red side.

White balance: A measurement of how pure the reproduction of white is accomplished in an image.

ACRONYM ALERT

CCD: Charge Coupled Device. A sensor consisting of an array of cells that interpolates a physical image and coverts it into a digital file.

MJPEG: Motion-picture Joint Photographic Experts Group. An organization that develops and maintains standards for digitizing images. Also a file format used for compressing and storing editable versions of motion pictures developed by that group.

MPEG: Motion Picture Experts Group. An organization that developed a standard for compressing and storing digital video. Their format is not as editable as MJPEG.

TIFF: Tagged Image File Format. An image file format used for storing digital images that does not result in any loss of quality.

CHAPTER 11

WORKING WITH REMOVABLE DISKS

In the first generation of the PC, there was no hard disk installed. In fact, it wasn't until the second generation that a hard disk was even supported. Information was stored on 8″ floppy disks and stored carefully away in cabinets.

These days, you would almost think the devices such as the floppy diskette could be donated to the historical society and life could move on. One simply saves the great American novel to hard disk, and when ready, it can spew out on the printer in perfectly formatted form. The fact of the matter is, most of us work with information that either travels with us or needs to travel to others that will work with it. In the modern age, this is frequently done over the Internet or by email.

Once in a while, however, there is simply no substitute for Sneakernet. Copy to a floppy and hop on over. Modern technology now offers far more sophisticated options than the floppy diskette for removable media, however. In this chapter, I'll take a look at some of the various options, how they work, and what might be the right choice for a given set of circumstances.

A+ EXAM OBJECTIVES

Those who are taking CompTIA's Core exam can look for the following items in this chapter.

1.1 Identify the names, purpose, and characteristics of system modules. Recognize these modules by sight or definition.

1.2 Identify basic procedures for adding and removing field-replaceable modules for desktop systems. Given a replacement scenario, choose the appropriate sequences.

1.4 Identify typical IRQs, DMAs, and I/O addresses and procedures for altering these settings when installing and configuring devices. Choose the appropriate installation or configuration steps in a given scenario.

2.1   Recognize common problems associated with each module and their symptoms, and identify steps to isolate and troubleshoot the problems. Given a problem situation, interpret the symptoms and infer the most likely cause.

THE FLOPPY DISK

The floppy disk drive was not actually invented as a device for the PC. The first floppy disk drives appeared as a storage device for IBM's mainframe computers in 1967. Alan Shugart led the team of engineers that developed the drive and after two years of development came out with the 8″ floppy. Following up on the suggestions of David Noble, they designed a fabric sleeve that enveloped a flexible mylar base coated with magnetic medium. A few years later, having established his own company, Al released the first 5.25″ drive as a product of Shugart Associates. The floppy disk drive went through several incarnations before it finally arrived at the 3.5″ drive common to computers today (see **Figure 11.1**). The 3.5″ medium is commonly known as the diskette. This was so that in the old days, when 5.25″ drives were still common, people could easily differentiate between the two.

There have been several variations on the various designs of floppy disk drives that have emerged through the years. However, a few things remain constant. The basic parts that make them work haven't changed a lot, and neither have the methods they use to access data. Conventional floppy drives contain the following basic components:

- A clamping mechanism holds the disk in place as it spins. Floppy disks have a tendency to be unstable at high rotational speeds.

- A spindle motor spins the disk. With the exception of the 5.25″ double-sided, high-density (DS-HD) drives, this motor spins at 300rpm. The 5.25″ DS-HD spins at 360rpm.

- One or two magnetic read/write (R/W) heads are mounted on an actuator arm that moves the heads over surface of the medium. The initial R/W head is positioned to read the bottom surface of the disk.

- A head actuator consisting of a stepper motor coupled to the floppy controller moves the actuator arm, positioning the R/W heads to the appropriate track and sector on the disk.

- A sensor detects the rotational position of the disk. 5.25″ drives use an index hole cut in the sleeve, while 3.5″ drives have a magnetic sensor inside.

Figure 11.1   The floppy diskette drive continues to be an important component in today's computer systems.

HOW THE FLOPPY DRIVE WORKS

When the drive is formatted, the magnetic medium is mapped out in circular paths known as *tracks*. These tracks get subdivided into 512-byte *sectors*. Diskettes make use of a hidden file stored on the first sectors of the diskette surface called the file allocation table (FAT) to keep track of where each file is located on the diskette. FAT records the starting track and sector number of each group of contiguous sectors used by the file. Unless a user has access to specialized software known as a *disk editor* (which allows the user to write directly to the disk on a bit-by-bit basis), FAT is invisible to the user and is seen only by the OS.

The recording head lays down data using a method known as *tunnel erasure*. Data is recorded in much the same manner as audiocassette recorders record music. Magnetic energy realigns magnetic particles embedded in the surface of the medium. As information is written to the surface, the erase heads, positioned directly behind the recording head, trim the track cleanly on the disk. This forces the data to reside within its specified track. This helps eliminate the possibility of cross talk between tracks, which could lead to corrupted data. It also provides for a method of organizing data on the diskette.

When it's time to retrieve that data from the diskette, the computer system's floppy controller generates a signal that directs the R/W heads to the appropriate area of the diskette, using FAT as a guideline. The first time you turn your computer on, the R/W heads of the drive position themselves to track 0, sector 1. An improperly calibrated drive might be slightly off kilter when this happens. If this happens, and the heads are not properly positioned over track 0, then every read/write operation that occurs from then on will be inaccurate.

Disks written by an improperly calibrated drive are usually readable by that same drive, because the read heads are off by the same degree as the write heads. However, when that disk or diskette is moved over to another drive, it can't be read.

When a request for data is made, a stepper motor attached to the actuator arms moves the heads across the diskette surface where they latch on to the appropriate track. *Stepper motors* work by ticking off small increments rather than moving smoothly across the platter. These increments are calibrated to the width of the track. Therefore each position of the motor will move the arms to the next track. Once the track is latched onto, the R/W heads can then begin streaming data over the controller to the I/O bus.

BUZZ WORDS

Sector: The smallest readable unit of data on a magnetic disk drive. A sector consists of 512 bytes.

Track: A virtual circle of sectors on a magnetic drive that makes a complete ring around the disk surface.

Disk editor: A piece of specialized software that allows a user to examine and alter the contents of a disk drive bit by bit. Disk editors even allow access to parts of the drive not normally accessible by the user, such as FAT.

Tunnel erasure: A technique of erasing the magnetic charge from the edges of a recorded track on a magnetic disk.

Stepper motor: A motor that has been designed in such a way that, rather than rotating smoothly, it jumps from one position to another in precisely measured increments.

FLOPPY FORMATS

Over the years, the floppy disk has seen service in several different sizes. The first of Mr. Shugart's floppy drives was the 8″ floppy. It stored a massive 250 kilobytes of data. As I mentioned earlier, this drive was originally developed while he was at IBM as an add-on to mainframe computers. However, it also appeared on several different computers aimed at the home market, including the venerable Radio Shack TRS-80. Despite this, the floppy disk drive didn't really achieve respectability until the release of the 5.25″ floppy in 1976. That's where I'll start.

THE 5.25″ FLOPPY DISK DRIVE

The first 5.25″ drive that appeared in the IBM PC could store 360KB. With the release of the PC-AT, the 360K drive was replaced with a 1.2MB drive. Either one of them used a disk similar to the one in **Figure 11.2**. This drive had a remarkably long lifespan. In fact, it is possible that you'll still occasionally stumble across a computer with one of these installed.

On the original 360K drives, there were forty tracks on each side of the disk. On the 1.2MB drive, this got bumped to eighty tracks per side. Additional capacity was made possible by increasing the number of sectors per track from nine to fifteen.

The magnetic media for these drives is encased in a flexible plastic sleeve that the user inserts into the drive. On the front bezel of the drive is a lever that moves the clamping mechanism into place, holding the disk firmly in position. This lever was euphemistically referred to as the door, and the name has stuck. If this lever is not positioned, the disk will not seat and you will get the message "Drive B: not ready."

The 5.25″ disk has a spindle hole in the center for aligning the disk to the spindle motor. Adjacent to that is another smaller hole called the *index hole*. This is what allows the actuator arm to locate Track 0, Sector 1. The write access window is what allows the R/W head access to the media. This is a narrow slot opening that exposes a small section of the disk surface the entire width of usable surface. If you are looking at the side of the disk with these openings exposed, there will be a notch cut into the plastic sleeve on the upper right-hand corner. This is the *write-protect* mechanism. As crude as it may sound, placing a small piece of transparent tape over this notch prevented you from accidentally overwriting the data on the disk.

Connectors on a 5.25″ floppy disk drive are pretty straightforward. The power is derived from a standard

Figure 11.2 A 5.25″ floppy disk

Molex connector, just like your hard drive or CD-ROM. The data cable connector is unique in that on the back of the drive there is an edge card connector. The data plug slips over that. It is notched off-center to prevent the cable from being applied backwards.

Figure 11.3   A 3.5″ diskette

3.5″ DISKETTE DRIVES

Several things make the 3.5″ diskette a significant improvement over the 5.25″ disk. For one thing, more data can be stored on a smaller disk. Second, a rigid plastic housing keeps the media more secure. Someone transporting a diskette from home to work in a pocket is less likely to do permanent damage. The smaller size assures that it can fit right into a shirt pocket. Now you won't be sitting on your sales presentation while you drive to work.

The drive itself doesn't differ all that much from the original 5.25″. Differences center on the media used. 3.5″ diskettes pack more sectors into each track, and as a result hold more data. The original 3.5″ floppy first developed by IBM in 1984 had a capacity of 720K. A couple of years later, its engineers upped that capacity to 1.44MB, and that's where it has stayed until today. Teac developed and introduced a 2.88MB version, but it never really caught on.

If you look carefully at a diskette (if you don't have one handy, look at **Figure 11.3**), you'll see that on the diskette itself, the spindle hole exposes a metal disk embedded in the center of the medium. This disk has a small rectangular hole notched in it for the spindle to engage. A plastic (or sometimes metal) sliding door covers the access opening for the R/W heads. On the top edge, opposite the sliding door, are either one or two square holes punched into the plastic cover. If there is only one, your diskette is one of the older 720K types. The presence of two holes identifies a 1.44MB diskette. One of these holes is fitted with a sliding cover. This is your write protection. You can flip that closed to prevent overwriting your diskette. The theory is that you can permanently write-protect a diskette by snapping this cover off. Of course, a piece of scotch tape judiciously applied over the opening will override the write protection. The second hole indicates to the drive that it is a 1.44MB diskette and not 720K.

Table 11.1 summarizes the specifications for 5.25″ and 3.25″ floppies.

THE FLOPPY CABLE

The connector that hooks the drive to the controller is a 34-pin ribbon cable. It is easy to distinguish the floppy cable from the hard drive cable. Not only is it narrower (the cable for hard drives generally has forty conductors, unless it's a SCSI drive), but there is a twist in the cable that is very difficult to miss. This twist is clearly visible in **Figure 11.4.**

As with all ribbon cables, the pink or red conductor on the cable is the "number one" conductor. On older cables, there might be three different types of connectors. The connector

Table 11.1 Floppy Disk Formats, Past and Present

5.25" Format		
Specification	Double Density	High Density
Bytes per sector	512	512
Sectors per track	9	15
Tracks per side	40	80
Tracks per inch	48	96
Number of sides	2	2
Capacity	360K	1.2MB
Track width	.33mm	.16mm
Default cluster size	1	2
FAT length (sectors)	2	7
Root directory length (sectors)	7	14
Total sectors per disk	720	2,400

3.5" Format			
Specification	Double Density	High Density (1.44MB)	2.88MB
Bytes per sector	512	512	512
Sectors per track	9	18	36
Tracks per side	80	80	80
Tracks per inch	135	135	135
Number of sides	2	2	2
Capacity	720K	1.44MB	2.88MB
Track width	.115mm	.115mm	.115mm
Default cluster size	1	2	2
FAT length (sectors)	3	9	9
Root directory length (sectors)	7	14	15
Total sectors per disk	720	2,400	5,760

A comparison of floppy disk formats, past and present

at one end plugs into the motherboard controller. One of the other types is a rectangular connector with holes for pins to plug in to. Those are for 3.5" drives. The third kind has a larger connector that is designed to fit over an edge card, for 5.25" drives. Most cables currently manufactured no longer have connectors for a 5.25" drive. Since people rarely use two floppy

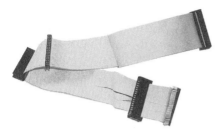

Figure 11.4 In order for a floppy disk drive to be a bootable device, it needs to be on the end opposite of the twist in the cable.

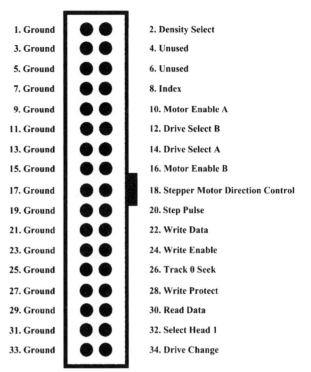

1. Ground			2. Density Select
3. Ground			4. Unused
5. Ground			6. Unused
7. Ground			8. Index
9. Ground			10. Motor Enable A
11. Ground			12. Drive Select B
13. Ground			14. Drive Select A
15. Ground			16. Motor Enable B
17. Ground			18. Stepper Motor Direction Control
19. Ground			20. Step Pulse
21. Ground			22. Write Data
23. Ground			24. Write Enable
25. Ground			26. Track 0 Seek
27. Ground			28. Write Protect
29. Ground			30. Read Data
31. Ground			32. Select Head 1
33. Ground			34. Drive Change

Figure 11.5 Standard pinouts for 34-pin floppy cable

drives anymore, it's also becoming more common to see floppy cables with only two connectors. One is for the motherboard controller and the other is for a single drive.

The reason for the twist is to identify the bootable drive. If there are two floppy drives on a system, the system BIOS identifies which is the bootable drive by its position relative to the twist. The drive on the side of the twist opposite of the controller is always the bootable drive. By default, this becomes Drive A. If you inadvertently plug your floppy into the connector on the same side of the cable as the controller, you will have no bootable floppy drive.

In the BIOS settings, there is a place where you can "swap floppies." Changing this setting from the default will make the drive on the controller side of the cable Drive A and the drive on the opposite end Drive B. It will not, however, change which device is bootable.

The thirty-fourth conductor, or the one on the opposite side of the color-coded wire, is the diskette change line. When a diskette is inserted into the drive, a signal called the drive change pulse will travel down this wire and tell the computer that a new diskette has been inserted into the drive. Naturally all the other conductors have a purpose, or they wouldn't be there. The pinouts for a standard floppy disk cable and its associated port are illustrated in **Figure 11.5**.

TROUBLESHOOTING FLOPPY DISK DRIVES

Floppy drive problems are probably misdiagnosed more often than any other device. Every time somebody inserts a diskette into the drive and the system returns some sort of error message, they automatically the drive is assumed to be defective. Much of the time, however, it's not the drive's fault. There are several different issues that will result in customers calling for help, claiming their floppy disk drive has failed.

DISKETTE PROBLEMS

Most of the time, when individuals are unable to read data from their floppies, it is the diskette itself that is to blame. Diskettes are notoriously vulnerable to environmental conditions. Excess temperature variation, exposure to magnetic radiation, or high doses of electromagnetic inter- ference (EMI) can wipe out portions of the data on the surface of the medium. Any contami- nation, such as dumping your coffee on your desk while a bunch of floppies are scattered about, will damage the diskette. A piece of lint from your shirt pocket working its way past the door can scratch the surface of the medium.

The type of error message generated by your computer when trying to access data will give you a good idea of where to start. You'll often see errors like these:

Data error reading Drive A:

Seek error writing Drive A:

Sector not found reading Drive A:

Abort, Retry, Fail?

Abort, Retry, Fail, Ignore?

These are all signs of defective diskettes, not defective drives. On these diskettes, if you're a Windows user, try running Scandisk in Thorough Mode. If there is sufficient free space on the diskette, many of them can be recovered.

The floppy cable itself might be the culprit. If you are working with a brand-new computer that just arrived and the floppy drive is not detected on bootup, one of two things might have happened. Is the drive light on the floppy drive constantly glowing? If so, whoever assembled your computer got the cable on backwards. One would like to think that a mistake like this would never happen, but one would be wrong. You'll also see this same symptom if, after doing some work on the system, you happen to plug it in backwards yourself.

If the light does not glow, and during the boot process, you don't hear the actuator arm trying to latch onto Sector 1, Track 0, then you have the second problem, and it's time to open the case. Floppy drive cables are good at coming off during shipping. If that's the case, simply put it back on and your computer should work.

Another diskette issue that occasionally appears is the repeating directory syndrome. You click the A: icon in Windows Explorer and get a list of files on that diskette. Since it didn't have the file you were looking for, you pop the next one in and click the icon once again. And get the same list of files. "Hmmm," you say. "I don't recall making a copy of that disk." So you pop in a third floppy and Explorer delivers the same list again.

Here's what is happening. When you run the first directory of the diskette, the file list is stored in the computer's cache memory. That way, if you need to review the list again, it's already there. The thirty-fourth wire on the floppy cable carries the drive change signal. When you replace the diskette in the drive with a new one, an electrical signal travels up that wire to a sensor in your drive, and a new directory is generated the next time the user requests it. If that wire gets crimped or broken, the signal never arrives, and the same directory listing appears over and over again. The solution is simple. Replace the floppy cable. In the meantime, you can force a directory update by alternating between drives while doing your search. After each search of a floppy, hit the C: drive. When you try the next floppy, your computer will have to do a new search.

Sometimes your problem lies in the CMOS. One of the settings you can change is what kind of floppy disk drives you have installed. Many versions of BIOS ship with the default setting of "None" for drive A. If the battery goes dead, your CMOS will revert to factory defaults. When this happens, if your default is "None," then the computer will not see a floppy drive on the next boot. Another thing that has been known to reset the CMOS is changing expansion cards. A sign that this might have happened is if you get error messages along the lines of "Not ready error reading Drive A:", "General failure reading Drive A:", and "Insert diskette for Drive A: and press any key when ready."

If all else checks out well, and you're still having problems, it's possible that the floppy drive has failed. They do have a relatively high failure rate, compared to other components, simply because of the nature of the abuse they receive. They are exposed to the elements more than any other device, and they're purely mechanical. Therefore, they fail. You will get most of the same messages as you get with CMOS issues, along with "Drive not Ready" and "FDD Controller Failure." Floppy drives are cheap. Don't try to fix it. Simply replace it.

OTHER REMOVABLE DISK DRIVES

It's been a long time since the floppy disk could claim to be the only removable medium. In fact, for the most part, it has found itself relegated to the role of an emergency boot drive, or simply a convenient method for moving small files from home to the office. For real data storage, there is any number of other technologies that have come along to make the floppy all but obsolete. These drives hold more data (by a long shot), but they also sit on faster interfaces. That's something you can't help but appreciate the next time you try running a PowerPoint presentation from a floppy disk.

ZIP DRIVES

The Zip drive very likely leads the way in removable media. Developed by Iomega, they are also available from numerous other manufacturers. These drives are available in 100MB (being phased out, but still available as of this writing), 250MB, and 750MB formats, so they offer a reasonable amount of space for storage. As far as users are concerned, these are nothing more than high-capacity floppy disks. They insert a Zip disk into the drive and copy their files over.

The drives have been available over the years in both internal and external versions. The internal drive mounts into your computer case no differently than a floppy. It's about the same size as a floppy and the opening differs only that it is wider to accept the thicker disk. (Even after all these years, I still try to stick a floppy disk into my Zip drive from time to time!) Internal drives are available with either an IDE or SCSI interface.

External drives can be picked up that hook up to a parallel port, to the external port of a SCSI adapter, or to a USB port. For the fastest data transfer, one of the newer releases with a FireWire interface will be preferable. (For a detailed explanation of the advantages of SCSI or FireWire, see Chapter Fourteen, The Many Faces of SCSI.)

There are some trouble-shooting issues that might arise when you're dealing with Zip disks. External drives that mount onto the parallel port, like the one in **Figure 11.6**, work best if the port is set to Enhanced Parallel Port (EPP) or Enhanced Capabilities Port (ECP) mode (see Chapter Seventeen, Printing Technologies, for detailed information on these modes and how to set them). The drives are built with pass-through par-

Figure 11.6   External Zip drives are great if you need to move from one computer to another on a regular basis.

allel ports for hooking up your printer. Some computers have been known to generate I/O errors in standard bidirectional mode because they think they're printing to themselves. I/O errors are almost a guarantee if you send a job to your printer and then decide you want to load a file from the Zip. Also, if you have other devices, such as a scanner or a copy-protection software key that plugs into a parallel port, performance can drop to a crawl if you try stacking more than three devices on the parallel port.

Another issue that has been repeatedly reported is the infamous "click of death." You insert a disk into the drive and it repeatedly clicks, over and over again. You can't make it stop and you can't abort the operation. The only solution is to restart your machine. Later on, the problem will spread to other disks that you use in that same drive. It acts just like a virus, except that it's hardware related and not a software issue. Therefore, if you are working with a Zip drive and it develops the click of death, whatever you do, don't insert a new disk to test the drive. The only thing you'll accomplish is that you'll now have two destroyed disks instead of one.

So what causes that to happen?

Haven't got a clue. (I was dying to say that somewhere in this book). Neither does Iomega. It suggests that a broken R/W head or torn media within the disk might cause the problem, but that's only a theory. Several other suggestions have been offered. The one that's easiest to believe is that the first disk to fail somehow throws the R/W head out of alignment. Subsequent disks then cannot be read and are damaged by the head coming in actual contact with the surface of the medium.

JAZ DRIVES

Jaz drives are another offering by Iomega. For the most part, Jaz and Zip drives are very similar. The interfaces are comparable; both are available in parallel, USB, or SCSI, with a FireWire option. Both use disks that go in and out of the computer with the ease of a floppy disk.

Jaz drives hold a lot more data, though. The drive supports up to 2GB disks, and the disks are available in either 1GB or 2GB densities. They're also somewhat faster than Zips. Jaz drives deliver access times in the vicinity of 10ms, which compares to some hard drives (good hard drives hover around 6.5ms to 10ms).

SUPER FLOPPY DRIVES

The so-called Super Floppy is a product that has been made by several manufacturers. For the most part, these are drives that support high-capacity removable disks, but will also read and write standard 1.44MB floppy diskettes.

The major player was the LS120 or SuperDisk, a format put out in a cooperative effort by Imation and Panasonic. Mitsubishi also made a line of these drives. They were available in internal and external versions, and there's even one for notebook computers. Interface options include parallel, SCSI, and USB.

The SuperDisk got its increased capacity by dramatically increasing the number of tracks per inch embedded on the media. A metal particle coating was used instead of the metal-oxide coating used by standard floppy diskettes. Onto this metal coating a laser beam etched 1736 tracks onto which data could be stored. Externally, the diskette didn't look that much different than a standard floppy diskette.

These drives weren't known for their blazing speed. Most users would consider them too slow for running an application from the disk. However, the convenience of having one drive read and write both 120MB disks and 1.44MB diskettes was something to be considered.

For a while, it looked like the death of the SuperDisk was imminent. Both Matsushita Corporation and Imation discontinued the manufacture of these drives in the waning months of the year 2000. However, when Apple Computer Corporation stopped installing floppy diskette drives into all of its computers, there was a sudden resurgence of interest. Their popularity today has surpassed what it was before they were "discontinued."

HiFD

A drive that lost its fight for recognition was Sony's HiFD (High Capacity Floppy Disk) drive. These drives supported a proprietary 200MB disk as well as standard 1.44MB diskettes. They offered decent performance, in the range of 3.6MB/s throughput, but did not have much to offer for interface options. They were only available in external form in the choice of either parallel or USB.

The HiFD diskette packed 2822 tracks per inch onto the tiny little diskette, and yet the same drive could read standard 1.44MB diskettes as well as 720KB versions. Needless to say, it wasn't possible to try to read the HiFD diskette in a standard drive. To prevent this from happening, the HiFD diskette was designed in such a way as to not fit into a standard 3.5″ drive.

The format was co-developed by Sony and Fuji Film Corporation and for a while looked like it might catch on. It received support from Sony, Teac, and Alps as far as the manufacture of drives was concerned. Fuji and Sony both offered media. However, heavy competition from Iomega in the form of the Zip drive was too much for the technology to overcome.

TAPE SOLUTIONS

Disks aren't the only domain of removable media. Tape drives have long been the primary choice of medium for the network administrator looking for a (relatively) fast and convenient way to back up servers and workstations. Tape drives were, in fact, the original "hard drive" of many computers that preceded the IBM PC. Commodore 64s, Radio Shack's TRS-80, the Texas Instruments TI-99, and many other home computing devices offered cassette tape storage mechanisms for both programs and data. Current product offerings are a bit more sophisticated than the cassette tapes used on these early machines.

QIC

For many years, the drive of choice for someone looking for a reasonably high-capacity storage mechanism for backup was Quarter Inch Cartridge (QIC). The cartridge itself was of a fixed size, and in order to increase capacity, manufacturers increased the length of the tape wound onto the spools and how much data could be crammed onto an inch of tape. This is known as the data density. Standards by which tapes and drives are manufactured are under the strict control of an organization called The Quarter Inch Committee. They make sure that tapes made by one manufacturer will work in the drives made by another.

Figuring out all those different numbers in the names of QIC tapes might look a little intimidating at first, but it's actually pretty straightforward. I'll take for an example a DC-9120 tape manufactured by Maxell. The number 9120 is Maxell's part identification number. The way it does it is to use the last three numbers as the native capacity of the tape. *Native capacity* is how much data the tape can hold if you do not use any compression. The 120 in the number tells me it is a 1.2GB tape. Now what does the DC mean?

There are actually two different formats for the tape used by QIC drives. There is the QIC-DC, or data cartridge, and the QIC-MC, or mini-cartridge. The data cartridge is a tape housed in a shell that measures 4″×6″×0.625″. The mini-cartridge measures 2.5″×3.5″×0.60″. Therefore, the DC-9120 is a Data Cartridge 1.2GB tape.

Data is encoded onto magnetic media in a manner similar to floppy disk drives. An iron oxide coating is written over by magnetizing the particles. Where a particle is magnetized, you have a 1; where it is not, you have a 0. The data is laid down onto the tape in tracks. Data density is derived by two methods. The first involves increasing the number of tracks that can be recorded onto a strip of tape. The other is simply squeezing more data onto each track. Between the tracks a thin strip of unrecorded medium insulates the data.

For a while, it looked like QIC was a dead technology. It was slow and didn't provide for much native storage capacity. A good QIC drive measured its data throughput in megabytes per minute, and not per second. Backing up a 36GB hard drive onto QIC tape was a job nobody volunteered for! However, the Quarter Inch Committee has revitalized the standard and is in the process of ratifying standards that would put it back onto a competitive level with some of the other "more modern" technologies. As of this writing this is now a 25GB native/50GB compressed drive capable of approximately 2Mb/s backup speeds.

While there were several dozen standards that developed over the years, relatively few became generally popular. While by no means an all-inclusive list, **Table 11.2** lists the most common QIC formats.

Table 11.2 Common QIC Formats

Format	Interface	Recording Method	Native Capacity	Tracks per Inch	Data Throughput	Data Density	Tape on Roll
QIC-40	Floppy or optional controller card	MFM	40MB/60MB	20	2MB-to-8MB/minute	10,000bpi	205ft to 307.5ft
QIC-80	Floppy or optional controller card	MFM	80MB/120MB	28	3MB-to-9MB/minute	14,700bpi	205ft to 307.5ft
QIC-120	SCSI or QIC-02	MFM	125MB	15	3MB-to-9MB/minute	10,000bpi	600ft.
QIC-150	SCSI or QIC-02	MFM	150MB/250MB	18	3MB-to-9MB/minute	10,000bpi	600ft.
QIC-525	SCSI or SCSI-2	MFM	320MB/525MB	26	12MB/minute	16,000bpi	1,000ft.
QIC-1000	SCSI or SCSI-2	MFM	1GB	30	18MB/minute	36,000bpi	760ft.
QIC-1350	SCSI-2	RLL	1.35GB	30	18MB/minute	51,000bpi	760ft.
QIC-2100	SCSI-2	RLL	2.1GB	30	18MB/minute	68,000bpi	875ft.
QIC-3010	Floppy or IDE	MFM	255MB	40	9MB/minute	22,000bpi	300ft.
QIC-3020	Floppy or IDE	MFM	500MB	40	9MB/minute	42,000bpi	400ft.
QIC-2GB	SCSI-2	MFM	2.0GB	42	18MB/minute	40,640bpi	900ft.
QIC-5GB	SCSI-2	RLL	5GB	44	18MB/minute	96,000bpi	1,200ft.
QIC-5010	SCSI-2	RLL	13GB	144	18MB/minute	68,000bpi	—

Some of the more common QIC formats, along with their capacity and transfer rates

DAT

Digital audiotape (DAT) has enjoyed a relatively long reign as the format of choice for most high-end tape backup units, although it is starting to feel the pressure of DLT (which I'll discuss in the next section of this chapter). DAT uses a different recording method than QIC. Unlike QIC, which laid data down in tracks, DAT records information using a *helical-scan* record head. The tape wraps around the head, much the same

> **Buzz Words** ───────────
>
> **Helical scan:** A recording technology that places data in diagonal tracks along the tape, as opposed to a linear track that follows parallel to the tape edge.

way your video recorder handles tape. Then the data is recorded onto the entire width of tape, treating it as one really wide track. The result is that a significantly larger amount of data can be recorded per square inch of tape. Because the same technology is used in both the computer industry and the audio industry, it is necessary for us to be technically correct in our terminology.

The first thing I need to do is try to eliminate some confusion as to what constitutes data and what constitutes audio. If you're recording a digital audio signal, it is correct to call it a DAT drive. However, when that same drive is put into a computer it becomes a data recorder, a digital data storage (DDS) drive. As with any other technology, DAT has evolved in the years that it has been out. With each new generation of DAT drive, more data could be squeezed onto the tape. These different generations appear as DDS numbers. The first DAT drives to come out were DDS-1. Current drives are now up to DDS-4. A comparison of these formats can be seen in **Table 11.3**.

DAT comes in both 4mm DAT and 8mm DAT. Since the latter is identical to the tape used in audio recorders, the inevitable question arises. Can I use DAT tape in a DDS drive? And the answer is a definitive maybe! Technically speaking, in order for a tape to be used in a DDS drive the tape must be manufactured to specifications outlined in the ISO-10777 standards and the ISO-12247 standards ratified by the International Standards Organization (ISO). Unless the tape you use meets those standards, many drive manufacturers will refuse to offer support. Tapes manufactured for use in audio systems is theoretically of lower quality.

Now, can you really do it or not? And once again, the answer is a definitive maybe. If the audio tape is of excellent quality, you will probably experience no difficulties. However, a tape

Table 11.3 DDS Standards

Standard	Native Format	Compressed Format	Tape Length	Data Transfer
DDS-1	2GB	4GB	90M	~1.35MB/s
DDS-2	4GB	8GB	120M	~1.35MB/s
DDS-3	12GB	24GB	125M	~2.65MB/s
DDS-4	20GB	40GB	150M	~2.65MB/s

A comparison of DAT formats

of lower quality will result in signal dropouts. In a musical tape, if you lose a bit of data here and there, it is of little or no consequence. Losing a few bytes of a Windows 2000 Service Pack would be a different issue altogether. I suggest that if you wish to save a couple of bucks here and there by using audio-grade tape that you test it thoroughly before you entrust your company's critical data to it.

DLT

A more recent technology to emerge in tape drives is the digital linear tape (DLT) drive. Developed by Digital Equipment Corporation, DLT abandons the helical-scan head in favor of a linear-record head. DLT drives use a pure metal tape coating rather than an oxide coating.

> **BUZZ WORDS** ────────
>
> **Signal saturation:** The maximum strength of a recording signal that a device can handle before the recording becomes unusable.

In a way, it almost looks as if DLT has taken a step backward in technology. Like the older QIC, it lays data down in parallel tracks. Instead of using a unified R/W head, though, as did QIC, the DLT drive has independent elements for read and write operations. Data throughput is significantly improved as a result. One of the advantages of DLT over DAT is a direct result of using linear technology. Because the tape does not have to be wrapped around the heads, far less tape tension is required. With less tension, there is less friction generated between the tape and the heads. As a result, both tape and drive last longer.

The use of metal tape, as opposed to metal-oxide tape, provides for significantly higher signal saturation. *Signal saturation* is the strength of signal that the tape can accurately record before distortion becomes so great that the recorded version of that signal becomes unusable. What this means to the engineer is that the signal used to record all those tiny little 1s can be much stronger than the signal used to record all the 0s. This allows for higher recording accuracy as well as faster recording speeds.

Another advantage of metal tape over metal-oxide tape is that the metal tape is far less susceptible to flaking off after extended use. It bonds more strongly to the base. When you combine this with the aforementioned fact that there is also less friction between the tape and the heads, a DLT tape lasts much longer than a DAT tape.

AIT

In some ways, the Advanced Intelligent Tape Drive (AIT) by Sony is just an extension of DAT. It uses the same helical scan R/W technology, but it adds a couple of new twists. A new technology called Memory-in-Cassette (MIC) architecture teaches the drive (and the tape) new tricks. The MIC chip consists of an EEPROM embedded in an 8mm cassette. Data access time and seek times in the event of specific file retrieval are reduced by as much as half that of either DAT or DLT. Data can be stored on the tape in partitions utilizing multiple load points (MLP). And a new write-once-read-many (WORM) feature allows data to be written to a drive permanently, with no ability to erase or write over that specific tape.

One of these features that deserves some extra attention is MLP. All tapes require a specific *load point*, which is the physical location where the actual data begins to be copied. Previous technologies allowed only one load point. If the load point was at the beginning of the tape, and a user wanted to

restore a specific file, the drive would have to start searching for that file from the very beginning of the tape. This could take several minutes. Some manufacturers sped up the process by using mid-load points (unfortunately also called MLP). Mid-load points placed the load point in the center of the tape, so searches could be done in either rewind or fast-forward mode. Multiple load points allow the user to preselect a specific point on the tape from which to start a search.

AIT native formats start at 25GB, with a theoretical potential of 2TB compressed. Higher compression ratios are made possible on AIT drives using adaptive lossless data compression (ALDC) technology. ALDC compresses data on an average of 2.6:1. Conventional compression technology is having a good day if it achieves 2:1.

Since one of the primary objections to helical scan technology was the wear and tear imposed on the media, AIT format makes use of metal-evaporated media with a proprietary Diamond Layer Coating to extend the life of the tape. In addition to a longer life, developers of AIT claim that much higher recording density can be achieved.

AIT-1

AIT-1, as the name implies, was the first generation of AIT tape drives and tapes. These drives were capable of a 35GB native capacity, and using ALDC could achieve 90GB compressed. Data throughput in native format was around 4MB/s (10MB/s compressed) on drives with an Ultra-SCSI LVD interface (see Chapter Fourteen, The Many Faces of SCSI). As of this writing, AIT-1 is still available. It can be considered the "entry level" AIT. In the event that a user should upgrade to one of the later generations of AIT somewhere down the line, media recorded by the AIT-1 drive can be read or written by all subsequent AIT generations.

AIT-2

The second generation of AIT drives increased both the capacity and the speed of the format. This was achieved through improvements in the quality of the recording heads, channel coding, and in how the media is manufactured. While remaining backwardly compatible with AIT-1, AIT-2 increases data transfer rates to 6MB/s (15MB/s compressed) and native capacity to 50GB (130GB compressed).

AIT-3

The most recent AIT offering boasts a native capacity of 100GB (260GB with compression) and a native data transfer rate of 12MB/s (31MB/s compressed). The increased capacity of AIT-3 was accomplished by doubling the number of recording tracks per inch of tape over the previous generations. Increased throughput is a result of improvements in the recording heads and controller circuitry.

SUPER-AIT

Super-AIT (SAIT) ups the ante in the AIT arena in areas of storage capacity, data transfer rate, and technological marvels. As of this writing, only the first generation of SAIT has reached the market. These drives offer the network administrator or user 500GB of native capacity, and when compressed, up to 1.3TB! Throughput in native mode approaches 30MB/s. By the time this book reaches the streets, SAIT-2 will most likely be available with a native capacity of 1TB (2.6TB compressed) and throughput of 60MB/s. On the drawing board is SAIT-3 and SAIT-4.

If initial research and development figures hold out, you can expect drives that store 4TB of data in native format, 10.4TB when compressed, and move it from your hard drive to tape, or vice versa, at 240MB/s.

SLR

Scalable Linear Recording (SLR) tape drives take the DLT to the next level. By incorporating multiple record channels across the breadth of the tape, storage capacity and throughput are increased. In order to assure that the heads are reading the correct tracks, a separate recording channel maintains channel synchronization.

When originally introduced, SLR drives were available as small as 525MB. Needless to say, today's drives are a bit larger. Current drives are available to 50GB in native mode, or 100GB compressed. Tandberg Data, the company that developed this technology, claims that a 30GB hard drive can be backed up in an hour our less. The small tape size allows for tape auto-changers to take up far less space than some of the competitors.

CHAPTER SUMMARY

A lot of the information presented in this chapter is actually targeted more toward the "real world" than it is the exam. Still, there is much exam material to be found here. Especially important is the section of floppy disk drives. Know their history and their evolution.

Don't, however, discount the importance of knowing about some of the other devices described in this chapter. Even some of the devices that have been discontinued are likely to show up on your bench someday after you become a professional. It wouldn't be all that impressive to have to ask the customer, "What in the world is that?"

BRAIN DRAIN

1. List as many forms of removable media as you can.

2. How did the Super Floppy drive differ from a Zip drive?

3. If you have an application that consists of 245MB worth of files, and you want to run it from removable media, what options would be best?

4. Describe how a helical-scan recording mechanism works.

5. Discuss as many differences as you can between DAT and DLT tape drives.

THE 64K$ QUESTIONS

1. 5.25″ floppy disk drives were available in _____ and _____ sizes. (Choose two)
   a. 360KB
   b. 720KB
   c. 1.2MB
   d. 1.44MB
   e. 2.88MB

2. 3.5″ floppy diskettes were available in what sizes?
   a. 360KB
   b. 720KB
   c. 1.2MB
   d. 1.44MB
   e. 2.88MB

3. Double-density floppies featured _____ sectors per track.
   a. 9
   b. 15
   c. 20
   d. 40

4. High-density floppies featured _____ sectors per track.
   a. 9
   b. 15
   c. 20
   d. 40

5. How many bytes are there per sector on a floppy disk?
   a. 9 (8 for data and 1 for parity)
   b. 256
   c. 512
   d. 1024

6. Repeating directories from multiple disks is most likely a result of _____.
   a. A bad diskette
   b. A stuck actuator arm
   c. A faulty cable
   d. Corrupted drivers

7. The "click of death" is a failure that appears on _____.
   a. Zip drives
   b. Syquest cartridges
   c. Floppy disk drives
   d. Tape drives

8. Two tape drives that use helical scan recording technology are _____ and _____.
   a. QIC
   b. DAT
   c. DLT
   d. AIC

9. Two tape drives that use linear recording technology are_____ and _____.
   a. QIC
   b. DAT
   c. DLT
   d. AIC

10. You just changed the battery on your motherboard and now the floppy drive isn't recognized. Why might this be?
   a. You accidentally unseated the cable.
   b. You damaged an IC with ESD.
   c. The CMOS reverted to default settings.
   d. A spurious electrical charge damaged the drive.

TRICKY TERMINOLOGY

Disk editor: A piece of specialized software that allows a user to examine and alter the contents of a disk drive bit by bit. Disk editors even allow access to parts of the drive not normally accessible by the user, such as FAT.

Diskette: A term typically applied to the 3.5″ floppy disk in order to distinguish it from the 5.25″ floppy disk.

Helical scan: A recording technology that places data in diagonal tracks along the tape, as opposed to a linear track that follows parallel to the tape edge.

Index hole: A small opening in the covering of a floppy disk that allows the R/W heads to properly align to Track 0, Sector 1.

Load point: The physical location on a tape where data begins to be stored.

Native capacity: How much data any given medium can store without benefit of compression. Various compression techniques allow data beyond native capacity to be recorded.

Sector: The smallest readable unit of data on a magnetic disk drive. A sector consists of 512 bytes.

Signal saturation: The maximum strength of a recording signal that a device can handle before the recording becomes unusable.

Stepper motor: A motor that has been designed in such a way that, rather than rotating smoothly, it jumps from one position to another in precisely measured increments.

Track: A virtual circle of sectors on a magnetic drive that makes a complete ring around the disk surface.

Tunnel erasure: A technique of erasing the magnetic charge from the edges of a recorded track on a magnetic disk.

Write protect: A process or mechanism that prevents the data on a disk or other medium from being erased or overwritten.

ACRONYM ALERT

AIT: Advanced Intelligent Tape. A tape format that incorporates a linear recording mechanism in conjunction with a memory chip embedded in the tape cartridge to allow for advanced features.

ALDC: Adaptive Lossless Data Compression. An advanced data compression algorithm that allows a greater degree of compression without any loss of data.

DAT: Digital Audiotape. A tape format that uses an 8mm recording tape and a helical scan recording mechanism very similar to that used by digital audio recorders.

DDS: Digital Data Storage

DLT: Digital Linear Tape. A tape format that records data in a straight line along the tape, parallel to the tape's edge.

ECP: Enhanced Capabilities Port. One of several different methods of configuring a parallel port.

EPP: Enhanced Parallel Port. One of several different methods of configuring a parallel port.

FAT: File Allocation Table. A file on a disk, hidden from the user, that identifies what file is using each sector on the disk. It is the disk's roadmap, if you will.

MIC: Memory In Cartridge. The embedded memory chip of an AIT.

MLP: Mid-Load Point. A tape drive technology that places the load point in the center of the tape.

MLP: Multiple Load Point. A tape drive technology that allows a single tape to be mounted from several different locations on the tape.

QIC: Quarter Inch Cartridge. A tape format so named because of the size of the tape used (not the size of the cartridge).

SLR: Scalable Linear Recording. A tape drive technology that uses linear recording technology and allows multiple channels of data to be stored across the width of the tape.

WORM: Write Once Read Many. A recording technology that write protects the contents of the medium in order to prevent that data from being erased or overwritten.

CHAPTER 12

HARD DISK DRIVE STRUCTURE AND GEOMETRY

The hard disk drive is one of those devices that has a good excuse if it suffers from a complex. Of all the devices in the system, the hard drive has seen as rapid and dramatic a pace of improvement as any other, including the CPU. Yet it never gets the fanfare. It does more physical work than any other component, and yet the user complains when it makes too much noise.

From the time the Winchester Hard Disk Drive was introduced in 1975 to the present, experienced computer users have considered a hard disk drive a necessity. A hard drive is the fundamental form of mass storage in use today. While all systems of today ship with one installed, this has not always been the case. Most early computers, such as the Timex Sinclair, the Commodore series of computers, and Radio Shack's TRS-80s used a tape drive for storage. Even after the release of the PC, hard disks remained an option (and an expensive one at that) for many years.

The Winchester was far from being the first hard disk, however. IBM developed the first true hard disk drive in 1956. It called it the 305 RAMAC. The letters stood for Random Access Method for Accounting and Control. It possessed fifty disks that were two feet in diameter, and stored a mind-boggling **five megabytes** of data.

To help you understand hard drives, I'll be taking you though a few other parts of the computer as well. I'll be discussing certain BIOS instructions as well as hard drive geometry. A key issue that impinges heavily on computer performance is how a particular computer deals with I/O operations.

A+ EXAM OBJECTIVES

Some exam objectives to be covered in this chapter include the following:

1.1   Identify the names, purpose, and characteristics of system modules. Recognize these modules by sight or definition.

1.2   Identify basic procedures for adding and removing field-replaceable modules for desktop systems. Given a replacement scenario, choose the appropriate sequences.

1.4   Identify typical IRQs, DMAs, and I/O addresses, and procedures for altering these settings when installing and configuring devices. Choose the appropriate installation or configuration steps in a given scenario.

1.5   Identify the names, purposes, and performance characteristics of standardized/common peripheral ports, associated cabling, and their connectors. Recognize ports, cabling, and connectors by sight.

1.6   Identify proper procedures for installing and configuring common IDE devices. Choose the appropriate installation or configuration sequences in given scenarios. Recognize the associated cables.

1.9   Identify procedures to optimize PC operations in specific situations. Predict the effects of specific procedures under given scenarios.

1.10 Determine the issues that must be considered when upgrading a PC. In a given scenario, determine when and how to upgrade system components.

2.1   Recognize common problems associated with each module and their symptoms, and identify steps to isolate and troubleshoot the problems. Given a problem situation, interpret the symptoms and infer the most likely cause.

3.1   Identify the various types of preventive maintenance measures, products, and procedures, and when and how to use them.

BASIC HARD DRIVE GEOMETRY

Every hard drive in use today traces its ancestry back to a form of design based on the CHS parameters. CHS stands for Cylinders, Heads, and Sectors per track. It is through this configuration that the system determines the storage capacity of the drive, and it is through this geometry that the file allocation table is able to properly map the information stored on the device. IBM first introduced CHS on the IBM PC.

I discussed the concepts of sectors and tracks in Chapter Eleven, Working with Removable Disks. With hard drives comes a new geometric structure. Hard drives also have cylinders. Hard drives are generally equipped with more than one disk onto which data is stored. These are called *platters*. On most hard drives, each platter also has two surfaces on which data is stored. (Some of the less expensive models save a few dollars per drive in production costs by not equipping the bottom surface of the platter closest to the drive's base with an actuator arm and R/W head.) If you take every track that is vertically aligned across every surface of each platter, you have a *cylinder*. **Figure 12.1** shows you the relationships between sectors, tracks, and cylinders.

BUZZ WORDS

Platter: One of two or more physical disk structures installed in a typical hard drive.

Cylinder: A virtual structure created by the tracks that line up vertically on the surface of each of the platters.

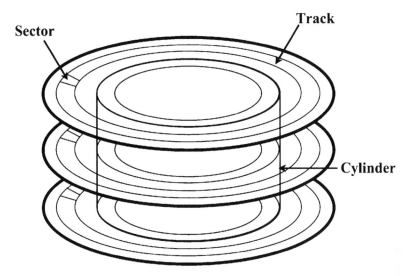

Figure 12.1   A simplified example of sectors, tracks, and cylinders

CHS reads are initialized by a routine in the BIOS known as Int13H. INT stands for interrupt and 13h is simply the hexadecimal for the number 19. Therefore, you could simply call it Interrupt 19, and you would be still correct. The Int13h routine provides for a three-dimensional address space. This space allocates a 10-bit address for tracking cylinders, an 8-bit address for heads, and a 6-bit address for sectors per track. As a result, Int13h supports 1024 cylinders, 256 heads, and 63 sectors per track. All hard drive calls must, in some way, shape, or form, conform to these parameters.

Herein lies the problem. If you do the math, you'll see that Int13h is limited to reading 16,515,072 sectors. Multiply that by 512 for the number of bytes in a sector and you see that Int13h provides support for hard drives up to and including 8GB hard disk drives. That's all, folks.

Now, obviously there are much bigger drives than this. Most computers shipping today have drives in the 40-80GB range. These larger drives are made possible through one of the drive translation methods that I will discuss later in this chapter. *Drive translation* takes disk space beyond what Int13h would typically be able to read and converts those locations into something it does understand. This is made possible by adding the *Int13h extensions* to the BIOS.

So why not just get rid of the Int13h altogether and replace it with something more modern and up to date? The problem there is that it isn't just hardware that addresses this interrupt. Any software that wants to read to the disk, which is any software written in the past twenty-five

> **BUZZ WORDS**
>
> **Drive translation:** A technique by which an address space beyond what Int13h can read is converted into something that it can understand.
>
> **Int13h extensions:** Additional instructions added to the BIOS that intercept hard disk I/O operations and provide the drive translation required by hard disks larger than 8GB.

years or so, also addresses the Int13h call. If Int13h suddenly disappears, none of that software will work. For some reason people get upset when they find the new computer they just bought won't run several thousand dollars' worth of software they've bought over the past few years.

To make sure this didn't happen, engineers simply added the extensions. Hardware and software make their calls to the to Int13h. The extensions intercept these calls and engage whatever drive translation method has been chosen. Newer extensions replace the 24-bit address space of Int13h with a 64-bit space. As a result, drives in the nine and a half trillion-gigabyte range are theoretically possible.

The long and short of it is that, no matter what kind of hard drive you have, it needs to be able to somehow translate all I/O operations into something that the antiquated concept of Int13h can comprehend. When data is requested from the hard drive, the controller will first locate the cylinder that holds the data. Then it will determine which specific track has the data so that the correct R/W head is activated. Once the track is located it will lock on to the first sector that holds the data the system needs.

Early hard drives also were afflicted by the requirement that each track has the same number of sectors, regardless of their position on the platter. The tracks toward the spindle had no fewer sectors than the outermost track. As a result, the tracks toward the outside consisted of wide, sweeping sectors, while the ones toward the inside were all bunched together. Western Digital developed a technology called *zone bit recording* that allowed the sectors to be approximately the same size. The outside tracks could contain a greater number of sectors than those near the spindle. This is illustrated in **Figure 12.2**.

How a Hard Drive is Constructed

The physical structure of the hard drive makes it one of the most complicated devices in your system. It is an electro-mechanical device that requires a large number of moving parts and a fair amount of logic circuitry to work. While the platters and read/write heads are the core of the hard drive, there is a lot

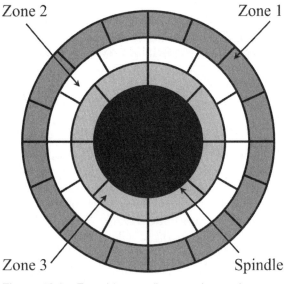

Figure 12.2 Zone bit recording permits much more efficient management of the platter surface. Without this technology, hard drives would be nowhere near the size they are today.

going on that makes them work together. And, as with any other chain, the whole thing falls apart at the weakest link.

DISK PLATTERS

The flat disks onto which data is stored are the platters. These consist of a rigid substrate material coated with some form of magnetic medium. Aluminum is the most common metal used for the substrate, although there are some companies who have taken to using glass. The platters must be very light and very rigid. Also, the surface of a hard disk must be machined to extremely tight tolerances, and aluminum is one of the easiest metals to work with. The magnetic medium has gone through a few changes over the years.

The magnetic medium is what actually holds the information you store on your drive. Zeros and ones are registered simply by the amount of magnetic charge stored by the magnetic particles. In a way, ours is an industry of sand and rust. The first material used was ferrous oxide, or plain old rust. Admittedly it was very refined rust, but when all the fancy terms are put aside, rust it was. Into the ferrous oxide was mixed an adhesive material, and it was applied to the platter using a spin-coating method. While the disk was rapidly spinning on a platter, the medium was applied. What managed to stick in spite of the forces of inertia was an incredibly even and extremely thin layer of the material.

Metal oxides had their problems though. The particles were somewhat large and didn't provide as smooth a surface as might be desirable. Read/write heads had to be positioned farther away in order to prevent impact with particles that might protrude slightly from the surface. The size of the particles meant that there could only be so many per square inch. This limited how much data could be stored on any given platter.

Newer drives, like the one in **Figure 12.3**, use *thin-film metal* media. This allows for greater storage capacities and a thinner surface. A thinner surface allows read/write heads to float closer to the surface. Between the refined media and this closer proximity less magnetic energy is required to magnetize the particle.

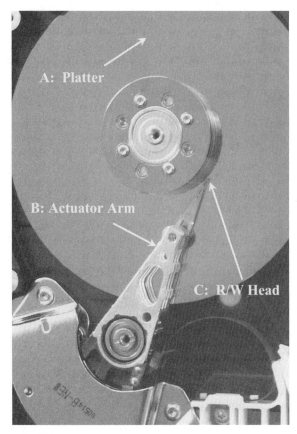

Figure 12.3 Thin-film metal platters have a surface as reflective as any mirror.

Thin-film media is also more efficient for the manufacturers. The material is applied to the platter in a process called *vapor deposition*. This process vaporizes the metal in a chamber. The aluminum platter attracts the molecules of the metal vapors until the surface has all it can hold. The end result is the thinnest and most uniform coating that, until recently, technology was able to offer.

Prior to selling its hard drive division to Hitachi, IBM developed a technology using glass platters instead of aluminum. It claims that glass allows for higher information density and tighter head-to-surface tolerances. IBM's designers must be onto something. One of their first releases was a tiny drive that housed 1.7GB of data per square inch.

It wasn't just the substance of the platter they changed. They also came up with a new technology for platter coatings. This new surface promises a surface that is far more uniform and holds up to a hundred times more data per square inch than conventional materials. To do this, they heat a mixture of iron and platinum. When deposited on the platter the mixture forms a nearly perfect matrix of submicroscopic crystals. These crystals are much smaller than the clusters of molecules conventional magnetic media requires to hold a single bit, and each crystal can store a bit.

Buzz Words ———————————

Thin-film metal: A metalized magnetic medium applied by evaporating metal and allowing it to "condense" back onto the surface being coated.

Vapor deposition: The process of applying a metal coating by the process of evaporation.

Bit cell: The collection of magnetized particles that comprise a single bit on magnetic media.

Read/Write Heads

Now that you have a surface on which to store your data, you need a way to put that data on and get it back off. For every advance in coating technology, there has to be a corresponding advance in read/write (R/W) heads. Their job is to take bits of information from the computer and convert them into magnetic pulses, which in turn magnetize the surface of the medium. When the computer asks for information to be returned, they have to read the magnetic patterns embedded on the platter and convert that energy into digital information.

The term read/write is actually a misnomer on modern hard drives. In the old days, a single head performed both read and write operations. Those days are long gone. Current drives have one transducer that handles write operations and another that reads data back. They are assembled into a composite assembly that is so small as to look like a single unit to the naked eye.

One of the problems that designers face in the rapidly advancing technologies of hard drives is that, the more data that gets packed onto the drive, the smaller the individual bit cells become. A *bit cell* is the tiny collection of magnetic particles that house a single bit. The size of the bit cell will determine the track width. As tracks become narrower, the R/W heads must focus on a correspondingly smaller target.

Also, as the bit cells become smaller, they form tighter clusters with much less distance between cells. It is rather important that the magnetic energy of one bit cell not interfere with that of its neighbor. To prevent this, modern drives put a substantially weaker charge into each bit cell. An amplifier boosts that signal to a level that the controller can convert into digital signals.

For each surface of a disk platter that stores information, there must be an R/W head. When I get to the section that discusses how data is actually located on a drive I will discuss a situation where an extra head is employed. But for now, I'll stick to the one surface/one head scheme.

A critical issue relating to R/W heads is their floating height. In operation, the head does not actually come in contact with the platter. It floats on a cushion of air just a few nanometers above the surface of the platter. That distance is called the *floating height*. To put this in perspective, if the head were the size of an average two-story house that floated above the ground (and just try getting that to happen!), you wouldn't be able to slip a sheet of paper between the house and the ground.

In fact, in the event that the head and platter should come in contact with one another, this results in the infamous *head crash*. Head crashes are disastrous in that not only is the medium damaged; the head, and therefore the hard drive, will almost certainly be destroyed. There are two things that can cause a head crash. The most common is the irate user kicking a misbehaving computer. The impact of foot against computer while the disk is spinning kills the drive. A more uncommon cause is a piece of foreign material that somehow makes its way into the drive. Modern drives are so well sealed that this is an extremely rare event.

> ## BUZZ WORDS
>
> **Floating height:** The distance above a hard drive's platter that the R/W heads hover as the platter spins beneath.
>
> **Head crash:** A disastrous event caused by the R/W head in a drive coming into physical contact with the platter while it is spinning.
>
> **Voice coil:** An extremely fast and highly accurate motor that works by applying an electrical current to a tightly wrapped coil of wires surrounding, but not touching, a permanently magnetized cylinder. When current is applied to the coil, the cylinder rotates. Negative voltage rotates the cylinder one direction, positive the other. The amount of voltage determines how far the cylinder moves.

ACTUATOR ARMS AND THE ACTUATOR MECHANISM

R/W heads can't move themselves across the platter. They've got to ride on something, and that is the job of the actuator arm. As I've pointed out, each platter has two surfaces, and each surface needs its own R/W head. If you look at **Figure 12.4**, you will see how all the actuator arms are mounted in as a group. All platters are mounted to the same spindle. There is one pair of arms associated with each platter. When the controller needs to locate information on a different track, it directs the actuator arms to move the heads to that track.

In the old days, the same type of stepper motor I described in Chapter Eleven was used to control the actuator arms. Newer hard drives use a *voice coil*

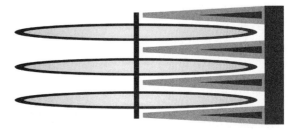

Figure 12.4 The actuator arms are responsible for getting the R/W heads where they need to be.

mechanism. This consists of a magnetic coil that moves the arm in a distance proportionate to how much energy is applied to the coil. It gets its name from the fact that this is the same technology that moves the diaphragm of a loudspeaker in a stereo system. The advantage of a voice coil mechanism is that it is more accurate and has few moving parts. Therefore, not only does it work better, it lasts longer.

A key reason manufacturers made the change from stepper motors to voice coils was because of how much data gets packed onto today's hard drives. I discussed earlier about the sectors on a hard drive being laid out in tracks. How much data can be squeezed onto a drive is directly related to the number of tracks per inch (TPI) the manufacturer can fit onto an individual platter. The first hard drives had only a couple of hundred TPI. Modern drives have now exceeded 28,000 TPI. Accurately positioning an R/W head over tracks that small would be impractical using a stepper motor.

The voice coil has no rigid steps over which it must move. Also, by providing some form of feedback mechanism, if the first attempt to position the head turns out to be inaccurate, a device called the servo dynamically repositions it in just a few milliseconds.

Head Parking

Earlier, I mentioned that the head floats on a microscopically thin layer of air above the spinning platter. I pointed out that if the head should come into contact with the platter, it would cause a head crash.

When you turn your PC off, and the platter stops spinning, that head is going to sit down on the platter no matter what you do. Manufacturers have accordingly created a *head parking* system, designing into the drive platters an area reserved solely for the purpose of providing the head a safe place to sit when the PC is not in operation. This is the *landing zone*. The location of the landing zone is one of the hard disk configuration settings of the BIOS. However, all modern hard drives are designed in such a way that the BIOS can automatically detect the necessary parameters.

In the early days of computer technology, it was up to the user to properly park the heads when the PC was powered down. MS-DOS had a head-parking utility just for that purpose. Fortunately for us, it has been many years since that's been necessary. Hard drives now automatically park themselves as part of their shutdown procedure. This is good, but IBM's approach is better.

It uses a process called load/unload. When a power-down is in process, the heads are lifted into the air. Instead of dropping the heads onto the surface of the platter, IBM drives slide the actuator arms onto a restraining mechanism, which prevents the heads from ever coming into contact with the platter.

Buzz Words

Head parking: A process of positioning R/W heads on a hard drive in a place where contact with the platter will do no harm.

Landing zone: An area on the hard disk's platter where the R/W heads can be safely parked.

HARD DRIVE PERFORMANCE AND I/O OPERATIONS

Manufacturers provide all kinds of specifications to show you just how fast their drives are and why they are so much better than the competition's. The specifications provided are indeed very valuable bits of information to use when selecting a drive. I will discuss in detail the most commonly advertised specs in detail. A important limitation of hard drive performance that is rarely, if ever, mentioned by hard drive manufacturers is the amount of time required to actually perform an I/O operation from beginning to end. But since I/O operations per second are a direct corollary of the basic specifications, I'll discuss those first.

ROTATIONAL SPEED

The easiest way to improve a hard drive's overall performance is to make it spin faster. In the next two sections I will be discussing the factors of latency and data transfer rate. Both of these are directly affected by how fast the disk is spinning.

Early disks spun at 4800rpm. However, recent technologies have pushed the limit to an amazing 15,000rpm. To put that in perspective, let's go back to the analogy of the R/W head being the size of a two-story house. I also said that if it were that large, the floating height was so minute, you wouldn't be able to fit a sheet of paper between the house and the ground. Now factor this into the equation. At 10,000rpm, the ground is moving beneath the house at a speed the equivalent of approximately 6000 miles per second!

Which brings us to one of the problems design engineers had to face when designing drives this fast. It is critical that the surface be as absolutely smooth as possible. Also, significantly more heat is generated by these drives, both from the more powerful motor and from friction, which needs to be dissipated. This is something that you need to consider when designing a system for yourself or a client. If you wish to use one of these faster drives, efficient cooling of the case isn't just an option. It's an absolute necessity. This is further exacerbated when several of these drives are used together for a drive array.

The impact of rotational speed on performance is rather critical. The faster a disk rotates, the faster the R/W heads can latch onto the first sector of data during a seek operation. Once data begins to be read from the surface of the disk, faster rotational speeds mean that data is moving beneath the heads that much faster. Therefore data transfer rates are improved as well.

AVERAGE ACCESS TIME

Frequently, manufacturers will advertise their average seek time. This is all fine and good, and it's a wonderful thing to know. However, average seek time is only half of the equation that yields average access time. *Average access time* is the time that

BUZZ WORDS ——————

Average access time: The amount of time required by a disk drive to lock on to the first sector that contains data requested by the controller.

Table 12.1   Average latency measurements based on rotational speed

Rotational Speed (rpm)	Rotations/sec	Milliseconds/ rotation	Latency
15,000	250	4ms	2ms
10,000	166.666	6ms	3ms
7,200	120	8.33ms	4.16ms
5,400	90	11.111ms	5.555ms
4,800	80	12.5ms	6.25ms

The impact of rotational speed is seen both in how many tracks per second can be read and in how long it takes to complete a single rotation.

elapses between a request for data and the instant that the first bit in information is picked up by the R/W head. The other half of the equation is the drive's latency.

Average seek time is a guess at how long it will take to move the R/W heads into position to lock onto the correct track. When the manufacturers make these measurements, they are based on moving the heads a distance equal to one third of the diameter of the platter. Obviously, if the actuator arm has to move from the first track to the last, this time will be longer. Conversely, if it is only moving from track one to track five, it will be much shorter. Still, this average provides a good comparison between two competing drives.

Latency is how long it takes for the R/W heads to lock onto the sector once the track has been located. This specification is calculated by taking rotational speed and calculating how much time one half of a complete rotation will take. Therefore a hard drive with a rotational speed of 10,000rpm will have a published latency of three milliseconds.

Of course, this is an inaccurate assessment of reality. Should the actuator arm lock onto the track a fraction of a rotation before the sector shoots past in its rotational path, it won't have time to lock onto the sector on that rotation. In effect, it would take in excess of a full rotation to actually locate the sector. **Table 12.1** compares rotational speed to latency.

Data Transfer Rate

Once the data has been located and begins to move from the surface of the platter, across the drive electronics, and finally into memory, the concept of data transfer rate (DTR) comes into play. As I mentioned earlier, this is directly affected by the rotational speed of the drive.

Unfortunately for the world of consumers, there are several different methods by which DTR is measured. Most commonly cited is *burst mode*. This is how fast data can move from the R/W head to the drive's buffer in a perfect world when the data is moving downhill with a tail wind. In other words, you're never going to see those speeds. You might see this listed as the *internal host transfer rate* as well. The *external host transfer rate* is a far more critical measurement, because this tells you how fast data gets moved from the controller to RAM.

Transfer rates are provided in megabytes per second (MB/s) ratings. In the next chapter, as I discuss the different interfaces hard drive use, I'll take a closer look at some of these ratings.

> **BUZZ WORDS** ─────────────
>
> **Burst mode:** The speed at which data moves from the R/W heads to a drive's buffer memory. Also known as internal host transfer rate.
>
> **Internal host transfer rate:** The speed at which data moves from the R/W heads to a drive's buffer memory. Also known as burst mode.
>
> **External host transfer rate:** How fast data moves from a drive's controller to RAM.

HARD DRIVE I/O OPERATIONS

Hard disk I/O operations result in one of the biggest bottlenecks of system performance, simply because of their complexity and how often they occur. When data that does not exist in memory is requested by the CPU, a very convoluted process begins in order to locate that data on the hard drive and transfer it to memory where it can be used. There are actually four steps to a hard drive I/O operation.

- *The Queuing Phase:* This is where all the commands required by the hard disk controller are issued and, when possible, lined up in the correct order for execution.
- *The Command Phase:* The commands are executed in the order in which they exist in the controller's cache memory.
- *The Access Phase:* The R/W heads locate and lock on to the first sector containing the requested data.
- *The Data Transfer Phase:* Data is copied from the surface of the drive, moved to the controller's cache RAM, and then to system RAM.

I/O OPERATIONS/SEC

After reading the previous section, it should be obvious that the number of clock cycles for a single I/O operation can be quite substantial. And remember that transferring even a small file may result in multiple I/O operations. When files get fragmented on the hard disk, they require multiple I/O operations. This is the key reason a badly fragmented disk hurts system performance so badly. **Table 12.2** summarizes I/O operations, providing a crude estimate of how long transferring a single burst of data can actually take.

Table 12.2 Estimating I/O Operations Per Second

I/O Phase	Est. Time (ms)	Est. Time (cc)[1]	Total CC Elapsed
Queuing Phase	30 to10,000[2]	30,000 to 10,000,000	30,000 to 10,000,000
Command Phase	.001 to .003	1 to 3	30,001 to 10,000,003
Access Phase[3]	14.2ms	14,200	44,201 to 10,014,203

Hard Drive I/O operations of a typical 7200rpm hard drive

[1] CC = clock cycles: based on a 100MHz front-side bus
[2] Time required for the queuing phase is dependant on the number of commands required to perform a specific I/O request.
[3] Access phase is one of the few delays you'll see published in the manufacturer's specs. This shows up as average access time.

DATA ENCODING MECHANISMS

The data that is stored on your hard drive isn't really data at all. You can't put a hard drive platter under a microscope and read off the zeros and ones stored there. The information is encoded into patterns of magnetically charged particles. The controller coverts a digital signal into electronic pulses which, in turn, magnetize the metal or metal-oxide particles on the platter. When the heads read data back, it is their task to interpret the pattern of charged particles and convert the magnetic fluxes into an electrical signal the controller can turn back into data. This is all part of the *data encoding mechanism*. All devices need some encoding mechanism.

> **BUZZ WORDS**
>
> **Data encoding mechanism:** The method used by a device to convert digital information into an electronic format recognizable by the target device.
>
> **Flux reversal:** A transition of magnetic charge from a positive to a negative state, or vice versa.

Binary data moves across the bus as positive and negative electrical charges. Moving from a positive to a negative state is known as a *flux reversal.* The hard drive has a chip on board known as the encoder-decoder (ENDEC) that has the job of taking these digital waveforms and converting them into electrical signals that get sent to the R/W heads. The heads apply the magnetic charges to the media surface. A single bit of data requires tens of thousands of molecules of media to create one of the bit cells discussed earlier

One of the limiting factors that determine the maximum capacity of a hard drive is how many times it is possible to change the magnetic polarity of individual particles in a square inch of drive surface. If the polarity changes overlap, they will impact on one another. Try this little experiment. Take two magnets and some iron filings. Sprinkle the iron filings onto a sheet of paper and put one of the magnets underneath the paper and watch the pattern that the filings assume. I'm sure you did this in grade school at some time or the other. Now take the other magnet and place it alongside the first magnet under the paper. Watch what happens to the filings. Rotate one of the magnets 180 degrees and see how this affects your little patterns. The closer you move the magnets to one another, the greater the confusion.

This is pretty close to what is going on when the R/W heads apply flux reversals to the media surface, except on a submicroscopic level. If the charged particles are too close to one another, the integrity of your data can be affected.

Another thing that can impact data integrity is the synchronization between the read heads and the write heads. In order to make sure that data is read back in exactly the same way as it was recorded, an accurate timing mechanism must be employed to assure synchronization. Then all read and write heads on the drive march to that same beat.

As data is written to the drive, it goes down in a series of electrical pulses that create transition cells. A *transition cell* is the minimum number of particles that can be affected by a single magnetic flux. Now if all data alternated evenly between zeros (-) and ones (+), then on playback, the data would look like -+-+-+-+ and there would be no issues. However, that would be like having a dictionary that read ABABABABABABAB from beginning to end. It wouldn't be interesting, informative, or accurate. In other words, it would be useless.

Real data will have varying numbers of zeros and ones clumped together. Therefore, the R/W head will encounter varying amounts of time in which is sees nothing but negative polarity, followed by equally varying amounts of time in which it sees nothing but positive polarity. Without a clocking mechanism in place it would appear to the controller as a -+-+-+ pattern, except that individual bits would take up widely varying amounts of hard drive space.

The clock ticks off read/write intervals. If eight zeros in a row come down the pipe, the clock counts off eight transition cells for the write head to mark down. When the read head comes along to read that data back, the clock will tick though the transition cells, and the read head will find eight zeros. It is critical that clock mechanisms be incredibly accurate. If, for any reason, the read heads were out of synch with the write heads, the results would be disastrous. **Figure 12.5** shows you what would happen. The arrows represent individual ticks of the clock. The square waves in the top half of the diagram represent positive and negative magnetic pulses. Since this is an analog electrical event, a timing mechanism needs to be in place to assure that consecutive identical bits are properly read. In order to have the system accurately interpret the magnetized surface as encoded data, read and write operations must be synchronized. If the clock ticks off four cycles while applying a negative pulse (rendering four zeros), and on the read cycle, it ticks off five cycles (rendering five zeros) all the data from that point forward will be corrupt.

The encoding mechanism determines how binary data is converted into charged particles, and then when read back, how the charged particles tell the controller to create a binary signal. The two encoding mechanisms used over the years have been modified frequency modulation (MFM) and run length limited (RLL).

MFM

MFM was one of the first methods of data encoding used in hard disk drives. An earlier method of simple frequency modulation continues to be used on floppy drives, but has never been used

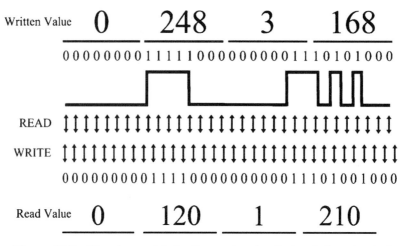

Figure 12.5   Were is possible for the read and write heads to get out of synch with one another, the results would be disastrous.

on hard drives. Using simple frequency modulation, each bit of data stored on the drive is generated by an individual flux reversal. A graphics image that sent 5000 ones in a row would send across 5000 flux reversals. For each bit, a separate clock transition would be recorded along with the bit of data.

MFM minimized the usage of clock transitions by only requiring one when a zero was preceded by another zero. That reduced the amount of physical space on the platter that was being used by timing information, and made more room available for data. Since less timing data was being generated, the clock frequency could be doubled. In other words, twice as many bits of data could be stored to surface medium per flux transition.

Many books on the subject include MFM as a form of interface. This is not entirely inaccurate, nor is it entirely accurate. MFM is an encoding mechanism, not an interface. However, it requires its own separate interface. The controller that reads and writes data based on MFM encoding will work with no other device. Therefore, the MFM controller could effectively be considered to be the MFM interface.

RLL

RLL encoding is a far more efficient means of encoding large amounts of data. Because of this, it is the method used by virtually all hard drives manufactured over the course of about twenty years. Instead of encoding and decoding data a bit at a time, it takes a cluster of data and encodes it all at once. A single flux transition can write a large block of data.

Two parameters are used to define RLL sequences. Those are run length and run limit. A run is simply the number of clock cycles (of the hard drive's controller) that data can be written to the drive without a flux reversal. The run limit represents the maximum number of bits the controller would allow to be written in a single flux without embedding a clock signal. The run length is the actual number of bits written.

Since data is moved in blocks, rather than a bit at a time, the timing that I discussed earlier is easier to maintain. Also, since there are significantly fewer clock transitions that needed to be recorded, much greater data densities were made possible. All else being equal, an RLL drive can hold twice as much data as an MFM drive using exactly the same medium.

> **BUZZ WORDS** ───────────
>
> **Areal density:** The total amount of storage capacity for a specific unit of area on the surface of the drive platter.
>
> **File system:** The mechanism used by a hard drive to map the specific sectors used by any given file.

PRML AND EPRML

Even RLL imposed some severe limitations on the amount of data that could be stored on the hard drive. Recent disk drives have been manufactured using an encoding mechanism called partial response/maximum likelihood (PRML). PRML doesn't try to read every single flux reversal that occurs. Instead, it uses a very sophisticated digital sampling algorithm. The electrical signal that is generated by the reading of magnetic impulses on the surface of the drive is scanned and samples of that signal are taken at precisely timed intervals. This is the "partial response" half of the equation. The controller then calculates the most likely sequence of bits that would occur as a result of those samples. That is the "maximum likelihood."

Doesn't sound very accurate, does it? The fact is, bit errors from this method are only one in every several trillion bits read. And because PRML permits up to thirty-five percent more storage capacity per platter (or *areal density*, as it's called) without changing the formulation of the medium, it is a logical choice for high-capacity drives.

Extended PRML (EPRML) works in exactly the same manner. However, improvements in the algorithms used and in the circuitry employed allow for faster write operations as well as faster reads. In addition it substantially increases areal density over that of PRML. This has been the method used for the last couple of generations of hard drives.

FILE SYSTEMS

Now that I've discussed the basics of how information is stored on a magnetic disk, it is time to take a look at how the computer manages how it's stored. The writing of data is complex enough, but before the drive can read that data back later on down the road, there needs to be some way of locating that information. This is the function of the file system.

The *file system* is a direct function of the operating system. As such, the OS a user chooses affects many different functions of the computer system. Many of the functions impacted are under the control of the file system. For example, these days, most people take it for granted that they can name a file My Business Proposal.doc and every computer of every user who will access that document can read it. Most people don't even realize that prior to 1995, most operating systems would have returned a message along the lines of "invalid file name" if a user attempted to use such a name.

OS Versus FS

Most operating systems these days support multiple file systems. A problem that is occasionally encountered is that a file system supported by one OS may or may not be supported by another OS. Over a network, this isn't a problem. But it is something that must be considered if you are attempting to configure a computer to dual-boot. Dual-booting consists of installing two or more different operating systems and allowing the user to select which OS to use when he or she starts the machine.

For the most part, a discussion of file systems is more appropriate in a book on operating systems. I consider this to be an area of understanding that is critical to the hardware technician, though, and therefore am including it in this book. The file systems I will discuss in depth will be the File Allocation Table (FAT) system and New Technology File System (NTFS). Another file system not frequently seen today is High Performance File System (HPFS). Even though not as common, it is worth taking a brief look. Your CD-ROM drive uses its own file system known as Compact Disk File System (CDFS), which I will take a closer look at in Chapter Sixteen, Multimedia. Users of Linux and Unix make use of the Unix File System, which is completely incompatible with any of the FAT-based systems.

FAT

File Allocation Table, or FAT as I'll call it from here, was the original file system used by the first IBM-compatible PCs. It works by creating a database of entries that the operating system uses to find data on the hard drive. In fact, two different copies of that database are maintained. If you read some of the articles out of the popular press, you might think that there are only two versions of FAT: FAT16 and FAT32. You would, of course, be wrong. The first version of FAT was FAT12. The numbers represented in these different versions of FAT indicate how many bits are allocated to the binary number that identified individual clusters. In other words, FAT12 uses a 12-bit number, FAT16 makes use of a 16-bit number, and not surprisingly, FAT32 allows for a 32-bit number. Obviously, the more bits used to create the number, the more numbers the file system can generate. It also dictates cluster sizes and the maximum size of volume that was possible using a particular system. **Table 12.3** lists the various versions of FAT and how they differed.

FAT17 FAT12 has lived a long and healthy life as a file system. It continues to be used on floppy disks and on very small partitions. Both FAT16 and FAT32 have no trouble reading and writing to FAT12 partitions.

FAT16 FAT16, for the longest time, was the file system of choice for nearly every computer in use. It allowed for partitions of up to 2GB, which at the time was considered to be unthinkably large. Four different primary partitions could be maintained on a single physical drive, allowing the user to create multiple logical drives or to install more than one OS on a single machine. If you were to open the FAT with a disk-editing tool (and I highly recommend you **not** do this unless you are either extremely capable, extremely careful not to edit anything, or have a strong desire to reformat your hard drive), you would see a list of every cluster on your

Table 12.3 Comparison of FAT Systems

File System	Size of FAT Entry	Range of Cluster Sizes	Max Clusters	Max Volume Size
FAT12	12 bits	.5K to 4K	4,086	16,736,256 bytes
FAT16	16 bits	2K to 32K	65,526	2,147,123,200 bytes
FAT32	28 bits[1]	4KB to 32KB	268,435,456	~2 terabytes[2]

The differences among the versions of FAT are clear.

[1] While the actual entry for FAT32 is 32 bits, 4 bits are reserved for OS use and not used for generating cluster numbers.
[2] Roughly 2 terabytes is the theoretical limit to volume size in FAT32. However, limitations in the file allocation tables prevent drives from reaching this size under current technology.

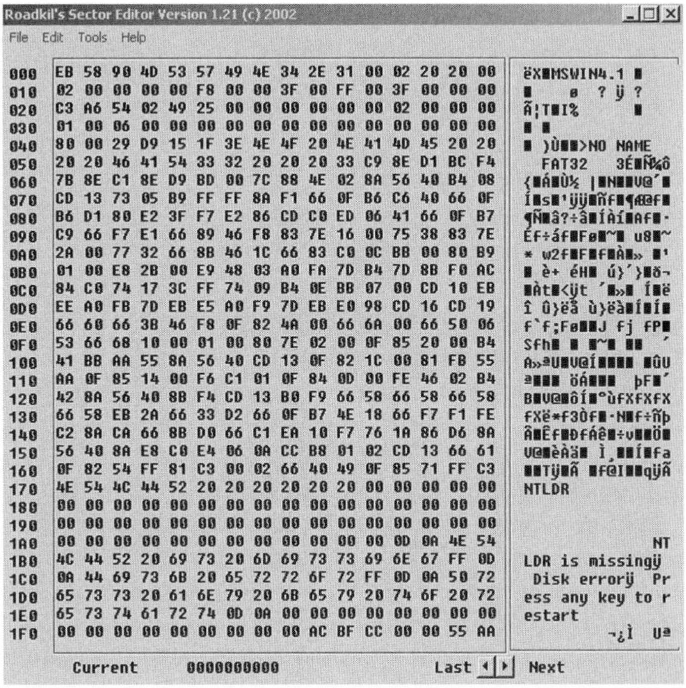

Figure 12.6 A disk editor is a tool that allows an experienced user to modify the contents of a drive, including areas normally not accessible by the user.

hard drive, like the one shown in **Figure 12.6**. Of course, it wouldn't look much like a list to you, since it would consist of a bunch of binary code all run together. But each entry would contain certain information that allows the OS to find every cluster that hold data for that file. This information includes the following:

- A designation whether the cluster is in use or not
- A point to the next cluster that contains data owned by that particular file
- A marker preventing it from being used if it has been marked bad

FAT16 is limited to a total of 512 entries in the root directory. This is due to a physical limitation of FAT16. The root directory has to start in the first sector immediately following the file allocation tables. Therefore, in order to make certain that the drive is efficiently used, the concept of directories was brought into play. As far as FAT is concerned, a directory is just another file. To allow the OS to distinguish between files and directories, FAT places a special marker in each directory. Directory entries contain information that directs the OS to the files or subdirectories that reside within it.

- 11 bytes identifying the name of the file or directory
- 8 bits defining the attributes of the file or directory
- 24 bits identifying the time the file was created
- 16 bits identifying the date the file was created
- 16 bits showing the last date on which the file was accessed
- 16 bits showing the time the file was last modified
- 16 bits showing the date the file was last modified
- 16 bits indicating the first cluster number occupied by the entry
- 32 bits indicating the size of the entry

I pointed out earlier that the hard drive's most basic element of storage is the sector. I also told you that hard drives no longer read single sectors, but rather file allocation units (FAUs) or clusters. FAT16 is not terribly efficient in its use of clusters. The larger the partition, the greater the number of sectors required to make a cluster. This is, of course, true of all file systems. It is simply more noticeable with FAT16.

The *cluster* is the smallest element into which the hard drive can actually store a file. As you can see in Table 12.4, the smallest cluster used by FAT16 is 2K. What that means is that no matter how small a file might be, it will occupy a minimum of 2K of hard drive space. An example of this is the Windows icon. Those little pictures you see floating on your desktop are frequently less than 800 bytes. However, since they are individual files, each one of them eats up an entire 2K cluster. And the larger the partition, the more sectors, and therefore the more hard drive space you will need for individual files. **Table 12.4** details the cluster sizes used by FAT16 with the different partition sizes it supports.

As you can see, when you start to get up into those larger partitions (as far as FAT16 is concerned, anyway), those clusters start to get really big. Let me give you an example of how this can impact your system.

Buzz Words

Cluster: The minimum number of sectors a specific file system can recognize as a single data unit. Another term for file allocation unit (FAU).

Table 12.4 FAT16 File Allocation Unit Size by Partition Size

Partition Size	FAT Type	Cluster Size
16MB to 128MB	12-bit	4 Sectors (Appx. 2K)
128MB to 256MB	16-bit	8 Sectors (Appx. 4K)
256K to 512K	16-bit	16 Sectors (Appx. 8K)
512K to 1GB	16-bit	32 Sectors (Appx. 16K)
1GB to 2GB	16-bit	64 Sectors (Appx. 32K)

Partition sizes and cluster sizes for FAT16

There is a CD I've seen in some of the discount bins that has 10,000 different Windows icons. As I mentioned before, a Windows icon is a very small file, as little as 800 bytes. Now what would happen if you had a 2GB hard drive partitioned to FAT16? As you see in Table 12.4, that 2GB partition is going to use clusters of 64 sectors, or 32K. That means that each and every one of those icons is going to take up 32K of space when you copy it to your hard drive, because each of them constitutes an individual file. One file equals one cluster. That's the rule.

Now if you look at the description of the files without knowing how FAT works, here is what you might think. There are 10,000 files of 800 bytes each. 10,000 × 800 = 8,000,000. Therefore, it's only going to require 8MB of hard drive space to store all of those files, right? As you can guess, it's not going to work that way. Since each cluster is 32K, it doesn't matter how small the file is. It needs its own cluster. Copying 10,000 icon files to the hard drive will require approximately 320MB of space.

FAT16 is also limited in the way it handles file names. It uses what is called the 8.3 file naming convention. This means that the file name can have eight characters, followed by a three-character extension. The extension is frequently used by applications to identify what kind of file it is. For example, a file with a .doc extension is a document file. Word processing programs know they can open this kind of file. Files that end in .txt are ASCII text files (usually). Programmers might create their own extensions for the particular data file created by their program. Microsoft's Excel uses an .xls extension. The file name itself can be anything you want it to be, as long as it is only eight characters long.

FAT32 FAT32 overcame a lot of these limitations. To start with, the root directory can be stored anywhere the operating system wants to store it, and it is not limited to a single sector. Therefore, the limitation of 512 entries to the root directory disappears. Each entry is also 32 bits wide, rather than the 16 bits of FAT16. Since there can be a lot more entries, and each entry is twice as large, the file allocation tables have the potential to be much larger in FAT32.

The master boot record (MBR) that I will discuss in detail later in this chapter was expanded from a single sector to two sectors in FAT32. This allows for extended BIOS information to be stored in this section.

Table 12.5 FAT32 File Allocation Unit Size by Partition Size

Partition Size	FAT Type	Cluster Size
<512MB-8GB	8 sectors	4K
8-16GB	16 sectors	8K
16-32GB	32 sectors	16K
32-2048GB	64 sectors	32K

FAT32 makes far more efficient use of hard drive space than previous file systems.

FAT32 supports long file names (LFN) as well. Instead of being limited to eight-character file names, the file name (including extension) can be up to 254 characters long. LFN will be discussed in detail in the next section.

As with FAT16, FAT32 uses different sized clusters as partition sizes increased. However, the 32-bit structure of the file system allows for much larger partitions to be created with each level of cluster. **Table 12.5** shows the effect of partition size on cluster size when using FAT32.

As you can see, FAT32 makes much more efficient use of hard drive space than does FAT16. If you want to store those 10,000 icons using FAT32, and your partition is 8GB or smaller, you will only eat up about 40MB of space.

NTFS

Users of Microsoft's Windows NT 4.0 or 2000 operating systems have the option of using the New Technology File System (NTFS). This is one of the more powerful file systems available today. There are some compatibility issues that you should be aware of. A FAT32 system cannot read NTFS files stored in the same system. Likewise, NTFS version 4.0 can't read FAT32 files. Version 5.0 can. As of this writing, there is an installable file system for Linux users that supports read-only capabilities for NTFS, but by the time you're reading this, that has probably been improved.

NTFS isn't simply a list of entries. It acts as a relational database of information and can provide far more than simply the location at which the data is stored. It allows for incredibly large volumes. It also allows for security to be imposed on specific files. This allows the operating system and those with permissions to administer the OS to allow or disallow access to files to specific users on an individual basis. In addition, it can generate a message log indicating successes and failures of accessing those files.

One unique talent possessed by NTFS is the ability to compress and decompress individual files on the fly (**Figure 12.7**). Compression allows the file to occupy far less hard drive space in storage than when in use. With some earlier compression techniques, there was always a danger of data corruption. Fortunately, with NTFS, compression and decompression don't carry that risk.

As far back as MS-DOS, computers had the ability to compress the contents of a hard drive and then have the OS decompress the files as they were used. This, however, was an all-or-none undertaking. You either compressed the whole drive, or nothing at all.

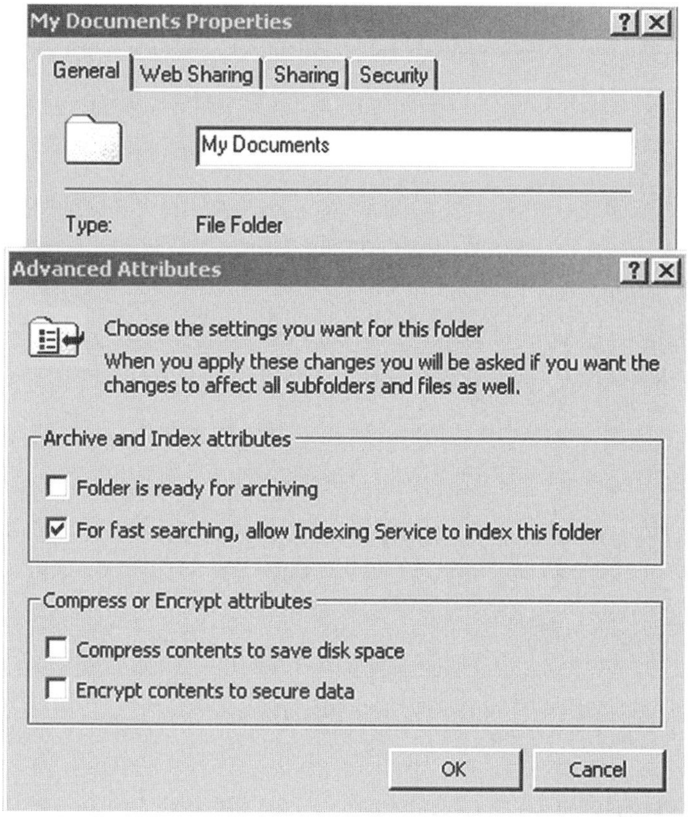

Figure 12.7 NTFS allows the user to individually compress or encrypt files on the fly.

With NTFS, you can compress individual files or directories on an as-needed basis. Files that are only infrequently used can be compressed for storage. Some types of files, especially graphics and audio files, are well suited for compression. A typical graphics file can be squeezed down to a fraction of its original size.

NTFS is also capable of using much smaller cluster sizes than FAT systems. Small NTFS partitions can read individual sectors. Yet, like FAT32, NTFS is capable of very large partitions and long file names. **Table 12.6** shows relative partition information for NTFS.

The versions of NTFS used with NT 4.0 and Windows 2000 are not the same. Windows 2000 uses a newer version. NTFS version 5.0 adds a few new bells and whistles that version 4 didn't support. It can handle the same functions as version 4, including individual file and folder security settings and compression. But in addition, it can also allow an administrator to set drive usage limits for individual users.

The newer version of NTFS also supports the Encryptable File System (EFS). The user is able to take files and render them unreadable to anyone who doesn't possess the decryption key. In order the make sure that hostile departing employees don't encrypt the entire system before

Table 12.6 NTFS File Allocation Unit Size by Partition Size

Partition Size	Number of Sectors/Cluster	Cluster Size
0–260MB	1 sector	512 bytes
261MB–8GB	8 sectors	4K
8–16GB	16 sectors	8K
16–32GB	32 sectors	16K
32–2048GB	64 sectors	32K

NTFS is very similar to FAT32 in terms of disk space usage, except for the fact that very small partitions can recognize a single sector as an FAU.

they move over to your competitors, Microsoft requires that there be an assigned EFS Recovery Agent delegated, or the process does not work. An EFS Recovery Agent has the necessary permissions to import and export encryption keys, so that the data can be recovered even if the employee is unable or unwilling to do it for you.

This new NTFS also has something called the Distributed File System (DFS) built into it. This actually isn't new to NTFS 5.0. It was available to NTFS 4.0 as an installable file system add-on. With 5.0, however, it's integrated into the file system. DFS allows an administrator to build up a collection of links to various resources, wherever they might happen to reside on the network, and locate them all in a singular server. Users can then browse to those links without having to know the location of the actual files. DFS finds the files for them.

HPFS

IBM and Microsoft actually worked together to design the High Performance File System for the OS/2 operating system. At the time this file system was released, the two companies were working together to co-develop an operating system that could compete with the Macintosh graphical interface. They were looking for a file system that was a little more user-friendly than FAT16, and might provide a little more horsepower.

It was the first of the PC-compatible file systems to support long file names. It also allowed for non-case-sensitive file names. If you named a file My Novel.doc, it would actually find your file even if you looked for my NoveL.doc. This was an improvement over HPFS's primary competitor, the Unix File System, which is case sensitive. It was pretty much everything that NTFS would eventually become (not surprising, since Microsoft co-developed it), but had a few minor issues.

It was incompatible with FAT. Installed onto a dual-boot system with OS/2, an MS-DOS or Windows system could not read the files from the HPFS. HPFS could read FAT, but not the other way around. A bigger problem with versions of MS-DOS prior to 4.01 was that MS-DOS couldn't see even FAT drives that existed downstream from an HPFS drive. For example, if you installed DOS onto drive C, and then OS/2 onto drive D using HPFS, drives E, F, and later couldn't be seen by MS-DOS, no matter what file system they used.

With MS-DOS 4.01 and later, you could see the FAT drives, but there was an additional problem. Since DOS couldn't see the HPFS drive, it effectively didn't exist. Therefore, in the system described above, under HPFS, drive C was MS-DOS, drive D was OS/2, and drives E, F, and later were whatever they happened to be. That same machine, booted to MS-DOS saw drive C, ignored the HPFS drive, and made the next drive it could see drive D. If drive E happened to be HPFS, then the next drive MS-DOS could see would be drive D. To HPFS, that same drive would be drive F. This played havoc on organization.

How did this affect your floppy drives? Not much, actually. By default, HPFS doesn't support removable media. Nobody has ever really considered the floppy disk drive to be a high performance device. Therefore only FAT12 is used with floppy drives. All other file systems can read it.

THE UNIX FILE SYSTEM

If you are reading this book specifically for the purpose of preparing for the A+ Core Exam, it is unlikely that you will get any questions relating to this file system. Still, there are a lot of computers out there in the real world that make use of the Unix operating system, and unless you know the basics of the file system used you're going to flounder like a duck on an oil slick.

The Unix File System (UFS) uses a tree structure for sorting directories, subdirectories, and individual files. In fact, I think it's safe to say that other OSs emulated Unix in this manner. With Unix, the root directory is represented by a single /. Beneath the root are several subdirectories. The most common subdirectories seen on a Unix system are as follows:

- */bin:* Commands and directories needed by the user
- */dev:* Files used to represent specific devices, either installed on the system or remotely connected
- */etc:* Commands and utilities used for system administration
- */lib:* Libraries used by various programs or programming languages
- */tmp:* Temporary files
- */usr:* Subdivided into subdirectories; includes the games that ship with Unix and the home directory for each user created on the system
- */Kernel File:* Home of the Unix operating system files

UFS breaks the hard drive down into *blocks*. Depending on the version of Unix being used, blocks will consist of one, two, or four sectors. Data is stored in the blocks.

The file system can be broken down into four distinct components: the boot block, the Super block, the i-node list, and the data blocks. The boot block

BUZZ WORDS

Block: The number of sectors on a hard drive that UFS uses as the smallest recognizable data unit.

contains the information needed to initialize the operating system from a cold start. The Super block defines the state of the file system. This would include such information as how many files are already stored, how much available space remains on the device, and permissions associated with the device. The i-node list, usually simply referred to as the i-list, keeps track of the locations of individual files stored on the device. And, as you might imagine, the data blocks are where the data is actually stored.

By default Unix is a network operating system. As such, it must support the ability to service multiple users at once. One of the methods it uses to accomplish this is to assign users their own home directories in the /usr directory. When a user logs onto the system, he or she is automatically directed to the home directory. Unix uses a different method of accessing files than the file systems I discussed earlier in the chapter. Instead of a file system table that maps out specific FAUs on the hard drive, Unix provides a unique file system for each user. The OS opens a separate instance of a root file system for each new user who logs on.

The i-list keeps track of the file systems that are mounted at any given time. The i-list is nothing more than a fixed memory location that contains a list of entries for each file system mounted. For each file system an i-node is generated. It is the i-node that contains the information used by UFS to locate files on the physical storage device. Each i-node can contain up to ten pointers. A *pointer* is a line of code that maps to a specific block. Each i-node can also contain one indirect pointer, one double-indirect pointer, and one triple-indirect pointer. An indirect pointer maps points to a cluster of pointers.

The ten pointers of an i-node can basically define a 5KB file. For a file larger than 5KB, an indirect pointer maps to a storage block that stores a table of additional block pointers. If an earlier version of Unix is installed, a block points to a single sector of 512 bytes. A pointer uses 4 bytes. Therefore, a table could contain 128 pointers. A 1024-byte block could contain 256 pointers and a 2048-byte block could contain 512. For the purposes of this discussion, I will stick to the 512-byte block. An indirect pointer adds 128 pointers per block, which would allow the system to manage a 64KB file.

Once file size exceeds 64KB a double-indirect pointer will be employed. A double-indirect pointer maintains a table of locations to up to 128 indirect pointers. Since an indirect pointer can map up to 64KB of storage space, a double-indirect pointer would map up to $128 \times 64KB$, or 8MB.

For files larger than 8MB, the system needs to make use of the services of the triple-indirect pointer. The triple-indirect pointer maps to 128 double-indirect pointers. This allows the UFS to support files up to a gigabyte in size.

As I mentioned earlier, the more recent versions of Unix make use of 2KB blocks. This means each block can contain up to 512 pointers. As a result, UFS can theoretically support up to 64GB files. However, a field contained in the i-node that defines file size is only 4 bytes long. This imposes a 4GB limitation on file size.

Other information stored in each i-node includes the following:

■   *File owner ID:* A number generated by the OS that is used by the security file to identify the specific user on the system who created the file.

- *Group ID:* This identifies a group of users that can be granted specific levels of access by the owner.
- *File type:* Files can be listed as any one of several file types. Among these are:
  - Regular file: a conventional data file
  - D file (directory file): a file that contains file names and their associated i-node numbers
  - L file (symbolic link file): a file that contains the path information needed to access a file
  - C file (character special file): a file that is intended to be accessed one character at a time. The file associated to your keyboard would be an example of a character file.
  - B file (block special file): a file that is accessed a block at a time. The file associated to your monitor is an example of a block special file.
  - P file (pipe file): A file associated to a device that streams data into a system, such as a modem or network card. This type of file is usually required by any device that needs to buffer data.
- *File access permissions:* There are three sets of permissions. User access is automatically granted to the person that owns the file. This is generally the creator, unless someone with administrative privileges has taken ownership. Group access is restricted access granted to any member of a specified group. Other access consists of whatever level of access has been granted to anyone not recognized by user or group access lists. Permissions come in three types as well. Read access allows a user to inspect the data stored in the file, but that user can make no changes or delete the file. Write access allows the user to make changes to the file. Execute access allows the user to run any executable code contained within the file.

An i-node can also keep track of various access times, including the following:

- *File access time:* This indicates when the file data last opened by the system. Events that will change this value include the following:
  - Displaying the contents of the file
  - Copying the file to a new location or file system
  - Editing the file

  These events will **not** change this value:
  - Moving the file to another directory in the current file system
  - Using redirection to append data to an existing file
- *File modification time:* This indicates when data contained within the file was last changed. Events that will affect this value include the following:
  - Creating the file initializes the value.
  - Editing a file and saving it will update this value.
  - Overwriting the file with new data will update this value.
  - Appending data to an existing file will update this value.

■ *I-node modification time:* This value shows when information in the i-node was last changed. Events that alter this value include the following:

    ■ Creating additional hard links to the file

    ■ Changes in file size

THE MASTER BOOT RECORD

In Chapter Five, Motherboards, BIOS, and the Chipset, I discussed in some detail the process of POST. I noted that the bootstrap loader locates and runs the Master Boot Record (MBR). The exact content of the MBR varies among operating systems, but the functionality remains the same. For the purposes of this discussion, I will use the FAT16 MBR used by MS-DOS.

In DOS, the MBR consisted of a single sector that held all of the information I will discuss throughout the rest of this section. This sector is located at Cylinder 0, Head 0, Sector 1 of the hard drive. In FAT16, that was the only place the MBR could be located. On the outset, this may seem to contradict what I said earlier about the hard drive reading clusters rather than sectors. Keep in mind, however, that this early in the boot process the file system has yet to be defined. In fact, it is this MBR that defines the file system. System BIOS reads sectors. Therefore, programmers had to fit all that information onto a single sector. One of the advances of different 32-bit file systems was that they could extend the MBR to two sectors, rather than just one.

The information stored on the MBR (see **Table 12.7**) tells the system several things. It defines the file system to be used. This is a string of executable code that once run, remains resident in memory. This code tells the computer which file system you chose when you first prepared your hard drive. This code is added to the MBR during the FDISK process in MS-DOS and Windows or by similar third-party utilities.

Table 12.7 Contents of the MBR

Process	Size of Process	Location on Drive
Boot Code (Defines file system and boots computer)	446 bytes	000h
First Partition Table	16 bytes	1BEh
Second Partition Table	16 bytes	1CEh
Third Partition Table	16 bytes	1DEh
Fourth Partition Table	16 bytes	1EEh
Executable Marker	2 bytes	1FEh

The MBR contains several specific pieces of information that the system requires in order to boot.

Next come the partition tables. If desired, a user can subdivide the available space on a disk into multiple logical sections called *partitions*. To the user, each partition appears as a separate hard disk, or *logical drive*.

Partition tables contain 16-byte blocks of data for each partition that exists on the hard drive. 16 bytes doesn't sound like a lot, but as you can see in **Table 12.8**, it manages to do a lot. A FAT16-formatted drive could contain up to four partition entries. The first would be the primary partition for that drive while the subsequent partitions will be extended partitions. There could be additional logical drive entries because each of the extended partitions contains an entry similar to the MBR called the volume boot record (VBR). The VBR is not limited to one sector and therefore can define as many logical drives as the user chooses to configure.

Following the partition tables is a marker that indicates the location of the first lines of executable code for the operating system. This is the *executable marker*, and it is only a 2-byte entry in MS-DOS.

> **BUZZ WORDS** ——————
>
> **Partition:** Logical sections on a hard disk that divide the overall disk space into multiple logical drives.
>
> **Logical drive:** A section of disk space isolated from the rest of the same physical disk so that it appears to the user as a separate disk drive.
>
> **Executable marker:** A pointer in the MBR that directs the boot sequence to the first line of code for the primary kernel file of the OS installed.

Table 12.8 Contents of a Partition Table (First Primary Partition)

Process	Size of Process	Location on Drive
Partition State (active/inactive)	1 byte	00h
Begin Partition (which head)	1 byte	01h
Begin Partition (cylinder/sector)	2 bytes	02h
Partition Type	1 byte	04h
End Partition (which head)	1 byte	05h
End Partition (cylinder/sector)	2 bytes	06h
Sectors between MBR and Partition	4 bytes	08h
Number of Sectors in Partition	4 bytes	0Ch

Relative location of data for 2nd, 3rd, and 4th partitions is offset by 16 bytes from these positions.

The reason boot sector viruses are so dangerous is that, as you can see from this table, changing just a single bit of data can make it impossible for the hard disk controller to accurately locate a partition.

FILE ALLOCATION TABLES

Once the file system has been loaded, the drive will now be read in clusters rather than individual sectors. The FAT occupies the sectors of the hard drive directly following the MBR. FAT16 generated two different copies of the tables, while FAT32 generates four. The purpose of the FAT is to identify the locations of all clusters that contain data for a specific file. Every single cluster on the drive is assigned a FAT entry, whether it initially contains data or not.

Each FAT entry will consist of a 16-bit entry (hence the name FAT16) that defines the usage of that particular cluster. That entry will have certain information telling the system whether or not there is data in the cluster, if the cluster has been marked bad, and if another cluster elsewhere also holds data relevant to that file. If so, the directory table will point the direction to the next cluster for that file. **Table 12.9** details the possible entries that would describe a cluster.

The directory tables and the file allocation tables are not the same thing. The *directory table* maintains a list of file names and all of the information associated with those files that lets the operating system know how to deal with them. Each file name takes up eight bits, the extension another three bits. *Directory attribute* information is stored in a single bit and will include such information as whether the file is hidden, or read only, whether it has been archived or not, and whether it constitutes a system file or not. A subdirectory is treated as if it is a file by the directory tables, except that it is assigned a directory attribute.

In addition to attribute information, the directory tables store information that tells the system the time and date that the file was created, what cluster to go to, and finally, the overall size of the file. This last bit of information sends the disk controller back to FAT to look up

Table 12.9 Defining Clusters

FAT Entry (range)	Definition
0000h	Cluster is empty.
0002h-FFEFh	Cluster is used; points to next cluster in file.
FFF0h-FFF6h	Cluster is reserved.
FFF7h	Cluster is marked "bad."
FFF8h-FFFFh	Cluster is used and is the last cluster in file. This is the End of File Marker.

The entries in the FAT have specific functions.

the next cluster in that file, if the End of File (EOF) marker has not been reached. The original FAT16 file system provided for a 32-bit entry for each file or directory, yet only made use of 22 bytes. The layout of a typical directory entry is detailed in **Table 12.10**.

When manufacturers made the move to FAT32, they opened up the possibility of those long file names I discussed earlier. The file allocation tables not only have to deal with much longer file names, but also create an 8.3 file name compatible with older applications. With FAT32, those 8.3 entries were redesigned to make use of all 32 bits available to the entry. This allowed the directory table to provide additional information, including far more refined time and date information, as well as the ability to tell when the file was last accessed and not simply when it was created.

Table 12.10 FAT16 Directory Table Entries

Table Entry Value	Size of Entry
File Name	8 bytes
File Extension	3 bytes
File Attribute	1 byte
Time	2 bytes
Date	2 bytes
Cluster Location	2 bytes
File Size	4 bytes

A listing of the functions in a file table entry for FAT16

CHAPTER SUMMARY

This chapter introduced you to the technology behind hard drives. As with most of the chapters of this book, I provided far more detail than is required simply to pass the A+ Exam. I discussed how hard drives are made and covered some of the key components of the hard drive. I also introduced you to some of the different file systems that have been used, past and present.

As hard drives evolve, so must file systems, system BIOS, and the operating systems. As you will see in the next chapter, hard drives haven't always been the humongous high-speed devices you enjoy today.

BRAIN DRAIN

1. Describe how CHS defines the capacity of a hard drive.

2. List as many critical components of a hard drive as you can think of and describe their function.

3. Describe how data is stored to a hard disk and then subsequently read back.

4. Describe the MBR of FAT16.

5. In as much detail as you can, define how the FAT works.

THE 64K$ QUESTIONS

1. The physical surface on which data is stored on a hard drive is known as a _____.

    a. Spindle

b.   Cylinder

c.   Disk

d.   Platter

2.   Int13h limits the maximum capacity that a computer can recognize to approximately _____.

   a.   512MB

   b.   2GB

   c.   8GB

   d.   137GB

3.   Modern hard drives use a _____ to move the actuator arms.

   a.   Voice coil

   b.   Servo motor

   c.   Stepper motor

   d.   Resistive coil

4.   The speed at which data can be moved from the surface of the medium to the hard drive's buffers is a direct function of _____.

   a.   Access time

   b.   Latency

   c.   The size of the buffer

   d.   Rotational speed

5.   Of the following encoding systems, which is most likely to be used on a hard drive purchased today?

   a.   EPRML

   b.   PRML

   c.   MFM

   d.   RLL

6.   What is the size of the MBR used by FAT16?

   a.   256 bytes

   b.   512 bytes

   c.   1024 bytes

   d.   There is no limit.

7.   As a systems administrator, you want to enforce as much security in your organization as you possibly can. Therefore, you have decided that all computers will run an OS that uses the _____ file system.

   a.   FAT16

   b.   FAT32

   c.   NTFS

   d.   HPFS

8.   File Allocation Tables are generated by _____.

   a.   FDISK

   b.   FORMAT

   c.   A low-level format that occurs at the factory

   d.   The OS when it is installed

9.   What part of the MBR is created and added during the OS installation?

   a.   File system

   b.   Partition tables

   c.   Boot ID

   d.   OS pointer

10. A partition created by FAT16 is limited to _____.

   a.   512MB

   b.   2GB

   c.   4GB

   d.   137GB

TRICKY TERMINOLOGY

Areal density: The total amount of storage capacity for a specific unit of area on the surface of the drive platter.

Average access time: The amount of time required by a disk drive to lock on to the first sector that contains data requested by the controller.

Average seek time: The amount of time it takes to locate and lock on to the first track that contains data requested by the controller.

Bit cell: The collection of magnetized particles that comprise a single bit on magnetic media.

Block: The number of sectors on a hard drive that UFS uses as the smallest recognizable data unit.

Burst mode: The speed at which data moves from the R/W heads to a drive's buffer memory. Also known as internal host transfer rate.

Cluster: The minimum number of sectors a specific file system can recognize as a single data unit. Another term for file allocation unit.

Cylinder: A virtual structure created by the tracks that line up vertically on the surface of each of the platters.

Data encoding mechanism: The method used by a device to convert digital information into an electronic format recognizable by the target device.

Directory attribute: A single bit that identifies an entry in the directory table as being a subdirectory rather than a file.

Directory table: A database of all file names on a hard drive and the partitions with which they are associated. Other information pertaining to file system security is also contained here.

Drive translation: A technique by which an address space beyond what Int13h can read is converted into something that it can understand.

Executable marker: A pointer in the MBR that directs the boot sequence to the first line of code for the primary kernel file of the OS installed.

External host rate: How fast data moves from a drive's controller to RAM.

File system: The mechanism used by a hard drive to map the specific sectors used by any given file.

Floating height: The distance above a hard drive's platter that the R/W heads hover as the platter spins beneath.

Flux reversal: A transition of magnet charge from a positive to a negative state, or vice versa.

Head crash: A disastrous event caused by the R/W head in a drive coming into physical contact with the platter while it is spinning.

Head parking: A process of positioning R/W heads in a hard drive in a place where contact with the platter will do no harm.

Int13h extensions: Additional instructions added to the BIOS that intercept hard disk I/O operations and provide the drive translation required by hard disks larger than 8GB.

Internal host rate: The speed at which data moves from the R/W heads to a drive's buffer memory. Also known as burst mode.

Landing zone: An area on the hard disk's platter where the R/W heads can be safely parked.

Latency: The amount of time that elapses between the instant the R/W heads lock onto the first track that contains information requested by the controller, and then lock onto the first sector.

Logical drive: A section of disk space isolated from the rest of the same physical disk so that it appears to the user as a separate disk drive.

Partition: Logical sections on a hard disk that divide the overall disk space into multiple logical drives.

Platter: One of two or more physical disk structures installed in a typical hard drive.

Pointer: A line of code used by UFS to map a cluster used by a specific file.

Thin-film metal: A metalized magnetic medium applied by evaporating metal and allowing it to "condense" back onto the surface being coated.

Transition cell: The minimum number of particles that can be affected by a single magnetic flux.

Vapor deposition: The process of applying a metal coating by the process of evaporation.

Voice coil: An extremely fast and highly accurate motor that works by applying an electrical current to a tightly wrapped coil of wires surrounding, but not touching, a permanently magnetized cylinder. When current is applied to the coil, the cylinder rotates. Negative voltage rotates the cylinder one direction, positive the other. The amount of voltage determines how far the cylinder moves.

Zone bit recording: A technology that allows the sectors on the outer tracks of a hard disk to be the same physical size as those toward the center. This allows for far more sectors per track on the outer tracks.

ACRONYM ALERT

CHS: Cylinders, Heads, Sectors-per-track. The parameters of hard drive configuration that define total capacity of the drive as well as specific locations on the drive.

DFS: Distributed File System. A subset of NTFS that allows users to browse to remote resources on a network without requiring the user to know the specific path information.

DTR: Data Transfer Rate. How fast information moves from one device to another.

EFS: Encryptable File System. A subset of NTFS that allows individual files to be scrambled on an as-needed basis and subsequently unscrambled only by a user with appropriate permissions.

ENDEC: Encoder/Decoder

EPRML: Extended PRML. A data encoding mechanism used by most hard disk drives currently being manufactured.

FAT: File Allocation Table

FAU: File Allocation Unit. The smallest usable amount of drive space in sectors used by a file system for a single file, regardless of how small that file may be.

HPFS: High Performance File System

IOPS: I/O Operations Per Second. The maximum number of times a device can receive and then execute either a request for data or a request to write data to the device, assuming the smallest block of data the device utilizes.

LFN: Long File Names

MFM: Modified Frequency Modulation. One of the early data encoding mechanisms used by hard disk drives.

NTFS: New Technology File System

PRML: Partial Response/Maximum Likelihood. A data encoding mechanism used by more recent hard disk drives.

R/W: Read/Write

RLL: Run Length Limited. One of the early data encoding mechanisms used by hard disk drives.

UFS: Unix File System

VBR: Volume Boot Record

CHAPTER 13

HARD DISK INTERFACING AND DISK MANAGEMENT

By now, you should have a pretty good understanding of how data is stored on the hard drive and how the computer system goes about locating that data. Getting data from the drive to memory is the next thing that I will discuss. This is done across the hard drive interface. There have been a fair number of different interfaces used over the years, and even now there are several to choose from. When people discuss the differences between IDE drives and SCSI drives, they're not talking about the kind of hard drive they have, but rather the interface across which data is moved. This chapter will cover the various interfaces that have existed over the years.

File maintenance and disk management are things that don't just take care of themselves. There's a lot going on in a hard drive, and failure to properly care for your drive can carry a severe penalty in overall system performance. The second half of this chapter will deal with those issues.

A+ EXAM OBJECTIVES

Exam objectives covered in this chapter include the following:

1.1 Identify the names, purpose, and characteristics of system modules. Recognize these modules by sight or definition.

1.2 Identify basic procedures for adding and removing field-replaceable modules for desktop systems. Given a replacement scenario, choose the appropriate sequences.

1.5 Identify the names, purposes, and performance characteristics of standardized/common peripheral ports, associated cabling, and their connectors. Recognize ports, cabling, and connectors by sight.

1.6 Identify proper procedures for installing and configuring common IDE devices. Choose the appropriate installation or configuration sequences in given scenarios. Recognize the associated cables.

1.9   Identify procedures to optimize PC operations in specific situations. Predict the effects of specific procedures under given scenarios.

1.10 Determine the issues that must be considered when upgrading a PC. In a given scenario, determine when and how to upgrade system components.

2.1   Recognize common problems associated with each module and their symptoms, and identify steps to isolate and troubleshoot the problems. Given a problem situation, interpret the symptoms and infer the most likely cause.

HARD DRIVE INTERFACES

In Chapter Twelve I described how much impact hard disk I/O operations have on overall system performance. As you may have noticed, it is rather significant. How fast the interface can move data from the drive to RAM is the next bottleneck to be considered. In an application that makes use of lots and lots of little tiny files, I/O operations per second (IOPS) will be the performance-limiting factor. Conversely, an application that consistently reads and writes large files will be more greatly impacted by the speed of the interface. Large chunks of data that are contiguously stored will require but a single I/O operation before data begins to be transferred. It is the interface that will limit the speed of that transfer.

> **BUZZ WORDS**
>
> **Command overhead:** The number of instructions that must be executed in order to carry out a specific request, combined with the speed at which the device can carry out those instructions.

Many factors influence overall performance of the hard drive interface. One of these is the system bus on which it resides. It should not come as a surprise that an interface on an 8MHz bus is going to be slower than one that sits on a 33MHz bus. Another aspect of the interface that affects performance is the hard drive's *command overhead*. All I/O operations begin when a command is issued by the chipset. The controller accepts this command and executes it. Executed commands will result in a variety of actions occurring, including moving the actuator arm to a specific position, or initiating the transfer of data to or from the surface of the platter to cache or the transfer of data to or from the cache to RAM. As interfaces evolved, their command structure became more sophisticated. As command cycles become shorter, it takes fewer commands to perform the same operation, and the process by which commands are moved through the system becomes more efficient.

What hard drive interface you choose directly impacts both the number of devices you can hang off the chain and the type of devices that are supported. For example, some of the early interfaces I will discuss could only handle hard disk drives and two connected devices. Later developments provide support for practically any device you can dream of. And it's theoretically possible to hang over a hundred devices onto some of the newer interfaces.

ST-506 AND ST-412

As I mentioned in Chapter Twelve, Hard Disk Drive Structure and Geometry, modified frequency modulation (MFM) can be considered to be both a data translation method and an interface.

This is because the MFM required a special adapter and cables that were unique to an MFM drive. Technically speaking, the interface is usually referenced by the two drives that made use of this method. Among the first hard drives manufactured for use in personal computers was the ST-506. Al Shugart released this drive back in 1980. It was a 5MB drive that required a separate controller card and two separate cables. IBM wanted something a little larger than 5MB and went with the ST-412, which was a 10MB version.

File data was carried across a 20-conductor ribbon cable, and a 34-conductor cable handled control data, including timing signals, commands, and so forth. Unlike modern drives, which house a lot of controller circuitry on the drive itself, these older drives relied exclusively upon the controller card.

> **BUZZ WORDS** ───────
>
> **Interleave ratio:** The number of sectors that must pass beneath the R/W heads between the reading of one sector and the time the heads will be ready to read the next sector. For example, on a 3:1 ratio, the heads will read or write one sector, two sectors will pass by completely ignored, then the next sector will be written. The unused sectors will be filled in during the next two rotations of the platter.

In order to make sure that the timing of drives was accurate, it was essential that the drive be properly configured. People complain about the work that goes into prepping a drive these days. Yet compared to what you used to have to go through, today's technology is a piece of cake.

Drives had to be not only manually configured for the number of cylinders, heads, and sectors per track, they also had to be set up with the proper interleave ratio. A modern hard drive finds the first sector that holds the data the controller seeks and starts streaming it across the interface. Sectors are read sequentially, one after the other. The older controllers used with the ST-506 and ST-412 weren't fast enough to keep up with that kind of data stream, however. They would miss the next sector every time.

Therefore, sectors were not written and/or read back sequentially. The interleave ratio reordered the way sectors were written to the track. These older drives only managed to squeeze seventeen sectors onto any given track. In a perfect world, when the controller could keep up with the spinning of the head, the sectors on track one would be numbered 1, 2, 3, . . . 17. That track would be read sequentially, and then the next track would begin. Since that wasn't possible, the drive and controller you purchased would tell you what *interleave ratio* to set. Really fast controllers might be able to handle a 1:2 interleave. In this case, the tracks would be numbered 1, 10, 2, 11, 3, 12, and so forth to the end of the drive. A 1:3 ratio would be numbered 1, 12, 7, 2, 13, 8, 3, 14, 9, 4, 15, 10, 5, 16, 11, 6, and finally 17.

Of course, it wasn't the users' responsibility to set up the sector number. They simply had to know the correct interleave. An improperly configured drive was a corrupted drive.

One reason you can't really call this an MFM interface is that some of the later drives that used exactly the same interface made use of the run length limited (RLL) data encryption. Yet the controllers and the cable remained the same.

EXAM NOTE: While these older interfaces may not seem relevant in today's context, CompTIA's A+ Core exam considers the history of the different components to be important. Make sure you know them.

ESDI

The next step in the evolution of the hard drive was the Enhanced Small Device Interface. This interface was the result of a cooperative effort among several manufacturers, led by Maxtor Corporation. ESDI drives were more complex devices than the ST-506 and ST-412s, in that some of the controller circuitry was housed directly on the drive. This assured better data integrity on the transfer cycle.

ESDI did enjoy a decent throughput. It had a theoretical top bandwidth of about 24Mb/s. Unfortunately, the interface didn't live long enough to see if manufacturers would ever be able to achieve these speeds. In terms of ease of installation and overall user-friendliness, it wasn't any better that the drives it was supposed to replace. Also, it had only been around for a very short while before the next standard hit the streets and pretty much blew ESDI off the pavement.

IDE

That next standard was Integrated Drive Electronics (IDE). IDE moved all of the controller circuitry onto the drive itself, leaving only an interface port on the computer. Early IDE-enabled computers had I/O cards that installed into a free ISA slot, but the port would eventually migrate onto the motherboard, where it remains to this day. Even though the port may be housed on an expansion card, it is important that you understand that the 40-pin plug on the card was nothing more than a port. The controller is on the drive.

Initially, IDE drives hooked up by way of a 40-pin ribbon cable. Beginning with ATA-4, which I will be discussing shortly, the number of conductors was increased to eighty, while the number of pins on the port remained forty. **Figure 13.1** and **Table 13.1** show the pinouts of the 40-pin IDE port.

IDE has got to be one of the most confusing terms in the industry, and that is primarily because it is such a generic term. There have been a myriad of different IDE standards, and more than a fair share of nonstandards. Still newer standards are on the horizon. To make matters worse, not everybody uses the same term to mean the same thing. Here are some of the different terms you hear that are associated with IDE:

- *ATAPI*: ATA Packet Interface
- *ATA*: Advanced Technology Attachment
- *EIDE*: Enhanced IDE; Western Digital's version of ATA-2
- *Ultra-ATA*: ATA device that is capable of using direct memory access
- *Ultra-DMA*: A form of direct memory access controlled by the device rather than the motherboard; often (incorrectly) used interchangeably with Ultra-ATA

ATAPI

Before I get into a detailed discussion of the different IDE modes the industry has seen over the years, it would be a good idea to have some understanding of the concept of the Advanced

Table 13.1   Pinouts of the 40-pin IDE port

Pin	Description	Pin	Description
1	Reset	21	DRQ 3
2	Ground	22	Ground
3	Data Bit 7	23	-IOW
4	Data Bit 8	24	Ground
5	Data Bit 6	25	-IOR
6	Data Bit 9	26	Ground
7	Data Bit 5	27	I/O channel ready
8	Data Bit 10	28	SPSYNC: Cable select
9	Data Bit 4	29	-DACK 3
10	Data Bit 11	30	Ground
11	Data Bit 3	31	RQ 14
12	Data Bit 12	32	-IOCS 16
13	Data Bit 2	33	Address Bit 1
14	Data Bit 13	34	-PDIAG
15	Data Bit 1	35	Address Bit 0
16	Data Bit 14	36	Address Bit 2
17	Data Bit 0	37	-CS1FX
18	Data Bit 15	38	-CS3FX
19	Ground	39	-DA/SP
20	Cable key (pin missing)	40	Ground

IDE connector pinout chart

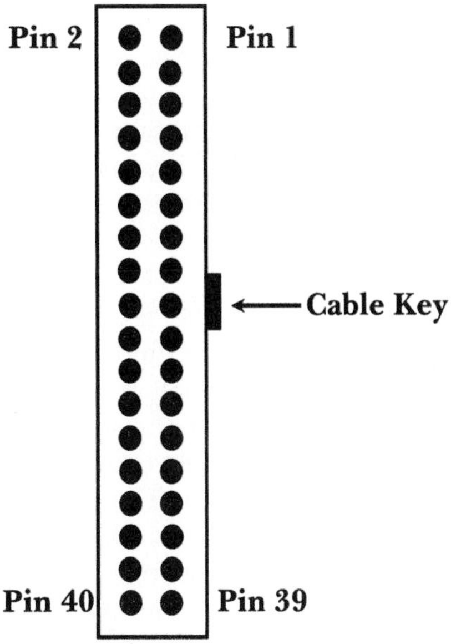

Figure 13.1   Pinouts for IDE connector

Technology Attachment Packet Interface (ATAPI). In the next chapter, I'm going to be discussing the Small Computer Systems Interface (SCSI) in great detail. But for now, one characteristic of SCSI I want to introduce is the fact that it has a command set that supports different kinds of devices on the same interface. Therefore, a single SCSI host adapter can control a hard drive, a CD-ROM drive, and a tape drive. This, combined with some advanced features that I will discuss in the next chapter, made SCSI the preferable interface for "serious" computer users.

ATAPI takes some of the features of SCSI and incorporates them into the IDE interface. As a result, it supports multiple devices. It also allows for devices other than hard drives to become bootable devices.

Devices that make use of ATAPI move data in a completely different way than the earlier IDE devices. Instead of moving information across the bus a bit at a time, the information is combined into packets and moved from device to device in little packages of data. This is where the name is derived. Starting with ATA-4, all ATA modes incorporated ATAPI.

> **Exam Note:** Disk capacity limitations imposed by the different versions of IDE are something that show up on the A+ Exam on a regular basis.

ATA

The Advanced Technology Attachment (ATA) was the first incarnation of IDE to appear. The debut of the interface supported only hard drives, allowed for but a single port per computer, and each port could only have two drives on it. To differentiate between drives, jumpers on the drive set them to either master or slave status. Only a master drive was bootable.

Data transfer could occur in one of three programmable input/output (PIO) modes: PIO-0, PIO-1, and PIO-2. This technique requires the CPU to get into the middle of things by executing commands that shuffle the data to or from RAM and the drive. The end result is that instead of spending its time processing instructions and data, the CPU is tied up playing go fetch. Another limitation of this data transfer method is that the time overhead involved in putting data in the cache, reading each byte into the CPU, sending it out to the cache again, and then routing, it limited the maximum throughput that was possible.

Later versions of ATA would support PIO-3 and PIO-4 as well. Each mode had a specific *cycle rate*, or amount of time it took to complete a cycle. In this case, I am referring to the clock cycles of the hard drive controller rather than that of the FSB. The controller's speed is dictated by the speed of the bus onto which it is installed. How is this different? An IDE controller installed in a standard PCI slot is going to be running at 33MHz. The system board onto which it is installed may have a 133MHz FSB.

A single cycle is both the rising edge and the falling edge of a single tick of the bus clock. I examined the sine-wave effect in Chapter Eight, Searching Your Memory. This cycle rate, in effect, dictates maximum data transfer rate. Unfortunately, hard drives can't keep up with the overall system clock, and therefore, the device must set its own pace. The different PIO modes worked on different clock cycles, as is illustrated in **Table 13.2**. For purposes of comparison, I have included FSB speeds of 100 and 133MHz.

You'll notice that the fastest of the PIO modes indicates a cycle rate of 120ns. If you're working with a computer with a 100MHz front-side bus (slow by today's standards), then a single cycle of the drive controller eats up twelve cycles of the front-side bus. On a 133MHz bus, that's sixteen clock cycles that go by simply waiting for the hard drive controller to run just one of its own cycles. And remember, your CPU is operating at speeds several times that of the FSB.

The ATA standards did define a data transfer method known as direct memory access (DMA). DMA had been around for a long time, and was nothing new. Floppy disk drives and sound cards both made use of DMA long before hard drives. With DMA, the CPU sets up the initial transfer of a given file, but once the transfer is set up, the data

> **Buzz Words** ————————
>
> **Cycle rate:** The amount of time it takes for a specific device under the control of a timing mechanism to complete one "tick" of that timer.

Table 13.2 Comparisons of PIO Modes

PIO Mode	Defining Standard	Cycle Rate	Theoretical Transfer Rate	Cycles/sec for		
				33MHz Bus	100MHz Bus	133MHz Bus
PIO-0	ATA	600ns	3.3Mb/s	~20	60	80
PIO-1	ATA	383ns	5.2Mb/s	~12.5	~38	51
PIO-2	ATA	240ns	8.3Mb/s	8	24	32
PIO-3	ATA-2	180ns	11.1Mb/s	6	18	24
PIO-4	ATA-2	120ns	16.7Mb/s	4	12	16

Each generation of PIO got increasingly faster, but it never caught up to ATA.

Table 13.3 Comparisons of ATA-1 DMA Modes

Mode	Standard	Cycle Rate	Theoretical Transfer Rate	Cycles/sec for		
				33MHz Bus	100MHz Bus	133MHz Bus
Mode 0	AT	960ns	2.1Mb/s	~32	96	128
Mode 1	AT	480	4.2MB/s	~16	48	64
Mode 2	AT	240	8.3MB/s	~8	24	32

ATA-1 was only marginally faster than PIO, but it was somewhat more efficient.

can move directly from the hard drive's controller to RAM, without having to make a pit stop at the CPU. The CPU goes back to work processing instructions and data, and the overall transfer of data is much faster.

Under original ATA standards, the only DMA modes supported were single-word DMA. The ATA interface was a 16-bit interface and therefore, on each transfer, it could move two bytes of data, or a word. Three modes of DMA were defined, as illustrated in **Table 13.3**.

In one respect, designers of the original ATA interface kind of shot themselves in the foot. Under the original Int13h CHS parameters that I discussed in Chapter Twelve, the addressing scheme called for 1024 cylinders, 256 heads, and a maximum of 63 sectors per track. If you do your math, you see that $1024 \times 256 \times 63$ equals 16,515,072. That is the maximum number of sectors that Int13h can recognize. Multiply that number by 512, which is the number of bytes in a sector, and you see that under Int13h is capable of seeing hard drives of up to 8,455,716,864 bytes, or 8GB.

ATA addressing standards call for 65,536 cylinders, 16 heads, and 256 sectors per track. Now, theoretically, this allows for drives up to 137,438,953,472 bytes, or 137GB. Unfortunately, in the

Table 13.4 ATA and Int13h

Standard	Cylinders	Heads	Sectors/Track	Maximum Address Space
Int13h	1024	256	63	~8GB
ATA	65,536	16	256	~137GB
Combined	1024	16	63	504MB

The first implementation of ATA actually resulted in a dramatic decrease in the maximum capacity of hard disks.

initial release, the effect this had on the system was that, for each of those parameters, the system would use the lower of either standard (see **Table 13.4**).

ATA-2

As computer bus speeds were increasing, the need for a more efficient means of moving data was becoming critical. This is where Multiword Direct Memory Access (MDMA) comes into the picture. With the release of ATA-2 in 1994, forcing the CPU to negotiate the transfer of data became unnecessary. Of course, everybody wanted to own the technology, so before ANSI finally stepped in with some defined standards, there was a bit of confusion as to what ATA-2 really was. Western Digital had its Enhanced IDE (EIDE), which still shows up in many publications as being a "standard." Seagate had Fast-ATA. Both of these were improvements on the original AT standards, but were never accepted in their entirety as true standards. Both of these technologies did possess features in common and contributed to what would eventually become the ATA-2 standards. I'll take a brief look at both of these after the official ATA-2 standards are clearly defined. There were some distinct improvements introduced by ATA-2, which include the following:

■ *PIO Modes 3 and 4*: The initial PIO modes supported by ATA were rather limited in their speed. As I mentioned earlier, Mode 2 topped out at 8.3Mb/s throughput. Mode 3 bumped this up to 11.1Mb/s, while Mode 4 achieved 16.7Mb/s. One thing I think I should point out here is that these are theoretical maximums. In the real world, no drive ever truly achieved these speeds.

■ *Multiword DMA*: DMA did prove to be a nice enhancement for data transfer, but moving information across the bus a single word at a time was a bit cumbersome and inefficient. Under multiword DMA, once the data transfer is set up, information is sent out in bursts. One word follows the other in rapid sequence, and there is no need to set up separate transfers for each word. These days, multiword DMA is accepted as the norm, and, in fact, there are no current interfaces that even support single-word DMA.

■ *Logical block addressing*: Prior to ATA-2, all drives used the standard CHS parameters that I discussed early in this chapter. This meant that there was a limitation of 528MB

(504MB in binary calculation) of address space visible to the hard drive. This was a limitation of the Int13h BIOS call trying to interface with the original ATA standards. A few companies had experimented with different extensions to Int13h that would allow for larger drives, including Extended CHS (ECHS). This still shows up in the BIOS settings of many computers as Large Mode. Logical block addressing (LBA) numbers each sector on the drive with its own unique number. This doesn't permit drives that use this method to address CHS parameters beyond the limitations described above. What it does is translate addresses down into something that fits CHS's comfortable little world. It does this through a process called LBA assist translation. This is a mathematical algorithm that takes actual cylinder numbers and translates them into expressions CHS can use. Theoretically, there is no limit to the size of hard drive LBA can address. However, ATA modes 2-5 are still limited to the 137GB ceiling dictated by their address space.

- *Block transfer:* In the same way that multiword DMA allows for more data to move across the bus on any given cycle, block transfer allows multiple commands to be moved from the CPU to the controller on a single interrupt. Prior to the introduction of this technology, every transfer of data and every command moved across the bus required the drive's controller circuitry to generate an interrupt to let the CPU know it was ready for activity. Moving one command across an interrupt meant that, until that command was executed and the results moved across the bus (requiring an additional interrupt for the data transfer), no other commands could be moved.

  When a hard drive uses *block mode*, it allows one interrupt to move several commands. This not only improves drive performance, but overall system performance as well. The drive can hold several commands in cache, executing them without needing to stop what the CPU is doing to ask for the next command. The CPU is no different than people in that respect. The more you interrupt it the slower it works.

- *Identify drive command:* Have you ever wondered how your system was able to automatically recognize your hard drive without you having to go in and configure anything? As much as it might seem like magic, it's really a result of the identify drive command (IDC). This is a simple command to which the hard drive can respond by spewing out information concerning the number of cylinders, heads, and sectors per track. System BIOS can use this to automatically configure the drive, and the OS can use it for file system management. You also see a lot of hard drive utilities on the market these days. Many of the functions of these applications would not be possible without the identify drive command.

I mentioned earlier in this section that there were some proprietary technologies used by certain manufacturers that occasionally get confused with ATA-2. These were EIDE and Fast ATA.

BUZZ WORDS

Block transfer: The movement of multiple commands over an interface on a single interrupt cycle.

Block mode: The data transfer setting that allows multiple commands to be moved over an interface in a single interrupt cycle.

■ **Exam Note:** Be able to differentiate between the UDMA modes and the ATA modes.

EIDE was merely an incorporation of some new technology onto the original ATA interface. It was never a standard. Western Digital had come up with a better mousetrap, and didn't want to wait around for the notoriously slow hand of the standards committees to approve its work. So it simply released product using that technology. It incorporated most of what would later become the ATA-2 standards. Among the new features, EIDE supported ATAPI.

Another improvement of EIDE over ATA was that it defined the use of two different IDE ports on a single machine: a primary port and a secondary port. This allowed for up to four different IDE devices to be installed on a machine. Interestingly enough, there was nothing about the original ATA standards that kept manufacturers from putting an additional channel onto a system board or I/O card. However, since there were no specific standards defined for how to go about doing this, it was rarely if ever done.

Fast ATA was Seagate's version of EIDE. Like Western Digital, Seagate had developed a better interface and was unwilling to wait out the standards committees, especially since WD was entering the market with its EIDE. Fortunately, for the most part, neither term, EIDE or Fast–ATA, is much in use any more.

ATA-3

This particular set of standards was really no more than a fine-tuning of ATA-2. The only real improvements over ATA-2 were the addition of SMART drive technology and the ability to password-protect IDE devices.

Self Monitoring Analysis and Reporting Technology (SMART) was a method by which a hard drive could self-administer a few simple tests and try to predict if it was about to fail. SMART kept track of several factors in its efforts to predict the future. Among the information monitored was the following:

■ *Remapped sectors*: If the drive is constantly being forced to move data from one location to another because of bad sectors, this is a sign of impending disaster.

■ *ECC error counts*: SMART drives use error correction code to detect and correct data errors on the fly. SMART can monitor error correction code (ECC) usage and if it seems to be called upon with increasing frequency, this is assumed to be a sign of a failing drive.

■ *Head flying height*: The drive's R/W heads are supposed to float on a cushion of air a certain distance above the spinning platter. If this height is slowly diminishing, this is a bad thing. You've got a head crash coming your way.

■ *Temperature*: Is the drive suddenly starting to run hotter? A motor bearing failure is imminent.

■ *Spin-up time*: If the drive is taking longer to reach the correct rotational velocity every time it spins up, the motor is starting to fail.

■ *Data throughput*: If the speed at which data can be moved from the drive to RAM is starting to diminish, this means something is going wrong. SMART has no way of knowing what the problem is, only that there is one.

SMART requires two components in order to work properly. First off, you obviously need a drive that supports it. Second, you need some sort of monitoring software. The drive doesn't perform these tricks by itself. Drives that support it usually ship with a utility that you can load to do this monitoring. If you didn't know why that floppy disk shipped with your new drive and you simply threw it away, most third-party hardware diagnostics programs, such as Norton Utilities, provide some form of SMART monitoring.

EXAM NOTE: Know what SMART technology is and how it works.

The security features introduced in ATA-3 allow the user to go into BIOS and set password protection on devices. A computer on a network can have a separate hard drive for sensitive data that, in order to be accessed, requires that the user input a specific password.

ATA-4

The release of ATA-4 in 1998 opened the way for much faster hard drives on the IDE interface. It was the first of the versions to fully incorporate ATAPI. ATA-4 was developed by Quantum and then freely licensed to the industry. There were several improvements introduced in this release:

- Ultra-DMA (UDMA) modes
- Cyclical redundancy checking (CRC)
- Command queuing
- Command overlapping
- An advanced command set, with obsolete commands cleaned up

UDMA differs from legacy DMA in several respects. The older ATA-2 and ATA-3 hard drives that made use of DMA used a method called *third-party DMA*. What this means is that a controlling device separate from that controlling the drive itself was in charge of DMA transfers. In the case of IDE hard drives, that third party was the DMA controller chip on the motherboard. A key issue here is that those chips are limited to the speed of the older ISA bus. UDMA allows the device controller to directly handle data transfer through a process called bus mastering. Under bus mastering, the device takes charge of the bus on which it and its companion device reside, and data moves directly from one device to another. The DMA controller chip is not involved, and transfers occur at the speed of whatever bus the system is using. These days, that would be the PCI bus, although in the past, both MCA and VLB were used (see Chapter Nine, Examining the Expansion Bus).

Later modes of UDMA also sped up data transfer through a process called *double-transition clocking*. As I discussed in Chapter Eight, every clock

BUZZ WORDS ——————

Third-party DMA: Direct memory access that is managed by a device other than the two devices utilizing DMA to exchange data.

Double-transition clocking: The movement of two transfers of data on a single clock cycle.

cycle has two stages, a rising end and a falling end. Conventional DMA could only propagate a transfer of data on the rising end of the cycle. Double-transition clocking permits the device to transmit or receive on both the rising end and the falling end of each clock cycle. This has the same effect as doubling the clock speed, without the side effect of having to worry about timing issues imposed by other devices that may be using that same clock signal for its timing.

UDMA has survived the last several years, but in that time it has undergone several developmental stages. To date, there have been six modes of UDMA. Each mode has provided for faster data transfers as well as adding new features. The following is a list of UDMA modes that have been developed. Note, however, that the list contains modes that are native to ATA-5 and 6 as well as ATA-4. I simply felt it better to keep the list together.

- *Mode 0*: This could almost be considered the "experimental" mode. This release did not provide for double-transition clocking and didn't operate at a faster clock speed than PIO modes. Most operating systems of the day didn't support UDMA modes, nor did most BIOS routines. Therefore, on many machines, it caused more problems than people were willing to endure for an almost insignificant gain in performance.

- *Mode 1*: Aside from a slightly faster clock cycle, there were no improvements over Mode 0.

- *Mode 2*: Here is the introduction of double-transition clocking. Data transfer is noticeably faster. By now BIOS manufacturers have caught on to the fact that UDMA is the direction the industry is moving, and support for it is almost universal. Windows 95 now provides support for it, and IDE hard drives are becoming almost respectable.

- *Mode 3*: This mode was released with ATA-5. It simply increased the clock cycle of Mode 2. The only other improvement was that it provided support for ATAPI-5.

- *Mode 4*: This mode was released with ATA-5. More frequently known as UDMA-66, this interface requires the use of an 80-conductor cable, otherwise it drops back into Mode 3 operation. A key improvement to this mode, aside from speed, is the introduction of cyclical redundancy check (CRC) error correction.

- *Mode 5*: UDMA-100

- *Mode 6*: UDMA-133. Available memory space was also increased to 64 bits.

CRC is a form of error correction that treats an entire packet of data as if it were one long binary number. It performs a mathematical calculation on that number and stores the results in a data field at the end of the packet. On the receiving end, that calculation is performed again on just the data set. If the value of the new calculation matches that in the trailer, the data is assumed to be good. If there is any discrepancy, the packet is discarded and sent again.

Since ATAPI sends data across the bus in packets, CRC can basically treat those ones and zeros that make up the data in the packet as a large binary number and then perform a mathematical calculation on that number. The results of this calculation are made a part of the packet in the CRC trailer. Before that data is stripped out of the packet and reassembled into a file, the same calculation is performed. If the same results are achieved, the data is accepted. If not, the packet is rejected and a request is sent out to the transmitting device to resend that packet. CRC substantially reduces the likelihood of data being corrupted as it is sent over the bus.

Command queuing is a concept that was borrowed from SCSI. Using PIO mode, commands sent to an IDE device had to be completely executed and the operation initiated by that command had to be completed before the next command could be sent to the controller. This wasn't exactly the most efficient way of doing things, but at the time, technology hadn't provided for a better way. Under *command queuing*, the device can store commands in a cache. Several commands can be ready to go as soon as the drive is ready to execute them. *Command overlapping* provides a method of letting the drive have more than one command be in the pipeline at a time. This is very similar to the pipelining function I discussed in Chapter Six, Understanding CPUs. The controller can be executing one command while the drive is performing the operation requested by the previous command. Meanwhile the I/O bus can be transferring the data generated by the command before that one. These concepts will be discussed in more detail in Chapter Fourteen, The Many Faces of SCSI.

ATA-5

ATA-5 is really nothing more than a tweak for ATA-4. When ATA modes 3 and 4 were introduced, speeds increased to 44.4 and 66.7Mb/s, respectively. An 80-conductor cable is required for the device to be able to approach these speeds. ATA-5 further bumps speed to 100Mb/s. There was a little tweaking of the command set. A few new commands were added; some obsolete ones were removed. For the most part, however, it is merely a faster ATA-4.

ATA-6

If you recall from the earlier discussion about the ATA interface, it had an address bus of 32 bits, only 28 bits of which were used for actual addressing. This imposes a limitation of 137GB as the largest drive it can support. We have now reached that limitation. ATA-6 standards define a 64-bit address bus and bump the speed to 133Mb/s. The address space handling sectors was increased from eight to sixteen. This allows for drives in excess of several hundred terabytes.

A new command set provides enhanced support for streaming audio-video data, something that until now has been almost the exclusive domain of SCSI drives. Several other changes improved timing control and overall data throughput.

SERIAL ATA

All of the IDA technologies that I've discussed so far have been varying forms of Parallel ATA (PATA). The latest standards to emerge in 2002 defined Serial ATA (SATA). SATA offers a number of improvements in areas of speed and ease of configuration. The initial specification,

SATA 1.0, came out of the gates at 150Mb/s throughput. While on paper that only represents a 14 percent improvement over ATA-6, the improvement is actually greater than it appears. If you recall, I've mentioned several times in this and other chapters that theoretical throughputs are rarely, if ever, achieved. SATA comes closer to achieving its maximum data transfer than other technology discussed so far.

Easier configuration comes about because only one device can be installed on each SATA channel. Since there is only one device per channel, there is no longer the confusion of managing master/slave relationships (more on that later). The reduced size of the cable means that there is far less "cable clutter" inside the enclosure. Airflow is improved, and accessing other devices inside the system is greatly facilitated.

So how is having one device per channel an advantage over the ATA modes that supported two devices per channel? The answer to that is several-fold. For one thing, two devices don't compete on the same cable for bandwidth.

Next, consider the interface. PATA used a 40-pin connector on the motherboard that was 2.3″ × .4″ in size. SATA uses a 7-conductor cable. Two connectors for these cables fit into an area that is .6″ × .4″. In other words, a controller card or motherboard that uses SATA can fit the same number of devices. While the initial offering of SATA controller cards offered only two ports for devices, there are now more advanced devices that support up to sixteen ports with onboard RAID architecture. I'll be discussing RAID in Chapter Fourteen, The Many Faces of SCSI.

SATA uses a high-speed differential signal using Gigabit technology. What this means is that for each data cable, there is a matching cable that carries an exact inverse of the data signal (see **Figure 13.2**). If the two signals were blended together, in theory, they would cancel each other out, resulting in zero voltage. As electrical signals travel over wire, they pick up noise. The farther they travel, the more noise they pick up. Noise shows up as voltage fluctuations. A device using *differential signaling* compares the matched pair of signals. Any voltage differences between the two are filtered out. This contrasts with *single-ended signaling*, in which the active signal wire is coupled with a ground. As a result, cable lengths can be longer.

A conventional 40-conductor IDE cable is limited to approximately 18″ in length. Any longer, and data corruption becomes a serious risk. SATA cables can be up to 1 meter in length, or nearly twice that of standard IDE.

Power consumption is also reduced. Standard 1″ IDE hard disks operate at 5V. SATA devices require a peak operating voltage of a mere 500mv.

SATA also borrows some technology that has been around for a while for SCSI users. One of these is tagged command queuing. Earlier in the chapter, I discussed how command queuing could line up commands in a row in the controller's buffer rather than being forced to feed the controller one command at a time. Tagged command queuing allows the controller to re-sort those commands into a different order if doing so will provide more efficient operation.

Buzz Words

Differential signaling: A method by which a single data wire on a parallel cable is matched up by a wire carrying the inverse of the signal being carried by the data wire.

Single-ended signaling: A method by which a single data wire on a parallel cable is matched up by a ground wire.

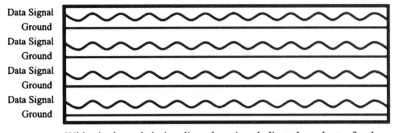

With single-ended signaling, there is a dedicated conductor for the signal, coupled to a ground.

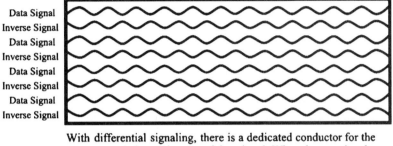

With differential signaling, there is a dedicated conductor for the signal, coupled to an inverse of that signal. When the two signals are measured together, the result should be 0. Any difference is assumed to be noise, and is filtered out.

Figure 13.2 A conceptual diagram of differential signaling

SATA-II became available to users in 2004. The primary difference is in bandwidth. SATA-II handles a full 300Mb/s. SATA-III, scheduled for a 2007 rollout, bumps that up to 600Mb/s. We can only hope that the rest of hard drive technology is able to keep pace with interface technology.

SCSI

Since the SCSI interface provides support for many devices other than hard drives and it is such a complex subject on its own, it is covered separately in its own chapter. It will be discussed in much greater detail in the Chapter Fourteen, The Many Faces of SCSI. In order to provide a complete discussion of hard drive interfaces, however, it is important to provide a simplified overview of SCSI.

Even the earlier releases of SCSI supported up to seven devices, plus the host adapter itself, on a single chain controlled by a single IRQ. In addition, SCSI supported more than just hard drives, so you could have a tape drive, a CD-ROM, and two or three hard drives hanging off the same cable.

From the start, SCSI provided support for functions that IDE wouldn't make available for several years. These included command queuing, command overlapping, and bus mastering.

Overall, SCSI is now, and has always been, a faster and more efficient interface. The thing that has always kept IDE alive and well has been the added expense and configuration difficulties imposed by SCSI. This will all be discussed in greater detail in the next chapter. Toward the end of Chapter Fourteen, I will take a look at the differences and similarities and consider when one interface or the other might be desirable.

THE NONSTANDARD INTERFACES

Most of the options I've discussed so far have described the interfaces for internally mounted hard disk drives for desktop computers or servers. However, sometimes it is convenient, or even essential, to make use of an externally mounted hard drive. Some other options for connecting a hard drive to a computer include the following:

- Parallel port
- Universal Serial Bus
- Personal Computer Memory Card International Association (PCMCIA)

All of these interfaces have special niches that they occupy and need to be addressed. With parallel port and USB devices, the drive itself uses one of the technologies previously discussed, usually IDE. The enclosure is equipped with the interface that will be used to interconnect with the computer and a logic board that will act as a translator. PCMCIA makes use of its own interface.

PARALLEL PORT HARD DRIVES

People frequently think of the parallel port as being the exclusive domain of printers. Yet as I pointed out in Chapter Eleven, Working With Removable Disks, it is used for a number of other devices. Hard drive manufacturers have long made use of the parallel interface for designing external hard drives. Relying on a parallel port has one advantage over either IDE or SCSI, and that is its portability. Not all computers have an external SCSI port. But have you ever seen a computer without a parallel port?

It is, of course, very slow compared to anything else you might use. Data throughput is limited to a maximum of 1.2Mb/s. Nobody will ever confuse it with a high-performance device.

The parallel port is rapidly losing ground to USB for an external interface, however. You will see why in the next section.

USB

In Chapter Nine, I discussed the features of USB. By default, it is Plug 'n Play. It loads and unloads drivers on the fly and automatically recognizes when a device has been added. You can add the drive while the computer is up and running, and it will automatically be recognized and introduced to the machine. And you won't have to unplug your printer to make room for the drive.

Even for people who need a permanently connected external drive, USB is a better choice than the parallel port. While stacking devices on the parallel port is definitely possible, it isn't all that desirable. An already slow interface suffers even more. Since USB 1.0 only supports a maximum throughput of 12Mb/s, which is a much faster interface than the parallel port, it's still no speed demon. That still only works out to about 1.5MB/s. USB 2.0 is the better choice (and by the time this book is in print, will probably be the only choice) with a throughput of 480Mb/s.

The USB enclosure of most of the drives being shipped these days also have a USB hub built in. This allows you to daisy chain additional devices off the back of the drive. You may recall from Chapter Nine that a USB chain can have up to 127 devices installed.

PCMCIA

While PCMCIA is technically the name of the association that developed the standard, it is also used as the name of the bus that the standard defines. PCMCIA devices are the small card-sized devices used in notebook computers. The bus offers reasonably good speed, combined with a very small interface. Hard disks on this interface are only 2.5″ across and only about a quarter of an inch high. As far as performance goes, they can be every bit as fast as conventional IDE drives.

The nice thing about PCMCIA drives is that they are easily removed from the host computer and added to a different machine. Several manufacturers make devices that install into an external drive bay in your home computer and allow you to insert the PCMCIA drive from your notebook. While not the easiest method of maintaining files, it assures you of having the data you need on whatever computer you need it on.

NOTEBOOK IDE

Internal hard disks for notebook computers these days are generally IDE drives. They differ physically in a couple of respects, however. The overall width is consistent at 2.5″. However, over the years, they have been released in heights of 9.5mm, 12.7mm, and 19mm. Putting a thinner drive in a larger bay is no problem as long as the drive is secured in some fashion. If the notebook was designed as a friction enclosure (pressure from the two sides and the top and the bottom), this is not a good idea. There is a risk of the drive bouncing around. Most if not all modern designs make use of the 9.5mm, and that's about all that's shipping today.

The cable is also different in a notebook. Instead of being a 40-conductor cable, it uses 44 conductors. There is no separate power plug for these drives, so power is supplied through the same cable as the data. The ends of the cable are extremely small and use spring clips to hold them in place. This prevents them from being dislodged as the computer is carried from place to place.

HARD DISK PREPARATION

Hard disk drives don't arrive at your doorstep from the factory ready to read and write data. A certain amount of preparation is involved. First off, you have to get the drive installed into your machine. Depending on what kind of drive you've selected the procedures for that will vary slightly. Once it is installed, you have to introduce the drive to the file system you intend to use. Most Microsoft operating systems use a utility called FDISK to perform that function. Finally, once the drive has been installed and prepared for a file system, it needs to be formatted to the particular operating system you have chosen to use. In the next few pages, I will take a detailed look at installing and configuring your hard drive.

INSTALLING A HARD DRIVE

Overall, this is actually a fairly easy task. Before you begin, you will want to make sure you have an available drive bay in which to seat the drive. You don't just want it hanging from the cables in the middle of the case. Second, you need to make sure you can get power to the drive. If you've used up all your Molex plugs from the power supply, you can get a Y-connector from any electronics supply house. You can see an example of one of these in **Figure 13.3**. Basically, these inexpensive little devices turn one Molex into two. However, before you do that, you might want to examine your system and the devices you have already installed carefully. If the system has a small power supply, say around 65 watts, and you start stacking too many devices onto it, you could cause a premature failure. Many power supplies, on the other hand, are perfectly capable of powering far more devices than they have plugs for, so this is usually a pretty safe solution.

The kind of computer case you're using will dictate how the drive physically mounts. Most cases these days have drive bays that can be removed from the case. This makes the process of mounting the drive a whole lot easier. While the drive is still outside of the case, the process of connecting cables is a much easier job.

While the drive is still outside of the case is also the time to be setting any jumpers there may be. PATA IDE devices need to be either a master or a slave. If you're installing an SATA device, this is not an issue.

If the drive is to be your primary boot device, it is best (and in many cases necessary) to make it the master device on the primary port. There is a jumper on the back of the drive that performs this function. Just put the shunt over the correct pair of pins and you're good to go.

SCSI devices may or may not have either jumpers or switches for setting the device ID. It is becoming more and more common for this function to be handled by the firmware of the host adapter card. I'll be addressing that in more detail next chapter.

One little detail that needs to be examined is directly related to the master/slave relationships on IDE devices. There is another setting on most drives that is labeled cable select (CS). If both drives are set for CS, the drive's position

Figure 13.3 If you run out of Molex plugs to supply power to devices in your system, perhaps a Y-connector is in order. Be cautious of using too many. You don't want to risk overstressing your power supply.

on the cable determines whether it is master or slave. This is done by having conductor number 28 disconnected from the end connector. Manufactures do this either by clipping a short length of the wire from somewhere between the middle and end connector, or by simply not connecting the twenty-eighth wire to the end connector. The first type is easy to recognize. There's a hole in the cable. The latter is not. The original idea was that this would make configuring IDE drives much easier. You put the slave drive in the middle of the cable and the master at the end.

> **EXAM NOTE:** Master/slave relationships of IDE devices can be presented in a number of ways. If you're lucky, you'll just get a multiple choice question of definitions. More likely, you'll get a scenario in which a drive isn't working and you have to explain why.

Unfortunately, it didn't. If either drive is not set to CS, it won't be recognized by the system if its jumper is set opposite of its position on the cable. For example, if a drive is set to be a slave, you cannot force your system to recognize it if you place it on the end connector. If all you have is a CS cable and you need the device on the end to be a master, then you're only solution is to manually solder a jumper between the thirty-ninth conductor on the cable over to the twenty-eighth. If conductor 28 was simply never connected at the factory, all this work will do you no good. You're better off spending a few bucks on a standard IDE cable. And along those lines, by default, all 80-conductor cables are CS.

Once the jumpers are set, the ribbon cable properly installed (and don't forget to make sure the pink or red wire is linked to pin number 1), and the power cable hooked up, you are ready to mount the cage back into the case and prepare the drive. I wouldn't recommend sealing up the case, however, until you know the system is booting properly. It's easy to forget to set a jumper or to inadvertently knock loose another cable while poking around inside the system.

FDISK

While operating systems written by companies other than Microsoft use their own utilities to prepare a hard drive for formatting, FDISK is far and away the most common utility used. FDISK is the utility that writes that master boot record that I discussed in Chapter Twelve. It assigns the file system to be used and creates the partition tables, based on selections you make while running the utility. In this section, I will look at the utility and how to effectively use it.

To start with, you should never run FDISK from the drive that you're actually working with. With newer OSs, that isn't possible, so it's a moot point. However, some older versions do not employ any fail-safe mechanisms to prevent you from doing this. As a standard operating procedure, I recommend preparing a boot diskette with both the FDISK.EXE and FORMAT.COM files copied on to it. It is particularly useful for users of the WIN95 or earlier operating systems to add CD-ROM support to that diskette as well. Detailed instructions on preparing this diskette can be found in Chapter Sixteen, Multimedia.

> **EXAM NOTE:** Be able to describe in detail what FDISK and FORMAT do, and how they affect the system.

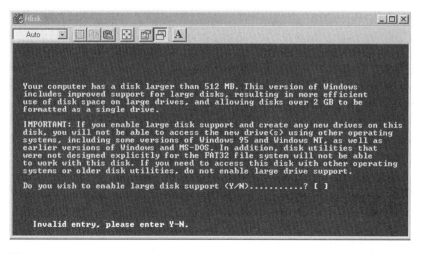

Figure 13.4 The opening screen of FDISK. And if you press the wrong key, such as the hot-key for your screen capture software, this is the message you'll get.

Figure 13.5 The FDISK Options screen. If you only have one physical hard drive installed, option 5 will not appear.

When you boot to that disk, you'll be at a DOS screen with an A:\ prompt. Type fdisk at the command prompt and you'll be presented with a screen that looks like the one in **Figure 13.4**. What this is telling you is that the version of FDISK you're running supports both FAT16 and FAT32. If you answer Yes (Y) to the question at the bottom, you are enabling FAT32. Answering No (N) puts you in FAT16.

This brings you to the FDISK Options screen shown in **Figure 13.5**. In this particular illustration, you are presented with five options. This is because the computer I'm using to create

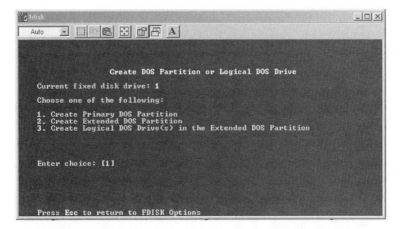

Figure 13.6   Creating partitions or Logical DOS Drives

the illustrations has more than one physical disk installed. If you run this utility on a machine with only one physical disk, option 5, Change current fixed disk drive, will not appear.

How you work with this first screen is entirely dependent upon whether this is a brand-new machine you're configuring for the first time or if it is an older computer that you are servicing. If you are working with a drive that already has an operating system installed and you're trying to blow it away, you will be better off if you work backward through the menu and then work forward. For the purposes of this discussion, however, I'll take the screens in order.

OPTION 1, CREATE DOS PARTITION OR LOGICAL DOS DRIVE

This option brings up the screen shown in **Figure 13.6**

If you select 1. Create Primary DOS Partition, then you are creating the partition that will begin on the physical sectors immediately following the file allocation tables. 2. Create Extended DOS Partition is where you further subdivide your drive into smaller pieces. Note that you cannot create an extended partition if no primary partition has been created. There is a specific order in which things must be done.

3. Create Logical DOS Drive(s) in the Extended DOS Partition allows you to further subdivide the extended partitions into even smaller chunks. Since the MBR only supports four partitions, these logical DOS drives are defined in the Volume Boot Record (VBR) contained within the extended partitions themselves. Every extended partition requires that at least one logical DOS drive be created.

OPTION 2, SET ACTIVE PARTITION

The second option shown in the FDISK Options screen is 2. Set active partition. If you have created a single large partition, this will be done automatically for you. If not, you will get the screen shown in **Figure 13.7**. The message you see in the illustration indicates that an active partition has already been set. This will not be the case on a newly installed drive. Users with

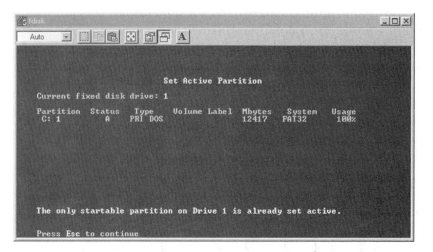

Figure 13.7   Setting the active partition

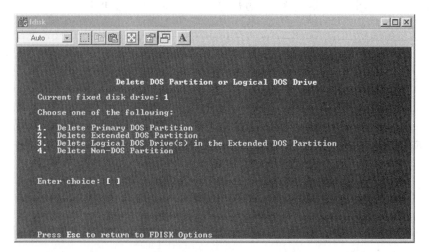

Figure 13.8   Deleting partitions

drives configured with more than one unformatted partition will be shown a list of all partitions on the drive. You select the one you want marked active by typing in its number.

Option 3, Delete Partition or Logical DOS Drive

Selecting 3. Delete partition or Logical DOS Drive brings up the screen shown in **Figure 13.8**. The options are as follows:

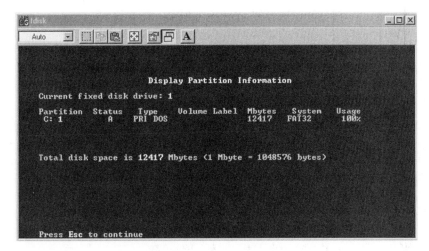

Figure 13.9 Viewing partitions

- *Delete Primary DOS Partition.* You cannot do this if there is an existing extended DOS partition. That's one of the reasons why on an existing machine you view the partitions first. That way you know there are extended partitions that need to be deleted.

- *Delete Extended DOS Partition.* You can't do this while there are logical DOS drives defined. Therefore, it is necessary to delete all logical DOS drives before you can delete the partition. That is the purpose of the next option.

- *Delete Logical DOS Drive(s) in the Extended DOS Partition.* It does exactly what it describes. Once you've done this, you can proceed to option 2.

- *Delete Non-DOS Partition.* This is the other reason you view partition information before you begin. Drives partitioned with NTFS, HPFS, or the Unix File System will not be seen by FAT. They'll only appear as non-DOS partitions.

OPTION 4, DISPLAY PARTITION INFORMATION

Back on the FDISK Options screen, option 4 brings up a screen that lists all DOS partitions, primary and extended, and all non-DOS partitions (**Figure 13.9**). In this particular image, there is only a single primary partition. You can't manipulate anything from this screen; you can simply view it. But on that machine that you're servicing for somebody else, knowing how the drive was originally prepared can save you several steps later on.

OPTION 5, CHANGE CURRENT FIXED DRIVE

Option 5 (**Figure 13.10**) allows you to redirect the actions of FDISK from your primary drive to any of the others installed on a system. This option has also caused more disasters than any other I've described. After installing a second physical hard disk into a computer, when you run

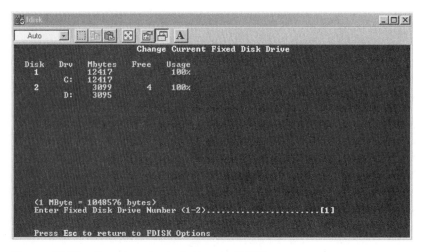

Figure 13.10 Changing physical drives in FDISK

FDISK it is essential that you switch over to the new drive before configuring partitions. You will be warned that a primary partition already exists if you try to create one on your existing drive. Unfortunately, it's all too easy for the beginner to simply go ahead and delete the primary partition after they read that message.

FORMATTING DRIVES

Now that you've got your partitions prepared and a file system selected, you are ready to format the drive for use. FDISK created the MBR, now the FORMAT command is going to prepare your file allocation tables for use. The format command is the utility that groups sectors into clusters, based on the file system and partition size selected. When you format a drive for the first time, it can seem to take forever. The bigger the drive, the longer it takes.

Interestingly, it only takes a few seconds to generate the file allocation tables. Effectively, that's all the drive really needs to have done before it's ready to be used. However, you don't want to be copying crucial and highly sensitive data, such as your saved games from *Redneck Rampage,* to a bad sector. Therefore, on an initial format, as the format command is creating the FAT, it is also scanning the hard drive, looking for bad or suspicious spots on the surface of the drive. It maps those sections as being bad sectors. Here's where a technology called *spare sectoring* comes into play. Virtually every hard drive manufactured, even under today's modern methods, has a certain number of sectors that can't be used to store data. Yet how often do you ever format a drive and have it tell you that it found a bunch of bad sectors?

BUZZ WORDS

Spare sectoring: A technique hard drive manufacturers use in which extra tracks of recordable space are included with each drive that ships. As bad sectors are discovered on the drive, new sectors are made available from this space to replace the bad ones.

Spare sectoring assumes that there will be bad sectors. However, it's bad PR to ship a drive that, fresh out of the box, starts spewing out a report of bad sectors when it's formatted. Every drive coming off the assembly line has a few extra tracks, over and above the rated capacity of the drive. At the factory, the drive undergoes a preliminary test, and defective sectors are already mapped and additional sectors made available from the spare tracks. To be on the safe side, the format routine is looking to see if the initial process missed any.

Once a drive has been formatted for the first time, it is possible to bypass the quality control stage. Typing in the FORMAT command with the /q trigger simply rewrites the file allocation tables without doing a surface scan.

HARD DISK MAINTENANCE

Okay, now it's been a while. For the last several months you've been using your hard drive daily and have given it a heavy workout. Several gigabytes worth of data have been added, deleted, edited, massaged, and manipulated. And all of a sudden your drive is becoming slower than death. What can you do about it? Several third-party software vendors offer basic utilities that help deal with this problem, as well as with the possibility that your drive may be developing bad sectors. Microsoft includes basic versions of these utilities in its product. These utilities are ScanDisk and Disk Defragmenter, usually called Defrag. ScanDisk can scour your hard drive for errors such as bad sectors, lost clusters, and invalid files. Defrag takes files that have been scattered all over your hard drive and puts them back together all in one place.

> **EXAM NOTE:** While the A+ Exam is supposedly vendor-neutral, the only disk maintenance tools you're likely to be asked about are ScanDisk and Defrag. Even if you're a Linux user, make sure you understand how these utilities work.

SCANDISK

ScanDisk is a utility that first appeared in Windows 95 and has been with Windows users since (**Figure 13.11**). When ScanDisk is run on a drive, there are two options. A standard check simply checks your files and folders for errors such as invalid names and/or date stamps. A thorough scan finds much more. A thorough scan scans the surface of the hard disk looking for bad sectors. It can also find other errors such as lost file fragments, cross-linked files, duplicate file names, and errors that occur when Windows converts a long file name to MS-DOS's more primitive naming conventions.

Two of these errors are worth taking a closer look at. These are the lost file fragments and cross-linked files. Many third-party utilities will refer to the lost file fragments as *lost clusters*.

Lost file fragments generally occur when there has been an unexpected system shutdown. If the OS suddenly crashes or if the user turns the machine off without going through the standard shutdown procedures, temporary files are left open, data that has been copied to virtual memory has not been saved, and open files are not properly closed. All of these can result in the FAT finding file allocation units (FAUs) on the hard drive that are occupied, but have no reference in FAT to a specific file. These unclaimed clusters are the ones that are being reported. When ScanDisk finds

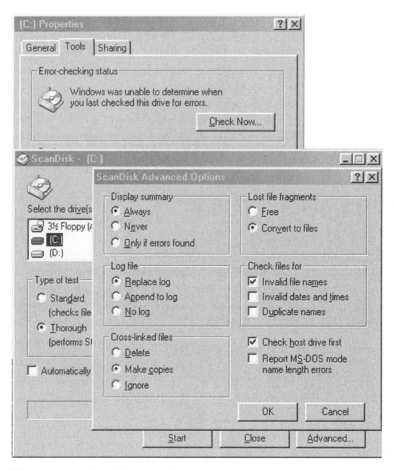

Figure 13.11 ScanDisk is a Microsoft utility that should be run on a regular basis. The Advanced Options allow the user to select a number of different errors to look for.

them, by default, they are converted to files in the system root directory with names of file0000.chk, file0001.chk, and so on. In most cases, these were temporary files the system still had open at the time of the shutdown. They have little or no impact on the permanent copy of that file still written to the hard drive. Still, from time to time, they are user data that was never written to file. In many cases, the data is corrupted, but if you can recognize what it is and where it goes, sometimes you can recover it. The vast majority of the time, your best bet is to delete the .chk files and free up the space.

BUZZ WORDS

Lost cluster: See Lost file fragment.

Lost file fragment: An FAU on the hard drive that contains data, but that has lost the pointers that identify the file to which it belongs.

Cross-linked file: An FAU that is claimed by two or more different files, and is therefore available to none.

Cross-linked files can be a more serious issue. You may recall when I discussed the formatting of hard drives, I pointed out that every single FAU on the hard drive is mapped, whether it is in use or not. When a file uses the FAU, the entry for that file in FAT marks that FAU as occupied and claims it. If two or more files mark the same FAU as being a part of that file, there is a problem. None of the files that claim those sectors can access the data on them. This situation can be caused by unexpected shutdowns, failure of a device controller, a glitch that occurred in the application that created the file, or any number of other things.

The way ScanDisk "fixes" these files is to compare the creation date in the file entry. The file with the most recent date gets the cluster. Most of the time this will be correct. That doesn't, however, mean that the other file didn't, at some time or the other, have data that occupied that file.

Other problems ScanDisk can find are invalid dates and invalid file names. No OS allows the user to create an invalid file name. But data corruption can cause it to happen. If the OS thinks that an invalid character exists, it will mark the file name as invalid. Invalid dates occur when the date of the file is later than the date the system reports as being current, or an invalid date format. ScanDisk fixes either of these problems.

DISK DEFRAGMENTER

When files are first copied to the hard drive, the controller attempts to find enough contiguous space for the entire file to fit. On a new drive, that's no problem. As time goes on and the drive fills, more files have been added to the FAUs following the end of any given file, the drive is fuller than it used to be, and there aren't as many really large spaces in which to fit data. When you open a file and edit it, and then subsequently save it back to disk, that file will be stored on the same FAUs it originally occupied. If that file can no longer fit into contiguous space, the controller will simply take the overflow and store it someplace else on the drive. The file now exists in two separate places on the drive. The more often a file is opened, edited, and resaved, the more different places it occupies.

The converse happens as files are deleted. That space becomes available. As the drive fills, contiguous space may become a premium. So new files get copied to wherever the controller can find space.

I pointed out in Chapter Twelve when discussing I/O operations that a contiguous file only requires one I/O operation to set up the data transfer, and then the data can move to memory in bursts. If the file has been fragmented, each fragment requires a new I/O operation, from setup to breakdown.

Another performance hit caused by a heavily fragmented drive comes as a result of the way Windows maintains its swap file. The swap file needs to be contiguous. You may have 2GB of free space, but if only 200MB of it is contiguous, then Windows effectively has a 200MB swap file. This is too small for optimum performance and can degrade overall system speed noticeably. Defrag (**Figure 13.12**) can put the files on your system back together again, and put all free space toward the end of the drive, where it belongs. Files are accessed much more quickly, and Windows can make a larger swap file.

Whenever possible, users should run Defrag in Safe Mode. This is because open files cannot be defragmented. In Safe Mode, critical system devices will obviously be running, but unused

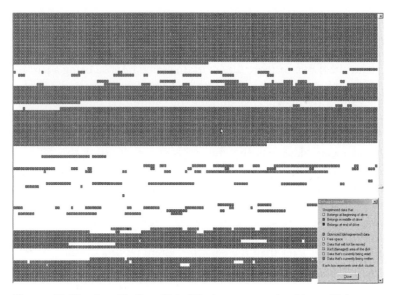

Figure 13.12 As with ScanDisk, Windows users should run Disk Defragmenter on a regular basis.

drivers, such as for a scanner, digital camera, printer, NIC, sound card, and so on, won't load, so those files can be relocated.

Linux and Unix users don't really have a need to defrag their drives. The file system used by these two OSs have code built in that relocates files to contiguous space when they outgrow their old living quarters.

TROUBLESHOOTING HARD DRIVES

Much of what will appear in this section is simply a reiteration of things I've said before. It's simply collected into one place for ease of use. There is also some additional material that you might find useful, however, so don't just automatically assume I'm just trying to make the book fatter.

Problems with hard drives will fall under one of two categories. They either don't work at all, or they seem to work when you start the machine, but they're acting up in some way, shape, or form. I'll cover both bases.

EXAM NOTE: Hard disk troubleshooting is one of the more prominent troubleshooting subjects on the entire exam. Rather than point out everything you are likely to encounter, suffice it to say that the next few pages are very important.

WHEN THE DRIVE ISN'T SEEN

If the drive isn't being seen at all by the system, nine times out of ten, it's a configuration issue. You boot the machine and all you have is drive A. You might know this is happening right off the bat if you get error messages like "No Fixed Disk Present," "Hard Disk Controller Failure," or any one of several numeric error messages in the 17** range, including 1701, 1780, 1781, 1790, and 1791. Other error messages that point to this include "Hard Disk Configuration Error," "Hard Disk 0 Failure," or "Invalid Drive Specification."

Ask this question: Was this drive just installed, or has it been in place for a while? If you just installed it, check the following:

- Is the power connector (Molex) hooked up? Drives have a tendency to not work as well when there is no electricity coming to them.

- Check the Molex to make sure there's current coming through it. This is where having a multimeter comes in handy.

- Did you use a Y-cable to get power to the drive? If so, try hooking it up directly to one of the cables coming straight out of the power supply. The Y-connector might be bad.

- Is the ribbon cable connected? Even if there's power going to the drive, the BIOS finds the drive on POST by sending signals down the cable. No cable, no signals. No signals, no drive.

- Is the ribbon cable connected to the proper port on the motherboard or I/O card? On older machines, it was necessary for the boot drive to be on the primary port, or it wouldn't be recognized.

- Check the jumpers for master/slave if it is an IDE drive. If the settings are right, check and see if you have a CS cable. Those can drive you nuts, too. A notch clipped out of the twenty-eighth conductor tells you it is CS, but not seeing a notch doesn't necessarily tell you it isn't. To be on the safe side, put the slave drive in the middle connector and the master on the end.

- Check device ID numbers on SCSI drives. Two devices can't share the same ID unless they're part of an array. I'll cover that in more detail in the next chapter.

- Check your CMOS settings. On many machines, it's possible to disable the IDE ports. Maybe the IDE port got disabled somehow. If the CMOS thinks there isn't a drive there, nothing else matters. The drive isn't there. On most machines, the default is "AUTO," so this shouldn't be an issue. But people do play with CMOS settings, even though they should know better.

- Is the drive any good? Hey, face it! Sometimes, you just get a bad drive. Make it the only device on the primary IDE port, set it to master, put it in the middle connector, make sure it's got power, and fire it up. Still not there? You might have a bad drive, but you also might have a bad port. Try a drive you know works.

WHEN THE DRIVE IS THERE, MORE OR LESS

While booting the machine, the POST routine usually displays its progress. On some brands of computer, these messages are concealed by the manufacturer's logo. You need to disable this screen if possible. The POST messages can contain information that helps with troubleshooting certain problems. Press the Esc key as soon as the promo screen appears, and you should see the POST messages. Usually. One of the messages displayed is a listing of IDE devices found.

If you can't clear that screen, or are a little late on the uptake, you should also get a message telling you what key to push to enter the CMOS Setup program. These are discussed in detail in Chapter Five, Motherboards, BIOS, and the Chipset. Many BIOS products have an IDE Autodetect utility that will tell you if it's finding a drive or not. Run that.

If the machine makes it all the way through the POST routine and then fails, there are several things to look at:

- Is the hard drive recognized by the BIOS, but not the operating system? Check the following:
  - Are the installation parameters set correctly?
  - Does your BIOS support the type of drive you're using? This is mostly a problem on older machines.
  - Are you using the correct translation mode? If the CMOS somehow got accidentally moved from LBA to Large or Normal, the OS is going to choke.
  - Did somebody accidentally FDISK or format the drive? Fix the problem, then take the machine away from the user!

- Did you get an error message saying "I/O error reading Drive C:"? This could be a bad thing. Many viruses attack the boot sector, and this is the message you're likely to get. Most reliable antivirus programs, such as McAffee or Norton AntiVirus, provide a bootable diskette that starts machines that are so affected. Maybe you'll get lucky and that can fix the problem. Then again, maybe you won't. If you prepared the drive using one of Microsoft's versions of FDISK, use that same version and try the command fdisk/mbr. That can sometimes repair a corrupted master boot record. That same error message can result from a damaged boot sector. If this is the case, the drive is dead. It might be possible to salvage the data from the drive.

- You get the message "No Operating System Found." If this happens, take that boot diskette you made earlier and boot to the A:\ prompt. Now log onto the C: drive by typing C:\ and pressing the <Enter> key. If you get a C:\ prompt, type CD WINDOWS or CD DOS depending on what you're using for an OS. Does your prompt change to C:\WINDOWS? If it does, it's unlikely you have a bad drive, but rather a corrupted installation of your OS. Before you get rash and FDISK the drive and start over, try reinstalling the OS over the previous installation. That way you don't blow away all of your other directories. Most of your data can be salvaged, although you will probably have to reinstall most, if not all of your applications.

- Your machine boots okay, but Windows always has to start a ScanDisk. This could be a sign of impending drive failure. Is ScanDisk finding a lot of bad sectors? If so, back up your data and replace the drive now, while you still have your data intact.

- "Invalid Command Interpreter," "No Boot Device Available," or "Missing Operating System" usually indicates that the MBR has become corrupted. Try the FDISK /MBR (which only occasionally works) or use one of several third-party utilities that are available for restoring MBRs.

■ "General Failure Reading Drive C:" can occur either on bootup or long after the system boots, while you're running an application. This indicates bad sectors on the drive. Run ScanDisk. Boot to a floppy and run it from there, if necessary.

Since hard drives have become so incredibly cheap (relatively speaking), it is becoming easier for an IT administrator to take a hard drive exhibiting any of the above symptoms, especially a drive that announces bad sectors, and circular file it, replacing it with a new drive. In a mission-critical installation, it is probably not a bad idea to replace the drive, but you might want to try something before you are too quick to throw away what might be a perfectly good drive.

Sometimes, the operating system has a hard time reading a particular cluster, so it relocates the cluster and marks it bad. That is a safety net programmed into the OS to protect your data. The cluster might not necessarily be bad, however. There may have simply been a temporary problem. Shutting down a system while the OS is still running can do that.

So before you discard the drive, FDISK it, format it, and put it to use in a less critical installation. It might continue to work for years.

THE DRIVE DOES NOT FORMAT TO CAPACITY

A problem that is gradually working its way out of modern installations occurs when a larger hard drive is installed, and then only formats to a fraction of its capacity. Years ago, it was possible to have your drive format to 508MB, regardless of how large it was. This was because the BIOS and/or chipset on the motherboard only supported the first generation of IDE devices. If it was just the BIOS that was the issue, the problem could be solved by installing an I/O card equipped with ATA-3 or later IDE, as long as it was equipped with supplemental BIOS. If the chipset was the limitation, the only solution was a new motherboard.

Next came the 8GB limitation. If the BIOS and/or chipset did not support the Int13h extensions that I discussed, then a 40GB drive might be easily identified by the system, but would only format to a maximum of 8GB. The problem and solution here was the same as described in the previous paragraph.

The problem most recently seen is a 32GB limitation. Once again, this may be a BIOS limitation. If the BIOS version is prior to 1998, this is most likely the problem. Once again, an adapter card with supplemental BIOS may fix the problem as long as it's not inherent in the chipset. If your BIOS version is after 1999, it's most likely an OS-related issue. Windows 2000 and XP will only allow FAT32 partitions of 32GB. If you require a larger partition using those operating systems, you need to use NTFS.

CHAPTER SUMMARY

That concludes my discussion of hard drives. Chapter Twelve dealt with the construction of hard disks and drive geometry, and in this chapter I discussed the various interfaces that have existed along the way, hard disk preparation and maintenance, and some troubleshooting issues.

The key points for exam candidates to take away from this chapter are the interfaces up to and including ATA-4. Also spend some extra time on disk preparation and maintenance and troubleshooting.

BRAIN DRAIN

1. List as many hard disk interfaces as you can think of.

2. You have installed a new 80GB hard drive in your computer and everything seems to be working fine, except it only formats to 32GB. What is the cause of this problem and what is a possible solution?

3. Discuss as many improvements in the second generation of IDE compared to the first generation as you can think of.

4. Describe in detail the preparation of a hard disk once it has been installed, assuming a FAT32 file system.

5. Based on the discussion generated by Question 4, describe what is happening to the hard disk on each step along the way.

THE 64K$ QUESTIONS

1. The ST-506 hard disk drive offered a maximum capacity of _____ MB.
   a. 2
   b. 5
   c. 10
   d. 20

2. The first release of the ST-506 used the _____ encoding scheme.
   a. RLL
   b. DRML
   c. MFM
   d. ESDI

3. Which of the following was not a feature of the first generation of IDE?
   a. It only supported drives up to 528MB.
   b. Only one IDE channel was allowed per system.
   c. It supported devices other than hard drives.
   d. Two devices could be put on each channel.

4. The maximum capacity limitation for ATA-5 devices is _____.
   a. 528MB
   b. 8GB
   c. 32GB
   d. 137GB

5. Most hard drives in use today use _____ addressing.
   a. ECHS
   b. Large
   c. CHS
   d. LBA

6. Notebook IDE devices use a _____ -pin cable.
   a. 32
   b. 40
   c. 44
   d. 50

7. The Microsoft utility that re-creates the MBR is _____.
   a. FORMAT
   b. SCANDISK
   c. RESTORE
   d. FDISK

8. Serial ATA devices operate on a maximum peak voltage of _____.

    a. 2.2V

    b. 5V

    c. 500mv

    d. 12V

9. A CS cable differs from a standard IDE cable in that _____.

    a. It has eighty conductors

    b. It automatically configures the drive for master/slave settings

    c. Conductor 39 is swapped with conductor 28

    d. The twenty-eighth conductor has been clipped between the center connector and the one on the end

10. Why does the /q trigger on the FORMAT command not work the first time you format a disk.

    a. Who are you kidding? It does!

    b. The sectors have not yet been mapped out.

    c. Format tests each FAU before registering its entry in AT.

    d. The File Allocation Tables have not yet been written.

TRICKY TERMINOLOGY

Block mode: The data transfer setting that allows multiple commands to be moved over an interface on a single interrupt cycle.

Block transfer: The movement of multiple commands over an interface on a single interrupt cycle.

Command overhead: The number of instructions that must be executed in order to carry out a specific request,

combined with the speed at which the device can carry out those instructions.

Command overlapping: The ability of a device to start processing a command even before the command issued prior to it has completed its cycle.

Command queuing: Allows a device to store a series of commands in a buffer area, assuring that as one command is completed another one is rolled up to the gate and ready to go.

Cross-linked file: An FAU that is claimed by two or more different files, and is therefore available to none.

Cycle rate: The amount of time it takes for a specific device under the control of a timing mechanism to complete one "tick" of that timer.

Differential signaling: A method by which a single data wire on a parallel cable is matched up by a wire carrying the inverse of the signal being carried by the data wire.

Double-transition clocking: The movement of two transfers of data on a single clock cycle.

Interleave ratio: The number of sectors that must pass beneath the R/W heads between the reading of one sector and the time the heads will be ready to read the next sector. For example, on a 3:1 ratio, the heads will read or write one sector, two sectors will pass by completely ignored, then the next sector will be written. The unused sectors will be filled in during the next two rotations of the platter.

Lost cluster: See Lost file fragment.

Lost file fragment: An FAU on the hard drive that contains data, but that has lost the pointers that identify the file to which it belongs.

Single-ended signaling: A method by which a single data wire on a parallel cable is matched up by a ground wire.

Spare sectoring: A technique hard drive manufacturers use in which extra tracks of recordable space are included with each drive that ships. As bad sectors are discovered on the drive, new sectors are made available from this space to replace the bad ones.

Third-party DMA: Direct memory access that is managed by a device other than the two devices utilizing DMA to exchange data.

ACRONYM ALERT

ATA: Advanced Technology Attachment

ATAPI: Advanced Technology Application Programming Interface

ECHS: Extended CHS

EIDE: Enhanced IDE

ESDI: Enhanced Small Device Interface. An earlier hard disk drive interface that preceded IDE.

PATA: Parallel ATA

PIO: Programmed Input/Output. A transfer of data in which each byte of data must be negotiated and managed by the CPU.

SATA: Serial ATA

SMART: Self Monitoring Analysis and Reporting Technology. Commands built into a hard disk interface that allows the drive to do some rather extensive self-diagnostics.

CHAPTER 14

THE MANY FACES OF SCSI

The Small Computer Systems Interface (SCSI), pronounced *skuzzy*, was another brainchild of Al Shugart and was initially released as Shugart Associated System Interface (SASI). It evolved from something called the OEM Bus, which had been developed by IBM to interconnect peripherals to the 360 mainframe computer. The idea is that multiple unrelated devices can interface together in a single chain.

The American National Standards Institute (ANSI) released the first set of standards in 1986 as ANSI X3.131-1986. ANSI defined an interface that would accept a number of peripheral devices on a single chain, using a parallel bus. SCSI-1, as it's now called, supported a total of eight devices, including the host adapter. Each device would carry a unique ID number to prevent conflicts. Unfortunately, very few technical specifications were provided and many of the commands included were considered optional. As a result many different devices and adapters appeared on the market that were incompatible with one another. The later release of SCSI-II alleviated much of the confusion, and eventually SCSI-III would define a cross-platform interface.

A+ EXAM OBJECTIVES

Interconnecting SCSI devices has long been a topic that intimidates novice hardware technicians. It shouldn't. This chapter will lead you through the ins and outs of SCSI. If you're taking the CompTIA Exam, it will also cover the following objectives.

1.5 Identify the names, purposes, and performance characteristics of standardized/common peripheral ports, associated cabling, and their connectors. Recognize ports, cabling, and connectors by sight.

1.7 Identify proper procedures for installing and configuring common SCSI devices. Choose the appropriate installation or configuration sequences in given scenarios. Recognize the associated cables.

2.1 Recognize common problems associated with each module and their symptoms, and identify steps to isolate and troubleshoot the problems. Given a problem situation, interpret the symptoms and infer the most likely cause.

How SCSI Works

The core of the SCSI chain is the *host controller*. This can either be a card that plugs into the expansion bus, or it can be built right onto the motherboard in many cases. The host controller is the device that is assigned the IRQ and I/O.

A single SCSI chain consists of the host controller and all the devices connected to it. This would include both internal and external devices. Many controllers provide an external connection that allows the user to hook up devices like scanners, external SCSI hard drives, and CD-ROMs.

Any given controller will be capable of controlling a set number of devices. SCSI-I and II support eight devices, including the controller. SCSI-III supports sixteen devices, including the controller. All internal devices, external devices, and the controller itself count toward this number. However, many adapters are equipped with two or more channels, allowing a separate SCSI chain for each channel.

Devices on the chain are subsequently assigned *device ID* numbers. Every device on the chain, including the host controller itself, must have a unique ID. The IDs need not go in order, and you can skip numbers in the sequence. Typically, the host adapter is assigned ID #7.

The reason for this is that ID numbers are assigned a priority. The highest priorities are assigned the highest numbers, therefore, with SCSI-I and SCSI-II, ID7 carried the highest priority. In order to maintain compatibility, SCSI-III devices place the order of priority, from highest to lowest, 7 through 0, followed by 14 through 8.

No two devices can share an ID number. To do so will result in one of two things. If the devices are designed to support logical unit numbers (LUN), and each device is assigned a different LUN, then all of those devices will be seen by the controller as a single device. If no LUNs are assigned, then the first device with that ID is recognized and subsequent devices with the same ID are ignored.

Internally, SCSI devices hook up on the same cable. If you have three devices, you need a cable with four connections: one for the host controller, one each for the three devices. It doesn't matter what order they are installed in the system. Device IDs will determine the order in which the system "sees" them. Externally, they hook up a little differently. The back of each external SCSI device has an input port and an output port. A cable goes from the external SCSI port to the device. Another cable goes from that device to the next one, and so on until you reach the end.

Any device that is on the end of the SCSI chain must be *terminated*. Any electrical signal that reaches the end of a wire will simply turn around and come back home unless there is something on the end of the cable to prevent this from happening. This is referred to as echo in computer networks and SCSI chains. Nearly all SCSI devices have been equipped with a termination circuit. This is generally done with resistors, although how those resistors are used varies with the equipment. Sometimes you need to physically plug them into the device; other times they are hardwired into the device and engaged by a switch. With some

BUZZ WORDS ————————

Terminate: To create a dead end for electrical signals traveling down a wire so that they do not echo back the other direction.

host adapters, termination can be accomplished through the software, and some older devices have a termination device that must be plugged in. Refer to your manual for the proper procedure for any device you're working with. You can also purchase SCSI cables with terminating resistors installed at one end.

Parallel SCSI has a serious problem with attenuation and noise. This problem is exacerbated as speeds increase, and is substantially greater with older devices. In Chapter Thirteen, Hard Disk Interfacing and Disk Management, I discussed the differences between single-ended (SE) and differential signaling. Early SCSI was single-ended. Each of the bits in the 8-bit signal travels over a pair of wires. One of these wire pairs carried the actual signal, while its partner acted as a ground. On the better cables, these wires were twisted together to reduce cross talk. One of these cables could effectively carry a signal about 6 meters, or 20 feet. Standard ribbon cables were even less than that. As speeds increase, and as the number of devices on the chain increase, this distance is shortened even more. **Table 14.1** compares cable lengths to SCSI standards.

Differential SCSI (now called HVD, for high-voltage differential) was developed to offset this limitation. Differential SCSI uses two wires per bit of information transmitted. This is referred to as a balanced signal, and is the same differential signaling discussed in Chapter Thirteen. It allows for up to 25-meter runs of SCSI devices.

However, that inverse signal wire takes the place of the ground on single-ended devices. As a result, single-ended and differential devices are not compatible on the same SCSI chain. Differential devices can fry any SE devices on the same chain. Also, a different controller is required to handle the signal differences. You can use differential devices in the same system as single-ended devices by adding a separate SCSI controller and creating an isolated differential chain. While differential SCSI was primarily a mainframe peripheral, there were a number of differential controllers and devices produced for the PC market.

Table 14.1   Cable Distance Limitations with Single-Ended SCSI

SCSI Level	No. of Devices	Distance
SCSI-I/II, 5MHz	1	6M
SCSI-I/II, 10MHz	3	3M
SCSI-I/II, 10MHz	>3	1.5M

Single-ended SCSI was severely limited in terms of cable length. The more devices on the chain, the worse it got.

Low-voltage differential (LVD) appeared in 1998. As the name implies, LVD devices operate on a much lower voltage than standard differential devices. They can also sense the presence of single-ended devices on the chain and automatically switch to single-ended operation themselves. If no other SCSI device is detected, or if all the other devices are also LVD devices, the device will operate as LVD. These devices can operate on up to 12 meters of cable. SCSI-III standards dictate that all devices must be LVD. Therefore, it's safe to assume that a device marked SCSI-III is LVD, and that if the device is HVD it is SCSI-II. As with SE devices, LVD and HVD cannot exist on the same chain without adapters in place.

> **NOTE:** One other way to get around the issue of SE and HVD on the same chain was to add an SE-HVD converter to the chain, instead of using a controller and an isolated chain. The problem there was that a new controller would only set you back $100 to $150. A converter can run upwards of $300 and effectively reduces the length of the HVD chain.

Aside from the voltage differences of the wires carrying the signals, differential SCSI was no different than standard SCSI in all other respects. All of the rules concerning termination and device IDs hold fast.

USING SCSI EXPANDERS

Even with LVD devices in place, there are times when more distance is needed. A device known as a *SCSI expander* allows this to be done. The expander takes the SCSI bus and splits it into up to three different segments. Each segment can support a run of cable equal to that of the bus that it's on. Therefore, if you have a bus of all LVD devices, three segments of 12 meters are possible. Also, if you are not adding any devices to the middle segment, a longer cable than would otherwise be acceptable can be used.

Expanders work by taking the signal, cleaning up the noise that has been picked up along the way, amplifying it back to its original signal strength, and then sending it along its way. The device and the process are completely invisible to the host adapter. In fact, it is not even considered a device, and therefore requires no device ID. **Table 14.2** shows how much extra distance one can achieve on a SCSI chain using expanders.

Another thing that makes the SCSI expander a very versatile device is that you can mix early SCSI modes with some of the more advanced modes. You can get devices that move a parallel interface across copper wire to a serial fiber-optics interface. There are even devices that move an HVD signal across to an SE interface.

Use of SCSI expanders, on its simplest level, allows someone to stretch a SCSI chain a little farther than he or she would otherwise be able to. This allows external devices to be installed at a greater distance from the host adapter. **Figure 14.1** shows how this might be done.

BUZZ WORDS

SCSI expander: A device that allows a technician to effectively increase the length of a SCSI chain without the risk of data corruption.

Table 14.2 Distance Extensions Using SCSI Expanders

Bus Type	Standard	Fast	Ultra	Ultra2
Single-Ended SCSI				
No Expander	6M	3M	1.5M	N/A
1 Expander	12M	6M	3M	N/A
2 Expanders (populated)	18M	9M	4.5M	N/A
2 Expanders (point to point)	24M	12M	6M	N/A
Low-Voltage Differential				
No Expander	12M	12M	12M	12M
1 Expander	Not Used	Not Used	Not Used	24M
2 Expanders (populated)	Not Used	Not Used	Not Used	36M
2 Expanders (point to point)	Not Used	Not Used	Not Used	48M
High-Voltage Differential				
No Expander	25M	25M	25M	N/A
1 Expander	50M	50M	50M	N/A
2 Expanders (populated)	75M	75M	75M	N/A
2 Expanders (point to point)	100M	100M	100M	N/A

Adding expanders can greatly extend the range of a single SCSI chain.

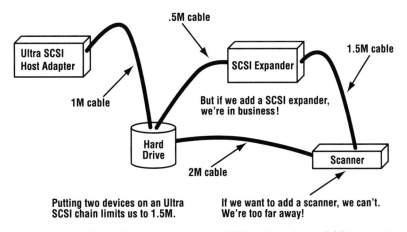

Figure 14.1 Extending the length of a SCSI chain using a SCSI expander

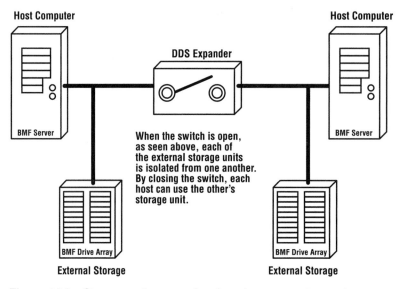

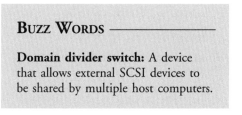

Figure 14.2 Storage systems can be shared among systems when a domain divider switch is used.

Another use of this device involves using it as a *domain divider switch*. For example, if you have two separate computers, each with its own array of hard drives in an external storage bank, it is possible to share those devices between the two host computers. By placing a SCSI expander between the two banks of drives, each computer has access to either array when the switch is closed. If for any reason you need to isolate them, you open the switch and they are separated. A diagram of this in **Figure 14.2** shows you how it works.

BUZZ WORDS ————

Domain divider switch: A device that allows external SCSI devices to be shared by multiple host computers.

TECHNIQUES OF SPANNING DISKS

While not the exclusive realm of SCSI, one key reason for wanting to use SCSI on a high-end system or network server is to facilitate the use of either RAID arrays or to create a single volume set from several drives. While those two concepts may at first sound redundant they really are not. I'm going to start with volume sets for a simple and very scientific reason. It doesn't take as long to discuss and it provides the foundation for later discussions.

VOLUME SETS

While it's true that hard drives are getting bigger every day, every once in a while you run into a situation where you just have too much data to fit onto a single hard drive. Yet for some

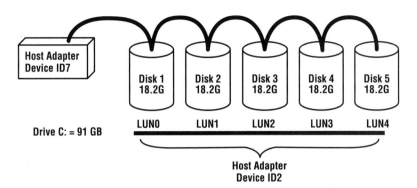

Figure 14.3 Putting five separate hard drives into a single volume set allows you to store much larger chunks of data than single hard drives allow.

reason, it is essential that this data be maintained as a single set. An example of this would be trying to fit a 240GB database onto a single drive. Even if you could find a drive that large, there is still one very good reason you would want to span it across multiple drives. If you have several hundred people accessing that data on a regular basis, a single drive will not be up to the task. A *volume set* takes multiple drives and combines them together to appear to the system and the user as a single drive.

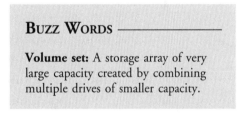

BUZZ WORDS

Volume set: A storage array of very large capacity created by combining multiple drives of smaller capacity.

Earlier in the chapter, I mentioned that if LUNs were used, two devices could be assigned the same ID and the controller would see those two devices as being one. A volume set is an example of where you would do this. Three 72GB hard drives given the same device ID but different LUNs will appear to the controller as a single 216GB drive. These drives become a single volume set.

When you set up a volume set, you are usually doing so with a small collection of hard drives that you are installing into the computer. In this situation, you would decide how many of your drives belong in the set and assign that set a device ID. On a unit level, each of the individual drives would receive its own LUN. From that point on, however many drives you assigned to that set are now all seen as a single drive by the operating system. **Figure 14.3** shows five 18.2GB hard disk drives configured as a single 91GB drive.

RAID ARRAYS

RAID is an acronym for Redundant Array of Independent Disks. RAID allows you to configure several disks to appear as one, similar to a volume set. Unlike a volume set, however, you can build in a certain degree of fault tolerance using RAID. Fault tolerance is a safety cushion that allows a system to keep running in the event of a single (or in some cases, even multiple) component failure.

There are several different levels of RAID, which provide varying degrees of fault tolerance from none to extremely high. I'm not going to discuss all levels of RAID here simply because some levels are proprietary to specific manufacturers and others just aren't used any more. Also, there are single RAID layers and nested RAID layers. Nested layers are when you combine two different single layers. Doing this generally requires more complex hardware, specialized software, or possibly both.

The levels I will discuss here include RAID levels 0, 1, 5, 10, and 50. These are the ones you might actually use some day. Levels 0, 1, and 5 are considered single layers, while 10 and 50 are the two nested layers I'll cover.

SINGLE RAID LEVELS

RAID can be fairly simple, or it can be pretty complex. On the most basic level are the single RAID layers. These are pretty simple and straightforward. Those layers include the following:

- *RAID 0*: Disk striping without parity
- *RAID 1*: Disk mirroring or Disk duplexing
- *RAID 2*: Disk striping with error correction code
- *RAID 3*: Disk bit striping with parity on a dedicated disk
- *RAID 4*: Disk block striping with parity on a dedicated disk
- *RAID 5*: Disk block striping with parity distributed across all disks
- *RAID 6*: Disk block striping with two parity sets distributed across all disks
- *RAID 7*: Proprietary

The difference between disk bit striping and disk block striping is simple. In disk bit striping, the data is striped across the disk in 512-bit sectors. This is the smallest increment that the disk can read. In block striping, there is a user-configurable "chunk" of data that goes onto each disk, dividing the file across disks. Data blocks generally are configured as 2K, 4K, 8K, or 16K blocks. For optimum performance, you want your data block to be the same size as your FAU (see Chapter Twelve, Hard Disk Drive Structure and Geometry).

RAID 0 RAID 0 is the one level of RAID that provides for no fault tolerance. It is simple disk striping without parity. This is one of the RAID levels that is supported by Windows NT 4.0 and Windows 2000 out of the box, as well as several versions of NetWare, Unix, and Linux. RAID 0 (shown in **Figure 14.4**) requires a minimum of two hard drives and can support up to as many drives as you can fit onto your controllers.

When you use RAID 0, you are taking your data and dividing it across multiple drives in stripes. Then, when your hard drive goes back looking for the data again, it can read it back off the drives, reading all the drives simultaneously. The advantage lies in the fact that I/O performance is greatly increased. The amount of performance increase is proportionate to the number of drives in the array. The more drives, the faster your computer will be. You also get to use all the space on all the drives for data storage.

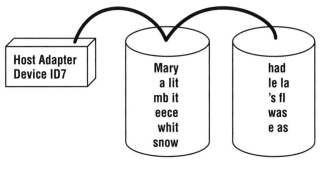

Disk striping without parity

Figure 14.4   RAID 0, disk striping without parity

Of course, the downside to all this is that there is no fault tolerance. If one drive dies, then all your data is gone unless you have developed an appropriate disaster recovery plan. Everything that I said about I/O operations increasing proportionately to the number of drives in your system also holds true to a hard drive specification called mean time before failure (MTBF). This basically is an average number of hours a particular model of drive will last before it dies. If you have five drives, each with an MTBF of 100,000 hours, you have a system MTBF of 20,000 hours.

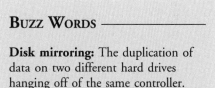

BUZZ WORDS

Disk mirroring: The duplication of data on two different hard drives hanging off of the same controller.

Disk duplexing: The duplication of data on two different hard drives hanging off of different controllers.

RAID 1   RAID 1 comes in two forms. There is *disk mirroring* and *disk duplexing*. They differ in only one minor respect. Both require two disks, and both make a duplicate volume. For every byte of data written to one disk, that identical byte is written to the second. This provides a reasonable level of fault tolerance. If one of the drives fails, the other will automatically take over.

The difference between mirroring and duplexing is in the number of controllers used (see **Figure 14.5**). On a mirrored system, there is a single controller for both disks. The argument against this technique is that your system is dead in the water in the event of a controller failure. Disk duplexing, on the other hand, puts each disk on a separate controller. If either a controller or a disk fails, its clone can take over. Logic dictates that this is the superior method, because it is unlikely that you would lose either both controllers, both hard drives, or one controller plus the opposite hard drive at the same time. Therefore your data is safer. Either way, performance suffers noticeably on write operations, but can actually be enhanced on read operations. Your actual storage capacity is cut in half, however.

RAID 5   RAID 5 is probably the most common form of RAID that you'll encounter on servers today. RAID 5 is disk striping with parity. RAID 5 requires a minimum of three hard drives. The maximum number of drives you can use depends on whether you are using a hardware

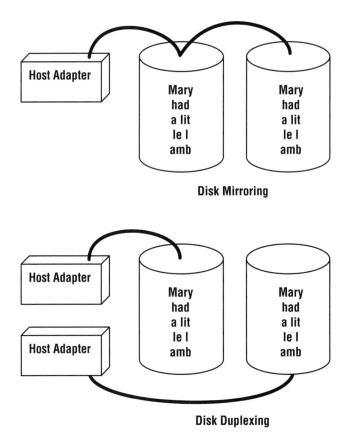

Figure 14.5 Disk mirroring needs only a single controller, while disk duplexing puts each hard drive on a separate controller.

controller or the software RAID included in NT or Novell. Software RAID can make use of up to thirty-two drives. Your hardware will dictate its own limitations.

RAID 5 (**Figure 14.6**) resembles RAID 0 in that it spreads the data across the drives equally. It adds fault tolerance because for each block of data

BUZZ WORDS ————————

Parity block: A data set that represents a mathematical image of data stored elsewhere in a RAID array.

copied to the array, it generates a mathematical image of that data called a *parity block*. The parity information is also distributed evenly across the drives. If a single drive fails, the system continues as if nothing had happened. The parity information is used to rebuild all data in its entirety.

The more drives you put into your system, the more efficiently your system will run. Not only does it have the same effect as more hard drives in a RAID 0 setup as far as performance is concerned, but there is the issue of storage as well. Using a larger number of drives will result in a larger percentage of total available drive space actually being used for data.

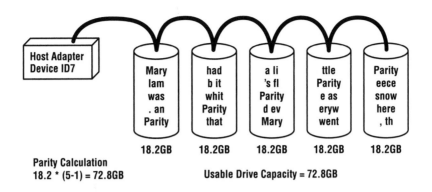

Figure 14.6   RAID 5 provides a high degree of fault tolerance but at the expense of storage capacity.

In order to store the parity information, your system will need space to hold that data. The partitions created on each drive will be no larger than the largest partition that can be created on your smallest drive. Therefore, if you're trying to create a RAID 5 using one 9.1GB and two 18.2GB drives, all three drives will be configured with 9.1GB partitions sewn into the array. You can use the following formula to figure out how much space you'll end up with on your final volume.

(Capacity of Smallest Drive) / (Total Number of Drives in System − 1)

Here's an example. You're going to build a RAID 5 array using five 18.2GB drives plus one 9.1GB drive. How much space will you have? The smallest drive is 9.1GB, and you have six drives. So the first value in the equation is 9.1. You will need the equivalent of one of those six drives for the parity information, leaving five for data. $9.1 \times 5 = 45.5$. Our final volume will be 45.5GB.

Now, what would happen if you took that 9.1GB drive out of the array and only used the five 18.2GB drives? Right away, overall system drive capacity jumps to 72.8GB. $18.2 \times (5 − 1)$ = 72.8GB. You actually lose capacity by including that 9.1GB drive in the array.

NESTED RAID ARRAYS

People being what they are, it doesn't matter how good you make something, there will always be somebody who thinks that it needs to be better. Nested RAID is a perfect example of that. The techniques for nesting RAID all involve large numbers of disk drives and either proprietary controllers or specialized software. Some require both. However, extremely high levels of fault tolerance can be achieved with these techniques.

RAID 0+1 and RAID 10   Trying to understand the difference between these two techniques is understandably confusing. Still, there is actually a difference between a true RAID 10 implementation and simply combining RAID 0 with RAID 1. You now know what RAIDs 0 and 1 can do. You get great performance with RAID 0 but no fault tolerance. You get fault tolerance with RAID 1, but the performance is slower than using a single hard drive. But what if you could have a combination?

A combined RAID 0/1 is a software-based solution, requiring some form of third-party volume manager. RAID 0 can conceivably be placed across a large number of disks, whereas a mirror requires that you use two. RAID 0/1 is a technique of mirroring a disk stripe set without parity. The RAID 0 portion of your system can be any number of drives that your controllers support. However many you use, that number must be exactly duplicated in the mirror. In other words, it would be possible to create a stripe across five disks, greatly enhancing I/O performance. Then, in order to make the system fault tolerant, that stripe set is duplicated to five more disks. While it is possible to set up this configuration on a single controller, it actually makes more sense to place each RAID 0 on its own controller, as seen in **Figure 14.7**. In the event that any single disk fails, that entire side of the mirror is broken and the system is dependent on the other side until the defective disk is replaced.

RAID 10 is stranger yet. RAID 10 requires a minimum of four hard disk drives. Two of these drives will be mirrored. The other pair will be striped in a RAID 0 array for performance. It requires specialized hardware and software support, which adds to the cost of implementation. The advantage is that the machine benefits from a performance standpoint as well as enjoying a certain degree of fault tolerance. The disadvantage to this scheme is that the cost is somewhat high for the limited protection it offers.

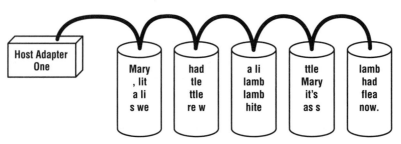

The first controller is used to set up a disk stripe without parity.

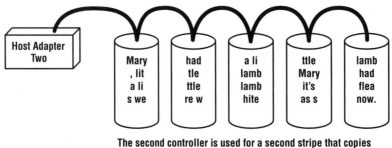

The second controller is used for a second stripe that copies the data from the first stripe set.

Figure 14.7 RAID 1/0 is a mirror of a stripe set without parity.

On the first adapter we configure a RAID 5 array.

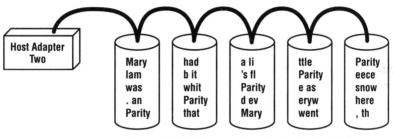

A second RAID 5 array precisely duplicates the first array.

Figure 14.8   You could have more fault tolerance than a RAID 50 array provides. You could have an identical backup server with another RAID 50 array!

RAID 50   This is the most expensive technique to implement of all the ones I will discuss; yet it is by far the most fault tolerant. First, you configure the first RAID 5 array, using anywhere from three to thirty-two disks. Then, on a separate controller, an identical collection of disks duplicates that array. Take a look at **Figure 14.8** and see how it's done. Due to the expense involved, this strategy would only be employed on critical systems. However, security of data is up there with the highest that can be obtained. For the system to fail completely, you would have to have four drives fail simultaneously. Failure of one drive in either array would not bring it down. Parity would simply rebuild the array. Failure of two drives in the same array would cause the second array to kick in. Even if two drives in one array fail, failure of a drive in the second array won't kill the computer. Parity rebuilds that array. Therefore, for total failure, two drives in each array would have to go down at the same time. I think it's safe to assume that if all that happens at once, you've probably got a bigger problem on your hands than a few hard drives.

THE EVOLUTION OF SCSI

Since Al Shugart first introduced his brainchild, SCSI technology has undergone two major evolutionary changes. SCSI-I and II were methods of parallel communication. SCSI-III introduced us to serial SCSI. The different technologies called SCSI have gone from a mere 5MB/s to speeds in excess of a gigabyte per second.

SCSI

The initial SCSI specifications defined an 8-bit, 5MHz bus. Since data could only be moved once per clock cycle, that provided for a 5Mbs throughput. These standards also called for every request for data made by the host adapter to be acknowledged by the target device. This assured accuracy of data transfer. SCSI-I defined only single-ended signaling. As an 8-bit parallel bus, it could never exceed 8MHz in speed.

One major problem that nearly prevented SCSI from ever getting off the ground was a lack of defined standards. Shugart Industries had provided a nice set of ideas with no instructions on how to implement them. There were no defined command sets. Manufacturers would pick and choose from the features and commands suited to the product they were designing and implement only those commands. Then they would ship the device with a controller card specific to their device. Of course, that meant that the card that controlled a hard drive didn't work with a CD-ROM, which in turn didn't work with a scanner, which in turn didn't work with the hard drive.

Another source of frustration for early SCSI users was the diversity of different connectors used. There were DB-25 and DB-50 connectors. The DB-25 appeared in two different sizes. External devices hooked up by way of a 50-pin low-density Centronics connector. This connection looked very similar the one on your printer.

SCSI-I did not provide for any error correction. One of the optional parameters of the original specification allowed for use of bus parity for error detection. Parity, however, does nothing to correct errors. It simply shuts down the system to prevent data corruption. Therefore, it was rarely used.

SCSI-II

The lack of uniform standards prompted the industry to another joint summit. A group calling itself The X3T9 Group met and hammered out the preliminary specifications for SCSI-II (X3.131-1990). One significant change in the SCSI-II standards was that the group defined a total of eighteen commands, called the Common Command Set (CCS), that must be supported by any SCSI-II device. CCS assured that any SCSI-II controller would work with any SCSI-II device.

X3T9 also defined some new bus specifications in the SCSI-II document. To address issues of speed, 16- and 32-bit busses, along with a 10MHz bus speed, were defined. The 10MHz bus was labeled *Fast SCSI*. The 16-bit versions became generically known as *Wide SCSI* (5MHz), and Fast/Wide SCSI (10MHz). In addition, 32-bit *Ultrawide* standards were written. **Table 14.3** shows the differences between these different bus specifications.

SCSI-II also introduced the concepts of command queuing and tagged command queuing that I described in Chapter Thirteen. Another technology introduced that has found its way to other devices on the system since then is that of *scatter-gather data*

> **Buzz Words**
>
> **Fast SCSI:** SCSI over a 10MHz bus.
>
> **Wide SCSI:** SCSI over a 16-bit bus.
>
> **Ultrawide SCSI:** SCSI over a 32-bit bus.
>
> **Scatter-gather data transfer:** The ability of a device to execute a command on one set of data and output the results to multiple devices.

Table 14.3 Comparison of the SCSI-II Standards

SCSI Type	5MHz	10MHz
SCSI-I 8-bit	5MB/s	N/A
SCSI-II 8-bit	5MB/s	10MB/s (Fast SCSI)
SCSI-II 16-bit	10MB/s (Wide SCSI)	20MB/s (Fast/Wide SCSI)
SCSI-II 32-bit	20MB/s (Wide SCSI)	40MB/s (Fast/Wide SCSI)

By today's standards, SCSI-II devices are slow. In their heyday, they were the fastest hard drives available.

transfer. This technology allows a device to execute a command on one set of data and output the results to multiple devices and/or addresses on the system.

SCSI-III

With the release of SCSI-III ANSI broke away from describing the bus in a single document. Instead, its approach involves a collection of documents, each of which describes a different aspect of SCSI-III. Different documents have been created to define protocols, commands, and interfaces. One of these papers defined what is now known as the SCSI Architectural Model (SAM) that covers the physical and electrical aspects of SCSI, including signal characteristics and physical terminations.

The thing that makes SCSI-III such an open standard is that, since it has been defined in a collection of papers instead of a single set of standards, work can be done independently on each layer of the suite. This has allowed for newer and faster technologies to emerge at a much faster rate. Published standards related to SCSI-III include the following:

- SCSI-III Primary Commands (SPC)
  - SCSI-III Primary Commands
    Commands common to all SCSI-III Devices
  - SCSI-III Block Commands
    Commands related to block-oriented devices, such as disk drives
  - SCSI-III Stream Commands
    Data-streaming commands for devices such as tape drives
  - SCSI-III Graphics Commands
    General input/output device commands for devices such as printers and scanners
  - SCSI-III Medium Changer Commands
    For devices such as CD-ROM carousels
  - SCSI-III Controller Commands
    Commands specific to the host adapter, to include hardware RAID controllers

- SCSI-III Protocols
  - SCSI-III Interlocked Protocol (SIP)
  - SCSI-III Fiber Channel Protocol (FCP)
  - SCSI-III Serial Bus Protocol
  - SCSI-III Serial Storage Protocol (SSP)
  - SCSI-III Interconnects
  - SCSI-III Parallel Interface (SPI)
  - Fiber Channel Physical and Signaling Interface (FC-PH)
  - IEEE-1394 High Performance Serial Bus (FireWire)
  - Serial Storage Architecture Bus (SSA)

The result of this division of labor is that new technologies can be developed much more quickly. If a company develops a new protocol, it won't have to wait for an entire new standard to be developed around it before the protocol can be implemented. Protocols can be developed independently of command sets and interfaces. Since this process became a reality, there has been a burst of new technologies released for high-end PCs.

The most significant changes that both computer technicians and end users have to deal with involve connections, so I think that's the best place to start.

SCSI-III INTERCONNECTS

From the start, SCSI has always been a parallel interface that depended exclusively on copper wires to carry the signals. Emerging technologies and speed limitations imposed by parallel communications has caused the industry to look beyond parallel communication over copper wire for the future of SCSI. SCSI interfaces are now being released that use fiber optics instead of wire and a serial data transfer instead of parallel. Therefore, separate sets of standards were developed for different ways of moving data. The modular approach to writing standards means that as new technologies emerge, products based on those technologies appear faster.

SPI Just because new ways of dealing with SCSI have emerged doesn't mean that the old ways are dead. The copper-based parallel interface is still alive and well. The SCSI-III Parallel Interface (SPI) defines the standards manufacturers use to make devices that sit on this interface. Currently, a lot of hard drives are still manufactured that use parallel data transfer. Also, it is still a favorite technology for external devices, such as scanners (although it is starting to lose ground to FireWire, which I will discuss later in this section). The different SPI standards are compared in **Table 14.4**.

Rounding off the list of improvements afforded by SPI is its approach to handling errors that may occur. Previous versions of SCSI were able to use parity in order to check for errors, but could do nothing to correct them. The SCSI-III standards defined a method of using cyclical redundancy checking (CRC) to detect errors and fix them on the fly. Since data is being moved across the bus in chunks, CRC treats the zeros and ones that make up the data as if they represented a very large binary number. It performs a rather complex mathematical algorithm

Table 14.4 Comparison of SCSI-III SPI Modes

SPI Level	SCSI Type	Narrow Mode	Wide Mode
SPI-1	Ultra-SCSI/Fast20	20Mb/s	40Mb/s
SPI-2	Ultra2-SCSI/Fast40	40Mb/s	80Mb/s
SPI-3	Ultra3 (or Ultra160)	N/A	160Mb/s
SPI-4	Ultra320	N/A	320Mb/s
SPI-5	Ultra640		640Mb/s

on each burst of data and includes the results of that calculation as part of the data packet. On the receiving end, the reverse of that calculation is performed. If the results are consistent, the data is accepted. If not, the controller will request that the data be resent.

> **BUZZ WORDS** ————————
>
> **Domain validation:** A process by which a SCSI host adapter sends out a series of commands to each device on the chain and calculates each device's maximum data transfer rate.

There's another feature that has become part of the SCSI-III architecture that should be noted. A process called *domain validation* occurs on boot up. The host adapter sends a series of I/O commands to each device on the chain, testing its throughput capabilities. At this time, a maximum data transfer rate is negotiated between the device and the controller, and that is the rate that will be used from there on out.

SCSI-III introduced the technology of double-transition clocking (DTC) that I discussed in Chapter 13, Hard Disk Interfacing and Disk Management. Previous parallel connections allowed for data to be transferred only on the rising edge of each clock cycle. DTC uses both the rising edge and the falling edge to effectively double throughput. Ultra 160 SCSI can deliver burst modes of 160 megabytes per second.

Ultra640 SCSI is the latest current standard, as of this writing, and was defined under the SP-5 standards released in October of 2002. It is really nothing more than an improvement on SPI-4, or Ultra320. Ultra320 requires that the device be low-voltage differential. It also isolates the host adapter from the interconductor interference by putting it on a separate 80MHz clock that controls data transfer. This clock controls all request (REQ) and acknowledgment (ACK) commands as well as a signal known as the P1 Gating signal. A change unique to SPI-5 is that data is moved in packets instead of a byte at a time.

FC-PH FC-PH (Fiber Channel Physical and Signaling Interface) is one of the three serial interfaces that were introduced with the SCSI-III standards. A serious problem facing the parallel interface is that as speeds get faster it gets increasingly difficult to synchronize the signals. Preventing data corruption becomes a problem.

Serial data, on the other hand, can be moved at incredibly high speeds. So what might be presumably lost in stepping back from the 8-bit bandwidth of parallel communications to moving data a bit at a time, as serial does, is more than made up for when the speed of the transmission is fifty to sixty times faster.

In addition to the significant boost in the speed limit, the serial bus is immune to attenuation and noise. Serial communications over fiber optics eliminates both factors. Therefore, much longer cable runs are possible. Even with copper-based transfer methods, such as FireWire (discussed in Chapter Nine, Examining the Expansion Bus), potential cable lengths are much longer. And because they contain far fewer strands per cable, the medium is much more manageable. More and more devices are moving to one of the different serial media as time moves on.

Of course, to move data in a serial fashion requires that data be packaged differently. The hardware needs to be able to interpret what constitutes the beginning and the end of a transmission, and then be able to assemble a mass of raw digital information back into usable form. In addition, in order to remain compatible with other SCSI-III devices, it needs to be able to accomplish that using the command set defined by SCSI-III standards. It accomplishes both goals by breaking data into packets and sending it across the medium. This is a concept that will become increasingly familiar to you, as this is how data is transferred over modems and across networks as well.

The most common implementation of this interface currently in use is Fiber Channel Arbitrated Loop (FC-AL). The name of this interface can be slightly deceiving. While the specifications were written with the intent of fiber optics, actual implementations use electronic (copper-base) media as well as optical. Media choices include twin-axial cable, coaxial cable, fiber optics, and an FC-AL backplane. Fiber optics promises to be an extremely high-speed bus. The specifications actually define throughput of 1.0625GHz, which would translate out to slightly over a billion bits per second if maximum efficiency could be extracted. Throughput could approach 135MB/s. On the table for consideration and review are proposals that would include 2.12GHz and 4.24GHz standards as well.

Current implementations support 100MB/s per second per loop on mass storage devices with standards already proposed for 200 and 400MB/s loops. FC-AL supports a number of different types of devices ranging from mass storage to network to multimedia. A single loop can support up to 126 devices with up to 30 meters between each device. Termination is not an issue with FC-AL, either. Therefore, it is a whole lot easier to configure an FC-AL loop than an SPI chain. Many manufacturers of high-end servers are already employing FC-AL RAID adapters in their premium lines.

The preferred method for installing FC-AL hard drives is to design the enclosure with a specialized backplane. The drives then fit directly to the backplane. This eliminates the confusion of having a lot of cables inside the box. In addition, FC-AL backplanes are equipped with a circuit called the Port Bypass Circuit (PBC). The PBC automatically detects any drive that has been removed from the loop and instantly re-creates the loop around the vacated connector.

FC-AL does not use device IDs in the conventional manner. Embedded in the device's circuitry is an IEEE Fiber Channel Address (IFCA). Every device manufactured is assigned a unique IFCA that is used by no other device in the world. When the device is plugged into the cable or backplane, the controller uses that ID to enter it into the loop. The user does not have to worry about setting any jumpers or switches. No special software needs to be run. The new device is simply there. This makes installing FC-AL devices the proverbial piece of cake.

One aspect of FC-AL that hard drives specifically benefit from is the fact that it has a greatly reduced processing overhead for commands. Devices hooked up to a traditional parallel SCSI chain can only transmit commands at their asynchronous bus speed. What this means is that, while these devices may be on a bus theoretically capable of 160Mbs (20MB) burst speeds, commands are limited to around 2Mbs. Installing multiple drives as a nonstriped single volume can have a negative impact on performance in many cases because of this.

Conversely, FC-AL transmits at full loop speed, or 100Mbs. This, coupled with high-speed cache ram on the controller for command queuing and controller-operated tagged command queuing, can increase throughput of small file transfer by as much as 200 to 600 percent!

Therefore, while the 160 megabytes per second of Ultra 160 appears on the outset to be faster than that of FC-AL, this is a classic case of looks being deceiving. FC-AL can be dual-ported for a total bandwidth of 200 megabytes per second. And even if this wasn't the case, its lower command overhead alone makes it a much faster interface.

IEEE-1394 (FireWire)   FireWire was discussed in detail in Chapter Nine. The reader should, however, note that IEEE-1394, or FireWire, is actually one of the serial SCSI interfaces.

SSA   Serial Storage Architecture (SSA) is a set of standards optimized specifically for mass storage devices and associated devices such as hardware RAID controllers. SSA does have a slower throughput than any of the other serial standards. The standard allows for bidirectional data transfer of 20Mbs in each direction, although a few high-end devices claim 80Mbs sustained throughput. SSA allows for up to 128 devices to be installed in a single loop. This allows for the construction of huge mass storage devices containing a large number of individual drives.

The physical connectors for an SSA device are quite a bit smaller than the standard SCSI interface. With hard drives and other internal storage devices becoming smaller with each generation, this is an important feature. Also, the cabling standards of SSA call for *hot-pluggable* devices. This means that an SSA device can be pulled from the system and replaced on the fly without the added expense of hot-swappable drive bays.

Because the interface does allow for full-duplex operation, several devices can be active on the bus simultaneously. Read/write operations are much faster, as data from one request can be streaming in at the same time as other requests are being generated.

SSA seems to be rapidly losing ground to FC-AL, however. One of the primary supporters, Conner, was purchased by Seagate, which was a strong supporter of FC-AL. And even IBM, the company that originally developed SSA, is shipping FC-AL product, but not SSA.

Of course, with all the different types of serial interfaces I've discussed, don't feel embarrassed if this seems a little confusing. On the outset, it might seem like the industry should just make it simple, stick to the fastest interface, and drop all the rest. However each of the standards has advantages over the other in specific implementations. **Table 14.5** outlines some of the different standards and how they get used.

Table 14.5   Comparison of Serial SCSI Standards

Serial Standard	Speed	No. of Devices	Max. Bus Length	Common Use
SSA	+/–80Mbs	128	25M	Mass storage arrays
FireWire	+/–400Mbs	63	72M	High-speed external devices
FC-AL	+/–1.06Gbs	126	10KM (theoretical)	A high-speed internal interface

While the three different serial SCSI standards exhibit varying performance, each one shines in a different set of implementations.

UNDERSTANDING ASPI

The Advanced SCSI Programmer Interface (ASPI) really doesn't do much in terms of making your system perform any faster. What it does do is make sure that each of your devices does what it's supposed to do properly and efficiently, without tying up immense amounts of memory using very large and complex drivers for each device. Still, to a certain extent, ASPI does have an impact on performance.

Initially, SCSI drivers and devices were extremely common causes of system lock-up and intermittent application failures. There were numerous reasons for this. For one, SCSI controllers often maintain onboard cache memory. Like any other memory in the computer, SCSI cache must be addressed by the address bus through the MCC (nowadays, part of the chipset). Also, a good many SCSI adapters use their own onboard BIOS chip that communicates with the system through a mini-driver. Many times, conflicting commands generated between the system BIOS and the SCSI BIOS or conflicts between device drivers loaded into upper memory would cause random and intermittent crashes. To solve this, a new standard for SCSI device drivers and command interpretation was developed.

ASPI functions in two layers. The ASPI-Manager is a set of files in the operating system that handles communication between the OS and the host adapter. These files reside within the Hardware Abstraction Layer (HAL) of the various Windows operating systems. The second layer is a device mini-driver for the specific component. This driver communicates with ASPI-Manager to link the specific device to the host adapter. This permits a uniform method by which all SCSI devices function. An advantage that shouldn't be overlooked is the fact that device manufacturers have a much simpler task of interfacing their device with the operating system. Lowering the costs of production effectively lowers the cost of the device.

INSTALLING SCSI DEVICES

Installing serial SCSI is so automatic it requires no discussion. As with USB, installation and configuration is fully Plug 'n Play. Installing parallel SCSI devices is only slightly more complicated than any other peripheral in your machine. Following a few simple rules will make installing even older devices simple. Failing to follow them can make you want an aspirin. There are three things you have to deal with in working with SCSI: the host adapter, the cable, and the device itself. Let's take a look at them one at a time.

HOST ADAPTERS

Host adapters come from many different companies and in many different forms. Things to consider are the level of SCSI you want the adapter to support, the level of support you want it to provide, and the bus on which it will reside. All of these contribute to whether or not the device does what you want it to or not. It is also possible to purchase motherboards with onboard SCSI host adapters.

SCSI adapters are available in both ISA and PCI buses. In the realm of PCI, many companies are providing cards for the 66MHz 64-bit PCI bus. This would be the adapter of choice if your requirements are the ultimate in performance. If you're planning on taking advantage of the performance gains offered by Ultra 160 or FC-AL, and your system has an appropriate slot, this is the way to go.

Any computer, however, will benefit by choosing a 32-bit PCI host adapter over an ISA adapter. An 8MHz bus is somewhat of a bottleneck for a 20MHz adapter, as you might imagine. Since the goal of SCSI is to push the limits of system performance, ISA should only be used if it is the only alternative. PCI will provide substantially better performance. The PCI bus also will make it a whole lot easier to install and configure the card.

Also, consider the devices you intend to install. Separate adapters are needed for HVD and SE devices (although, admittedly, HVD devices are becoming rare). This is a nonissue if your system will be equipped with SCSI-III devices. Some SCSI adapters also provide hardware RAID control. If the goal is to build a high-end server, hardware RAID can greatly enhance performance.

Once you've selected the host adapter, it's time to put it in the system. Plug 'n Play has made this pretty easy with most of the major brands. On older systems using an ISA adapter, PnP might not be an option. Non-PnP devices will need to be configured for an IRQ and an I/O address. On some cards (the majority of them, these days), this is done in software. Some, on the other hand, are configured by way of DIP switches or jumpers. In this case, you'll need to know in advance what one of your available IRQs is. If you know you must manually configure the card, then prior to bringing the system down for the installation, identify what resources are available. In Windows, this can be done in Device Manager. That covers about 80 percent of the systems in use today.

THE COMPONENTS OF A SCSI CARD

If you look at most SCSI adapters, you see that there is a BIOS chip on them. For simple SE SCSI signaling, it is possible to include into the BIOS of the system the total command set required. Supporting any of the protocols that require balanced signaling or make use of advanced SCSI functions requires a little more help than that. The BIOS chip on the adapter provides the full command set for that specific card. In the old days, computers didn't recognize a SCSI hard drive as a bootable device. There is information in the host adapter BIOS that allows the machine to boot to SCSI. This BIOS information is shadowed to memory on boot and supplements BIOS information provided by the computer.

SCSI host adapters usually include as part of the BIOS a configuration utility that can be initialized on system boot. This program also provides some decent diagnostics utilities that can come in very handy with a SCSI device that doesn't want to install. It will identify any device IDs it finds on the chain, helping to locate conflicts. From here, a SCSI hard drive can be low-level formatted.

Like motherboards, SCSI host adapters are equipped with chipsets that control their functions. This chipset will determine the host adapter's capabilities and performance levels, so picking a brand that uses a decent chipset is important. The manufacturers of host adapters frequently make chipsets as well. For example, Adaptec makes its own chipsets. Some brands get their chipsets from third-party manufacturers and what you're getting can turn into a guessing game. When it comes to SCSI adapters, it's really a good idea to stick with manufacturers you know and trust.

There will also be a small amount of memory built into each host adapter. This is the memory that is used for command queuing. Most adapters also include a certain amount of cache memory. Some adapters allow you to add more memory for additional cache. These adapters will have empty SIMM or DIMM sockets on board for this purpose.

As far as users are concerned, the most significant component on the card is the place where they plug the cable. Some cards provide only a single interconnect for the standard they support. Others support multiple interfaces. For example, a SCSI III adapter might be equipped with both a 50-pin SCSI II interconnect and a 68-pin or 80-pin connector for the SCSI III devices. While both can be used, you should keep in mind that unless the card specifically states that it is a dual-channel card, all devices on that adapter card, regardless of the port they're connected to, are part of the same chain, and therefore cannot have duplicated IDs anywhere on the device.

SCSI Connectors and Cables, Past and Present

As I've mentioned before, there have been a number of SCSI connectors used throughout the years. Different devices might have different connectors, so it's important to pay attention to what you've got. There are adapters to go from one type to the other, but you'll never have one when you need it.

The most common cables you'll run into are the A cable and the P cable. The A is for 8-bit SCSI signals, and comes in two different varieties: 50-pin shielded and 50-pin unshielded. The unshielded cable will be a ribbon cable similar to the one you used with your IDE hard drive. It is commonly used for internal devices. Shielded cables are used for external devices and are round, somewhat thick cables with the individual wires clustered in layers. **Figure 14.9** shows the pinouts for a 50-pin A cable.

16-bit signals are carried over a P cable and connector. This is a 68-pin interface. One notable difference is that with the P connector, even- and odd-numbered wires are not on opposite sides of the connector, as they are with the A-connector. Side A of the interface carries

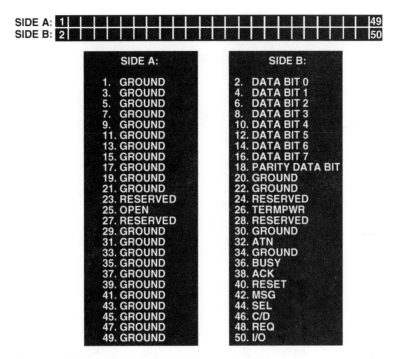

SIDE A: 1 |||||||||||||||||||||||| 49
SIDE B: 2 |||||||||||||||||||||||| 50

SIDE A:	SIDE B:
1. GROUND	2. DATA BIT 0
3. GROUND	4. DATA BIT 1
5. GROUND	6. DATA BIT 2
7. GROUND	8. DATA BIT 3
9. GROUND	10. DATA BIT 4
11. GROUND	12. DATA BIT 5
13. GROUND	14. DATA BIT 6
15. GROUND	16. DATA BIT 7
17. GROUND	18. PARITY DATA BIT
19. GROUND	20. GROUND
21. GROUND	22. GROUND
23. RESERVED	24. RESERVED
25. OPEN	26. TERMPWR
27. RESERVED	28. RESERVED
29. GROUND	30. GROUND
31. GROUND	32. ATN
33. GROUND	34. GROUND
35. GROUND	36. BUSY
37. GROUND	38. ACK
39. GROUND	40. RESET
41. GROUND	42. MSG
43. GROUND	44. SEL
45. GROUND	46. C/D
47. GROUND	48. REQ
49. GROUND	50. I/O

Figure 14.9   Pinouts for 50-pin A connector

wires 1 through 34, while Side B carries 35 through 68. The pinouts for this connector are illustrated in **Figure 14.10**.

There are also some proprietary SCSI connectors that you might occasionally run into. Two notable examples are the 60-pin IBM connector used on certain PS/2 models of its line. There were also 25-pin connectors used on both Macintosh computers and some PCs. Since this book does not target proprietary standards, I mention them only in passing to make you aware of their existence. In the modern world of computers it is unlikely that you will run into them.

SCSI DEVICES

Installing an actual device onto a SCSI chain works just like any other interface. The one thing that can cause a small amount of initial confusion occurs when all you've ever worked with are IDE devices. SCSI drives can look very similar to IDE at a casual glance. However, if you look closer, you'll find that they're quite different.

The socket where you plug the cable has a lot more pins for one thing. Admittedly, unless you happen to have one of each in your hand, a 50-pin SCSI socket doesn't look that much different from a 40-pin IDE. An IDE device, however, will have the jumpers for setting master/slave relationships. A SCSI drive either has no jumpers, if it is a software-configurable device, or a lot more than just three if you have to set the device ID by jumpers.

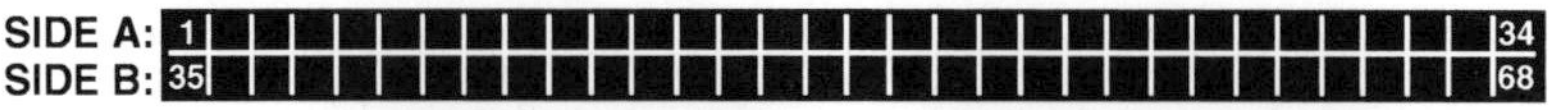

SIDE A:	SIDE B:
1. GROUND	35. DATA BIT 12
2. GROUND	36. DATA BIT 13
3. GROUND	37. DATA BIT 14
4. GROUND	38. DATA BIT 15
5. GROUND	39. PARITY BIT 0
6. GROUND	40. DATA BIT 0
7. GROUND	41. DATA BIT 1
8. GROUND	42. DATA BIT 2
9. GROUND	43. DATA BIT 3
10. GROUND	44. DATA BIT 4
11. GROUND	45. DATA BIT 5
12. GROUND	46. DATA BIT 6
13. GROUND	47. DATA BIT 7
14. GROUND	48. PARITY BIT 1
15. GROUND	49. GROUND
16. GROUND	50. GROUND
17. TERMPWR	51. TERMPWR
18. TERMPWR	52. TERMPWR
19. RESERVED	53. RESERVED
20. GROUND	54. GROUND
21. GROUND	55. ATN
22. GROUND	56. GROUND
23. GROUND	57. BUSY
24. GROUND	58. ACK
25. GROUND	59. RESET
26. GROUND	60. MSGL
27. GROUND	61. SEL
28. GROUND	62. C/D
29. GROUND	63. REQ
30. GROUND	64. I/O
31. GROUND	65. DATA BIT 8
32. GROUND	66. DATA BIT 9
33. GROUND	67. DATA BIT 10
34. GROUND	68. DATA BIT 11

Figure 14.10   Pinouts for a 68-pin P connector

SETTING UP THE SCSI CHAIN

With today's lineup of Plug 'n Play host adapters, terminated cables and auto-configuring devices, this section is almost unnecessary. However, not everything you're going to see is modern. So it is a good idea to be familiar with the concepts for those times you're doing work on an older Pentium-based server with SCSI II devices. One of the very first sections of this chapter mentioned that two essential factors of setting up SCSI are termination and device IDs. Both are crucial, or the chain won't work properly, if at all.

TERMINATION

An electrical anomaly that all circuits have to deal with is reaching the end of the wire. Where does the signal go after that? It might be easy to imagine that it simply stops at the end of the wire, and then disappears. Unfortunately (or fortunately, depending on which viewpoint you want to take) the universe doesn't operate that way. The signal I keep discussing is created by the movement of electrons along a piece of wire. When those electrons reach the end of the wire, they can't just jump out into air. There has to be something there to accept them, otherwise they will simply turn around and go back the other way, which can be a problem for the next signal that was sent. The two collide and the SCSI chain goes down.

To stop this, you simply place a resistor in the chain at the last device you install. The resistor absorbs those electrons and the signal stops. This terminating resistor must be in place at both ends of the chain. On the host adapter, there is a resistor built in. Most adapters these days are auto-terminating. If there is no device hooked up to the external port, the terminator is activated. Plugging a device onto that port acts to disconnect the terminating resistor.

It's on the other end of the chain that you need to be careful. There are terminators that can be installed onto the cable itself. Also, SCSI devices are equipped with their own terminating circuits. How these are employed vary from device to device. On some internal drives, it consists of a jumper. There is a shunt that goes over the jumper to engage termination; it is removed to disable it. Most external devices use a simple switch.

One mistake that almost everyone who works with older SCSI devices makes eventually is to add a device onto the chain without removing the termination from the device that had previously been on the end. The new device, as a result, is farther downstream than the terminating resistor and is simply not recognized. Before you spend several fruitless minutes trying to troubleshoot the device, check termination. That's most likely your problem. This is SCSI's equivalent of getting the master/slave configuration wrong. If you find that termination is set correctly and the new device still can't be recognized, then your problem may be because of a duplicate device ID on the chain.

DEVICE IDs

The final SCSI concept that I need to discuss is that of device IDs. I mentioned earlier that each device on the chain has to have a unique device ID. This is how the host adapter keeps track of what is transferring data. The exception to this rule is when you're putting multiple devices into an array, such as the volume sets or RAID arrays that I talked about a few pages back. In this case, the array owns the device ID and each device is given its own LUN.

That seems pretty straightforward, but just how do you go about doing it? On newer devices, it's about as simple as anything you'll ever do in this industry. Most devices that ship these days have their device IDs and/or LUNs set by software. When you run the SCSI setup utilities of a host adapter, device IDs are dolled out. If the adapter is one that supports RAID arrays from within the hardware itself, you will be given the opportunity to identify those devices that you wish to be part of the array. The adapter will then configure LUNs for those drives.

Older drives aren't always so easy. The majority of drives were built with a set of jumper switches on the back of the drive, and setting the device ID is done through those jumpers. Different manufacturers had different settings to achieve specific IDs. So it's a good idea to have the manual available when setting up your drive. If none is available, you can take the trial-and-error approach, or you can be more scientific about it.

Table 14.6 SCSI Settings: MSB to the Right

Device ID	SW1	SW2	SW3
0	Off	Off	Off
1	On	Off	Off
2	Off	On	Off
3	On	On	Off
4	Off	Off	On
5	On	Off	On
6	Off	On	On
7	On	On	On

This table shows switch settings for a device whose most significant bit is located on the right.

Table 14.7 SCSI Settings: MSB to the Left

Device ID	SW1	SW2	SW3
0	Off	Off	Off
1	Off	Off	On
2	Off	On	Off
3	Off	On	On
4	On	Off	Off
5	On	Off	On
6	On	On	Off
7	On	On	On

This table shows switch settings for a device whose most significant bit is located on the left.

With three switches, you have a total of eight different combinations in which they can be set. It's simple mathematics; you have two positions in which a switch can be set, and three switches. Two raised to the power of three gives you a total of eight. That should sound like a familiar number to you if you've already made it this far into the book (and I know I have). All you're doing when you set those switches is setting the binary pattern for the number of the device ID you're choosing. There are two different methods that these drives can be figured. Some manufacturers put the most significant bit (MSB) to the right, others to the left. **Table 14.6** and **Table 14.7** identify switch positions for these settings.

There were also some brands of hard drive that had a bank of pins over which you placed shunts. These are easier to figure out. There are eight banks of two pins each. They represent the ID numbers 0 through 7. Counting from zero up, put the shunt over the pair that represents the number you want to use.

The beauty of some of the newer standards, such as FireWire and FC-AL, is that they require neither device IDs nor termination. They are Plug 'n Play all the way through. Installing a device onto either of these busses is easier than programming your microwave. The downside for the technician is that people no longer have to pay a technician a hundred bucks an hour to come in and set up their hardware.

COMPARING IDE AND SCSI

Which of the two different interconnects to use in your hard drive subsystem can be a critical decision for certain types of computers. The overall performance of a computer is largely dependant upon the hard drives. After reading this chapter, you should have come to the realization that SCSI is definitely the faster interface, especially with some of the newer incarnations of SCSI.

There is no denying that is the truth. Yet UDMA-66 and UDMA-100 drives continue to dominate the marketplace. Why is that?

Cost is a big reason. Right now IDE hard drives are dirt-cheap. Immense amounts of storage can be purchased for small amounts of jingle. And these drives are pretty darned good in terms of performance as well. The same size drive on the SCSI interface will cost more than double that of an IDE, and you have to purchase an additional host adapter card as well.

In that case, why do people continue to buy SCSI? Because of the advanced capabilities of SCSI and the fact that it remains moderately faster than IDE, SCSI still has a loyal following. And for hot-swapping devices in RAID arrays, there is no equal.

THE ADVANTAGES OF SCSI

With SCSI, you can have up to fourteen devices on a chain, and if necessary, you can add another host adapter and double that. For computers with huge storage requirements, such as a server with a secure RAID 5 array, this is key. Overall speed is superior to IDE, as I've already pointed out, but the ways it goes about being faster come into play as well.

On a server where many different users will be asking for files at the same time, SCSI's tagged command queuing is a distinct advantage. Multiple requests for I/O operations are handled much more quickly and efficiently. And the data from those requests gets moved on and off the bus at a much faster rate. Set up a striped set, as I discussed earlier, and the benefits are even greater.

People who regularly work with large files that need to be transferred quickly will also appreciate the SCSI interface. Anybody who's ever done any computerized video editing appreciates that fact. A streaming video file needs to move from the drive to RAM and then to the graphics adapter much more quickly than any word processing document would need to move through a system. Poor data throughput will result in a jittery image and most likely a grainy effect as well.

SCSI is also not as limited to platform as other interfaces. SCSI works on PCs, MACs, and other systems with equal ease. An administrator who has to use multiple platforms can make life easier if all computers are on SCSI. That way a few spare drives can be kept in stock without worrying about which computer they may eventually be used on.

Therefore, a good place to consider SCSI usage would include the following:

- Network servers
- Graphics workstations
- Digital audio-video workstations
- Mixed platform environments
- Any system on which large numbers of devices need to be installed

Obviously, any time excellent performance is the key issue, and cost is not a consideration, you should go with SCSI. However, there are times when users simply won't appreciate the advantages of SCSI. That's when you should consider...

The Advantages of IDE

First and foremost, the biggest advantage of IDE is cost. Anytime you can pick up 40GB of storage space for just about a day's pay, that's a real advantage. It wasn't that long ago that I wanted a 1.2GB drive so bad it hurt. But it was going to set me back two weeks worth of pay. It was really hard to justify that kind of expense. SCSI has dropped quite a bit in price as well, but a 32GB Ultra 160 plus the controller can still make you say "Ouch!"

Performance isn't all that bad, either. The newer ATA-5 drives can move some data across the bus. These drives won't handle the multiple hits that drives on a server can expect, but for a single user on a single machine, that's not an issue. Even large files open quickly with a 7,200rpm UDA-100 drive. The machine I'm using for this book has a 20.4GB drive with those specifications and a 40MB Photoshop image opens in a couple of seconds.

For the novice, IDE can be a lot easier to configure as well. Even though SCSI has gone a long way in this respect, it can still require a little knowledge on the part of the person setting up the system. IDE isn't completely without issues, but on the whole, it is a lot easier for the beginner than SCSI.

Summary of Comparisons

If you're building a server, a high-end graphics workstation, or audio-video editing workstations, by all means go with SCSI. You'll need the performance. But for most single-user computing applications, there is no reason in the world to avoid IDE. Any time you're putting a system together for home use, or a number of systems to sit on corporate desktops or in a school environment, go with IDE. **Table 14.8** compares and contrasts some of the differences between the two interfaces in order to help you better understand them.

Table 14.8 Comparing IDE and SCSI

Comparison Factor	SCSI	IDE
Number of devices supported	High	Low
Type of devices supported	High	Moderate
Device availability	Fair	Excellent
Device cost	High	Moderate
Overall performance	High in most cases	High in single user, single application environments. Low in multiuser environments or with applications requiring extremely high throughput.
Ease of configuration	Moderate to low	High
Cross-platform usage	Good	Poor

By comparing the most significant factors side-by-side, it is easier to decide if a system should use SCSI or IDE devices.

I think it becomes pretty clear from all of this that SCSI and IDE shouldn't be considered competing interfaces, but rather complementary options. Each has a special set of circumstances in which it shines. Until such time as an interface such as FireWire becomes as inexpensive as IDE, I don't think you'll be attending IDE's funeral any time soon.

CHAPTER SUMMARY

For years, understanding the concepts of SCSI has been a major roadblock to novice technicians. Hopefully after reading this chapter, you realize just how difficult it isn't. There are some issues on older SCSI devices that need to be taken into consideration, such as manually setting ID numbers and properly terminating the chain. But for the most part, on modern devices, even these procedures have become automated.

For the exam, understand the concepts of device IDs, LUNs, and termination. But also know the evolution of SCSI. CompTIA likes to make sure you know the differences between Fast SCSI and Wide SCSI. Also understand the different signaling methods discussed in this chapter.

BRAIN DRAIN

1. You've just installed an older SCSI card you pulled from another machine. It was working fine in the other machine, but now the only device the system recognizes is the hard drive. The tape drive and CD-ROM are ignored. What are some of the things that may have caused this?

2. Discuss the differences between single-ended and differential SCSI. Include in your discussion advantages and disadvantages, and discuss how LVD has addressed some of these issues.

3. What was the one thing lacking from the very first release of SCSI specifications that caused so much confusion? What was one of the problems caused and why did this omission cause the problem?

4. You want to configure three hard drives on a chain to be seen by the system as a single larger volume. How can you go about doing this?

5. Discuss why termination of a SCSI chain is necessary. What happens if you don't terminate the chain properly and why is it this happens?

THE 64K$ QUESTIONS

1. How many devices could a SCSI-I chain support?
   a. 5
   b. 7
   c. 8
   d. 14

2. What device ID does the host controller typically occupy?
   a. 0
   b. 1
   c. 7
   d. 14

3. What are two methods of terminating a SCSI chain?
   a. Placing a null device on the last connector of the cable.

b. Installing a resistor into a specially designed socket.

c. Clipping the twenty-eighth wire of the last device.

d. Setting a jumper on the last device on the chain.

4. If you want three devices on the chain to be seen as a single device on the system you would set each device to the same _____.

   a. Device ID

   b. Device Unit Number

   c. Channel

   d. Logical Unit Number

5. How many devices can be supported by a parallel SCSI-III chain?

   a. 5

   b. 7

   c. 8

   d. 14

   e. None of the above

6. A high-voltage differential chain consisting of the controller and a single device can be as much as _____ meters long.

   a. 1.5

   b. 6

   c. 12

   d. 25

7. High-voltage differential devices cannot be on the same chain as a single-ended device.

   a. True

   b. False

8. What are two methods of combining multiple disk drives into a single larger volume without any loss of available storage capacity?

   a. RAID 5

   b. Volume set

   c. RAID 10

   d. RAID 0

9. Which of the following is an example of serial SCSI?

   a. Ultra 640

   b. SPI-5

   c. FireWire

   d. USB

10. A two-layered device driver scheme incorporated by SCSI is called _____.

    a. HAL

    b. ASCI

    c. PLM

    d. ASPI

TRICKY TERMINOLOGY

Device ID: A unique number assigned to each device on a SCSI chain, including the host adapter, that identifies it to other devices on the chain.

Disk duplexing: The duplication of data on two different hard drives hanging off of different controllers.

Disk mirroring: The duplication of data on two different hard drives hanging off of the same controller.

Domain divider switch: A device that allows external SCSI devices to be shared by multiple host computers.

Domain validation: A process by which a SCSI host adapter sends out a series of commands to each device on the chain and calculates each device's maximum data transfer rate.

Fast SCSI: SCSI over a 10MHz bus.

Host controller: The adapter installed on a system or embedded in the motherboard that manages SCSI devices.

Hot-pluggable: Another term for hot-swappable. A hot-pluggable device can be added or removed to its bus without the necessity of bringing the computer down.

Parity block: A data set that represents a mathematical image of data stored elsewhere in a RAID array.

Scatter-gather data transfer: The ability of a device to execute a command on one set of data and output the results to multiple devices.

SCSI expander: A device that allows a technician to effectively increase the length of a SCSI chain without the risk of data corruption.

Terminate: To create a dead end for electrical signals traveling down a wire so that they do not echo back the other direction.

Ultra wide SCSI: SCSI over a 32-bit bus.

Volume set: A storage array of very large capacity created by combining multiple drives of smaller capacity.

Wide SCSI: SCSI over a 16-bit bus.

ACRONYM ALERT

ACK: Acknowledgment

ASPI: Advanced SCSI Programmer Interface. A two-tiered device driver scheme employed by SCSI.

CCS: Common Command Set. Eighteen specific commands that must be included for every device that carries the SCSI-II label.

FC-AL: Fiber Channel Arbitrated Loop

FCP: Fiber Channel Protocol

FC-PH: Fiber Channel Physical and Signaling Interface

HAL: Hardware Abstraction Layer. A layer of the operating system that intercepts all calls to the hardware to prevent the applications from actually accessing the hardware.

HVD: High-Voltage Differential

IFCA: IEEE Fiber Channel Address. A unique address assigned to all FC-AL devices at the factory that allows them to be automatically configured onto the FC-AL loop.

LUN: Logical Unit Number. A setting on SCSI devices that allows multiple devices to be seen by the controller as a single device.

LVD: Low-Voltage Differential

MTBF: Mean Time Before Failure. An average of the number of hours a particular model of device is expected to operate before it dies.

PBC: Port Bypass Circuit. A circuit that manages an FC-AL loop and automatically detects when a device has been removed.

REQ: Request

SE: Single-Ended

SIP: SCSI Interlocked Protocol

SPC: SCSI Primary Commands

SPI: SCSI Parallel Interface

SSA: Serial Storage Architecture

SSP: Serial Storage Protocol

CHAPTER 15

YOUR COMPUTER AND GRAPHICS

I commented earlier in the book that people don't buy a computer because they want something that computes. They buy a computer because they want a word processor or a $2000 deck of cards or an in-house video arcade. Any one of these functions requires that the user have a nice pretty display for all those fancy pictures or a crisp, clear screen for displaying the austere prose they are composing.

That image doesn't just magically appear on the screen. In this chapter, I'll show you a little more about how it really gets there. I'll take you on a tour of different monitor types, and I'll show you what makes a $300 adapter better than a $50 one. I'll also explain why, for some people, that more expensive video card might not be the better choice. Also, even though this is not a book that is intended to instruct you on matters of software, when it comes to video, it is rather important that you understand certain issues dealing with operating systems, graphic file formats, and user applications specific to computer graphics. So, with that in mind, let's dive into the hardware end.

A+ EXAM OBJECTIVES

For those of you studying for the exam, objectives covered will include the following:

1.1 Identify the names, purpose, and characteristics of system modules. Recognize these modules by sight or definition.

1.2 Identify basic procedures for adding and removing field-replaceable modules for desktop systems. Given a replacement scenario, choose the appropriate sequences.

1.5 Identify the names, purposes, and performance characteristics of standardized/common peripheral ports, associated cabling, and their connectors. Recognize ports, cabling, and connectors by sight.

1.8 Identify proper procedures for installing and configuring common peripheral devices. Choose the appropriate installation or configuration sequences in given scenarios.

1.10 Determine the issues that must be considered when upgrading a PC. In a given scenario, determine when and how to upgrade system components.

2.1 Recognize common problems associated with each module and their symptoms, and identify steps to isolate and troubleshoot the problems. Given a problem situation, interpret the symptoms and infer the most likely cause.

4.2 Identify the types of RAM (Random Access Memory), form factors, and operational characteristics. Determine banking and speed requirements under given scenarios.

COMPUTER MONITORS

While this may sound like a gross oversimplification, there are only two types of monitors in general use by the PC-using public these days. The most common is the cathode-ray tube (CRT). These are relatively inexpensive and frequently are bundled with a computer when you purchase a complete system. Moving in on the CRT's space (both literally and figuratively) is the flat panel display. Flat panels are elegant little creatures that take up a fraction of the desktop space required for a standard CRT and still manage to deliver an image that is arguably superior to that of the CRT. The method by which each type delivers an image to the screen is different; therefore, the different types of monitor require separate discussions.

This chapter is devoted to the various forms of Video Graphics Array (VGA) standards that have evolved over the years. Toward the end of the chapter, I will include a short section on the Enhanced Graphics Adapter (EGA) and the Color Graphics Adapter (CGA) as historical references. If you see any of these displays today, it'll either be at a flea market on in a museum somewhere.

CATHODE-RAY TUBE MONITORS

So far, it's safe to say that the cathode-ray tube (CRT) is by far the most popular monitor in use today. The primary reason for its popularity is price. Over the years, the quality has improved dramatically as well. **Figure 15.1** illustrates a 19″ CRT monitor in use.

The design of a CRT is virtually identical to that of a television. As such, it has many similarities. However, since it's dealing with information coming in from a computer rather than over the air or cable, there are some key differences as well.

The CRT monitor consists of several different components that make it work. First off is the CRT itself. It's what makes the picture. Toward the back of the tube is a grouping of three electron guns. In control of the entire operation is a bank of electronics. Finally, since the monitor requires more power than anything else in a typical computer system, there is a rather large power supply.

THE CRT

The CRT is one of the last remaining vacuum tubes to be used on a regular basis in modern electronic technology. It consists of a large glass tube from which all the air has been evacuated.

The front of the tube is the flat surface visible to the user, while toward the rear, it stretches out into a long point (see **Figure 15.2**).

The inner surface of the front panel is coated with a compound consisting primarily of phosphorous. This is essentially the same substance that fireflies use to produce their remarkable display. Toward the back of the tube are mounted three electron guns. *Electron guns* are electrical components called cathodes. These are negatively charged devices that, when heated, emit a barrage of electrons. The stream of electrons is directed toward the front panel of the monitor, exciting the phosphorous and making it glow. The graphics adapter controls the rate at which the electron guns fire. I'll get to that in a bit.

In order to make sure that the electrons don't overlap each other, causing the

Figure 15.1 The venerable CRT is still the most popular monitor on the market today.

colors of the image to bleed into one another, a *shadow mask* is placed against the back surface of the front panel, over the phosphorous layer. Frequently, you will hear manufacturers talk about the Invar mask that they use in their product. This isn't a type of mask as much as it is the kind of metal from which the mask is made. Invar is a metal that can handle extremely high temperatures without having its shape distorted. Since the steady barrage of electrons hitting the mask does result in the mask getting hot, this is a characteristic that is prized by manufacturers.

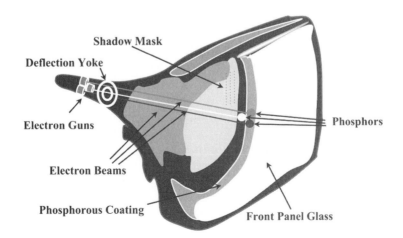

Figure 15.2 The anatomy of a standard CRT makes it an extremely complex apparatus.

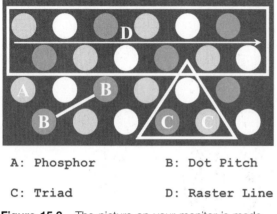

A: Phosphor   B: Dot Pitch

C: Triad   D: Raster Line

Figure 15.3   The picture on your monitor is made up of several million little dots of phosphorous that glow when struck by electrons.

This mask allows only specifically defined areas of phosphorous to be exposed to the electron beams. There are different layers of phosphorous, each compounded with a different substance to make it glow in a different color. The phosphorous compound is known as a *phosphor*. Each phosphor will always be exposed by the same electron beam and will always glow in one of the three primary colors: red, green, or blue. **Figure 15.3** illustrates this concept, as well as some of those to follow. The intensity at which the electrons strike the phosphor determines how brightly that phosphor glows. In order to produce the myriad of colors that you perceive on your computer screen, it takes three of those phosphors, one of each primary color, working together to produce a hue. These three phosphors working together form a *triad*.

Once struck by the electrons, however, that phosphor doesn't glow very long. A few hundredths of a second is all it's good for until it fades away. Therefore, the electron gun has to keep redrawing the screen over and over again to keep a stable image. How frequently it redraws the screen is the monitor's refresh rate. Refresh rates are measured in hertz and range from a low end of around 48Hz to as high as 200Hz on some brands. Maximum refresh rate is directly linked to the monitor's selected resolution. The maximum refresh rate advertised by a manufacturer can rarely be used in conjunction with the maximum resolution advertised. To get higher resolutions, a lower refresh rate must usually be used.

An advertised specification of computer monitors is the *dot pitch*. While dot pitch and resolution are directly related, they are not the same thing. Back in Figure 15.3 I illustrated the individual phosphors that make up the image. Dot pitch is the distance between two adjacent like-colored phosphors. This will be measured in some fraction of a millimeter. Dot pitch limits the absolute maximum resolution that a particular monitor can display.

The graphics adapter, and how the user has set it up, dictates actual display resolution. This is defined by how many pixels it takes to fill a line that moves across the screen, along with how many of these lines, called *raster lines*, it takes to produce the entire screen from top to bottom. Note that there is a big difference between pixels and phosphors or even triads. Or not, depending on the resolution you've selected.

A *pixel* is an individual colored dot that consists of several phosphors. A computer image is built up from thousands or millions of these pixels. Let's take a look at a typical color monitor and put some of these terms to use. I'll use a 19″ monitor capable of 1600×1200 resolution, with a maximum refresh rate of 200Hz as an example. If you set that monitor at its maximum resolution of 1600×1200, then each pixel consists of a single triad. Lower resolutions simply absorb more phosphors per pixel.

BUZZ WORDS

Raster line: A single row of pixels that make a horizontal line across an image.

Pixel: The collection of phosphors that collectively generate a single dot of color in a monitor's image.

Bezel: The plastic frame that masks off the unusable part of a monitor's image.

Now, consider the size. The advertised size of the display is a diagonal measurement from one corner of the tube to the opposite corner, for example, from upper right to lower left. On a CRT, unfortunately, maximum size does not equate to usable size. As the image progresses toward the outer perimeters of the tube, sharpness and contrast drop off dramatically. The *bezel*, or the plastic frame that makes up the front of your monitor's external case, masks off a portion of the tube so you won't see the fuzzy, murky part. What's left is the viewable area. The 19″ monitor I'm using has a viewable area of 18″.

The maximum resolution of 1600×1200 comes from the fact that there are a total of 1600 triads that make up each line going from left to right. These are the raster lines I mentioned. From top to bottom, there are 1200 of these lines. As the monitor creates the image you see, the electron guns scan from left to right, drawing a single line. The time it takes for the guns to finish one line and then return to start the next line is known as the horizontal refresh rate (HFR). Since there are a lot of lines to draw, HFR is usually a fairly high number. In fact, it is this number that limits the maximum vertical refresh rate (VFR) that a monitor can produce.

VFR is the number of times per second an entire screen can be drawn. VFR has a direct impact on the quality of image. It also can have a dramatic impact on the comfort level of the user. Way back in the day, when color monitors were first becoming the rage, many people who sat in front of a computer for hours on end complained that their computers gave them headaches. Many people insisted that the CRT was emitting some form of radiation that was harmful to human health.

Millions of dollars were spent researching this problem, and this was the conclusion. Yes, computer monitors do emit varying levels of low-level radiation. This isn't the same kind of radiation caused by nuclear bombs or power plants, but rather more akin to the radiation emitted by your radio station. There was no evidence whatsoever that this radiation had any impact on human health.

They did find, however, that VFR was directly responsible for the headaches people experienced. Most offices are illuminated by fluorescent lights. These lights are powered by a device called a ballast and flicker at a rate of sixty times per second, or 60Hz. This is a high enough frequency that most people don't even notice it. It also happens to be the refresh rate for standard VGA. Therefore, people were being bombarded by ambient light flickering at sixty times per second, while sitting in front of a computer screen doing the same thing. Enough hours of that would result in a headache. The solution was simple. You simply redesign VGA standards so that a higher VFR is used. 72Hz is a good starting point and higher is better, although there is some argument that 120Hz is not a good thing because it supposedly sets up another synchronization with the 60Hz cycle of the fluorescents.

BUZZ WORDS

Deflection yoke: A circular array of powerful magnets that act to deflect a beam of electrons from its natural path.

Cathode: A negatively charged device that emits a stream of electrons when heated.

Convergence: The accuracy with which multiple beams of electrons or light can focus on the same point.

CONTROLLING THE ELECTRON BEAMS

Since the image is actually created by the electron beams, it only stands to reason that controlling the electrons is key to controlling the image. There are actually several components within the monitor that contribute to this task. There are, first off, the electron guns that initially emit the electrons. The electrons are distributed across the rear surface of the front panel by a circular array of magnets called a *deflection yoke*. The shadow mask makes sure phosphors don't overlap. If you look back, Figure 15.2 illustrates the key components to a CRT monitor.

CAUTION: When discussing the internal components of a computer system, I suggested you peek inside and follow along as you read. Even though I am discussing some of the internal components of a computer monitor, I highly recommend that you not go inside of a monitor unless you have been properly trained. There are capacitors inside of monitors and television sets that can hold a lethal charge for weeks, or even months, after the unit has been unplugged. Accidentally coming in contact with a charged circuit inside the monitor could easily be the last mistake you ever make!

Electron Guns Color monitors have three of these devices, one for each of the primary colors. The gun consists of a cathode, some form of heat source, and a method by which the electrons can be focused. As I mentioned earlier, a *cathode* is a negatively charged device that, when heated, emits a stream of electrons. This is the purpose of the heating device. The higher the temperature, the more electrons that spew out of the cathode. The three electron guns are arranged in a triangular pattern toward the back of the tube. The three guns work in synchronization with one another and fire their beams simultaneously, all focused on precisely the same point. How well those three beams focus on the same point is a factor known as *convergence*. The better convergence is controlled, the sharper the image will appear.

The electron guns are devices that maintain a fixed position. This is, of course, not very conducive to 19″ screens, because unless there is a way of scattering those electrons across the entire surface of the monitor, our image will consist of one tiny little circle so small an electron microscope would have trouble finding it. Since manufacturers can't move the electron guns, they move the electron beams.

The Deflection Yoke Also occasionally called the deflection plates or the deflection coil, this device consists of an array of electromagnets distributed around the circumference of the tube. These magnets create a strong magnetic field that the beam of electrons must pass through on its way to the front panel. By varying the strength of the field generated by specific magnets, the beam of electrons can be deflected in a very precise pattern. This rapid changing of magnetic fields causes the horizontal and vertical movement I discussed earlier.

Since the electrons are spewing out of the electron guns continuously, and since the magnetic fields are merely moving the beam, there needs to be some way of sorting out the blue dots from the red dots from the green dots. In order to do that the designers put a "template" between the layers of phosphorous and the electron guns.

The Shadow Mask The shadow mask is what separates the individual phosphors. It is also what determines dot pitch. The shadow mask is an extremely thin sheet of metal perforated with millions of tiny little holes. Since this metal is going to be subjected to a constant barrage of electrons, it's going to get very hot, as I mentioned earlier. That is why it needs to be manufactured with a metal that can handle the stress without changing the size and shape of the holes.

One of the things that happens when any substance gets hot is that it expands. The shadow mask can't be doing that. Otherwise, the individual phosphors would change size as the mask heated up. This would result in image distortion. Invar is a type of metal that resists this distortion better than most other materials. Therefore, it is frequently used on high-quality monitors.

The Monitor Cable The signals that control how all of the above devices do their job actually come from the display adapter installed in the computer. In order to get that signal from the computer to the monitor, you use a cable. Standard VGA cables use the 15-pin connector you've grown to know and love. Each conductor in the cable has a specific job to do, as is illustrated in **Figure 15.4**. One of the easiest troubleshooting jobs you'll ever get is when somebody complains that the color on his or her monitor has suddenly changed radically. Each of the three primary colors moves down a specific wire. If the pin connecting that wire to the display adapter gets broken or bent, it will no longer transmit its signal and the image the user sees will be composed of only the remaining two colors. It isn't a pleasant sight.

LCD MONITOR

A technology that is seeing increasing popularity is the LCD monitor. The display gets its name from the fact that the pixels are formed from a liquid crystal display (LCD) instead of glowing phosphorous. As you might imagine, the technology is somewhat different. There are some distinct advantages to LCD displays over the more conventional CRTs. The one most

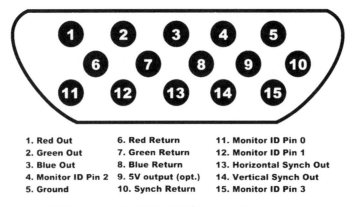

1. Red Out   6. Red Return   11. Monitor ID Pin 0
2. Green Out   7. Green Return   12. Monitor ID Pin 1
3. Blue Out   8. Blue Return   13. Horizontal Synch Out
4. Monitor ID Pin 2   9. 5V output (opt.)   14. Vertical Synch Out
5. Ground   10. Synch Return   15. Monitor ID Pin 3

Figure 15.4 A standard 15-pin VGA connector

immediately noticeable is how much of your desktop you get back when you migrate from a CRT to an LCD. The LCD takes up a whole lot less space.

Another distinct advantage they have is in the amount of power they consume. A typical CRT can pull between 120 and 200 watts of electricity from the wall, even more for some of the bigger displays. An LCD requires between 30 and 50 watts. For the individual user, that may not amount to much. A corporation, on the other hand, that has hundreds or thousands of computers in use can see significant savings on its electrical bill if it makes the move.

A difference between CRTs and LCDs that might take a little longer for some people to appreciate is the fact that, because there are no electron guns at work here, image refresh is handled in a completely different manner. The result of this is a much more solid image with virtually no measurable flicker.

LCDs come in three different packages. On the most basic level, that of your handheld games, PDAs, and such, a common-plane display is used. Notebook computers of the past used either a passive matrix or an active matrix design. The differences among the three are significant.

COMMON-PLANE LCDS

As I mentioned, this is the display commonly used in handheld games, advanced calculators, and pocket computers. You also see them on watches, panel displays for household appliances, and on the dashboards of automobiles. These displays offer a very limited number of colors and can create graphic images that are composed of certain predefined shapes. Almost any shape is possible, but creating a graphic from scratch is inordinately slow.

Common-plane displays can be either backlit or reflective. This means that the manufacturer can either project light through the display from a source behind the crystals, or it can simply require the user to make use of available light to see the image.

PASSIVE MATRIX DISPLAYS

The passive matrix display is a complex and cumbersome display. It starts with two glass panels, or substrates. A *substrate* is simply a solid surface of some sort, over which an active material can be applied. The substrates work together to form a grid consisting of rows and columns. These panels receive a coating that contains a conductive material that is transparent to the naked eye. On one of the panels, the coating is laid out in rows; on the other, it is laid out in columns.

The liquid crystal material is added between the substrates, and a thin coating of polarizing material is applied to the outer surface of the panel. Each of the rows and columns of conductive material is connected to an integrated circuit (IC). The graphics controller sends a signal down a particular row and column. Where two signals intersect, the material is activated.

The technology works well enough for very simple applications, but is too slow to be of any use in streaming video. For example, I used to own an older notebook computer that used a passive matrix display. As I moved the mouse cursor along the screen, I could see a little trail of pointers following the cursor itself, and I didn't have mouse trailers enabled. My new notebook uses an active matrix display.

ACTIVE MATRIX DISPLAYS

Another way you'll see these displays described is TFT displays. This comes from the fact that the active matrix makes use of thin film transistors (TFT) in order to generate the image. The term is slightly misleading, because the TFT actually consists of a transistor coupled to a capacitor. TFTs are arranged in rows and columns, each of which is under the control of an IC.

To make a specific pixel glow, the IC activates a particular row. Then a charge is sent down the column where the pixel is supposed to reside. Since all of the other rows on the display are turned off, there is only one pixel on that particular column that can be made active. Its capacitor is charged and as long as the charge lasts, the pixel will glow. As with CRT monitors, there is a separate element for each primary color. The millions of colors available are derived by having the elements glow in varying intensity.

GRAPHICS ADAPTERS

The second part of the graphics subsystem is the graphics adapter. This is the device that generates the signals that created the images I discussed in earlier sections of this chapter. It is the job of the graphics adapter to convert a series of zeros and ones into all those pretty pictures you see on the tube in front of you.

Graphics adapters can appear as either independent devices that you install into a computer, or they can be onboard devices that are a part of the motherboard, as I pointed out in Chapter Five, Motherboards, BIOS, and the Chipset. However the device is packaged, the way it functions is going to be the same.

The user's perception of how well a system performs can be a direct function of the graphics adapter. It doesn't matter how quickly the CPU, RAM, and hard drives are doing their jobs. If you have a seriously slow video card, then the results of all that processing is taking its own sweet time getting to you and, as far as you're concerned, you have a slow computer!

In this section, I'll take a closer look at how video cards do their job and what differentiates a really good card from a mediocre one. I'll even discuss reasons why even a mediocre adapter might be able to provide more horsepower than many people will ever need. Finally, I'll examine some compatibility issues specific to video cards.

> **Buzz Words** ————————
>
> **Co-processed:** Any adapter or device that is equipped with a microprocessor that offloads some of the work of the PC's CPU.

The Mechanics of Graphics Adapters

Today's video cards are *co-processed* adapters. A microprocessor on board the video card relieves the computer's CPU of the task of processing graphics. In addition, VGA cards all ship with a fairly substantial amount of memory installed on the card itself. These days it is fairly difficult to find any product on the market with anything less than about 8MB of RAM installed. Later in this chapter, I'll be taking a look at what that memory is used for.

Modern graphics adapters feature a chipset and a video BIOS. As with motherboards, these two collections of commands dictate what functions the card can perform. Graphics functions have gotten far too complex and change too rapidly to be included as a subset of system BIOS and/or chipsets.

The Video Chipset

The chipset is a collection of integrated circuits in which all the instructions specific to a particular card are housed. Therefore, if two different brands of graphics adapter both have the same chipset, it can be safely assumed that they will share most, if not all, features and will have nearly identical specifications. By embedding a video chipset onto a motherboard, and programming the system BIOS accordingly, it is relatively easy to include video as an onboard function.

As with the system, the video chipset will determine basic hardware functions. If a video chipset does not support 3D functions, you do not have a 3D video card. (See later in this chapter for how graphics adapters simulate 3D effects and a discussion of different 3D algorithms used.) The type and amount of memory supported by a specific adapter is a direct function of the chipset.

Video BIOS

The video BIOS performs exactly the same function as the system BIOS, except that it is specific to the graphics adapter. As with system BIOS, it consists of a set of instructions permanently encoded onto a ROM chip. On some video cards, this ROM chip is removable, allowing users to upgrade their BIOS if necessary. On most modern cards, it can be flashed with new instructions using an executable program.

The video BIOS has two important services that it provides. First and foremost is that, while the system is booting and prior to video drivers being installed onto the system, it provides rudimentary video support so that you can read the messages your system spits out while it is spinning up. Without this most basic function, you wouldn't be able to read the error messages that might be generated.

> **NOTE:** The instructions on a video BIOS are generally specific to a chipset. The chipset isn't going to be changed during the life of the card; therefore, be cautious about burning new instructions to video BIOS. About the only time this should be necessary would be when the manufacturer has discovered a flaw in the original programming. In some cases, it might be necessary to flash new BIOS in order to accommodate a newly released operating system, but for the most part, this is rarely necessary. Unless you have a real issue that can only be addressed by a new BIOS, don't experiment with video BIOS!

The second function that video BIOS provides is to act as a translator between the instructions and data handed off between the graphics adapter and the system board. As I mentioned earlier, it isn't possible to include BIOS instructions for every graphics adapter ever made on the system BIOS. Therefore, manufacturers provide their own instruction sets that are written to interact with the system BIOS.

VIDEO MEMORY

When computers first became available, everything was monochrome. All these fancy color monitors hadn't been invented yet. All there was to display on the screen was plain text. There were no elaborate graphics to contend with. As a result, there was very little memory required to produce screen shots, and the processor had no problems whatsoever putting information up on the screen. IBM allocated the first 128K of upper memory to video usage. That was all designers figured users would ever need.

These days, the GUI of our operating systems and the full-motion graphics of games makes video one of the biggest bottlenecks on the computer. One component of graphics adapters that has more impact on performance than anything else is the kind of memory installed on the card. Not the amount of memory, mind you, but rather the type. There have been several forms of memory used in video cards over the years. The most commonly used were VRAM, WRAM, and SGRAM. VRAM is the faster of the three because it is dual-ported and can be receiving data from an outside source and outputting data to either the video processor or the I/O stage on the same clock cycle. WRAM is a form of VRAM tuned exclusively to Microsoft's Windows functions. SGRAM works in a manner very similar to that used by the computer as main system memory, but its designers have fine-tuned the read/write operations specifically around graphics functions.

One additional technology is a type of memory called Multibank DRAM (MDRAM). As the name indicates, grouping larger numbers of smaller banks of memory is how the module is designed. Typically 32KB banks are used. Since each bank can be read to or written from independently, and I/O operations can occur across multiple banks simultaneously, data retrieval is much faster. However, it is a much more expensive alternative and, while it's been around for a while, hasn't been greeted by the industry with much enthusiasm.

Table 15.1 Memory used in Graphics Adapters

Type	Description	Relative Speed	Relative Cost	Relative Usage
FPM	Fast Page Mode	Very slow	N/A	Obsolete
SDRAM	Extended Data Out	Slow	Cheap	Obsolete
SGRAM	Synchronized Graphics RAM	Moderate	Cheap	Midrange and OEM
WRAM	Windows RAM	Fast	N/A	Obsolete
VRAM	Video RAM	Fast	Fairly expensive	Upper range; becoming obsolete
DDRAM	Double Data RAM	Extremely fast	Moderate	High-end cards
MDRAM	Multibank DRAM	Extremely fast	Extremely expensive	Rarely used

Types of video memory and their relative usage

Note: It is not unheard of for some high-end video cards to make use of two different types of memory on one card. Fast memory will be used for functions related to video processing, while a slower type, typically EDO, might be used for storing texture maps.

Many other types of memory have been embraced, and types that you might normally associate with conventional memory are used in graphics adapters today. These include FPM, EDO, SDRAM, and DDRAM. (See Chapter Eight for detailed discussions on how each of these types of memory works.)

So which of these types is the best memory to use, and why can't the manufacturers just pick a technology and stick with it? The answer to both is in the end user. What is the machine going to be used for? It would be senseless to always use an expensive high-end technology on every device you run off your assembly line. For many users, that would be prohibitively expensive. Also, the applications that will be run on the computer will determine your needs. Someone running word processing applications and spreadsheets all day won't need anything all that fancy. It is primarily the gaming world that drives the high-end market. **Table 15.1** groups the types of memory used by video cards in the order of their speed and relative price.

The main reason you need memory on a video card is that it acts as the *frame buffer*. Every time the monitor draws a screen (which, if your refresh rate is 80Hz, will be 80 times per second), the video card needs to be able to throw enough pixels up on the screen to create the image. Video memory acts as a place to assemble the next screen while the current screen is being drawn. The amount of memory you need on your graphics adapter is related to both the color depth and resolution you've selected. A simple formula is

Horizontal resolution × Vertical resolution × Color depth (in bits) / (8 × 1,048,576)

Let's do an example. How many megabytes do I need for my 1600×1200 monitor set for 24-bit color?

$$1600 \times 1200 \times 24 = 46,080,000$$

This is how many bits are required to generate a single screen. Now, to break that down into megabytes, complete the equation. There are 8 bits to a byte and 1,048,576 bytes to a megabyte, therefore

$$8 \times 1,048,576 = 8,388,608$$

To finalize the answer, simply divide the results of the first equation by the results of the second.

$$46,080,000 / 8,388,608 = 5.4931640625$$

Therefore, in order to create each frame that a video card must produce at that color depth and resolution, I need 5.5MB of RAM just to act as a frame buffer. The first commercially available video card that would suit these needs would be equipped with 8MB of RAM.

Now, if life were only that simple, no one would ever need anything more than 8MB installed on video cards. However, several of the functions that I will discuss later in the chapter also require dedicated memory, and those will impact on the total requirements.

THE RAMDAC

Key to the video subsystem is a chip called the random access memory, digital analog converter (RAMDAC). This is the microprocessor that processes the video signals. To do its job it has to be able to perform a few key tasks. One of the main ones is to take the digital information produced by the video card and convert it into an analog signal. While virtually all of today's graphics adapters feature a RAMDAC, this hasn't always been the case. Early ISA and some PCI video cards relied on the CPU of the computer to handle all video processing. As you might imagine, there was a tremendous performance hit that resulted from using cards of this nature.

Refresh rate, resolution, and the speed of video reproduction is all directly limited by the speed of the RAMDAC. Your screen has a lot of pixels that it has to reproduce. The higher the resolution setting, the more pixels there are that are being generated. Higher refresh rates mean that they have to be reproduced more times per second. That's a lot of data that's being processed by the RAMDAC. **Table 15.2** lists some common resolution and refresh rates and shows just how much data is being reproduced per second.

While the numbers shown in Table 15.2 represent millions of pixels per second, they also provide a good measure of the speed of the RAMDAC a card would need in order to use those settings. As the table footnote indicates, since the entire screen is not actually being used by the image, you would need to apply a conversion factor of some sort to calculate the actual number of pixels being reproduced. Once you've done that, you know how fast of a RAMDAC you will need. For example, if I figure my monitor is using approximately 80 percent of the total CRT,

Table 15.2   Resolution and Refresh Rate Data Generation

Resolution	43.5Hz (87 interlaced)	60Hz	72Hz	80Hz	85Hz	90Hz	100Hz
800x600	20.1	28.8	34.6	38.4	40.8	43.2	48
1024x768	34.2	47.2	56.6	62.9	70.8	93.4	78.6
1280x1024	57	78.6	94.4	104.9	111.4	118	131.1
1600x1200	83.5	115.2	138.2	153.6	163.2	172.8	192

Data throughput is a direct function of resolution and refresh rate.

Numbers in each cell represent millions of pixels per second that are being reproduced. The amount of data being transmitted is dependent on the color depth selected.

Values represent only pixels in visible area of screen. To accurately calculate exact values, one would need to know the exact percentage of screen not being used by image. A good rule of thumb is to multiply these values by a factor of 1.2 to 1.35 to generate actual data throughput.

if I set it at 1600×1200 with a 100Hz refresh rate, I'm going to need a RAMDAC slightly faster than 240MHz. My card actually has a 250MHz RAMDAC, so I'm all set.

COLOR DEPTH AND RESOLUTION

BUZZ WORDS —————

Color depth: The number of individual hues that can be generated by a given display setting.

Technically speaking, controlling the color depth and resolution of a monitor is a combined function of the display adapter and monitor in unison. The monitor has to support the resolution you've selected on your graphics adapter, and your adapter has to be able to generate signals usable by the monitor. For that to happen, certain characteristics of the monitor will determine your capabilities.

Any individual phosphor is capable of glowing on only a single color. Yet the world around us is a bit more varied than that—on the outside, anyway. In reality, the colors of nature aren't that much different than digitized color. Three primary colors make up every one of the colors humans can perceive. The myriad of hues we see all around us are created by mixing these three colors. The intensity of any one color in relation to the other two determines the color we perceive.

The colors that come out of a computer monitor are derived in exactly the same manner. There are three phosphors per triad, and the three of them work together to create a hue. How many bits of data are used to generate colors is known as the bit depth. *Color depth* is the number of colors offered by a particular bit depth. If you look at the standard Windows settings for color depth, you'll see 256 Colors, High Color (16-bit), True Color (24-bit), and True Color (32-bit). You can find these settings in the Display Properties dialog box shown in **Figure 15.5**.

The original 256-color VGA was based on three separate 6-bit digital/analog converters, one for each of the primary colors. That is a total of 18 bits of data for the triad. As a result, you

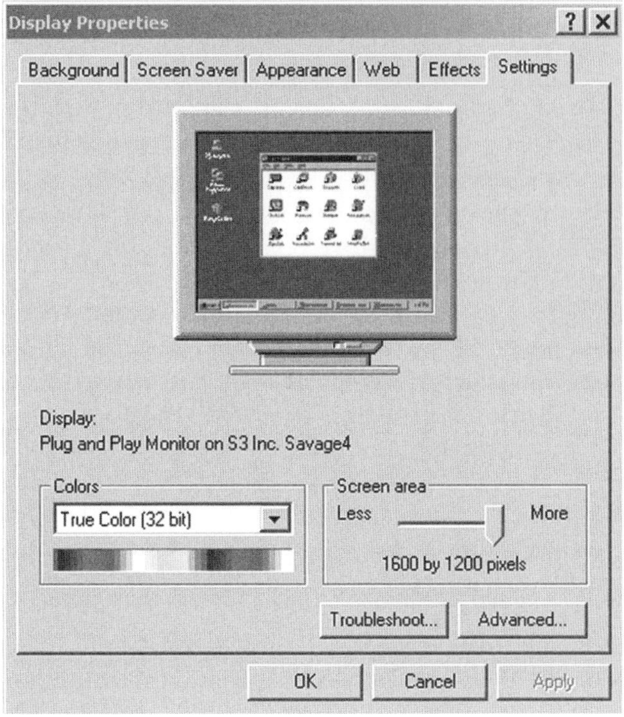

Figure 15.5   Windows Display Properties panel

had a total palette of 2^{18}, or 262,144 colors that could be generated. The VGA standard allowed users to select a total of 256 colors from that overall collection of colors that they could use at any one time. This became the working palette.

High Color, as described above, provides up to 16 bits of data for each triad. There are two ways a card manufacturer can allocate those bits of data. This is a function of the driver that ships with the card. One method is to evenly allocate five bits for each of the primary colors and drop the sixteenth bit. This allows for a display of 32,768 colors. The other, more commonly used, method is to allocate 5 bits each for red and blue, plus 6 bits for green. This provides the 65,536 colors promised by Windows.

True Color (24-bit) allows for the maximum number of colors displayed by any of today's graphics adapters. Each phosphor of the triad is allotted 8 bits to determine its intensity. As I pointed out in my discussion of binary, an 8-bit block of data provides for up to 256 combinations. By having three different primary colors working in synch, that allows for 256^3 colors. That is a total of 16,777,216 colors.

True Color (32-bit) is 24-bit true color with an added 8-bit alpha channel. The *alpha channel* allows programmers to add effects other than raw

BUZZ WORDS —————

Alpha channel: Eight bits used by 32-bit True Color to apply effects such as translucency and fogging.

color to the digital video. These extra 8 bits of data are used for generating the effect of translucency, or how well you can see through the color, to the overall image. It does not, however, increase the number of colors available.

Other terms you see thrown about a lot include SVGA, XGA, and UVGA. SVGA stands for Super VGA, and generally refers to resolution settings of 800x600 and up. Less frequently seen is the Extended Graphics Array (XGA). This was a favorite term of IBM for its 1024x768 setting available on certain onboard PS/2 computers. Ultra VGA (UVGA) refers to a resolution of 1280×1024. These particular options have been pretty much universally accepted by the industry as part of the SVGA set.

To the beginner, making the move to higher resolutions can have a disconcerting affect. Something about human psychology makes people want to have everything be the same, even after they change it! Changing resolution settings on a monitor does make the overall image sharper. It also expands the desktop so that you see more of your work. Someone accustomed to an 800×600 setting could expect to see something along the lines of the screen capture shown in **Figure 15.6**.

Making the move to 1280×1024, as shown in **Figure 15.7**, makes for an image with much lower granularity and overall sharpness. It also allows for more of the page to be seen at once. However, the letters are really tiny. You're squeezing more onto the monitor, but the monitor isn't getting any bigger. Since it can't get bigger, information displayed on it has to get smaller.

All is not lost, however. Windows users can go into the Display Properties, click on the appearance tab and bring up a screen like the one in **Figure 15.8**. The Item field shown in this image only displays one of many different elements you can manually resize, customizing the display to your liking.

Figure 15.6   A Windows Desktop set at 800×600

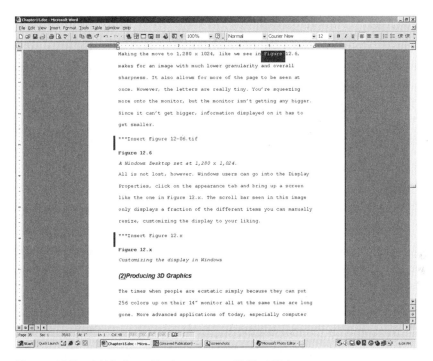

Figure 15.7   A Windows Desktop set at 1280×1024.

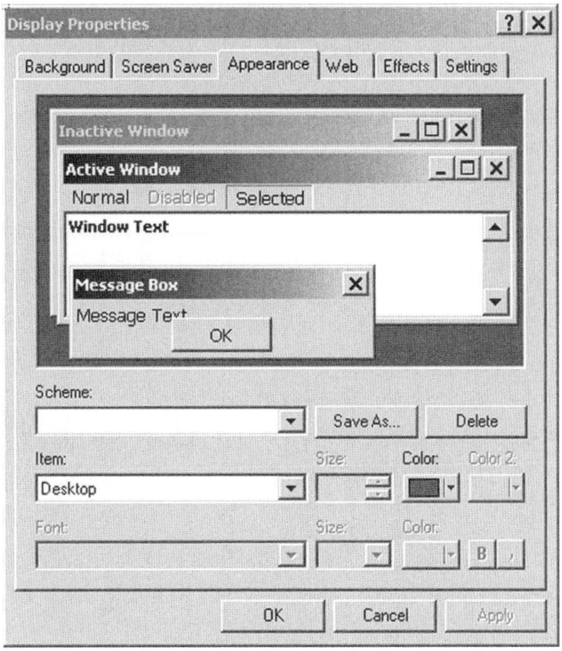

Figure 15.8   Customizing the display in Windows

Producing 3D Graphics

The times when people were ecstatic simply because they could put 256 colors up on their 14″ monitor all at the same time are long gone. More advanced applications of today, especially computer games and graphics applications, require a much greater semblance of realism and finer degrees of color management. To achieve that degree of realism, programmers are trying to make their images look as three-dimensional as possible. As 3D technology has developed, different techniques have been used to produce this effect. Some of these techniques involve hardware and driver technology while others fall under the category of Application Programming Interfaces (API). An API is a library of programming functions that can be applied as a unit.

Hardware and Driver 3D

Some of the tricks your computer needs to be able to perform must occur on the hardware level. Some of these happen on the chip level, while the device driver handles others. For the purposes of this discussion, I can pretty much bundle those together. However, it should be noted that while I will be discussing APIs separately, it is a function of the chipset that determines whether or not a particular API is supported, because it is the API that will be calling on the functions I'll be discussing here.

Hardware Triangle Setup On the most basic level, the graphics that appear on your screen consist of a collection of triangles and polygons. 3D effects are generated by constantly repositioning these fundamental shapes. In order to do this, a tremendous amount of mathematical work has to be done in order to calculate new angles and vectors. This can seriously drag down the performance of your computer if your CPU has to do all the work.

Many video cards provide an onboard 3D graphics processor, which offloads these functions from the CPU to itself. This dramatically improves the performance of both the computer and the video subsystem.

Double Buffering One of the biggest obstacles of moving animation is the jittery effect that slower video cards create. This is a result of the frame buffer being called upon to supply an image before it is completely assembled. Since the digital world can't wait, the buffer sends through what it has.

Double buffering sets up two completely separate frame buffers for image generation. While one buffer is spitting out its contents to the RAMDAC, the other has already starting compiling the next frame. That frame will be complete by the time the RAMDAC comes back for it, and the other buffer will already be at work on the next frame. The result is very smooth animation.

This doesn't require any additional video processing overhead to speak of, but it does require a

Buzz Words ──────────

Double buffering: The use of two separate buffers, so that as a frame is displayed on the monitor, another frame is the queue, ready for display, while yet a third is being assembled by the graphics adapter.

memory address space double that of what you need for simple frame buffering. This is the first of several reasons why today's video cards ship with such huge amounts of memory.

Texture Mapping One of the most basic methods of creating realism is to apply texture to the objects on the computer screen. To see why this is important, simply go to your clothes closet. A brown leather jacket doesn't look at all similar to a brown silk skirt, even if the shade of brown is identical. If you hold them up side by side, you might see that the colors match perfectly, but the surface is completely different. The leather jacket has a slightly rough, almost pebbled surface, while the silk skirt has that sensuous, soft, and slinky look and feeling. The skirt also gives off a slight shimmer if the light is just right.

Another example would be a brick house with a stone façade. Even if the stone and brick are the same color, you don't have any trouble telling them apart. They have different textures. Programmers use texture to make things look more real. Therefore, an image on your screen consists of two parts. First, there are the geometric shapes that make up the image. On a most basic level, images consist of a complex collection of triangles, circles, and polygons. Over the geometric pattern, colors and textures are applied.

The process of *texture mapping* creates the textures as separate bitmaps and stores them in memory. These bitmaps consist of very small images, ranging from 32×32 pixels up to 256×256 pixels. A term you might see used for these bitmaps is *texels*. As a new screen is drawn, the texture won't have to be redrawn for each new screen. The bitmaps can simply be poured over the corresponding patterns.

Keeping these textures resident on the video card is essential for maximizing performance. Therefore, texture mapping is reason number two for having extra memory. The more memory you have available on your card, the more of these texels you can store.

Bump Mapping Closely related to texture mapping is bump mapping. And it isn't any more complicated than the name makes it sound. A key aspect of texture is the collection of tiny (or not so tiny) bumps scattered across any given surface. The stone surface I talked about doesn't have an evenly spaced collection of texels, the way your computer is going to reproduce it. There will be randomly spaced bumps scattered across the surface.

Bump mapping placed raised surfaces here and there across the surface of the texture map and can even generate the illusion of tiny little shadows made by the bump. This adds an even greater sense of realism. It also requires additional memory. Reason number three.

Anti-aliasing One of the problems inherent with a separate bitmap for textures becomes apparent as soon as the image starts to move. To keep a sense of perspective, as the character in your game moves closer to an object, that object needs to get bigger. Conversely, as she moves

---

BUZZ WORDS

Texture mapping: A process by which predrawn textures are stored in memory and applied to an image as needed.

Texel: A small clip that serves as the sample of a texture used in texture mapping.

farther away, it needs to get smaller. If the object gets smaller, but the texture bitmaps stay the same size, there's going to be a problem, isn't there?

As you approach an object, you have to add more detail if you want a realistic affect. Otherwise, the screen starts filling in the extra space with randomly generated pixels. Moving away from the object isn't any better. If you're starting with a 256 × 256 texel and start moving away, the only way to make it look smaller is to start stripping away pixels. As a result, the textures started to show either a granulated or interlaced effect. The latter problem is solved by anti-aliasing.

Anti-aliasing samples the image size for each frame and recalculates texture maps. The recalculated bitmap provides a much more accurate rendition than the one originally stored in memory. This does not specifically require adding more memory, but the technique does place an additional burden on the RAMDAC. Therefore, a faster RAMDAC than would be estimated by the simple resolution and refresh rate calculation will be in order. Hmmm. Maybe my 250MHz RAMDAC isn't fast enough after all!

Buzz Words

Anti-aliasing: A process through which textures in an image are redrawn to more accurately reflect perceived distance.

Fogging: A technique of implying distance in an image by making objects that are farther away less distinct.

Depth queuing: A mathematical algorithm that recalculates the hue and intensity of colors in respect to increasing distances.

MIP Mapping The problems caused by moving the character closer to an object can be solved through a technique called MIP mapping. The acronym comes from a Latin phrase, *multium in parvo*, which means "many in one." Programmers who use this technique create multiple versions of the same bitmap.

They produce a bitmap that represents a texture for the largest object they intend to represent. This is stored as one bitmap. Then this bitmap is scaled down in size by increments of 50 percent, 25 percent, and so forth. A mathematical algorithm selects the appropriate version of the bitmap, based on distance to the object. This technique not only represents reason number four for having more memory, it's also an argument for a faster RAMDAC.

Fogging and Depth Queuing In the real world, as you move farther away from an object, atmospheric haze starts to make details of the object less distinct. It becomes softer and the colors start to shift toward blue. Graphics cards reproduce this affect through various forms of *fogging* techniques.

Properly applied, as objects or characters become closer to your point of view, they will become more and more distinct. Details will appear that you hadn't noticed before and colors will become more saturated. Fogging intensity can be increased or decreased, based on the affect the programmer is trying to achieve.

Fogging can be used in conjunction with another technique called *depth queuing*. This process takes the color shift I was just talking about and uses a mathematical algorithm that generates an exponential curve that is used to calculate both the hue and intensity of the color.

Dithering One of the problems of earlier computer games was that a character's face or costume was all one color and then abruptly ended. The leaves in the trees and where the mountains touched the sky were the same way. That is what make them look like the cartoons you watched when you were a kid.

In nature, we like to see colors run together. *Dithering* is a technique that simulates that effect. From a limited palette of colors, blending two existing colors creates a completely new color. By dithering transition lines between colors a more natural appearance can be created.

Another use for dithering is the ability to work with a 256-color palette and generate more colors than are provided by that palette. Conversely, you can take a 16K color image and drop it down to 256 colors without generating overly harsh cutoffs. This allows programmers to worry less about the kind of video their end users will have available and spend more time creating useful programs.

Filtering Techniques By now, you're starting to get the idea that a lot is going on in order to create the image on your screen. Because objects are constantly moving around and changing positions, they also need to change their appearance. One of the problems that must be addressed is not just in changes to the color hues based on distance, but deciding just what the new color needs to be. There are four filtering techniques that are commonly used to generate colors in 3D graphics engines.

- *Point-sampled filtering:* The most basic method of generating a new pixel is point sampling. This technique simply copies the color of the adjacent pixel to the position of the new pixel. All video cards are capable of this method, but it is the least desirable of the filtering methods. It results in a very "blocky" appearance to the image. For some images, however, this is not a major issue, and because it is the fastest of the methods, it is the one that will be used.

- *Bilinear filtering:* This technique goes a long way in eliminating the blocky appearance of point filtering. It does so because it samples the four adjacent pixels, the ones to the right, to the left, above it, and below it, and then interpolates a new value based on what it sees. This is a much smoother filtering method and allows for a more realistic color pattern to emerge when an image needs to be resized. The downside to this is that this is a memory intensive technique. It greatly increases the amount of memory you need to have available for texture mapping. Add this to the list of reasons you need a 32MB video card.

- *Trilinear filtering:* This basically applies bilinear filtering to a moving object. The information from two separate MIP maps (see MIP mapping) is extracted and bilinear filtering applied to each map. This literally doubles the amount of memory required, over and above that needed for bilinear filtering. Therefore, this is usually an option that can be turned on and off in the driver settings of video cards that support the technique. Now let's start looking for a 64MB card!

■ *Anistropic filtering*: Of course, characters and objects in a moving image don't always move at 90- or 180-degree angles to everything around them. When you come in from all sides of an object, or if an object needs to be rotated at an odd angle, you need to be able to calculate pixels based on new angles as well. Otherwise, angled and curved lines will take on a "stair-stepped" appearance that most people find quite unattractive. This effect is quite apparent in early computer games. Anistropic filtering takes multiple samples from multiple MIP maps and interpolates values to smooth out these lines and angles. This technique provides the best moving images so far available, but requires some pretty intense overhead on the part of your video card and system overall. If you've got the video card that supports it and the horsepower in your system to support the video card, then by all means give it a try. The worst-case scenario is that the graphics slow down to a crawl and you hate it. That's why it's an option that can be turned on and off on video cards that support the feature.

3D APIs

These days, everything is modular. It's all built up from preassembled blocks. You have modular homes, modular stereo systems, and modular exercise equipment. Programmers have modular programming languages. One of these modules is the API. The API can also function as part of the hardware abstraction layer (HAL) for the operating system. When a video card manufacturer includes support for a particular API, it does so by incorporating that support into the chipset of the video card. As long as the appropriate version of the API is installed into the operating system, that video card will now support all of the functions the particular API supports. The more APIs a card supports, the more choices a user has.

OpenGL   OpenGL is an API that was originally developed by Silicon Graphics. The idea was to produce a 3D graphics API that could be used across multiple platforms. Therefore, a graphics adapter that supported OpenGL could be designed to work on PCs, Macs, or Silicon Graphics workstations. The interface is completely independent of operating system.

OpenGL can be implemented with either an installable client driver or a mini client driver. An installable client driver provides all of the support that the current version of OpenGL as released by Silicon Graphics offers. Not all applications require this much horsepower. Games, for example, might only make use of a small collection of the functions supported by OpenGL. That's where a mini client driver comes into play. This is a stripped-down version of the driver that provides only the level of support required by the application. The functions supported by OpenGL include the following:

■ Modeling
■ Directional lighting
■ Smooth shading
■ Color transformation
■ Texture mapping
■ Alpha blending

- Fogging
- Motion blur

The various ways in which these functions are implemented are beyond the scope of this book, but a white paper can be downloaded from Silicon Graphics' Web site at www.sgi.com.

DirectX DirectX is actually a collection of different APIs that support both audio and video functions that was developed by Microsoft. One of the key limiting factors to multimedia in a Windows environment has been the separation of applications from the system's hardware by the HAL. While the HAL provides for a more stable computing environment, it has proved to be a hindrance to multimedia performance. DirectX provides a much thinner layer between the hardware and the applications that use it. While some of the components of DirectX are specific to audio reproduction, others are specific to video. The ones that deal with video are listed here:

- *DirectDraw*: This function of DirectX is responsible for accelerating the generation of two-dimensional images. Applications that require no 3D modeling can make use of this API for smoother 2D animations and faster screen draws in more conventional applications, such as word processors and spreadsheets.
- *Direct3D*: Here, Microsoft has provided an API that simulates direct access to hardware. 3D acceleration can be handled on a software level, providing enhanced 3D animations. A computer that is not blessed with a dedicated accelerator card can benefit from the affects of acceleration as long as the software being run, as well as the graphics adapter, both support the API.
- *DirectPlay*: Some games are best played over the Internet. Internet connections, however, are not exactly conducive to fast video response. DirectPlay is an API that provides enhanced response for games played in this fashion.
- *DirectShow*: Of course, in order to really enjoy the overall experience of a multimedia presentation, both the graphics and the sound are involved. DirectShow is an API that allows for a smooth blending of audio and video information.

Glide This API was developed by 3dfx for its line of high-end video cards. Originally developed for its Voodoo2 and Banshee chipsets, it had previously been considered a proprietary API. However, in 2001, 3dfx released the API to the public for open-source development. It differs from the more common APIs discussed above in two respects. It uses on-chip lookup tables for textures. While this technique isn't currently enjoying much support from the gaming industry, now that the API has been open-sourced, that may change. The second major difference is that it supports higher frame rates than are currently supported by either OpenGL or DirectX.

VIDEO CARD BUS CONSIDERATIONS

With any add-on device the I/O bus on which it resides has a serious impact on the performance of that device. In Chapter Nine, Examining the Expansion Bus, I discussed the significant differences that exist among the different technologies. One of the things I also pointed out was that graphics performance was a driving element in the development of faster busses. With graphics adapters, however, you have to take two different busses into consideration. They work on both an internal and an external bus.

THE EXTERNAL VIDEO BUS

The external graphics bus is the interface between the graphics adapter and the motherboard. Add-on graphics adapters are installed onto the expansion bus and are therefore going to be subject to the limitations of whatever choices are available on a particular computer. This is information I covered in detail in Chapter Nine and therefore, I will only briefly recap the essentials in this chapter. In the early days of computing, an OS such as MS-DOS placed no heavy burden on the graphics subsystem at all. The advent of the GUI changed all that. As Windows 3.x began to gain popularity the public began to demand faster and faster graphics. For purposes of clarity, I'm going to repeat in this chapter a table I used in Chapter Nine to compare the different evolutionary stages of the expansion bus. This information can be seen in **Table 15.3**.

For maximum performance, you're going to want to make use of the fastest bus your system has available. In most cases, this will be AGP, but which version of AGP your computer can handle will be determined by its particular chipset.

THE INTERNAL VIDEO BUS

Here the situation becomes a little more convoluted. While the external bus may be limited to 32-bit or, if you're lucky, 64-bit architecture, inside, the graphics adapter might be steaming along on a completely different stream. The chipset of the video card might produce 32-bit, 64-bit, 96-bit, or 128-bit data paths internally.

However, don't automatically assume that a 128-bit video card is going to be faster than a 64-bit card. Other factors that I discussed earlier have just as strong of an impact on performance. Overall performance takes into account the following factors:

- Chipset features and performance
- Type of memory installed on adapter
- Speed of RAMDAC
- Bit width
- How much process is offloaded to system processor
- Type of interface (PCI or AGP)
- Quality of device driver

Each of these factors contributes to performance. However, all else being equal, if the character in your game is trying to escape a burning building, a chipset operating with a 128-bit data path will kick ash.

Table 15.3 The Evolution of the Expansion Bus

BUS	Year Released	Bus Width	Maximum Speed	Address Space	Available Memory	Bandwidth	CPU Release
PC1	1981	8-bit	4.77MHz	8-bit	1MB	7.9MB/s	8088
ISA	1984	16-bit	8MHz	20-bit	16MB	15.9MB/s	80286
MCA	1987	32-bit	10MHz	20-bit	16MB	~38.6MB/s	80386
EISA	1988	32-bit	8MHz	32-bit	4GB	31.8MB/s	80386
PC Card	1990	16-bit	8MHz	24-bit	64MB	~15.8MB/s	80386
VLB	1991	32-bit	33MHz	32-bit	4GB	127.2MB/s	80486
PCI 1.0	1992	32-bit	33MHz	32-bit	4GB	127.2MB/s	80486
PCI 2.1	1995	32- or 64-bit	66MHz	32-bit	4GB	~510MB/s	Pentium
AGP 1.0	1996	32-bit	66MHz	32-bit	4GB	254MB/s	Pentium
AGP 2.0	1998	32-bit	66MHz	32-bit	4GB	~533MB/s	Pentium
PCI-X 1.0	2000	64-bit	133MHz	64-bit	N/A	~1.2GB/s	Pentium II
PCI-X 2.0	2002	64-bit	<533MHz	64-bit	N/A	~4.3GB/s	Pentium IV

Each new release of a PCI bus is not only faster, but can also have increased bit width and more efficient transfer of data in each clock cycle.

Another thing to consider is that two different manufacturers might design their video cards completely differently and still be able to call them 128-bit cards. A "true" 128-bit card will have a 128-bit chipset and graphics engine as well as a 128-bit path from chipset to video memory. Another less expensive card might call itself 128-bit but have a 64-bit engine. Only the path from chipset to memory is 128 bits wide. The latter implementation would have only a negligible effect on performance. The reason they design it this way is that advertising an inexpensive 128-bit card can have a substantial impact on sales.

A Discussion of Obsolete Display Modes

I promised in the introduction of this chapter that I would provide some information on earlier display modes as a historical reference. This is important to the exam candidate because CompTIA rightfully insists that a properly trained technician knows the history of the industry and not just current events.

In the earliest days of computing everybody worked on monochrome displays that were one of two types. The least expensive, and therefore most common, examples displayed cyan type over a very dark green background. For the writer or desktop publisher, a "deluxe" paper white monitor was available. These placed dark type over a bright background.

In 1981, IBM introduced the first color displays in the form of the Color Graphics Adapter (CGA). CGA monitors offered an amazing 320×200 resolution and the user could enjoy four whole colors! A proprietary implementation of CGA was introduced by Tandy Corporation that provided 640×480 resolution and up to sixteen colors, but it was a classic case of too little, too late. VGA had already established a strong foothold.

The Enhanced Graphics Adapter (EGA) was another development of IBM that was released in 1984. EGA was capable of sixteen colors at a resolution of 640×350. While this was a great improvement over CGA, sitting in front of one of these monitors for eight hours a day was no treat.

CGA and EGA both used the computer's system memory for drawing screens. At those resolutions and color depths, only a small amount of memory was required. I mentioned earlier that in the old days, the first 128K of high memory located directly above the 640K of conventional memory was dedicated to video. In fact, that 128K block was subdivided into two separate 64K address spaces. One of these spaces was dedicated to CGA and the other to EGA.

When IBM released VGA in 1987 the 640×480 resolution was just enough of an improvement to make text less painful to read. The real improvement was realized in how many colors could be displayed. While there were still only sixteen colors possible at the maximum resolution, if the user was willing to sacrifice resolution in exchange for more colors, at 320×200, up to 256 colors could be displayed at once.

Chapter Summary

Now that you have a better understanding of the graphics subsystem of a computer, you should be able to make more informed decisions about how to equip computers, based on their intended use. It's interesting how graphics cards receive so much attention, especially in the gaming market, when monitors don't. Both work together to create the image the user sees.

Certification candidates should take special note of issues such as resolution, color depth, and basic memory requirements. A great deal of emphasis is placed on display settings and what they mean. If I seemed to spend a lot of time discussing video memory, it's because it is such an important component. But it is no more important than the quality of the chipset and the speed of the RAMDAC.

BRAIN DRAIN

1. Describe in as much detail as possible how an image is generated on a typical CRT monitor.

2. You have just purchased a new 21″ monitor that can provide an 1880×1400 display and you want to use 32-bit True Color. Assuming you need no texturizing or other advanced features, what is the minimum memory your graphics card will require?

3. Why are TFT displays considered better than passive matrix displays?

4. What are three critical components for a graphics card and what are their functions?

5. What are the factors that contribute to the overall speed of a graphics card?

THE 64K$ QUESTIONS

1. In a CRT monitor, the phosphors are separated from one another by _____.
    a. The electron guns
    b. A shadow mask
    c. The deflection yoke
    d. A RAMDAC

2. In a CRT, the beams of electrons are redirected across the screen by _____.
    a. The electron guns
    b. A shadow mask
    c. The deflection yoke
    d. A RAMDAC

3. Smoother animation is made possible by a technique called _____.
    a. Texture mapping
    b. Anti-aliasing
    c. Frame buffering
    d. Dithering

4. Diagonal lines are made smoother and less jagged by employing _____.
    a. Texture mapping
    b. Anti-aliasing
    c. Frame buffering
    d. Dithering

5. If a programmer wants her colors to appear more natural with smoother blending, she will take advantage of a technique called _____.
    a. Texture mapping
    b. Anti-aliasing
    c. Frame buffering
    d. Dithering

6. The best way to speed up a video card is to add more memory.
    a. True
    b. False

7. The LCD display most likely used on a PDA is a _____.
    a. Common plane

b. Diagonal crystal

c. Passive matrix

d. TFT

8. If you were to purchase a high-end video card today, it would most likely be equipped with _____ memory.

a. VRAM

b. WRAM

c. MDRAM

d. DDRAM

9. Programmers can add extra effects to graphics without changing the actual color by using _____.

a. Anti-aliasing

b. A frame buffer

c. The alpha channel

d. Dithering

10. Which of the following is not an example of a graphics API?

a. DirectX

b. Glide

c. Cg

d. OpenGL

Tricky Terminology

Alpha channel: Eight bits used by 32-bit True Color to apply effects such as translucency and fogging.

Anti-aliasing: A process through which textures in an image are redrawn to more accurately reflect perceived distance.

Bezel: The plastic frame that masks off the unusable part of a monitor's image.

Cathode: A negatively charged device that emits a stream of electrons when heated.

Color depth: The number of individual hues that can be generated by a given display setting.

Convergence: The accuracy with which multiple beams of electrons or light can focus on the same point.

Co-processed: Any adapter or device that is equipped with a microprocessor that offloads some of the work of the PC's CPU.

Deflection yoke: A circular array of powerful magnets that act to deflect a beam of electrons from its natural path.

Depth queuing: A mathematical algorithm that recalculates the hue and intensity of colors in respect to increasing distances.

Dithering: A process of blending the colors of adjacent areas in an image to make the appearance more natural.

Dot pitch: The distance separating two like-colored phosphors that are adjacent to one another.

Double buffering: The use of two separate buffers, so that as a frame is displayed on the monitor, another frame is in the queue, ready for display, while yet a third is being assembled by the graphics adapter.

Electron gun: A cathode that, when heated, emits a stream of electrons from the positive pole.

Fogging: A technique of implying distance in an image by making objects that are farther away less distinct.

Frame buffer: Dedicated memory used by a graphics adapter to build the next image frame to be displayed in the time that the current image frame is on the screen.

Phosphor: A single dot of color created when the phosphorous layer of a CRT is excited by electrons.

Pixel: The collection of phosphors that collectively generate a single dot of color in a monitor's image.

Raster line: A single row of pixels that make a horizontal line across an image.

Shadow mask: A thin metal sheet perforated with tiny holes that outlines the individual phosphors in a CRT monitor.

Substrate: The supportive material over which an active substance can be applied.

Texel: A small clip that serves as the sample of a texture used in texture mapping.

Texture mapping: A process by which pre-drawn textures are stored in memory and applied to an image as needed.

Triad: The three separate phosphors, each of a separate primary color, that when combined form the separate hues of color perceived by the user.

ACRONYM ALERT

API: Application Programming Interface

CRT: Cathode-Ray Tube. A video display that uses a device called a cathode to fire a beam (or ray) of electrons towards a phosphorus-coated surface.

HAL: Hardware Abstraction Layer

HR: Horizontal Refresh. The speed at which a monitor can draw individual raster lines.

LCD: Liquid Crystal Display. An imaging device that consists of transistors suspended in a liquid emulsion.

MDRAM: Multibank DRAM. A form of memory that can be accessed in blocks, rather than sequentially.

MIP: *Multium in Parvo*. Latin for "many in one." It is a technique by which several samples of the same texture are created in different sizes.

TFT: Thin Film Transistor. An LCD that utilizes microscopically thin layers of transistors laid out in a grid pattern in a liquid crystal emulsion.

UVGA: Ultra VGA. High resolution VGA.

VR: Vertical Refresh. The number of times per second a monitor regenerates the image on the screen.

XGA: Extended Graphics Array. A proprietary display created by IBM.

CHAPTER 16

MULTIMEDIA: COMPUTERIZED HOME ENTERTAINMENT

In the early days of computing, the entire concept of streaming video coupled with high-quality sound coming from a computer was not even a designer's fantasy. Keep in mind that in those days, the best audio systems derived the maximum sound quality from a turntable dragging a diamond needle across a vinyl platter. Computers had a 1″ speaker through which a single beep could be played. As programmers learned fancier tricks, they could vary the frequency of that beep to the point that rudimentary tunes could be played.

Tandy Corporation took that a step further with Tandy Sound. A more advanced sound chip on the TL2000 series of computers allowed for some relatively sophisticated audio, including music and sound effects combined. About the only thing that kept this from really taking off was the nearly simultaneous release of the Ad Lib brand of sound card. The Ad Lib allowed the user to hook up higher-quality external speakers and even get stereo.

Multimedia, these days, has taken on near-theater-like qualities. 5.1 Digital Audio, MPEG II, and the 3-D graphics enhancements I introduced in Chapter Fifteen, Your Computer and Graphics, now allow *Terminator IV* to play in a window on your monitor while you're working on your spreadsheets. Today's computer games combine animation with actual video clips of live actors. (And frighteningly enough, this is still being done with a constant stream of zeros and ones.)

In this chapter, I will introduce you to two different elements of multimedia. Because the majority of these applications are now housed on some variation of optical medium, I have chosen to include the various members of the CD family in this chapter and show you how music is stored on a CD. Then, I'll discuss sound cards and their role in the overall process.

A+ EXAM OBJECTIVES

Some exam objectives that will be covered include the following:

1.1 Identify the names, purpose, and characteristics of system modules. Recognize these modules by sight or definition.

1.2 Identify basic procedures for adding and removing field-replaceable modules for desktop systems. Given a replacement scenario, choose the appropriate sequences.

1.4 Identify typical IRQs, DMAs, and I/O addresses, and procedures for altering these settings when installing and configuring devices. Choose the appropriate installation or configuration steps in a given scenario.

1.6 Identify proper procedures for installing and configuring common IDE devices. Choose the appropriate installation or configuration sequences in given scenarios. Recognize the associated cables.

2.1 Recognize common problems associated with each module and their symptoms, and identify steps to isolate and troubleshoot the problems. Given a problem situation, interpret the symptoms and infer the most likely cause.

THE COMPONENTS OF MULTIMEDIA

Three pieces needed to complete the multimedia puzzle are decent storage media, good sound reproduction, and a way to create cinematic quality graphics. Since I discussed the reproduction of graphics in Chapter Fifteen, I need not rehash that here. But one thing you need to keep in mind is that all those audio clips and graphics files require some CPU horsepower in addition to as much available memory as you can provide. Since they also take up a lot of space, some sort of portable storage mechanism is in order. For these files, the floppy disk just isn't going to cut it.

THE CD-ROM

The CD-ROM has almost universally been accepted as storage medium of choice for multimedia (see **Figure 16.1**). While it started out as an acronym for Compact Disc/Read Only Memory, CD-ROM is one of the few acronyms that has made the successful migration to the status of a "real word." CD-ROMs have made a few evolutionary advances in the years since they were first released. For one thing, they continually get faster.

Manufacturers have a unique method of measuring speed. When shopping for a CD-ROM drive, you find a range of speeds starting these days at about 32x and moving upward to 56x. Just what do those numbers mean? The first CD-ROM released had a maximum data throughput of 150KB/s. That's incredibly slow, by today's standards. When the first bump from 150 to 300KB/s was released, the marketing hype was "Two times the speed of regular CD-ROMs." Advertising slicks labeled them as "2x" CD-ROMs and the convention has stuck. **Table 16.1** compares the speeds of CD drives over the years.

> **EXAM NOTE:** Make sure you know the throughput of the initial release of the CD-ROM and how that relates to the speed factors the industry uses to rate CD-ROM speed.

Figure 16.1   The CD family has grown a lot since that first 150KB/s device. This machine is equipped with a 16X DVD/40X CD-ROM as well as a 52X CD-RW.

Table 16.1   Conventional CD-ROM Specifications Past, Present, and Future

Speed	Classification	Actual Bits per Second	Transfer Rate (KB/s)
1x	Single speed	153,600	150
2x	Double speed	307,200	300
4x	Quad	614,400	600
6x	Six speed	921,600	900
8x	Eight speed	1,228,800	1200
12x	Twelve speed	1,536,000	1500
16x	Sixteen speed	1,843,200	1800
24x	Twenty-four speed	2,457,600	2400
32x	Thirty-two speed	3,686,400	3600
40x	Forty speed	4,915,200	4800
48x	Forty-eight speed	7,372,800	7200
56x	Fifty-six speed	8,601,600	8400
72x*	Seventy-two speed	11,590,200	10,800

Each generation of CD drive has a speed based on a multiple of the original CD-ROM drive.

*Don't try finding a 72x drive at this point in time. For a short while, a proprietary technology known as TrueX provided this speed. TrueX has been subsequently abandoned. It is included here for informational purposes.

Until the release of DVD (I'll get into that), the one thing that didn't change with time was the amount of data stored on the disc. To understand that, let's take a look at how the data is stored. The first thing that is important is that CDs are not magnetic media like your hard drive, floppy disks, or Zip disks. They're an optical medium. Information is extracted from a disc by a laser beam.

HOW THE CD WORKS

A standard CD is a disc 120mm in diameter and consisting of three layers. The back layer (where the label is traditionally printed) is made of polycarbonate, a fairly durable plastic. However, that is an extremely thin layer of about .002mm. If you're

BUZZ WORDS

Pit: A tiny hole embedded in the recording layer of optical media that prevents the laser from reflecting back into the photoelectric sensor.

Land: All of the reflective surface of the recording layer in optical media that has not been burned or punched into a pit.

Optical stylus: A mechanism consisting of a laser-emitting diode coupled to a beam splitter.

worried about scratches on your CD (and you should be), worry most about the label side. Do not use standard felt-tip markers to write on this side, as many of those inks contain a solvent. Over time, they can actually eat into the plastic and damage the data on recordable CDs. Use only labels designed for CDs or specially designed felt markers for writing on that surface.

> **EXAM NOTE:** While this section admittedly gets more involved in how data is written to and read back from the surface of the CD-ROM than CompTIA requires, it's still good information to know. What CompTIA does expect is that you be able to describe the purpose of split beams and the function of pits and lands.

Onto that back surface of a conventional CD a .002mm layer of aluminum is deposited. The metal coating acts as a mirror onto which billions of little tiny *pits*, one-sixth of a micron wide, have been stamped. These pits vary in length from slightly under a micron to about three microns and are only one-sixth of a micron deep (see **Figure 16.2**). These pits are put onto the disc in a concentric spiral moving from the center of the disc to the outside. The area of disc surface outside of the pits is known as the *lands*. Data is grouped in sectors, similar to the way hard disks manage data, except that the sector size is 2KB (on data CDs) rather than 512 bytes. Track density on CDs is much higher than that of hard drives as well. CD manufacturers squeeze in excess of 16,000 tracks into every inch of the CD. That's roughly 400 times the density of magnetic media.

When your CD player reads the data off the disc, it shines an infrared laser, 780 nanometers wide, past a prism that splits the beam into three separate beams. This laser/beam-splitter combination is known as the *optical stylus*. On the first-generation CD-ROMs and most current audio CD players, the disc spins under the beam at 200 to 500rpm, the speed increasing as the laser reaches the outside edge of the disc. Higher throughput for data CDs requires that the disc spin faster. Rotation speeds have exceeded 11,000rpm on several models.

Light reflecting from pits is polarized 180 degrees from the light reflected from the lands. The difference in intensity between lands and pits results in a flickering beam of light that is

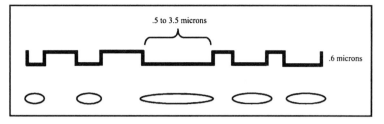

The top diagram represents a cross-section of a CD track, with its pits and lands. Beneath is a representation of the pits seen from above.

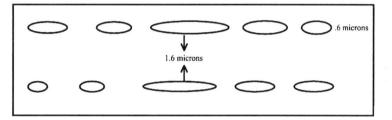

All pits are uniformly .6 microns wide and .6 microns deep, but they vary in length. All tracks are separated by 1.6 microns of land.

Figure 16.2   The pits etched into a CD are microscopically small, yet are all that is needed to store large amounts of data onto a relatively small surface.

picked up by a very sensitive photoelectric cell. This cell converts the beam into a pulsating electronic signal, which is translated by the controller into a series of zeros and ones.

As you might imagine, keeping a laser beam that tiny accurately focused on a stream of microscopic holes in plastic is a formidable task. It wouldn't be quite as difficult if disc surfaces were always mathematically flat, and spindle holes were punched into the absolute center of the CD so that as it rotated there would be no positional deviation of the tracks. Manufacturing CDs to such perfect standards would most likely drive their price out of the range of most users. Therefore, some fail-safe measures have to be taken.

A common approach to this problem is the technique of beam splitting. The CD reader doesn't focus the beam directly onto the disc itself. Instead, it is focused on a diffraction grid, which divides the original laser beam into three different light sources. The beam splitter is designed in such a way that the three outbound beams are passed through to the medium. The reflected light coming back from the CD is bounced ninety degrees to the photoreceptor diode, where the signals are interpreted.

Of the three beams directed at the CD, the center one is supposed to remain focused on the track containing the data. The two outside beams focus on the land surface on either side of the track (**Figure 16.3**). Since there are no pits in this area, the reflections that bounce back from either of these two beams should always be constant. Any flickering of these reflected beams generates electrical signals that cause the servomotor that positions the laser to adjust its focus accordingly.

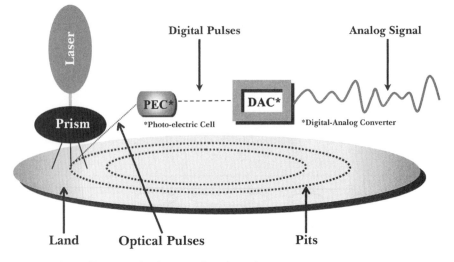

Figure 16.3 Diagram of a beam splitter in action

STORING DATA ON CDs

In order for a CD reader to accurately interpret what the CD burner created, there are standard file formats. Digital audio discs require very little in the way of error correction, and the original compact disc/digital audio (CD-DA) format is still used for audio CDs. Executable programs and critical data require error-free translations. For this, the International Organization for Standardization (ISO) wrote a series of standards for the CD data format called ISO 9660. This is the file format currently used in the manufacture of CD software. It allows approximately 650MB to be stored on a single compact disc.

AUDIO CD RECORDING

As I mentioned, audio CDs have completely different requirements than those used for storing digital data. Error correction is not as much of an issue. Accurately reproducing musical pitch is the requirement. To do so, the musical waveform being recorded is sampled many thousands of times per second. How many times per second a sample is extracted is the sample rate. The industry standard for CD-quality sound is 44,100 times per second. Sample rates for the sound track on computer games can vary. The conversion of analog waveforms into a digital file format is known as Pulse Code Modulation (PCM).

The sample taken is a 16-bit chunk of data called a *chop*. 147 chops can be stored in each 2352-byte sector. Typically, audio files end with a .wav extension. A standard WAV file is made of a sequential series of chops. If you recall your binary, you will be able to calculate that a 16-bit sample is

BUZZ WORDS

Chop: A 16-bit piece of data generated when music is sampled once during the digital recording procedure.

capable of generating 65,536 levels of sound. In order to record a stereo signal, two separate audio channels are simultaneously recorded onto individual tracks. Reading 44,100 16-bit samples simultaneously across two tracks yields an effective data transfer rate of 176,400 bytes per second. On playback, the digital signal passes through a circuit called the Digital-Analog Converter (DAC). This conversion is called Signal Quantisation.

Standards for audio CD recording are published and updated regularly in a publication known as the Red Book. This set of standards defines standard methods for manufacturing CDs, the specifications for PCM, how to manufacture and calibrate the optical stylus, and many other technical standards. As new or updated standards emerge, this book is updated.

DATA CD-ROM

The structure of a CD-ROM drive designed to read data differs very little from what I described for audio CD players. How data is stored is significantly different, though. Data CDs make use of the Compact Disc File System (CDFS). Whereas the audio CD creates a large file of 16-bit chops, typical computer data isn't so evenly structured. As a result, the file format used by data CDs uses a file system similar to that of other media. It differs in the size of sectors from magnetic media. While a hard drive contains 512-byte sectors, a CD-ROM uses those 2352-byte sectors I mentioned earlier. The CD/DA file system uses the entire sector to store data. CDFS can store 2000 bytes into each sector and reserves the remaining bytes for file system overhead.

While losing a byte of Beethoven now and then isn't critical, losing a byte of WINWORD.EXE can keep the program from running. Therefore, Error Detection Code (EDC) is incorporated into the data CDFS file structure. EDC works in conjunction with traditional ECC to assure that data integrity is maintained. Another 304 bytes, known as *synchronization bits*, assures that data is delivered in the correct order. Altogether, this results in a data CD being able to store only 650MB, as opposed to the 680MB of the audio CD. Data transfer, due to the additional overhead of EDC, was 150KB/s on the first generation of CD-ROMs. This is the root transfer that became the basis for the speed multipliers I discussed earlier in the chapter. One of the ways manufacturers have achieved higher throughput has been by increasing the rotational velocity of the disc.

> **EXAM NOTE:** Know why synchronization bits are necessary for data CDs but not for musical CDs. Also be aware that this is why data CDs format to a different capacity than music CDs.

Another key difference is reflected in how the different discs need to be able to access data. An audio disc is frequently played from beginning to end. Even if only selected tracks are being played there are very few files (relatively speaking) on an audio CD. Random access of data is rarely an issue, and even when it is, speed of that access isn't that critical. A data CD, conversely, can have tens of thousands of files. The reader needs to be able to access any one of these files

BUZZ WORDS ——————

Synchronization bits: Data included on each sector of a data CD that assures that the information will be processed in the correct sequence.

as quickly as possible when requested by the system. How the drive moves the laser head across the disc directly affects how quickly data can be extracted from the drive. Different methods for reading the data from the surface of the disc have emerged over the years.

CLV The first CD-ROM drives for computers were identical to those used in the audio industry. Manufacturers employed a technology called constant linear velocity (CLV) to read data from the disc. Unlike early hard drives, where every track across the drive has the same number of sectors, the number of sectors per track increases from the center of the CD to the edge. CLV drives use a mechanism called a servo to constantly adjust the rpm of the disc rotation in order to make sure that data throughput remains constant.

On audio CDs and the first-generation data CDs, this velocity changed from 210 rpm to 539 rpm. Audio CD players still use this method and spin the disc at these speeds. The method by which data throughput was increased on early generation CD-ROM drives was to increase the maximum rotational velocity of the disc. 4x drives would spin faster than 2x, 8x spun faster than 4x, and so on up the line.

The problem with this technique was that in order to randomly access data, the head not only has to locate the appropriate track, but it also has to adjust to the correct rotational speed for that track. This led to rather poor access times for data. Drives of this era were afflicted with access times of 400ms and some exceeded 500ms. As you might imagine, this did not exactly enhance the effect of trying to play an interactive game directly from a CD. Pioneer was the first company to abandon this approach in 1986 when it released its 10x CD-ROM drive.

CAV These drives developed by Pioneer incorporated a new technology called constant angular velocity (CAV). This approach keeps rotational speed constant and requires that the controller adapt to different speeds of data throughput as the heads move from center to edge. Now, when data needs to be accessed randomly, the laser head can find the track it needs and doesn't have to wait for the disc to settle into its new speed. Most drives currently manufactured actually employ both CAV and CLV modes. They use CAV to read data toward the middle of the disc and switch to CLV to read data from the perimeter.

The inclusion of digital signal processors (DSP) offloads much of the work of the DACs to these chips and provides much faster data transfers. A DSP is a microprocessor whose only reason for existence is to scan a nondigital signal and convert it to a digital stream of data.

Since CAV drives don't actually have a fixed data throughput, where do the manufacturers arrive at their published speeds? In some cases, the published speed ratings frequently represent only the inside track. Most reputable manufacturers actually publish the speed of their drives as a dual-speed rating; for example, you might be looking at a 24/48x CD-ROM drive. These numbers represent the speed obtained at both the outside track and the innermost track. In other words, your fancy new 56x CD-ROM only works at that speed when it's reading the inside track, then gets slower from there.

DATA TRANSFER AND THE REAL WORLD

As I have already pointed out, data throughput was increased primarily by way of increasing rotational speed of the disc. The question that needs to be asked is when do users realize the benefit of these gains? A blind answer to this question would be that faster is always better. The fact of the matter is that high transfer rates are rarely utilized in the majority of applications that CDs are put to.

As I said earlier, digital audio requires a mere 178KB/s to maintain CD-quality sound. Recorded video files (in compressed format) will not benefit from anything greater than about 300KB/s. Therefore, higher speeds really only strut their stuff if you're installing an application from the CD. For example, many of the office suites shipped by software companies these days fill from four to as many as eight CDs! Installing one of these applications from a 2x CD is not high on my list of pleasures. In order to provide a rough comparison, I did a very unscientific little experiment. I happened to have an old 4x CD-ROM lying around. I installed it on the same IDE port as a 48x CD-ROM. I then proceeded to install Office 2000 Small Business Edition. This application resides on two CDs for a complete installation. (The things I do for my readers!)

From the 4x drive the installation took an hour and forty-eight minutes. I then uninstalled the application, made sure the registry was cleaned of any entries generated by the first installation, and then repeated the installation from the 48x. I was finished in seventeen minutes. Based on raw speed measurements alone, the installation should have been eight times faster. If you do the math, you'll see that the actual improvement I realized was in the range of 6.35x.

Several factors can account for the discrepancy. Command overhead on the controllers is one of these (See Chapter Twelve, Hard Disk Drive Structure and Geometry, for a discussion of command overhead). The 48x drive would have also benefited greatly had the system I used for the experiment allowed me to use the UDMA mode supported by that drive. But the presence of the older PIO drive on the same channel forced the newer drive into PIO mode as well. Another factor that undoubtedly affected the different times was how much time I sat in a daze while the setup routine waited for me to either input data it was requesting or to click the Next button. (I told you it was a very unscientific experiment!)

Games that are played directly from the CD benefit very little from this extra speed, however. In time, you can expect the best computer games to ship in DVD format in order to be able to take advantage of MPEG-II technology that I'll be discussing later in this chapter.

THE CD INTERFACE

Modern CD-ROM drives will ship as either SCSI or ATAPI devices. In terms of performance, neither standard currently can claim an advantage over the other. Data throughput is still lower than the slowest of the available interfaces. However, it is still possible, even in this enlightened day and age, to stumble across computers that use one of the proprietary interfaces of yesteryear. At one time, the user had to choose among Sony, Mitsumi (or Panasonic, which is the same thing), and IDE. Eventually everybody gave way to IDE.

It can be pretty hard to tell the difference between the IDE and the early proprietary drives. The connectors looked identical. Unfortunately, the pins on those connectors didn't perform identical functions, and your CD-ROM drive would not work if plugged into the wrong connector. It didn't do any harm; it just didn't work. Differentiating SCSI from IDE can prove difficult if you look too quickly. The connectors look the same. However, SCSI will have fifty pins, while IDE only has forty. Also, the IDE device has to have a way of determining whether its role is master or slave on the port. On the back of the IDE drive will be three or four jumpers that perform that function. The manufacturers are pretty good about labeling these jumpers on the drive itself, so figuring it out shouldn't be too tough.

People sometimes get a little confused about SCSI versus ATAPI when it comes to CD-ROMs. As far as the interface goes, I pointed out when discussing the SCSI interface that in most cases, SCSI is the faster of the two. That's no different with CD-ROM drives than it is with any other devices. However, before rushing out and converting everything you own, including the CD-ROM, to SCSI, there are a few things you should consider.

The SCSI interface is a shared bandwidth. Any device on the chain is competing for space on that bandwidth. Raw performance of CD-ROM drives, at this point in technology anyway, doesn't even begin to approach the bandwidth available across the ATAPI interface. Therefore, even if you're using the fastest CD-ROM drives available, they won't become any more of a bottleneck than they already are if put them on the IDE interface. In fact, if the CD-ROM and the hard drives are both being hit constantly, such as in a server environment that accesses data from CDs a lot, then having the CD-ROM on the SCSI chain can actually hinder the performance of the hard drives and other father SCSI devices.

EXTERNAL CD-ROMs

External CD-ROM drives have always enjoyed a certain degree of popularity. You can add one to the system without having to open the case. Fighting with master/slave relationships is not an issue, and the drive can be moved from one machine to another. As a result, external devices are as popular today as they were a few years ago. Putting them onto the machine has been accomplished basically in one of several ways: external SCSI (including FireWire), parallel port operation, and, more recently, USB. Hooking up a SCSI CD-ROM drive differs in no way from hooking up any other SCSI device, which is covered in Chapter Fourteen, The Many Faces of SCSI.

Putting the drive on the parallel port is simple. It hooks up the same way as any printer. Operating systems that support PnP will automatically detect the new drive and load the appropriate drivers. To make the drive work properly, however, you must make sure that your BIOS is set to use the IEEE-1284 ECP/EPP mode. While the older bidirectional modes will work, performance will be really, really bad. ECP supports up to 1200KB/s throughput, as opposed to the 530KB/s that bidirectional can handle. (I'll be discussing these different modes in greater detail in Chapter Seventeen, Printing Technologies.)

Even with ECP enabled, parallel CD-ROM drives do not approach a decent internal drive in performance levels. They can also create compatibility issues with other parallel devices. Even though the CD-ROM drive is equipped with a pass-through parallel port for attaching a printer, some older printers don't coexist peacefully on the same port as another device.

USB or FireWire are far more desirable interfaces for external drives of any nature. USB provides throughput of up to 12Mb/s and is fully Plug 'n Play. USB is not afflicted with the compatibility issues of the parallel port and is also hot-pluggable. FireWire shares all of the above and has a much faster 400Mb/s throughput. That means when you're done using the drive on one machine and want to use it on another, you just pop it off the port and off you go. There is no need to shut down either machine.

Of course, for this to work, your machine must be able to accept USB or FireWire devices. As I discussed in the chapter on the expansion bus, both of these technologies require BIOS that supports them, along with the physical interface.

THE LOADING MECHANISM

Most CD-ROM drives currently manufactured utilize a tray-loading mechanism for inserting the CD. However, this isn't true for all drives. Loading mechanisms that have been used, past and present, fall into one of three types. They will be a tray, a caddy, or a slot. There are advantages and disadvantages to each. Each has it own little quirks, so understanding the differences can be important.

The tray is far and away the most common mechanism seen today. Its advantages are that it is the simplest to manufacture, and therefore the least expensive. On the other hand, the disc gets a lot of handling and, if loaded incorrectly into the tray, may get damaged.

The caddy gets a lot of use with multi disc changers, but has appeared in the past on a few single-disc drives. With the caddy, the disc must be inserted in a carrier (the caddy), which is inserted into the drive. Discs get the most protection in this manner. For the user, on the other hand, changing between discs is much more inconvenient.

The slot has become popular with some manufacturers, and many customers like them as well. With a slot-loading drive, the user simply inserts the disc into the slot and a loading mechanism draws the disc into the drive and seats it properly. When the user pushes the eject mechanism, the disc is pushed back out. Unfortunately, this approach puts the maximum amount of wear on the disc.

INSTALLING CD-ROM DRIVES

Installing a CD-ROM drive into a computer couldn't be easier. The drive itself simply slides into any available externally accessible 5$\frac{1}{4}$″ drive bay. It's generally a good idea to attach the cables before you attach the screws. In many enclosures, these bays back up to the power supply. The cables can be pretty difficult to access once the drive is in position. Another tip is to determine in advance which is the #1 connector so you get the IDE cable on right. Plug one of the Molex power connectors in and then make sure the audio cable is in place. Feed the wires down through the case the way you want them and then slide the drive back into place. It's probably not a good idea to tighten the screws down until you know the system is up and running.

Usually, if you can't get your new CD drive to work, it's because you have it on the same port as your hard drive and there's a master/slave conflict. The rules for CD-ROM drives are the same as the rules I discussed in Chapter Thirteen.

One short note on port/drive relationships: computers these days have two IDE ports, as I've already discussed. Theoretically, there's no reason the CD drive can't be either the master drive on the secondary port or the slave on the primary port. The only time this might come into play is when it comes time to add other ATAPI devices. Some CD-RWs won't operate as a slave. The only way to get the drive to work is if the CD-RW is the master device on the port. With Windows

98 (or earlier) operating systems, the primary system hard drive must be the master device on the primary port in order to boot. With many older systems, this is the case regardless of the OS in use. These situations limit the CD-RW to being installed on the secondary port. If you're having trouble getting a CD-RW to install correctly, check to see if this is your problem.

DEVICE DRIVERS

Any contemporary operating system will generally have support for CD-ROM drives built in. For example, Microsoft Windows detects the existence of a CD drive and loads the appropriate device drivers, virtual drivers, and DLLs automatically. Linux does the same. However, you might discover that, when you restart your computer to the command prompt, your CD-ROM drive disappears. For the drive to work from the command prompt, the appropriate drivers must be loaded on boot from the config.sys file, and a crucial program called MSCDEX must load from the autoexec.bat file. Most manufacturers make this a pretty simple task by including a floppy disk with an installation program for creating the necessary entries. Of course, that's usually the disk your client threw away because he or she didn't think it was necessary.

Since this will probably happen to you at least once in the course of your career, it's a good idea to be prepared. While it is true that CD-ROM manufacturers have never standardized on a universal DOS driver, CD-ROM drives operate over a very simplified command set. Because of this, a CD-ROM driver for one drive will usually work pretty well for another.

Generally, DOS drivers end in a .sys extension. For example, Toshiba drives ship with a file called toshiba.sys included on their installation disks. Mark the location of this file, and edit your config.sys file to include a line to load the driver, just as shown in **Figure 16.4**. In order to identify the device created as being a drive, a /D: parameter must be included. The line for a typical config.sys file would look something like Figure 16.4.

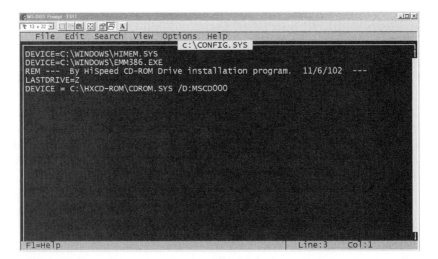

Figure 16.4 Standard config.sys command to load CD-ROM device driver

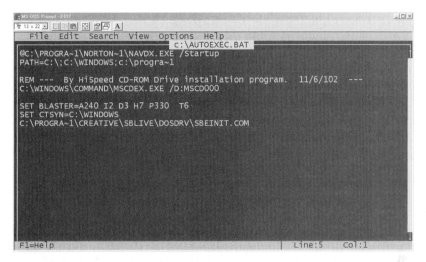

Figure 16.5   Standard autoexec.bat line to load mscdex.exe

In the autoexec.bat file, a related line must also be added, loading the MSCDEX program and identifying the driver and device it will control. The proper syntax for this line can be seen in **Figure 16.5**. The critical aspect of this line is that the /D: parameter must be identical to that in the line loaded by config.sys. If you do not do this, then when the autoexec.bat file loads, it won't find any devices under the control of the device driver.

A side note is that the device identification is not really critical. As long as the device ID in both autoexec.bat and config.sys are identical, you can use whatever you want. I could have written in the config.sys

```
DEVICE=C:\TOS\TOSHIBA.SYS  /D:RABBIT
```

as long as the line in autoexec.bat read

```
C:\WINDOWS\MSCDEX  /D:RABBIT
```

I would then have a CD-ROM drive loaded with the device name of Rabbit, under the control of toshiba.sys. My system would hop right along.

What is critical is that the files toshiba.sys and mscdex.exe really exist, and that they are where you say they are. If you want to make a bootable floppy disk with CD-ROM support, you can simply run the SYS command on the floppy, as such SYS A: This copies critical system files to the floppy disk. Then copy the files toshiba.sys (or whatever your brand requires) and mscdex.exe to the floppy. Create a file called config.sys in your text editor and add the line

```
DEVICE=TOSHIBA.SYS   /D:MSCD001
```

Then create one called autoexec.bat and add

```
MSCDEX   /D:MSCD001
```

The Descendants of CD-ROM

The CD-ROM drive has lived a long and fulfilling life, but it may be coming to an end. Recordable CD (CDR), Rewritable CD (CD-RW), Digital Video Disc (DVD), and the Recordable DVD (DVD-R) drives threaten its existence more and more each day with declining prices and increasing performance. Most manufacturers offer combo drives that incorporate features of all of the above. Currently installed in my system is a CD/DVD along with a CD/CDR/CD-RW. And lately, I've been getting an acquisitive itch for one of those drives that incorporate DVD-R/-RW, DVD+RW/+R, and even run CDR/CD-RW discs.

CDR and CD-RW

CD-ROMs were wonderful devices and enthusiastically embraced by the industry. By about 1997 it had reached the point that a computer without a CD-ROM drive was a special order item. It had become standard equipment. Long before that was the case, users were already clamoring for a device that would let them make their own CDs. Philips answered that demand in 1993 with the CDR. Naturally, consumers in general were unhappy that they could not overwrite the contents of a disc with an updated version. Therefore, CD-RW became the next must-have toy.

The CDR

CDR drives allow the end users to create their own compact discs. Conventional CDs use an aluminum base on which the pits are stamped. Considering that the melting point of aluminum is 1220 degrees, it's a pretty sure bet that you're not going to make CDs by melting pits in aluminum.

Therefore, a special medium had to be developed to make this work. The standard CD would obviously not be something the average person was going to make on his or her home computer. Therefore, a new disc emerged that made use of dyes in the recording layer that were easily melted by a low-power laser beam. A spiral track on the CDR blank is imprinted onto the blank at the factory at the time of manufacture. This is known as the *pregroove*, and it is the target area for the pits that will be eventually burned by the CDR drive. The dye is poured over the grooved base in a very thin layer. To simulate the reflectance of the aluminum layer of standard CDs a microscopically thin layer of metal is placed over the dye. If you look at **Figure 16.6**, you'll see a simplified illustration of how this is done.

CDR drives are equipped with a dual-powered laser. The lowest power is similar to that of a conventional CD. However, when the user wants to record data to a CDR, the write power of the laser is sufficiently powerful to burn a hole in the dye layer. The burned area becomes opaque, effectively duplicating the function of a pit in the read process.

The first dye used in CDRs was *cyanine dye*. More recent discs make use of *pthalocyanine dye*. Pthalocyanine is better than cyanine in two respects. First of all, it lasts longer. Cyanine dye is not archival, in that it has a life expectancy of twenty years or less. Certain light frequencies, including UV and other frequencies found in normal sunlight, can degrade the dye. Leaving the

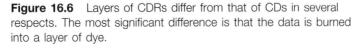

A. Protective Coating
B. Reflective Layer
C. Recording Layer
D. Substrate
E. Pregroove

Figure 16.6 Layers of CDRs differ from that of CDs in several respects. The most significant difference is that the data is burned into a layer of dye.

CDR that contained the overheads for a critical presentation on the dashboard of your car in the middle of July could result in unemployment. Pthalocyanine is not nearly as susceptible to photo-sensitivity and can be expected to last in excess of a century.

Another benefit of pthalocyanine is that a much higher degree of accuracy can be achieved when burning the pits, which in turn allows for higher speeds. When cyanine-based CDR media is used at high speeds, the pits are not nearly as deep and can be poorly defined, rendering the disc unreadable to many conventional CD-ROM players, especially those of an earlier vintage.

The metal layer is usually silver or gold. It is pretty easy to tell which has been used by the color of the disc. Gold is considered preferable to silver simply because it is far more resistant to corrosion. Either works equally well as a reflectance material, and due to cost considerations nearly all media currently manufactured use silver.

BUZZ WORDS

Cyanine dye: A bluish-colored dye that was used in the recording layer of early generations of CDR media.

Pthalocyanine dye: A more stable dye used in recent generations of CDR that is less sensitive to UV light and lasts for up to a 100 years.

Pregroove: A spiral track engraved on CDR and CD-RW media at the factory that acts as a target for the recording laser.

Multisession: The ability to record data onto a CDR or CD-RW in several stages without closing out the TOC.

For CDRs to work, a different method of formatting had to be developed. ISO 9660 did not provide for addition of data after the initial master was made. To make the CDR attractive to the average user, data would need to be added in increments. Most people don't have 650MB they want to submit to disc in one session. Manufacturers put the standards for *multisession* CD burning into a group of specifications known as the Orange Book. Companies that make CD mastering software have incorporated these features into their product, making it a simple matter for users to leave a CD open for future data to be added. Part of this procedure involves writing a Table of Contents (TOC) for each CDR, which can then be updated when new files are added. The TOC performs a similar function to that of the file allocation table on your hard drive.

The CD-RW

CDRs became very popular, very fast. Still, there was something missing. If you're working on a large project that takes a long time to complete, say this book, for example, the data changes on a constant basis. CDRs allowed for archiving data, but not modifying it. The CD-RW solved this problem.

In place of dyes on which to record data, the CD-RW blank has a layer of a rather exotic material made out of silver, antimony, tellurium, and indium. This compound reacts to different intensities of heat in different ways. Like all metals, it has a melting point. Unlike most metals, however, this compound also has a crystallization point. Melting point occurs at a moderately low temperature. Intense heat crystallizes it.

Therefore, in order to do its job, the CD-RW drive has a laser beam capable of three different intensities. The lowest is for reading back data. This is known as *read power*. *Erase power* is the next setting, because it actually requires less power to melt the material than it does to crystallize it. *Write power* is the setting that generates sufficient heat to crystallize the material. When data is written to the medium, the laser burns a crystalline pit.

Buzz Words

Read power: The lowest power setting for the optical stylus of a CD-RW, which it uses to read data from the surface.

Write power: The highest power setting for the optical stylus of a CD-RW, which it uses to record data onto the surface.

Erase power: A medium power setting for the optical stylus of a CD-RW, which it uses to melt the crystals generated by the previous recording session back into the uncrystallized recording layer.

Phase change layer: The recording layer of a CD-RW disk.

Dielectric layer: A transparent layer of material above and below the recording layer of a CD-RW that dissipates the heat built up in the CD during the recording process.

The CD-RW has a layer of this material called the *phase change layer*. This layer is located between two other layers of material that dissipate excess heat during the write process. These are the *dielectric layers*. The remainder of the disc is similar to the CDR.

The Orange Book had allowed for multisession recording, but it hadn't provided for rewriting the Table of Contents to allow for changes in the location of data on the disc. This was added with the release of the Orange Book III.

DVD

Digital Video Discs (also known as Digital Versatile Discs, depending on who you want to listen to) are actually a different technology all together. The disc looks the same; it's the same size, refracts light into pretty colors, and all that. But there, the resemblance ends.

DVD didn't get off to the most auspicious of starts. There was a rather bitter battle over control of the technology among several different companies, each with its own idea of how it should be done. The end result was five different file formats. See **Table 16.2** for an overview.

A major technological difference is that DVD can be pressed in layers, and both sides of the disc can contain data. Combine that with a file format that fits more information onto a

Table 16.2 DVD File Formats

Format	Description
DVD-ROM	High-capacity data storage
DVD Video	Use for full-length motion pictures
DVD Audio	Audio-only content
DVD-R	Recordable DVD
DVD-RAM	Rewritable DVD

DVD actually needs to support five different file formats.

Table 16.3 DVD Formats

Format	Description	Capacity
DVD 5	Single sided, single layer	4.7GB
DVD 8	Single sided, double layer	8.5GB
DVD 10	Double sided, single layer	9.4GB
DVD 18	Double sided, double layer	17GB

DVD capacities vary with the number of layers embedded.

single layer, and you have a disc that can store several gigabytes of data. This is done by creating the first layer on one side, coating it with a microscopically thin, transparent gold layer, and then pressing the second layer. If you do that to the second side you can have four layers of data. Multilayer discs are easily discernible from regular ones by their gold color. Discs are made as shown in **Table 16.3**.

The way capacity was increased so dramatically was managed on several levels. To start with, the lands created during the creation of masters were reduced in width from 1.6 microns to about .75 microns. By itself, this change allowed for double the number of tracks. The relative lengths of the pits were also cut by half. Now manufacturers can fit twice the number of pits onto four times as many tracks.

DVD 8 and DVD 18 further increase storage by allowing for two separate data storage layers on the medium. A microscopically thin layer of semireflecting material separates these layers. When the optical stylus needs to read the lower layer, it simply changes its focus to that layer. The bottom layer can't hold quite as much data as the top. Therefore, capacity isn't quite doubled.

It's interesting to note that double-sided discs are actually two separate discs bonded together by adhesive. The fact is, all DVDs are two layers. The layers actually required by a single-sided DVD are only half as thick as a standard CD. Manufacturers were concerned about the durability and stability of such thin material and bonded a layer of polycarbonate plastic to the back of the disc to make it the same thickness as a CD. By bonding two DVD discs, back-to-back, you get the double-sided variety.

As you might imagine, new file formats had to be developed to support this medium. As I mentioned earlier, the race to develop DVD resulted in five different formats. The call to arms led the Optical Storage Technology Association (OSTA) to develop the Universal Disc Format (UDF). This format merges video, audio, and data, allowing a file to support any of the three, or to mix any two or even all three into a single file. UDF also permits any type of optical disc to access any of these types of file, even if made by another medium.

Most DVD drives double as CD-ROM drives. In other words, they'll read either format. Manufacturers do this by mounting two separate optical styli on a swivel mount. Once the drive has detected the type of medium that has been inserted, the proper head moves into place and the fun begins. However, to take advantage of the motion picture capabilities of DVD, you need to have a video card capable of MPEG II standards. (See Chapter Fifteen, Your Computer and Graphics.)

SOUND CARDS

Until the early 1980s, the only sound you could get out of your computer was that which came from the built-in speaker. Unless, of course, you had one of several different models of Tandy computer made by Radio Shack. Tandy developed onboard 3-voice sound and 16-color CGA graphics. (If you recall from Chapter Fifteen, CGA was four colors!) Then a company out of Canada released a PC expansion card called the Ad Lib that provided FM quality sound through a pair of external speakers. It offered a total of *eleven* voices.

Confused about what is meant by "voices" in a sound card? Basically, a *voice* is a collection of sampled frequencies that simulate the sound of a particular instrument. In the real world, sound occurs in waves. These waves are measured in cycles per second, or hertz. The more cycles per second, the higher the perceived pitch. In order to convert sound to a digital computer file, the sound is sampled thousands of times per second. CD-quality sound (audio quality equal to that of a Compact Audio Disc) is generally sampled 44,000 times per second. FM quality, or that of a decent radio broadcast, is considered to be around 11,000 samples per second.

If two instruments play the same note, say a guitar and a trumpet, even though the pitch may be the same, the two instruments still sound dramatically different. This is because, along with the base frequency, which is what determines pitch, there is a very complex collection of additional sound frequencies that the instrument produces that are generated along with the root frequency of the note. The *root frequency* is the single frequency that makes a C sharp a C sharp, regardless of the instrument playing that note.

The additional frequencies generated by specific instruments are called harmonics and subharmonics. *Harmonics* are frequencies of sound that are higher than the root frequency of the note being played. *Subharmonics* are frequencies lower than root.

The harmonics of a stringed instrument differ greatly from those of a brass instrument, which differ greatly from those of a woodwind. It's the harmonics that make them sound different. By preprogramming a sound card to play a root frequency, along with a predetermined set of harmonics, that sound card can simulate the sound of a guitar or a trumpet or a saxophone. The magic of the sound card is that it takes this wide range of harmonics and re-creates it using only the zeros and ones that your computer can understand. The more preprogrammed sets of harmonics a sound card has, the more voices it is said to have. A basic sound card these days has a minimum of sixty-four voices, and it can reach into the thousands if you have a lot of money to spend (**Figure 16.7**).

However, before you get too carried away, keep in mind that, just as your eye can't determine even a tiny fraction of the colors your video card can synthesize, neither can your ear distinguish between more than a few hundred voices. The frequency range that a finely tuned human ear can consciously detect is about 20Hz to 20,000Hz. The older a person gets, the narrower this range becomes. In addition, musical instruments are capable of a very narrow range of root frequencies. For example, the root frequencies on a grand piano range from 27.5Hz on the very lowest note to 4186Hz on the highest. Harmonics, on the other hand, have been measured to extend far beyond the capabilities of human hearing.

The original file format for sound was the WAV file (it is still the most commonly used). If you've ever opened up the actual files on an audio CD to see what they look like, you'll see that they are basically just WAV files. Very big WAV files. A five-minute song can run upwards of 80MB in size. That's what makes the

Figure 16.7 Modern sound cards are capable of reproducing sounds that make first- and second-generation audio CD players sound positively primitive.

CD-ROM format so essential to multimedia. These files may be big, but they don't change. A CD can hold about seventy minutes of music in .wav format.

These days, other file formats are becoming increasingly popular for computerized music files. MP3s fill the Internet, and many emerging artists offer free samples of their work for the cost of a simple download. Be careful, however, that you are actually downloading the file with the artist's consent. Any other use would be an infringement of copyright.

An MP3 (which stands for MPEG Layer III, not MPEG Version III) of that same five-minute song will only be four or five megabytes. The music is still nothing more than a collection of zeros and ones. MP3 is simply an advanced compression algorithm. The sound card takes these data files and converts them from digital format to an analog waveform that can be amplified and sent to speakers.

How the Sound Card Works

The typical sound card takes the functions of a CD player and adds them to your computer system. If you look carefully at a sound card, you see that it's covered with different chips. The back has plugs unlike any other in your system. There will be either three or four eighth-inch mini-plugs for microphone, speaker out, and line in. Many cards also provide for line-out functions. The large 15-pin female connector can actually serve two purposes. It can be used to hook up a joystick or to hook up musical instrument device interface (MIDI) devices.

The speaker-out plug is fairly self-explanatory. It's where you plug the speakers into your sound card. Line in and Line out are for hooking up external audio devices, such as a tape player. Line in brings the signal of the device into the sound card, while line out sends the output of the sound card to the external device. The microphone connector allows the user to hook up a microphone to the sound card, and, with many applications, provide voice overlays to other types of files, including presentations, Web sites, and anything else where a little human explanation might not hurt.

These plugs will pass their signals to, or receive their signals from, one of two chips. The analog-digital converter (ADC) is the chip that processes incoming analog signals. This device samples the signal anywhere from 8000 to 48,000 times every second and takes that mini-slice of sound and converts it to a 16-bit chop, exactly as the CD player described earlier in the chapter handles sound waves. Sound leaving the computer passes through the digital-analog converter (DAC), which is pretty much identical to the ones used in CD players.

There is an amazing amount of mathematics involved in handling these conversions, and on most good sound cards a DSP identical to the one I described when discussing audio CD players handles this task. To further enhance the sound card's capabilities, wave table synthesis maintains common voices, including most musical instruments and human voice samples on a ROM chip. Whenever a violin is played, the ROM already has a sample of that instrument and all the harmonics that make that instrument sound unique precalculated. The DSP, in effect, has less work to do.

Sounds that are not stored in ROM can be either generated by an application or piece of hardware or can be encapsulated into a file. Usually when you're playing the latest version of

Kill the Alien Slime, the sounds unique to the game are stored in files, although many manufacturers keep them on the CD and require that the user play them directly from there.

INSTALLING AND TROUBLESHOOTING SOUND CARDS

With the possible exception of network cards, there is no device anywhere that has greater potential for problems. Nor is there any device easier to install when things work the way they should. Most of the problems you encounter can be traced right back to the "good old days" when sound card manufacturers all had to make their products SoundBlaster-compatible in order to be marketable.

IRQ CONFLICTS

IRQ conflicts are a primary source of trouble. Plug 'n Play was supposed to eliminate these hassles. A good PnP BIOS coupled with a PnP sound card and you never have conflicts, right? If only life were so easy! It's the history of the sound card that became its biggest headache. While Ad Lib may have invented the sound card, it was Creative Labs that made it popular. It did so by making its product so easy to install that the average user could easily do it with little technical background. Creative Labs did this by creating a software installation method that automatically created all the lines in the users' autoexec.bat and config.sys files for them. What Creative Labs realized was that LPT2 was rarely used in most computers. Therefore, that particular combination of IRQ and I/O address was available for the sound card on most installations. This installation routine worked on 95 percent of the IBM-compatible DOS-based computers in existence at the time. The five percent that gave people headaches were those that had second parallel ports installed.

Naturally, there were options for those computers on which LPT2 was actually in use. Installation was far less automatic, however. In any case, there were several generations of the Creative Labs SoundBlaster line of sound cards that defaulted to IRQ5. Subsequent crops of sound cards that followed had to be SoundBlaster-compatible in order to be marketable. One of the things that required was the use of IRQ5, IO 0220, and DMA1. In essence, Creative Labs succeeded in taking a reserved IRQ and essentially claiming it as its own. The majority of resource conflicts you'll encounter are when legacy sound cannot install onto IRQ5.

Worse yet, many sound cards will frequently try to claim two IRQs. The one currently installed on the machine I'm using right now has IRQ10 as a base IRQ and IRQ5 for Creative SB16 emulation. If a sound card doesn't want to install smoothly, check to see what resources it's trying to use. When possible, use the techniques described in the section on the PCI bus to resolve the issues. Sometimes, you'll have no choice but to manually reallocate resources. Windows users can do this in the Properties screen for any given device in Device Manager. Be careful in doing this, however. As you recall, manual resource allocation takes those resources out of the hands of Plug 'n Play. This can compound issues later on when it comes time to install the next device.

DMA CONFLICTS

Conflicts across DMA channels are far more rare than IRQ conflicts. They do, however, occur. Usually, it is because the user just reconfigured a parallel port to use ECP (extended capabilities port) mode. ECP requires that the parallel port be assigned a DMA channel. The problem is that when you are in the BIOS Setup program of the CMOS reconfiguring devices, the rest of the system hasn't booted yet. Therefore, whatever DMA channel your sound card is using appears to be available to the parallel port. This usually isn't a problem, but if the parallel port decides to grab the one you happened to have chosen for your sound card, a conflict will develop.

It's an easy fix. Simply find out what you configured your sound card to use and go back to the CMOS and change the ECP configuration to a different DMA. Problem solved.

CHAPTER SUMMARY

When discussing multimedia, there are a number of different components that are involved in the overall equation. No one would call it multi-anything if there weren't

This chapter covered primarily optical storage mechanisms and sound reproduction. However, there were a number of discussions in previous chapters that could have been just as easily included in this chapter. In Chapter Ten, Input Devices, I discussed various tactile feedback game controllers. Of special note was the tactile feedback computer chair my wife is supposed to get me for our anniversary.

In Chapter Fifteen, Your Computer and Graphics, I discussed several different video functions that would be completely unnecessary without multimedia applications. Among these were the various 3D effects and specialized memory designed specifically for streaming media files.

And if you think all the way back to Chapter Six, Understanding CPUs, you will recall that there were discussions of embedded instruction sets specific to multimedia functions. Among these were MMX, Streaming SIMD, and 3D-Now!

So as you see, true multimedia applications do more to stress a computer system than any other function, with the possible exception of certain specialized server operations. Improving on multimedia performance requires an understanding of the complete system.

BRAIN DRAIN

1. Discuss in as much detail as possible how data is written to a conventional CD and subsequently read back. Include in your discussion as many components of the CD-ROM drive as you can recall.

2. Discuss some different ways in which the CDR drives and media differ from the drives and media that are considered CD-RW.

3. Describe how it is possible to have a double-sided, double-layered DVD.

4. Why are harmonics important in recorded music? How do modern sound cards deal with harmonics in a way that reduces processing overhead for both the CPU and the sound card?

5. In as much detail as you can muster, describe how each component of a computer system contributes to the overall multimedia process. Don't

confine your thinking to just this chapter, but consider what you've learned from previous chapters as well.

THE 64K$ QUESTIONS

1. The first CD-ROMs designed for use on a computer provided data throughput of _____.
   a. 1.2Mb/s
   b. 150Kb/s
   c. 512Kb/s
   d. 20Mb/s
   e. None of the above.

2. A 2x CD-ROM provides data throughput of _____.
   a. 1.2Mb/s
   b. 250Kb/s
   c. 512Kb/s
   d. 20Mb/s
   e. None of the above

3. The recording layer on a CDR consists of _____.
   a. Pthalocyanine dye
   b. Aluminum
   c. Gold
   d. An alloy of four different metals

4. Which of the following drives requires a laser beam that can operate at three different power levels?
   a. CD
   b. CDR
   c. CD-RW
   d. DVD

5. Which of the following media separates two separate recording layers with a microscopically thin layer of gold?
   a. CD
   b. CDR
   c. CD-RW
   d. DVD

6. It is the root frequency of a note played by a piano that makes it sound different than when that same note is played on a guitar.
   a. True
   b. False

7. The 15-pin connector on the back of a sound card is used for what device? Choose all that apply.
   a. Joystick
   b. 5.1 Surround Sound speaker setups
   c. Multimedia devices
   d. MIDI devices

8. Which chip can directly sample an electronic current and extract digital information from that current?
   a. DAC
   b. PROM
   c. RISC
   d. DSP

9. The conversion of an analog waveform into a digital signal is known as _____.
   a. Pulse Code Manipulation
   b. Frequency Spectrum Sampling
   c. Pulse Code Modulation
   d. Digital Encapsulation

10. A voice on a sound card is _____.
    a. A prepackaged sound byte
    b. A frequently used chop
    c. A preencoded selection of harmonics unique to a specific instrument
    d. The chip that modifies sound files as they come in from an application

TRICKY TERMINOLOGY

Caddy: On a CD-ROM (or similar) drive, it is a form of loading mechanism that consists of a plastic CD holder that encases the CD while it is in the drive.

Chop: A 16-bit piece of data generated when music is sampled once during the digital recording procedure.

Cyanine dye: A bluish-colored dye that was used in the recording layer of early generations of CDR media.

Dielectric layer: A transparent layer of material above and below the recording layer of a CD-RW that dissipates the heat built up in the CD during the recording process.

Erase power: A medium power setting for the optical stylus of a CD-RW, which it uses to melt the crystals generated by the previous recording session back into the uncrystallized recording layer.

Harmonics: Sound frequencies above the root frequency that are generated by an instrument or voice when a certain note is generated.

Land: All of the reflective surface of the recording layer in optical media that has not been burned or punched into a pit.

Multisession: The ability to record data onto a CDR or CD-RW in several stages, without closing out the TOC.

Optical stylus: A mechanism consisting of a laser-emitting diode coupled to a beam splitter.

Phase change layer: The recording layer of a CD-RW.

Pit: A tiny hole embedded in the recording layer of optical media that prevents the laser from reflecting back into the photoelectric sensor.

Pregroove: A spiral track engraved on CDR and CD-RW media at the factory that acts as a target for the recording laser.

Pthalocyanine dye: A more stable dye used in recent generations of CDR that is less sensitive to UV light than cyanine dye and lasts for up to a 100 years.

Read power: The lowest power setting for the optical stylus of a CD-RW, which it uses to read data from the surface.

Root frequency: The single frequency of any given musical note that makes that note sound the way it does, regardless of what instrument plays it.

Slot: On a CD-ROM (or similar) drive, it is a form of loading mechanism that engages a CD when it is inserted into the opening and draws the disc into the drive.

Subharmonics: Sound frequencies below the root frequency that are generated by an instrument or voice when a certain note is played.

Synchronization bits: Data included on each sector of a data CD that assures that the information will be processed in the correct sequence.

Tray: On a CD-ROM (or similar) drive, it is a form of loading mechanism that consists of a platform that ejects when the user pushes a button, and retracts with the CD in place.

Voice: A collection of preprogrammed harmonics that are used to simulate the sound made by a particular instrument.

Write power: The highest power setting for the optical stylus of a CD-RW, which it uses to record data onto the surface.

ACRONYM ALERT

ADC: Analog-to-Digital Converter

CAV: Constant Angular Velocity. A data reading mechanism used by optical drives that allows the rotational velocity of the disc to remain constant, forcing the controller to interpret the data at faster speeds as the optical stylus moves from the center to the edge.

CDAD: Compact Disc, Audio Disc. The file system used by CD-ROMs to store music.

CDFS: Compact Disc File System. The file system used by CD-ROMs to store computer data.

CDR: Recordable CD

CD-ROM: Compact Disc-Read Only Memory

CD-RW: Rewriteable CD

CLV: Constant Linear Velocity. A data reading mechanism used by optical drives in which the rotational velocity of the disc must slow down as the disc is tracked from center to edge, thus assuring that the relative number of tracks per millisecond that passes beneath the optical stylus always remains the same.

DAC: Digital-to-Analog Converter

DSP: Digital Signal Processor. A microprocessor that can sample an electronic current and convert it into a digital signal.

DVD: Digital Video Disc, or Digital Versatile Disc

DVD-R: Recordable DVD

DVD-RW: Rewriteable DVD

EDC: Error Detection Code. Code embedded in a file system that enables the system to detect that an error in the transmission of that data has occurred, and where possible alerts the system to take corrective action.

ISO: International Organization for Standards. One of several groups that oversees the development and ratification of standards in the computer industry, as well as many other industries.

MIDI: Musical Instrument Device Interface

PCM: Pulse Code Modulation. The process of converting electrical current into a digital signal.

CHAPTER 17

PRINTING TECHNOLOGIES: GETTING IT ALL ON PAPER

The previous chapters have all dealt with the various technologies of the computer. I've discussed how the computer processes data and how it stores data. I've talked about various ways users can interact with the computer and how all sorts of pretty pictures are made by a series of ones and zeros. Now I will tackle the various ways data can be moved from a digital file stored on a magnetic or optical disk surface to the surface of a piece of paper.

These days, there is a tremendous variety of printers on the market, ranging from incredibly inexpensive machines to devices that make my mortgage seem paltry. Across the board, capabilities vary, but you can break them down into two categories to start the decision making process. There are printers that print color and printers that don't.

In terms of technologies, there are six that I'll be discussing in this chapter. I'll start with the impact printers, then move on to inkjets. Because monochrome laser printers receive the most attention on the exam, these devices will get a bit more detailed coverage. This is where many books stop. You picked this book over all the rest, so you also get a discussion on color laser printers and thermal and phase-change inkjet printers (sometimes called dye sublimation printers).

A+ EXAM OBJECTIVES

Exam objectives that will be covered in this chapter include the following:

1.5   Identify the names, purposes, and performance characteristics of standardized/common peripheral ports, associated cabling, and their connectors. Recognize ports, cabling, and connectors by sight.

1.8   Identify proper procedures for installing and configuring common peripheral devices. Choose the appropriate installation or configuration sequences in given scenarios.

2.1   Recognize common problems associated with each module and their symptoms, and identify steps to isolate and troubleshoot the problems. Given a problem situation, interpret the symptoms and infer the most likely cause.

3.1   Identify the various types of preventive maintenance measures, products, and procedures and when and how to use them.

3.2   Identify various safety measures and procedures, and when/how to use them.

4.4   Identify the purpose of CMOS (Complementary Metal-Oxide Semiconductor) memory, what it contains, and how and when to change its parameters. Given a scenario involving CMOS, choose the appropriate course of action. (Printer, Parallel Port)

5.1   Identify printer technologies, interfaces, and options/upgrades.

5.2   Recognize common printer problems and techniques used to resolve them.

IMPACT PRINTERS

Impact printers can be safely broken down into three categories. Among the first printers to come out was the line printer. These were ungainly devices that hung off of the old mainframe computers. However, don't call the line printer old-fashioned. It's a technology that refuses to die, and they are still around today. A similar technology that is also still with us is the dot matrix printer. Finally, I'll take a look at daisy wheel printers and see why they had a short but lucrative life span.

LINE PRINTERS AND DOT MATRIX PRINTERS

The technology behind these two types of printer is so similar that it will be easier simply to discuss them together. The primary difference between the two lies in how they handle an image. Early line printers, or line matrix printers, as they're often called, printed just a single line at a time. As such, they could only reproduce standard ASCII characters and were incapable of generating graphics beyond simple boxes and borders created with these characters. In 1996, Tally Corporation introduced a technology called Page Segment Architecture that divided the page into zones before sending the data to the printer. This allowed the devices to create more complex graphics. Dot matrix printers compile the entire page before sending it to the printer, so very complex graphics are possible, including rudimentary color on printers equipped with four-color ribbons and the appropriate device driver.

The driving technology behind producing the printed output is fundamentally the same, however. Therefore, for the remainder of this section, when I refer to a dot matrix printer, you should automatically think of both. The way they transfer an image to a sheet of paper is to thrust steel pins against a ribbon saturated in ink. The impact of the pin against the ribbon forces the ink onto the paper where it was struck.

Everywhere the pin strikes the ribbon a single dot is formed. By collecting enough dots into a familiar pattern, you can make it look like letters, numbers, punctuation marks, or even a crude facsimile of your spouse's favorite pet. Sounds simple enough, but there's a lot that has to go on in order to make the dots appear on paper in the right order to reproduce the image

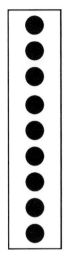

Figure 17.1 Alignment of pins on a 9-pin printer

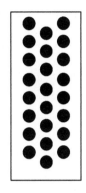

Figure 17.2 Alignment of pins on a 24-pin printer

you see on screen onto paper. This starts with the *print head*. On the dot matrix printers, there were a few choices in this respect. The most basic printers had a simple 9-pin print head. The nine pins were aligned vertically, as you see in **Figure 17.1**.

In order to achieve higher resolution, manufacturers developed the 24-pin printer. The idea was the same, except that by having a greater number of pins, which were made of a finer wire, a document could be printed that exhibited much finer resolution and detail. The print head squeezed twenty-four wires onto a single print head by arranging them into three rows of eight pins, as you can see in **Figure 17.2**. 24-pin printers were a bit slower, but that was a sacrifice people were willing to make in order to produce "letter-quality" documents.

> **BUZZ WORDS** ————
>
> **Print head:** The mechanism on any impact or inkjet printer that is responsible for depositing the pigment onto the paper.

These weren't the only options offered. Some manufacturers also came out with 18-pin and 48-pin printers. These really never caught on all that well. The 9-pin and 24-pin printer is still alive and well, thanks to the fact that many people still need to be able to print out multipart forms. The impact printer is able to do this.

THE DOT MATRIX PRINTING PROCESS

The key to printing a readable document is getting all those pins to hit the paper at just the right moment in time. Also, the pin has to hit the ribbon with enough impact to force ink onto the paper.

The way the print head is manufactured, the pins are seated into sleeves, linked to strong springs. The natural position of the spring is such that the pin would be in contact with the

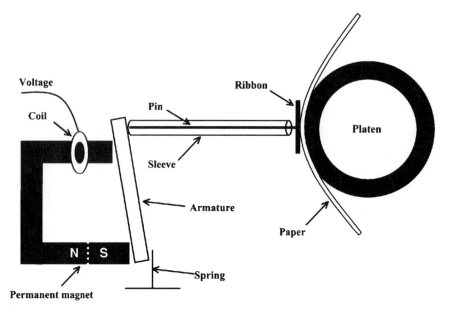

Figure 17.3 A diagram of a dot matrix print head

paper at all times, were a very strong magnet not holding it back. An electrical coil is wrapped around one pole of the magnet that forms an electromagnet. When current is applied to the electromagnet, it neutralizes the energy from the fixed magnet. The spring releases, and the pin

pops back to its natural position. The dot is pressed into the paper and the electromagnet is turned back off. The fixed magnet pulls the pin back away. **Figure 17.3** is a rough diagram of the process that takes place.

Therefore, the printing process consists of sending electrical signals down wires attached to the magnets. Every time a dot is needed, the electromagnet is turned on for a very brief instant. The real trick here is timing. The print head needs to move across the paper at exactly the right speed, and the paper transport mechanism needs to be able to advance the paper at precisely the right time and precisely the right distance.

The paper feed mechanism isn't all that complicated. The core component is a stepper motor. The paper is fed through a geared assembly that has little teeth that move the paper. This assembly is coupled to a platen. The *platen* is the hard rubber-encased cylinder against which the paper rests. Gears on either end of the platen core engage with a stepper motor that advances or feeds the paper. The stepper motor is user adjustable so that whoever is using the printer can have it advance the paper in different increments to approximate single-spacing and double-spacing. Most also provide for space-and-a-half, and some provide even more options.

If you've seen paper designed for dot matrix printers, you already know that there are holes running along each side of the paper. These are needed because the paper transport method used by dot matrix printers is a *tractor feed*. The teeth on the paper feed assembly fit into these holes. There is a geared belt that keeps the print head moving in synch with the motor. All of this is under the control of commands sent by the printer driver.

DOT MATRIX MAINTENANCE

Since dot matrix printers are almost purely mechanical devices, they require significantly more care

> **BUZZ WORDS**
>
> **Tractor feed:** A paper transport mechanism that uses a set of gears on a printer to advance the paper by engaging in perforations along each side of the paper.

and feeding than most other components in a system. Unfortunately, they're all too often the devices that get the least attention. As a result, many dot matrix printers don't enjoy nearly as long a life span as they should be able to expect. That they last as long as they do is a tribute to the manufacturers!

First and foremost, these printers need regular cleaning. The condition of both the platen and the print heads directly impacts print quality. If too much dried ink and print fiber gets jammed into the print head, the pins might not be ejected by the springs. This would result in sketchy print quality. A dirty or damaged platen can be just as harmful. Never let somebody send a print job onto a dot matrix printer when there's no paper installed. Pay attention to the warning the printer issues saying it's out of paper. On dot matrix printers, if you send a print job despite the warning, the print head will stream along, sending the print job to the platen, polluting it with ink and perhaps even punching holes into the hard rubber. If there are holes in the platen, the pins will punch through the paper, putting holes in your page. If there is ink on it, the back of your page will be covered with stray marks.

Both the print head and the platen need to be in proper alignment as well. If they're not, individual characters will shade from light to dark. **Figure 17.4** illustrates what can happen if the print head itself is out of alignment. The illustration illustrates a vertical alignment problem, but print heads can be offset either vertically or horizontally.

If the platen itself goes out of alignment the entire line will be affected. It will go from light to dark from the beginning of the line to the end, or vice versa. **Figure 17.5** shows you what I mean.

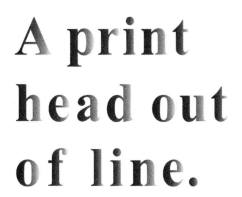

A print head out of line.

Figure 17.4 A print head out of alignment affects individual letters.

A Platen out of line.

Figure 17.5 A platen out of alignment throws the whole line out of whack!

As far as realigning either the head or the platen, how that is done or even whether or not it can be done is dependent on the make and model of your printer. Most print heads can be aligned. With many models, aligning the platen is a factory service job. If you can get your hands on a service manual for your model, it should give you instruction on how to perform these tasks.

Daisy Wheel Printers

Daisy wheel printers were one of the most simplified of the printer designs that were sold. They did produce very high output quality, but were abysmally slow and extremely noisy. The letters themselves were

Figure 17.6 The only way to change fonts on an old daisy wheel was to change the type wheel.

molded onto a disk made of a springy material, usually steel or plastic. Each character was on a separate tab. In a way, it made the whole thing look like a high-tech flower (See **Figure 17.6**). This disk spun at high speed. In order to produce a particular character, a piston hammered that particular tab against a ribbon and onto the paper. The technology behind this goes all the way back to Johannes Guttenberg, except Mr. Guttenberg didn't have the benefit of electricity to speed up the process. Printers such as these are referred to as fully formed character printers. As you might imagine, these were text printers. Generating complex graphics was far beyond their capability.

Two types of ribbons were available for the venerable daisy wheel. You could get the standard inked-cloth ribbon. A printer equipped with one of these produced quality akin to a decent typewriter. ("Typewriter?" you ask, "What's a typewriter?") Another ribbon consisted of a coating of ink on a Mylar ribbon. Print quality from these ribbons exceeded that of many typesetters. Because of this quality difference, despite the array of disadvantages, the daisy wheel printer was an incredibly popular device for anyone who required top-quality output but couldn't afford the two grand that a laser printer cost at the time.

Inkjet Technologies

Inkjet printers fall under one of three categories. There are thermal, piezoelectric, and phase-change printers. In spite of the diverse sounding nature of their names, they actually work in a very similar manner. Ink flows into a tiny little tube and some force of nature ejects it onto the paper at exactly the right moment. It's the force of nature chosen by the manufacturer that makes the technologies different. Oddly enough, the methods that inkjet printers use to select when and where to place ink is very similar to dot matrix printers. Instead of magnets and pins, they have tubes of ink and the force of nature.

The paper transport mechanism on inkjet printers is very similar to that of the laser printer that will be discussed later in the chapter. Because the exam tests on laser printers in this regard, but not inkjets, I have chosen to defer the discussion of this topic to the section on laser printers.

THERMAL INKJETS

As you might imagine from the description, the force of nature used by *thermal inkjet printers* is heat. Heat brings ink up to the boiling point, and forces it through a very small nozzle and onto the paper. In order to assure that the ink can be brought to boiling at precisely the right instant, a thermal inkjet printer keeps the reservoir of ink at a temperature just under the critical point. At the instant a droplet of ink is needed, a heating circuit applies a sudden burst of heat. Poof! Out comes a bubble of ink. This is one of the reasons this type of printer is sometimes called a *bubblejet*. **Figure 17.7** is a conceptual diagram of how the thermal print head works.

While Canon discovered the technology back in 1977, it wasn't until 1984 that HP came to market with its Thinkjet. This first-generation product was capable of 96 dots per inch (DPI) and could pump out 150 characters per minute. This doesn't sound like much by today's standards, but keep this in mind. A dot matrix printer, at best, could manage 72dpi. The dot matrix might have been a little faster, but the inkjet beat it by a long shot in terms of print quality.

A key issue with thermal inkjets is that heating the nozzle constantly shortens its life. HP gets around that problem by making the print head part of the ink cartridge. When you change the ink cartridge, you're automatically changing the print head as well.

> **BUZZ WORDS**
>
> **Thermal inkjet printer:** A printer that ejects ink onto a page of paper by heating the fluid.
>
> **Bubblejet printer:** Another term for a thermal printer.

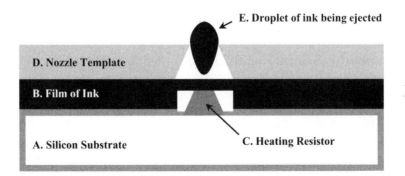

Figure 17.7 Conceptual diagram of a thermal inkjet head in action. A piezoelectric head would look very similar to this one, except that the entire nozzle of the print head is a piezoelectric device. A microscopic filament toward the back vibrates and the tube contracts.

Piezoelectric Inkjets

Have you ever decorated a birthday cake? If so, you might have used one of those devices that squeezes frosting onto the cake through a nozzle, so you can put pretty shapes on the top. As strange as it may seem, this is how the piezoelectric inkjet printer does its thing.

The nozzles are made from a *piezoelectric crystal* (PEC). A PEC has the unique characteristic that when given a shot of electricity, it changes shape. PECs squeeze inward. A combination of gravity and surface tension keeps a droplet of ink in place inside the nozzle. When the printer needs to eject it onto the paper, it zaps the nozzle with a charge of electricity. The nozzle squeezes inward and the ink is forced out onto the paper.

> **Buzz Words**
>
> **Piezoelectric crystal:** A substance that changes shape when exposed to electricity.
>
> **Phase-change printer:** A printer that liquefies solid inks before applying them to paper.
>
> **Cold fusing:** A process used by some phase change printers that uses pressure rollers to press the ink into the paper.

Proponents of piezoelectric inkjets claim that this method forms a cleaner image than does the thermal inkjet. Their reasoning is that when the bubble produced by a thermal inkjet printer strikes the page, it is going to burst, producing a halo effect. The piezoelectric printer is putting a solid droplet of ink onto the page, they claim, and that won't happen. I'm not getting involved in that argument. All I know is that I've used both Hewlett Packard and Epson inkjet printers. HP uses thermal technology and Epson uses piezoelectric. I have never been dissatisfied with either one. Long live competition!

Phase-Change Inkjets

Phase-change inkjet printers use a radically different technology than either of the above. The phase-change inkjet starts with a stick of solid ink. The print head melts the ink and holds the melted ink in a specially designed reservoir. When the print head is called upon to apply ink to the paper, it uses a mechanical mechanism to eject the ink. The ink then hardens almost immediately.

These printers have an amazing capability of producing a more photo-realistic image for one simple reason. Ink applied by either thermal inkjets or piezoelectric inkjets is going to adhere to the paper in an extremely thin layer. Phase-change printers result in a much thicker coating. So thick, in fact, that Tekronix, one of the leading manufacturers of this kind of printer, uses a final process called *cold fusing*. That is where the paper is run through a pressure roller to flatten the droplets of hardened ink.

This has two different but complimentary side effects. The surface of the image takes on a more photographic nature. This is because conventional photographic prints are produced on a gelatin surface that is much thicker than a layer of ink. It gives the image a greater feeling of depth. The thicker coating of the phase-change printer more closely simulates that surface.

The second thing that provides a subtle improvement is that the pressure of the fusing roller creates a blending effect between adjacent droplets of ink. There is less pixelization of the image.

A NOTE ON RECYCLING INK CARTRIDGES

There is a thriving business that has developed around the ecologically sound principle of recycling ink and toner cartridges. There is also a bit of controversy over the idea. Since you are unlikely to get an unbiased discussion from either the printer manufacturers (who want to sell you their new cartridges) or the recyclers (who want you to buy their product), I thought I'd throw in my two cents' worth.

The cost savings of refilling your own ink cartridges or purchasing remanufactured toner cartridges are substantial. However, along with those savings come some inherent tradeoffs. With ink cartridges, in order to make the process work, the ink must have the same drying time as the manufacturer's original ink, and it must exhibit the same mixing characteristics. Inkjets use cyan, magenta, yellow, and black inks (CMYK). In the printing industry, these are known as subtractive colors. This is as opposed to the additive colors of red, green, and blue used by monitors. A chemical anomaly that liquid pigments possess is that different formulas do not necessarily produce the same hue when two of the subtractive colors are mixed. Another factor relating to color quality is that the inks used in the remanufacturing process are, by necessity, thinner than the original inks. As a result of the above factors, the print quality delivered by remanufactured ink cartridges can range from fairly decent (but not as good as the original) to abysmal.

Manufacturers claim that the use of these remanufactured cartridges shortens the life of the printer. While I have located no detailed research along these lines, I can see how this is theoretically possible. The inkjet process centers around the ink, and since the ink used in the remanufacturing process is thinner, this would have an impact on the rest of the printing mechanism. And since the seals must be punctured in order to insert the inks into the cartridge, if the seals are not properly restored, the cartridge can burst, spewing ink into the printer. This is rare, but I have seen the results of this happening, and it isn't pretty.

There are fewer risks involved in the use of remanufactured toner cartridges, and with one notable exception, these risks all center around print quality and not the life of the printer. As laser printers have evolved over the years, they have become capable of increasingly fine resolution. In order to produce that finer resolution, the particles used in the manufacture of the toner must be correspondingly smaller. Many remanufacturers take the "one size fits all" approach to toner refills. As a result, your fancy new 1200dpi laser printer may not be able to perform to that level. This will show up in the reproduction of graphics. Other issues affecting print quality involve the proper replacement of different components in the cartridge. A damaged imaging drum that isn't properly replaced will result in print defects on the page.

The one risk of recycled toner cartridges that can affect the life of the printer is in how well the remanufacturer refitted the seals. As with the inkjet cartridges, if a seal in a toner cartridge bursts, the effects can be disastrous.

However, the risks involved are low-percentage risks. Disaster is extremely rare, so it's like the reverse of playing the lottery. If lower print quality is not an issue, recycling toner and ink cartridges can save money and is friendly on the environment. But before you make the jump to recycled products on a newer printer, check and see if there is any fine print in the warranty concerning their use.

Optical Printers

There are two different forms of optical printer that dominate the market today. The lion's share goes to the laser printer that everyone knows and loves. Another competing technology that has only a small portion of market share is the LED printer. For the most part, these printers differ only in the light source they use for generating images, and therefore will be considered as one. Therefore, for the rest of the chapter, unless I say otherwise, when I refer to a laser printer, you can apply whatever it is I'm saying to an LED printer as well.

Laser printers involve a combination of mechanics, optics, and electronics that so closely borders on magic as to make Merlin shiver. Yet at the heart, it's all relatively simple. First of all, I'll give you a look at the key components that make the process of laser printing do what it does. Then I'll follow a sheet of paper through a print job.

Components of the Laser Printer

As you read this next section, it might help to refer to **Figure 17.8** to see the relationship of the parts to one another. The parts that a typical laser printer uses to generate the image include a photosensitive drum, the laser itself, the formatter, a special roller known as the charging roller (in the old days, an array of wires called the transfer corona was used for this), a developing roller, a transfer roller, and finally a fusing roller. A key ingredient, of course, is the toner itself.

The photosensitive drum consists of a roller made of milled aluminum. Onto the surface of the aluminum, a coating of a special organic compound is applied. This compound has the unique nature of electrical photosensitivity. Unlike photographic film or paper that has a mixtures of substances that change color when exposed to light, the photosensitive drum changes electrical charge. The drum can hold very high charges of electricity, but when exposed to light, that charge will dissipate. A conductor at the core of the drum carries away that dissipated charge.

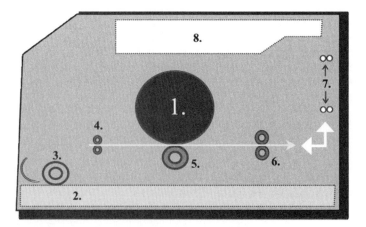

1. Photosensitive drum
2. Paper tray
3. Pickup roller
4. Registration roller
5. Transfer roller
6. Fuser assembly
7. Output rollers
8. Output bin

Figure 17.8 Cutaway diagram of a typical laser printer

The light source that a printer uses to dissipate charge in selected areas on the photosensitive drum is a laser-emitting diode. The diameter of this laser beam directly affects the resolution of the printer. For higher resolutions, smaller beams are required. The laser flashes on and off at a high rate of speed exposing "dots" onto the surface of the photosensitive drum. This is where the LED printer differs from the laser, in that it does not use a laser beam.

The image is assembled in the printer by a device called the formatter. You'll also see this referred to as the raster image processor. This is the logic of the system. In many respects it is much like the motherboard of a computer. A laser printer needs to have enough RAM to hold an entire image, and it needs a processor to assemble all the zeros and ones that comprise the print job into an order that will create the final image. On a monochrome printer, a one causes the laser to fire while a zero does not.

In order to start the print job the photosensitive drum has to have a uniform charge across the entire surface. Otherwise, there might be irregularities in the image. It is the task of the charging roller to apply this charge. The developing roller brings an even layer of freshly charged toner from the toner cartridge and makes it available to the surface of an electrically charged sheet of paper.

In order to attract the toner from the developing roller to the paper, the paper needs to have a charge opposite of that of the toner adhered to the photosensitive drum. The transfer roller applies a positive charge to paper as it is fed through the printer. In older printers a wire called the transfer corona did this job.

Once the toner has been applied to the paper, there needs to be a way to make it stick. The fusing roller heats the paper, along with its coating of toner, to the melting point of certain materials within the toner. Toner used by laser printers is a finely powdered mixture of three main ingredients. First and foremost is the powder that gives it color. On monochrome printers, this is predominately carbon. Carbon, however, is not very conducive to either taking an electrical charge or melting at any temperature to which paper could be exposed. To allow the mixture to take a charge a small amount of iron oxide is added. To make it melt at a lower temperature a powdered plastic is used.

A couple of ancillary parts important to the overall process are the erase lamp, the static discharge unit, and the cleaning blade. The erase lamp is used to eliminate any residual charge from the last print job, allowing the photosensitive drum to start from a clean charge. The cleaning blade scrapes away any residual toner left on the drum. The static discharge unit is responsible for draining away the charge from the paper before it gets sucked up around the photosensitive drum. Now that you have a good idea of the parts that are used by the printer, take a look at the printing process.

THE LASER PRINTING PROCESS

The whole process of creating a laser image can be broken down into six steps. Each of these is going to make use of one of the components I described in the previous section. As you go through the next few paragraphs, you will follow a typical print job from start to finish. The first thing that's going to happen is that the computer is going to send the print job to the printer driver, which in turn converts the data to the format supported by whatever printing language you've selected. (Printer languages will be discussed later in the chapter.) When this happens, the printer starts heating up the fuser assembly. While the next two steps are being performed, the formatter will be assembling the image.

CLEANING

By the time you get to the end of this, you'll see that you are looking at an endless cycle. But for the sake of discussion, I have to assume that the process starts somewhere. The first thing you have to do is remove any vestiges of the previous print job. Therefore, the first stage of the image formation process consists of preparing the photosensitive drum to accept a new image. This involves both physical and electrical cleaning. Before a new image is formed on the drum, leftover toner from the previous image must be removed. In order to get rid of all the electrical charge left over by the last job, the erase lamp gives the drum a strong dose of light. A rubber cleaning blade scrapes toner off the drum into a debris cavity.

CONDITIONING

Now that the mess from the last job is cleaned up, it's time to prepare the photosensitive drum for the next one. First off, it must be conditioned. The charging roller, or on some older printers, the primary corona, applies a very strong negative charge. How much of a charge depends entirely upon the make and model of printer, but typically this charge can be in the range of −800 to −1200V. Now the printer has a blank sheet of "electronic paper."

WRITING

By now, the formatter has finished processing the image. It will send the data from that image as a series of on/off pulses to the laser assembly. The beam turns on and off very rapidly. Everywhere that the beam exposes the photosensitive drum, a fairly large portion of the charge on the drum's surface is bled away. A wire in the center of the imaging drum carries the dispersed charge to ground. Once this job has been completed, you'll have a surface that consists of a −800 to −1200V sheet of virtual paper sprinkled with −200 to −400V dots that make up the letters and graphics.

DEVELOPING

Meanwhile, a small amount of toner is moved from the storage reservoir of the toner cartridge to a smaller charging reservoir. The toner in the charging reservoir receives a charge of approximately −600V. Notice that so far, everything has been given a negative charge. However, if you go back to Chapter Three, Basic Electricity and the Power Supply, you will recall that voltage is simply the difference in charge between two objects. Therefore, while all of these different charges may be negative relative to ground, relative to one another, these surfaces will contain positive charges as well as negative charges. A positively charged object will try to attract objects that are negatively charged relative to itself. The toner will be attracted to the exposed areas of the drum because, relative to the toner, these dots represent a positive differential. The more strongly charged unexposed areas are going to repel the toner.

TRANSFER

At this point in time, were you to stop the print process and look inside the toner cartridge, you would see perfectly shaped letters and images on the photosensitive drum, although they would appear in reverse. While the above steps were going on, the sheet of paper that this toner is intended for has been passing under the transfer roller (or transfer corona on older printers). The transfer roller applies a strong positive charge to the paper. The negatively charged toner particles adhering to the imaging drum are attracted to the paper. As the paper moves through the transport mechanism, the static discharge unit drains away the positive charge. This unit consists of a row of metal teeth that carry a strong negative charge. This separates the photosensitive drum and paper. Were the static discharge unit to fail, the paper, along with the accompanying image, would be magnetically sealed to the imaging drum.

THE FUSING ROLLER

You now have a perfectly formed image on the paper. However, at this point in time the only thing keeping that toner on the page is the love the toner and paper feel for one another, with the help of inertia, gravity, and some slight residual electrical charge. If you want the image to stay, you're going to need to do something to fix it there permanently. That is the job of the fusing roller. The paper rolls between the fusing roller and a pressure roller. The fusing roller heats the paper and toner up to the melting point of the plastic in the toner and the pressure roller squeezes it onto the paper. You now have a final print job. Congratulations.

MOVING PAPER

A part of the process that was not described in the previous sections involves how the paper gets from the paper tray (usually located at the base of the printer) to all the places it needs to be, when it needs to be there. That is the responsibility of the paper transport mechanism. The following discussion is going to be based on Hewlett Packard's line of printers. While different brands may have variations on the process here and there, for the most part, it will be pretty much the same.

The process of paper transport starts when a pickup roller rotates around and snatches the top sheet of paper from the stack loaded in the paper tray. The paper tray itself is a fairly complex component. It needs to be able to keep the top sheet in the stack properly aligned in order for the pickup roller to find anything to grab. In order to prevent more than one sheet of paper from being fed into the mechanism, a separation roller (or separation pad on some models) keeps two sheets from sticking together.

The paper moves into the registration rollers. At this point in time, a mechanism called the DC controller causes the paper to pause momentarily while it makes sure the leading edge of the paper proper lines up with the image written to the photosensitive drum. You can easily hear this part of the process while it is taking place. Once proper alignment is achieved, the paper can move on.

The paper then moves between the photosensitive drum and the transfer roller. From here, the paper moves into the fuser assembly. As I discussed earlier, this assembly consists of a fusing roller heated to the melting point of the toner and a pressure roller. As the paper exits the fuser assembly, the leading edge activates the exit photo sensor. This notifies the DC controller that the paper is leaving the fuser assembly, and when the trailing edge passes the sensor, the DC controller is notified that Elvis has left the building. On a printer that only does single-sided printing, the paper moves from the fuser assembly and into the exit rollers, which move the printed page into the output bin.

Printers capable of duplex printing still have more work to do before they allow the paper to move into the exit rollers. Duplex printing is where the printer can print onto both sides of the page. In order to do that, the printer has to be able to get the paper turned over and sent through the printing process a second time.

With duplex printing, instead of moving from the fuser assembly into the exit rollers, a deflection pawl directs the paper into the duplex feed rollers. The duplex feed rollers carry the paper into the switchback station, where the leading edge of the paper activates the switchback photo sensor. When the trailing edge passes the sensor, the DC controller knows the paper is fully loaded into the switchback station, and the reverse side is ready for printing. The trailing edge of the paper now becomes the leading edge. It is moved back into the registration rollers, where the image and paper are properly aligned and the reverse side goes through the printing process. This time, however, as the page exits the fuser assembly, the deflection pawls are retracted and the paper is allowed to move into the exit rollers. Out comes your page, printed on both sides.

COLOR LASER PRINTING

The theoretical concepts of color lasers are really no different that those of monochrome printers. The complexity of the process is somewhat greater, but the technology is the same. Instead of having a single toner cartridge with an associated transfer roller, the color laser has four cartridges. For standard text printing, there is the conventional black toner cartridge, and for full-color printing, there is a cartridge for each of the subtractive colors: magenta, cyan, and yellow.

A full-color image has a portion of itself printed by each of these four cartridges onto an intermediate transfer surface. This usually consists of a belt assembly. When the image has been assembled in its entirety, the intermediate transfer belt moves the image to the paper and then the fuser does its thing. **Figure 17.9** is a conceptual diagram of the process at work, and not a diagram of the actual mechanism.

MAINTAINING AND TROUBLESHOOTING LASER PRINTERS

The beauty of laser printers is that they actually vary very little from one brand to another. Since I'm trained on Hewlett Packard's line of LaserJet printers, I'll be using them as an example throughout this section, but there isn't anything I'll say here that doesn't directly apply to other brands as well.

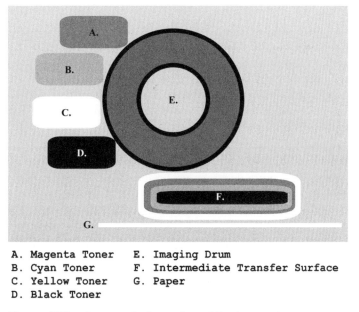

A. Magenta Toner   E. Imaging Drum
B. Cyan Toner   F. Intermediate Transfer Surface
C. Yellow Toner   G. Paper
D. Black Toner

Figure 17.9   A conceptual overview of the laser color printing process

Printer errors will generally fall under one of four categories:

- Communication errors
- Processing errors
- Paper transport errors
- Imaging errors

Communication errors occur when the computer can't find the printer. Obviously, the first thing to check is the cable itself. If the printer is hooked up directly through the parallel port, this is generally no problem. A networked printer has its own issues related to networking that do not fall within the scope of this book. Assuming that the cable is properly installed and is not defective, and that the printer is hooked up to the parallel port, your next step is to bypass the driver. You can do this by opening a command prompt and copying an ASCII text file directly to LPT1. As an example, you could open Notepad, type out a few characters, and save the file as C:\document\test.txt. Now, at the command prompt, type copy c:\document\test.txt LPT1 and see if the printer fires up and spits out the document. If it does, you have physical connectivity to the printer. The problem is in the configuration. Reinstall the drivers, and use the correct ones this time.

Processing errors occur when the data gets to the printer, but nothing but gobbledygook comes out. Frequently this is simply a corrupted printer driver, and can be fixed easily by reinstalling the drivers. On laser printers, there are two other things that can cause this. One is bad memory. As I mentioned earlier, the laser printer relies on RAM in much the same way as a computer. The second thing is a chip failure on the formatter board. The latter is relatively rare, in that when formatter boards fail, they usually fail completely. Other processing errors include insufficient memory to process a given job, or in the case of older printers, the data might be coming in so fast the printer can't keep up. Most laser printers are able to generate an error message to the front panel. The service manual for the printer will interpret the error messages that are delivered.

Paper transport errors can come in the form of paper jams or the paper not being picked up out of the delivery tray. This is the result of worn rollers. On laser printers, the rollers that receive the most wear and tear are generally user-replaceable. Paper rollers are a lot like good snow tires. To properly work, they need some decent tread. If your rollers are smooth, they won't generate the friction they need to move paper. Another cause of paper jams is simply using a medium that is not supported by the printer. Stock that is either too light or too heavy can result in jams when the rollers are perfectly good. If you have checked the rollers and know them to be good, compared the stock in use to the manufacturer's specifications and found it acceptable, but you are still getting a jam in the input area of the printer, you might have either a bad paper tray or a defective paper sensor. The paper tray needs to be properly adjusted for the type of paper installed. Putting 8.5″ × 11″ paper in a legal-sized tray can cause jams. The sensors on the trays indicate what kind of paper is installed in multiformat trays. If the sensor reports the wrong size, paper jams will result.

Imaging errors can be defined in many ways. Unwanted marks on the page, smearing, a totally black page, or a skewed image are all examples of imaging errors. Defects that repeat themselves at regular intervals down the page are generally the result of a roller gone bad or defects on the imaging drum. Transfer rollers, developing rollers, and the rollers in the fusing assembly can all leave marks on the page if they're damaged. Most printer service manuals have a repetitive defect guide to help you troubleshoot what roller is causing what defect. If you don't have a manual at your disposal, start with the easy ones. Pull the toner cartridge, and in dim light open the shutter and rotate the imaging drum around. If there is a defect on the drum that matches that on the page, you've solved the problem. Change out the toner cartridge. Nothing there? Try the same thing on the fuser assembly. Turn the printer off and wait for it to cool down before pulling a fuser assembly. Those things get hot!

There are literally hundreds of other issues related to laser printers. Enough to fill a book by itself. Any certified (or certifiable) technicians out there could point at any one of these issues and say, "Yeah, but it could also be this, this, this, or this!" What I have provided here are some of the most common problems and the most common solutions. For more detailed information on printers, there are a number of good books that have been written. Also, each of the major manufacturers provides technical training on their products at very reasonable cost.

Printer Languages

All those dots don't just magically appear. They are created as a result of zeros and ones being converted into pulses of laser light, electrical signals that release the charge of an electromagnet, or the signal that ejects the ink. All printers, whether they're impact, inkjet, or optical, require a fixed set of instructions that tell them when to put a dot onto paper. In the case of color printers, it also has to inform the printer which color of ink to eject. Printer languages provide those instructions. Three commonly used languages include HP's Printer Control Language (PCL), Adobe's Postscript, and the Microsoft Windows Graphical Device Interface (GDI). Each of these languages works in a slightly different manner and different versions of each have appeared over the years.

ASCII

In Chapter One, PC Basics, I provided a detailed explanation of the American Standard Code for Information Interchange, (ASCII), and there are tables of both printable and nonprintable characters in Appendix C. It's easy to overlook ASCII as being a printer language simply because it is frequently considered to be simply a character set. However, the early line printers depended on ASCII to provide the common commands that controlled the printer as well. It should be noted that, while ASCII is considered to be old technology, it is still alive and well. In fact, as you will see a little later in this chapter, continued support of ASCII is a requirement for maintaining IEEE 1284 standards.

PCL

HP developed the original PCL as a language by which dot matrix printers could be controlled. By the time the first laser printers appeared, the language was already in its third generation. PCL versions one and two first appeared back in the 1980s. PCL3 was the first of the versions to provide support to laser printers. The original HP LaserJet, released in 1984, used this language.

As a language, PCL is considered to be an escape code language. In other words, the ASCII escape character precedes specific commands. These commands are embedded in the document. An example of this would be in how PCL would print a specific word on a specific position on the page. ESC *p75x150Yprinter would start at the printable edge of the page and count off 75 units. It would then drop down 150 units and print the word "printer."

When the Laserjet Plus was released in 1985, PCL was modified to allow fonts and graphics to be generated as bitmaps. While these bitmaps provided relatively primitive output by today's standards, they handled simple word processing, along with simple graphics tasks, such as box drawing, relatively well. Later versions improved upon the ability to generate and output graphical information, and current generations are capable of near photographic output.

PCL5 added another embedded language called the Hewlett Packard Graphics Language (HPGL) to PCL. This provided for the ability to use outline fonts instead of bitmap fonts. Outline fonts are much more easily scaled to different sizes. It also supplies support for vector graphics. Vector graphics allows for the mathematical calculation of dot position. A printer that can do that can produce virtually any form or shape you might imagine.

The most recent implementation of PCL is (not surprisingly) PCL6. This language incorporates a new modular architecture that can be easily modified for future HP printers. The benefits to the user include a faster return to the application after sending a job to the printer.

The language uses a more efficient data stream. This allows for faster printing of complex graphics and can substantially reduce network traffic generated by network print jobs.

POSTSCRIPT

Apple Computer Corporation's Laserwriter first implemented Adobe's Postscript on its Macintosh. It came out at a time when PCL was still limited to crude bitmap drawings of the overall image. The fact that Postscript supported outline fonts and vector graphics gave the Laserwriter a huge advantage in terms of print quality. Many people, myself included, credit the incorporation of Postscript into its printers for the massive acceptance of Macintosh computers as the platform of choice for graphic artists.

Postscript, however, is platform independent. As a language, it can be incorporated into virtually any printer design. The original release of Postscript, Postscript Level One, was very processor intensive and required much more memory to be installed into the printer. For someone to whom output quality was of primary importance, this was an acceptable sacrifice.

Postscript Level Two was the next step. It did everything Level One could do, along with several major enhancements. These included the ability to add a Postscript driver to the display. This allows the image on the monitor to more closely resemble the final output. It also provided support for image typesetters. Users of Postscript could transport their files, regardless of platform, to the typesetter and have the final product precisely duplicate the document they originally created.

Postscript Level Three made further improvements. It allows for up to 4096 levels of gray in monochrome printing. When printing color, different levels of transparency can be applied to any given hue. In addition, the blending of adjacent colors is considered to be more natural.

WINDOWS GDI

One thing of which many Windows users are no doubt unaware is that there is a significant difference between a "printer" and a "print device." The key to understanding Windows is that it never allows hardware to directly interact with applications. That is all done through the Hardware Abstraction Layer (HAL) that I've mentioned several times throughout this book. To Windows, the printer is the collection of files the OS uses to communicate with the print device. The print device is the actual machine that spits out the final page.

Part of the Windows GDI is the inclusion of its own printer language. Since that language is embedded into the OS, it allows printer manufacturers to write simplified device drivers. Applications developers have a single interface to which they can write their code as well. Like Postscript, the language is independent of the printer hardware. Unlike Postscript, it is specific to the Windows platform. As such, the GDI language is considered to be host-based.

A key issue to consider here is whether or not the printer supports any languages other than GDI. A printer that supports only GDI can only be used in the Windows environment. The language is compatible with neither PDL nor Postscript. Also, GDI requires that your computer build and process the images. This places a fairly large burden on the CPU and memory.

Therefore, it is essential that you take into consideration the performance hit such a printer will impose on your system as well as the overall speed of the printing process. If you have a slow computer, print jobs will take longer to send to the printer. And while that is happening, trying to run any other application will be greatly hampered by the overhead imposed by the GDI language. Most users will find trying to use their computer for another application while a large print job is being processed is impractical.

On the plus side, GDI offers a much richer set of features than the more conventional languages. N-plus printing allows smaller versions of multiple pages to be printed onto a single sheet of paper. People who want the ability to do duplex printing without the necessarily high cost of a duplex printer can take advantage of manual duplexing.

The advantage that appeals to most people, however, is the inherently lower cost of GDI printers. Since they offload most of the work to the computer, a slow processor and small amounts of RAM (used for buffering) are all that the printer needs. As a result, a plethora of inexpensive yet highly functional printers are now available on the market.

IEEE 1284

If you've gotten this far through the book, by now you've realized that the Institute of Electrical and Electronic Engineers (IEEE) plays a key role in keeping the industry as near to "standard" as it can possibly be. IEEE 1284 was ratified as a standard in March of 1994 and defines several aspects of the printing process. Among these, any device bearing the IEEE 1284 standard must support five different printer modes, as follows:

- *Compatibility mode*: A unidirectional signal that is used to send data to the printer. This is also known as Centronix mode. Very slow, at approximately 150KB/s.

- *Nibble mode*: Sends the 8-bit byte of data to the printer in two cycles, each of which carries four bits, or a nibble of data. This method requires software support and more overhead on the part of the host computer. Even slower than compatibility mode, ranging from 50KB to 65KB/s.

- *Byte mode*: Like nibble mode, it provides bidirectional communication between the printer and the computer. Unlike nibble mode, it sends eight bits on each cycle. Speeds in byte mode are comparable to those of compatibility mode.

- *Enhanced parallel port (EPP)*: Because it provides for different types of signals to be transferred on any given clock cycle, EPP provides for faster and more efficient communication between peripherals. EPP allows continuous data transfer of around 500KB/s with burst rates of up to 2MB/s.

- *Extended compatibility port (ECP)*: Provides for both data and command cycles, therefore supporting more advanced devices, including scanners, storage devices, and such. Data throughput is similar to that of EPP. However, since DMA is used, there is less delay imposed on the application.

CONFIGURING PARALLEL PORTS

Pay special attention to the latter settings, EPP and ECP. In the CMOS of your computer, usually in the Integrated Peripherals section, is a place where you can configure your parallel port. Many versions of BIOS ship with bidirectional or byte mode enabled. For maximum performance, nearly every user will benefit by reconfiguring the parallel port to EPP. If you wish to control more than one device from your parallel port, ECP is the better choice. ECP can actually set up virtual channels for each device.

Note, however, that ECP requires a DMA channel. Since you are configuring the parallel port directly from the CMOS, any sound cards or other devices that may be using DMA will not yet be initialized. Therefore, there is a possibility that ECP will grab a DMA channel that another device is configured to use. This will only cause problems if both devices are active at the same time. For example, if ECP and the sound card are both on DMA3, and you like to play music while you work, the first time you attempt to print a document while playing Pachelbel, your computer is going to lock up like a tomb. The fix is easy. Simply reboot the machine, go into CMOS, and select a different DMA channel for ECP.

In addition to defining the minimum printing modes supported, IEEE 1284 devices also must follow certain other standards as well. For one thing, there are certain restrictions to any defined methods by which the printing mode that is to be used is negotiated. A byte of data is sent from the peripheral to indicate the mode for which it is configured, and the computer moves into that mode. **Table 17.1** shows the bytes sent during the negotiation for each mode.

Other aspects of parallel printing under the auspices of IEEE include the structure of the connectors used. There are some specific parameters that must be met before "IEEE 1284" can be stamped on the cable or device. These include, but are not limited to, the following:

- All signals move across a twisted pair and must provide for a signal and ground return.
- The cable will have a minimum of 85 percent optical braid coverage over foil.
- Signal and ground returns must have an unbalanced impedance of 62 ohms (+/- 6 ohms) over the frequency band of 4 to 16 MHz.
- Crosstalk between wires can be no greater than 10 percent.
- Cable shielding must be connected to the connector back shell using a 360-degree concentric method. Pigtail connections are not acceptable.
- Compliant cable assemblies shall be marked with "IEEE Std. 1284-1994 Compliant."

The connectors defined include the standard 25-pin connector described in Chapter Two. In order to maintain IEEE-1284 compliance, cables used to connect peripherals other than printers must be wired with a standard Type A cable. These cables can be male-to-male or male-to-female.

Table 17.1 Bit Values Used for Determining Printing Mode

Bit	Description	Valid Bit Values
8	Request extensibility link (REL)	1000 0000
7	Request EPP mode	0100 0000
6	Request ECP mode with REL	0011 0000
5	Request ECP mode without REL	0001 0000
4	Reserved	0000 1000
3	Request device ID	Nibble mode—0000 0100; Byte mode—0000 0101; ECP mode without REL—0001 0100; ECP mode with REL—0011 0100
2	Reserved	0000 0010
1	Byte mode	0000 0001
none	Nibble mode	0000 0000

Printers don't automatically know what printing mode an application has chosen. Information contained in the print job identifies the mode.

Most printers will require a cable that goes from the 25-pin male to a connector that in the past has been called the Centronix port. The IEEE description for the connector is the Type C connector.

The final parameters defined by IEEE had to do with the way in which printer drivers and interfaces were defined. These include voltage levels of specific signals, output signal impedance, and other electrical signals that are generated on a driver level. Manufacturers are expected to follow these standards when designing their product.

While this may seem to be a little on the dictatorial side on the part of IEEE, the end result is that if you buy a device stated to be IEEE 1284 compliant and an IEEE 1284 compliant cable, you know your new toy is going to work. There are many devices on the market today that will not work unless the cable is IEEE 1284.

CHAPTER SUMMARY

This chapter provided only the briefest overview of how printers work. A more detailed discussion would require an entire book in and of itself. The key details to remember from this chapter are primarily in the overall construction of a printer. Modern printers are modular devices and just knowing what makes them tick puts you halfway toward learning how to fix them.

Brain Drain

1. Describe in as much detail as possible the differences between how a line printer and a dot matrix printer compile images.

2. How does the print head of an impact printer deliver a single dot to the printed page?

3. What are the key differences between thermal inkjet printers and piezoelectric inkjet printers?

4. From beginning to end, describe in detail the monochrome laser printing process.

5. List as many different things as you can that define an IEEE 1284 compliant device and/or cable.

The $64K Questions

1. Two different forms of impact printer include (pick two) _____.
   a. LED
   b. Thermal
   c. Dot matrix
   d. Daisy wheel

2. Bubblejet printers use piezoelectric print heads.
   a. True
   b. False

3. During the laser printing process, the paper is charged by _____.
   a. The primary corona
   b. The charging roller
   c. The developing roller
   d. The transfer roller

4. The imaging drum typically receives a _____ charge during the conditioning cycle.
   a. 200 to 400V
   b. −800 to −1200V
   c. −400 to −600V
   d. 400 to 600V

5. What component prevents the paper from adhering to the print drum after the toner is transferred?
   a. The separation pad
   b. The transfer roller
   c. The static discharge unit
   d. The fuser input assembly

6. Color laser printers apply the image from each toner cartridge _____.
   a. Directly to the paper
   b. To the imaging drum
   c. To an intermediate transfer belt
   d. To a film surface

7. If you wished to hang a scanner, an external CD-ROM, and a printer all off the same parallel port, which mode would be most suitable?
   a. Compatibility mode
   b. Nibble mode
   c. EPP
   d. ECP

8. There are _____ conductors on a standard parallel cable.
   a. 18
   b. 25
   c. 32
   d. 40

9. A printer capable of duplex printing does what?

    a. It prints on both sides of the page.

    b. It prints both color and black-and-white images.

    c. It can print thumbnails of several pages on a single sheet of paper.

    d. It can collate multiple print jobs into separate output bins.

10. A deflection pawl is unique to _____.

    a. Line printers

    b. Daisy wheel printers

    c. Color laser printers

    d. Duplex printers

TRICKY TERMINOLOGY

Bubblejet printer: Another term for a thermal printer.

Byte mode: Like nibble mode, it provides bidirectional communication between the printer and the computer. Unlike nibble mode, it sends eight bits on each cycle. Speeds of byte mode are comparable to those of compatibility mode.

Cold fusing: A process used by some phase-change printers that uses pressure rollers to press the ink into the paper.

Compatibility mode: A unidirectional signal that is used to send data to the printer. This is also known as Centronix mode. Very slow, at approximately 150KB/s.

Nibble mode: Sends the 8-bit byte of data to the printer in two cycles, each of which carries four bits, or a nibble of

data. This method requires software support and more overhead on the part of the host computer. Even slower than compatibility mode, ranging from 50KB to 65KB/s.

Phase-change printer: A printer that liquefies solid inks before applying them to paper.

Piezoelectric crystal: A substance that changes shape when exposed to electricity.

Platen: The hard cylinder that supports the paper on impact printers.

Print head: The mechanism on any impact or inkjet printer that is responsible for depositing the pigment onto the paper.

Thermal printer: A printer that ejects ink onto a page of paper by heating the fluid.

Tractor feed: A paper transport mechanism that uses a set of gears on a printer to advance the paper by engaging in perforations along each side of the paper.

ACRONYM ALERT

DPI: Dots Per Inch

ECP: Extended Compatibility Port. A parallel mode that provides for both data and command cycles, therefore supporting more advanced devices, including scanners, storage devices, and such. Data throughput is similar to that of EPP. However, since DMA is used, there is less delay imposed on the application.

EPP: Enhanced Parallel Port. Because it provides for different types of signals to be transferred on any given clock cycle, EPP provides for faster and more efficient communication between peripherals. EPP allows continuous data transfer of around 500KB/s with burst rates of up to 2MB/s.

GDI: Graphical Device Interface. A subset of Microsoft's Windows operating systems that manages imaging devices such as printers, scanners, and graphics cards. Printers that use this interface as their printer language are referred to as GDI printers.

HAL: Hardware Abstraction Layer. A subset of Microsoft's Windows operating systems that provides a virtual barrier between the computer's hardware and the applications and upper-level OS functions.

HPGL: Hewlett Packard Graphics Language. A printer language developed by HP to add complex graphics to the printer's toolset.

PCL: Printer Control Language. Hewlett Packard's printer language, originally developed for dot matrix printers and later adopted for use with laser printers.

CHAPTER 18

GETTING ON THE NETWORK

Once you have a number of computers in a business, or as is increasingly common, within the family, it becomes a very appealing thought to be able to access the files on one computer while you're working on another. In the business environment, this isn't just a luxury; it can be critically important. Oddly enough, as complicated as it may appear on the outset, setting up a small network doesn't have to be an overwhelming ordeal. In fact, it can even be fun! There are a few things that will make the job go much easier if you know them up front, rather than learning them along the way. That's what this chapter is all about. Also, while I won't be examining network infrastructure in any great detail (that could entail an entire series of books, and not simply a single chapter in one book), I will be taking a look at some of the hardware used in more advanced networks.

Along these lines, I will also be covering the different ways a network can be laid out. On the simplest level, two computers could be hooked up with a serial cable connecting them and that would constitute a network. On a much wider scale, the Internet itself comprises a very large worldwide network. This chapter will feature a brief discussion of some of the more commonly implemented local area topologies used, both past and present.

Since this is a book on hardware, I won't be getting into a detailed discussion of protocols. However, I would be remiss in not providing an introduction to the most commonly used protocols and where you might see them in use. Also, they get some exposure on the exam.

A+ Exam Objectives

Exam objectives that will be covered in this chapter include the following:

1.2   Identify basic procedures for adding and removing field-replaceable modules for desktop systems. Given a replacement scenario, choose the appropriate sequences. (NIC)

1.5   Identify the names, purposes, and performance characteristics of standardized/common peripheral ports, associated cabling, and their connectors. Recognize ports, cabling, and connectors by sight.

1.8 Identify proper procedures for installing and configuring common peripheral devices. Choose the appropriate installation or configuration sequences in given scenarios.

6.1 Identify the common types of network cables, their characteristics and connectors.

6.2 Identify basic networking concepts including how a network works.

6.3 Identify common technologies available for establishing Internet connectivity and their characteristics.

WHY BUILD A NETWORK?

The first question an individual needs to ask before taking on the project of networking a home or business is simply, "Why am I doing this?" For the aspiring computer professional, the answer could be as simple as wanting the practice before taking the job for a paying customer. For a business, a little deeper analysis might be in order. For a business or individual with multiple computers, any one of the following reasons might offer sufficient justification to take on the challenge of building a network:

- *Sharing files*: Keeping multiple copies of the same file is neither efficient nor convenient. Security can also become an issue. With a network, management of resources becomes easier.

- *Sharing peripherals*: Devices that get relatively infrequent use can be installed in a convenient location and shared out to those who require their services.

- *Communications*: Email, intra-office communications, and even global communication are made substantially easier when those in contact with one another have a mutually accessible network link.

- *Managing resources*: While this may sound like a rehash of the first two listings, it isn't really. A well-designed network allows resources, such as the user accounts, to be managed by a single administrative entity.

- *Security*: A properly administered network can be rather precisely controlled in respect to who has access to what information or resources, or who has access to whom.

- *Software management*: Rolling out new software is dramatically easier if it is done over the network. In addition, managing all of those licenses is easier if all software is maintained in a single location, along with records of what licenses were used where.

PEER TO PEER, OR CLIENT/SERVER

On the most basic level, a network is achieved as soon as you get two computers to talk to one another. As networks grow and become more complex, a certain degree of organization becomes necessary. There has evolved two basic types of network: the peer to peer and the client/server.

PEER TO PEER

Peer-to-peer (P2P) networks are the easiest, and by far the least expensive networks to set up. However, they can turn into an administration nightmare. By definition, a peer is an equal. Therefore, your P2P network is a collection of equals. Every computer on the network is both a client machine and also performs the role of server.

A couple of key definitions are in order here. A *client* is not the end user. The end user is referred to as the user. A client is any device or software that requires the services of another device or piece of software in order to perform a function. A *server* is any device or software that doles out services to those that need them.

On a P2P network, since every computer is acting in both roles, both security and resource administration become serious issues. Whoever happens to be logged on to a computer at any given time is the administrator. Therefore, he or she can set permissions on files, create passwords, share or unshare resources, and so on and so forth.

As a result, P2P networks are really unsuitable for larger networks. They're basically good for very small networks, where not a lot of information gets shared among users and security is not an issue. Somebody creating a home network so she can hook her computer up to her roommate's computer can easily get by with this level of network. Even smaller offices can survive on P2P as long as there is some organized methodology for managing information.

BUZZ WORDS

Client: Any device or software that requires the services of another device or piece of software in order to perform a function.

Server: Any device or software that provides services to other devices or pieces of software that need them.

Credentials: On a network, these consist of the user ID and password that provide network access for the user.

Permissions: Resource access or actions that a particular user is allowed.

CLIENT/SERVER

Once security and data integrity become more important than ease of implementation, the client/server network becomes more attractive. In this design, the network has one or more computers that become dedicated servers, running a specialized network operating system (NOS). One person or a group of people will be assigned the responsibility of managing the network. Depending on the NOS selected, this person might be called the administrator, the supervisor, or even the superuser. Throughout this chapter I'll be using the term administrator.

People who need to have access to the network will be assigned a user account with a user ID and (usually) a password that they use to confirm their identities when they log onto the network. These are the user's *credentials*. The NOS uses the combination of user ID and password to determine what a person may or may not do while logged on. These are the user's *permissions*.

The administrator can centrally control all the resources on the network, which might include files, peripherals, and access to external communications. The beauty of this setup is two-fold. First off, each user only needs to know one password to access everything on the network to which he or she has been given permission. Second, a single individual or group of individuals controls all security. This allows for a much higher degree of both organization and security.

The Hardware of Networking

I said earlier that, on the most basic level, two computers could be hooked together over a serial cable. And that is true. The most basic need of computer networking is that the devices that are to communicate over the network be equipped with some form of transceiver and the media over which they will communicate.

A *transceiver* is any device which can both transmit and receive a signal, hence the name. Media can consist of wire, light beams, or radio waves, or any combination thereof. As a network grows in size and complexity, other devices become either necessary or desirable in order to help manage the network. These include hubs, repeaters, switches, bridges, routers, and brouters. Don't worry if some of these terms are unfamiliar to you. Each will be discussed in further detail in this chapter.

Networking Transceivers

In order to communicate on the network a device must be able to transmit and receive data. To do this, it must be equipped with a transceiver. The most basic transceiver is the network interface card (NIC). A modem is also a valid networking transceiver. However, modems will be discussed in more detail in Chapter Nineteen, Telecommunications.

More specialized transceivers also exist. A print server is a small device that sits alongside a printer and connects it directly to the network. This way users access it the same way they would any computer on the network without causing some unfortunate user the inconvenience of having the office printer hanging off of his or her computer.

Network Interface Cards

The NIC stands alone as the most commonly used networking transceiver in use today (**Figure 18.1**). When choosing a NIC, there are a couple of things to take into consideration:

- *Bus type*: NICs typically come on a PCI card. Some high-end cards are available on a 64-bit, 66MHz PCI 2.01 compliant bus. This will be the fastest, but make sure your computer supports the standard. Usually, it's only the high-end servers that do. If absolutely necessary, it is still possible to get NIC on an ISA card.

- *Network interface type*: The older 10Mb cards were available with the RJ-45 connector and/or a BNC connector for coaxial cable. 10/100 cards will come with only the RJ-45. There are also cards for the various wireless media that will be discussed later in this chapter, as well as those for fiber-optic cabling.

- *Networking standard*: Typically, this will be some form of Ethernet. Some older networks are still on 10Mb/s Ethernet. Most, however, are running 100Mb/s and a growing

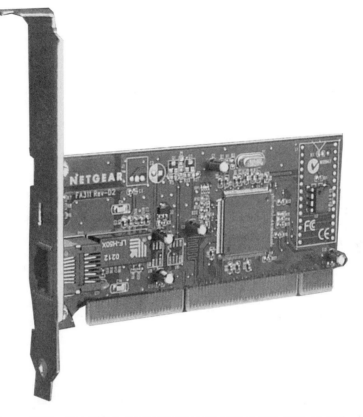

Figure 18.1 The NIC is the basic transceiver that gets data on and off the network for the vast majority of computers.

number of organizations have migrated to Gigabit Ethernet (1000Mb/s). While Ethernet dominates the market, it is still, as of this writing, possible to get cards that support token ring, even though the standard is all but dead.

On the back of the NIC, in addition to the interface for the medium, there will generally be two lights. One is a link light and the other is the activity light. The link light tells you that you have connectivity between the host and the rest of the network and should glow constantly. The activity light will flicker when data is being transmitted.

It isn't at all uncommon to see the NIC installed onto the motherboard itself. It may also show up as a combo card, sharing the same circuit board with another peripheral. There are some interesting variations in this respect. Hewlett Packard has included on some of its systems a combination of a SCSI adapter and NIC on one card. It's not at all uncommon for manufacturers of PCMCIA cards to ship a modem/NIC combo. There are even a few of these types of cards available that can be installed into a PCI slot.

Installing and Troubleshooting NICs

NIC installation, in the past, has rightfully earned a reputation as being one of the more challenging tasks. Thankfully, Plug 'n Play has started to make this a thing of the past. Still, when things go wrong, these devices can quickly make a day turn sour.

When a NIC fails to be recognized by the system after a fresh installation, chances are extremely good that you are experiencing an IRQ conflict (see Chapter Nine, Examining the Expansion Bus). If the device is PnP, it may mean that none of the IRQs that it has been programmed to accept is available. If you recall from Chapter Nine, sometimes simply swapping positions with another device on the PCI bus will solve the problem. If not, you may have to go into the CMOS and reserve one of the IRQs the NIC will use. This is very likely to cause the conflicting device to stop being recognized on the next boot, but at least you know which device needs reconfiguring.

On some older NICs, it is also possible that it is not an IRQ conflict, but rather an I/O address conflict. A good memory mapping utility can help you resolve what device is trying to use what addresses in memory. Most operating systems have ways in which you can manually reconfigure devices to use another I/O address. In Windows, you would go into Device Manager, select the afflicted device, and click the Properties button. On the window that pops up, click the Resources tab and deselect the Use automatic settings checkbox (see **Figure 18.2**). Select another option, if possible. If there are no other options available for that device, try the same procedure on the other conflicting device. If neither device can be reconfigured, it may be necessary to replace one or the other of the devices.

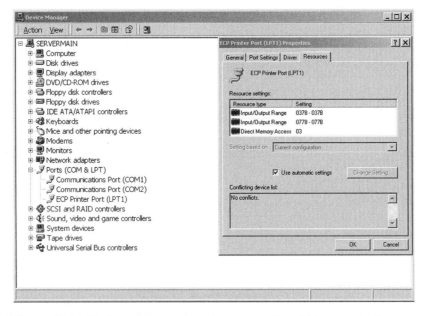

Figure 18.2 Most operating systems have a way by which many devices can be configured to use a different I/O address or IRQ than the one handed out by the BIOS.

NETWORKING MEDIA

Once the signal has been generated by the computer and is ready to be transmitted to the intended recipient, the data is going to need a path over which it can travel. This path is known as the *media*. In terms of media, there are two forms. *Bounded media* is any transmission method that physically links the two devices. It doesn't matter what the material is made of. All that matters is that it be a tangible medium. Something you can touch.

Unbounded media is anything that travels across space (or the airwaves) to get where it's going. This can include radio waves, light waves, microwaves, or any other method that technology may have invented in the meantime. It is the electronic equivalent of telepathy.

BUZZ WORDS

Media: The substance or energy wave over which a data signal is transmitted.

Bounded media: Any medium that physically connects a device to the network by way of a tangible cable.

Unbounded media: Any medium that connects the device to the network using energy forms that travel through air and/or space.

BOUNDED MEDIA

The majority of networks that are in existence today consist of some form of bounded media. They are hooked up by way of copper wire or fiber-optic cables. While copper currently enjoys the advantage, fiber optics is gradually moving in on its turf. Fiber optics has the advantage of being able to carry light waves, and light waves are more easily modulated for high-speed connections.

Local area networks are almost exclusively the domain of twisted-pair cabling. However, there are still a large number of older networks out there that make use of coaxial cable. Each type of media has its own unique set of advantages and disadvantages.

TWISTED PAIR

Twisted-pair cable is available in two different physical packages, as well as several different categories. Physically, there is unshielded twisted pair (UTP) and shielded twisted pair (STP). UTP is the most commonly used and shows up on the majority of networks. Shielded twisted pair has the advantage of being more resistant to outside influences exerted by electromagnetic interference and radio frequency interference. However, its higher cost frequently keeps it from being used in most installations.

Twisted-pair cabling consists of four pairs of 22- to 24-gauge strands of wire. Each pair is twisted together across the length of the cable. Oddly enough, this is where it gets its name. The insulation around each of the strands consists of different colors; some are solid, some are striped. See **Table 18.1** for the color combinations.

Patch cables are generally terminated with connectors knows as RJ-45 connectors (like the one shown in **Figure 18.3**). They look very similar to the ends of your telephone wires, only larger. The telephone line uses an RJ-11 connector, which only has four connectors at the most. (Many telephone cables only make use of two of them.) The Electronic Industry Association

Figure 18.3 The RJ-45 connector is easily confused with a telephone jack by the beginner.

Table 18.1 Twisted-Pair Cabling Color Codes

Pair	Color Combinations
Pair 1	Orange-white/orange striped
Pair 2	Green-white/green striped
Pair 3	Blue-white/blue striped
Pair 4	Brown-white/brown striped

Twisted-pair cabling consists of eight strands of wire separated into four pairs.

(EIA) and the Telecommunications Industry Association (TIA) worked together to ratify color-coding standards to assure that uniform wiring was used from installation from installation. There were two different standards adopted for twisted-pair wiring, EIA/TIA 568A and 568B. The most commonly used method follows the color-coding standard in 568B. Both standards are explained in **Table 18.2**.

Buzz Words ——————

Crossover cable: A network patch cord that routes the transmit signal from one device to the receive terminals on the other device.

An accessory that comes in extremely handy for the computer technician is the crossover cable. A *crossover cable* is connected in such a way that the transmit+ and transmit- signals from one end of the cable are routed to the receive+ and receive- on the opposite end. This cable allows two devices to be directly hooked together without the need for a hub. Should you need to connect two computers, or should you wish to hook your notebook computer up to a router in order to be able to configure it, the crossover cable will be necessary. Crossover cables are most frequently based on 568B standards and are wired in the manner illustrated in **Table 18.3**.

Table 18.2 Wiring Pinouts for EIA/TIA 568A and 568B Twisted-Pair Cabling

Pin No.	Signal Carried	568A	568B
1	Transmit (+)	White/green	White/orange
2	Transmit (−)	Green	Orange
3	Receive (+)	White/orange	White/green
4	Not used	Blue	Blue
5	Not used	White/blue	White/blue
6	Receive (−)	Orange	Green
7	Not used	White/brown	White/brown
8	Not used	Brown	Brown

Note that the two standards differ only in the colors used for the wire that actually transmits signals.

Twisted-pair cable is designated by its category. In each case but one, the cables are structurally the same, but each category is capable of handling different signal speeds. Category Five (Cat5) is the most commonly used, although a newer implementation, Cat5e, is quickly passing it by.

Increased signal speed can be achieved by increasing the number of twists per inch placed onto each twisted pair. Increasing the number of twists acts to reduce crosstalk between cables. Crosstalk occurs anytime you lay two runs of cable side-by-side. A portion of the signal carried by each strand will leak over to the other strand. This affects both the accuracy and the speed of data transmissions. If you can reduce crosstalk, you can increase data throughput. **Table 18.4** compares the most common twisted-pair cable types.

Table 18.3 Wiring Diagram for Crossover Cable

Pin no. End 1	Sending Device	Color Coding	Pin no. End 2	Receiving Device
1	Transmit (+)	White/orange	3	Receive (+)
2	Transmit (–)	Orange	6	Receive (–)
3	Receive (+)	White/green	1	Transmit (+)
4	Not used	Blue	4	Not used
5	Not used	White/blue	5	Not used
6	Receive (–)	Green	2	Transmit (–)
7	Not used	White/brown	7	Not used
8	Not used	Brown	8	Not used

Crossover cables work by reversing the transmit and receive data signal carriers.

Table 18.4 Twisted-Pair Categories

Category	Max. Frequency	Usage
1	Voice only, no data	Telephone or modem
2	4MHz	Localtalk/ISDN
3	16MHz	Ethernet
4	20MHz	Token ring
5	100MHz	Fast Ethernet
5e	100MHz	Gigabit Ethernet/ATM to 622MB/sec
6*	250MHz	Gigabit Ethernet/ATM to 2.4GB/sec
7*	600MHz	Not typically used in U.S.

Twisted-pair cabling is available in many different incarnations. Be sure you use the correct wire for the job.

*Not yet officially ratified as of this writing.

COAXIAL CABLING

An older style of cabling used in networks that is still seen frequently enough to merit discussion is coaxial cable. If you've ever hooked up a VCR to your television, you've used a form of *coaxial* cable, or coax. However, be aware that the coax used in video applications and that used in computer networks are not the same. Coaxial cable gets its name from the fact that the data signal travels along the same axis as the ground. As is shown in **Figure 18.4**, coax consists of a center core, an inside insulator, a mesh shielding (or ground), and an outside insulator.

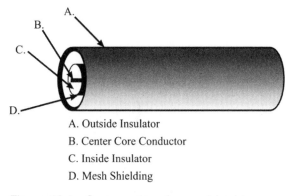

A. Outside Insulator
B. Center Core Conductor
C. Inside Insulator
D. Mesh Shielding

Figure 18.4   Cross-section of a coaxial cable

The form of coax most commonly used in networking is RG-58U. This is a 50-ohm cable that meets all standards for Ethernet. It is frequently referred to as *thinnet*. It is capable of carrying an Ethernet signal for a distance of 185 meters without help. RG-59 is what you use in television installations and is a 75-ohm cable. They are not interchangeable.

Another coaxial cable used in networks is RG-8, or *thicknet*. RG-8 can be a bit difficult to manage, but because it can carry a signal for up to 500 meters, it was the medium of choice for any connection that had to run a longer distance. None of the coaxial cable types was able to keep up with contemporary twisted-pair categories. **Table 18.5** compares different coax types to different twisted-pair types.

The connector that RG-58U cable hooks up to is not called a coaxial connector, however. It is a BNC connector. A typical coaxial connector is either a push-on or screw-on type of assembly. **Figure 18.5** shows the push-on type. The BNC connector is a bayonet assembly.

BUZZ WORDS

Coaxial: A cable over which the signal and ground both follow the same axis.

Thinnet: A name commonly given to RG-58U coaxial cable.

Thicknet: A name commonly given to RG-8 coaxial cable.

Table 18.5   An Overview of Copper Media

Cable Type	Bandwidth	Max. Segment Length
RG-58	10Mb/s	180M
RG-8	10Mb/s	500M
CAT3	10Mb/s	100M
CAT5	100Mb/s	100M
CAT5e	1000Mb/s	100M
CAT6*	1000Mb/s	100M

A knowledge of maximum bandwidth and maximum segment length is essential both for the exam and for work in the field.

*CAT6 has not been ratified as of this writing and the specifications are subject to change.

Figure 18.5 This particular NIC is equipped with both a BNC and an RJ-45 connector.

Many books and articles define BNC as an acronym for British Naval Connector, or Bayonet Nut Connector. Technically speaking, although both definitions have become accepted, neither is correct. It's actually an acronym for Bayonet Neil-Conselman, in respect to the engineers who developed the connector.

RG-8 is connected to the network by way of a device called a *vampire clamp*. The rather macabre

> **BUZZ WORDS**
>
> **Vampire clamp:** A device consisting of two halves that screw together. One half is fitted with sharp teeth that bite through the insulation of RG-8 cable.

name of this device comes from the fact that it consists of two halves that are drawn together around the cable by tightening some screws. Sharp teeth sink in through the insulation and make contact with the conductor. On the outside of the clamp, a 15-pin D-shell connector, called an AUI connector (AUI is an acronym for attachment unit interface) hooks up to the patch cable.

Depending on whether your network is going to be based on a bus topology or a star topology (both of which will be discussed later in this chapter), you may or may not need a couple of other little devices. A bus network basically consists of all the computers hooked up in a line. In order to do that, a T-connector, similar to the one shown in **Figure 18.6**, is fitted to the BNC on the back of the network card. You simply run cables from one T to the next.

At the end of the chain, you need to do something to stop the signal. As I've mentioned before, when an electrical current reaches the end of the wire, it doesn't simply stop dead in its tracks. If there isn't something there to absorb it, it will simply turn around and go back the way it came. This, of course, stops the network dead in its tracks. Therefore, you need to put a terminating resistor on each end of the bus to absorb the signal.

Figure 18.6 T-connectors link computers together in a chain. The cable coming in from one computer goes on one side of the T, the cable going to the next computer down the line hooks up to the other side.

FIBER-OPTIC CABLE

When you move into the high-tech world of fiber optics, you start learning a whole new vocabulary. You don't have a network card, you have an optical transmitter and an optical receiver, collectively referred to as the optical transceiver. The cable is different as well, in that light can only travel in one direction. Therefore, for a device that is capable of full duplex operation, there must be an incoming fiber and an outbound fiber that carry signals in their respective directions. Fiber optics is available in single-mode and multimode designs.

Single-mode fiber is a single strand of optical glass encased in a reflective tube and surrounded by a very tough PVC coating. The glass strand is typically between 8 and 10 microns in diameter and carries a single signal in one direction.

> **BUZZ WORDS**
>
> **Single-mode fiber:** A fiber-optic strand that moves only a single signal through the core.
>
> **Multimode fiber:** A fiber-optic strand that moves multiple signals through the core.

Multimode fiber (**Figure 18.7**) is also a single strand, but is typically 50 to 100 microns in diameter and is designed to have several different signals traveling over the fiber. Using different light frequencies for each channel and then bouncing the signal along the fiber at varying angles enables this to happen.

Fiber-optic cable can be packaged in two different ways as well. Tight buffered cabling bundles a single strand of fiber optic into the cable. This is frequently used for LANs and inter-device connections. However, large numbers of signals can be collected together in a single run

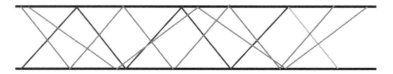

Figure 18.7 Multimode fiber sends multiple signals down the fiber, using different light frequencies and bouncing each beam at a different angle.

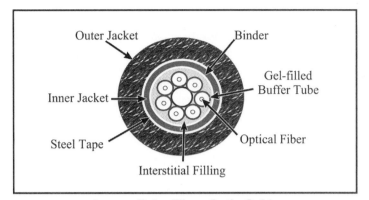

Loose-Tube Fiber-Optic Cable

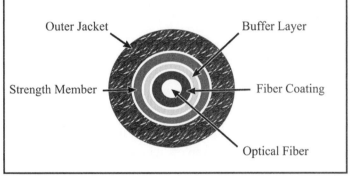

Tight Buffered Cable

Figure 18.8 Tight buffered cable runs a single optical strand, or in the case of duplex fiber, a pair of strands. Loose-tube cable carries many strands.

by using loose-tube cabling. This consists of several strands of optical glass in a single cable. **Figure 18.8** shows a loose-tube and a tight buffered cable side-by-side. Either one can be used for single-mode or multimode fiber. Loose-tube cable is generally used as a backbone between larger data centers.

Fiber optics carries several advantages over conventional copper cabling. For one thing, much faster throughput is possible. It's already being used to carry data in the range of several gigabits per second, and that is just beginning to tap its potential. Fiber optics can also carry a signal for much greater distances than copper before attenuation begins to degrade the signal.

Because it is not an electrical signal, it is immune to most of the forms of electrical interference that hamper copper-based digital systems. Neither RFI nor EMI has any effect on it. It could care less if you lay it directly along a high-voltage power line. The photons moving along the fiber optics will not be affected. Since it isn't made of metal, but rather glass, it does not corrode. As a result, it is not affected by the elements.

Fiber optics is also the best medium to use in an installation requiring a high degree of security. It is virtually impossible to tap into the medium without bringing the network down. People have a tendency to notice an event of this nature, and the disruption alerts them to the fact that something is going on.

If there is any downside to the use of fiber optics at all, it is in the higher cost of both the medium and the devices needed by the medium to move data. It is also somewhat more difficult to install. This results in a high cost for the initial installation.

UNBOUNDED MEDIA

A detailed discussion of the ins and outs of wireless telecommunications is quite beyond the boundaries of this book. Therefore, I will limit this section to a brief overview of the different forms of wireless networking that are available and when you might want to use which one. The different wireless technologies I will discuss will fall into three categories of signal transmission. There is radio, optical, and microwave transmission. Each has its advantages and disadvantages. Optical transmission is the most commonly used around the home and office, so I'll start there.

OPTICAL NETWORKING

Depending on what you're trying to accomplish, you might find yourself exploring one of two different network technologies that employ light waves traveling through air as a method of transmitting signals. One uses infrared light waves, while the other takes advantage of a laser beam.

INFRARED NETWORKING

If you've ever used a remote control to change the channel on your TV set, you've employed the technology used by infrared networks. Infrared networks can be one of four different types:

- *Line-of-sight networks*: Each device needs to have a direct and unobstructed path over which the beam can travel.
- *Reflective networks*: A transmission redirector is located in a spot common to all devices on the network. It, in turn, sends the signal to the appropriate location.
- *Scatter infrared network*: The signal bounces off of reflective surfaces and therefore can go around corners.
- *Broadband optical telepoint*: By far the fastest of infrared technologies, this method supports multimedia and streaming video. Unlike other methods of infrared wireless technology, multiple signals can be carried at once, each in a separate channel.

In all cases, zeros and ones are encoded into a unique series of light pulses. This series of pulses is picked up by the receiving devices and decoded back into digital form.

NETWORKING OVER LASER

One of the key disadvantages of infrared is speed. Or lack thereof, I should say. Also, distances between devices are seriously limited using infrared technology. While a laser connection can prove to be a little more difficult and expensive to install at the outset, it can provide very fast transmission rates over much greater distances between stations. Despite its initial outlay, laser technology can provide a much more efficient and cost-effective means for interconnecting offices, compared to high-speed dedicated lines leased from a telecommunications provider, assuming a line of sight can be maintained.

The technology involved in converting and transmitting data by way of optical means is very similar to that used by fiber optics. The key difference is that you don't have a contained medium over which data is sent.

The most common conventional laser systems provide speeds of either 155Mb/s or 622Mb/s. Distances of up to 4km are supported, although this can be affected by a number of factors. Inclement weather (such as a dust storm), atmospheric conditions (pollution), and physical obstructions (a flock of pigeons flying through the beam) all can affect your signal. Another thing that affects distance is the speed of the signal being transmitted. A 622Mb/s ATM transmission would be limited to about half the transmission distance of a 155Mb/s signal.

Some technologies, such as LightPointe Teledata Communications' Lightstation Multilink Series, use multiple beams to minimize the distance-limiting factors listed above. Therefore, if a bird should interrupt one beam, another beam will pick up the slack. In either case, most networking protocols have error correction mechanisms that will cause the offending or lost packets to be resent.

The laser interconnect is protocol-transparent. This means that, whatever networking protocols you might be using, the signal can be sent and received. Therefore, a 10BaseT network can move over the beam just as easily as a 622Mb/s ATM. If you're new to networking and don't know what 10BaseT and ATM are, they will be discussed in more detail later in the chapter.

NETWORKING OVER THE RADIO

For most people, the only exposure to radio transmissions is listening to Q99 acid rock as they navigate the freeway on the way to work. Even that is going away, as everyone adds twelve-disc CD changers to their SUVs. Still, radio frequencies are alive and well, even in the high-tech world of computer networking.

Radio waves fall into three categories: shortwave, very high frequency (VHF), and ultra-high frequency (UHF). In the U.S., these frequencies fall under the jurisdiction of the Federal Communications Commission (FCC). If you want to use radio waves, you must first be licensed to operate your equipment, and then you need to be assigned your frequency.

There are some frequencies that do not fall under the watchful eye of the FCC. These are the public bands. The public bands are in the range from 902 to 928MHz and from 5.72 to 5.85GHz. However, since anyone can use these, two factors impact on their usefulness. First of all, you are severely limited in the amount of power you use to broadcast. This is intended to reduce geographical overlap of the signals. Second, you do not have exclusive control of the frequency and if somebody else jumps in, that signal gets mixed with yours. If you are simply exchanging pleasantries with the trucker on I-89 about the smokies on the prowl, that's no big deal. However, when that signal is your precious data, you don't want it getting corrupted by unwanted signals, and just as importantly, you don't want just anybody picking it out of the air.

Networking over radio is generally done with either single-frequency or spread-spectrum. Single-frequency transmission is just what it sounds like. You are assigned a single frequency and that is what you use to transmit your data. When you use spread-spectrum, you are assigned several frequencies and you "hop" from one to the other. This provides for a greater degree of security.

SINGLE-FREQUENCY TRANSMISSIONS

As I stated in the last paragraph, the concept is simple. You have one frequency. Your data is converted from digital to analog radio waves and transmitted over the air. Installation of a single-frequency radio network will be one of two types:

- *Low power, single frequency (LPSF)*: You are permitted an extremely limited broadcast power. As a result, you have an operating range of between 20 and 25 meters between devices. Speeds (depending on choice of equipment) range from as low as 1Mb/s to a maximum of about 10Mb/s. These networks are useful for small offices where it is impractical to run wiring for any reason.
- *High power, single frequency (HPSF)*: This technology is useful for setting up low-speed wide area network (WAN) links where conventional bounded media are not an option. The broadcast equipment is permitted to operate at a higher power, allowing for line-of-sight telecommunications. In some cases, a controlled atmospheric bounce can extend the range of the network beyond the horizon. Speed limitations are similar to that of LPSF.

Whichever single-frequency model you choose, both are going to share some limitations. While virtually impervious to conditions such as smoke, smog, or birds, anything that generates EMI can degrade or interrupt the signal. A lightening strike, a radio transmitter, and almost anything else you can think of may inadvertently generate signals that overlap yours. The signals are also easily picked out of the air and intercepted. Therefore security can become a very real issue.

SPREAD-SPECTRUM RADIO

Spread-spectrum transmission addresses the issue of security. Because the broadcast signal is continually bouncing from one frequency to another, it is far more difficult to intercept the data. This, of course, is not without its drawbacks. In order to make sure the transmitting station and the intended recipient get all the data that was sent, and receive it intact, some form of synchronization has to take place. Two different methods are used:

- *Direct-sequence transmission* is the faster of the two methods. A predefined sequence of radio frequencies is employed, and both sending and receiving devices jump from one to the other in that sequence, using a predefined timing sequence as well. This is the less secure of the two methods. While it will keep out the casual eavesdropper, a dedicated hacker will have no problem cracking either the frequencies in use, the hop sequence, or the timing sequence.

- *Frequency hopping* uses a far more complicated timing scheme for switching from frequency to frequency. Also, there can be no alternating patterns in the hop sequence. This makes it far more difficult to hack, since both the timing and the sequence change. This is a far more secure method of sending data; however, it comes at the cost of speed.

NETWORKING OVER MICROWAVES

No, we haven't come up with a scheme forcing everybody in the world to interconnect their microwave ovens. However, the same technology that bakes your potato or heats up your frozen burrito can also be used to send data. And it can send that data across extremely long distances. The key here is that microwave transmission requires that the sender and the receiver have a direct line-of-sight communications link. And unlike radio, you can't bounce the signal off the atmosphere.

Microwave networking comes in two flavors, terrestrial microwave and satellite microwave. As the names suggest, terrestrial microwave is ground-based, while satellite microwave bounces the signal off of a satellite orbiting in space.

- *Terrestrial microwave*: This is the technology that results in all those parabolic antennae that sit on top of the roof of all those federal agencies, such as NSA or the CIA. They are also used on the corporate level as a replacement for bounded WAN media. Microwave transmission requires direct line of sight, so the height of the antenna directly affects distance of transmission.

- *Satellite microwave*: You've all seen those spy movies where the good guy rolls out of his or her inflatable raft and sets up the little tiny antenna that looks like an umbrella. He or she points it at the sky and in mere moments is in contact with headquarters. This is the director's sorry attempt to accurately represent satellite microwave technology at work. All you need in order to set up a satellite link is to have the appropriate frequency assigned to you and the right equipment. Since there are multiple satellites in orbit that are capable of bouncing your signal, there are precious few (if any) places on the surface of the planet that you won't be able to receive the signal. The distances involved will generate something called a propogation delay. This is the amount of time that elapses from the time you send your signal out, have it travel 50,000 miles to the nearest satellite, bounce off and travel 50,000 miles to your intended recipient, get the reply, and follow the same path back. This results in delays of up to several seconds. Also, unlike in those movies I mentioned, the lock on the satellite must be accurate. You can't really just point the cute little antenna at the sky and automatically find a signal.

Whichever method you choose, you're going to spend a pretty good chunk of change on the hardware you need, an assigned frequency, and the licensed operators you need to keep the system up and running. This is not "basic" networking technology and your average network engineer is going to give you a very blank, or possibly horrified, look if you ask him or her to troubleshoot a downed link.

OTHER NETWORKING HARDWARE

Throughout this discussion, I have mentioned that networks can grow almost infinitely if the right equipment is used. When discussing the different media types, I pointed out the distance limitations of each type. Yet, if those limitations were etched in stone, with no way of extending these boundaries, the Internet would not exist. Corporations would not be interconnected across continents. The following is a brief overview of some other networking components you might bump into from time to time.

REPEATERS

One of the more basic devices is the repeater. Since copper-based media has relatively short maximum runs, there needed to be a way of extending that distance. A *repeater* is a device that intercepts the signal, filters out any noise that has been picked up along the way, and then amplifies the signal back to its original strength. There is a bit of a limitation to the number of repeaters that can be used on a network, however. The 5-4-3 rule states that there can be up to five network segments interconnected, using four repeaters or active hubs (see the next section), as long as only three of those segments actually have devices installed. Still, they're good when you need to run twisted-pair cable beyond the 100 meters for which it is capable.

HUBS

Hubs are devices that interconnect several other devices on a star network. They generally consist of a rectangular box with several RJ-45 sockets (or BNC on some older models). **Figure 18.9** is an example of a small office/home office (SOHO) hub that can interconnect four computers on a network.

Hubs can be either passive or active. The passive hub is the most basic hub available. It simply takes a signal coming in from any one of its ports and broadcasts that signal out all ports, including the one from whence it came. An active hub doubles as a repeater. Therefore, before rebroadcasting a signal, it cleans it up and amplifies it back to original strength.

While this may superficially seem to be a minor difference, it can have a great impact on the

Buzz Words

Repeater: A device that cleans up, amplifies, and retransmits a signal, effectively increasing the distance data can travel over any given medium.

Hub: A device that interconnects multiple hosts on a star network over a single segment.

maximum physical dimensions of a network. With a passive RJ-45 hub, two devices can only have 100 meters of wire separating them. Therefore, if one device is 75 meters from the hub and the other device is 50 meters from the hub, the total distance exceeds the capabilities of the medium. They won't see each other. With an active hub, each device can be up to 100 meters from the hub and still communicate.

Figure 18.9   A four port hub

SWITCHES

Superficially, *switches* don't look that much different than hubs. From an engineering standpoint, they're quite different. As I said earlier, a hub simply rebroadcasts any signal it receives out through all ports. It can't pick and choose. Also, a hub is shared bandwidth. If I have twenty-four devices hooked up to a 24-port 100Mb/s hub, those twenty-four devices are competing for the same 100Mb of bandwidth. On a 100Mb switch, each port represents a separate 100Mb segment. Also, the switch maintains a database of all host addresses that exist downstream of any given port. When the switch receives a signal from one port, it scans its database, locates the correct port for the intended host, and transmits that signal only through that port. Devices on the other ports don't have to deal with transmissions not intended for them.

As a result, network congestion can be significantly decreased when switches are used in place of hubs whenever possible. A relatively large network can be created using switches as well. On a 24-port switch, each port can host a 24-port hub. You now have up to 576 devices on the network, but only twenty-four of them will be competing for bandwidth on any given segment. Each port would represent a separate collision domain. A collision domain is simply a segment of the network on which it is possible for the devices on that segment to interfere with one another.

If you tried that same trick using a hub in place of the switch, you would have all 576 devices competing for the same bandwidth, and the entire network is a single collision domain. The lack of overall bandwidth and the frequency of collisions will result in an unbearably slow network. Replacing the central hub with a switch will greatly improve performance.

BRIDGES

Bridges are devices that interconnect two or more unlike networks. The networks may differ in topology or in platform. For example, if your network still has a couple of token ring segments in use, a bridge

BUZZ WORDS

Switch: A device that breaks a larger network down into smaller segments, isolating each segment into its own collision domain.

Bridge: A device that interconnects two networks or segments of a network with different topologies or different platforms together.

will be necessary to interconnect the token ring segments to the Ethernet network. Also, a bridge might be in order if a Macintosh network is trying to interconnect with a PC network.

A bridge can be a dedicated piece of hardware or it can be a piece of software running on a server. In order to reduce the performance hit that a software-based implementation will incur, it is best to use a hardware solution whenever possible.

ROUTERS

Routers are used to interconnect two or more completely different networks to one another. As with

BUZZ WORDS ————————

Router: A device that interconnects two autonomous networks into a single larger network.

Default gateway: The route through which all packets that contain addresses that the transmitting device cannot resolve will be sent.

Topology: The method through which a network is physically wired.

switches and hubs, routers will have several different interconnects. Unlike switches and hubs, these interconnects are likely to be of different types. RJ-45 jacks will be required for the internal LAN, but different connections may be required in order to interconnect with telecommunications equipment and/or other routers in the network.

Each port can be configured to a different network address. Internally, the router maintains a list of all network addresses that exist downstream of each port. This list is known as the routing tables. When the router receives a packet, it examines the header for the network address and then compares that address to its tables. If it finds the address listed, it simply forwards the packet through the appropriate port. If not, it forwards the packet through the port that the administrator has configured to be the default gateway. The *default gateway* is the path to the next router downstream. It then becomes the responsibility of the next router to figure out what to do with that packet.

When discussing switches, I pointed out that each port on a switch was an independent collision domain. With routers, each port becomes an independent broadcast domain. Devices on a network are constantly sending out broadcasts to all devices on the network for many different reasons. The larger the network becomes, the more congestion is caused by these broadcasts. Routers (unless configured to do so by the administrator) do not forward broadcasts. Therefore, a very large network can be subnetted into several smaller networks using routers. The broadcasts generated by any given subnet will not interfere with the other subnets.

NETWORK TOPOLOGIES

Networks themselves vary widely in how they are laid out, both logically and physically. The way a network is physically wired is its *topology*. No matter how complex the physical layout may look, it is actually going to fall under one of four categories. There are bus networks, ring networks, star networks, and mesh networks. This is the way they would be defined in that perfect world I keep fantasizing about. In the real world, you're going to find that many networks are mixtures of topologies. These are called hybrid networks.

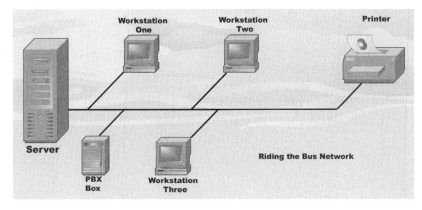

Figure 18.10   Layout of a typical bus network

BUS NETWORKS

These are the simplest networks to set up and the simplest to bring down. They're also among the simplest to understand. In the bus network, each computer is connected in a chain, just like that string of Christmas tree lights you had when you were a kid. The network cable runs from one computer or device to the next until you get to the last computer (see **Figure 18.10**).

This is a topology that is falling from favor for a couple of reasons. First off, in order to implement this network, you need to use coaxial cable. As I pointed out earlier in this chapter, this will limit you to 10Mb/s on your transmission speeds. Also, this network resembles that string of lights in more ways than just the symbolic. Remember how the whole string went out whenever one bulb died? That's what happens when one computer goes off the network. If Bob kicks his network cable off the back of his computer, the whole network goes down. Now nobody can print to the printer and nobody can share files. The computers themselves are working fine as stand-alones; you simply no longer have a network.

One of the things you have to keep in mind is that both ends of the network have to be terminated. Lose the termination, and you lose the network. Therefore, in Figure 18.10, the network adapters in the server and the printer will need terminating resistors plugged into the outbound ports of their T-connectors. On all other devices, both ends of the T-connections have cables hooked up.

Bus networks were reasonably efficient for small networks. Whether you were working with a peer-to-peer network or a client-server network was of no consequence. However, the larger the network becomes, the more cumbersome it is to manage. With one hundred people on a network, you have two hundred feet potentially kicking out connectors.

RING NETWORKS

For a while, it looked like the ring topology was on its way out as well. The most widely supported networking standard that made use of it was token ring, and token ring was going

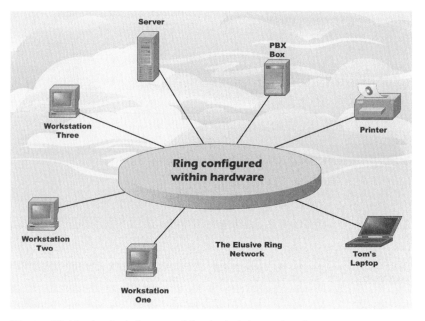

Figure 18.11 Logical diagram of the typical ring network

the way of the dinosaur. However, a newer technology, the fiber distributed data interface (FDDI), also makes use of the ring topology. (These different technologies will be discussed in detail later in the chapter.) Therefore, new life has been pumped into the topology.

The concept of the ring network is more logical than it is physical. **Figure 18.11** illustrates the physical implementation of a ring network. However, in the real world, the ring is incorporated into the hardware. Physically, the network more strongly resembles the star network that I will be discussing next.

Were the computers laid out in a physical ring, it would be just like a bus network. Bringing one computer off-line would bring down the network. However, in actual implementation, devices called multistation access units (MAUs) interconnect the devices. They look, feel, smell, and taste just like a typical hub in most respects. A cable runs from the computer to the MAU, just like it would to a hub. Internally, however, they are wired in a ring. The circuitry of an MAU can detect when a computer goes off-line and redirect the signal around the port that went down. Also, MAUs have two additional ports on the back, a ring in and a ring out. These aren't for hooking up telephones. They are the input and output connectors for interconnecting MAUs. They allow the network to be expanded without losing the logic of the ring.

STAR NETWORKS

Star networks are by far the most commonly implemented topology in today's networking environment. On the simplest level, as shown in **Figure 18.12**, a star can consist of a single hub

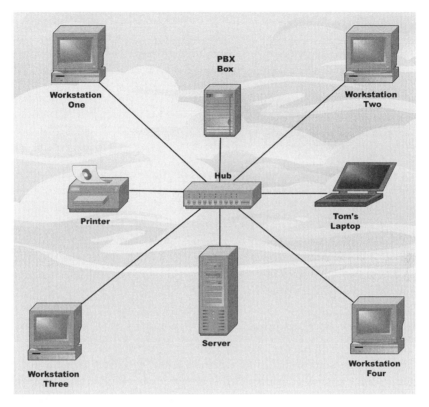

Figure 18.12 Layout of a typical star network

interconnecting devices. The beauty of the topology is that by using additional devices, such as routers and switches, networks can be as large and complex as necessity dictates.

Most administrators favor star networks because, regardless of geographic location of workstations and devices, the servers, hubs, routers, and so on can be centrally located. This greatly eases the administrative burden of larger networks. Troubleshooting is made easier as well. One of the easiest ways to tell if a workstation is physically connected when it is having trouble seeing the network is to check for "blinky lights." If both the NIC in the computer and the interface light at the hub are showing a link light, you have connectivity.

Star networks do require a more complex cabling scheme. Each workstation or other networked device needs to be wired to either a hub or switch. Hubs, switches, routers, and other devices all need to be interconnected. And somehow, you're expected to keep track of it all. A good topology map is a network administrator's best friend.

THE MESH NETWORK

The mesh network is one in which every single device in the network is directly linked by a dedicated circuit to every other device on the network. As you might imagine, the cabling infrastructure in a network of this nature would be extremely complex and confusing. Fortunately, it's really only used in a couple of places. The internal wiring of a router is basically a mesh network in a box. Also, there are certain network operating systems that allow the administrator to configure multiple servers to work together as though they were a single machine. This is known as a server cluster. Server clusters are frequently interconnected in a mesh.

THE OSI LAYERS AND IEEE

Networks are very complex and complicated mazes of computers, wires, and software. If every manufacturer was left to its own devices and allowed to make its own rules, there would be chaos. Fortunately, that is not the case. Two different organizations work hard to maintain standards that you can count on the manufacturers to follow. The International Organization for Standardization (ISO) came up with the Open Systems Interconnect (OSI) specifications. The Institute of Electrical and Electronic Engineers (IEEE) developed the 802 Standards Committees. These two organizations concentrate on different sets of standards that make the networking world a much nicer place to work.

THE OSI LAYERS

When you're looking at a network from a distance, especially a very complicated one such as the Internet, one thing stands out. It doesn't much matter what kind of computer you have, you still have access to the network. And all those files are there for you to use. One of the reasons this is possible is that data doesn't go across the wire as files. It is broken down and sent across as a stream of individual bits. In order to make sure the data gets put back together the right way, those bits are assembled into various packages that can be disassembled at one computer and reassembled at the next. ISO provided us with a set of standards that allows different platforms to break data down and put it back together in similar fashion. This is known as the OSI model. The OSI model is broken down into seven layers, as follows:

- *The Application Layer:* This layer provides a uniform interface for the applications running on a computer system to gain access to the network.
- *The Presentation Layer:* Here, the computers decide on what format they will use to transfer data. File formats such as JPEG, MP3, TIF, and others are managed at this layer. File compression is managed at this level as well.
- *The Session Layer:* Here is where the two computers set up and maintain a virtual connection while data is being exchanged.
- *The Transport Layer:* In this layer, data is broken down into smaller chunks called segments. In order to make sure the data goes from host to host without corruption, error-checking mechanisms are put into place. Another mechanism, called flow control, makes sure that both devices are sending and/or receiving data at a speed that is acceptable.

- *The Network Layer*: If you want to send somebody a letter, you need to know his or her address. Computers are the same way. The network layer handles addressing functions and makes sure a good route between hosts is maintained. It takes the segments made by the Transport Layer and packages them into frames.

- *The Data Link Layer*: You want to make sure that when you break data into a series of pieces, the pieces get put back together in the right order. You also want to make sure that every single piece got there. This is the job of the Data Link Layer. The Data Link Layer has been subdivided into the Logic Link Control (LLC) Layer and the Media Access Control (MAC) Layer.

- *The Physical Layer*: Of course, you don't send data over wires. You send electrical signals, or perhaps bursts of light. The Physical Layer takes the information and turns it into the signals that move across the wire.

The key to understanding the OSI layers is that they control neither how the hardware is manufactured, nor how software is written. Rather, they set specific rules as to how either one will communicate across a network.

THE IEEE 802 STANDARDS

In February of 1980, a group of engineers from several different areas of the industry got together to define networking standards. Because it was month two of year eighty, the standards that evolved from that conference have become known as the 802 standards. It should be noted that the numbers relate to the number of the committee assigned to research and implement standards under their jurisdiction. Each topology will fall under one of the following 802.x standards, as do certain key issues common to all topologies.

802.1   *AN/MAN Bridging and Management*: Covers different internetworking standards as well as the Spanning Tree Algorithm.

802.2   *Logic Link Control*: As its name suggests, this committee oversees the standards used by the LLC sublayer of the Data Link Layer. (Inactive)

802.3   *CSMA/CD Access Method*: Sometimes simply called Ethernet. This committee keeps up with the different advances in Ethernet technology.

802.4   *Token Passing Bus Access Method*: A bus network that used a token passing method of media access. (Inactive)

802.5   *Token Ring Access Method*: A ring network that uses a token passing method of media access. (Inactive)

802.6   *DQDB Access Method*: Distributed Queue Dual Bus access to media. (Disbanded)

802.7   *Broadband LAN*: A technology for building LANs using broadband technology instead of baseband technology. (Disbanded)

802.8   *The Fiber Optics Technical Advisory Group*: Oversees development of fiber optics solutions. (Disbanded)

802.9   *Isosynchronous LANs*: Frequently referred to as Integrated Voice/Data communications. (Inactive)

802.10 *Integrated Services*: Also known as Security. Administers development of methods by which access to the network and the transmission of data can be made secure. (Inactive)

802.11 *Wireless Networking*: Defines various methods of moving data without wires.

802.12 *Demand Priority Access*: Allows access to network media based on message priority. (Inactive)

802.14 *Standard Protocol for Cable TV-based Broadband Communications* (Disbanded)

802.15 *Working Group for Personal Area Networks*: Very short-range wireless networks.

802.16 *Broadband Wireless Access Standards*

802.17 *Resilient Packet Ring Working Group*: Uses fiber-optic ring networks and packet data transmission.

802.18 *Radio Regulatory Technical Advisory Group*

802.19 *Coexistence Technical Advisory Group*

802.20 *Mobile Broadband Wireless Access Working Group*

NAVIGATING THE HARDWARE PROTOCOLS

Once you enter the wild world of networking, you start getting a lot of strange names and acronyms thrown at you. Among these are things called protocols. A protocol is simply the collection of instructions that provide two devices a common method of talking to one another. One way you might look at this is what you might encounter if you were to take an international vacation. Once you got to Tibet, if you didn't understand the language, you couldn't communicate. But just as importantly, if you didn't understand their customs, you could find yourself in serious trouble, and fast!

Computers have the same problem. A Macintosh can't talk to a PC without a little help. Not only do the different platforms use a different language, but they also do things differently. Protocols act as your computer's translator. Protocols are employed on both a hardware level and a software level. Some of the various hardware protocols that I will discuss in this section include Ethernet, token ring, and FDDI. There are many others, but these are the most common, and this is a book on computer hardware, not networking.

ETHERNET

Ethernet started out in 1972 at Xerox Corporation when David Boggs and Robert Metcalfe worked out a method by which multiple devices could send signals across the same wire without interfering with each other. Xerox called on the expertise of Digital Equipment Corporation and Intel to help it in developing something that could be looked at as industry standard. They were fairly successful. In fact, you can still find references to the old DIX network (short for Digital, Intel, Xerox) in modern literature.

Ethernet, as we know it, looks a little different than it did back then. IEEE expanded on the DIX specifications and came up with the 802.3 standards of Carrier Sense, Multiple Access/ Collision Detection (CSMA/CD). It provided specifications for moving data across both twisted-pair cable and coaxial cable and also defined the terminators still used today. Later revisions of Ethernet include Fast Ethernet, which is a 100Mb/s system, and Gigabit Ethernet, a 1000Mb/s standard. But the key to Ethernet is CSMA/CD. Understanding just what that is will be easier if I break the phrase down into its components.

- *Carrier sense*: The computer gains access to the wire by listening for a moment of silence. It's the same thing you do when you're trying to merge onto a busy highway from the on-ramp. You wait for an empty spot and jump in.
- *Multiple access*: The freeway I'm talking about is designed for a lot of cars to travel on it, but only one can be in the lane at a time. Fortunately, they travel at the speed of light, just like that red convertible that cut me off this morning.
- *Collision detection*: If that red convertible jumps into the lane ahead of you just as you're moving in, you're going to have a collision. A collision on a network isn't quite so messy, however. The data is simply discarded. The offending computers send out a backoff algorithm, telling both computers to wait a randomly generated amount of time before sending again. That way, they will not collide with each other again. They'll probably collide with another computer, but at least they won't be exchanging phone numbers with each other again.

There are several Ethernet standards to choose from, ranging from 10Mb/s to the newer Gigabit Ethernet. The standards go by some rather arcane names, but once you understand the structure of the name, are actually pretty easy to understand (see **Figure 18.13**).

Here are some of the more commonly seen Ethernet types:

10BaseT   10Mb/s, Baseband, Twisted pair

10Base2   10Mb/s, Baseband, Thinnet (2 = 200 meters, which is rounded up from the actual 185 meters RG-58 cable will support)

10Base5   10Mb/s, Baseband, Thicknet (5 = 500 meters)

100BaseT   100Mb/s, Baseband, Twisted pair

100BaseT

100	**Base**	**T**
Bandwidth Kb/sec	Baseband Technology	Medium Used

Figure 18.13 Understanding Ethernet standards doesn't have to be that hard.

100BaseTX	100Mb/s, Baseband, Twisted pair using two data-grade pairs
100BaseFL	100Mb/s, Baseband, Fiber-optic cable
1000BaseT	1Gb/s, Baseband, Twisted pair

> **Buzz Words** ───────
>
> **Beaconing:** A process that occurs on a token ring network in which each station on the network sends a signal to its upstream neighbor and its downstream neighbor asking if it has seen the token lately.

Anyone planning to set up a home network or a SOHO network is going to be looking at Ethernet as the basis for that network. The equipment is the most reasonably priced and most widely supported of all the hardware protocols. Any of the major office-supply chains and/or consumer electronics chains carries two or more lines of each of the main components you'll need for setting up a network. Read on, and once I make my way through the technical folderol, I'll explain how to set up a small Ethernet star network, using Windows 98 and Windows 2000-based machines.

TOKEN RING

Token ring had its day in the sun, but for the most part, it is becoming a forgotten standard. As a networking standard, token ring started out as a brainchild of IBM back in the early 1970s. While there are some minor differences that are not even worth discussing, the IEEE 802.5 standard and IBM's token ring is pretty much the same thing.

While the ideology of the token ring network is based on the concept of a ring network, actual implementation is achieved in a physical star. In place of a hub, an MAU (described earlier) is used, which is wired internally to achieve a ring topology.

On a token ring network, the first computer to come on during the day becomes the token generator. In the event that a token is lost or discarded, it is up to the token generator to figure out that this has happened, and then generate a new token. The way it figures out that a problem has occurred is through a process called *beaconing*.

When a computer has gone an inordinately long time without its chance at the token, it sends a broadcast signal down the wire. This is the beacon. It is basically a message saying "Who is hogging the token!!??" In reply, each computer on the network, in turn, replies, "not me," "not me," "not me," until all of a sudden, there's a computer that doesn't respond. This usually means that either some user has turned off the machine without properly shutting it down or that the system simply crashed. The MAU will bypass the offending port, the token generator will generate a new token and send it down the wire, and all will be well again.

FDDI

Fiber distributed data interface takes up where token ring left off. Like token ring, it uses a token-passing deterministic approach to media access. FDDI, however, uses a dual-ring topology. A primary ring sends data in one direction, while a secondary ring provides for an alternate path in the event of a failure in the first ring. It was designed to use fiber optics as the transmission medium, which is where it gets its name. There are, however, implementations of FDDI that use copper cable as well. The latter is known as the copper distributed data interface (CDDI).

Stations on an FDDI network can be either dual-attached or single-attached stations. A dual-attached station is connected to both rings, while a single-attached station is connected only to the primary ring.

Dual-attached stations will be connected to the network via at least one A port, where they attach to the primary ring, and one B port, where they attach to the secondary ring. They may or may not also have one or more M ports installed. The M port is the port that a single-station unit uses to attach to the network. These hook up only to the primary ring.

When using fiber optics as a medium, very large networks over great distances are possible. There is a maximum distance of 2km (nearly a mile) that is permissible between stations. While current implementations of FDDI are 100Mb/s, the potential is there for much higher speeds.

NETWORKING PROTOCOLS

In order to get data to move from application to application and from one platform to another over the network, it is also necessary that the software have its own protocol. Software makes use of one of many different networking protocols. However, since this is simply an overview, I will cover only the ones commonly seen. Those will include NetBEUI, IPX/SPX, and TCP/IP.

NETBEUI

The term stands for NetBIOS Extended User Interface. Of course, understanding that presupposes that you already know that NetBIOS stands for Network Basic Input Output System. But then, you already knew that, didn't you?

NetBEUI is by far the easiest protocol to implement and to administer. It requires no specialized setup by the end user other than making sure that every computer on the network has its own unique computer name, and that each of the computers that are supposed to talk to each other are all on the same workgroup. You can do this in Windows 9x by going to the Control Panel, double-clicking Network, and clicking Identification. You'll get a screen like the one shown in **Figure 18.14**. In Windows 2000, you get here by going to the System applet in Control Panel. The screen looks slightly different, but not enough to create confusion. All else being correctly set up, your computer is now on the network.

One of the biggest limitations of NetBEUI is that it is not a routable protocol. When a NetBEUI packet hits a router it's like hitting a brick wall. It goes no further. Therefore, as an internetworking protocol, it's useless. It can only be used on networks that are limited to single physical locations.

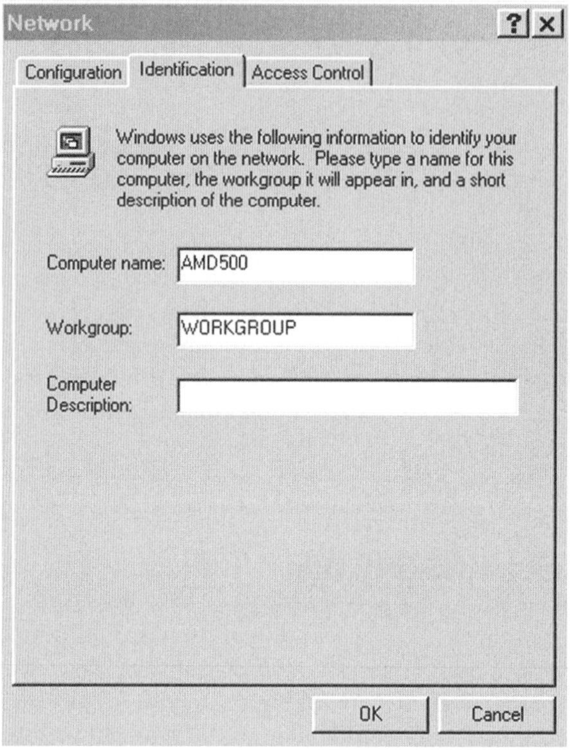

Figure 18.14 Setting the Identification and Workgroup in Windows

IPX/SPX

The Internet Packet Exchange/Sequenced Packet Exchange (IPX/SPX) was for several years the default protocol for Novel's NetWare. Like NetBEUI, it is very easy to install and configure. Since it makes use of the actual hardware address of your network card for addressing, there are no special configurations required. The only thing you really have to watch for is if you have multiple adapters on a single machine. Then, the internal address needs to be unique for each adapter. Microsoft users will find an IPX compatible protocol in the form of NWLink.

As I mentioned before, every network card in the world has (or is supposed to have, anyway) a hardware address that is unique to it and only it. This is a 48-bit address. 24 bits are used as the manufacturer's ID and will be the same for everything that manufacturer puts out. (I would be remiss in my duties were I not to mention that some of the larger manufacturers, such as 3Com, have multiple manufacturer ID numbers.) The other 24 bits are used for a unique serial number for that particular card.

IPX makes use of a 32-bit network address and adds the 48-bit hardware address to make a computer's overall address. This 80-bit address becomes the computer's official identification on the network. Because there is not a great deal of address/name resolution required, IPX has very little memory and CPU overhead. Therefore, it's a fast protocol. It's also fully routable.

TCP/IP

The Transmission Control Protocol/Internet Protocol (TCP/IP) is the protocol of choice for the Internet. There are a good many reasons for this. The biggest reason of all is that it provides a hierarchical scheme for addressing that allows for very large networks with a minimal number of hop points to get to a given host on the network.

BUZZ WORDS ———————

Subnet mask: A configuration setting within TCP/IP that identifies to the system what part of an IP address is the network address and what part is the host address.

TCP/IP uses a logical address known as the IP address rather than a physical one. This logical address consists of a 32-bit address that is broken down into four octets (an octet being the eight bits that make up that particular byte). These octets appear to the end user in decimal form, as shown in **Figure 18.15**. The address is divided into two sections. One part of the IP address is the network address and the other half is the host address. When data is transmitted from one computer to the other, TCP/IP breaks the information down into packets before sending it across the wire. Each packet contains the sending computer's IP address as well as the intended recipient's address.

Another component of the TCP/IP configuration is called the *subnet mask*. This tells the computer which part of the address is the network address and which part is the host address. The part of the subnet mask represented by the number 255 covers the network address.

For every IP address, there must be an associated subnet mask. A subnet mask basically tells the system what part of the IP address is the network address and what part is the host address.

There are five different classes of TCP/IP address, but networks use only three of them. The other two types of address are for specialized purposes. The three types commonly used are Class A, Class B, and Class C addresses.

- *Class A addresses*: In a Class A address, only the first octet is used for a network address. The remaining three octets are used for host addresses, and the default subnet mask is 255.0.0.0. The range of addresses starting with 10.*.*.* are reserved for private addressing and cannot be exposed to public traffic.

- *Class B addresses*: Class B addresses use the first two octets for the network address and the last two for a host address. The default subnet mask is 255.255.0.0. All addresses between 172.16.0.0 and 172.31.255.255 are set aside for private use.

- *Class C addresses*: The first three octets identify the network and the last octet identifies host addresses. The default subnet mask is 255.255.255.0 The range of addresses reserved for private use is 192.168.0.0 to 192.168.255.255.

$$192 \quad 168 \quad 144 \quad 17$$
$$11000000 \ 10101000 \ 10010000 \ 00010001$$

Figure 18.15 This is what a 32-bit TCP/IP address looks like. It's a series of binary numbers that represent groupings of zeros and ones.

This is only the briefest overview of TCP/IP. As a subject, the protocol has been the subject of many books, some of them quite huge. In my view, the best of these books is Craig Zacker's *TCP/IP Administration*.

CHAPTER SUMMARY

While this may have seemed like a long and complex chapter, in truth, I merely exposed you to the proverbial tip of the iceberg when it comes to networking. Because this is a book on hardware, my greatest concentration was in that arena. Still, I thought it would be a good idea if you had at least a basic introduction to the protocols of networking as well.

Protocols are divided into hardware protocols and networking protocols. Don't be fooled into thinking I covered all of them in this chapter. That would require a textbook in and of itself. I introduced you to the most commonly used protocols, both in the area of hardware and networking. If you're interested in a more complete discussion, refer to my book *The Complete Guide to Networking and Network+*, also from Thomson/Delmar Learning.

BRAIN DRAIN

1. Should you desire to set up a small network in your home, what would be the bare necessities you would need to get up and running?

2. Describe the difference between bounded and unbounded media and give examples of each.

3. In detail, discuss the difference between a collision domain and a broadcast domain.

4. Define the term beaconing and describe the process in detail.

5. Discuss the differences between hardware protocols and networking protocols.

THE 64K$ QUESTIONS

1. The maximum distance twisted-pair cable can be run without assistance is

   _____.

   a. 100 feet

   b. 100 meters

   c. 185 meters

   d. 500 meters

2. The maximum distance coaxial cable can be run without assistance is

   _____.

   a. 100 feet

   b. 100 meters

   c. 185 meters

   d. 500 meters

3. The proper device for interconnecting a token ring network segment to an Ethernet segment is a _____.

   a. Repeater

   b. MAU

   c. Switch

   d. Bridge

4. A(n) _____ doubles as a repeater.

   a. Passive hub

   b. Switch

   c. Router

   d. Active hub

5. In order to interconnect two autonomous networks into a single larger network, you would need a _____.

   a. Passive hub

   b. Switch

   c. Router

   d. Active hub

6. The term CSMA/CD stands for _____.

   a. Collision sensing media access/Carrier detection

   b. Carrier secured multiple access/Collision detection

   c. Carrier sense multiple access/Collision detection

   d. Common sensing media access/Collision detection

7. Two hardware protocols that make use of a ring topology are _____ and _____. (Pick two.)

   a. CSMA/CD

   b. Ethernet

   c. FDDI

   d. Token ring

8. Bus networks typically made use of STP cabling.

   a. True

   b. False

9. The protocol of choice for the Internet is _____.

   a. NetBEUI

   b. IPX/SPX

   c. TCP/IP

   d. FDDI

10. 192.168.0.110 is an example of a _____ address.

    a. Class A

    b. Class B

    c. Class C

    d. Class D

TRICKY TERMINOLOGY

Beaconing: A process that occurs on a token ring network in which each station on the network sends a signal to its upstream neighbor and its downstream neighbor asking if it has seen the token lately.

Bounded media: Any medium that physically connects a device to the network by way of a tangible cable.

Bridge: A device that interconnects two networks or segments of a network of different topologies or different platforms together.

Client: Any device or software that requires the services of another device or piece of software in order to perform its function.

Coaxial: A cable over which the signal and ground both follow the same axis.

Credentials: On a network, these consist of the user ID and password that provides network access for the user.

Crossover cable: A network patch cord that routes the transmit signal from one device to the receive terminals on the other device.

Default gateway: The route through which all packets that contain addresses that the transmitting device cannot resolve will be sent.

Hub: A device that interconnects multiple hosts on a star network over a single segment.

Media: The substance or energy wave over which a data signal is transmitted.

Multimode fiber: A fiber-optic strand that moves multiple signals through the core.

Permissions: Resource access or actions for which a particular user is allowed.

Repeater: A device that cleans up, amplifies, and retransmits a signal, effectively increasing the distance data can travel over any given medium.

Router: A device that interconnects two autonomous networks into a single larger network.

Server: Any device or software that provides services to other devices or pieces of software that need them.

Single-mode fiber: A fiber optics strand that moves only a single signal through the core.

Subnet Mask: A configuration setting within TCP/IP that identifies to the system what part of an IP address is the network address and what part is the host address.

Switch: A device that breaks a larger network down into smaller segments, isolating each segment into its own collision domain.

Thicknet: A name commonly given to RG-8 coaxial cable.

Thinnet: A name commonly given to RG-58U coaxial cable.

Topology: The method through which a network is physically wired.

Tranceiver: Any device that is designed to be able to either transmit or receive data.

Unbounded media: Any medium that connects the device to the network using energy forms that travel through air and/or space.

Vampire clamp: A device consisting of two halves that screw together. One half is fitted with sharp teeth that bite through the insulation of RG-8 cable.

ACRONYM ALERT

AUI: Attachment Unit Interface

CDDI: Copper Distributed Data Interface

CSMA/CD: Carrier Sense, Multiple Access/Collision Detection

DIX: Digital, Intel, Xerox

EIA: Electronics Industry Association

FCC: Federal Communications Commission

FDDI: Fiber Distributed Data Interface

HPSF: High Power Single Frequency

IPX/SPX: Internetwork Packet Exchange/ Sequenced Packet Exchange. An early Novell networking protocol.

ISO: International Standards Organization

LAN: Local Area Network

LLC: Logic Link Control

LPSF: Low Power Single Frequency

MAC: Media Access Control

MAU: Multistation Access Unit. A device similar to a hub that interconnects hosts on a token ring network.

NetBEUI: NetBIOS Extended User Interface. An early Microsoft networking protocol.

NIC: Network Interface Card

OSI: Open Standards Interconnect. A seven-layer model for developing networking standards.

P2P: Peer to Peer. A network on which all hosts are equals.

STP: Shielded Twisted Pair

TCP/IP: Transmission Control Protocol/ Internet Protocol. The protocol of choice for the Internet.

TIA: Telecommunications Industry Association

UHF: Ultrahigh Frequency

UTP: Unshielded Twisted Pair

VHF: Very High Frequency

WAN: Wide Area Network

CHAPTER 19

TELECOMMUNICATIONS

These days people take the Internet for granted. In fact, while I haven't taken any formal surveys, based on the service work I've done, I would guess that well over half the PCs owned by individuals are used more as Internet appliances than they are as work tools. Corporate culture has learned to rely on electronic communications as well. People want to get on the Internet, and companies want all their offices to talk to one another. So one of the questions that was raised in the early days of computing was, "How can we get computers on different sides of the country to talk to one another?"

The government had been connecting computers over secure telephone lines for several years by the time Dennis Hayes invented the first PC modem in 1977. In 1978 they began to ship in quantity. From that day forth, the world as we knew it changed. It wasn't too long after that before there were electronic bulletin boards, and then electronic mail. Now the Internet owns everything, or so it seems. How many times have you purchased an item that carried a rebate, and found that you had to process it online? My friends, we've only seen the beginning!

A+ EXAM OBJECTIVES

In this chapter, I'm going to address several different technologies used by computers in order to remotely communicate. In doing so, the following A+ objectives will be covered:

1.2 Identify basic procedures for adding and removing field-replaceable modules for desktop systems. Given a replacement scenario, choose the appropriate sequences. (Modems)

1.4 Identify typical IRQs, DMAs, and I/O addresses and procedures for altering these settings when installing and configuring devices. Choose the appropriate installation or configuration steps in a given scenario. (Modems)

1.5 Identify the names, purposes, and performance characteristics of standardized/common peripheral ports, associated cabling, and their connectors. Recognize ports, cabling, and connectors by sight. (RJ-11)

1.8   Identify proper procedures for installing and configuring common peripheral devices. Choose the appropriate installation or configuration sequences in given scenarios. (Modems)

2.1   Recognize common problems associated with each module and their symptoms, and identify steps to isolate and troubleshoot the problems. Given a problem situation, interpret the symptoms and infer the most likely cause. (Modems and sound card)

Modems

The term modem (**Figure 19.1**) is derived from its original name of modulator/demodulator. It is a device that takes digital data in binary form and sends it over a telephone wire as electrical signals. In order to accomplish this, a modem has two tricks to perform. First of all, it has to be able to convert data from digital form to analog waveforms. Second, since the modem is moving data over the line using serial communications, the data needs to be converted from parallel to serial. A device called the Universal Asynchronous Receiver Transmitter (UART) handles the serial/parallel conversions. A DAC, very much like the one I introduced in Chapter Sixteen, Multimedia, is responsible for digital/analog and analog/digital conversions.

As a device, the computer treats the modem pretty much like any other I/O device. In the early days, because modems are serial devices, they were assigned a COM port. Therefore, a preset IRQ and I/O allocation was standard for most modems. Over the years that has changed, and it isn't uncommon to see modems grabbing resources not common to the standard COM port settings.

In all other respects, it's a typical I/O device. But it's one that has to convert data from serial format to parallel and from digital to analog. Let's say you're chatting with a friend over the Internet. You type a letter and the keyboard turns the action into a series of zeros and ones that are processed and sent to the modem. The UART breaks the bytes down into bits and the DAC converts the bits into the frequencies outlined above. **Figure 19.2** shows the waveforms of two modems working in duplex mode.

Figure 19.1   Today's modems transfer data at rates that approach 200x that of the one Dennis Hayes gave to the public back in 1978. And people still are not happy.

Converting Data to Electrical Signals

Early modems worked by using a frequency-shifting key. Using this technique, the modem that initiates communication became the *originate modem*. The modem that answers the call was called, oddly enough, the *answer modem*. The two modems operated across separate frequency ranges. The originate modems sent zeros at 1070Hz and ones at 1270Hz. The answer modem used 2.025Hz and 2225Hz, respectively.

Because frequencies between the two modems were different, it was possible to design modems that could transmit and receive at the same time. This is known as *full duplex* operation. Any device that can only send or receive at any given time is *half duplex*. There have been in the past some specialized devices that were designed to send data only or to receive data only. They could not do both. This type of communication is known as *simplex*. **Figure 19.3** represents signals transferring back and forth between two modems using duplex operation.

Unfortunately, this method wasn't very conducive to high-speed communications. Something a

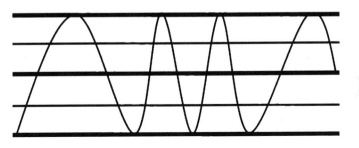

Figure 19.2 Frequency shifting in modem transmissions results in waveforms that look something like this.

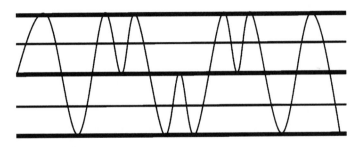

Figure 19.3 Phase-shifting modulation keeps the frequencies the same but changes the time of the phases to encode data.

little more sophisticated was needed. From frequency-shift keying, modems moved into phase-shift keying. As you saw in Figure 19.2, the electrical signal in a typical frequency-shifting scheme transmits a signal over a nice clean sine wave. Each wave cycle has two phases. One of those phases is the time in which the signal represents positive voltage. This is known as the rising end of the signal. The other phase is when the signal dips down into the negative range. Under phase-shift keying, the frequency of the signal doesn't change. The modem alters the waveforms in order to manipulate the phases.

The phases can be a full phase, a three-quarter phase, a half-phase, or a one-quarter phase. Each of the phases possible on the positive end of the frequency range represents four bits, and as you might imagine, the other four bits come from the negative spectrum.

Quadrature amplitude modulation (QAM) is a 24-carat term that simply describes a hybrid of frequency shift and phase-shift keying. Because phase and frequency can both be modified, more data can be crammed into a single wave cycle.

THE UART

The other job the modem has is to get the data from the native parallel format used by the computer into serial form so it can go out over the wire. On the receiving end, it has to do the opposite. That is the function of the universal asynchronous receiver transmitter. That's a bit of a mouthful for just about anybody, so it is simply called a UART (pronounced you-art).

Every serial device needs a dedicated UART in order to do its job. Later in the chapter, when I discuss ISDN and DSL, you can rest assured that a UART is handling serial/parallel conversions. Your computer generally comes with two serial ports, although in recent models, there has been a propensity to ship systems with only a single serial port. On the earliest PCs, the UART was a chip soldered onto the motherboard. The first IBM PC used an 8250 chip for each serial port. This chip had no buffering capability and therefore was painfully slow. Also, it had enough bugs in the design to populate the Amazon River basin and was quickly replaced by the 8250A. Which wasn't a whole lot better, by the way. **Table 19.1** lists the UARTs commonly used by serial modems or other telecommunications devices.

UARTs are very common chips and are used on a wide variety of serial devices. It would be a misrepresentation to let you think that only the few that I discussed when talking about modems are all that ever existed. A quick search of the Internet turned up over 300 different models of UART by a number of different manufacturers.

Most current modems ship with 16550A UARTs. It isn't uncommon for system boards and supplemental I/O cards to have 16750, 16850, or even 16950 chips installed. The device will dictate the type of UART required.

TRANSMITTING DATA OVER THE WIRE

Which brings me to the difference between bits per second (bps) and baud rate. In the days of frequency-shift keying, transmission speeds were limited to the frequency of the signal traveling across the telephone wire. The telephone companies, for some reason, were resistant to changing the way they sent voice across the wire just so users could have faster modems. The frequency

Table 19.1   UART Comparison Chart

UART	Buffer	Throughput	Comments
8250	None	19.2Kbps	Very buggy and short-lived
8250A	None	19.2Kbps	Fixed some of the bugs, but not all; slightly faster than the 8250
8250B	None	19.2Kbps	Finally got the 8250 series to work just in time for the 16450 to come out
16450	None	38.4Kbps	16-bit UART; buggy and still no buffer
16550	16 bytes	115.2Kbps	Problems with chip
16550A	16 bytes	115.2Kbps	Fixed bugs from the 16550; still commonly used today
16650	32 bytes	460.8Kbps	Programmable flow control and high speed throughput
16750	64 bytes send/56 bytes receive	921.6Kbps	Developed by Texas Instruments
16850	128 bytes	1.5Mbps	Has onboard infrared serial decoder
16950	128 bytes	3Mbps	Found on high-end multiport serial devices

The speed of the UART directly dictates the maximum speed of a serial device.

they chose was ~3400Hz. That is referred to as the *baud rate*. That's the actual frequency of the carrier signal going over the wire.

For several years, baud rate and bps were, for all intents and purposes, the same thing, because frequency-shift keying could only send one signal per wave cycle. The old 300bps modems were simply not making use of the full frequency spectrum available on the telephone line. When manufacturers made the move from 300 baud to 1200 baud, they started using half of the bandwidth available, and at 2400bps, while they weren't using the full bandwidth of the telephone line, they were going as fast as they could go using the binary values by which data is measured. At that point in time frequency-shift modulation was no longer an option if they wanted faster speeds.

That's where phase shift and QAM come into play. They both allow for more than one bit of data to be transmitted on a single wave cycle. This means that it is no longer accurate to refer to your modem as 56,000 baud. It isn't. It is still only 2400 baud, but it is theoretically capable

BUZZ WORDS —————

Baud rate: The electronic frequency over which data is transmitted.

Bit rate: The speed at which data travels over the wire, usually expressed in bits per second (bps) or kilobits per second (Kbps). Don't confuse this with bytes per second, and don't confuse it with baud rate.

Transmission rate: The number of bits per second that is being transmitted.

of transmitting 56,000 bits per second. In practical use, modems can't reach the theoretical maximum. But I'll get into that a little later.

This makes it sound like your data is moving over the telephone wire as individual bits. In reality, modems work a lot like network cards. Data is broken up into pieces and sent across the wire. What kind of pieces get sent depends entirely upon the communications session that is established between two modems. The two types of session are asynchronous and synchronous transmission.

ASYNCHRONOUS TRANSMISSION

Asynchronous mode is sometimes referred to as a connectionless communication. This doesn't mean you don't have some form of connection established between the two hosts. Obviously, that is not the case, or you wouldn't be able to communicate. It simply means that the originate modem throws its data onto the wire and assumes it will reach its intended destination.

In asynchronous mode, each byte of data is sent, one byte at a time. It is packaged into an "envelope" that consists of the data tucked in between a start bit and a stop bit. Accompanying each byte of data are another two bits that keep the clock cycles of the sending and receiving modems synchronized.

A key disadvantage to asynchronous transmission is that there are no error correction mechanisms in place to assure the integrity of the data. Parity (see Chapter Eight, Searching Your Memory) can be used to detect an error, but nothing can be done to correct it.

The reason it continues to exist as a transmission method is that some forms of communication work best in this manner. If you're just chatting with a friend over the Internet or browsing, it works fine. On the other hand, if you download a service pack for your NOS, you probably want to be sure that your data is arriving intact. For this type of communication you are much better off using. . .

SYNCHRONOUS TRANSMISSION

That service pack might be 30MB long, and it's going to take a long time to move it across the telephone wires to get it from one computer to the other. You can rest assured that quite a large number of blocks of data will be lost along the way. You need a way of determining when that happens and also a way of fixing the problem.

Synchronous transmission sends data across the wire in *message blocks*. A file is broken down into smaller chunks and sent out over the wire. On the receiving end, those piece are reassembled into the correct order. Each message block consists of several portions, as shown in **Figure 19.4**.

Direction of Data Travel

Figure 19.4 A synchronous message block is broken down into several key sections.

SYN: *Synchronization character.* This makes sure all the bytes in the frame stick together as they move across the wire and then get reassembled in the right order at the other end. If no data is being transmitted, SYN blocks can be transmitted to keep the session alive.

SOH: *Start of Header.* A header is not always used, but is an important part of most protocols.

HEADER: Placed into message block by protocol and can include information such as the sending computer's IP address, the intended recipient's IP address, and so forth.

STX: *Start of Text.* Pretty self-explanatory. It tells you that the next series of bits is the data being sent.

TEXT: The data

ETX: *End of Text.* Okay, I'm done sending text in this block. The next bytes are more control information.

BCC: *The Block Check Character.* Includes error detection and correction data, which may include parity (rarely used these days), checksum (on its way out), or cyclical redundancy check (the most common method in use today).

EOT: *End of Transmission.* I hope I don't have to explain that one.

All of this additional information is used by the system to make sure data gets where it's going and gets there intact. Two key sections that I will take a closer look at are the SYN and BCC blocks.

The primary purpose of the SYN block is synchronization of the session. It carries information that allows the two modems to keep the session alive. A key issue in telecommunications is packet loss. You spend all that money on a nice fast modem and then discover you're leaving behind 20 to 30 percent of the data you send, only to have to resend it. Packet loss kills bandwidth. For every message block that gets corrupted in transit, the intended recipient must send a NACK. While this makes sure the data is resent, it adds even more congestion to the session.

The BCC blocks carry information that allow for error detection and correction. Over the years there have been three major error correction mechanisms used, but only two remain commonplace in synchronous communication. An older method, still used by asynchronous communication, is parity checking. The two methods commonly used in synchronous sessions are checksum and cyclical redundancy check (CRC).

Parity Checking   I discussed parity checking in Chapter Eight, Searching Your Memory. Unlike RAM, however, which uses only odd parity, modems can be set to use either even parity or odd parity. If odd parity is selected, the number of ones in a byte are counted. If there is an even number of ones, the parity bit is set to one, making it an odd number. If there is already an odd number of ones, the parity bit is set to zero. In either case, with odd parity, at the

Odd Parity

Figure 19.5   Parity checking at work

receiving end there should always be an odd number (see **Figure 19.5**). With even parity, there should always be an even number of ones.

Unlike the parity checking mechanism used by early RAM, errors detected by modems do not shut the computer down. They result in a NACK packet being returned to the originating computer, requesting that the corrupted packet be resent.

The problem inherent with parity checking across telephone lines is that noisy lines have a tendency to cause a lot of distortion. It is quite possible for a message block to drop a one here and gain a one somewhere else. The parity checks out fine, but you've got two corrupted bits and not just one. In asynchronous transmissions, where only a byte at a time is going across the wire, parity can still be an effective error checking mechanism.

Checksum and CRC   Checksum and CRC are error checking and correction schemas that work well with large blocks of data. Under *checksum*, the number of ones in the message block is simply added up. The result is stored in the BCC and off goes the data. On the receiving end, your computer adds up the ones and if the answer it gets matches what is stored in the BCC, all is considered to be well. The packet is accepted and an ACK is sent out.

Buzz Words ————

Checksum: An error detection/correction mechanism that works by counting the number of ones present in the payload and storing that value in the BCC block of the packet.

Of course, if along the line the message block picked up two ones someplace and lost two ones someplace else, then the checksum results are "accurate" and a corrupt packet is accepted. This is not good. Another possibility is that the data in the checksum itself might become corrupted and report perfectly good packets as being bad. At least in the latter case, the worst that happens is that the packet is unnecessarily resent.

CRC performs a complex mathematical equation on the block. It treats the entire message block as if it were a single very large binary number. A rather complex mathematical equation is performed on the number the message block represents and the results of that equation are stored in the BCC. On the receiving end, the process is repeated. If the results match, the packet is accepted. The mathematical possibilities of any bits being shifted and still yielding the same CRC are rather minute. In fact, you could consider them to fall somewhere between slim and nonexistent.

SOH AND THE HEADER

Another key issue is that the protocol of the Internet is TCP/IP. In order to move data across the wire, TCP/IP encapsulates the message block into a TCP/IP packet. TCP/IP packets have their own header and trailer information that is required in order to get data from one place to another.

The SOH block indicates that the following bits of data are going to be a header of some sort (not specifically TCP/IP, but across the Internet it will usually be). A little earlier I was talking about the futility of having a high-speed connection if too many of your packets were being lost. One feature designed into TCP/IP is the ability to detect packet loss. The two primary reasons for packet loss are congestion and poor line conditions. In either case, it's better to slow the transmission down than to lose too many packets. Lower transmission rates where the data is accurately sent are much more efficient than having to fill a high-speed wire with the same messages over and over again.

SOME MODEM TERMINOLOGY

Modem aficionados have their own collection of buzz words that set them apart from normal people. Unless you know some of the terms they use, figuring out what the guy on the other line is trying to tell you can be pretty challenging. While the following list of terms is by no means all encompassing, it should give you a pretty decent start.

- *Bell 103*: 300 bps U.S. standard
- *Bell 212A*: 1200 bps U.S. standard
- *Compression*: The process of reducing information in data storage or transmission by the elimination of redundant elements. Various compression protocols have evolved over the years. Most current modems use V.90bis as the data compression method of choice.
- *Firmware*: Similar to the computer's BIOS, this is built-in software stored on a ROM chip that controls the operation of a dedicated, microprocessor-based device.

- *Flash ROM*: A type of memory used for firmware in modems and other digital devices. Unlike conventional ROM (read-only memory), flash ROM can be erased and reprogrammed, making it possible to update a product's firmware without replacing memory chips.

- *International Telecommunications Union (ITU)*: The agency in charge of overseeing telecommunications sponsored by United Nations. The ITU is charged with establishing and coordinating standards for electronic communications worldwide.

- *ISDN*: Integrated Services Digital Network; an all-digital replacement for analog telephone service. ISDN provides two 64 kbps channels, which can be combined or used independently for both voice and data.

- *K56flex*: A protocol, jointly developed by Lucent Technologies and Rockwell International Corp., to achieve 56 kbps modem transmissions over ordinary phone lines. K56flex requires that the host device (at an ISP or online service) be connected to a minimum of an ISDN or preferably a T1 line. K56flex allows downloads at up to 53.3 kbps, uploads are limited to the normal V.34 speed of 33.6 kbps. See x2.

- *MNP*: Microcom Networking Protocol (Proprietary)

- *T1*: A digital phone line that provides up to twenty-four channels of data at 64 kbps. A fractional T1 is one or several of those channels connected to form a singular link. T1 lines can carry data or digital telephone signals and are commonly used for high-speed WAN connections between offices.

- *V.32*: 9600bps, 4800bps

- *V.32bis*: 14.4kbps, 12kbps, 9600bps, 7200bps, 4800bps

- *V.32terbo*: Pseudo-standard extending V.32bis to 16.8 and 19.2kbps. Never really took off.

- *V.34*: An ITU standard for data transmission at up to 33.6 kbps. V.34 is the successor to several earlier ITU standards, and modems using this standard are designed to be backwardly compatible with older, slower modems.

- *V.42*: MNP 4 and Link Access Protocol/Modems (LAP/M) modem-to-modem error correction

- *V.42bis*: LAP/M and 4-to-1 data compression

- *x2*: A technology developed by U.S. Robotics for achieving modem transmissions at close to 56 kbps over ordinary phone lines. In most respects, it is similar to K56flex.

THE AT COMMAND SET

In the good old days, modems were operated in the same manner as your computer. You had to issue specific commands to perform a specific function. Since these commands were used only for modems, they were not DOS commands. You had to be running some form of terminal emulation software. These days, you double-click your favorite Web browser and the software does all that for you. However, it is still a good idea to know your way around a modem, should you ever find yourself in the position of having to manually communicate with another device or needing to troubleshoot a modem. The standard modem command set is called the AT Command Set and is modeled after the original Hayes Command Set. There are the basic command set and the extended set. **Table 19.2** lists the Basic AT Command Set, along with descriptions of what each one does.

The Extended Command Set provides for far more control of modem functions and performance. Using these will require fairly substantial knowledge of modem registers and other aspects that are beyond the scope of this book.

Table 19.2   The Basic AT Command Set

Command	Function
AT	Attention (precedes all commands except A/ and +++)
A/	Repeat previous command (does not require a <CR>)
A	Takes the modem off hook while inactive; otherwise, the modem will try to answer all incoming calls
B0	Select CCITT V.22 (1200 bps)
B1	Select Bell 212A (1200 bps)
B2	Select CCITT V23 — Originate modem will transmit data at 75 bps and receive data at 1200 bps; answer modem will transmit data at 1200 bps and receive data at 75 bps; the command N0 (disable auto mode) must be selected
D	Takes the modem off-hook and waits for a dial tone, allowing the modem to dial out (see X command for exceptions)
Dmn	ATDmn will dial a phone number where "m" is a modifier: L, W, ,, ;, @, or S; "n" represents a number dialed by the user
L	Dial last number
W	Wait for dial tone; if you have selected X0 or X1 (disable dial tone detection), then you can use this modifier to override that setting
,	Pause during dial; the amount of time the modem waits is determined in register S8
;	Return to command mode after dialing; it does not wait for carrier or hang up
@	Wait for 5 seconds of silence (used for systems that do not provide a dial tone)
!	Hook flash; forces the modem to go on-hook for a half second; used in PBX systems and for certain voice features such as call waiting
S=(0-9)	Dials a stored number; up to ten numbers can be stored, and the addresses are from 0 to 9; to store a number into one of these addresses, use the "&Z" command

(Continued)

Table 19.2 The Basic AT Command Set *(Continued)*

Command	Function
E0	Turns Echo off; commands issued to the modem are not displayed on the screen
E1	Turns Echo on; commands issued to the modem are displayed on the screen
H0	Hang up modem
H1	Bring modem on-line
I0	Return numeric product code
I1	Return hardware variation code
I2	Report internal code
I3	Report software revision number
I4	Report product feature listing
L0	Speaker volume off
L1	Speaker volume low
M0	Speaker always off
M1	Speaker on until carrier detected, then turns speaker off
M2	Speaker always on
M3	Speaker on during answering only
N0	Disable automode; this will fix the speed at which the modem connects to the speed specified in register S37
N1	Enable automode; the modem will negotiate the highest available line speed and ignore any ATBn command
O0	Return to data mode
O1	Retrain the modem; line conditions may change after the original connection; retraining the modem will force a renegotiation of speed based on the current line conditions
P	Some older telephone systems still support only pulse dialing, this forces the modem to dial in pulse mode
Q0	Enable response to DTE
Q1	Disable response to DTE; the modem does not respond to the terminal; issuing a command will not produce a response (unless the command is something like ATZ, which will restore this setting to default)
Sn	Set default S-register; any subsequent = or ? commands will modify the default S register
Sn=m	Set register n to value m
Sn?	Return the value of register n
T	Touch-tone dialing; the default on nearly all modems
V0	Result codes will be sent in numeric form (stored in a file called the result code table)

(Continued)

Table 19.2   The Basic AT Command Set *(Continued)*

Command	Function
V1	Result codes will be sent in work form (see the result code table)
W0	Report DTE speed only; Error Correction or Data Compression methods in use will not be reported
W1	Report DCE speed; Error Correction/Data Compression protocol and DTE speed will be reported
W2	Report DCE speed only
X0	Send OK, CONNECT, RING, NO CARRIER, ERROR, and NO ANSWER; busy and dial tone detection are disabled
X1	Send X0 messages and CONNECT speed
X2	Send X1 messages and NO DIAL TONE
X3	Send X2 messages and BUSY and RING BACK; dial tone detection is disabled
X4	Send all responses
Y0	Prevents disconnections caused by long spaces
Y1	Forces a disconnect after a long space; with error correction, hang up after sending 1.6-second long space; without error correction, hang up after 4-second long space
Z0	Reset modem to profile 0
Z1	Reset modem to profile 1
+++	Escape sequence; transfers the modem from data mode to command mode; must be preceded by at least 1 second of no characters and followed by one second of no characters; O0 (ATO0 or ATO) returns the modem to data mode
=n	Sets the value of the default S register

The AT Command Set is starting to go the way of the platypus. Still, there are enough modems running around that having a reference of the commonly used commands might be useful.

INITIALIZATION STRINGS

When a modem first initiates contact with another modem, there are certain parameters that must be set simply in order to initialize communications. In order to accomplish this, the modem is programmed with the *initialization string*. This tells the modem on the other end precisely what the originate modem is capable of doing in terms of compression and speed. Modems ship with a default string that works most of the time. Sometimes fine-tuning the string will do wonders for modem performance. How you go about doing this is determined by the operating system you're running.

BUZZ WORDS

Initialization string: A series of AT commands that are issued by the originate modem during the connection process.

Windows 95/98

1. Double-click My Computer, then double-click Dial-Up Networking. (If a Dial-Up Networking folder is not present in My Computer, try this: From the Start button, choose Programs, and then Accessories. There you will see Dial-Up Networking.)

2. Right-click your connection icon and choose Properties.

3. Click the Configure button.

4. Click the Connection tab.

5. Click the Advanced button.

6. Enter the init string in the Extra Settings field.

7. Click OK to save changes.

WINDOWS NT 4.0\2000

1. Click the Start Menu, then click Settings, and then select Control Panel.

2. Double-click the icon labeled Modems.

3. Select the modem you wish to configure and click the Properties button

4. On the window that pops up, select the Connection tab.

5. Click the button that says Advanced.

6. Type the initialization string in the Extra Settings box.

7. Click OK repeatedly until you are at back the Control Panel window.

Some of the problems that can be solved by editing the initialization string include dropped connections, poor connect speeds, and many others. Each brand of modem will have initialization strings specific to that modem, and therefore, you will need to be able to access the documentation for your particular model. If you've thrown away or lost the documentation that shipped with your modem you can usually retrieve that information off of the technical support area of the manufacturer's Web page. Also, specific ISPs might suggest initialization strings different from the default.

INSTALLING AND TROUBLESHOOTING MODEMS

All that said and done, just what is going to be involved when you go to install a modem and what kinds of problems can you expect on down the road? The answers are, "That depends," and "More than you care to think about." But I'm willing to bet you're looking for a little more detail than that. So I'll start with installing a modem.

INSTALLING MODEMS

First off, there is a fairly wide variety of modems available to choose from, ranging from incredibly inexpensive to outrageously expensive. A better way to break them down would be into external modems and internal modems. Which way you go is an entirely personal decision, but having some insight into the differences will make that decision easier to make intelligently. In many respects, the decision you make here will affect you later on down the road when you're trying to troubleshoot problems that will inevitably arise.

- *Internal modems*: These install into an available expansion slot inside the computer. While ISA modems are becoming increasingly hard to find, they do still exist. PCI modems will fall into two different categories. There are software dependent, or soft, modems, and then there are real modems. I'll talk about the pros and cons of software-dependent modems at great length a little later on.

- *External modems*: While the most commonly available external modems are those that install onto a serial port, there is an increasing number of USB modems becoming available. Serial modems can be the easiest to troubleshoot because of the function lights that are easily seen on the front panel of the device. USB modems are generally more limited in the number of function lights, if any, that are available.

Installation of external modems is usually pretty straightforward. There isn't really a whole lot that can go wrong. You simply have to make sure that you have an available serial port, or USB port in the case of USB modems, and the correct cable. Once the system detects the new device, it is simply a matter of installing the software drivers.

Two things that can cause an external modem installed on a serial port to not be detected are IRQ conflicts and/or a disabled serial port. With Plug 'n Play, IRQ conflicts are pretty rare these days, but they can still occur. An external modem is going to want one of the standard COM ports. Whether it is COM1, COM2, COM3, or COM4 usually doesn't matter, as long as one of them is available. Plug 'n Play will usually detect other devices that occupy COM ports and give the modem one that isn't occupied.

If, for some reason, Plug 'n Play isn't working, it could be because of one of two things. Either the serial port is disabled, or another device in the system is occupying the same base I/O address as the modem. External modems hook up to an existing serial port; therefore, IRQ conflicts are incredibly rare.

I/O conflicts are equally rare, but there is one notable case where this can become an issue. Some motherboards are shipping with tertiary and quaternary IDE ports on board. By default, they are disabled. However, should you choose to activate these ports, they need I/O base addresses the same way everything else does. The base address for a tertiary IDE port happens to overlap with COM3. Therefore, installing an external modem set to COM3 on a system with a tertiary IDE enabled is going to cause a conflict. And it's one that can be difficult to diagnose.

The more likely cause for a serial modem failing to be recognized is that the serial port to which it is attached has been disabled. If you were previously using a soft modem that was installed at the factory, there is a very strong possibility that, in order to get the soft modem to work, one of your serial ports was disabled. Murphy's Law dictates that the disabled port will be the port you're trying to use. Go into the CMOS settings and enable the port and all should be well.

Internal modems have their own set of problems. Once again, for the most part, Plug 'n Play minimizes these problems. However, you can occasionally bump into IRQ problems with internal modems. If you're installing a PCI soft modem, the issue I discussed in the previous

Table 19.3 Modem Light Functions

Marking	Meaning	Modem function
PWR	Power On	Lights when power is applied to the modem
MR	Modem Ready	Lights when the modem self-check has satisfactorily completed
TR (DTR)	Terminal Ready	Lights when Data Terminal Ready (DTR) signal from the PC is present
SD (TD)	Send (Transmit) Data	Lights while modem is transmitting data to a remote modem
RD	Receive Data	Lights while modem is receiving data from a remote modem
OH	Off Hook	Lets you know the modem is off hook
HS	High Speed	Lights when connected to high-speed link
AA	Auto Answer	Indicates that modem is set to accept calls
CD	Carrier Detect	Lights when remote carrier has been detected
RS	Request to Send	Lights when an RTS signal is being generated
CS	Clear to Send	Lights when a CTS signal is being generated

The lights on an external modem aren't just for show. They indicate whether or not certain functions are working.

paragraph applies to you in reverse. It is possible that the reason you can't get the system to see your new modem is that the serial port is claiming the IRQ. Serial and parallel ports grab their resources during POST, long before PCI devices get their shot. The only way to get the soft modem to work is to disable the serial port. This can be a bummer if you have something attached to that port.

TROUBLESHOOTING MODEMS

One of the beauties of external modems is that collection of pretty lights on the front. You should know, however, that those lights weren't put there just for show. They have some very important functionality. While not all external modems have the same collection of lights, the ones most commonly seen are outlined in **Table 19.3**.

Having all those lights out in plain sight makes the work of troubleshooting modem problems a lot easier. Internal modems don't give you benefit of any visible lights, but the problems you face will be the same. I've put together a list of some of the more commonly seen problems modem users experience and possible solutions.

- *Windows doesn't see the modem*: Check for IRQ conflicts. Does it show up in Device Manager at all? If so, is there either a yellow exclamation point or a red X? A yellow exclamation point tells you it sees the modem but the device is not working. This is usually a driver issue. A red X means you told Windows there is a modem installed, but Windows disagrees.

■ *Windows sees the modem, but it won't dial*: Won't even go there. Way too many things cause that, but you can tell if it's the modem's fault. Open a Hyperterminal session (Start, Programs, Accessories, Communications, Hyperterminal), and at the prompt, type the command AT. If the echoed response is "OK," then the modem itself is working. Next you follow the procedures in the previously described symptom.

■ *You get a "No Dial Tone" message*: Is the phone line hooked up to the modem? If it is an external modem, is it actually plugged in and turned on? If both answers are yes, check and see if you have dial tone on a voice phone. You may be having a service outage. If so, did you pay your bill?

■ *My 56K modem only connects at 28.8K*: Don't be surprised to hear that you're not alone. In some localities, the quality of the phone lines is too poor to maintain any speeds higher than that. If you know the phone lines are not the issue, check and see if your settings are correct. If the COM port settings are set to 28.8Kbps, that's all you're ever going to get, regardless of what modem you use or line quality.

■ *My Connection Status tells me I'm hooked up at 49.2K but I'm only downloading at 4.3K*: That's not a problem. For one thing, the 4.3K represents bytes per second, while the 49.2 is bits per second. Therefore, that 4.3K translate out to 35,225 bits per second. Since your modem is also sending out ACK and SYN messages all the time, 4.3K is actually a good rate.

■ *I'm having problems with downloads*: This could include corrupted files or files that won't open (basically the same thing). Usually caused by a data overrun. The remote computer is sending data faster than your modem is able to process it. This usually means your flow control is set incorrectly. In the Advanced Settings you will see settings for Xon/Xoff as well as RTS/CTS. If you have a fast modem, you don't want to be using Xon/Xoff. Make sure you and the other computer are in agreement on which setting you're supposed to be using.

■ *My connection is constantly being dropped for no apparent reason*: Most frequently this is a result of poor line quality. Keep in mind that line quality is not a constant thing. Electrical signals that are perfectly good on a nice sunny day pick up a lot of noise during a thunderstorm. However, if the line is not to blame, it could be that the modem is causing a timeout generated by a DTR signal not arriving in time. On most modems, adding a parameter to the initialization string can rectify this. Check with your manufacturer for the correct string.

■ *My modem keeps getting slower the longer I remain connected*: This is a result of the retraining I discussed earlier. Either line conditions or congestion is preventing high-speed connection and the two modems keep renegotiating slower speeds.

■ *I click on a site that contains data for a project I'm doing at work and I get football scores instead*: This is a problem?

Soft Modems

Throughout this chapter I've made references to soft modems and real modems. Another term you might see thrown about is Winmodem. Please note that Winmodem is a registered trademark of 3Com/USRobotics, and should not be used interchangeably. The term soft modem is derived from the fact that the device is dependent on the OS to function. These modems typically hand off many of the functions that I've discussed in this chapter onto the computer itself.

Soft modems will fall into two categories: those with onboard digital signal processors (DSP) that provide both UART and DAC functions, and those that make the computer do everything. If a modem has its own DSP, it will perform the functions of both signal processing and that of the UART. This modem will be relatively easy to install and offer little or no performance degradation.

Conversely, the modem that lacks a DSP will make the computer's CPU handle all data processing. It will require one of the UARTs resident on the motherboard in order to function. And every time it is in use, other programs will suffer because the modem is using a substantial amount of CPU time for its own purposes.

A real modem has an onboard controller, its own UART, and its own DSP to handle all those functions. They are much easier to install and to troubleshoot than soft modems. That is not to say, however, that there is not a time and a place to use soft modems. They are inexpensive, for one thing. This can become a big issue for a lot of people.

Also, if the primary reason for the computer's existence is to hook the household up to the Internet, then it is less likely that large numbers of applications are going to be running in the background. For someone like me, however, who routinely has two or three Internet connections active at once, a word processor, a desktop publisher, a photo-editing program, and a drawing program all running at once, soft modems can become an issue. They key here is to know what your computer is intended to do and buy appropriately.

ISDN

For some people, the speed of a modem is simply too slow. Yet some of the faster technologies that I will discuss in the next section are simply too expensive. If you happen to fall into that category, you might want to see if any providers in your area provide for an Integrated Services Digital Network (ISDN). This is a service that, on its most basic level, provides noticeably faster throughput in both directions.

Unlike a telephone line, an ISDN signal stays digital from beginning to end. The only conversion necessary is to move from parallel to serial and back again. As with modems, this is done through a UART.

Basic Rate ISDN (BRI) provides the user with two 64K channels for carrying data (although some service providers drop that to 56K due to the type of switches they use). These are the *B-channels*.

Buzz Words

B-channel: A carrier channel used by ISDN for transmitting user data at 64Kbps. Multiple B-channels can be combined for higher transmission rates.

These carry nothing but user information. This can include digital data, digitized voice communications, and so forth. A third channel, the *D-channel*, is a 16K connection that carries the transmission control signals.

Primary Rate ISDN (PRI) provides even higher speeds. Up to twenty-three channels can be combined to provide the user with up to 1536K of throughput. In Europe, ISDN services can provide for up to thirty channels for 1920K. Another difference between BRI and PRI is that with PRI, you get a 64K D-channel as well.

For those who need speeds in between the high and low bandwidths of BRI and PRI, the International Telegraph and Telephone Consultation Committee (CCITT) defined the H-channels. These channels (listed in **Table 19.4**) provide speeds from 384K up to 1920K.

How you interconnect your system to the ISDN line will be determined by where you live. In the U.S., the signal is going to enter the

Table 19.4 Summary of ISDN Services

ISDN Service	Structure	Maximum Speed
H0	6B, 1D	384K
H10	23B, 1D	1472K
H11	24B, 1D	1536K
H12	30B, 1D	1920K

The H channels define intermediate ISDN speeds.

Note: H11 and H12 service is available in Europe

building by way of a U interface. The U interface only supports a single device, and that device is going to be the Network Termination-1 (NT1). All the NT1 really does is convert the incoming 2-wire circuit to a 4-wire S/T interface. The S/T interface provides access to more than one device. It is possible to get S/T interfaces that support up to seven different devices. It is also possible that your provider might install equipment that has the NT1 and S/T interface designed into the device, making it impossible to add other devices.

The signal must also pass through a Network Termination-2 (NT2) interface. It's unlikely that you'll have to deal with that interface directly because it is built into the ISDN equipment, and not a separate device. From here, the circuit can now be interconnected with the user's equipment. It sounds pretty complicated, but since much of this can be integrated into the equipment supplied by your provider, it need not be intimidating. **Figure 19.6** shows a block diagram of a complete ISDN circuit.

This equipment will fall under one of two categories. Devices that are designed around ISDN are Terminal Equipment-1 (TE1) devices. Those devices that were originally designed to interface with conventional telephone lines are designated Terminal Equipment-2 (TE2). In order to interconnect TE2 devices, you're going to need a terminal adapter (TA). A TA brings the ISDN into your building and provides either RJ-45 ports or a standard serial port for interconnecting to your computer. An ISDN modem is a prime example of a TA.

By using a channel aggregation protocol, the two incoming channels can be combined into a single 128K connection. The two protocols most commonly used are Bonding (Bandwidth on Demand) and Multilink-PPP. The latter is the more recently introduced protocol and is supposedly superior in its error handling capabilities.

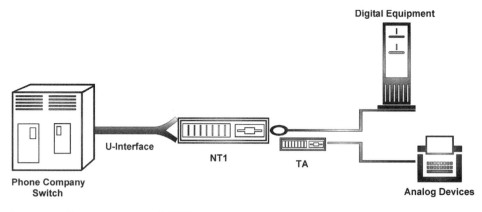

Figure 19.6 The makings of ISDN

It isn't necessary to combine the two channels if your requirements are not purely data transmission. The signals can be separated, allowing voice over one and data over the other.

CAUTION: While the TA provides an RJ-45 connection, you must pay attention to the type of TA installed. Plugging an analog device into a digital circuit will kill that device. If a TA is designed for analog circuits, it will have a port labeled either A/B or POTS (an acronym for plain old telephone service). Along those same lines (figuratively speaking), it is essential that, in an office environment, you know if a digital telephone system is in place. If you plug the analog modem in your laptop into a digital line, you'll be shopping for a new modem that afternoon. The one you plugged into a digital line will be fried.

Throughout this book, I've made mention of specific programming interfaces for different types of hardware. The Common ISDN Advanced Programming Interface (CAPI) is the one used by Windows to interface with ISDN. CAPI intercepts programming calls made directly to the ISDN and directs them to the correct port. This is how multiple applications can access the device.

DSL

An increasing number of people are finding that Digital Subscriber Lines (DSL) are the answer to their bandwidth needs. The beauty of DSL is that it comes in over your regular telephone wires. Therefore, you don't have a bunch of people coming into your building, ripping and tearing. And since it comes in on a different frequency than standard telephone service, you can make a phone call while your DSL connection is active, without having to pay for a second telephone line.

DSL has a lot of advantages over standard telephone service or ISDN. Then again, there are some disadvantages as well. I'll look at both, starting with the advantages.

- *Speed*: A DSL line, depending on your provider and the distance you are from its central office, can provide up to 1.5Mbps.
- *Cost*: In order to approach that speed with ISDN, you would need a PRI with the maximum number of available channels. This would cost substantially more than typical DSL rates.
- *Convenience*: No new lines need to be run into your building. Existing telephone lines work fine.
- *Multifunction access*: The DSL connection and the telephone lines can be simultaneously active.
- *One-stop shopping*: In most cases, your provider comes in with all the hardware you'll need to make the connection.

But as I mentioned, DSL is not without its shortcomings. It isn't for everyone, and quite frankly, at this point in time, it isn't available to everyone. Some of the disadvantages include:

- *Availability*: Currently, DSL is only being offered in higher-population centers.
- *Location*: You have to be within a certain distance from the main office or the company can't hook you up. Under ideal circumstances the maximum distance from the switching station is 18,000 feet.
- *Consistency*: The farther you get from the main office, the slower your connection gets. You might get 1.5Mbps at work, but less than 400K at home.
- *Disparity between incoming and outgoing signals*: The connection from your ISP to you is four to six times faster than the connection from you to them.

The concept behind DSL is that the wires used by your telephone are severely under-utilized. The copper wires are perfectly capable of carrying signals of several gigahertz, yet the telephone line is lazing along at 3.4K. DSL takes advantage of the rest of that bandwidth. It is technically possible to provide bandwidth in excess of 8Mbps over a DSL link (although current FCC regulations limit service to 1.5Mbps).

However, as I mentioned earlier, there are some distance limitations involved. The maximum distance that a signal can be run is around 18,000 feet, or slightly more than three miles. As that distance increases, throughput drops.

Even if you live with 18,000 feet of the main office, you might find that you can't get DSL service. There are several factors that can knock you out of the loop:

- *Distances can be deceiving*: The main office may be less than 18,000 feet away as the crow flies. But the wires may loop up and down several blocks, back and forth, before they reach your location. Therefore, there might be more than 18,000 feet of cable separating you from it.

- *Fiber-optic cables*: DSL signals can't do the digital-to-analog, analog-to-digital conversions needed to send the signal over fiber-optic cables. Therefore, a fiber-optic circuit is a glass wall that blocks the signal.

- *Bridge taps*: These are circuits that are inserted into the line that route service to other customers. They add to the total length of the circuit and can force you to logically be more that 18,000 feet away.

- *Loading coils*: These are small devices that clean up and regenerate the analog signal that carries voice over the telephone wire. DSL is incompatible with loading coils. They are like a brick wall that blocks the signal.

There are two devices that make DSL work. One of these, the DSL transceiver, is installed on the subscriber's end. Sometimes you'll see this device referred to as the DSL modem, but that is an inaccurate term. In that the data that passes over DSL is purely digital, no modulation or demodulation is necessary. This device will accept the incoming signal and send it out to either an RJ-45 port or a USB port. Many times, you will find devices that combine the functions of either a hub, switch, or router with the transceiver, making it a multifunction device.

On the service provider's end, a device called a DSL Access Multiplexer (DSLAM) is installed to combine the incoming signals from all the customers into a single huge connection to the Internet. The DSLAM will provide other services, such as dynamic IP assignment and routing functions.

One of the things that you'll see about cable modems in the next section is that, under that technology, as you add users to the loop, performance drops. The DSLAM prevents this from happening. As long as the total bandwidth used by users currently active does not exceed the ISP's connection to the Internet backbone, all will be well.

CABLE MODEMS

Another increasingly popular connection to the Internet merges your cable TV services with your Internet service. To understand how cable modems do their thing, it is probably a good idea if you understand how basic cable television service works.

In the good old days, you were lucky if you had two channels that your TV could pick up, unless you lived in or near a big city. Then you might be able to get four or five. Because standard network television is freely available to the public, it has to be supported through the commercials that you've all grown to know and love. Also, content is carefully monitored.

The alternative that was offered involved piping in as many signals as possible into a central location and sending them out over wires to those who were willing to help pay for the service. This became known as cable TV. With cable, it became possible to combine hundreds of different channels over a broadband connection. It also became possible to pick and choose what signals a service provider sent out to a specific household, and subscription services became possible.

It was a logical move from providing television service to providing Internet access. After all, you've already got the infrastructure laid out. A coaxial cable can carry bandwidth approaching nearly a gigahertz, and each TV channel only occupies 6MHz. Even with 150 channels, there's plenty of bandwidth still available on the wire. So why not use it for Internet access? The biggest obstacle was getting the FCC to approve it. Once FCC approval was obtained, the way was cleared for any cable TV provider to add Internet access as an option.

The device that makes it possible is the cable modem. And in this case, it really is a modem. The cable modem is broken down into the following components:

- *The tuner*: This makes sure that the Internet stays the Internet and that the History Channel stays the History Channel.

- *The modulator/demodulator*: This performs the same function as your analog modem.

- *A Media Access Control (MAC) interface*: This provides access to the wire for your computer. (See Chapter Eighteen, Getting on the Network, for more information on this subject.)

- *A microprocessor*: Prevents the process of converting a cable signal to a computer signal from overloading the computer's CPU.

- *A network interface*: Provides access to the signal by your computer. Typically, this is a standard RJ-45 connector.

When I was discussing DSL services, I talked about the function of the DSLAM. On a cable network, a device called the Cable Modem Termination System (CMTS) handles that function. It is the CMTS that bundles all of the customers' Internet connections and pipes them to the backbone. The service provider uses standard DHCP services (see Chapter Eighteen, Getting on the Network) to hand out IP addresses.

The CMTS takes a single 6MHz channel and uses it to pipe Internet services to customers. This provides bandwidth that can approach 40Mbps. Up to 1000 customers can be bundled into a single channel. The more people on the channel, the less bandwidth there is available for each user.

This also opens up a potential security issue. Since all the users on a channel are sharing bandwidth, it is pretty much the same thing as putting them all on the same network. Let's assume for a moment that you're one of the growing number of people out there that have several computers in their home and have decided to network them. In order to make your network functional, you needed to share out files and directories that needed to be accessed by the machines on your network. So you've shared out the My Documents directory on computer A. Now you can go to computer B or computer C and double-click Entire Network and see those folders.

And so can your neighbors if they happen to be online at the same time as you. Therefore, it is imperative that you install some form of firewall to protect your computer from intrusion by others. A *firewall* is a logical barrier that allows people on

BUZZ WORDS ————————

Firewall: A hardware or software barrier that allows access to external networks for users inside the firewall, but denies access from the outside.

your side to get out to the outside world, but keeps the outside world from getting in. You can create a firewall in one of two ways. Some companies, like Bay Networks, manufacture cable modem routers that have a hardware firewall built in. This is the method that will provide the fastest performance, and quite frankly, the devices aren't that expensive. It is the method I most strongly recommend.

If your security needs aren't that stringent, there are software firewalls that can be installed on your local machines that do the same job. However, because they are software based, they are using memory and CPU resources that could be put to better use elsewhere. My experience with software firewalls is that, while they can be every bit as effective as a hardware firewall, the commercial versions can cost every bit as much as an inexpensive hardware device, and the hardware device won't result in a degradation of performance.

HIGH-SPEED WAN CONNECTIONS

The aforementioned technologies pretty much cover the range available to household communications. Business-to-business connections can be substantially more complicated and are the subject of several different books all by themselves. I thought it would be useful to include a list of options along with some of the speeds you can expect. While no means an all-inclusive list, **Table 19.5** covers the vast majority of telecommunications links in use today.

CHAPTER SUMMARY

In this chapter I have provided a brief overview of the ways different computers can link together remotely. You can clearly see that this technology has come a long way from the days of 300bps modems to the present situation of DSL links in every home (well, a lot of homes, anyway).

Still, this is only scratching surface of this technology. Some companies are predicting that before this decade is out, the vast majority of computers across the world will have a capacity for communication over high-speed wireless links at speeds we can only dream of now. It's going to be fun to watch.

Table 19.5   Overview of High-Speed Telecommunications Links

Technology	Appx. Speed	Description
ISDN-BRI	128.0K	BRI (Basic Rate Interface) 2x64K B-channels, 1x64K D-channel
Euro-ISDN	144.0K	128K usable. Allows full transparent internetworking between all European countries
B-ISDN	1.500M	Broadband Integrated Services Digital Network
G.lite	1.500M	18,000 feet Asymmetric Digital Subscriber Line, sends at 512K, receives at 1.5M
IDSL	1.500M	18,000 ft, DSL over ISDN, sends 64K-1.5M, receives 1.5-9M
Cable Modem	1.500M	Sends at 10M, receives at 56M (on a good day, with a tailwind)
DS1	1.544M	Digital Signal Level 1, 24 Channels (1xT1)
HDSL	1.544M	12,000 ft, High bit-rate DSL, sends at 2.048M, receives at 1.544M
SDSL	1.544M	12,000 ft, Symmetric DSL, sends at 2.048M, receives at 1.544M
T1	1.544M	Digital Trunk Line 1, 24 Channels (1xT1)
ISDN-PRI	1.544M	Primary Rate Interface 23x64K B-channels, 1x64K D-channel on T1, 23B+D
Euro-ISDN/PRI	2.048M	Primary Rate Interface 30x64K B-channels, 1x64K D-channel on E1, 30B+D
16C952	3.000M	Dual-channel version of the 16950 UART
DS1c	3.152M	Digital Signal Level 1c, 48 Channels (2xT1)
T1c	3.152M	Digital Trunk Line 1c, 48 Channels (2xT1)
UMTS	3.500M	Universal Mobile Telephone System
DS2	6.312M	Digital Signal Level 2, 96 Channels (4xT1)
T2	6.312M	Digital Trunk Line 2,96 Channels (4xT1)
ADSL	8.000M	Asymmetric DSL, sends at 1.500M, receives at 8.000M
E2	8.448M	120 Channels, Europe & Japan
CAIS bus	10.000M	Common Airborne Instrumentation System
RS-485	10.000M	4000ft, Balanced line interface, 2-wire, half-duplex, differential.
RS-530	10.000M	30km, Fiber-optic point-to-point
Wireless LAN	11.000M	Limited Range Wireless Ethernet
DS3	44.736M	Digital Signal Level 3, 672 Channels (28xT1)
T3	44.736M	Digital Trunk Line 3, 672 Channels (28xT1)
V-ADSL	51.000M	51.00M at 1000 feet, drops to 25.600Mbps from 3000-4000 feet

(Continued)

Table 19.5 Overview of High-Speed Telecommunications Links

Technology	Appx. Speed	Description
STS-1	51.840M	Synchronous Transport Signal, Level 1
OC1	51.840M	Optical Carrier 1, fiber-optic networks
VDSL	52.000M	Very high speed DSL, upstream data = 1.5-2.3M, downstream data = 13-52M
DS3c	89.472M	Digital Signal Level 3c, 1344 Channels (56xT1)
T3c	89.472M	Digital Trunk Line 3c, 1344 Channels (56xT1)
DS3d	135.000M	Digital Signal Level 3d, (87xT1)
T3d	135.000M	Digital Trunk Line 3d, (87xT1)
OC3c	155.520M	Optical Carrier 3, fiber-optic internet backbone
DS4	274.176M	Digital Signal Level 4, 4032 Channels (168xT1)
T4	274.176M	Digital Trunk Line 4, 4032 Channels (168xT1)
STM-3	466.560M	Synchronous Transport Module, Level 3
STS-9	466.560M	Synchronous Transport Signal, Level 9
OC9	466.560M	Optical Carrier 9, fiber-optic networks
ATM	622.000M	Asynchronous Transfer Mode
STM-4	622.080M	Synchronous Transport Module, Level 4
STS-12	622.080M	Synchronous Transport Signal, Level 12
OC12c	622.080M	Optical Carrier 12
OC18	933.120M	Optical Carrier 18
WidebandATM	1.000G	Gigabit Ethernet over fiber-optic cable.
OC24	1.244G	Optical Carrier 24
OC36	1.866G	Optical Carrier 36
SONET	2.488G	Synchronous Optical Network
STM-16	2,488G	Synchronous Transport Module, Level 16
STS-48	2,488G	Synchronous Transport Signal, Level 48
OC48c	2.488G	Optical Carrier 48
OC96	4.976G	Optical Carrier 96
FLAG	5.300G	Fiber-optic Link Around the Globe, 27,300km linking Great Britain and Japan.
OC192c	9.953G	Optical Carrier 192, fiber-optic networks
OC256	13.271G	Optical Carrier 256, fiber-optic networks
OC768	39.813G	Optical Carrier 768, fiber-optic networks
OC3072	159.252G	Optical Carrier 3072, fiber-optic networks

The variety of different broadband communications options used around the world is actually staggering.

BRAIN DRAIN

1. Describe in detail two main tricks a modem must perform to transmit data over a telephone wire.

2. In your own words explain why, if a modem is connected at 53.2K, data is only moving at 4.2K.

3. Describe in detail how asynchronous communication works and where it might be used.

4. Describe in detail how synchronous communication works and where it might be used.

5. What are some limitations of DSL?

THE 64K$ QUESTIONS

1. What device on a modem is responsible for serial/parallel conversions?
   a. The UART
   b. The DAC
   c. The RAMDAC
   d. The RJ-11

2. What device on a modem is responsible for digital/analog conversions?
   a. The UART
   b. The DAC
   c. The RAMDAC
   d. The RJ-11

3. A device that can only transmit data, but not receive it, is working in _____ mode.
   a. Duplex
   b. Condominium
   c. Simplex
   d. Half duplex

4. A V.92 modem is capable of 53,200 baud.
   a. True
   b. False

5. When transferring large files, most modems manufactured today use _____ as their error correction method.
   a. Parity
   b. Checksum
   c. CRC
   d. NACK

6. You just finished installing a Plug 'n Play soft modem and the computer doesn't even see it during POST. What is the most likely cause of the problem?
   a. An IRQ conflict
   b. An I/O address conflict
   c. A COM port is not available
   d. A UART is not available

7. Basic Rate ISDN provides _____.
   a. Two 64K B-channels and one 64K D-channel
   b. Twenty-three 64K B-channels and one 64K D-channel
   c. Two 64K B-channels and one 16K D-channel
   d. Two 64K B-channels and two 16K D-channels

8. A key reason DSL has not achieved greater market penetration than it has is because _____.
   a. It costs too much
   b. It is too difficult to configure
   c. It is too severely regulated
   d. The subscriber has to be within 18,000 feet of the central office

9. Cable modem users should ALWAYS install a _____.

    a. Tuner

    b. Firewall

    c. HSDL

    d. Security password

10. Which of the following services is purely digital, end to end?

    a. POTS

    b. ISDN

    c. Cable

    d. DSL

Tricky Terminology

Answer modem: The device that is being called.

B-channel: A carrier channel used by ISDN for transmitting user data at 64Kbps. Multiple B-channels can be combined for higher transmission rates.

Baud rate: The electronic frequency over which data is transmitted.

Bit rate: The speed at which data travels over the wire, usually expressed in bits per second (bps) or kilobits per second (Kbps). Don't confuse this with bytes per second, and don't confuse it with baud rate.

Checksum: An error detection/correction mechanism that works by counting the number of ones present in the payload and storing that value in the BCC block of the packet.

D-channel: A 16Kbps or 64Kbps channel used by ISDN for control data, including synchronization, ACKs and NACKs and other nonuser data.

Duplex: A communications method by which a device can be transmitting and receiving at the same time.

Firewall: A hardware or software barrier that allows access to external networks for users inside the firewall, but denies access from the outside.

Half duplex: A communications method by which a device can either transmit or receive, but not both at the same time.

Initialization string: A series of AT commands that are issued by the originate modem during the connection process.

Message block: A piece of data being transmitted by a modem that represents a portion of the overall data being sent.

Modem: Modulator/demodulator. A device that converts parallel digital signals into serial analog signals for transmission over a wire.

Originate modem: The device that initiates a call.

Simplex: A communications method by which a device can either transmit or receive but cannot do both.

Transmission rate: The number of bits per second that is being transmitted.

Acronym Alert

BCC: The Block Check Character. Includes error detection and correction data, which may include parity (rarely used these days), checksum (on its way out), or cyclical redundancy check (the most common method in use today).

BRI: Basic Rate ISDN. Two 64K B-channels and one 16K D-channel.

CMTS: Cable Modem Termination System. A device on the ISP's end that combines all incoming cable modem signals into a single channel for transmission over the Internet backbone.

DSL: Digital Subscriber Line. A broadband high-speed data connection that moves over standard telephone cable.

DSLAM: DSL Access Multiplexer. A device on the ISP's end that combines all incoming DSL signals into a single channel for transmission over the Internet backbone.

DSP: Digital Signal Processor. A chip that performs multiple processing functions on a signal. For example, the DSP on a modem combines the functions of a UART and a DAC.

EOT: End of Transmission. I hope I don't have to explain that one.

ETX: End of Text. Okay, I'm done sending text in this block. The next bytes are more control information.

ISDN: Integrated Services Digital Network. A telecommunications technology that provides high-speed data transfer over standard telephone lines.

PRI: Primary Rate ISDN. Twenty-three 64K B-channels and one 64K D-channel.

QAM: Quadrature Amplitude Modulation. A method of encoding data sent over a modem using a combination of frequency-shifting and phase shift-keying.

SOH: Start of Header. A header is not always used, but is an important part of most protocols.

STX: Start of Text. Pretty self-explanatory. It tells you that the next series of bits is the data being sent.

SYN: Synchronization character. This makes sure all the bytes in the frame stick together as they move across the wire and then get reassembled in the right order at the other end. If no data is being transmitted, SYN blocks can be transmitted to keep the session alive.

CHAPTER 20

PORTABLE COMPUTING

All too often when a hardware technician first makes the move from fixing desktop systems to fixing his or her first laptop, it is hard not to feel a bit intimidated. After all, this is a laptop and not a regular computer! Laptops are *different*!

Well, I hate to be the one to break the news to you, but laptop computers really aren't that much different than their larger counterparts. They're just tinier is all. In fact, a vast majority of the technology that goes into the manufacture of portable computers has already been discussed in previous chapters.

Therefore, I'm going to start this chapter by reviewing material already covered that relates to portable computing before I dive into new material.

A+ Exam Objectives

Along the way, candidates for the A+ exam are going to see several objectives:

1.3   Identify basic procedures for adding and removing field-replaceable modules for portable systems. Given a replacement scenario, choose the appropriate sequences.

1.10 Determine the issues that must be considered when upgrading a PC. In a given scenario, determine when and how to upgrade system components.

2.1   Recognize common problems associated with each module and their symptoms, and identify steps to isolate and troubleshoot the problems. Given a problem situation, interpret the symptoms and infer the most likely cause.

4.2   Identify the types of RAM (Random Access Memory), form factors, and operational characteristics. Determine banking and speed requirements under given scenarios.

4.3   Identify the most popular types of motherboards, their components, and their architecture. (Bus structures)

If this list seems to induce a strong sense of déjà vu, that's probably because you've seen these same objectives over and over again. Here, I'm going to be concentrating on how these objectives relate to portable computing.

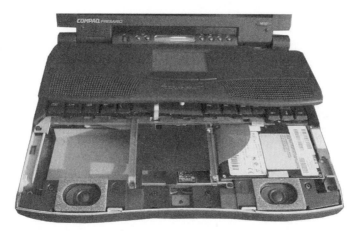

Figure 20.1 Pulling the palmrest off of this notebook shows just how small the components really are. The sound system, trackpad, and hard disk all fit underneath where your hands rest.

A LITTLE REVIEW

Laptop computers, as I said earlier, are nothing more than desktops with a hormone deficiency in most respects. They follow the same computer model that I introduced in Chapter One, PC Basics. Where they differ is in how the individual components are packaged. **Figure 20.1** shows just how many things fit under something as simple as the palmrest. Everything must be smaller, and where possible, designed to consume less power. When each individual component is designed to consume less power, then the overall system consumes less power. That means the battery lasts longer. And the one aspect in which laptops differ the most from desktops is in the fact that they frequently don't have the luxury of that little umbilical cord that attaches them to a power outlet in the wall.

With that in mind, I would like to spend the next few pages going over the basic components required by a computer system and discussing how they are designed differently for laptops. Where relevant, I'll also discuss commonly used methods of assembling laptops so that you will have a head start in figuring out how to take one apart.

CPUs

In the early days of computing, up into the release of the first generation of Pentium by Intel, CPUs were almost universally designed to be 5V devices. As a result, early laptop computers (behemoths by today's standards) could only run for short periods of time between battery charges.

Intel first addressed this issue with the 80386SLC. This was a processor designed with portable computing in mind that operated on 3.3V. Since then, most CPU manufacturers have maintained separate lines of CPUs for desktops and notebooks. The CPU capabilities are similar, if not identical, but CPUs designed for portable computing are designed to consume less power.

Another difference that stands out is in how the CPU is mounted to the motherboard. Many designs featured a CPU that was soldered onto the main system board. In fact, some early models used a gold-plated tape to actually tape the processors into their sockets. That kind of put a crimp in the upgrading process. Most current designs allow the CPU to be swapped out, but you might have to get used to a different type of socket. Instead of the ZIF socket common to most desktops, many laptops incorporate Very Low Insertion Force (VLIF) sockets.

If you're looking for the release handle on one of these sockets, you can stop searching. In its place is a small screw. Turning the screw one way releases the CPU, while turning in the other direction locks it in place.

MEMORY

In Chapter Eight, Searching Your Memory, I discussed a memory package called the SO-DIMM (small outline dual inline memory module, in case your memory has failed you). Laptop manufacturers are by far the largest consumer of this particular memory package.

Generally, laptops will feature one of two designs. The first of these designs makes use of motherboards on which a base amount of memory is integrated right onto the motherboard. Then, for purposes of upgrades, one or two SO-DIMM sockets are provided. The second method is to simply put SO-DIMM sockets on the motherboard and ship the unit with one socket populated.

Upgrading or replacing memory on notebooks isn't any more difficult than it is on desktop systems. You just have to know where to look for the sockets. On some models, such as the one in **Figure 20.2**, you flip the laptop over and on the base of the unit is a small door held shut by a single screw. Remove the screw, pop the door open with a small flat-bladed screwdriver, and there are the sockets.

Other manufacturers weren't so friendly. On some models, the memory sockets are located under-neath the keyboard. In order to re-place or upgrade the memory, you must remove the keyboard. I'll dis-cuss how you go about that a bit later in the chapter.

HARD DRIVES

The vast majority of laptops released today incorporate standard IDE drives in a 2.5″ form factor. As you can see in **Figure 20.3**, these drives

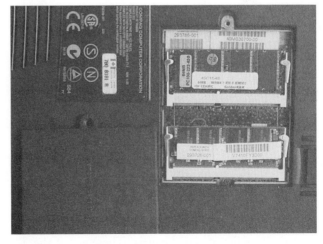

Figure 20.2   One of two common places to put the memory on laptops is beneath a door on the base of the computer. The other place is under the keyboard.

are much thinner that their 3.5″ counterparts and consume far less power. The cable is typically a 2″ 44-conductor cable, rather the 40 conductors used on desktop drives. The extra four conductors provide power to the drive. One conductor provides power to the motor, another provides power to the logic, and then there is a ground for each of them.

Changing out a hard drive in a notebook requires a bit more dexterity than does a desktop computer. In most cases, it is necessary to remove the keyboard, and in a few isolated models, the palmrest must come off as well.

Figure 20.3 The only real difference between hard drives used by laptops and those used in PCs is the size. And that's quite a difference.

Most laptop computers also offer the benefit of allowing the user to install hard drives in a PCMCIA slot (see Chapter Nine, Examining the Expansion Bus). These generally fit into a Type II slot and can be installed and removed as needed.

VIDEO DISPLAYS

The one thing you won't see on a laptop computer is a CRT display. Wouldn't that be fun to carry around? Some of the very first "portable" computers were equipped with CRT monitors and weighed nearly twenty pounds. Not exactly unnoticeable weight to be carrying around, but for the professional in the field who needed a computer, it was a way to go.

Figure 20.4 Even a venerable old classic like Windows 98 looks pretty decent on today's laptop displays.

Today's laptops all come equipped with one of the LCD displays I discussed in Chapter Fifteen, Your Computer and Graphics. **Figure 20.4** shows an example of an LCD display. While many earlier models of laptops sported passive matrix displays, these days even the cheapest models give the user the benefits of active matrix. These are of the TFT variety discussed in Chapter Fifteen, Your Computer and Graphics.

Because of the rough usage laptops are subjected to, their displays are all too frequently damaged or broken. While it's not an inexpensive part to replace, on a perfectly usable computer, it might be a less expensive option to replace a damaged LCD panel than to go out and buy a new computer. And on most models, it isn't all that complicated a repair.

With some models, the screen must be replaced separately and is a rather complex process that involves removing and disassembling the display. How you do this varies greatly from model to model. On most units shipping today, the display is an integrated component consisting of the display, the bezel, and the circuitry involved. A hinged bracket assembly usually holds this assembly in place. Two screws on the back of the computer (or on the bottom on some models) hold the display in place and the bracket slides backward away from the laptop. There are a few models that have additional screws on the bottom of the laptop that must be removed before the bracket can come out. But most have just those two screws.

The tricky part is not damaging the ribbon cable that interconnects the display to the motherboard. The terminals used are a bit different than the ones you get used to in desktop designs. They're actually a smaller implementation of the Sub-D assembly. The end of the cable slides into a slot on the motherboard. The slot is equipped with two tabs that lock the cable into place when pressed down.

Finally, there will be two other wires that need to be disconnected. These are the high-voltage wires and generally coexist in a single plug-in terminal that makes removal and replacement an easy task.

REMOVABLE DISK DRIVES

The two most commonly seen removable media used by laptop computers are the floppy diskette and the CD-ROM. The key limitation to many laptop designs is the distinct lack of space for installing lots and lots of drives. Early on, one solution to this problem was to make the floppy and the CD interchangeable.

Here is another area in which PCMCIA shows its forte. Disk drives can be designed into PCMCIA Type III devices and then subsequently inserted and removed on the fly, as needed. Also, many manufacturers of laptops include a module bay that is used to swap out various devices, including floppy drives, CD/DVD drives, and even an extra battery if necessary.

DEVICES UNIQUE TO PORTABLE COMPUTING

Now that the review is out of the way, it's time to move on to some items you'll only see used in conjunction with laptop computers. Among these are the types of batteries used, AC adapter/chargers, PC cards, pointing devices unique to portables, and the docking station. Another device that deserves mention is a little toy called the port replicator. While it's true that most if not all of these devices see a certain degree of use outside the arena of portable computers, since it is with portables that they get the most exposure, this is where I've chosen to discuss them.

BATTERIES AND CHARGER/ADAPTERS

One of the key issues that had to be resolved when the first portable computers were developed was how to keep a constant and reliable supply of electricity available. A 250-mile extension cord didn't seem to be the answer, so batteries became the power source of choice. Some early models used standard alkaline batteries like you buy at the grocery store. When they were dead you put in some new ones and threw the old ones out.

This was neither cost-effective nor ecologically sensible. But rechargeable batteries of that era, like the one in **Figure 20.5**, were not very efficient for the purpose of laptop computers. The earliest of these batteries used an alloy of nickel and cadmium to generate and store current. These were called NiCad

Figure 20.5 The battery is sole reason you can take your laptop on the road. Show it some respect.

batteries and had a couple of rather serious inherent problems. The first of these was efficiency. It could take three hours of charging to give the batteries enough oomph to power a typical notebook computer of that time for half an hour. Second, NiCads exhibited a phenomenon called *battery memory*. Unless they were frequently discharged completely before recharging, they would "remember" how much of a charge they took in the last few recharging cycles and the amount of charge became its total capacity. The battery lost its ability to take a full charge.

> **EXAM NOTE:** Of all questions relating to portable computing, questions regarding the different types of batteries are the most common. Know your battery types.

NiCads were eventually replaced by Nickel Metal Hydride (Ni-MH) batteries. They really weren't a significant improvement over NiCads, but they helped a bit. While they still suffered from battery memory, it wasn't anywhere near as severe as it had been with NiCads. The recharge-to-usage ratio was a lot friendlier as well, giving slightly more usage time than it required to fully charge them. The most serious downside to Ni-MHs was that if overcharged, they could be permanently damaged.

Still, there was a lot of room for improvement. Today's notebooks all ship with Lithium-Ion (Li-Ion) batteries. Li-Ions don't suffer from battery memory, you can plug them in for hours, or even days at a time and they won't overcharge, and it only takes about an hour of charging to get three to five hours of use.

The AC adapter/charger that ships with a particular unit will be specific to that computer/battery combination. Just because the connector tip of another adapter seems to fit your computer is not an indication that it will work properly. You could even destroy a notebook computer by using the wrong AC adapter/charger. If you examine the terminal that plugs into the computer, you see a small pin in the center, while the outside resembles a

BUZZ WORDS ————————————————

Battery memory: A phenomenon exhibited by rechargeable batteries where the pattern of recent charge cycles affects the maximum charge the battery will accept.

barrel. The pin is considered the tip. On adapters that output DC voltage, the adapter may be tip-positive or it may be tip-negative. What this means is that the tip is carrying either the positive or the negative current. Needless to say, they're not interchangeable.

Output voltages of different adapters also vary. A quick perusal of one online source of replacement AC adapters for notebooks turned up a range between 9V and 20V.

Figure 20.6 Putting this PCMCIA NIC on the keyboard gives a good idea of just how small a PC card really is.

PC CARDS

The *PC card* (**Figure 20.6**) is basically another way of describing devices designed for the PCMCIA slots. While the PCMCIA bus was discussed in detail in Chapter Nine, I have chosen to reserve a discussion of the cards themselves for this chapter.

For the most part, PC cards are truly PnP. In general, they require no intervention on the part of the user as far as installation and configuration of a device, other than providing the driver disk when needed during the first installation of a new device.

As was mentioned in Chapter Nine, PCMCIA slots are either Type I (3.3mm), Type II (5mm), or Type III (10.5mm). Type I and II slots are generally used for accessory cards such as NICS or modems. Type III slots see more use when designing drives.

One thing unique to PC cards is the typical structure of the device drivers used. PC cards use a two-tiered device driver. The first level is the *socket driver*. The socket driver notifies the computer when the device has been either inserted or removed and provides I/O operations. The second level is the *card service*. The card service interprets the command set for a particular device. As a result of this multitiered approach, PC cards can be added and removed on the fly as needed. However, before you simply start yanking devices out of your notebook, you might want to check with the manufacturer's instructions in this respect. There are some model-specific recommendations in this regard.

> **EXAM NOTE:** A good understanding of PC card drivers is useful even if you're not taking the exam. If you are planning to take the exam, it's essential. That's another popular subject.

BUZZ WORDS ————

PC card: Any auxiliary device designed to be plugged into a PCMCIA slot.

Socket driver: The portion of a PC card driver that is responsible for I/O services and insertion/removal notification.

Card services: The portion of a PC card driver that interprets the command set for a specific device.

POINTING DEVICES USED ON PORTABLES

The three most common pointing devices used on laptops are the trackpad, the trackpoint, and the trackball (discussed in Chapter Ten, Input Devices). The trackball is rarely used on modern computers and has already been discussed, so in this section I'll concentrate on the trackpad and the trackpoint.

Trackpads (**Figure 20.7**) work by sensing the electrostatic energy generated by the user's finger. An array of transistors tracks the movement of the finger as it moves across the surface and relays vector information to the device driver. The driver converts this information into the data needed to display the mouse cursor in the proper position on the screen.

Because of this, the sensitivity of a trackpad is directly proportional to the amount of electrostatic energy emitted by the person using the computer. For example, if you have long fingernails, and try to operate the trackpad with the tip of a nail, in most cases, it won't work. A technician who has just finished servicing a laptop and is still wearing an antistatic wristband is often surprised to find that the trackpad either responds poorly, or not at all.

In general, the trackpad is part of the palmrest. A small ribbon cable that uses an LIF connector similar to the one used by the display connects to the motherboard. With some models, the trackpad can be replaced, if necessary, separately from the palmrest. With other models, it is necessary to replace the entire palmrest.

A *trackpoint* uses technology similar to trackballs, except that it is a scaled-down version, usually embedded in the keyboard. It is very small, operated by the tip of a single finger, and sports a textured rubber surface. These characteristics earned it the nickname eraser-point. The signals generated by the trackpoint are sent through the ribbon cable interconnected the keyboard to the motherboard. Should a trackpoint fail, it will be necessary to replace the entire motherboard.

Since many people dislike both trackpads and trackpoints, most manufacturers provide some way of hooking up a standard mouse or trackball to their models of laptop. This can consist of either a USB or a PS2 port. While this does add one more accessory to be carting around in the carrying case, many people find that minor inconvenience far less annoying than the inconvenience of fighting with one of these other devices.

Figure 20.7 The trackpad is one of the more commonly used pointing devices on notebook computers.

DOCKING STATIONS

More people are deciding that owning and maintaining two separate computer systems is more trouble than it's worth. (I don't know why! I have half a dozen!) Today's laptop designs are every bit as powerful as their desktop counterparts. The only drawback is that you can't install as many toys.

The *docking station* eliminates even that argument. The docking station is a device to which a portable computer is attached that allows full-sized components to be installed. A portable computer designed for docking station use will have an interface called a docking connector on the back of the computer.

Docking stations provide all the standard I/O connectors of a desktop computer and also allow additional drives and/or PCI cards to be installed that are not part of the original laptop's configuration. I went to Dell Computer Corporation's Web site and examined the specifications for one of its docking stations. It offers the following:

- Standard I/O ports installed include serial, parallel, video, two PS/2, four USB, VGA, DVI, S-Video, and audio ports
- One half-height standard PCI slot and one internal media bay with battery charging support
- RJ-45 and RJ-11 jacks for network and modem hookups
- Cable lock security with latch

This is not intended as a promotion for Dell's products, it is just an example of the array of options available. All notebook manufacturers offer similar options for their line of portable products.

One issue involved with using docking stations is the fact that the device list that the operating system must support changes between portable and docked configurations. This isn't really a problem, but each change does require that the OS detect and install drivers for the appropriate devices. This slows the boot process. The Windows user can get around this by creating a separate hardware profile for each configuration. In Device Manager, there is a tab called Hardware Profiles that allows you to copy the existing profile. You then highlight the devices unique to the docking station and for each of these devices select the option "Disable in This Profile." Save that profile as Portable and rename the original as Docked. The next time you boot the computer, you will be asked which profile you wish.

PORT REPLICATORS

A *port replicator* is actually nothing more than a scaled-down docking station. In fact, with most models, the replicator attaches to the docking connector. A port replicator provides all the I/O

> **BUZZ WORDS**
>
> **Docking station:** A device to which a laptop computer can be attached that provides additional hardware support, including I/O ports, PCI slots, and drive bays.

ports of the docking station, but lacks additional PCI slots and/or drive bays. For many portables that lack integrated network support, it is usually possible to get a port replicator with a built-in NIC. As with docking stations, it is possible for the user to create separate profiles for each configuration to speed up the boot process.

Exam Note: Another pair of devices that see their share of coverage on the A+ exam are the docking station and the port replicator. Know the differences between the two and the issues that arise when using either one.

The PDA

The personal digital assistant (PDA), like the one illustrated in **Figure 20.6**, is a device that is currently enjoying tremendous popularity. While not a full-blown computer system by most people's standards, the PDA can take many day-to-day applications and put them in a shirt pocket. These applications include schedules, expense records, small database applications, and literally hundreds of others. Some models can interconnect to a cellular modem and allow for full Internet or networking capability while on the road.

Data is usually input with a stylus. The PDA makes use of the touchscreen technology I discussed in Chapter Nine. The user opens the appropriate application and taps the surface of the display with the stylus. Text is usually entered in one of two ways. Some incorporate little teeny keyboards. The keys are depressed either with the tip of a fingernail or with the stylus if the user possesses sufficient coordination. Touch typing is not much of an option. Other models bring up a display of a typical keyboard layout and the user taps the desired character with the stylus.

An emerging technology that has become incredibly popular is handwriting recognition. A popular implementation of this technology is called Graffiti. The user scrawls the message onto the space provided and the PDA converts it to text format. The problem that I see with that technology is that nothing exists that can recognize my handwriting. Not even my wife.

PDAs generally have their own specific and unique operating system. Currently the two most popular are the Palm

Figure 20.8 I often take short trips without a notebook computer. But I don't leave home without my PDA!

OS, used by Palms, most Sony models of PDA, and many others, and Windows CE, used by many of the HP models as well as others.

Whichever way the user chooses to go, the PDA will offer some method by which he or she can interconnect the PDA to a standard PC and migrate data back and forth. Most PDAs also feature a slot into which external accessories can be connected. These accessories include memory cards, cellular modem hookups, and many others. As a technician, you probably won't see too many PDAs; they aren't really serviceable. When they die, generally the only option is to buy a new one.

CHAPTER SUMMARY

As you can see from this chapter, working with portable computers need not be intimidating. They're just smaller versions of the desktops you're already familiar with. The few differences that do exist are not technically challenging and are easy enough to understand and remember. The one thing that nobody tells you before you start servicing laptops is that your hands can't be more than an inch or so wide, but your fingers must be fourteen inches long with at least five sets of knuckles.

BRAIN DRAIN

1. How many different components can you think of that are designed differently for laptops than they are for desktops?

2. Explain the purpose of having a 44-conductor IDE cable in a laptop computer.

3. Describe the three main forms of battery used by laptops over the years and how they differ.

4. Describe how a docking station differs from a port replicator.

5. You own a laptop computer and a docking station. Nearly every time you boot your machine it goes through the Plug 'n Play process. Why is this and how can you stop this from happening?

THE 64K$ QUESTIONS

1. The memory package typically used by notebook computers is the _____.

   a. SDRAM

   b. SO-DIMM

   c. DIMM

   d. RDRAM

2. Modern laptop computers typically use _____ displays.

   a. Passive matrix

   b. CRT

   c. TFT

   d. NRF

3. However, many older laptops were equipped with _____ displays.

   a. Passive matrix

   b. CRT

   c. TFT

   d. NRF

4. An optional hard drive available for laptop computers fits into a _____ PCMCIA slot.

   a. Type I

   b. Type II

c. Type III

d. Either Type II or Type III

5. Two characteristics that might prevent two different AC adapters from being interchangeable are _____ and _____. (Pick two.)

    a. The AC outlet

    b. The type of connector used to interconnect the adapter to the laptop

    c. Input voltage

    d. Output voltage

6. A type of battery used in laptops that exhibits no battery memory whatsoever is a _____ battery.

    a. NiCad

    b. Ni-MH

    c. Li-Ion

    d. Alkaline

7. Which layer of a PC card driver notifies the computer when a device has been removed or inserted?

    a. Card service

    b. SCSI services

    c. ASPI

    d. Socket services

8. Which layer of a PC card driver handles the interpretation of the device's command set?

    a. Card service

    b. SCSI services

    c. ASPI

    d. Socket services

9. What pointing device is most sensitive to the person's individual electrostatic charge?

    a. The trackball

b. The mouse

c. The trackpoint

d. The trackpad

10. Two major differences between a port replicator and a docking station are _____ and _____.

    a. PCI card support

    b. External SVGA support

    c. Additional PS2 connectors

    d. Support for additional drives

TRICKY TERMINOLOGY

Battery memory: A phenomenon exhibited by rechargeable batteries where the pattern of recent charge cycles affects the maximum charge the battery will accept.

Card services: The portion of a PC card driver that interprets the command set for a specific device.

Docking station: A device to which a laptop computer can be attached that provides additional hardware support, including I/O ports, PCI slots, and drive bays.

PC card: Any auxiliary device designed to be plugged into a PCMCIA slot.

Port replicator: A device to which a laptop computer can be attached that provides additional I/O services to the computer.

Socket driver: The portion of a PC card driver that is responsible for I/O services and insertion/removal notification.

Trackpad: A pointing device used on laptop computers that makes use of an electrostatically sensitive surface. The user runs a finger across the surface and the trackpad tracks the movement of the electrostatic charge.

Trackpoint: A small pointing device used on laptop computers, similar to a trackball, but much smaller.

ACRONYM ALERT

PDA: Personal Digital Assistant. Any one of several computing devices designed for maximum portability.

NiCad: Nickel Cadmium. A type of rechargeable battery.

Ni-MH: Nickel Metal Hydride. A type of rechargeable battery.

Li-Ion: Lithium Ion. A type of rechargeable battery.

CHAPTER 21

BASIC TROUBLESHOOTING PROCEDURES

Now that you know everything there is to know about how computer hardware works (or at least have glimpsed beneath the tip of the iceberg), fixing one of these babies should be a piece of cake, right? Oh, if it were only that simple. Throughout this book, I have discussed troubleshooting tips unique to specific pieces of hardware. In this chapter, I'm going to look at troubleshooting techniques, tools, and procedures in general.

One thing I would like to point out is that troubleshooting is as much art as it is science. Some people have a talent for it and others don't. Still, even those with only a rudimentary talent for troubleshooting can succeed if they learn to use a well-thought-out procedure. But I'll warn you right now: while a mathematical model for troubleshooting allows you to solve many problems, a little creative thinking is what separates the wanna-bes from the pros.

A+ EXAM OBJECTIVES

As far as the A+ Core exam is concerned, this chapter really covers just two objectives:

2.1   Recognize common problems associated with each module and their symptoms, and identify steps to isolate and troubleshoot the problems. Given a problem situation, interpret the symptoms and infer the most likely cause.

2.2   Identify basic troubleshooting procedures and tools, and how to elicit problem symptoms from customers. Justify asking particular questions in a given scenario.

THE COMPTIA TROUBLESHOOTING METHOD

Scour the books on computer hardware and networking and you'll find as many variations on this theme as there are books. Since some of the people who wrote these books are like me and actually worked on computers before they sat down to write a book, they provide some pretty good approaches. They all boil down to basically the same approach, once you strip away the veneer. Here are the steps, in order:

- Identify the problem
- Re-create the problem
- Isolate the cause of the problem
- Decide on a possible solution
- Test your idea
- Fix the computer
- Follow up

EXAM NOTE: The following pages outline the CompTIA approach to troubleshooting. The exam is rather insistent that you be able to describe the procedure in detail.

IDENTIFY THE PROBLEM

The customers walk in, slam their systems down on the counter, and say in a disgusted voice, "This thing don't work!" They seem to think they have just given you all the information you'll ever need to fix the problem. Some people think that hardware technicians have this magic wand hidden in back, and as soon as the door closes behind them, we pull it out, wave it a few times, and the computer is miraculously fixed. I hate to disillusion you, but the magic wand only has so many uses in it, so I only bring it out in dire emergencies.

A few leading questions will usually help you target the real problem. Several of the books I read when I was in training all suggested that first question you should ask a client is, "What changed since the last time it worked?" It took a couple of years for me to figure out that this was a useless question. The answer was always, "Nothing." This evidences the difference between an open-ended question and a closed-ended question. A *closed-ended question*, such as the one above, elicits a response that ends the conversation right there.

You need to be more specific. If the computer still works, but is exhibiting problems, a good question might be, "What were you doing at the moment the problem first appeared?" This represents an *open-ended question*. The answer provided by the user has a strong potential of leading to other questions. And it may even lead to a solution.

If a specific device, such as a sound card or a modem, is exhibiting peculiarities, you might ask if any new software has been installed, or if another device was installed on the system. Once in a while, you get lucky and the customer is able to be specific about the problem. That's always a nice head start.

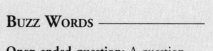

BUZZ WORDS

Open-ended question: A question that will provide further insight into the discussion as a result of the answer provided.

Closed-ended question: A question that leads to an answer that provides no further insight or leads to an abrupt dead end to the discussion.

RE-CREATE THE PROBLEM

The next thing you want to do is make the problem happen for you. If you are able to replicate the error or device failure, there might be an error message associated with the problem that you can use to point you in the right direction. Many messages will provide the memory address at which the error occurred and if you can find out what was running at that address, it might give you some ideas. For example, device drivers frequently load to the same memory address each time. Therefore, if the error repeats itself over and over and the address is always the same, it might be a device driver that is generating the error. It could also mean that the RAM stick is bad as well.

In any case, in order to successfully analyze a problem, you need to be able to re-create it. If the problem won't raise its ugly head for you, then the problem might not be with the computer. User errors are not so easily fixed by technicians. However a good technician can gently point out the errors and show the user how to correct them.

ISOLATE THE CAUSE OF THE PROBLEM

There is where the troubleshooting session frequently turns into a turkey-shooting session. If the address of the error points to a specific device, you have a head start. If not, you might find yourself resorting to one of the several hardware and software diagnostic tools that I'll discuss later in the chapter. The last thing you want to do is to arbitrarily start replacing parts, hoping you'll eventually get lucky. For one thing, that's not a very cost-effective approach, and for another, you run the risk of damaging good parts.

But what if all your diagnostic tools unearth nothing? You've successfully re-created the problem on the computer and now you and your colleagues are standing around scratching your heads and saying, "Never seen anything like that before!" And in this industry, the longer you work at your job, the more likely it is that will happen to you.

That's when it's time to find somebody who has seen the problem before. A good start is online technical support if you are working on a name-brand computer. Most manufacturers maintain an extensive knowledge base. If it's a known problem, they'll be familiar with it.

Even if the computer is a white-box clone made by the Mom and Pop operation that went out of business last year, all hope is not lost. Mom and Pop had to have bought the parts they used somewhere, and those parts came from a manufacturer. Once you've isolated the component that is giving you a hard time, see if you can find anything on the Internet that relates to the problem you're having. Later in this chapter, I will be going through each component, one at a time, and providing some of the more commonly seen issues and possible solutions.

DECIDE ON A POSSIBLE SOLUTION

Now that you think you know what's causing the problem, you probably already have a possible solution in mind. This is your *hypothesis*. Think about that solution carefully before you implement it. For

BUZZ WORDS ————————

Hypothesis: Any theory that can be tested to be proven either true or false.

example, if your solution involves formatting the customer's hard drive, you might want to make sure there are backups of any critical data. If backups don't exist, you might want to think about possible ways of getting that data off before you destroy it permanently.

Also keep in mind that some symptoms are generated by multiple components. Memory errors can be caused by the memory itself, a faulty chipset, or even a bad power supply. Therefore, you need to be thorough in your analysis before you jump into the next step.

TEST YOUR IDEA

You think it's a bad CPU, but you're not 100 percent certain. If you have another computer lying around that uses a CPU your sick computer will support, you might try installing a known good CPU in the system. One of the things I do is to keep a collection of "known-goods." These are parts that I can use to test a sick computer. I have several CPUs, at least one example of each of the most commonly used memory sticks, and a couple of motherboards. I keep both an AT and an ATX power supply just for testing purposes.

One thing you probably want to avoid doing is simply ordering in new parts randomly. Distributors are justifiably reluctant to take back opened computer components. They have no way of knowing what precautions you may or may not have taken to protect those components from ESD while they were in your possession. By testing your idea first, you eliminate a lot of unnecessary hassles.

FIX THE COMPUTER

Once you're comfortable that your hypothesis is correct and that it fixes the problem, go ahead and implement your solution. Install new parts that the customer can keep and then test the solution. Run the customer's applications for a while. Do your best to replicate the original problem, but keep watching for new problems while you're doing that. It is not at all uncommon for a new problem to appear once the original problem has been fixed. Whatever you do, don't just fire the machine up and say, "This, my friend, is why they pay me the big bucks!" and hand it off to the user. That's a good way of having it come flying back in your face.

FOLLOW UP

You also need to provide customers with proof that you've fixed their problem. And by this, I don't simply mean an invoice that lists what you did and how much it's going to cost them. When they pick up their system, show them it's fixed. Let them poke around on it and try to re-create the original problem themselves. Once they're satisfied the problem has gone away, then you can give them the invoice and watch their eyes glaze over.

Doing this accomplishes two things. First off, you demonstrate to the customer that your solution has worked. That greatly eases the pain of seeing the bill. Second, in the event that the problem recurs, you will be able to point out the fact that it was working when it left. While this admittedly does provide for a very good method of covering your own bases (in the industry, that's called the CYA solution; don't ask why), it also might be providing some insight into what might be going on over on the customer's side. Is there an environmental issue causing the problem? I once had a computer system that kept coming back with bad power supplies. I finally got on my horse and rode over to the customer's site. I tested the outlet and found that it required immediate attention. You're not supposed to get 140V out of those things!

Just because the computer is now working perfectly doesn't mean your job is done. One of the things they teach you in the military is that no job is complete until the paperwork is done. That holds true of computer repair as well. You need to document exactly what you did. There are some pretty nifty help-desk software solutions that allow you to create a searchable database of problems and their solutions. The larger that database becomes, the more frequently you can simply turn to it for solutions.

TROUBLESHOOTING TOOLS

An auto mechanic wouldn't even consider trying to drop a transmission if he or she didn't have the right set of tools. As unbelievable as it may sound, there are problems that can't be fixed with a 16-ounce ball peen hammer. While a vast number of computer problems can be fixed with a keen wit and a Phillips screwdriver, sometimes you need a little extra help. The computer industry is blessed with a large number of troubleshooting aids that come in very handy. Some are pieces of hardware that perform certain functions, while others are software-based solutions. Somebody who wants to fix computers for a living should assemble a collection of necessities.

HARDWARE-BASED TROUBLESHOOTING TOOLS

There are certain tools you can't live without. Every technician needs a good set of screwdrivers, a pair of needle-nosed pliers, a 16-ounce ball peen hammer, and some duct tape. You may think I'm kidding about the hammer, but I'm not. Maybe I'm exaggerating about needing 16 ounces, but you'll find out what I'm talking about the next time you try to install a double-height drive into a pair of 5.25″ bays. That little shelf they put in to keep the drives properly seated really gets in the way. The duct tape is useful for taking specific items such as drive rails or drive bay covers and securing them to the inside of the case where they will be easy to find the next time you need them.

But then, these aren't really troubleshooting tools are they? Troubleshooting tools are the ones that help you solve problems. And there are some good ones on the market.

THE POST CARD

Unfortunately, this is not the one you send to your mother-in-law when you go on vacation. These are a bit expensive for that. The *POST card* I'm talking about is used to diagnose problems that occur during the boot process that prevent the computer from starting properly. It mounts into an empty expansion slot and while the computer is booting

BUZZ WORDS ———————————

POST card: A device that follows each step of the POST procedure and reports the results. Should the POST fail, the last successful process will be indicated in an encoded display.

Figure 21.1 This POST card, by Ultra-X, is one of the most formidable tools you can have in your arsenal. It identifies problems that occur during the POST process.

(or trying to, anyway), it's zipping off light patterns on an LED readout so fast that you can't possibly read them. Don't worry about that. The ones you can't read are the ones you don't care about. They represent components that passed.

At the point that the boot process fails, the readout will display a pattern of lights that represents a specific component. The POST card ships with a booklet that itemizes all of those error messages. All you have to do is look up the number displayed, and it tells you what part of the POST process failed. JDR Microdevices in San Jose, California, offers four different options. It has standard POST cards in both PCI and ISA form. But it also has ISA and PCI versions that test the BIOS as well as the POST process.

A more advanced version of this card is available from Ultra-X, Inc. in Santa Clara, California. It can go beyond the POST test (which it does rather extensively) and continue to test RAM, drive operation including CD-ROM drives, and much more. The Professional Kit includes an impressive array of diagnostics software utilities, a collection of loopback plugs, and the PCI card. This is the card illustrated in **Figure 21.1**. A rather interesting option, offered by PCWiz out of Clearwater, Florida, offers a single card that has an ISA connector on one edge and a PCI connector on other.

THE MULTIMETER

Sometimes simply testing for power or continuity can tell you a lot about what's going on. A simple and inexpensive tool for that is a multimeter. I recommend that you spend a few extra bucks on this and get a digital version. They're easier to work with.

The multimeter will tell you if you have proper power coming out of the connectors coming from your power supply. You can use them to test a wire for continuity. They're also useful for testing those ceramic fuses that don't let you see the wire.

LOOPBACK ADAPTER

Testing a port can sometimes be a matter of having that port talk to itself. By doing this, you are verifying the functionality of the port itself and taking external variables, such as device drivers or cables, out of the equation. In order to do that, you'll need a specialized plug called a *loopback adapter* that wraps the signal back to the computer rather than sending it out to a device. This takes the device out of the loop and tells you whether or not it is the port that is bad rather than a device or cable. Loopback adapters are available for either serial ports or parallel ports (**Figure 21.2**).

There are also software variations on the loopback test. Most modems ship with a disk that has their diagnostics software. This will usually include some form of loopback test. In Microsoft products, a loopback adapter is available as an option when installing network cards.

LOGIC PROBES

The problem with a data signal is that it only lasts for a few nanoseconds. Most of us have a bit of difficulty in seeing an event that only lasts that long. Therefore, in order to detect the presence of one of these signals, you need a logic probe. A logic probe locks onto a signal and the display holds what it finds. These are good for testing a totally dead system to see if anything at all is happening on the board.

MEMORY TESTERS

In Chapter Eight, Searching Your Memory, I pointed out that sometimes it is very difficult to identify

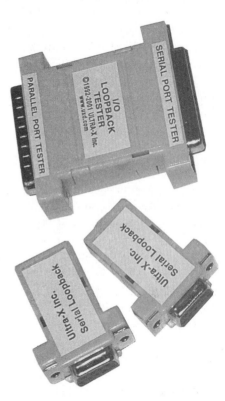

Figure 21.2 Loopback adapters help you diagnose problems with the serial and parallel ports on a machine.

memory simply by looking at it. It is also very difficult to test memory. Even computer systems that have built-in diagnostics programs tell you that there is a problem, but they don't tell you where the problem resides. It's all fine and good if you only have one stick of memory installed. But a lot of trial and error is going to be involved any time you have more than one module installed.

Specialized devices designed just to test memory are a valuable addition to your collection of troubleshooting tools, if you can afford one. The problem is that they tend to be pretty expensive. And RAM is getting to be where it isn't. However, if you can justify the expense, a memory tester is able to identify memory by type, speed, and density. However, they can also do more specialized tricks. Some of the better ones can detect and locate broken solder joints, bad cells on DRAM chips, and more. Cool toys, if you can afford one.

THE ADVANCED CABLE TESTER

This is actually more of a networking tool than it is a hardware technician's tool. It can, however, come in handy. An advanced cable tester can test for continuity, do a signal test on each conductor along the cable, and even detect a break in the cable. Some of them not only detect the break, but also tell you how far down the cable from the tester that the break occurs. This greatly enhances your ability to fix the problem.

The cable tester may or may not come with a remote unit. If it doesn't, there will be two sockets for plugging the cable into. These can be of limited use when testing an installed cable. One with a remote unit provides a second smaller unit that can be plugged onto the cable at the user's end. Then, from the hub or patch panel, you can perform your tests.

SOFTWARE TROUBLESHOOTING ESSENTIALS

There are also some excellent software applications on the market that assist in the task of troubleshooting. These range from individual task-specific utilities to entire suites of programs that perform a myriad of tricks for the hardware technician. While I would like to emphasize that, throughout this book, it has never been my intention to promote or disparage any particular product, this happens to be one of those areas in which there really is no choice but to shine the spotlight on specific products. However, I should point out that the inclusion of a particular product in this chapter does not represent an endorsement. Conversely my failure to mention a competing product most likely means simply that I am not familiar with the product. I'm not a testing lab.

THE HARDWARE MANUFACTURERS' UTILITIES

One of the first places you might turn for help should be the company that made the computer. And that doesn't always mean calling its tech support line and seeing who can keep you on hold the longest. Many of the tier one manufacturers ship their systems with a CD that contains a plethora of diagnostics utilities specific to that machine. Among these are Compaq, Dell, Hewlett Packard, and IBM.

Many of IBM and Compaq's machines ship with a diagnostics program that can be initialized during the boot sequence that will perform an exhaustive test on every component in the system if you ask it to. It can also do simpler tasks, such as run a diagnostics on the hard drive. On the server end, some of these diagnostics are so sophisticated they not only detect faulty memory, they tell you specifically the slot in which the memory is installed.

Even if a specific machine doesn't ship with a diagnostics utility on board, it is likely that there is one available. Check the manufacturer's support site. I have found that a number of different manufacturers offer model-specific troubleshooting utilities. Some of these are specific to certain machines while others are more generic. Dell even provides an excellent "Ask Dudley" troubleshooting guide that leads you through most of the common problems. You will find that most of the manufacturers offer something similar to that. These manufacturers don't just offer these services out of the goodness of their hearts. They have millions of machines out there in the world, and eventually all of them need support. If everybody had to depend on telephone support, there wouldn't be enough people in the world to staff the support lines.

TASK-SPECIFIC UTILITIES

Earlier in the chapter, I mentioned that some symptoms might be induced by more than one component. One of the options I offered at the time was basically a trial-and-error method of replacing suspected parts with known good parts. While, personally, I don't think there's any substitute for testing with the real thing, I have been known to be guilty of taking shortcuts. Certain utilities exist that perform tests on just one component. The reason I don't put all my faith in them is because they are not a 100 percent accurate. However, I find them very useful in telling me which component to swap out first. Some of these are shareware, and you have the opportunity to try them for a while before you shell out your bucks. The following is a short list of some of the ones I've tested and think you might find useful. There are about a gazillion others.

- *Burnin Test*: Shareware, requires registration for continued use. If you build your own systems, a program of this nature is a necessity. Once a system is built, this program will perform stress tests on each component for a preset period of time.

- *CPUCheck*: Shareware, requires registration for continued use. Identifies the CPU and detects internal and external bus speeds.

- *CTBios*: Freeware. Identifies the manufacturer of your motherboard.

- *CTPCI*: Freeware. Identifies and reports all PCI devices installed in your system.

- *DocMemory*: Freeware. Detects bad memory and tells you which stick is defective.

- *FindIRQ*: Freeware provided by *PC Magazine*. No charge to download. Tests to see which IRQs are in use and returns a report on available IRQs.

- *Look RS232 Pro*: Shareware, requires registration for continued use. Tests each line on the serial cable to make sure it's doing what it's supposed to be doing.

- *Modem Doctor*: Shareware, requires registration for continued use. Does loopback testing, detects and reports conflicts, and helps you fine-tune your initialization string. Excellent tool to have.

- *RST*: Commercial program from Ultra-X. Short for the RAM Stress Test, this program works from a bootable floppy diskette and is completely independent of the operating system. It can detect the precise DRAM chip on which a failure occurred, allowing the tech to isolate the problem on a very granular level.

- *WhatChanged*: Commercial Program, costs $29.95. Finds changes in the Windows Registry. When the customer tells you nothing changed, you can clear your throat meaningfully and say, "Uh-huh."

Utility Suites

Here's where I take a risk of offending some company or the other by leaving it out, but as before, my list is not all-inclusive. It only lists those with which I'm familiar enough to be able to accurately describe them.

Many companies have put together complete suites of utilities that can diagnose pretty much every component in your system. Some of the more basic ones do fairly simple tests and only report which component is faulty. They don't go so far as to identify a specific problem. Still, this is better than nothing. Others perform exhaustive diagnostics and probably tell you far more than you need to know.

- *BCM Diagnostics*: Shareware. Similar to Norton Utilities, except that it is hardware-specific. Runs diagnostics on processor, RAM, graphics adapter, modem, sound card, and attached drives. Doesn't do much for motherboard issues, however.

- *Checkit Professional by Smith-Micro*: Commercial program. Does extensive tests on all hardware components and identifies specific problems. Includes a DOS-based boot diskette that provides for troubleshooting when Windows won't boot. Extremely detailed and extremely powerful.

- *Dr. Hardware*: Commercial program. Doesn't actually perform diagnostics, but is an inexpensive way to do a total inventory of a system and generate a list of all hardware installed on a system.

- *Norton Utilities*: Commercial program. Provides simpler diagnostics as well as options for fine-tuning a system. Tends to be more OS-oriented with only a few simpler hardware diagnostics.

- *QuickTech Pro by Ultra-X*: Commercial program. An even more potent analysis program than Checkit Professional, in my opinion. This is the armored tank of all the programs that I've used. This even ships with a FAT editor and an IDE low-level format as part of the package. I'm still trying to find a problem that it can't diagnose. Tests can be run in either quick mode or detailed mode. In detailed mode, you get over sixty-five pages of information about your system.

TROUBLESHOOTING ROADMAPS

Most of the components in a computer system have been around for so long that that are some pretty straightforward approaches to troubleshooting problems with them. In the following sections, I will take a look at some common approaches to finding out what's wrong so you can fix it.

BOOT FAILURE OR POST-BOOT PROBLEMS

When the system won't even boot, your problems are exacerbated by the fact that you can't run most of the diagnostics utilities. That's when you want one of those POST cards I described earlier. Lacking one of those, try the following:

- *Are you plugged in?* Computers don't run without juice. Make sure there are no loose connections.

- *Are you plugged into a surge suppressor?* (I certainly hope so.) Make sure it is plugged in and turned on. And while this may sound like a no-brainer, check to make sure it isn't plugged into itself. Twice (not just once, but twice), I've gone on site to a "dead" computer and found the power strip looped back to itself.

- *Are you getting power from the power supply?* Use your multimeter to check voltage on one of the free Molex connectors. If there is no current, you most likely have a bad power supply.

- *Do you get any display at all?* Obviously POST messages won't show if you don't and you'll be counting on beep codes.

- *Does it beep?* Even a successful POST will send out a single beep through the PC speaker, indicating that the speaker works. No video combined with no beeps is a good sign that the problem exists on the motherboard. If you're getting more than one beep, check Appendix D: BIOS Beep Codes and Error Messages.

You've tried all of the above and still have no idea what's going on. Now it's time to strip the system down to just the motherboard and processor connected to the power supply and front panel connectors. In this state, there should be resounding beep codes generated. If not, either the motherboard and/or processor is bad. (Sorry I can't be more specific as to which it is.) If you do get a beep, add each component one at a time. Start with memory. If there is more than one RAM stick installed, add them each, one at a time. If, when RAM is added, the machine goes back to being a doorstop, you've found the problem. Next add expansion cards, one at a time. And finally hook up the drives, one at a time.

Sometimes the problem appears after a successful POST. The computer thinks it's working; you simply disagree. The following list itemizes some of the more common post-boot malfunctions that can occur.

- *Disk boot failure*: You may get a message telling you to "Insert system disk and press any key to continue." This means that Int19h failed to find a useable MBR and could not boot the system. This could mean a hard drive failure or a corrupted OS. In either case, use a boot diskette to boot the system and see if you can access the hard drive from there.

- *Diskette drive failure*: During POST, the CMOS reported a floppy diskette drive as being present, but one is not being detected. Check cables first. If the cable is properly seated and intact, replace the drive.

- *Diskette drive mismatch*: Your CMOS is reporting one type of drive, but POST is finding another. Check the CMOS settings. This is especially true if you recently replaced the system board battery.

- *FDD controller error*: This isn't necessarily a hardware problem. If you're booting to a defective diskette you will also get this message.

- *Fixed disk controller failure*: This error is generated when POST sends a query to the hard drive controller and the drive either fails to respond or responds improperly. If it is a

SCSI drive the problem could exist on either the controller or the drive. If it is an IDE drive, the controller is on the drive.

■ *Fixed disk failure*: One of the drives on the system is not working properly. This message will also be generated from a corrupted MBR, so an FDISK and format frequently fixes this problem. There is, of course, the issue of what to do about all that data before you perform these steps.

■ *Fixed disk read fail*: Found the hard drive, all right. But now it can't read the MBR. See above.

■ *Floppy disk controller fail*: See Diskette controller failure.

■ *Floppy disk fail*: See Diskette drive failure.

■ *Gate A20 failure*: While Gate A20 is actually the twenty-first line off the address bus, and therefore the gateway to high memory, this error is most often reported because of a bad keyboard.

■ *Hard drive (or HDD) controller failure*: See Fixed disk controller failure.

■ *Invalid configuration information, please run setup*: That's pretty self-explanatory. During POST, the BIOS detected something that did not agree with the configuration settings in CMOS. For example, if you just installed new memory, it is common for this message to be displayed on the first boot following the install. On some models, new IDE devices have the same effect.

■ *Invalid media type*: This is usually the message displayed directly after an FDISK, but prior to a format. It finds the hard drive, but finds no MBR whatsoever.

■ *Invalid partition table*: You don't want to see this message. It means the information stored in the partition tables of the MBR does not correspond with the geometry of the hard drive. So now it can't read the hard drive. One time you might see this message without it meaning disaster is if you recently ran a third-party disk portioning utility and inadvertently set more than one partition as being active. A utility called Partition Doctor may get you out of this mess.

■ *Keyboard not found, press any key to continue*: And who thought up that message, I wonder. If it didn't find a keyboard, what the heck good is it going to do to press a key? I say that in jest, but in many computers, it's the case. However, on some systems, you can reseat the keyboard connector, press a key, and the boot process will continue.

■ *Keyboard locked – unlock*: This is another one of those nicely worded errors that doesn't mean what it says. It's really referring to a key lock on the system case that needs to be unlocked before you're allowed to use the system.

■ *Memory failure at xxxx xxxxx*: During POST, when the system memory test was run, the R/W operation wrote one set of data to RAM but got back something different when trying to read it back.

■ *Memory test fail*: See Memory failure at xxxx xxxxx.

■ *Missing operating system*: The system booted just fine, but never found an operating system. If you know the OS is installed, and it is the MBR that is corrupted, you might be able to get away with running a SYS command on the drive. Or it might mean that key files in the OS are corrupted. You will need to reinstall the OS in that case.

- *No boot device found, press F1 to retry*: Int19h failed to find a device with a suitable MBR. Check your CMOS settings to see if the boot order has been changed. Otherwise check to see if your drive has failed.

There are many, many others from the different BIOS manufacturers. These are the key ones that you're likely to see on most systems. There might be slight wording variations, but they'll amount to the same thing.

TROUBLESHOOTING RAM

I covered memory troubleshooting in detail in Chapter Eight, Searching Your Memory. But a few brief pointers might be in order. Check the following list to see if your problem appears here.

- *My computer is not reporting the correct amount of memory*: What OS are you running? DOS can't see past 64MB by itself. You can have 2GB of RAM installed and DOS will only report 64MB. On an older system, make sure the larger RAM sticks are in the lower banks. Some early BIOS routines would not recognize larger memory that was detected after a smaller stick was initialized. Do you have onboard video? If so, your system is most likely grabbing some of your system RAM to use as video memory.

- *I just installed new memory and now my system doesn't work!*: Don't panic. This is a common problem. Most likely, you simply installed the wrong type of memory. EDO and SDRAM don't get along, nothing but FPM gets along with FPM, and so forth and so forth. Chapter Eight goes into this in great detail. If there is not a memory type mismatch, perhaps the new stick is simply defective. On newer systems, this will usually result in a successful boot, and the new memory will simply be ignored. On some systems, however, especially earlier ones, defective RAM will cause the whole system to go down in flames (figuratively speaking) when you try to boot it.

- *I'm getting a memory mismatch error on boot*: If you just installed memory, it is common to have to run the setup utility in order to introduce the new RAM to the CMOS. Let it do its thing. If the message repeats itself over and over again, even after you've run the setup utility, there's a pretty good chance one of the RAM sticks is defective. Use one of the diagnostic utilities I discussed earlier.

- *My system boots fine, but I get intermittent memory errors while I'm working*: Have fun. This could be defective memory, a corrupted system file, a corrupted device driver, or even a flaky power supply. Start with simplest to fix first. Run one of the diagnostics utilities I keep harping on and see if you have bad RAM. If not, start documenting the memory addresses reported by the error messages and use the memory map supplied by your OS to find out what's running at that address. If it's a device driver, try reinstalling the driver. If that doesn't work, if possible, pull the device from the system and see if the error persists. If it goes away, you've found the problem. If the RAM checks good, and all devices test out good, start thinking seriously about replacing your power supply.

- *My system says I'm out of memory and I've got lots of memory*: These messages don't always refer to physical memory. In fact, most often they refer to your swap file. Check your virtual memory settings. Maybe they need to be increased. In Windows, it's usually best to just let Windows manage its own. You also might need to run Defrag. Even if there's lots of free memory, the swap file needs a large contiguous space.

- *I added more memory and my system actually slowed down*: This is a chipset-related issue, and I'm willing to bet you've got an Intel 430FX, VX, or TX chipset. The reason for this is that a minor design issue (It's not a flaw. Intel never has flaws.) only allows data from the lower 64MB to be stored to cache. Anything stored in addresses above 64MB must be retrieved in multiple independent I/O operations. As I pointed out in Chapter Eight, this can add large numbers of clock cycles to each I/O operation.

TROUBLESHOOTING HARD DRIVES

Hard drive failures occur in a wide range of situations. Sometimes it's not found, sometimes it's the wrong size, and sometimes it's just too slow! In any case, hard drives have resulted in more gray hairs on my head than just about anything else, except of course, for my children. So let me try to break down some of the simpler problems and see which ones can be fixed.

- *I'm getting a general failure of the hard drive*: Sometimes this is a failure of the drive and other times it's a failure of the MBR. If it's an IDE drive, it's easy to tell. As you're booting the machine, enter the CMOS Setup utility. Most BIOS manufacturers provide a hard disk detection utility of some sort. If the utility can't find the drive, it is not being electrically detected. This could be as simple as a faulty or loose cable. Were you just working inside the machine? If either the ribbon cable or the Molex got knocked loose, you'll get this failure. If your CMOS detects your drive, the problem is most likely the MBR.

- *My CMOS found the drive, but it still won't boot*: Did you just now install the drive? Don't forget that drives don't work all by themselves right out of the box. You need to partition and format the drive before an MBR is generated. It won't work until you do that. If it is a drive that has been in the system for a while, you may have either a corrupted MBR or a file in the OS. Try booting the machine to a bootable floppy and accessing the drive that way. If that works, you may have picked up a boot sector virus or perhaps the drive has simply failed. Get your hands on a good antivirus software, such as Norton Antivirus or McAffee, and see if it finds anything.

- *I ran an antivirus program and it 1) found nothing and the system still won't boot or 2) it found a virus and claimed it fixed it, but the system still won't boot*: Now you're looking seriously at a corrupted MBR. In the old days of DOS, you would simply boot to a DOS boot diskette and run FDISK /MBR, which would regenerate a new MBR. This doesn't work on new systems and newer OSs. A good disk partitioning utility like Partition Magic might be able to bail you out. Most likely, you're going to wind up retrieving what data you can salvage from the drive and starting over from scratch.

- *I just installed a new 40GB drive on my computer and it tells me it's only 8GB*: This is a BIOS and/or chipset issue. If the system won't recognize past 8GB, it's only operating in Int13h mode. It recognizes none of the drive translation mechanisms you've grown to know and love (see Chapter Thirteen, Hard Disk Interfacing and Disk Management. It may be that a BIOS upgrade and a supplemental I/O controller will solve your problem. If you do not have a flashable BIOS, then a new motherboard is probably in order. Just as well. It probably means you're using an outdated CPU and RAM as well.

- *I just installed a new 80GB hard drive and it only formats to 32GB:* See above. It is a more recent BIOS limitation with the same solution.

- *I just installed a new hard drive and my computer doesn't see it at all:* If the drive you just installed was an IDE drive, check your jumpers. If it's the only drive on the cable, it needs to be set to Master. Some drives also have a setting for Single, and in this situation, that would work as well. If it is the second drive on the cable, one of the drives has to be Master and the other one needs to be Slave. Most drives also have a setting called Cable Select. For this setting to properly work, you need a cable-select cable. The position on the cable determines master/slave relationship. If a drive is jumpered to be a master and is placed on the slave position, it won't be seen.

- *My hard drive is making funny noises:* Without going into a lengthy explanation of everything that could be going wrong, it all boils down to the same thing. You're about to need a new drive. Back everything up and see what your local electronics store has on sale. The one exception to this is a light tapping sound that is common to all drives. They will periodically perform a thermal recalibration, especially shortly after bootup. A slight tapping sound is commonly heard while the drive is performing this task.

- *Every time I boot to a floppy, my 20.4GB hard drive is only seen as 504MB and I can't access it:* The most likely cause for this is that, at the time the hard disk was installed and configured, either you or the person that installed it used something called dynamic overlay software. This is a disk that ships from the manufacturer that provides for some proprietary drive translation mechanism that isn't loaded when you boot from a floppy. Nothing is intercepting the hard drive calls for Int13h and you can find out why that is a problem in Chapter Thirteen.

- *My machine keeps running ScanDisk on bootup and finding new bad sectors each time:* Several things can lead to this, and not all of them lead to the conclusion that your drive is failing. An IDE cable longer than 18″ can cause bits of data to be corrupted, which, when accessed, will show up as bad sectors, even though it's the data that's bad and not the drive. Another thing that can lead to this is that some BIOS manufacturers provide for manual control of the drive translation method used by your drive. If this is set too fast, data corruption will occur. See above. Then there is always the possibility that the disk itself is starting to fail. Far too many people assume it is because of surface damage, but this is unlikely. Hard drives are sealed devices, so dust and dirt can't get in. If your drive head impacted with the surface, you wouldn't be getting drive errors. You would have a dead drive. It can be caused by one of the chips on the drive controller getting zapped by ESD. The computer may be located too close to some device or object emitting high amounts of magnetic energy (such as a loudspeaker designed for home stereo systems or a poorly shielded monitor).

- *My computer says, "Error Reading Sector 0" and freezes up on bootup*: One of two things has most likely happened. A primary cause for this error is that you have picked up a boot sector virus and it has not only wiped out the master boot record, it has rendered it unreadable. Many of these can be detected and cleaned by an antivirus program that can be loaded from a bootable floppy. The other problem is that you truly do have a bad sector on that spot. In either case, before you attempt any repair, try to boot from a floppy and see if you can access the drive. Just because the hard drive won't boot doesn't mean you can't still get the data off the drive. If possible, copy all critical files to another location. Norton Disk Doctor or one of the other utilities might be able to repair the sector (but probably not). If it can't, FDISK the hard drive and reformat. If FDISK returns the same error message, go see what your local electronics store has on sale.

- *I'm getting a message that says "Not ready reading drive D:" on my second drive*: Most likely, this is a software issue and not a hardware issue. You may have recently installed a new toy on your system that forced a re-enumeration of the drive-lettering scheme. Your second drive changed letters, but your software doesn't know that. So it's trying to access what is now your CD-ROM drive, which has nothing in it. If you check and Drive D: truly is your second hard drive, that indicates a problem with the volume boot record. See "Error Reading Sector 0" for possible remedies.

- *I'm getting a "Runtime Error" reading when I try to perform an FDISK on my drive*: Don't tell me. Let me guess. You have a Western Digital hard drive. This results from the FDISK program being unable to read Track 0. Western Digital has a possible solution to this problem on its Web site at www.westerndigital.com called Data Lifeguard Tools. One of the options is to run a pseudo low-level format. (As we all know, pseudo means fake. You don't perform low-level formats on IDE drives, so even if your CMOS offers that option, don't use it.) Under the *diagnostics* menu, select "Write Zeros." When it's done, restart your machine and attempt FDISK again. When this fails, Western Digital recommends you contact its technical support. But what it really means is, it's time to see what the electronics store has on sale.

TROUBLESHOOTING MOTHERBOARD-RELATED ISSUES

Problems with your motherboard can sometimes be more challenging to diagnose, simply because they can appear to be so random. In fact, it would be a great idea if somebody put together a book just on that subject. In this section, I will touch on some of the basics and try to cover the more commonly seen problems relating to motherboard and component-level products on the motherboard.

- *My machine fails to boot and returns a bunch of beeps. What do they mean?*: This was covered in Boot Failure or POST problems earlier. See Appendix D: BIOS Beep Codes and Error Messages.

- *I'm trying to boot my machine, but it tells me about an "Invalid Checksum" and hangs*: Your CMOS settings went south for the winter on you. Perhaps the battery went dead or maybe you took a voltage hit and are lucky your system isn't totally fried. Either way, you can usually run the BIOS Setup program from boot and reset the configuration to Factory Defaults. This will get the system up and running and you can tweak the settings either now or later.

- *Okay, wise guy. I went to try that, but my computer won't tell me what buttons to push to get into the CMOS Setup. What now?:* I can only say, "Been there, done that." Sometimes the brand-name computers don't provide an opening screen telling you where to go. If they've got a flash screen advertising a product you've already bought, try hitting the ESC key. That will usually clear the flash screen and you'll see POST messages. This might possibly tell you how to enter setup. If that doesn't work, try the following key sequences:

  - Del If it is an Award or an AMI BIOS this will probably work.
  - F1 Many of the "custom" Phoenix BIOS programs run from this.
  - F2 In recent years, Phoenix moved to this key. F1 was getting too easy to remember. Dell also uses this key sequence.
  - F10 This the key used by most Compaq products.
  - Alt + Esc Some proprietary BIOS chips used this.
  - Ctrl + Alt + Esc See above.
  - Insert Another proprietary alternative used by some manufacturers.
  - Ctrl + Alt + S Yet another proprietary alternative.

- *None of these work:* Yeah, well, that's why manufacturers have technical support. Give them a call, or better yet, check their Web sites. That's usually faster.

- *Oh, no! I made some settings to my CMOS and now my system won't boot:* Let that be a lesson to you. Don't ever change more than one parameter at a time. Wait till you see what affect that has before you make other changes. In this case, simply reset the system back to factory defaults and start over from scratch.

- *Every time I boot my machine it tells me that it's "Updating the ESCD" even though I didn't add any new devices:* The ESCD is your extended system configuration data, and on Plug 'n Play machines it tells the BIOS how to configure the devices. If you have an OS that is Plug 'n Play, such as Windows 95 or later, it might disagree with your BIOS on how to configure the settings. In most cases, it can do this without any problems and the BIOS accepts and remembers the changes. In some cases, however, the ESCD isn't permanently changed, but the device configuration was. So it resets the device on boot up. Windows sees this and says, "Hey, I'm the boss around here," and once again resets the configuration. And on and on it goes, a never-ending cycle. It isn't hurting anything, so you can simply ignore it. On the other hand, if it is annoying you to no end, you might see if your manufacturer supplies a BIOS upgrade to your computer. On some early Pentium machines (and just about anything made prior to that), that will involve replacing the BIOS chip. If your BIOS is flashable, you can burn the new code to your BIOS chip.

- *Thanks for the tip buddy! I just flashed my BIOS and now my system is an oversized doorstop!*: One of two things happened here. You either chose, or were supplied, the wrong version of BIOS for your particular motherboard, or you downloaded the software from the Internet and got a corrupt download. If your computer is relatively recent, it will include a feature called boot block. When it encounters corrupted BIOS, it automatically checks the floppy for a new version to flash. Yet one more reason not to retire your floppy diskette drive! Get a correct or clean version, pop it in the floppy drive, and restart. You're back up and running. If your machine does not support boot block, then pray that you have a removable BIOS chip. Better yet, only purchase motherboards that do feature removable BIOS. You can order in a new chip from the manufacturer. (that'll be fifty bucks please. Will this be MasterCard or Visa?) If the BIOS is soldered on, why don't you see what is new in the world of CPUs while you're shopping for your new motherboard? And by the way—it wasn't my fault. I only told you what to do. I didn't download the flash for you!

- *Somebody entered a password on one of the computers in our office and now nobody can access the system*: It's hard to get good help these days, isn't it? All is not lost. Many motherboards have a jumper for disconnecting the onboard battery from the CMOS chip. After a couple of minutes, put the jumper back on. Your BIOS settings will be back to factor defaults and you're good to go. If you can't find a jumper that does this, or aren't sure which one, just pull the battery out. Don't get any fingerprints on the battery, though. That will substantially shorten the life of the battery.

I've intentionally made this a short list, because a vast majority of chipset-related problems aren't easily detected as being a motherboard issue. It is the device under control of the chipset that exhibits the symptoms and not the motherboard. Some of the more common ones will be listed in the appropriate sections.

Diagnosing Processor-Related Failures

First off, if it is an outright processor-related failure, then the machine is doing nothing. You might hear the power supply spin up, but that's about it. Therefore, if your "blue screen of death" is telling you that the tragedy occurred in processor registers x and y, that really isn't indicating a processor failure. It is simply reporting at what register addresses the error occurred. That tells you the processor is doing its job, right up to the very end, and not that it's failing. However, ESD or a voltage surge could possibly damage a processor to the point that it is flaky but not outright dead. I would have to say, however, that this would be a pretty rare occurrence. Watch for the following, however.

- *I turn the machine on and nothing happens. No video, no beeps, not a darn thing. Is that my processor?*: Maybe. Probably not. Did you have cause to reinstall the processor for any reason, or is this a system you have just finished building? If so, it's possible the processor is defective, but more likely it is simply seated incorrectly. If you are using a socketed processor, check to see if it is correctly oriented. Always remember some advice I gave you earlier in the book. Read the manual! Check for bent pins. If you find one, you might be lucky enough to be able to straighten it without snapping it off (I hate it when that happens). Many times, however, this same symptom is generated by bad or incorrect memory, a hard drive improperly configured, or one of several other possible causes that are not processor related.

- *I get five short beeps when the machine starts to boot, and then that's all she wrote*: You have an AMI BIOS and it's telling you the processor failed. Buy a new one.

- *I'm getting two short beeps followed by two long beeps when the machine starts to boot, and then that's all she wrote*: You have a Phoenix BIOS. See above.

- *My machine boots fine, but after a few minutes the screen goes blank/blue screens*: See if the processor's cooling fan bit the bullet. If the CPU overheats, this will happen. If this happens too frequently, or if the machine fails to shut down, permanent damage can occur. I was once standing next to a Pentium 66 when the cooling fan died. That processor literally exploded! Customer wanted to know if I could fix it.

- *I've got a* CPU *that is supposed to be a 600MHz, but it only shows up as 450MHz after the machine starts*: Check your motherboard for manual jumper settings or the CMOS for BIOS-controlled settings. The CPU will run at whatever speed you tell it to. Consistently running a processor faster than the speed for which it was designed can result in overheating and data corruption. Overclockers beware!

Sorry if this section seems short, but as I said, most processors are all or none. They either work or they don't. And most problems that the processor gets blamed for really aren't its fault. So let's just move on to the next section.

FIXING FLOPPIES

This is another subject that was pretty thoroughly covered in its respective chapter (Chapter Eleven, Working With Removable Disks). To keep everything consistent, I'll recap here.

- *My computer reports "Floppy Drive Not Found. Press F1 to continue"*: Generally this is a result of a cable that has come loose, either the power connector or the ribbon cable. This is a common occurrence on new computers that were shipped by a commercial carrier service. If you were recently poking around in the machine, you may have knocked the cable loose. Check both the drive and the motherboard connection. Either one can come loose. If the cables are all intact, it's possible you do have a bad drive. I keep a known-good floppy around just for testing purposes. And no, you can't have it. Get your own.

- *I'm not getting any error messages, but my floppy isn't detected*: Check the CMOS settings. On some machines "None" is the factory default. If you just replaced the battery, or if it just failed, the CMOS will revert to factory defaults. If the CMOS says you don't have a floppy, then by golly, you don't have a floppy. If there is a floppy disk enabled in this setting, dig a little deeper in the CMOS settings. There might be a security setting that disables the floppy controller in order to prevent unauthorized use. You might want to check with your boss before changing that one.

■ *My system doesn't detect the floppy and the drive light stays on all the time*: This one's easy. Your ribbon cable is reversed on one side or the other. Swap it around and all will be well.

■ *I've got a 1.44MB drive but it thinks it's only 720K*: Check your CMOS settings. On an older machine, this might be the factory default. If you recently changed the battery, or if your battery just died, this will be a symptom.

■ *I can't boot from my floppy drive, but once the machine is up and running, it's always available and ready to use*: Check the boot order in your CMOS. If the floppy drive isn't selected as a potential boot device then this is normal. On some versions of BIOS, it is not uncommon for the machine to not recognize the floppy if it is set last in the order. Move it up a notch in the pecking order and it will most likely boot.

■ *I'm trying to format a floppy diskette and it keeps telling me it found a bad Track 0. These are brand-new diskettes*: This is a problem that should have gone away by now. In the days of 720K drives, it was common to get this message when trying to format a high-density diskette.

■ *I'm getting "I/O Error Reading Drive A:" messages more and more often lately*: This is most likely a problem with the diskettes themselves. How and where do you store them? Underneath the monitor is not a good place. EMI or proximity to magnets can cause the tracks to get corrupted on the diskettes. While ScanDisk can most likely restore the data, I highly recommend that you copy the diskettes over to new ones and throw the old ones away.

■ *Data Error Reading Drive A: (or B:)*: See above

■ *Sector Not Found Drive A: (or B:)*: See one step above above.

■ *Not Ready Reading Drive A: (or B:)*: Duh! Put a diskette in, for gosh sakes! If there is a diskette in, try formatting it. If there is a diskette in the drive that supposedly already had data on it, you can rephrase that as, "a diskette that used to have data on it." Run a thorough ScanDisk on it and see if you can fix the problem. If ScanDisk asks if you want to format the diskette, that's a sure sign the FAT was corrupted. Bye-bye, data.

■ *Invalid Drive Specification*: Either you're like me and type 128 mistakes per minute and there really is no Drive W: on the system, or the system didn't recognize the floppy during the boot process and you just didn't notice. It is not uncommon for CMOS settings to have a setting that says "Halt ON:" and give several options for errors that it will ignore. Floppy drive errors are one of those, and some manufacturers, in their infinite wisdom, chose to make this setting the factory default.

■ *I got a diskette stuck in my floppy and I can't get it out! What will I do?*: Call me. I'll get it out for $50.00 plus travel and lodging expenses. Or you can do it yourself pretty easily. What happened is that the metal door on the diskette is jammed in the drive mechanism. Shut the machine down and unplug it. Take something long and skinny, a butter knife usually works pretty well, and gently pry it out. But, while it's in there, you might want to copy its contents to a temporary directory on your hard drive so you can make a new copy.

- *The metal door on the diskette is bent/deformed/missing and I have to have the data stored on it*: The metal door is there to protect the medium. It isn't required for the drive to read the data off the diskette. Pop the door off, copy the data to a temporary directory on your hard drive, and make a new copy. An unfortunate side affect to this problem is frequent I/O or Data Error messages once the drive is seated. Refer to those sections for those problems.

- *I've got a lot of really tiny files that I want to store to a floppy diskette, but I get the diskette about halfway full and my system tells me the diskette is all the way full*: The solution is to not copy the files to the root directory. Diskettes use FAT12 as a file system, and as such, it uses 2 sectors per cluster. Therefore, it is technically possible to fit a hair over 1400 files onto the diskette, if they're all under 1K. However, the root directory is limited to 224 total entries. This includes file names and directory names. Entries in directories don't count, just the root directory. So by having a couple of directories, you can copy as many files as you can fit on the diskette.

- *I just ran a directory of a diskette and didn't find what I wanted. After I inserted a new diskette and tried to read the directory, I got the same list of files*: When you run a directory on the diskette, the contents of the directory are stored in cache RAM. That way, if you need to read the directory a second time, the drive doesn't have to hit the file allocation tables again, it just reads back the contents from cache. The thirty-fourth conductor on your floppy cable is the drive change indicator. It sends a signal from the drive itself to the controller, telling the system that you have changed the diskette in the drive. That clears the cache and forces a new read. If the thirty-fourth conductor is crimped or broken, the signal doesn't arrive at the controller. The solution is to replace the cable. In the meantime, you can force the cache to clear by reading a different drive and then going back to the A: drive.

TROUBLESHOOTING GRAPHICS ADAPTERS

If you're having trouble with a video card, chances are extremely good that you're having a driver-related issue or are having an argument with your OS (you'll never win, by the way). If the graphics card is letting you see the screen, it is most likely doing its job. There are some little quirks here and there that are related to the video card. Some can be easily fixed, and others can be easily fixed by replacing the video card.

- *The system goes through the whole boot process (or seems to) without ever once giving me a screen, but I don't get any beeps*: Check your cable. It helps to have the monitor hooked up to the computer.

- *I get a long series of short beeps (usually eight) and the boot process stops*: You have an AMI BIOS and a video card failure. Try a new one. If you have an Award BIOS, this could mean bad memory instead.

- *I get one long beep and two short beeps and the boot process stops*: You have an Award BIOS and see above.

- *The computer boots fine, but all I can ever get is standard VGA*: This is a driver issue. Reload the drivers and try again. And this time try loading the correct drivers.

- *The computer boots fine until Windows starts to load and then the screen goes blank*: See above.

- *Windows loads fine, and I can select all the settings I want, but I keep getting sparkly little crystals all over the place, or black specks everywhere*: This is usually caused by bad video memory. If your card has replaceable memory, swap it out. Since video cards these days usually have it soldered on, it's a good excuse to get that new 256MB X-Force Accelerator Card you've been begging your significant other for.

- *My picture is a lovely shade of puke green/fuchsia/magenta/olive drab/cyan/whatever*: Check the pins on the monitor cable. One of them is probably bent. And then stop blaming the video card. It has nothing to do with it.

That's pretty much it for troubleshooting video. Almost everything else video related is a software or driver issue.

Troubleshooting Keyboards

Keyboard problems are, amazingly enough, fairly simple to diagnose. And they're usually easy to fix as well. A broken keyboard is simply replaced. The devices are way too cheap to justify spending a lot of time trying to repair them. There aren't that many issues to deal with, so let me get them out of the way.

- *I'm getting the message "Keyboard Not Found. Press Any Key to Continue"*: Check where you have it plugged in. The PS2 mouse and the PS2 keyboard connectors look, feel, smell, and taste alike. It's easy to get them reversed. Swap the cables and try again. Sometimes, it's simply a matter of reseating the cable. Keyboard cables are usually two inches shorter than you need them to be (even if they're ten feet long).

- *No matter what I do, I can't get the system to recognize my keyboard and I know it's good. I tried it on another machine*: You have two possibilities here, one of which you won't like. If you recently set up your machine to use the USB ports, you may have inadvertently told it to look for a USB keyboard. Whoops. Try again. If that's not the case, you may have a keyboard controller chip failure. And since that's part of the chipset these days, it's time to go shopping for a new motherboard.

- *My husband/wife spilled coffee onto the keyboard. I, of course, didn't do it because I never bring beverages near my computer. (Honey, could you refill my cup please? I'm busy working on my book.)*: This might be an exception to my "disposable" theory. Or it might not be, depending on how successful you are. Unplug the keyboard from the computer and shake out as much of the liquid as you can. Rinse it thoroughly in distilled water. Don't use tap water, as that can leave residues that cause problems. Then rinse it in alcohol. Let it dry for several hours before you try to use it again, or you stand the risk of frying the keyboard when you turn the computer on. It'll either work or it won't. Which means you'll either be shopping for a new keyboard or you won't.

- *The keys are sticking*: Clean the keyboard.

- *When I turn my computer on, I get a Keyboard Failure message and the thing keeps on beeping*: One of the keys is stuck. Either that, or your cat is sitting on the space bar. See above.

I told you it was short.

TROUBLESHOOTING OPTICAL DRIVES

For the most part, unwell CD-ROM drives exhibit symptoms similar to those of hard drives, except that they generally will not prevent your computer from booting properly. Unlike the hard drive, a CD-ROM is totally dependent on software drivers to work right, so a majority of the problems you face are either configuration or software issues. There are a few things, however, that can drive you nuts. Since CD-ROMs, CD-RWs, and DVDs all exhibit the same hardware issues, in the following section just consider CD-ROM to mean any of the above. If the issue is unique to a type of optical drive, then it's more likely to be a software or driver issue.

- *I just installed a new CD-ROM and my system doesn't recognize it*: Check your jumpers first. They're just like hard drives in that they need to be either master or slave. Everything I talked about in the section on hard drives holds true here as well.

- *I just installed a new CD-ROM and my system doesn't recognize it. I've checked all the jumper settings and they're correct, and I've even checked to see if I have a cable-select cable. I still can't make it work*: Check and see if the IDE port onto which you are trying to install it has been disabled. Some CMOS setup programs allow for the disabling of ports for security reasons or simply in order to reclaim the IRQ.

- *I just installed a new CD-RW and my system doesn't recognize it. I've checked all the jumper settings and they're correct, and I've even checked to see if I have a cable-select cable. I still can't make it work*: Some CD-RWs only work if they're the Master drive on the port. Since most systems require the bootable drive to be on the primary port, the solution is to move the CD-RW to the secondary port and let it be the master of its domain.

- *My CD-ROM works fine in Windows, but when I restart in DOS mode, it disappears*: Like I said, CD-ROM drives are totally dependent on software drivers. Windows loads its own drivers from the registry. When you boot in DOS mode, you need an autoexec.bat and config.sys file, just like in the old days.

- *My CD-ROM drive letter keeps changing*: That probably means that you're also using some form of removable medium that hooks up either to the parallel port or a USB port. When that drive is present, it reassigns drive letters.

- *My CD-ROM won't read CDRs or CD-RWs*: This is usually only a problem with older drives, but there are a couple of things that can cause this problem. One is that the older CD-ROM isn't capable of reading a multisession table of contents (see Chapter Sixteen, Multimedia: Computerized Home Entertainment). You need a drive that is "multisession compliant" to read the newer media. The second thing that could be causing the problem lies in the mechanism itself. Early models of CD-ROM expect a certain contrast between the pits and lands. They simply can't extract the data off the disc if the contrast is too subtle.

■ *I'm getting an inordinately high number of I/O errors on discs that other computers have no problem with*: Try running one of those cleaning discs made specifically for CD players. If the lens on the optical stylus gets dirty, this will happen. If this doesn't work, check your CMOS settings for the drive and make sure it is correct. Many CD drives only work in PIO mode. If the drive is on the same cable as your UDMA hard drive, it may be forcing the CD-ROM into UDMA mode. Next, check the IDE cable. It shouldn't be longer than 18″, but many manufacturers cheat this length and ship 24″ cables. While this usually doesn't cause major problems, it can. Finally, if bus mastering has been set up on your machine, make sure you have a CD-ROM drive that is bus mastering capable. Pretty much any newer CD-ROM drive should be able to handle it, but if you brought an older drive into service for any reason, this can become an issue.

■ *My kid (dog, husband, wife, best friend, but never me) scratched up one of my most critical CDs and now my drive won't read it*: The best solution is to replace the disc. If this isn't possible, try smearing a little toothpaste onto the surface of the disk. Take a moistened soft cloth and, in a circular motion, buff the scratched surface. Never do this on the label side! Once you've done this, rinse the disk and dry it with a soft cloth. This doesn't always work, but it has saved many a disc that my kid (dog, husband, wife, best friend, but never me) scratched for me.

FIGURING OUT THE I/O PORTS

Many of the devices you use with your computer aren't internal. They hang off of one of the externally accessible ports. Most of the time, that makes it much easier to add and remove devices, because you don't have to take the computer apart in order to access the device. Once in a while, though, you get something that just doesn't want to cooperate. How are you supposed to tell if it's the device that's flaky or the port you're trying to use? That's what I'll look at in this section.

■ *No matter what I plug onto my serial device, I can't make it work*: With serial devices, one of the first things you should do is make sure the port is enabled in your CMOS. Many systems these days ship with soft modems installed (see Chapter Nineteen, Telecommunications). With most of these, in order to get them to work one of the serial ports had to be disabled. My law of shifting reality specifically states that this will be the port you're trying to use, whichever one that happens to be. If you get into the CMOS and find that both of the serial ports are assigned COM ports, you might want to check the port itself. That's where one of those loopback connectors that I discussed earlier in the chapter comes in real handy. If the port tests good and is enabled in the CMOS, you've pretty much narrowed it down to the device configuration. Check and see if its settings agree with those in your CMOS. If the port is set to COM1 and the device to

COM2, they won't communicate. That's like having the postman knock on the front door and you answering the back door. You won't get your mail.

■ *I'm still using a serial mouse. Every time I use any programs that access the modem, my system freezes*: That's an easy one. They're both on the same COM port. The mouse is usually easier to change over than the modem (but not always), so try a different COM port. I'll bet the problem goes away.

■ *I had a parallel Zip drive and a printer hooked up together and they worked fine. But then I added a scanner and now it takes forever to print anything and I can type a letter faster than I can copy it from the Zip. What happened?*: There are several parallel modes. If you want to use your parallel port for more than just a printer, you need to be using ECP mode. For more information on this, refer to Chapter Seventeen, Printing Technologies.

■ *I bought a new printer, and for the life of me, I can't make it work*: As with the above problem, the parallel mode selected in your CMOS may be the culprit. Many new printers require that either EPP or ECP mode be selected in order to function properly. On the very minimum, they're going to need bidirectional mode. If you have Centronics, ASCII, or Compatibility Mode selected, they just won't work. Also check the type of cable you're using. With many printers, if it isn't IEEE 1284 compliant, forget about it.

■ *I just set my parallel port to ECP like you told me to, and now my sound card doesn't work. Who made you the computer guru?*: My boss, so live with it. What happened there is that ECP requires a DMA channel. It decided to take the same one your sound card uses, and since the parallel port grabs the DMA channel before the sound card gets a chance, guess which one wins. Put one or the other on a different DMA channel. That's one resource where there's plenty to go around.

■ *Since I've got two printers, I thought it would be a good idea to add a second parallel port. But I can't make it work*: That's probably because you need to configure LPT2 for the second port. By default, LPT2 is looking for IRQ5. If you've got a sound card, there's a pretty good chance it grabs IRQ5 also. See if you can reconfigure the sound card to another IRQ.

■ *I've got USB ports on the back of my machine, but they don't work*: Check your CMOS. This is another one of those things that can be disabled in order to get the IRQ back. I've seen quite a few systems shipped with the USB option disabled by default.

TROUBLESHOOTING POWER SUPPLIES

I saved this section for last because it's the most fun. What makes troubleshooting power supplies such a challenge is that they rarely die a fast, clean, respectable death. They always do it the hard way. And when that happens, the errors they cause can get interpreted as almost anything but a power supply. So let me see if I can make some sense of this.

■ *I push the power button on my machine and nothing happens. No lights, no fan—nothing*: First off, check and see if you're plugged in. Hopefully, you're on a surge suppressor, so see if it's plugged in and turned on. Sometimes the switch on the surge suppressor gets inadvertently switched to the off position. Now look around you. Are the lights on? Is there power coming into the house? You wouldn't be the first person in the world to simply be unaware that there was a power outage, and you certainly won't be the last. If there is power coming into the house, check the outlet for voltage. Maybe a circuit breaker kicked out. If all of these tests come out positive, pull the power supply and check to see if the fuse popped. Most power supplies these days do not have externally accessible fuses, so that will require popping the cover. Be careful of those capacitors. They can hold a charge for quite some time and if you touch a charged capacitor it can cause a nasty surprise. If the fuse is good and you still can't get power, then sorry, my friend. It's time for a new power supply. Fortunately, they're not that expensive. And in a way, that makes you one of the lucky ones. Your power supply died abruptly and was pretty easy to diagnose.

- *You would not believe what my computer sounds like when I turn it on. It scares my neighbors off!*: That's probably the fan in the power supply. When the bearing starts to go out, it will develop weird sounds ranging from that of a crying baby to a screeching banshee. I had one that sounded like far off in the woods, a woman with the most beautiful voice was singing with the wind. I didn't want to change that one, it sounded so nice. But I figured the data on the computer deserves respect, too.

- *I'm getting power to the computer, but the fan stopped making noise*: Check and see if there's air blowing out of the back of the power supply. If not, replace the power supply. Before you do that, however, you might want to peek inside the power supply. Some of those fans are the same type they sell at electronics stores for about five bucks and simply plug right in. That would be a cheap and easy fix if the power supply is otherwise good.

- *When I turn my machine on, it doesn't start up right away and hangs in the middle of the boot process. Yet when I try it a second time, it starts up just fine*: The capacitors in your power supply are beginning to lose their ability to take a charge. They're not powering up in time to provide power to all the devices on your PC. There is supposed to be a power good signal that the power supply delivers when it's up to speed, but failing capacitors tend to fool that circuit. I suggest you replace your power supply ASAP.

- *I'll be working along in on my computer and all of the sudden, it'll just reboot itself*: That sucks, doesn't it? There are actually a couple of things that can cause this. The power supply is the most likely culprit. It's delivering rated voltage for 99.9999999999999% of the time and for that tiny fraction of a second that it doesn't, your RAM and CPU lose everything that used to be in them. That causes a reboot.

- *More and more lately, I seem to be getting blue screens of death. I've been monitoring the memory addresses reported by the messages and they're random. I can't find a single address or program that seems to be causing the problem*: See above. Except instead of a reboot, you're getting a blue screen. I'm not sure which is worse. They have about the same effect on your data and they're both equally irritating.

- *None of my power management functions works right. How come?*: 1) Power management is not properly configured in the CMOS, 2) power management is not properly configured in the OS, or 3) you have one of those AT/ATX combo boards that were so popular for a while. They're actually an AT-style board that happens to be designed along the lines of an ATX board, so they have all the peripherals on board. There were also hybrid cases so that you could use either style of board. So on the outside, it looks like an ATX, but in reality it's an AT power supply. And AT power supplies don't support power management.

CHAPTER SUMMARY

Well, that's about it for troubleshooting and that's about it for this book. There is one more chapter that covers an overview of operating systems, but it's optional reading for the A+ Core Exam. I simply thought it would be a good idea to show how the OS interfaces with the hardware.

Hopefully, reading this book was as good for you as writing it was for me. I'd hate to think I was the only one in the world having this much fun. One thing I should point out, as if you didn't already know this, is that this is a rapidly changing industry. Some technology that was state of the art when I began writing was already passé by the time I finished. So I polished the manuscript up a bit before sending it along to press. And by the time it hits the bookshelves, something else will have become obsolete.

There's nothing we can do about the industry except try to keep up. So don't ever stop reading and learning new things. And watch for future revisions of this book that take up changes in the industry. Hope to see you then.

BRAIN DRAIN

1. Discuss the differences between open-ended questions and closed-ended questions. Make up a list of open-ended questions that you might ask a client who is having computer problems.

2. Why is it so necessary to re-create the problem before attempting to fix it? Why can't you just take the customer's word?

3. How many different places can you think of that might provide documentation and/or troubleshooting help for a problem you can't diagnose?

4. Why are memory errors so hard to diagnose?

5. Why is a slowly failing power supply such a problem?

THE $64K QUESTIONS

1. Which of the following issues is addressed by re-creating a problem before trying to fix it?
   a. Hard disk errors
   b. Memory errors
   c. Motherboard errors
   d. User errors

2. Which of the following is an example of a software-based troubleshooting tool? (Select all that apply.)
   a. A RAMDISK
   b. A POST Card
   c. A memory mapper
   d. A partition manager

3. Of the following list, which one will test a serial port without having either the device or the cable affect the test?

a. A loopback adapter

b. A partition manager

c. A multimeter

d. A POST Card

4. You think that the hard drive might actually still be good, but you want to test it. Which might be of use?

a. A partition manager

b. FDISK

c. Disk Doctor

d. All of the above

5. Boot failure problems are rarely the result of _____ failure.

a. CPU

b. Motherboard

c. Software

d. Hard disk

6. Memory errors can actually be generated because of a failing

_____.

a. CPU

b. Hard disk

c. Power supply

d. Floppy disk drive

7. The twenty-eighth wire on a floppy disk cable is the _____ wire.

a. Power

b. Drive change indicator

c. Master/slave indicator

d. Null

8. You have a machine with 256MB of RAM installed, but once it is booted it only recognized 64MB. Why is this?

a. You are running OS2.

b. This is known as a Gate 20 failure.

c. The memory is bad.

d. You are running MS-DOS.

9. What two drive size limitations appear as a result of older BIOS?

a. 2.5GB

b. 8GB

c. 32GB

d. 128GB

10. What is a common cause of intermittently changing drive letters on a system?

a. A failing disk drive

b. A bad cable

c. A failing controller

d. An external removable disk that is not always present on the system.

TRICKY TERMINOLOGY

Closed-ended question: A question that leads to an answer that provides no further insight or leads to an abrupt dead end to the discussion.

Hypothesis: Any theory that can be tested to be proven either true or false.

POST Card: A device that follows each step of the POST procedure and reports the results. Should the POST fail, the last successful process will be indicated in an encoded display.

Loopback adapter: A piece of hardware that routes an output signal directly back to the computer, giving the impression that a device is present.

Open-ended question: A question that will provide further insight into the discussion as a result of the answer provided.

ACRONYM ALERT

Sorry. No new ones in this chapter.

CHAPTER 22

AN INTRODUCTION TO OPERATING SYSTEMS

In this final chapter, I'll be going over the fundamental basics of what an operating system (OS) is, what it does, and how it does what it does. Since this is a hardware book, in this section, I'll be concentrating mostly on how the OS relates to the hardware.

A+ EXAM OBJECTIVES

Because this book is about the Core Hardware Exam, this chapter has no relevant exam objectives.

JUST WHAT IS AN OS?

One of the first things I ask students coming into a class on operating systems is to define an *operating system* (OS). About ninety percent of the answers I get are variations on, "It's what makes the computer work."

At first blush, this may seem like a fairly accurate answer. But consider this. If you install a newly formatted hard drive into a system, with no OS installed, and attempt to boot the machine, you will receive some variation on the message "Operating system not found." The very existence of this message proves that the computer is working. It knows enough to tell you that the OS doesn't exist.

Therefore, while the computer may not be doing what you want it to do, it is indeed working. So a more accurate reply to my question would be, "The OS is what makes the computer do what you want it to do." Of course, CompTIA and the rest of the world want technicians to be a wee bit more technical than that when spewing out definitions, so the technical definition I'll offer is this.

An OS is the program running on the computer that manages all of the services required by applications that are to run on the system and interfaces with the hardware. These services include the following:

■ The file system

■ Processor control

■ Memory management

■ Device control

■ Security

Different OSs handle these functions in different ways, and some of these factors become part of my later discussions. For now, I'd like to give brief descriptions of each one before I move on.

FILE SYSTEMS

Since I covered file systems in some detail in my discussion of hard disk drives, I won't go over all that material again. What I'd like to point out in this section is that the file system is not just under the control of the hard disk controller, but is actually managed by the OS. One of the steps taken by the OS during installation is to write a short piece of executable code into the MBR of the hard disk. From that point forward, the OS and the hardware know to use a command set based on that specific file system. To briefly review file systems, **Table 22.1** lists the various file systems and some of their characteristics.

Table 22.1 A Comparison of File Systems

Feature	FAT16	FAT32	NTFS
Filename convention	DOS 8.3	LFN system	LFN unicode
Filename size	232 bytes	232 bytes	264 bytes
Maximum volume size	2GB	2TB	16 exabytes
Directories	Unsorted	B-tree*	B-tree*
Compression	No	No	Yes
Security	None	None	Yes
Management	None	None	Disk quotas

A comparison of the file systems

*B-tree is a data searching algorithm that uses a storage architecture similar to a tree, with "branches" and "leaves" representing paths and objects.

PROCESSOR CONTROL IN THE OS

A key concept to keep in mind is that operating systems are written to specific microprocessors. While it is true that various OSs have been written to multiple platforms (Linux is a good example), the version written for Intel processors doesn't run on Power PC processors and vice versa. There are a number of powerful reasons this is the case, but two primary reasons are the command structure built into the processor itself and how many threads of code a processor is capable of handling. A thread is any particular series of instructions that must be run from beginning to end.

When an application is running on the system, the entire OS is not running along with that entire application all at the same time. That wouldn't be possible. Instead, a program runs in a series of smaller strings of code called *processes*. A process is simply a single grouping of code that must be run from beginning to end. Processes can include strings of code from the application, device driver routines, strings of data, or even commands issued by the firmware of devices installed on the system.

> **BUZZ WORDS** ───────
>
> **Process:** A single grouping of code from an application that must run from beginning to end.
>
> **Virtual memory:** A section of hard disk space that is set aside and used by the OS as though it were memory. Also called a swap file or a paging file.

When multiple applications are running simultaneously on a system, the processor is going to be bombarded with many different requests to process this line of code or that. It is up to the OS to decide what processes are going to run at any given time. The OS is capable of initiating a process, canceling a process, or suspending one until a later time. In the event that two processes start to repeatedly call one another, it is up to the OS to break the infinite loop that will result if nothing is done.

MEMORY MANAGEMENT

A modern computer system is equipped with massive amounts of memory these days. And not all of it is conventional RAM. In addition to RAM, the OS has to keep track of video memory, cache, and buffer memory installed on devices. From the mechanical side of memory management, it is up to the OS to allocate memory for each application or process that starts, and when each one is finished that space must be freed for use. This is one area where some OSs have been notoriously inefficient and is the cause of many system crashes.

In order to accomplish the above task, the OS needs to keep track of what memory is being used for what process and what memory addresses are available for use. Another area of "memory" managed by the OS is something called a swap file (or paging file by some OSs). Since this isn't really memory, another term is *virtual memory*. This is an area of hard disk space that is treated by the OS as if it were memory. If physical RAM fills up and a new process needs to be opened, then processes not currently running on the system will be moved over to the swap file, freeing physical RAM for the new process.

A critical function of the OS is to protect the memory space allocated to specific processes. Individual processes running on the system need to think that they're the only process running. If another process or application invades their space, both processes will crash and burn.

But memory mechanics isn't the only thing the OS has to be concerned with. It also needs to set and enforce certain rules for memory usage. The OS will dictate when a process can be loaded into memory and how much memory that process will be allowed to use. And when the process is no longer needed by the application, the OS needs to unload it from memory.

Device Control

Now let's take a look at all those fancy new toys you installed on your system. How does the OS deal with those? The answer to that question is two-fold. It gets some of its instructions from the computer hardware and other instructions from the device driver installed on the system.

For a device to work, it must be supported by the system BIOS and the chipset on the motherboard. If the computer won't support a device, it doesn't matter how many device drivers you install on the OS, it won't work.

The *device driver* provides the advanced command set specific to that particular device. The OS will have a set of files that are general command sets for specific types of drivers. Windows makes use of an Application Programming Interface (API) for each device type. For example, most modern IDE hard disks, CD-ROMs, CD-RWs, DVDs, and the like are all under the control of ATAPI. For some devices, such as a simple CD-ROM, this is all that is needed. For more sophisticated devices, like an IDE tape drive, a device driver may need to be installed. The device driver, as stated earlier, provides the command set specific to that device.

When an application running in the OS has need of the services of a particular device, the application will initiate a *system call* to the OS. A system call is simply a request for a service not directly provided by the application. The OS will then initiate an I/O operation to the specific device.

In order to keep track of where specific devices are located, the OS and the hardware make use of IRQs and DMA channels. These concepts were discussed in detail in Chapter Nine, Examining the Expansion Bus.

Security

Security really amounts to who gets to do what and when they get to do it. Different OSs offer vastly different levels of security. Some are OS specific and some are dependent on the file system in use.

The types of security that are available include the following:

- Password authentication
- File access
- Application access
- OS control and management
- System control and management

Since the levels and degrees of security vary from OS to OS, I would suggest that you turn to the sister volume of this book, *The A+ Guide to Operating Systems*.

OPERATING SYSTEM STRUCTURE

That's a lot of responsibility for just one program. As such, the programmers of an OS must make sure that the OS gets priority over all system resources. Over the years, a layered approach to designing OSs has emerged. And in fact, you can effectively say that your entire computer is a layered structure. Before breaking the OS down, I think it would be a good idea to examine how the system structure works.

The first thing that you need to understand is that the average user isn't the least bit interested in running the OS. For them, the OS is a minor convenience running in the background that occasionally comes in handy, but usually gets in the way. The average user is only interested in running programs.

But as I pointed out earlier, the programs depend on the OS in order to run. Each program needs the hardware on the system in order to do its thing, and it kind of needs the OS to help it out in that respect. In fact, in most modern OSs, the applications aren't allowed to access the hardware at all. It must pass its requests on to the OS, which in turn manages hardware functions. **Figure 22.1** shows the basic model of a computer system broken down from the applications down to the basic hardware.

A modern OS such as Windows 2003 is broken down into several layers:

- User interface
- Executive kernel
- Microkernel
- Hardware abstraction layer

The user interface these days is that pretty little screen that appears when your machine boots up. The term generally used for this is the graphical user interface (GUI). When the user interfaces with the GUI, either by clicking on an icon or typing something into a command line, the OS will issue a series of instructions to the OS *kernel*. In the old days of MS-DOS, the kernel consisted of three very small files. Modern OSs are much more sophisticated. The kernel is broken down into two layers. There is the executive kernel and the microkernel. The executive kernel derives its name from the fact that it is the portion of the OS executing commands. When the executive kernel receives a command, it will issue a system call to one or more of several of its subcomponents. While the names and

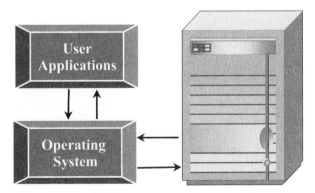

Figure 22.1 A computer system is a complex interaction between the applications, the OS, and the hardware.

variety of these subcomponents vary from OS to OS, there will inevitably be components that manage I/O, memory, process and processor control, and security. More sophisticated OSs add additional components.

The subcomponent processes the requests it has received and passes the request on to the microkernel. The *microkernel* on most OSs is a single file (or a very small set of files) that provides basic I/O functions and command interpretation. If those requests are requests for more services to be provided on the OS level, they are passed on to the appropriate component. If it is a hardware request, then the appropriate device driver is called upon for its services.

In the days of DOS, this amounted to a direct access of the hardware by the application. Of course, DOS was not a multitasking OS. There were, however, programs written for DOS that emulated multitasking and provided more attractive and (sometimes) more efficient user interfaces. These were referred to as DOS shells. If two programs attempted to access the hardware at the same time, there was a complete and total system crash.

Today's OSs are all multitasking, so they can't let that happen. Therefore, the application isn't allowed to directly access the hardware. Hardware requests are passed onto the hardware abstraction layer (HAL). HAL is the only layer of the OS allowed to communicate with the hardware.

Defining HAL is more complex than a simple one-line description. HAL is a very complex layer of any modern OS. It consists of a collection of *virtual device drivers,* the APIs that I described earlier in the chapter. The virtual device driver is a file native to the OS that is designed to interface with a particular piece of hardware. In Microsoft OSs, the virtual device drivers are easily recognized by the fact that they end in a .vxd extension.

> ## Buzz Words
>
> **Kernel:** The microcode running on the system that provides the most fundamental OS services.
>
> **Microkernel:** A single file (or a very small set of files) that provides basic I/O functions and command interpretation.
>
> **Virtual device driver:** A set of files that intercepts hardware calls from applications in order to prevent direct access of hardware by the applications.

Seeing the OS at Work

In order to show how the OS interfaces with the PC hardware, I am going to provide a brief overview of the Windows XP architecture. However, for some of the new features in XP to be truly appreciated, the reader will have to have some understanding of the evolution of OS/hardware interfaces.

In the "good old days" of MS-DOS, the hardware, the OS, and the applications quite literally exchanged chatter among themselves. While the OS was predominately in control, firmware embedded in device drivers was able to make direct calls to the applications and vice versa. Device drivers interfaced with the OS, and the OS was responsible for making or fulfilling requests for data. But it was not at all uncommon for some devices to issue commands directly to hardware.

This did not provide for the most stable of operating environments. Starting with Windows 95, Microsoft started employing the HAL that I discussed earlier in the chapter, and with each subsequent version the technology has gotten more and more sophisticated.

Today's OSs are built in layers. XP is derived from the Windows 2000/NT architecture and consists of two primary layers, with the bottom layer subdivided into further layers (**Figure 22.2**). The two primary layers are defined as User mode and Kernel mode. As the names imply, *User mode* is where all the functions dealing with logons, the user interface, running applications, and accessing the network occur. *Kernel mode* handles security, I/O requests and executions, and hardware interfaces.

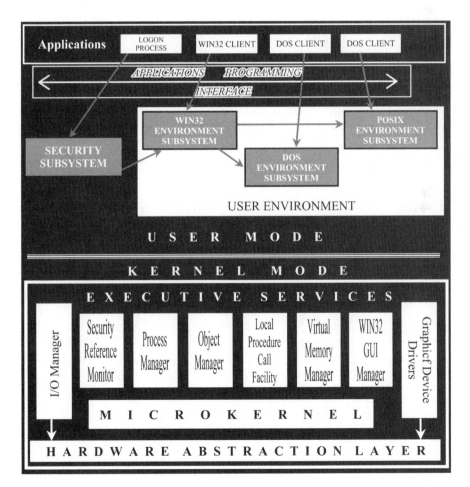

Figure 22.2   The layers of XP

In XP, when an application or user request involves making a hardware call, XP does not allow direct access to the hardware (Figure 22.2). The software running on the user's desktop may *think* it's accessing the hardware. In reality, it's accessing a group of files that make up the hardware abstraction layer. There are two basic pipelines for hardware requests. Those involving a graphical device, such as the video card or monitor, or perhaps a printer, will pass through the graphics device driver's interface. All other hardware calls go through the I/O manager.

These two pipelines hand off the request for hardware services to a set of files associated with the specific device. Each device installed on the system will have an associated virtual device driver. In addition to the .vxd file, groups of devices that share a common command set will have one or more dynamic link library (DLL) files that manage the common commands. These files carry a .dll extension.

The .vxd file and the .dll files associated with a specific device are what the applications running on the system "see" as being the actual hardware. These files communicate with the actual hardware device driver to control the specific device being called on for service.

CHAPTER SUMMARY

While it is not the intent of this book to discuss operating systems in detail, the OS and the computer are so tightly intertwined that it is virtually impossible to discuss either subject without having to make frequent references to the other. This chapter offers a very brief look at how the OS and the hardware interact with one another. For a more detailed discussion of various operating systems, see the author's companion reference, *The A+ Guide to Operating Systems.*

BRAIN DRAIN

1. List the five primary functions of the OS as they relate to the hardware and applications on the system.

2. List as many different file systems supported by Microsoft OSs as you can. What are some of the differences?

3. What are some of the responsibilities of the OS in terms of controlling the microprocessor?

4. What are some of the responsibilities of the OS in terms of controlling memory?

5. Describe how HAL fools the applications into thinking they're talking to the hardware, while all the while it is actually blocking direct access.

THE 64K$ QUESTIONS

1. Which of the following is not a function of the OS?
   a. Memory management
   b. BIOS control
   c. Security
   d. Device management

2. The file name portion of a FAT16 filename could be up to _____ characters long.
   a. 8
   b. 11
   c. 32
   d. 255

3. What was the largest partition allowed by FAT16?

   a. 512MB

   b. 1GB

   c. 2GB

   d. 64TB

4. An individual line of code from within an application that is running on the processor is called a _____.

   a. String

   b. Process

   c. Thread

   d. Stream

5. A part of the hard disk treated as if it were physical memory is called _____.

   a. Virtual memory

   b. The swap file

   c. The paging file

   d. All of the above

6. Which of the following notifies the CPU that the OS wants to communicate with a specific device?

   a. System call

   b. IRQ

   c. DMA

   d. I/O address

7. Which of the following is not an example of an OS?

   a. MS Word

   b. MS-DOS

   c. Windows 3.1

   d. OS2

8. An FAU on a 2GB partition located on a FAT16 drive takes up _____ of space.

   a. 4KB

   b. 8KB

   c. 16KB

   d. 32KB

9. Windows uses a(n) _____ to prevent the applications from directly accessing the hardware.

   a. InF

   b. RPG

   c. .vxd

   d. DLL

10. The two operating modes in XP are _____ and _____.

    a. System

    b. User

    c. Kernel

    d. Executive

TRICKY TERMINOLOGY

Device driver: A piece of software running on the system that provides the command set for a specific piece of hardware.

Kernel: The microcode running on the system that provides the most fundamental OS services.

Kernel mode: OS functions dealing with security, I/O requests and executions, and the hardware interface.

Microkernel: A single file (or a very small set of files) that provides basic I/O functions and command interpretation.

Operating system: A program running on a computer system that manages all of the services required by applications that are to run on the system and interfaces with the hardware.

Paging file: A file on the hard disk that holds the information stored in virtual memory. Also called a swap file.

Process: A single section of code from an application that must run from beginning to end.

System call: A request for a service not directly provided by the application.

Swap file: A file on the hard disk that holds the information stored in virtual memory. Also called a paging file.

User mode: OS functions dealing with the user interface, logons, services needed to run applications and provide network access.

Virtual device driver: A set of files that intercepts hardware calls from applications in order to prevent direct access of hardware by the applications.

Virtual memory: A section of hard disk space that is set aside and used by the OS as though it were memory. Also called a swap file or a paging file.

ACRONYM ALERT

API: Application Programming Interface. A collection of files used by Microsoft OSs that maintains and translates the basic command set required by all devices of a particular type.

ATAPI: Advanced Technology Application Programming Interface

DLL: Dynamic Link Library. A file that contains shared code that can be used by more than one application.

GUI: Graphical User Interface. The pretty point-and-click interface common to OSs today.

HAL: Hardware Abstraction Layer. A set of files that plays the part of hardware for applications running on the system so that those applications never have direct access to the hardware.

OS: Operating System

RAM: Random Access Memory. The physical memory installed on a computer system.

GLOSSARY

Address bus: A bank of wires running throughout the system and into the CPU that specifies specific locations. The total addressable space is calculated as 2x, where x represents the total number of wires in the bus.

Alpha channel: Eight bits used by 32-bit True Color to apply effects such as translucency and fogging.

Alternating current: An electrical current that reverses the direction of current flow many times each second.

Answer modem: The device that is being called.

Anti-aliasing: A process through which textures in an image are redrawn to more accurately reflect perceived distance.

Areal density: The total amount of storage capacity for a specific unit of area on the surface of the drive platter.

Arithmetic logic unit: A subcomponent of a microprocessor responsible for executing simple mathematical calculations, such as add, subtract, multiply, and divide. It cannot perform floating point calculations.

Asynchronous communication: A form of serial communication that transmits data a byte at a time over a single conductor.

Asynchronous timing: A device on a bus can deliver its data at any speed it sees fit to a reserved area of memory called a buffer. Data is then fed to the CPU at a rate optimal to the CPU.

Average access time: The amount of time required by a disk drive to lock on to the first sector that contains data requested by the controller.

Average seek time: The amount of time it takes to locate and lock on to the first track that contains data requested by the controller.

Back-side bus: A portion of the EDB. It is the path that data takes as it moves from cache loaded on the CPU's die into the CPU's registers.

Battery memory: A phenomenon exhibited by rechargeable batteries where the pattern of recent charge cycles affects the maximum charge the battery will accept.

Baud rate: The electronic frequency over which data is transmitted.

B-channel: A carrier channel used by ISDN for transmitting user data at 64KB/s. Multiple B-channels can be combined for higher transmission rates.

Beaconing: A process that occurs on a token ring network in which each station on the network sends a signal to its upstream neighbor and its downstream neighbor asking if it has seen the token lately.

Benchmarking: A method of measuring the base performance of a device or system before any load is placed on it.

Bezel: The plastic frame that masks off the unusable part of a monitor's image.

Binary: A Base2 counting system that consists of the two characters 0 and 1.

Bit cell: The collection of magnetized particles that comprise a single bit on magnetic media.

Bit rate: The speed at which data travels over the wire, usually expressed in bits per second (bps) or kilobits per second (KB/s). Don't confuse this with bytes per second, and don't confuse it with baud rate.

Bit: A single zero or one, resulting in a single transition between off and on.

Blackout: A complete loss of power to an entire area.

Block mode: The data transfer setting that allows multiple commands to be moved over an interface on a single interrupt cycle.

Block transfer: The movement of multiple commands over an interface on a single interrupt cycle.

Block: The number of sectors on a hard drive that UFS uses as the smallest recognizable data unit.

Boot block: A feature present on most modern system boards that allows the system to boot to a minimal configuration, including floppy drive support, in the event that the BIOS is corrupted or destroyed by a virus.

Bootstrap loader: A program that resides on the BIOS chip that is responsible for locating and initializing the Master Boot Record.

Bounded media: Any medium that physically connects a device to the network by way of a tangible cable.

Branch prediction: The ability of certain CPUs to be able to predict a situation where either one of two separate subroutines may be run, depending on the results of processing code not yet completed. A CPU capable of branch prediction will load a few lines of code from each subroutine.

Break code: A signal generated by a keyswitch when the key is released.

Bridge: A device that interconnects two networks or segments of a network of different topologies or different platforms together.

Bridge: A specialized circuit that moves data between two disparate devices or busses in a such a manner that both devices become compatible.

Brownout: A drop in voltages that lasts a noticeable period of time.

Bubblejet printer: Another term for a thermal printer.

Burst mode: The speed at which data moves from the R/W heads to a drive's buffer memory. Also known as internal host transfer rate.

Bus mastering: A technology that allows two compatible devices to exchange data directly without requiring arbitration or processing of that data by the CPU.

Byte mode: Like nibble mode, it provides bidirectional communication between the printer and the computer. Unlike nibble mode, it sends eight bits on each cycle. Speeds of byte mode are comparable to those of compatibility mode.

Byte: Any combination of eight zeros or ones.

Caddy: On a CD-ROM (or similar) drive, it is a form of loading mechanism that consists of a plastic CD holder that encases the CD while it is in the drive.

Capacitor: An electrical component that stores electrical current and provides it to the circuit as needed.

Capacity: The total number of bits a memory chip holds.

Card services: The portion of a PC card driver that interprets the command set for a specific device.

CAS latency: The delay that occurs between RAS and CAS. Also known as RAS/CAS delay.

Cascade: A process by which multiple circuits are linked together in such a way that they appear to the system as a single device.

Cathode: A negatively charged device that emits a stream of electrons when heated.

Central Arbitration Point: A circuit that offloads the responsibility for refereeing and processing the transfer of data between two bus-mastering devices.

Channel: A dedicated path for data to take that prevents other data from competing for time on the bus.

Character set: The code used to generate printable symbols that human users can understand.

Checksum: An error detection/correction mechanism that works by counting the number of ones present in the payload and storing that value in the BCC block of the packet.

Chipset: A matched set of two (three on some of the older systems) ICs that control critical system functions, including bus speeds, memory types and capacity, and the type of hardware supported by a motherboard.

Chop: A 16-bit piece of data generated when music is sampled once during the digital recording procedure.

Client: Any device or software that requires the services of another device or piece of software in order to perform its function.

Clock cycle: A timing signal generated by an electrical current that synchronizes data movement throughout the system. As an electrical current, a clock cycle resembles a sine wave with a rising half of the signal and a falling half.

Closed-ended question: A question that leads to an answer that provides no further insight or leads to an abrupt dead end to the discussion.

Cluster: The minimum number of sectors a specific file system can recognize as a single data unit. Another term for file allocation unit.

CMOS setup: One of the programs loaded on the BIOS chip. This particular program allows user-defined parameters relating to BIOS settings to be configured.

Coaxial: A cable over which the signal and ground both follow the same axis.

Codec: A coined term derived from two other terms, coder and decoder. A codec is an IC that has been programmed to convert data from one form to another. An example of this would be a chip that takes analog signals and converts them to digital, and vice versa.

Coil: An electrical component consisting of tightly wound wire that is used to filter out AC current and low-frequency signals.

Cold fusing: A process used by some phase-change printers that uses pressure rollers to press the ink into the paper.

Color depth: The number of individual hues that can be generated by a given display setting.

COM port: A predefined combination of an IRQ and an I/O address configured for communications devices.

Command overhead: The number of instructions that must be executed in order to carry out a specific request, combined with the speed at which the device can carry out those instructions.

Command overlapping: The ability of a device to start processing a command even before the command issued prior to it has completed its cycle.

Command queuing: Allows a device to store a series of commands in a buffer area, assuring that as one command is completed another one is rolled up to the gate and ready to go.

Compatibility mode: A unidirectional signal that is used to send data to the printer. This is also known as Centronix mode. Very slow, at approximately 150KB/s.

Computer: Any device that can accept the input of user data, process that data according to a specific set of instructions, and then provide the results of that processing in the form of output to the end user.

Conductor: Any substance that encourages the flow of electricity. Also the man at the podium that waves a white stick in front of the musicians.

Continuity module: A null memory module that fills the empty banks on a system using Rambus memory.

Conventional memory: The first 640K of any computer system. In the old days of DOS, the only place where programs could run was in conventional memory.

Convergence: The accuracy with which multiple beams of electrons or light can focus on the same point.

Cool: A shift in the color of an image toward the blue side.

Co-processed: Any adapter or device that is equipped with a microprocessor that offloads some of the work of the PC's CPU.

Credentials: On a network, these consist of the user ID and password that provides network access for the user.

Cross-linked file: An FAU that is claimed by two or more different files, and is therefore available to none.

Crossover cable: A network patch cord that routes the transmit signal from one device to the receive terminals on the other device.

Current: The number of electrons that flow through a circuit in a fixed amount of time.

Cyanine dye: A bluish-colored dye that was used in the recording layer of early generations of CDR media.

Cycle rate: The amount of time it takes for a specific device under the control of a timing mechanism to complete one "tick" of that timer.

Cylinder: A virtual structure created by the tracks that line up vertically on the surface of each of the platters.

Data cache: A set of registers used for storing data loaded by the prefetch until such time as the CPU is ready to use it.

Data encoding mechanism: The method used by a device to convert digital information into an electronic format recognizable by the target device.

Data phase: The portion of an I/O operation that performs the actual transfer of data from device to device.

D-channel: A 16KB/s or 64KB/s channel used by ISDN for control data, including synchronization, ACKs and NACKs and other non-user data.

Decimal: A Base10 counting system that consists of ten characters, 0 through 9.

Decode unit: The subcomponent of a microprocessor that takes complex instructions and breaks them down into a series of simpler instructions that the CPU is able to understand.

Default gateway: The route through which all packets that contain addresses that the transmitting device cannot resolve will be sent.

Deflection yoke: A circular array of powerful magnets that act to deflect a beam of electrons from its natural path.

Depth queuing: A mathematical algorithm that recalculates the hue and intensity of colors in respect to increasing distances.

Device driver: A piece of software running on the system that provides the command set for a specific piece of hardware.

Device ID: A unique number assigned to each device on a SCSI chain, including the host adapter, that identifies it to other devices on the chain.

Dielectric layer: A transparent layer of material above and below the recording layer of a CD-RW that dissipates the heat built up in the CD during the recording process.

Differential signaling: A method by which a single data wire on a parallel cable is matched up by a wire carrying the inverse of the signal being carried by the data wire.

Digital noise: Unwanted color artifacts introduced into a digitized image during capture and/or by imaging software during the processing of that image.

Diode: An electrical component that freely permits the flow of electrons in one direction, but resists electron flow in the opposite direction.

Direct current: An electrical current that exhibits a steady directional flow from a source of relative positive voltage to a target of relative negative voltage.

Directory attribute: A single bit that identifies an entry in the directory table as being a subdirectory rather than a file.

Directory table: A database of all file names on a hard drive and the partitions with which they are associated. Other information pertaining to file system security is also contained here.

Disk duplexing: The duplication of data on two different hard drives hanging off of different controllers.

Disk editor: A piece of specialized software that allows a user to examine and alter the contents of a disk drive bit by bit. Disk editors even allow access to parts of the drive not normally accessible by the user, such as FAT.

Disk mirroring: The duplication of data on two different hard drives hanging off of the same controller.

Diskette: A term typically applied to the 3.5″ floppy disk in order to distinguish it from the 5.25″ floppy disk.

Dithering: A process of blending the colors of adjacent areas in an image to make the appearance more natural.

Docking station: A device to which a laptop computer can be attached that provides additional hardware support, including I/O ports, PCI slots, and drive bays.

Domain divider switch: A device that allows external SCSI devices to be shared by multiple host computers.

Domain validation: A process by which a SCSI host adapter sends out a series of commands to each device on the chain and calculates each device's maximum data transfer rate.

Dot pitch: The distance separating two like-colored phosphors that are adjacent to one another.

Double buffering: The use of two separate buffers, so that as a frame is displayed on the monitor, another frame is in the queue, ready for display, while yet a third is being assembled by the graphics adapter.

Double-transition clocking: The movement of two transfers of data on a single clock cycle.

Drive bay: A metal frame within a computer enclosure (which may or may not be removable) that supports disk drives.

Drive rails: Devices that attach to the side of a disk drive that allow the user to install or subsequently remove it without needing any tools.

Drive translation: A technique by which an address space beyond what Int13h can read is converted into something that it can understand.

Duplex: A communications method by which a device can be transmitting and receiving at the same time.

Edge triggered: Any response that elicited and/or is controlled by a direct electrical signal coming from a pin or wire on a device. The voltage is applied and the device depends on the interrupt controller to "remember" that it sent the signal.

Electron gun: A cathode that, when heated, emits a stream of electrons from the positive pole.

Ending delimiter: A single bit at the end of a byte of data being transmitted asynchronously that marks the end of a byte.

Enhanced I/O controller hub: The IC in the newer Intel chipsets that manages all function other than memory and AGP.

Erase power: A medium power setting for the optical stylus of a CD-RW, which it uses to melt the crystals generated by the previous recording session back into the uncrystallized recording layer.

Executable marker: A pointer in the MBR that directs the boot sequence to the first line of code for the primary kernel file of the OS installed.

Expanded memory: Memory beyond the first megabyte of RAM that can be used for storing data. Expanded memory could not be used for executing programs.

Expansion bus: A circuit on a motherboard that allows accessory devices to be added to the system. The expansion bus straddles several of the primary system busses.

Extended memory: Memory beyond the first megabyte of RAM that can be used for data storage and the execution of program code.

External data bus: The wires that move data from outside the CPU to the internal registers of the CPU.

External host rate: How fast data moves from a drive's controller to RAM.

Farad: The major measurement of a capacitor's ability to store energy.

Fast SCSI: SCSI over a 10MHz bus.

Fatal exception: Any event that stops the CPU completely. These can include programming errors, such as a request to divide any number by zero, or a hardware event that returns a non-maskable interrupt.

Faux parity: A null chip that fools a system into thinking parity memory was installed, when in fact, it was not.

File system: The mechanism used by a hard drive to map the specific sectors used by any given file.

Firewall: A hardware or software barrier that allows access to external networks for users inside the firewall, but denies access from the outside.

FireWire: A high-speed serial SCSI connection originally developed by Apple Computer Corporation that is capable of 400Mb/s throughput.

Floating height: The distance above a hard drive's platter that the R/W heads hover as the platter spins beneath.

Floating point unit: A subcomponent of a microprocessor that is responsible for more complex mathematical calculations.

Flux reversal: A transition of magnet charge from a positive to a negative state, or vice versa.

Fogging: A technique of implying distance in an image by making objects that are farther away less distinct.

Form factor: A preconfigured size, orientation, and design layout for a particular component used in order to assure compatibility among manufacturers.

Frame buffer: Dedicated memory used by a graphics adapter to build the next image frame to be displayed in the time that the current image frame is on the screen.

Frame: The metal skeleton that provides the primary support for a computer enclosure.

Front-side bus: A portion of the EDB. It is the path that data takes from outside locations to make its way into the CPU.

Full-height bay: A term that describes a disk drive that is 3^1/$_2$″ from top to bottom.

Fuse: An electrical component that consists of a filament that vaporizes when more than a certain amount of current tries to pass.

Gauge: A measurement of the thickness of a substance such as sheet metal or wire. Larger numbers indicate smaller sizes.

Half duplex: A communications method by which a device can either transmit or receive, but not both at the same time.

Half-height bay: A term that describes a disk drive that is 1.62″ from top to bottom.

Harmonics: Sound frequencies above the root frequency that are generated by an instrument or voice when a certain note is generated.

Head crash: A disastrous event caused by the R/W head in a drive coming into physical contact with the platter while it is spinning.

Head parking: A process of positioning R/W heads in a hard drive in a place where contact with the platter will do no harm.

Helical scan: A recording technology that places data in diagonal tracks along the tape, as opposed to a linear track that follows parallel to the tape edge.

Hexadecimal: A counting system that uses Base16 as it root. As such, this system requires a total of sixteen different characters to represent base values.

Host controller: The adapter installed on a system or embedded in the motherboard that manages SCSI devices.

Hot swap: The ability to replace or remove a device from a computer system without having to shut the system down.

Hot-pluggable: Another term for hot-swappable. A hot-pluggable device can be added or removed to its bus without the necessity of bringing the computer down.

Hub: A device that interconnects multiple hosts on a star network over a single segment.

Hyperthreading: The ability of certain CPUs to execute multiple lines of code at the same time.

Hypothesis: Any theory that can be tested to be proven either true or false.

i386 instruction set: The basic CPU-level instructions embedded in the 80386 microprocessor. These instructions went on to become the core instructions for subsequent generations of Intel-compatible microprocessors.

Index hole: A small opening in the covering of a floppy disk that allows the R/W heads to properly align to Track 0, Sector 1.

Initialization string: A series of AT commands that are issued by the originate modem during the connection process.

Initiator: The device in a bus-mastering chain that is to act as the source of the data being transferred.

Input: Any data that is intended and/or ready to be sent to the CPU for processing.

Instruction cache: A set of registers used for storing instruction code loaded by the prefetch until such time as the CPU is ready to use it.

Instruction pipelining: The ability of certain CPUs to be loading the next set of instructions or data at the same time they process the current set.

Insulator: Any substance that tends to resist the flow of electricity.

Int13h extensions: Additional instructions added to the BIOS that intercept hard disk I/O operations and provide the drive translation required by hard disks larger than 8GB.

Interleave ratio: The number of sectors that must pass beneath the R/W heads between the reading of one sector and the time the heads will be ready to read the next sector. For example, on a 3:1 ratio, the heads will read or write one sector, two sectors will pass by completely ignored, then the next sector will be written. The unused sectors will be filled in during the next two rotations of the platter.

Internal host rate: The speed at which data moves from the R/W heads to a drive's buffer memory. Also known as burst mode.

Inverter: A device or circuit that converts DC current to AC current.

Kernel mode: OS Functions dealing with security, I/O requests and executions, and the hardware interface.

Kernel: The microcode running on the system that provides the most fundamental OS services.

Key matrix: The specific geometric layout of the keyswitches on a keyboard.

Key: A null space on an edge card connector or memory module that is used for properly aligning the device into its slot.

Keycap travel: The actual distance a user must press a key on a keyboard in order to produce results.

Keycap: The plastic button the user presses down when typing on a keyboard.

Keyswitch: The electromechanical connection that informs the keyboard controller circuitry that a key has been pressed.

Land: All of the reflective surface of the recording layer in optical media that has not been burned or punched into a pit.

Landing zone: An area on the hard disk's platter where the R/W heads can be safely parked.

Latency: The amount of time that elapses between the instant the R/W heads lock onto the first track that contains information requested by the controller, and then lock onto the first sector.

Latency: The delay that occurs from the time the CPU makes a request for data and the time that information can be accessed from the device holding the data. All devices, including memory and hard drives, exhibit latency.

Level triggered: A response that is arbitrated by a control circuit and/or device driver that allows the same device to make use of one of several interrupt channels. The level-triggered interrupt raises the voltage on the appropriate wire and holds it until the expected response is received.

Line conditioner: A device that is able to filter out transient noise, such as EMI, from the current.

Linewidth: The actual thickness of traces used within the CPU.

Load point: The physical location on a tape where data begins to be stored.

Logic gate: Two or more transistors whose position will direct the positioning of the next bank of transistors downstream.

Logical drive: A section of disk space isolated from the rest of the same physical disk so that it appears to the user as a separate disk drive.

Loopback adapter: A piece of hardware that routes an output signal directly back to the computer, giving the impression that a device is present.

Lost cluster: See Lost file fragment.

Lost file fragment: An FAU on the hard drive that contains data, but that has lost the pointers that identify the file to which it belongs.

LPT port: A predefined combination of an IRQ and an I/O address configured for line printers.

Make code: A signal generated by a keyswitch when the key is first pressed down.

Media: The substance or energy wave over which a data signal is transmitted.

Megabyte: Depending on whether you are calculating a value in binary or decimal, a megabyte is either 1 million bytes (decimal) or 1,048,576 bytes (binary). A binary megabyte is used in virtually every circumstance except when calculating hard drive capacity. Hard drive manufacturers typically define capacity in decimal values.

Memory bank: The total number of memory modules required to assure that the bit width of available memory matches the bit width of the CPU in use.

Memory controller hub: The IC in the newer Intel chipsets that manages RAM and AGP bus.

Message block: A piece of data being transmitted by a modem that represents a portion of the overall data being sent.

Microfarad: The minor measurement of a capacitor's ability to store energy.

Microkernel: a single file (or a very small set of files) that provides basic I/O functions and command interpretation.

Miniconnector: A smaller four-pin connector coming off a power supply that delivers current to devices such as floppy disk drives.

Modem: Modulator/demodulator. A device that converts parallel digital signals into serial analog signals for transmission over a wire.

Molex: The larger four-pin connector coming off a power supply that delivers current to devices such as CD-ROM drives or hard drives. Technically speaking, it is the name of the company that invented the plug.

Multimode fiber: A fiber-optic strand that moves multiple signals through the core.

Multisession: The ability to record data onto a CDR or CD-RW in several stages, without closing out the TOC.

Native capacity: How much data any given medium can store without benefit of compression. Various compression techniques allow data beyond native capacity to be recorded.

Nibble mode: Sends the 8-bit byte of data to the printer in two cycles, each of which carries four bits, or a nibble of data. This method requires software support and more overhead on the part of the host computer. Even slower than compatibility mode, ranging from 50KB to 65KB/s.

Nibble: Any combination of four zeros or ones.

Northbridge: The faster of the ICs in the chipset that is responsible for managing RAM, cache, and AGP functions.

Open-ended question: A question that will provide further insight into the discussion as a result of the answer provided.

Operating system: A program running on a computer system that manages all of the services required by applications that are to run on the system and interfaces with the hardware.

Optical stylus: A mechanism consisting of a laser-emitting diode coupled to a beam splitter.

Optomechanical mouse: A mouse that uses perforated wheels passing in front of an LED to generate pulses of light that are used to track movement along the X and Y axis.

Originate modem: The device that initiates a call.

Output: Data that is being transmitted by one device to another once that data has been processed.

Overclocking: A technique of forcing a CPU or system bus to run faster than its rated speed in order to extract maximum performance.

Page: The amount of data that can be moved on a single memory read/write cycle; usually between 1 to 20KB.

Paging file: A file on the hard disk that holds the information stored in virtual memory. Also called a swap file.

Parallel communications: The act of transferring an entire byte of data on a single cycle, using eight separate conductors.

Parity block: A data set that represents a mathematical image of data stored elsewhere in a RAID array.

Parity: A form of error detection used by serial communications and some forms of memory to detect the presence of a single-bit error.

Parity: An error checking mechanism that simply counted the number of 1s in a byte of data. A ninth bit is available on a parity chip for the parity bit. With odd-parity checking, if an even number of 1s is found in the byte, a 1 is placed in the parity bit to keep the number of 1s odd. With even parity, a 0 would be placed in that position to keep the number of 1s even.

Partition: Logical sections on a hard disk that divide the overall disk space into multiple logical drives.

PC card: Any auxiliary device designed to be plugged into a PCMCIA slot.

Permissions: Resource access or actions for which a particular user is allowed.

Phase change layer: The recording layer of a CD-RW.

Phase-change printer: A printer that liquefies solid inks before applying them to paper.

Phosphor: A single dot of color created when the phosphorous layer of a CRT is excited by electrons.

Piezoelectric crystal: A substance that changes shape when exposed to electricity.

Pit: A tiny hole embedded in the recording layer of optical media that prevents the laser from reflecting back into the photoelectric sensor.

Pixel: The collection of phosphors that collectively generate a single dot of color in a monitor's image.

Platen: The hard cylinder that supports the paper on impact printers.

Platter: One of two or more physical disk structures installed in a typical hard drive.

Plenum: An architectural term referring to the space between the ceiling of one floor in a building and the floor of the one above it.

Pointer: A line of code used by UFS to map a cluster used by a specific file.

Polarity: The characteristic of an electrical circuit to have one point of relative positive charge (or pole) and another point of relative negative charge (or pole).

Port replicator: A device to which a laptop computer can be attached that provides additional I/O services to the computer.

POST Card: A device that follows each step of the POST procedure and reports the results. Should the POST fail, the last successful process will be indicated in an encoded display.

P-rating: short for performance rating, this was a labeling method that, instead of designating a CPU by its clock speed, labeled it as the Intel CPU that it could be compared to, even though the actual clock speed and bus speed were both lower.

Prefetch: The subcomponent of a microprocessor that is responsible for retrieving data and moving it into the CPU.

Pregroove: A spiral track engraved on CDR and CD-RW media at the factory that acts as a target for the recording laser.

Print head: The mechanism on any impact or inkjet printer that is responsible for depositing the pigment onto the paper.

Process: A single section of code from an application that must run from beginning to end.

Processing: Any manipulation of data that can occur between the time the data has been inputted into the computer and the time that is provided as output. Processing can consist of calculations performed on the data, replication of that data to alternative locations, and the comparison of one data set to another. Not all processing is done by the CPU.

Protected mode: A function of a CPU that prevents two separate programs from seeing each other's code or from attempting to use overlapping memory addresses. Should either event occur, the CPU would lock up.

Pthalocyanine dye: A more stable dye used in recent generations of CDR that is less sensitive to UV light than cyanine dye and lasts for up to a 100 years.

Quad-pumped: A technique of moving four bits of data over each wire on each clock cycle of the front-side bus.

RAS/CAS delay: The delay that occurs between RAS and CAS. Also known as CAS latency.

Raster line: A single row of pixels that make a horizontal line across an image.

Read power: The lowest power setting for the optical stylus of a CD-RW, which it uses to read data from the surface.

Rectifier circuit: A specialized series of components that converts AC current to DC current.

Refresh rate: The number of columns of memory cells per cycle that the MCC will recharge.

Refresh: The process of recharging the capacitors that link to the transistors of each memory cell on a chip.

Register: A bank of transistors grouped together to perform a specific function.

Repeater: A device that cleans up, amplifies, and retransmits a signal, effectively increasing the distance data can travel over any given medium.

Resistance: The tendency for a substance to block the flow of electrons.

Resistor: An electrical component that restricts the flow of current by a precisely measured amount.

Riser: A specialized expansion card that supports other expansion devices such as PCI or ISA cards horizontally, parallel to the motherboard, in order to save space.

Root frequency: The single frequency of any given musical note that makes that note sound the way it does, regardless of what instrument plays it.

Router: A device that interconnects two autonomous networks into a single larger network.

Sag: A sudden transient decrease in voltage.

Scatter-gather data transfer: The ability of a device to execute a command on one set of data and output the results to multiple devices.

SCSI expander: A device that allows a technician to effectively increase the length of a SCSI chain without the risk of data corruption.

Sector: The smallest readable unit of data on a magnetic disk drive. A sector consists of 512 bytes.

Segment register cache: Separate cache locations maintained by Pentium II (and later) for keeping 16-bit code running separately from 32-bit code.

Semiconductor: A substance that exhibits the characteristics of both a conductor and a resistor, depending on the amount of voltage passing through.

Serial communications: The act of transferring data a single bit at a time over a single connection.

Server: Any device or software that provides services to other devices or pieces of software that need them.

Shadow mask: A thin metal sheet perforated with tiny holes that outlines the individual phosphors in a CRT monitor.

Sideband addressing: The ability of a device to send and receive data in a single memory access.

Signal saturation: The maximum strength of a recording signal that a device can handle before the recording becomes unusable.

Simplex: A communications method by which a device can either transmit or receive but cannot do both.

Single-ended signaling: A method by which a single data wire on a parallel cable is matched up by a ground wire.

Single-mode fiber: A fiber optics strand that moves only a single signal through the core.

Slot: A mounting assembly designed to support edge card-mounted devices.

Slot: On a CD-ROM (or similar) drive, it is a form of loading mechanism that engages a CD when it is inserted into the opening and draws the disc into the drive.

Socket driver: The portion of a PC card driver that is responsible for I/O services and insertion/removal notification.

Socket: A mounting assembly designed to support pin-mounted devices.

Southbridge: The slower of the ICs that make up the chipset. The southbridge manages serial and parallel communications, USB, and most of the expansion slots.

Spare sectoring: A technique hard drive manufacturers use in which extra tracks of recordable space are included with each drive that ships. As bad sectors are discovered on the drive, new sectors are made available from this space to replace the bad ones.

Speculative execution: When two different subroutines have been loaded by branch prediction, speculative execution will actually process the lines of each branch loaded.

Speed mismatch compatibility: A technology that allows two devices on the same bus to operate at different speeds and still successfully communicate with one another.

Spike: A sudden transient increase in voltage.

Standby power supply: A device that uses a generator to provide electrical current to a room or building in the event of a total power failure.

Starting delimiter: A single bit at the beginning of a data byte being transmitted asynchronously that marks the beginning of the byte.

Stepper motor: A motor that has been designed in such a way that, rather than rotating smoothly, it jumps from one position to another in precisely measured increments.

Streaming SIMD: The ability of certain CPUs to execute an instruction only once, but apply that instruction to several sets of data.

Subharmonics: Sound frequencies below the root frequency that are generated by an instrument or voice when a certain note is played.

Subnet Mask: A configuration setting within TCP/IP that identifies to the system what part of an IP address is the network address and what part is the host address.

Substrate: The supportive material over which an active substance can be applied.

Surge suppressor: A device that is able to filter out voltage surges and prevent them from reaching the devices plugged into its outlets.

Swap file: A file on the hard disk that holds the information stored in virtual memory. Also called a paging file.

Swap file: The file on the hard disk that stores the data reserved in virtual memory.

Switch: A device that breaks a larger network down into smaller segments, isolating each segment into its own collision domain.

Synchronization bits: Data included on each sector of a data CD that assures that the information will be processed in the correct sequence.

Synchronous communication: A form of serial communication that transmits large amounts of data at once in packets.

Synchronous timing: Bus speeds are a sub-multiple of the CPU's clock speed, and data is delivered at a steady rate based on that speed.

System call: a request for a service not directly provided by the application.

Target: Any device that is to be the intended recipient of data.

Terminate: To create a dead end for electrical signals traveling down a wire so that they do not echo back the other direction.

Texel: A small clip that serves as the sample of a texture used in texture mapping.

Texture mapping: A process by which pre-drawn textures are stored in memory and applied to an image as needed.

Thermal printer: A printer that ejects ink onto a page of paper by heating the fluid.

Thicknet: A name commonly given to RG-8 coaxial cable.

Thin-film metal: A metalized magnetic medium applied by evaporating metal and allowing it to "condense" back onto the surface being coated.

Thinnet: A name commonly given to RG-58U coaxial cable.

Third-party DMA: Direct memory access that is managed by a device other than the two devices utilizing DMA to exchange data.

Threshold voltage: The amount of electrical differential required to move a semiconductor from a state of resistance to a state of conductance.

Topology: The method through which a network is physically wired.

Trace: The fine copper path seen on printed circuit boards that acts as a conductor for a signal.

Track: A virtual circle of sectors on a magnetic drive that makes a complete ring around the disk surface.

Trackpad: A pointing device used on laptop computers that makes use of an electrostatically sensitive surface. The user runs a finger across the surface and the trackpad tracks the movement of the electrostatic charge.

Trackpoint: A small pointing device used on laptop computers, similar to a trackball, but much smaller.

Tractor feed: A paper transport mechanism that uses a set of gears on a printer to advance the paper by engaging in perforations along each side of the paper.

Tranceiver: Any device that is designed to be able to either transmit or receive data.

Transistor: A microscopic on/off switch that uses the electrical characteristics of a semiconductor to reverse positions.

Transition cell: The minimum number of particles that can be affected by a single magnetic flux.

Transmission rate: The number of bits per second that is being transmitted.

Tray: On a CD-ROM (or similar) drive, it is a form of loading mechanism that consists of a platform that ejects when the user pushes a button, and retracts with the CD in place.

Triad: The three separate phosphors, each of a separate primary color, that when combined form the separate hues of color perceived by the user.

Tunnel erasure: A technique of erasing the magnetic charge from the edges of a recorded track on a magnetic disk.

Ultra wide SCSI: SCSI over a 32-bit bus.

Unbounded media: Any medium that connects the device to the network using energy forms that travel through air and/or space.

Uninterruptible power supply: A device that uses batteries to provide electrical current to another device in the event of a total power failure.

USB device: Any component designed to be operated on the USB.

USB host: Any computer or other device equipped with USB-compatible BIOS, firmware, and controller.

USB hub: A device that manages the I/O for two or more USB device chains.

User mode: OS Functions dealing with the user interface, logons, services needed to run applications, and network access.

Vampire clamp: A device consisting of two halves that screw together. One half is fitted with sharp teeth that bite through the insulation of RG-8 cable.

Vapor deposition: The process of applying a metal coating by the process of evaporation.

Virtual device driver: A set of files that intercepts hardware calls from applications in order to prevent direct access of hardware by the applications.

Virtual memory: A section of hard disk space that is set aside and used by the OS as though it were memory. Also called a swap file or a paging file.

Virtual memory: A slice of hard drive space that is reserved for the OS for temporary storage of data needed by dormant programs that is treated as if it were system memory.

Virtual real mode: A technique of creating separate address spaces and time slicing the CPU time so that legacy applications think they're the only programs running on the machine, even though there may be several running at once.

Voice coil: An extremely fast and highly accurate motor that works by applying an electrical current to a tightly wrapped coil of wires surrounding, but not touching, a permanently magnetized cylinder. When current is applied to the coil, the cylinder rotates. Negative voltage rotates the cylinder one direction, positive the other. The amount of voltage determines how far the cylinder moves.

Voice: A collection of preprogrammed harmonics that are used to simulate the sound made by a particular instrument.

Volatile: Unstable or changeable. Requires constant power in order to continue to exist.

Voltage: The difference in charge between two objects or surfaces. This is sometimes referred to as electrical pressure.

Volume set: A storage array of very large capacity created by combining multiple drives of smaller capacity.

Warm: A shift in the color of an image toward the red side.

White balance: A measurement of how pure the reproduction of white is accomplished in an image.

Wide SCSI: SCSI over a 16-bit bus.

Word: The amount of data that can move across the CPU's external data bus in one clock cycle; usually between two and four bytes.

Write power: The highest power setting for the optical stylus of a CD-RW, which it uses to record data onto the surface.

Write protect: A process or mechanism that prevents the data on a disk or other medium from being erased or overwritten.

Zone bit recording: A technology that allows the sectors on the outer tracks of a hard disk to be the same physical size as those toward the center. This allows for far more sectors per track on the outer tracks.

GLOSSARY OF ACRONYMS

AC: Alternating Current. Current that reverses direction many times in a second.

ACK: Acknowledgment

ACR: Audio Communications Riser. A specialized card that takes the concept of the AMR and adds networking functionality as well.

ADC: Analog-to-Digital Converter

AGP: Advanced Graphics Port. A high-speed bus designed exclusively for graphics.

AIT: Advanced Intelligent Tape. A tape format that incorporates a linear recording mechanism in conjunction with a memory chip embedded in the tape cartridge to allow for advanced features.

ALDC: Adaptive Lossless Data Compression. An advanced data compression algorithm that allows a greater degree of compression without any loss of data.

ALU: Arithmetic Logic Unit. The subcomponent of a CPU that handles rudimentary mathematical functions.

AMR: Audio Modem Riser. A specialized card found on certain motherboards that supports either a modem, a sound card, or a device that combines both functions.

ANSI: American National Standards Institute. This term refers to an organization charged with establishing standards for several different industries, including the computer industry. It also refers to an early character set developed by that organization.

API: Application Programming Interface. A collection of files used by Microsoft OSs that maintains and translates the basic command set required by all devices of a particular type.

ASCII: American Standard Code for Information Interchange. An early character set used by computers.

ASPI: Advanced SCSI Programmer Interface. A two-tiered device driver scheme employed by SCSI.

AT: Advanced Technology. A form factor promoted by IBM in the early days of personal computing.

ATA: Advanced Technology Attachment

ATAPI: Advanced Technology Application Programming Interface

ATX: Advanced Technology Extended. An improvement of the older AT form factor that provided greater accessibility to components and far more efficiency in the use of space.

AUI: Attachment Unit Interface. A 15-pin female connector used by some early network cards and sound cards.

BCC: Block Check Character. Includes error detection and correction data, which may include parity (rarely used these days), checksum (on its way out), or cyclical redundancy check (the most common method in use today).

BIOS: Basic Input Output System. Basic instruction, usually (but not always) loaded onto a Read Only Memory chip that leads the system through the process of startup and provides instructions as to how to communicate with different forms of hardware.

BNC: Bayonet Neil-Conselman. A barrel-shaped connector named after the two engineers involved in the design.

BRI: Basic Rate ISDN. Two 64K B-channels and one 16K D-channel.

BSB: Back-Side Bus. The portion of the EDB that moves data back and forth between onboard cache and the CPU.

CAS: Column Access Strobe. A circuit that is part of the MCC, responsible for locking onto the first column in a memory module in which the target data is located.

CAV: Constant Angular Velocity. A data reading mechanism used by optical drives that allows the rotational velocity of the disc to remain constant, forcing the controller to interpret the data at faster speeds as the optical stylus moves from the center to the edge.

CCD: Charge Coupled Device. A sensor consisting of an array of cells that interpolates a physical image and converts it into a digital file.

CCS: Common Command Set. Eighteen specific commands that must be included for every device that carries the SCSI-II label.

CDAD: Compact Disc, Audio Disc. The file system used by CD-ROMs to store music.

CDDI: Copper Distributed Data Interface

CDFS: Compact Disc File System. The file system used by CD-ROMs to store computer data.

CDR: Recordable CD

CD-ROM: Compact Disc-Read Only Memory

CD-RW: Rewriteable CD

CHS: Cylinders, Heads, Sectors-per-track. The parameters of hard drive configuration that define total capacity of the drive as well as specific locations on the drive.

CLV: Constant Linear Velocity. A data reading mechanism used by optical drives in which the rotational velocity of the disc must slow down as the disc is tracked from center to edge, thus assuring that the relative number of tracks per millisecond that passes beneath the optical stylus always remains the same.

CMOS: Complimentary Metal-Oxide Semiconductor. The type of chip that houses the user-configurable parameters needed by BIOS.

CMTS: Cable Modem Termination System. A device on the ISP's end that combines all incoming cable modem signals into a single channel for transmission over the Internet backbone.

CNR: Communications Network Riser. A specialized card that takes the concept of the AMR and adds networking functionality as well.

CPU: Central Processing Unit. The primary microprocessor on a modern computer that is responsible for executing programs and processing user data.

CRT: Cathode-Ray Tube. A video display that uses a device called a cathode to fire a beam (or ray) of electrons towards a phosphorus-coated surface.

CSMA/CD: Carrier Sense, Multiple Access/Collision Detection

DAC: Digital-to-Analog Converter

DAT: Digital Audiotape. A tape format that uses an 8mm recording tape and a helical scan recording mechanism very similar to that used by digital audio recorders.

DC: Direct Current. A unidirectional current that flows from the positive side of the circuit to the negative side.

DDR: Dual Data Rate. A form of memory that is capable of executing two transfers of data on each clock cycle.

DDRAM: Double Data-rate RAM. A form of memory that moves two bits of data for each clock cycle.

DDS: Digital Data Storage

DFS: Distributed File System. A subset of NTFS that allows users to browse to remote resources on a network without requiring the user to know the specific path information.

DIMM: Dual Inline Memory Module. A 168- or 184-pin memory module that allows the connection on either side of the base to perform disparate functions.

DIX: Digital, Intel, Xerox

DLL: Dynamic Link Library. A file that contains shared code that can be used by more than one application.

DLT: Digital Linear Tape. A tape format that records data in a straight line along the tape, parallel to the tape's edge.

DPI: Dots Per Inch

DRAM: Dynamic Random Access Memory

DSL: Digital Subscriber Line. A broadband high-speed data connection that moves over standard telephone cable.

DSLAM: DSL Access Multiplexer. A device on the ISP's end that combines all incoming DSL signals into a single channel for transmission over the Internet backbone.

DSP: Digital Signal Processor. A chip that performs multiple processing functions on a signal. For example, the DSP on a modem combines the functions of a UART and a DAC.

DSP: Digital Signal Processor. A microprocessor that can sample an electronic current and convert it into a digital signal.

DVD: Digital Video Disc, or Digital Versatile Disc

DVD-R: Recordable DVD

DVD-RW: Rewriteable DVD

Dword: Double Word

EBX: Embedded Board Expandable. One of several form factors whose objective was to keep the system as small as possible.

ECC: Error Correction Code. An error correction method that stored a mathematical image of data being moved on a nibble chip and could correct single-bit errors as they were detected.

ECHS: Extended CHS

ECI: Extended Capabilities ID. Information programmed onto a PCI card that defines any enhanced functions that device can perform beyond the basic functions defined by its device class.

ECP: Enhanced Capabilities Port. One of several different methods of configuring a parallel port.

ECP: Extended Compatibility Port. A parallel mode that provides for both data and command cycles, therefore supporting more advanced devices, including scanners, storage devices, and such. Data throughput is similar to that of EPP. However, since DMA is used, there is less delay imposed on the application.

EDB: External Data Bus. The path that data uses to move from the CPU to an outside circuit, or vice versa.

EDC: Error Detection Code. Code embedded in a file system that enables the system to detect that an error in the transmission of that data has occurred, and where possible alerts the system to take corrective action.

EDO: Extended Data Out. A form of memory that replaced FPM and that allowed the RAS/CAS operations for the next I/O operation to be performed at the same time as data from the previous operation is being moved out of the chip.

EEPROM: Electronically Erasable Programmable Read Only Memory. A more modern implementation of an IC that can be wiped clean and rewritten if necessary.

EFS: Encryptable File System. A subset of NTFS that allows individual files to be scrambled on an as-needed basis and subsequently unscrambled only by a user with appropriate permissions.

EIA: Electronics Industry Association

EIDE: Enhanced IDE

EISA: Enhanced ISA. A 32-bit 8.33MHz bus released by a coalition of manufacturers led by Compaq. VLB was designed to be backwardly compatible with ISA.

ENDEC: Encoder/Decoder

EOT: End of Transmission. I hope I don't have to explain that one.

EPP: Enhanced Parallel Port. Because it provides for different types of signals to be transferred on any given clock cycle, EPP provides for faster and more efficient communication between peripherals. EPP allows continuous data transfer of around 500KB/s with burst rates of up to 2MB/s.

EPP: Enhanced Parallel Port. One of several different methods of configuring a parallel port.

EPRML: Extended PRML. A data encoding mechanism used by most hard disk drives currently being manufactured.

EPROM: Erasable Programmable Read Only Memory. An IC that can be wiped clean and rewritten if necessary.

ESDI: Enhanced Small Device Interface. An earlier hard disk drive interface that preceded IDE.

ESN: Electronic Serial Number. On Pentium III CPUs (and later) this is a number embedded by Intel at the factory that identifies that specific CPU.

EXT: End of Text. Okay, I'm done sending text in this block. The next bytes are more control information.

FAT: File Allocation Table. A file on a disk, hidden from the user, that identifies what file is using each sector on the disk. It is the disk's roadmap, if you will.

FAU: File Allocation Unit. The smallest usable amount of drive space in sectors used by a file system for a single file, regardless of how small that file may be.

FC-AL: Fiber Channel Arbitrated Loop

FCC: Federal Communications Commission

FCP: Fiber Channel Protocol

FC-PGA: Flip Chip Pin Grid Array. A CPU socket designed for easy CPU installation or replacement used in modern machines.

FC-PH: Fiber Channel Physical and Signaling Interface

FDDI: Fiber Distributed Data Interface

FPM: Fast Page Mode. An early form of memory that eliminated the RAS cycle from any read operation retrieving data from the same row as the previous operation.

FPU: Floating Point Unit. The subcomponent of the CPU that handles more advanced mathematical functions.

FSB: Front-Side Bus. The portion of the EDB that moves data in and out of the CPU from external locations.

GDI: Graphical Device Interface. A subset of Microsoft's Windows operating systems that manages imaging devices such as printers, scanners, and graphics cards. Printers that use this interface as their printer language are referred to as GDI printers.

GPF: General Protection Fault. A failure of an application (and possibly the CPU) that results from one program invading another program's address space.

GUI: Graphical User Interface. The pretty point-and-click interface common to OSs today.

HAL: Hardware Abstraction Layer. A subset of Microsoft's Windows operating systems that provides a virtual barrier between the computer's hardware and the applications and upper-level OS functions.

HPFS: High Performance File System

HPGL: Hewlett Packard Graphics Language. A printer language developed by HP to add complex graphics to the printer's toolset.

HPSF: High Power Single Frequency

HR: Horizontal Refresh. The speed at which a monitor can draw individual raster lines.

HVD: High-Voltage Differential

Hz: Hertz. A measurement for frequency, or the number of times during any given timing cycle that the measured event occurs.

I/O: Input/Output. The process of sending or receiving data between devices.

IC: Integrated Circuit. A single microchip onto which the code necessary to provide several different functions has been burned.

iComp: Intel Comparative Microprocessor Index. A benchmarking method developed by Intel.

IDE: Integrated Drive Electronics. A method of managing hard drives and other devices that takes the controller circuitry off the motherboard or separate controller card and places it on the device itself.

IFCA: IEEE Fiber Channel Address. A unique address assigned to all FC-AL devices at the factory that allows them to be automatically configured onto the FC-AL loop.

IOPS: I/O Operations Per Second. The maximum number of times a device can receive and then execute either a request for data or a request to write data to the device, assuming the smallest block of data the device utilizes.

IPS: Instructions per Second. An early measurement of CPU performance that was based solely on how many times in one second the device could execute commands.

IPX/SPX: Internetwork Packet Exchange/ Sequenced Packet Exchange. An early Novell networking protocol.

ISA: Industry Standards Architecture. An 8- or 16-bit expansion bus designed by IBM.

ISDN: Integrated Services Digital Network. A telecommunications technology that provides high-speed data transfer over standard telephone lines.

ISO: International Organization for Standardization. One of several groups that oversees the development and ratification of standards in the computer industry, as well as many other industries.

JEDEC: Joint Electron Device Engineering Council. An organization that oversees standards for many of the electronic devices in use, including memory modules.

L1: Level 1. A small amount of extremely fast memory used to store data or instructions that the CPU expects it will need within a few clock cycles, or that it uses frequently.

L2: Level 2. A secondary level of slower cache memory. This is usually a larger amount of memory than the L1 and is the second place the CPU looks for needed instructions or data.

L3: Level 3. A third layer of cache supported only by a select few CPUs.

LAN: Local Area Network

LCD: Liquid Crystal Display. An imaging device that consists of transistors suspended in a liquid emulsion.

LFN: Long File Names

Li-Ion: Lithium Ion. A type of rechargeable battery.

LLC: Logic Link Control

LPSF: Low Power Single Frequency

LPX: Low-Profile Extended. A form factor designed to take up a minimum of desktop real estate that puts the expansion slots onto a single riser card that supports the cards parallel to the motherboard. Most LPX designs were proprietary.

LUN: Logical Unit Number. A setting on SCSI devices that allows multiple devices to be seen by the controller as a single device.

LVD: Low-Voltage Differential

MAC: Media Access Control

MAU: Multistation Access Unit. A device similar to a hub that interconnects hosts on a token ring network.

MB: Megabyte. In binary, this would be 1,048,576 bytes. In decimal, it would be 1 million bytes.

MBR: Master Boot Record. The first one or two sectors of a bootable medium that contains information about the file system, the partition tables, and a pointer to the OS.

MCA: Micro Channel Architecture. A proprietary 32-bit 12MHz bus released by IBM shortly after Intel's release of the 80386 CPU.

MCC: Memory Controller Chip or Memory Controller Circuit. The chip or circuitry on the chipset that manages memory mapping and refresh functions.

MDRAM: Multibank DRAM. A form of memory that can be accessed in blocks, rather than sequentially.

MFM: Modified Frequency Modulation. One of the early data encoding mechanisms used by hard disk drives.

MIC: Memory In Cartridge. The embedded memory chip of an AIT.

MIDI: Musical Instrument Device Interface

MIP: *Multium in Parvo*. Latin for "many in one." It is a technique by which several samples of the same texture are created in different sizes.

MJPEG: Motion-picture Joint Photographic Experts Group. An organization that develops and maintains standards for digitizing images. Also a file format used for compressing and storing editable versions of motion pictures developed by that group.

MLP: Mid-Load Point. A tape drive technology that places the load point in the center of the tape.

MLP: Multiple Load Point. A tape drive technology that allows a single tape to be mounted from several different locations on the tape.

MMX: Multimedia Extensions. A set of instructions targeted specifically at multimedia.

MOV: Metal Oxide Varistor. An electrical component that can absorb abrupt spikes in current.

MPEG: Motion Picture Experts Group. An organization that developed a standard for compressing and storing digital video. Its format is not as editable as MJPEG.

MRH-S: SDRAM Memory Repeater Hub. A chip in newer Intel chipsets used to arbitrate memory requests between multiple banks of memory.

MTBF: Mean Time Before Failure. An average of the number of hours a particular model of device is expected to operate before it dies.

MTH: Memory Translator Hub. A chip in newer Intel chipsets that replaces the northbridge chip used by contemporary chipsets.

NetBEUI: NetBIOS Extended User Interface. An early Microsoft networking protocol.

NIC: Network Interface Card

NiCad: Nickel Cadmium. A type of rechargeable battery.

Ni-MH: Nickel Metal Hydride. A type of rechargeable battery.

NLX: New Low-profile Extended. One of several form factors whose objective was to keep the system as small as possible.

NMI: Nonmaskable Interrupt. Similar to the IRQs used by devices, an NMI is an interrupt to the CPU indicating that immediate action is required. If the CPU cannot resolve the issue, the NMI will cause the CPU to lock up.

NTFS: New Technology File System

OS: Operating System

OSI: Open Standards Interconnect. A seven-layer model for developing networking standards.

P2P: Peer to Peer. A network on which all hosts are equals.

PATA: Parallel ATA

PBC: Port Bypass Circuit. A circuit that manages an FC-AL loop and automatically detects when a device has been removed.

PCI: Peripheral Components Interconnect. A 32- or 64-bit expansion bus designed by Intel.

PCI-X: PCI Extended. A recently released 133MHz version of the PCI bus.

PCL: Printer Control Language. Hewlett Packard's printer language, originally developed for dot matrix printers and later adopted for use with laser printers.

PCM: Pulse Code Modulation. The process of converting electrical current into a digital signal.

PDA: Personal Digital Assistant. Any one of several computing devices designed for maximum portability.

PGA: Pin Grid Array. A pin-mounted CPU on which the pins are arranged in perfectly symmetrical patterns of squares.

PIO: Programmed Input/Output. A transfer of data in which each byte of data must be negotiated and managed by the CPU.

POST: Power On, Self Test. A program run from the BIOS chip that initializes system hardware and handles the Plug 'n Play scans.

PPB: PCI to PCI Bridge. The circuitry that arbitrates data transfer between two different PCI busses on the same system.

PRI: Primary Rate ISDN. Twenty-three 64K B-channels and one 64K D-channel.

PRML: Partial Response/Maximum Likelihood. A data encoding mechanism used by more recent hard disk drives.

PROM: Programmable Read Only Memory. An IC that can be programmed once.

QAM: Quadrature Amplitude Modulation. A method of encoding data sent over a modem using a combination of frequency shifting and phase shift keying.

QIC: Quarter Inch Cartridge. A tape format so named because of the size of the tape used (not the size of the cartridge).

R/W: Read/Write

RAM: Random Access Memory. A device used for short-term storage of data or instructions that are or will soon be required by the CPU in order for it to do its job.

RAS: Row Access Strobe. A circuit that is part of the MCC responsible for locking onto the first row in a memory module in which the target data is located.

RDRAM: Rambus Dynamic Random Access Memory. A specialized form of memory manufactured by Rambus, Inc.

REQ: Request

RLL: Run Length Limited. One of the early data encoding mechanisms used by hard disk drives.

ROM BIOS: Read Only Memory-Basic Input Output Services. A chip on the motherboard that contains all the necessary code for jumpstarting a computer from a dead off condition to the point where the OS can take over.

RTC: Real Time Clock. The chip that keeps actual time, as humans keep track of it, on the systems.

SATA: Serial ATA

SCSI: Small Computer Systems Interface. An interface that allows several different types of device to hook up to the same controller circuit.

SDRAM: Synchronous Dynamic Random Access Memory

SE: Single-Ended

SECC: Single Edge Contact Cartridge. A type of CPU package that makes use of an edge card connector and mounts in a slot.

SIMD: Single Instruction, Multiple Data. A process by which a CPU can execute an instruction once, but apply that instruction to several sets of data simultaneously.

SIMM: Single Inline Memory Module. A 30- or 72-pin memory module on which two opposing pins on the base perform the same function.

SIP: SCSI Interlocked Protocol

SIPP: Single Inline Pin Package. An earlier memory module that put eight or nine DRAM chips on a single IC and mounted into the system board by way of a single row of pins protruding from the base.

SLR: Scalable Linear Recording. A tape drive technology that uses linear recording technology and allows multiple channels of data to be stored across the width of the tape.

SMART: Self Monitoring Analysis and Reporting Technology. Commands built into a hard disk interface that allow the drive to do some rather extensive self-diagnostics.

SO-DIMM: Small Outline Dual Inline Memory Module. A compact form of memory used primarily in notebook computers, but also seen in some video cards.

SOH: Start of Header. A header is not always used, but is an important part of most protocols.

SPC: SCSI Primary Commands

SPGA: Staggered Pin Grid Array. A pin-mounted CPU on which the pins are arranged in offsetting rows of pins that results in a pattern of diagonal rows.

SPI: SCSI Parallel Interface

SPS: Standby Power Supply. A device that uses a generator to continue to provide power to an entire room or building after a total loss of electricity.

SRAM: Static RAM. A form of very high-speed memory typically used for cache.

SSA: Serial Storage Architecture

SSE: Streaming SIMD Extensions. The set of instructions that supports the execution of a single instruction on several sets of data at once.

SSP: Serial Storage Protocol

STP: Shielded Twisted Pair

STX: Start of Text: Pretty self-explanatory. It tells you that the next series of bits is the data being sent.

SYN: Synchronization character. This makes sure all the bytes in the frame stick together as they move across the wire and then get reassembled in the right order at the other end. If no data is being transmitted, SYN blocks can be transmitted to keep the session alive.

TCP/IP: Transmission Control Protocol/Internet Protocol. The protocol of choice for the Internet.

TFT: Thin Film Transistor. An LCD that utilizes microscopically thin layers of transistors laid out in a grid pattern in a liquid crystal emulsion.

TIA: Telecommunications Industry Association

TIFF: Tagged Image File Format. An image file format used for storing digital images that does not result in any loss of quality.

UFS: Unix File System

UHF: Ultrahigh Frequency

UPS: Uninterruptible Power Supply. A device that uses a bank of batteries to continue to provide current to the devices plugged in when there has been a total loss of electricity.

USB: Universal Serial Bus. A moderate-speed bus that allows 127 devices to share a single chain and a 12Mb/s bandwidth.

UTP: Unshielded Twisted Pair

UV: Ultraviolet. Wavelengths of light beyond the upper range of the visible light spectrum.

UVGA: Ultra VGA. High-resolution VGA.

VBR: Volume Boot Record

VC-SDRAM: Virtual Channel SDRAM. A newer form of memory that gives each operational application its own address space and path to move data back and forth, so that they don't compete for bandwidth.

VESA: Video Electronics Standards Association. The organization charged with maintaining standards surrounding graphics adapters and monitors.

VGA: Video Graphics Array. The most commonly used video display in use today.

VHF: Very High Frequency

VID-VRM: Voltage Identifier, Voltage Regulator Module. A device that automatically locks on to the correct voltage of the installed chip and configures the device accordingly.

VLB: VESA Local Bus. A 32-bit 33MHz bus designed by VESA to address issues surrounding the transfer of large amounts of graphics data. VLB was designed to be backwardly compatible with ISA.

VR: Vertical Refresh. The number of times per second a monitor regenerates the image on the screen.

WAN: Wide Area Network

WORM: Write Once Read Many. A recording technology that write protects the contents of the medium in order to prevent that data from being erased or overwritten.

WTX: Workstation Technology Extended. One of several form factors whose objective was to keep the system as small as possible.

XGA: Extended Graphics Array. A proprietary display created by IBM.

REFERENCE CHARTS: PINOUTS AND CHARACTER SETS

PINOUTS OF COMMON COMPONENTS

Throughout the book, I discussed in detail some of the different packages used by device manufacturers, both past and present, in assembling their product. For most readers, knowing the actual use of any given pin on a module is of limited use. Someone going into engineering or design, however, might find it useful. Therefore, rather than cluttering up the chapters with the pinouts of specific devices, I have chosen to provide them in the form of an appendix.

Pinouts of Common Components
- Pinouts for 30-pin SIMM
- Pinouts for 72-pin SIMM
- Pinouts for 168-pin DIMM
- 184-pin Nonregistered DIMM
- Pinouts of 144-pin SO-DIMM
- Floppy Disk Cable (nonmedia sense)
- Cable Pinouts
- Floppy Disk Cable (media sense)
- Serial Cable Pinouts
- Pinouts for Parallel Cable
- Pinout Descriptors for Centronics Connector

Expansion Bus Pinouts
- Pinouts for the 8-bit PC Bus
- 16-bit ISA Extensions
- 32-bit PCI Pinouts
- 64-bit PCI Extensions

Character Set Charts
- The ASCII Character Set (Control Characters)
- The ASCII Character Set (Printed Characters)
- ISO Latin Character Set

Pinouts for 30-pin SIMM

Pin Number	Pin Name	Description
1	VCC	+5VDC
2	/CAS	Column Address Strobe
3	DQ0	Data 0
4	A0	Address 0
5	A1	Address 1
6	DQ1	Data 1
7	A2	Address 2
8	A3	Address 3
9	GND	Ground
10	DQ2	Data 2
11	A4	Address 4
12	A5	Address 5
13	DQ3	Data 3
14	A6	Address 6
15	A7	Address 7
16	DQ4	Data 4
17	A8	Address 8
18	A9	Address 9
19	A10	Address 10
20	DQ5	Data 5
21	/WE	Write Enable
22	GND	Ground
23	DQ6	Data 6
24	A11	Address 11
25	DQ7	Data 7
26	QP	Data Parity Out
27	/RAS	Row Address Strobe
28	/CASP	Parity Bit Column Access Strobe
29	DP	Data Parity In
30	VDC	+5VDC

Pinouts for 72-pin SIMM

Pin Number	Pin Name (Non-parity)	Pin Name (Parity)	Description
1	VSS	VSS	Ground
2	DQ0	DQ0	Data 0
3	DQ16	DQ16	Data 16
4	DQ1	DQ1	Data 1
5	DQ17	DQ17	Data 17
6	DQ2	DQ2	Data 2
7	DQ18	DQ18	Data 18
8	DQ3	DQ3	Data 3
9	DQ19	DQ19	Data 19
10	VCC	VCC	+5VDC
11	Not connected	Not connected	Not connected
12	A0	A0	Address 0
13	A1	A1	Address 1
14	A2	A2	Address 2
15	A3	A3	Address 3
16	A4	A4	Address 4
17	A5	A5	Address 5
18	A6	A6	Address 6
19	A10	A10	Address 10
20	DQ4	DQ4	Data 4
21	DQ20	DQ20	Data 20
22	DQ5	DQ5	Data 5
23	DQ21	DQ21	Data 21
24	DQ6	DQ6	Data 6
25	DQ22	DQ22	Data 22
26	DQ7	DQ7	Data 7
27	DQ23	DQ23	Data 23
28	A7	A7	Address 7
29	A11	A11	Address 11
30	VCC	VCC	+5VDC
31	A8	A8	Address 8
32	A9	A9	Address 9
33	RAS 3	RAS 3	Row Address Strobe 3
34	RAS 2	RAS 2	Row Address Strobe 2
35	Not connected	PQ3	Parity bit 3
36	Not connected	PQ1	Parity bit 1

(Continued)

Pinouts for 72-pin SIMM *(Continued)*

Pin Number	Pin Name (Non-parity)	Pin Name (Parity)	Description
37	Not connected	PQ2	Parity bit 2
38	Not connected	PQ4	Parity bit 4
39	VSS	VSS	Ground
40	CAS 0	CAS 0	Column Address Strobe 0
41	CAS 2	CAS 2	Column Address Strobe 2
42	CAS 3	CAS 3	Column Address Strobe 3
43	CAS 1	CAS 1	Column Address Strobe 1
44	RAS 0	RAS 0	Row Address Strobe 0
45	RAS 1	RAS 1	Row Address Strobe 1
46	Not connected	Not connected	Not connected
47	WE	WE	Read/Write
48	Not connected	Not connected	Not connected
49	DQ8	DQ8	Data 8
50	DQ24	DQ24	Data 24
51	DQ9	DQ9	Data 9
52	DQ25	DQ25	Data 25
53	DQ10	DQ10	Data 10
54	DQ26	DQ26	Data 26
55	DQ11	DQ11	Data 11
56	DQ27	DQ27	Data 27
57	DQ12	DQ12	Data 12
58	DQ28	DQ28	Data 28
59	VCC	VCC	+5 VDC
60	DQ29	DQ29	Data 29
61	DQ13	DQ13	Data 13
62	DQ30	DQ30	Data 30
63	DQ14	DQ14	Data 14
64	DQ31	DQ31	Data 31
65	DQ16	DQ16	Data 16
66	Not connected	Not connected	Not connected
67	PD1	PD1	Presence Detect 1
68	PD2	PD2	Presence Detect 2
69	PD3	PD3	Presence Detect 3
70	PD4	PD4	Presence Detect 4
71	Not connected	Not connected	Not connected
72	VSS	VSS	Ground

Pinouts for 168-pin DIMM

	SIDE ONE				
Pin	Parity	NonParity	72bit	80bit	Description
1	VSS	VSS	VSS	VSS	Ground
2	DQ0	DQ0	DQ0	DQ0	Data 0
3	DQ1	DQ1	DQ1	DQ1	Data 1
4	DQ2	DQ2	DQ2	DQ2	Data 2
5	DQ3	DQ3	DQ3	DQ3	Data 3
6	VCC	VCC	VCC	VCC	+5VDC or +3.3VDC
7	DQ4	DQ4	DQ4	DQ4	Data 4
8	DQ5	DQ5	DQ5	DQ5	Data 5
9	DQ6	DQ6	DQ6	DQ6	Data 6
10	DQ7	DQ7	DQ7	DQ7	Data 7
11	DQ8	DQ8	DQ8	DQ8	Data 8
12	VSS	VSS	VSS	VSS	Ground
13	DQ9	DQ9	DQ9	DQ9	Data 9
14	DQ10	DQ10	DQ10	DQ10	Data 10
15	DQ11	DQ11	DQ11	DQ11	Data 11
16	DQ12	DQ12	DQ12	DQ12	Data 12
17	DQ13	DQ13	DQ13	DQ13	Data 13
18	VCC	VCC	VCC	VCC	+5VDC or +3.3VDC
19	DQ14	DQ14	DQ14	DQ14	Data 14
20	DQ15	DQ15	DQ15	DQ15	Data 15
21	CB0	Not connected	CB0	CB0	Parity Check Bit or Input/Output 0
22	CB1	Not connected	CB1	CB1	Parity Check Bit or Input/Output 1
23	VSS	VSS	VSS	VSS	Ground
24	Not connected	Not connected	Not connected	CB8	Parity Check Bit or Input/Output 8
25	Not connected	Not connected	Not connected	CB9	Parity Check Bit or Input/Output 9
26	VCC	VCC	VCC	VCC	+5VDC or +3.3VDC
27	WE0	WE0	WE0	WE0	Read Write Input
28	CAS0	CAS0	CAS0	CAS0	Column Address Strobe 0
29	CAS1	CAS1	CAS1	CAS1	Column Address Strobe 1
30	RAS0	RAS0	RAS0	RAS0	Row Address Strobe 0
31	OE0	OE0	OE0	OE0	Output Enable
32	VSS	VSS	VSS	VSS	Ground

(Continued)

Pinouts for 168-pin DIMM *(Continued)*

Pin	Parity	NonParity	72bit	80bit	Description
33	A0	A0	A0	A0	Address 0
34	A2	A2	A2	A2	Address 2
35	A4	A4	A4	A4	Address 4
36	A6	A6	A6	A6	Address 6
37	A8	A8	A8	A8	Address 8
38	A10	A10	A10	A10	Address 10
39	A12	A12	A12	A12	Address 12
40	VCC	VCC	VCC	VCC	+5VDC or +3.3VDC
41	VCC	VCC	VCC	VCC	+5VDC or +3.3VDC
42	Not connected	Not connected	Not connected	Not connected	Not connected
43	VSS	VSS	VSS	VSS	Ground
44	OE2	OE2	OE2	OE2	
45	RAS2	RAS2	RAS2	RAS2	Row Address Strobe 2
46	CAS2	CAS2	CAS2	CAS2	Column Address Strobe 2
47	CAS3	CAS3	CAS3	CAS3	Column Address Strobe 3
48	WE2	WE2	WE2	WE2	Read Write Input
49	VCC	VCC	VCC	VCC	+5VDC or +3.3VDC
50	Not connected	Not connected	Not connected	CB10	Parity Check Bit or Input/Output 10
51	Not connected	Not connected	Not connected	CB11	Parity Check Bit or Input/Output 11
52	CB2	Not con-	CB2	CB2	Parity Check Bit or Input/Output 2
53	CB3	Not con-	CB3	CB3	Parity Check Bit or Input/Output 3
54	VSS	VSS	VSS	VSS	Ground
55	DQ16	DQ16	DQ16	DQ16	Data 16
56	DQ17	DQ17	DQ17	DQ17	Data 17
57	DQ18	DQ18	DQ18	DQ18	Data 18
58	DQ19	DQ19	DQ19	DQ19	Data 19
59	VCC	VCC	VCC	VCC	+5VDC or +3.3VDC
60	DQ20	DQ20	DQ20	DQ20	Data 20
61	Not connected	Not connected	Not connected	Not connected	Not connected
62	Not connected	Not connected	Not connected	Not connected	Not connected
63	Not connected	Not connected	Not connected	Not connected	Not connected
64	VSS	VSS	VSS	VSS	Ground

(Continued)

Pinouts for 168-pin DIMM *(Continued)*

Pin	Parity	NonParity	72bit	80bit	Description
65	DQ21	DQ21	DQ21	DQ21	Data 21
66	DQ22	DQ22	DQ22	DQ22	Data 22
67	DQ23	DQ23	DQ23	DQ23	Data 23
68	VSS	VSS	VSS	VSS	Ground
69	DQ24	DQ24	DQ24	DQ24	Data 24
70	DQ25	DQ25	DQ25	DQ25	Data 25
71	DQ26	DQ26	DQ26	DQ26	Data 26
72	DQ27	DQ27	DQ27	DQ27	Data 27
73	VCC	VCC	VCC	VCC	+5VDC or +3.3VDC
74	DQ28	DQ28	DQ28	DQ28	Data 28
75	DQ29	DQ29	DQ29	DQ29	Data 29
76	DQ30	DQ30	DQ30	DQ30	Data 30
77	DQ31	DQ31	DQ31	DQ31	Data 31
78	VSS	VSS	VSS	VSS	Ground
79	Not connected	Not connected	Not connected	Not connected	Not connected
80	Not connected	Not connected	Not connected	Not connected	Not connected
81	Not connected	Not connected	Not connected	Not connected	Not connected
82	SDA	SDA	SDA	SDA	Serial Data
83	SCL	SCL	SCL	SCL	Serial Clock
84	VCC	VCC	VCC	VCC	+5VDC or +3.3VDC

SIDE TWO

Pin	Parity	Non-Parity	72-bit ECC	80-bit ECC	Description
85	VSS	VSS	VSS	VSS	Ground
86	DQ32	DQ32	DQ32	DQ32	Data 32
87	DQ33	DQ33	DQ33	DQ33	Data 33
88	DQ34	DQ34	DQ34	DQ34	Data 34
89	DQ35	DQ35	DQ35	DQ35	Data 35
90	VCC	VCC	VCC	VCC	+5VDC or +3.3VDC
91	DQ36	DQ36	DQ36	DQ36	Data 36
92	DQ37	DQ37	DQ37	DQ37	Data 37
93	DQ38	DQ38	DQ38	DQ38	Data 38
94	DQ39	DQ39	DQ39	DQ39	Data 39

(Continued)

Pinouts for 168-pin DIMM *(Continued)*

Pin	Parity	Non-Parity	72-bit ECC	80-bit ECC	Description
95	DQ40	DQ40	DQ40	DQ40	Data 40
96	VSS	VSS	VSS	VSS	Ground
97	DQ41	DQ41	DQ41	DQ41	Data 41
98	DQ42	DQ42	DQ42	DQ42	Data 42
99	DQ43	DQ43	DQ43	DQ43	Data 43
100	DQ44	DQ44	DQ44	DQ44	Data 44
101	DQ45	DQ45	DQ45	DQ45	Data 45
102	VCC	VCC	VCC	VCC	+5VDC or +3.3VDC
103	DQ46	DQ46	DQ46	DQ46	Data 46
104	DQ47	DQ47	DQ47	DQ47	Data 47
105	CB4	Not connected	CB4	CB4	Parity Check Bit or Input/Output 4
106	CB5	Not connected	CB5	CB5	Parity Check Bit or Input/Output 5
107	VSS	VSS	VSS	VSS	Ground
108	Not connected	Not connected	Not connected	CB12	Parity Check Bit or Input/Output 12
109	Not connected	Not connected	Not connected	CB13	Parity Check Bit or Input/Output 13
110	VCC	VCC	VCC	VCC	+5VDC or +3.3VDC
111	Not connected	Not connected	Not connected	Not connected	Not connected
112	CAS4	CAS4	CAS4	CAS4	ColumnAddressStrobe4
113	CAS5	CAS5	CAS5	CAS5	ColumnAddressStrobe5
114	RAS1	RAS1	RAS1	RAS1	Row Address Strobe 1
115	Not connected	Not connected	Not connected	Not connected	Not connected
116	VSS	VSS	VSS	VSS	Ground
117	A1	A1	A1	A1	Address 1
118	A3	A3	A3	A3	Address 3
119	A5	A5	A5	A5	Address 5
120	A7	A7	A7	A7	Address 7
121	A9	A9	A9	A9	Address 9
122	A11	A11	A11	A11	Address 11
123	A13	A13	A13	A13	Address 13
124	VCC	VCC	VCC	VCC	+5VDC or +3.3VDC
125	Not connected	Not connected	Not connected	Not connected	Not connected

(Continued)

Pinouts for 168-pin DIMM *(Continued)*

Pin	Parity	Non-Parity	72-bit ECC	80-bit ECC	Description
126	Not connected	Not connected	Not connected	Not connected	Not connected
127	VSS	VSS	VSS	VSS	Ground
128	Not connected	D not connected	Not connected	Not connected	Not connected
129	RAS3	RAS3	RAS3	RAS3	Column Address Strobe 3
130	CAS6	CAS6	CAS6	CAS6	Column Address Strobe 6
131	CAS7	CAS7	CAS7	CAS7	Column Address Strobe 7
132	Not connected	Not connected	Not connected	Not connected	Not connected
133	VCC	VCC	VCC	VCC	+5VDC or +3.3VDC
134	Not connected	Not connected	Not connected	CB14	Parity Check Bit or Input/Output 14
135	Not connected	Not connected	Not connected	CB15	Parity Check Bit or Input/Output 15
136	CB6	Not connected	CB6	CB6	Parity Check Bit or Input/Output 6
137	CB7	Not connected	CB7	CB7	Parity Check Bit or Input/Output 7
138	VSS	VSS	VSS	VSS	Ground
139	DQ48	DQ48	DQ48	DQ48	Data 48
140	DQ49	DQ49	DQ49	DQ49	Data 49
141	DQ50	DQ50	DQ50	DQ50	Data 50
142	DQ51	DQ51	DQ51	DQ51	Data 51
143	VCC	VCC	VCC	VCC	+5VDC or +3.3VDC
144	DQ52	DQ52	DQ52	DQ52	Data 52
145	Not connected	Not connected	Not connected	Not connected	Not connected
146	Not connected	Not connected	Not connected	Not connected	Not connected
147	Not connected	Not connected	Not connected	Not connected	Notconnected
148	VSS	VSS	VSS	VSS	Ground
149	DQ53	DQ53	DQ53	DQ53	Data 53
150	DQ54	DQ54	DQ54	DQ54	Data 54
151	DQ55	DQ55	DQ55	DQ55	Data 55
152	VSS	VSS	VSS	VSS	Ground
153	DQ56	DQ56	DQ56	DQ56	Data 56
154	DQ57	DQ57	DQ57	DQ57	Data 57

(Continued)

Pinouts for 168-pin DIMM *(Concluded)*

Pin	Parity	Non-Parity	72-bit ECC	80-bit ECC	Description
155	DQ58	DQ58	DQ58	DQ58	Data 58
156	DQ59	DQ59	DQ59	DQ59	Data 59
157	VCC	VCC	VCC	VCC	+5VDC or +3.3VDC
158	DQ60	DQ60	DQ60	DQ60	Data 60
159	DQ61	DQ61	DQ61	DQ61	Data 61
160	DQ62	DQ62	DQ62	DQ62	Data 62
161	DQ63	DQ63	DQ63	DQ63	Data 63
162	VSS	VSS	VSS	VSS	Ground
163	CK3	CK3	CK3	CK3	
164	Not connected	Not connected	Not connected	Not connected	Not connected
165	SA0	SA0	SA0	SA0	Serial Address 0
166	SA1	SA1	SA1	SA1	Serial Address 1
167	SA2	SA2	SA2	SA2	Serial Address 2
168	VCC	VCC	VCC	VCC	+5VDC or +3.3VDC

184-pin Nonregistered DIMM

SIDE ONE							
PIN	SYMBOL	PIN	SYMBOL	PIN	SYMBOL	PIN	SYMBOL
1	VREF	16	CK1	31	DQ19	46	VDD
2	DQ0	17	CK1#	32	A5	47	DNU
3	VSS	18	VSS	33	DQ24	48	A0
4	DQ1	19	DQ10	34	VSS	49	DNU
5	DQS0	20	DQ11	35	DQ25	50	VSS
6	DQ2	21	CKE0	36	DQS3	51	DNU#
7	VDD	22	VDDQ	37	A4	52	BA1
8	DQ3	23	DQ16	38	VDD	53	DQ32
9	NC	24	DQ17	39	DQ26	54	VDDQ
10	DNU	25	DQS2	40	DQ27	55	DQ33
11	VSS	26	VSS	41	A2	56	DQS4
12	DQ8	27	A9	42	VSS	57	DQ34
13	DQ9	28	DQ18	43	A1	58	VSS
14	DQS1	29	A7	44	DNU	59	BA0
15	VDDQ	30	VDDQ	45	DNU	60	DQ35

(Continued)

184-pin Nonregistered DIMM *(Concluded)*

PIN	SYMBOL	PIN	SYMBOL	PIN	SYMBOL	PIN	SYMBOL
61	DQ40	69	DQ43	77	VDDQ	85	VDD
62	VDDQ	70	VDD	78	DQS6	86	DQS7
63	WE#	71	NC	79	DQ50	87	DQ58
64	DQ41	72	DQ48	80	DQ51	88	DQ59
65	CAS#	73	DQ49	81	VSS	89	VSS
66	VSS	74	VSS	82	NC	90	NC
67	DQS5	75	CK2#	83	DQ56	91	SDA
68	DQ42	76	CK2	84	DQ57	92	SCL

SIDE TWO

PIN	SYMBOL	PIN	SYMBOL	PIN	SYMBOL	PIN	SYMBOL
93	VSS	116	VSS	139	VSS	162	DQ47
94	DQ4	117	DQ21	140	DNU	163	NC
95	DQ5	118	A11	141	A10	164	VDDQ
96	VDDQ	119	DQS11/DM2	142	DNU	165	DQ52
97	DQS9/DM0	120	VDD	143	VDDQ	166	DQ53
98	DQ6	121	DQ22	144	DNU	167	NC
99	DQ7	122	A8	145	VSS	168	VDD
100	VSS	123	DQ23	146	DQ36	169	DQS15/DM6
101	NC	124	VSS	147	DQ37	170	DQ54
102	NC	125	A6	148	VDD	171	DQ55
103	NC	126	DQ28	149	DQS13/DM4	172	VDDQ
104	VDDQ	127	DQ29	150	DQ38	173	NC
105	DQ12	128	VDDQ	151	DQ39	174	DQ60
106	DQ13	129	DQS12/DM3	152	VSS	175	DQ61
107	DQS10/DM1	130	A3	153	DQ44	176	VSS
108	VDD	131	DQ30	154	RAS#	177	DQS16/DM7
109	DQ14	132	VSS	155	DQ45	178	DQ62
110	DQ15	133	DQ31	156	VDDQ	179	DQ63
111	DNU	134	DNU	157	S0#	180	VDDQ
112	VDDQ	135	DNU	158	NC	181	SA0
113	NC	136	VDDQ	159	DQS14/DM5	182	SA1
114	DQ20	137	DNU	160	VSS	183	SA2
115	NC/A12	138	DNU	161	DQ46	184	VDDSPD

Note: Abbreviations in this table are identical to those on other tables. For clarity, due to the number of entries, they have been left out of this table.

Pinouts of 144-pin SO-DIMM

	SIDE ONE		
Pin	Normal	ECC	Description
1	VSS	VSS	Ground
2	VSS	VSS	Ground
3	DQ0	DQ0	Data 0
4	DQ32	DQ32	Data 32
5	DQ1	DQ1	Data 1
6	DQ33	DQ33	Data 33
7	DQ2	DQ2	Data 2
8	DQ34	DQ34	Data 34
9	DQ3	DQ3	Data 3
10	DQ35	DQ35	Data 35
11	VCC	VCC	+5VDC
12	VCC	VCC	+5VDC
13	DQ4	DQ4	Data 4
14	DQ36	DQ36	Data 36
15	DQ5	DQ5	Data 5
16	DQ37	DQ37	Data 37
17	DQ6	DQ6	Data 6
18	DQ38	DQ38	Data 38
19	DQ7	DQ7	Data 7
20	DQ39	DQ39	Data 39
21	VSS	VSS	Ground
22	VSS	VSS	Ground
23	CAS0	CAS0	Column Address Strobe 0
24	CAS4	CAS4	Column Address Strobe 4
25	CAS1	CAS1	Column Address Strobe 1
26	CAS5	CAS5	Column Address Strobe 5
27	VCC	VCC	+5VDC
28	VCC	VCC	+5VDC
29	A0	A0	Address 0
30	A3	A3	Address 3
31	A1	A1	Address 1
32	A4	A4	Address 4
33	A2	A2	Address 2
34	A5	A5	Address 5
35	VSS	VSS	Ground

(Continued)

Pinouts of 144-pin SO-DIMM *(Continued)*

Pin	Normal	ECC	Description
36	VSS	VSS	Ground
37	DQ8	DQ8	Data 8
38	DQ40	DQ40	Data 40
39	DQ9	DQ9	Data 9
40	DQ41	DQ41	Data 41
41	DQ10	DQ10	Data 10
42	DQ42	DQ42	Data 42
43	DQ11	DQ11	Data 11
44	DQ43	DQ43	Data 43
45	VCC	VCC	+5VDC
46	VCC	VCC	+5VDC
47	DQ12	DQ12	Data 12
48	DQ44	DQ44	Data 44
49	DQ13	DQ13	Data 13
50	DQ45	DQ45	Data 45
51	DQ14	DQ14	Data 14
52	DQ46	DQ46	Data 46
53	DQ15	DQ15	Data 15
54	DQ47	DQ47	Data 47
55	VSS	VSS	Ground
56	VSS	VSS	Ground
57	Not connected	CB0	Parity Check Bit 0
58	Not connected	CB4	Parity Check Bit 4
59	Not connected	CB1	Parity Check Bit 1
60	Not connected	CB5	Parity Check Bit 5
61	Not connected	Not connected	Not connected
62	Not connected	Not connected	Not connected
63	VCC	VCC	+5VDC
64	VCC	VCC	+5VDC
65	Not connected	Not connected	Not connected
66	Not connected	Not connected	Not connected
67	WE	WE	Read/Write
68	Not connected	Not connected	Not connected
69	RAS0	RAS0	Row Address Strobe 0
70	Not connected	Not connected	Not connected
71	RAS1	RAS1	Row Address Strobe 1

(Continued)

Pinouts of 144-pin SO-DIMM *(Continued)*

	SIDE TWO		
Pin	Normal	ECC	Description
72	Not connected	Not connected	Not connected
73	OE	OE	Output Enable
74	Not connected	Not connected	Not connected
75	VSS	VSS	Ground
76	VSS	VSS	Ground
77	Not connected	CB2	Parity Check Bit 2
78	Not connected	CB6	Parity Check Bit 6
79	Not connected	CB3	Parity Check Bit 3
80	Not connected	CB7	Parity Check Bit 7
81	VCC	VCC	+5VDC
82	VCC	VCC	+5VDC
83	DQ16	DQ16	Data 16
84	DQ48	DQ48	Data 48
85	DQ17	DQ17	Data 17
86	DQ49	DQ49	Data 49
87	DQ18	DQ18	Data 18
88	DQ50	DQ50	Data 50
89	DQ19	DQ19	Data 19
90	DQ51	DQ51	Data 51
91	VSS	VSS	Ground
92	VSS	VSS	Ground
93	DQ20	DQ20	Data 20
94	DQ52	DQ52	Data 52
95	DQ21	DQ21	Data 21
96	DQ53	DQ53	Data 53
97	DQ22	DQ22	Data 22
98	DQ54	DQ54	Data 54
99	DQ23	DQ23	Data 23
100	DQ55	DQ55	Data 55
101	VCC	VCC	+5VDC
102	VCC	VCC	+5VDC
103	A6	A6	Address 6
104	A7	A7	Address 7
105	A8	A8	Address 8
106	A11	A11	Address 11
107	VSS	VSS	Ground

(Continued)

Pinouts of 144-pin SO-DIMM *(Concluded)*

Pin	Normal	ECC	Description
108	VSS	VSS	Ground
109	A9	A9	Address 9
110	A12	A12	Address 12
111	A10	A10	Address 10
112	A13	A13	Address 13
113	VCC	VCC	+5VDC
114	VCC	VCC	+5VDC
115	CAS2	CAS2	Column Address Strobe 2
116	CAS6	CAS6	Column Address Strobe 6
117	CAS3	CAS3	Column Address Strobe 3
118	CAS7	CAS7	Column Address Strobe 7
119	VSS	VSS	Ground
120	VSS	VSS	Ground
121	DQ24	DQ24	Data 24
122	DQ56	DQ56	Data 56
123	DQ25	DQ25	Data 25
124	DQ57	DQ57	Data 57
125	DQ26	DQ26	Data 26
126	DQ58	DQ58	Data 58
127	DQ27	DQ27	Data 27
128	DQ59	DQ59	Data 59
129	VCC	VCC	+5VDC
130	VCC	VCC	+5VDC
131	DQ28	DQ28	Data 28
132	DQ60	DQ60	Data 60
133	DQ29	DQ29	Data 29
134	DQ61	DQ61	Data 61
135	DQ30	DQ30	Data 30
136	DQ62	DQ62	Data 62
137	DQ31	DQ31	Data 31
138	DQ63	DQ63	Data 63
139	VSS	VSS	Ground
140	VSS	VSS	Ground
141	SDA	SDA	Serial Data
142	SCL	SCL	Serial Clock
143	VCC	VCC	+5VDC
144	VCC	VCC	+5VDC

Cable Pinouts

Floppy Disk Cable (nonmedia sense)

Pin	Signal	Pin	Signal	Pin	Signal
1	Ground	13	Ground	25	Ground
2	HD select	14	Reserved	26	Track 0
3	+5v DC	15	Ground	27	Ground
4	Drive Type ID 1	16	Motor enable	28	Write protect
5	Ground	17	Ground	29	Ground
6	+12v DC	18	Direction in	30	Read data
7	Ground	19	Ground	31	Ground
8	Index	20	Step	32	Head 1 Select
9	Ground	21	Ground	33	Ground
10	Reserved	22	Write data	34	Diskette change
11	Ground	23	Ground		
12	Drive select	24	Write enable		

Floppy Disk Cable (media sense)

Pin	Signal	Pin	Signal
1	Ground	18	Direction in
2	Data rate select	19	Ground
3	+5v DC	20	Step
4	Drive type ID 1/Drive Status1	21	Ground
5	Ground	22	Write data
6	+12v DC	23	Ground
7	Ground	24	Write enable
8	Index	25	Ground
9	Drive type ID 0	26	Track 0
10	Reserved	27	Media type ID 0/ Drive status 2
11	Ground	28	Write protect
12	Drive select	29	Ground
13	Ground	30	Read data
14	Security Command	31	Ground
15	Ground	32	Head 1 select
16	Motor enable	33	Data rate select
17	Media type 1/ Drive status 3	34	Diskette change

Serial Cable Pinouts

DB-25	DB-9	Signal Direction	Signal Name
1			Protective Ground
2	3	DTE-to-DCE	Transmitted Data
3	2	DCE-to-DTE	Received Data
4	7	DTE-to-DCE	Request To Send
5	8	DCE-to-DTE	Clear To Send
6	6	DCE-to-DTE	Data Set Ready
7	5		Signal Ground
8	1	DCE-to-DTE	Received Line Signal Detector (Carrier Detect)
20	4	DTE-to-DCE	Data Terminal Ready
22	9	DCE-to-DTE	Ring Indicator

On DB-25 cables, pins 9-19 are not used.

Pinouts for Parallel Cable

PIN	Purpose	PIN	Purpose
Pin 1	-Strobe	Pin 14	Auto Feed -
Pin 2	Data Bit 0 +	Pin 15	Error -
Pin 3	Data Bit 1 +	Pin 16	Initialize Printer -
Pin 4	Data Bit 2 +	Pin 17	Select Input -
Pin 5	Data Bit 3 +	Pin 18	Data Bit 0 Return (ground)
Pin 6	Data Bit 4 +	Pin 19	Data Bit 1 Return (ground)
Pin 7	Data Bit 5 +	Pin 20	Data Bit 2 Return (ground)
Pin 8	Data Bit 6 +	Pin 21	Data Bit 3 Return (ground)
Pin 9	Data Bit 7 +	Pin 22	Data Bit 4 Return (ground)
Pin 10	Acknowledge -	Pin 23	Data Bit 5 Return (ground)
Pin 11	Busy +	Pin 24	Data Bit 6 Return (ground)
Pin 12	Paper End +	Pin 25	Data Bit 7 Return (ground)
Pin 13	Select +		

Pinout Descriptors for Centronics Connector

Pin #	Function	Pin #	Function
1	Strobe	19	Ground
2	Data 0	20	Ground
3	Data 1	21	Ground
4	Data 2	22	Ground
5	Data 3	23	Ground
6	Data 4	24	Ground
7	Data 5	25	Ground
8	Data 6	26	Ground
9	Data 7	27	Ground
10	ACK	28	Ground
11	Busy	29	Ground
12	Paper Out	30	Ground
13	Select	31	Input Prime (Spare)
14	Auto Line Feed	32	Error
15	PI	33	Ground
16	Ground	34	N/C (Spare)
17	Frame Ground	35	+5V
18	+5V	36	Select In (Spare)

EXPANSION BUS PINOUTS

Pinouts for the 8-bit PC Bus

Pin #	Pin Function	Direction	Pin #	Pin Function	Direction
A1:	CHANNEL CHECK	Card-to-PC	B1:	Ground	N/A
A2:	DATA SIGNAL 7	Bidirectional	B2:	RESET DRIVER	PC-to-Card
A3:	DATA SIGNAL 6	Bidirectional	B3:	+5V	N/A
A4:	DATA SIGNAL 5	Bidirectional	B4:	IRQ 2	Card-to-PC
A5:	DATA SIGNAL 4	Bidirectional	B5:	-5V	PC-to-Card
A6:	DATA SIGNAL 3	Bidirectional	B6:	DMA CHANNEL 2	Card-to-PC
A7:	DATA SIGNAL 2	Bidirectional	B7:	-12V	PC-to-Card
A8:	DATA SIGNAL 1	Bidirectional	B8:	NO WAIT STATE	Card-to-PC
A9:	DATA SIGNAL 0	Bidirectional	B9:	+12V	PC-to-Card
A10:	CHANNEL READY	Card-to-PC	B10:	Ground	N/A
A11:	ADDRESS ENABLE	PC-to-Card	B11:	SYSTEM MEMORY WRITE	PC-to-Card
A12:	ADDRESS SIGNAL 19	PC-to-Card	B12:	SYSTEM MEMORY READ	PC-to-Card
A13:	ADDRESS SIGNAL 18	PC-to-Card	B13:	I/O WRITE	PC-to-Card
A14:	ADDRESS SIGNAL 17	PC-to-Card	B14:	I/O READ	PC-to-Card
A15:	ADDRESS SIGNAL 16	PC-to-Card	B15:	DMA ACKNOWLEDGE CHANNEL 3	PC-to-Card
A16:	ADDRESS SIGNAL 15	PC-to-Card	B16:	DMA CHANNEL 3	Card-to-PC
A17:	ADDRESS SIGNAL 14	PC-to-Card	B17:	DMA ACKNOWLEDGE CHANNEL 1	PC-to-Card
A18:	ADDRESS SIGNAL 13	PC-to-Card	B18:	DMA CHANNEL 1	Card-to-PC
A19:	ADDRESS SIGNAL 12	PC-to-Card	B19:	REFRESH	Bidirectional
A20:	ADDRESS SIGNAL 11	PC-to-Card	B20:	BUS CLOCK	PC-to-Card
A21:	ADDRESS SIGNAL 10	PC-to-Card	B21:	IRQ 7	Card-to-PC
A22:	ADDRESS SIGNAL 9	PC-to-Card	B22:	IRQ 6	Card-to-PC
A23:	ADDRESS SIGNAL 8	PC-to-Card	B23:	IRQ 5	Card-to-PC
A24:	ADDRESS SIGNAL 7	PC-to-Card	B24:	IRQ 4	Card-to-PC
A25:	ADDRESS SIGNAL 6	PC-to-Card	B25:	IRQ 3	Card-to-PC
A26:	ADDRESS SIGNAL 5	PC-to-Card	B26:	DMA ACKNOWLEDGE CHANNEL 2	PC-to-Card
A27:	ADDRESS SIGNAL 4	PC-to-Card	B27:	TERMINAL COUNT	PC-to-Card
A28:	ADDRESS SIGNAL 3	PC-to-Card	B28:	BUS ADDRESS LATCH ENABLE	PC-to-Card
A29:	ADDRESS SIGNAL 2	PC-to-Card	B29:	+5V	PC-to-Card
A30:	ADDRESS SIGNAL 1	PC-to-Card	B30:	OSCILLATOR	PC-to-Card
A31:	ADDRESS SIGNAL 0	PC-to-Card	B31:	Ground	N/A

16-bit ISA Extensions

Pin #	Pin Function	Direction	Pin #	Pin Function	Direction
C1	System bus high enable	Bidirectional	D1	Memory 16-bit chip select	Card-to-PC
C2	Address bit 23	Bidirectional	D2	I/O 16-bit chip select	Card-to-PC
C3	Address bit 22	Bidirectional	D3	Interrupt Request 10	Card-to-PC
C4	Address bit 21	Bidirectional	D4	Interrupt Request 11	Card-to-PC
C5	Address bit 20	Bidirectional	D5	Interrupt Request 12	Card-to-PC
C6	Address bit 19	Bidirectional	D6	Interrupt Request 15	Card-to-PC
C7	Address bit 18	Bidirectional	D7	Interrupt Request 14	Card-to-PC
C8	Address bit 17	Bidirectional	D8	DMA Acknowledge 0	PC-to-Card
C9	Memory Read*	Bidirectional	D9	DMA Request 0	Card-to-PC
C10	Memory Write†	Bidirectional	D10	DMA Acknowledge 5	PC-to-Card
C11	Data bit 8	Bidirectional	D11	DMA Request 5	Card-to-PC
C12	Data bit 9	Bidirectional	D12	DMA Acknowledge 6	PC-to-Card
C13	Data bit 10	Bidirectional	D13	DMA Request 6	Card-to-PC
C14	Data bit 11	Bidirectional	D14	DMA Acknowledge 7	PC-to-Card
C15	Data bit 12	Bidirectional	D15	DMA Request 7	Card-to-PC
C16	Data bit 13	Bidirectional	D16		PC-to-Card
C17	Data bit 14	Bidirectional	D17	Used with DRQ to gain control of system	Card-to-PC
C18	Data bit 15	Bidirectional	D18	Ground	N/A

*Active on all memory read cycles.
†Active on all memory write cycles.

32-bit PCI Pinouts

Pin	Signal	Description	Pin	Signal	Description
A1	TRST	Test Logic Reset	B1	−12V	−12 VDC
A2	+12V	+12 VDC	B2	TCK	Test Clock
A3	TMS	Test Mode Select	B3	GND	Ground
A4	TDI	Test Data Input	B4	TDO	Test Data Output
A5	+5V	+5 VDC	B5	+5V	+5 VDC
A6	INTA	Interrupt A	B6	+5V	+5 VDC
A7	INTC	Interrupt C	B7	INTB	Interrupt B
A8	+5V	+5 VDC	B8	INTD	Interrupt D
A9	RESV01	Reserved VDC	B9	PRSNT1	Reserved
A10	+5V	+V I/O (+5 V or +3.3 V)	B10	RES	+V I/O (+5 V or +3.3 V)
A11	RESV03	Reserved VDC	B11	PRSNT2	Reserved
A12	GND03	Ground or Open (Key)	B12	GND	Ground or Open (Key)
A13	GND05	Ground or Open (Key)	B13	GND	Ground or Open (Key)
A14	RESV05	Reserved VDC	B14	RES	Reserved VDC
A15	RESET	Reset	B15	GND	Reset
A16	+5V	+V I/O (+5 V or +3.3 V)	B16	CLK	Clock
A17	GNT	Grant PCI use	B17	GND	Ground
A18	GND08	Ground	B18	REQ	Request
A19	RESV06	Reserved VDC	B19	+5V	+V I/O (+5 V or +3.3 V)
A20	AD30	Address/Data 30	B20	AD31	Address/Data 31
A21	+3.3V01	+3.3 VDC	B21	AD29	Address/Data 29
A22	AD28	Address/Data 28	B22	GND	Ground
A23	AD26	Address/Data 26	B23	AD27	Address/Data 27
A24	GND10	Ground	B24	AD25	Address/Data 25
A25	AD24	Address/Data 24	B25	+3.3V	+3.3VDC
A26	IDSEL	Initialization Device Select	B26	C/BE3	Command, Byte Enable 3
A27	+3.3V03	+3.3 VDC	B27	AD23	Address/Data 23
A28	AD22	Address/Data 22	B28	GND	Ground
A29	AD20	Address/Data 20	B29	AD21	Address/Data 21
A30	GND12	Ground	B30	AD19	Address/Data 19
A31	AD18	Address/Data 18	B31	+3.3V	+3.3 VDC
A32	AD16	Address/Data 16	B32	AD17	Address/Data 17
A33	+3.3V05	+3.3 VDC	B33	C/BE2	Command, Byte Enable 2
A34	FRAME	Address or Data phase	B34	GND13	Ground
A35	GND14	Ground	B35	IRDY	Initiator Ready
A36	TRDY	Target Ready	B36	+3.3V06	+3.3 VDC
A37	GND15	Ground	B37	DEVSEL	Device Select

(Continued)

32-bit PCI Pinouts *(Continued)*

Pin	Signal	Description	Pin	Signal	Description
A38	STOP	Stop Transfer Cycle	B38	GND16	Ground
A39	+3.3V07	+3.3 VDC	B39	LOCK	Lock bus
A40	SDONE	Snoop Done	B40	PERR	Parity Error
A41	SBO	Snoop Backoff	B41	+3.3V08	+3.3 VDC
A42	GND17	Ground	B42	SERR	System Error
A43	PAR	Parity	B43	+3.3V09	+3.3 VDC
A44	AD15	Address/Data 15	B44	C/BE1	Command, Byte Enable 1
A45	+3.3V10	+3.3 VDC	B45	AD14	Address/Data 14
A46	AD13	Address/Data 13	B46	GND18	Ground
A47	AD11	Address/Data 11	B47	AD12	Address/Data 12
A48	GND19	Ground	B48	AD10	Address/Data 10
A49	AD9	Address/Data 9	B49	GND20	Ground
A50		Connector Key	B50	(OPEN)	Ground or Open (Key)
A51		Connector Key	B51	(OPEN)	Ground or Open (Key)
A52	C/BE0	Command, Byte Enable 0	B52	AD8	Address/Data 8
A53	+3.3V11	+3.3 VDC	B53	AD7	Address/Data 7
A54	AD6	Address/Data 6	B54	+3.3V12	+3.3 VDC
A55	AD4	Address/Data 4	B55	AD5	Address/Data 5
A56	GND21	Ground	B56	AD3	Address/Data 3
A57	AD2	Address/Data 2	B57	GND22	Ground
A58	AD0	Address/Data 0	B58	AD1	Address/Data 1
A59	+5V	+V I/O (+5 V or +3.3 V)	B59	VCC08	+5 VDC
A60	REQ64	Request 64-bit	B60	ACK64	Acknowledge 64-bit
A61	VCC11	+5 VDC	B61	VCC10	+5 VDC
A62	VCC13	+5 VDC	B62	VCC12	+5 VDC

64-bit PCI Extensions

Pin	Signal	Description	Pin	Signal	Description
A63	GND	Ground	B63	RES	Reserved
A64	C/BE[7]#	Command, Byte Enable 7	B64	GND	Ground
A65	C/BE[5]#	Command, Byte Enable 5	B65	C/BE[6]#	Command, Byte Enable 6
A66	+5V	+V I/O (+5 V or +3.3 V)	B66	C/BE[4]#	Command, Byte Enable 4
A67	PAR64	Parity 64 ???	B67	GND	Ground
A68	AD62	Address/Data 62	B68	AD63	Address/Data 63
A69	GND	Ground	B69	AD61	Address/Data 61
A70	AD60	Address/Data 60	B70	+5V	+V I/O (+5 V or +3.3 V)
A71	AD58	Address/Data 58	B71	AD59	Address/Data 59
A72	GND	Ground	B72	AD57	Address/Data 57
A73	AD56	Address/Data 56	B73	GND	Ground
A74	AD54	Address/Data 54	B74	AD55	Address/Data 55
A75	+5V	+V I/O (+5 V or +3.3 V)	B75	AD53	Address/Data 53
A76	AD52	Address/Data 52	B76	GND	Ground
A77	AD50	Address/Data 50	B77	AD51	Address/Data 51
A78	GND	Ground	B78	AD49	Address/Data 49
A79	AD48	Address/Data 48	B79	+5V	+V I/O (+5 V or +3.3 V)
A80	AD46	Address/Data 46	B80	AD47	Address/Data 47
A81	GND	Ground	B81	AD45	Address/Data 45
A82	AD44	Address/Data 44	B82	GND	Ground
A83	AD42	Address/Data 42	B83	AD43	Address/Data 43
A84	+5V	+V I/O (+5 V or +3.3 V)	B84	AD41	Address/Data 41
A85	AD40	Address/Data 40	B85	GND	Ground
A86	AD38	Address/Data 38	B86	AD39	Address/Data 39
A87	GND	Ground	B87	AD37	Address/Data 37
A88	AD36	Address/Data 36	B88	+5V	+V I/O (+5 V or +3.3 V)
A89	AD34	Address/Data 34	B89	AD35	Address/Data 35
A90	GND	Ground	B90	AD33	Address/Data 33
A91	AD32	Address/Data 32	B91	GND	Ground
A92	RES	Reserved	B92	RES	Reserved
A93	GND	Ground	B93	RES	Reserved
A94	RES	Reserved	B94	GND	Ground

Note: On older 5V PCI systems, there were a few differences. This section concentrates on 3.3V, but points out areas common to both systems.

CHARACTER SET CHARTS

Here is the complete ASCII character set discussed in detail in Chapter One and referred to often in the book. The first chart lists the control characters, and the second lists the printed characters. The third chart lists the Extended Latin Character set.

The ASCII Character Set (Control Characters)

Char	Oct	Dec	Hex	CNTL Key	Control Action
NUL	0	0	0	^@	Null character
SOH	1	1	1	^A	Start of heading, = console interrupt
STX	2	2	2	^B	Start of text (maintenance mode in HP command set)
ETX	3	3	3	^C	End of text
EOT	4	4	4	^D	End of transmission, not the same as ETB
ENQ	5	5	5	^E	Enquiry, goes with ACK (from HP Command Set)
ACK	6	6	6	^F	Acknowledge, clears ENQ logon hand
BEL	7	7	7	^G	Bell, rings the bell...
BS	10	8	8	^H	Backspace (From HP Command Set)
HT	11	9	9	^I	Horizontal tab, move to next tab stop
LF	12	10	a	^J	Line feed
VT	13	11	b	^K	Vertical tab
FF	14	12	c	^L	Form feed, page eject
CR	15	13	d	^M	Carriage return
SO	16	14	e	^N	Shift out, alternate character set
SI	17	15	f	^O	Shift in, resume default character set
DLE	20	16	10	^P	Data link escape
DC1	21	17	11	^Q	XON, with XOFF to pause listings; ":okay to send"
DC2	22	18	12	^R	Device control 2, block-mode flow control
DC3	23	19	13	^S	XOFF, with XON is TERM=18 flow control
DC4	24	20	14	^T	Device control 4
NAK	25	21	15	^U	Negative acknowledge
SYN	26	22	16	^V	Synchronous idle
ETB	27	23	17	^W	End transmission block, not the same as EOT
CAN	30	24	17	^X	Cancel line, MPE echoes
EM	31	25	19	^Y	End of medium, Control-Y interrupt
SUB	32	26	1a	^Z	Substitute
ESC	33	27	1b	^[	Escape, next character is not echoed
FS	34	28	1c	^\	File separator
GS	35	29	1d	^]	Group separator
RS	36	30	1e	^^	Record separator, block-mode terminator
US	37	31	1f	^_	Unit separator

The ASCII Character Set (Printed Characters)

Char	Octal	Dec	Hex	Description	Char	Octal	Dec	Hex	Description
SP	40	32	20	Space	;	73	59	3b	Semicolon
!	41	33	21	Exclamation mark	<	74	60	3c	Less-than sign (< in HTML)
"	42	34	22	Quotation mark (" in HTML)	=	75	61	3d	Equals sign
#	43	35	23	Crosshatch (number sign)	>	76	62	3e	Greater-than sign (> in HTML)
$	44	36	24	Dollar sign	?	77	63	3f	Question mark
%	45	37	25	Percent sign	@	100	64	40	At-sign
&	46	38	26	Ampersand	A	101	65	41	Uppercase A
'	47	39	27	Closing single quote (apostrophe)	B	102	66	42	Uppercase B
(	50	40	28	Opening parenthesis	C	103	67	43	Uppercase C
)	51	41	29	Closing parenthesis	D	104	68	44	Uppercase D
*	52	42	2a	Asterisk (star, multiply)	E	105	69	45	Uppercase E
+	53	43	2b	Plus	F	106	70	46	Uppercase F
,	54	44	2c	Comma	G	107	71	47	Uppercase G
-	55	45	2d	Hyphen, dash, minus	H	110	72	48	Uppercase H
.	56	46	2e	Period	I	111	73	49	Uppercase I
/	57	47	2f	Slant (forward slash, divide)	J	112	74	4a	Uppercase J
0	60	48	30	Zero	K	113	75	4b	Uppercase K
1	61	49	31	One	L	114	76	4c	Uppercase L
2	62	50	32	Two	M	115	77	4d	Uppercase M
3	63	51	33	Three	N	116	78	4e	Uppercase N
4	64	52	34	Four	O	117	79	4f	Uppercase O
5	65	53	35	Five	P	120	80	50	Uppercase P
6	66	54	36	Six	Q	121	81	51	Uppercase Q
7	67	55	37	Seven	R	122	82	52	Uppercase R
8	70	56	38	Eight	S	123	83	53	Uppercase S
9	71	57	39	Nine					
:	72	58	3a	Colon					

(Continued)

The ASCII Character Set (Printed Characters) (Concluded)

Char	Octal	Dec	Hex	Description	Char	Octal	Dec	Hex	Description
T	124	84	54	Uppercase T	k	153	107	6b	Lowercase k
U	125	85	55	Uppercase U	l	154	108	6c	Lowercase l
V	126	86	56	Uppercase V	m	155	109	6d	Lowercase m
W	127	87	57	Uppercase W	n	156	110	6e	Lowercase n
X	130	88	58	Uppercase X	o	157	111	6f	Lowercase o
Y	131	89	59	Uppercase Y	p	160	112	70	Lowercase p
Z	132	90	5a	Uppercase Z	q	161	113	71	Lowercase q
[	133	91	5b	Opening square bracket	r	162	114	72	Lowercase r
\	134	92	5c	Reverse slant (Backslash)	s	163	115	73	Lowercase s
]	135	93	5d	Closing square bracket	t	164	116	74	Lowercase t
^	136	94	5e	Caret (Circumflex)	u	165	117	75	Lowercase u
_	137	95	5f	Underscore	v	166	118	76	Lowercase v
`	140	96	60	Opening single quote	w	167	119	77	Lowercase w
a	141	97	61	Lowercase a	x	170	120	78	Lowercase x
b	142	98	62	Lowercase b	y	171	121	79	Lowercase y
c	143	99	63	Lowercase c	z	172	122	7a	Lowercase z
d	144	100	64	Lowercase d	{	173	123	7b	Opening curly brace
e	145	101	65	Lowercase e			174	124	7c	Vertical line
f	146	102	66	Lowercase f	}	175	125	7d	Closing curly brace
g	147	103	67	Lowercase g	~	176	126	7e	Tilde (approximate)
h	150	104	68	Lowercase h	DEL	177	127	7f	Delete (rubout), cross-hatch box
i	151	105	69	Lowercase i					
j	152	106	6a	Lowercase j					

ISO Latin Character Set

Decimal Value	Character	Description	Decimal Value	Character	Description	Decimal Value	Character	Description
32	Space	Standard space	56	8	Number eight	81	Q	Capital Q
33	!	Exclamation	57	9	Number nine	82	R	Capital R
34	"	Quotation mark	58	:	Colon	83	S	Capital S
35	#	Number sign	59	;	Semicolon	84	T	Capital T
36	$	Dollar sign	60	<	Left carat	85	U	Capital U
37	%	Percent sign	61	=	Equal sign	86	V	Capital V
38	&	Ampersand	62	>	Right carat	87	W	Capital W
39	'	Apostrophe	63	?	Question mark	88	X	Capital X
40	(	Left parenthesis	64	@	At sign	89	Y	Capital Y
41	)	Right parenthesis	65	A	Capital A	90	Z	Capital Z
42	*	Asterisk	66	B	Capital B	91	[	Left bracket
43	+	Plus sign	67	C	Capital C	92	\	Reverse solidus
44	,	Comma	68	D	Capital D	93	]	Right bracket
45	-	Minus sign/dash	69	E	Capital E	94	^	Carat
46	.	Period	70	F	Capital F	95	_	Underscore
47	/	Solidus (slash)	71	G	Capital G	96	`	Acute accent
48	0	Number zero	72	H	Capital H	97	a	Lowercase a
49	1	Number one	73	I	Capital I	98	b	Lowercase b
50	2	Number two	74	J	Capital J	99	c	Lowercase c
51	3	Number three	75	K	Capital K	100	d	Lowercase d
52	4	Number four	76	L	Capital L	101	e	Lowercase e
53	5	Number five	77	M	Capital M	102	f	Lowercase f
54	6	Number six	78	N	Capital N	103	g	Lowercase g
55	7	Number seven	79	O	Capital O	104	h	Lowercase h
			80	P	Capital P	105	i	Lowercase i

(Continued)

ISO Latin Character Set (Continued)

Decimal Value	Character	Description
106	j	Lowercase j
107	k	Lowercase k
108	l	Lowercase l
109	m	Lowercase m
110	n	Lowercase n
111	o	Lowercase o
112	p	Lowercase p
113	q	Lowercase q
114	r	Lowercase r
115	s	Lowercase s
116	t	Lowercase t
117	u	Lowercase u
118	v	Lowercase v
119	w	Lowercase w
120	x	Lowercase x
121	y	Lowercase y
122	z	Lowercase z
123	{	Left curly brace
124	|	Vertical bar
125	}	Right curly brace
126	~	Tilde
127-159		Nonprinting
160		Nonbreaking space
161	¡	Inverted exclamation
162	¢	Cent sign

Decimal Value	Character	Description
163	£	Pound sterling
164	¤	General currency sign
165	¥	Yen sign
166	¦	Broken vertical bar
167	§	Section sign
168	¨	Umlaut (dieresis)
169	©	Copyright
170	ª	Feminine ordinal
171	«	Left angle quote, guillemot left
172	¬	Not sign
173		Soft hyphen
174	®	Registered trademark
175	¯	Macron accent
176	°	Degree sign
177	±	Plus or minus
178	²	Superscript two
179	³	Superscript three
180	´	Acute accent
181	µ	Micro sign
182	¶	Paragraph sign
183	·	Middle dot
184	¸	Cedilla
185	¹	Superscript one
186	º	Masculine ordinal
187	»	Right angle quote, guillemot

Number	Character	Description
106	j	Lowercase j
188	¼	Fraction one-fourth
189	½	Fraction one-half
190	¾	Fraction three-fourths
191	¿	Inverted question mark
192	À	Capital A, grave accent (A-grave)
193	Á	Capital A, acute accent (A-acute)
194	Â	Capital A, circumflex accent (A-circ)
195	Ã	Capital A, tilde (A-tilde)
196	Ä	Capital A, dieresis or umlaut mark (A-uml)
197	Å	Capital A, ring (A-ring)
198	Æ	Capital AE dipthong (ligature) (AE-lig)
199	Ç	Capital C, cedilla (C-cedil)
200	È	Capital E, grave accent (E-grave)
201	É	Capital E, acute accent (E-acute)
202	Ê	Capital E, circumflex accent (E-circ)
203	Ë	Capital E, dieresis or umlaut mark (E-uml)
204	Ì	Capital I, grave accent (I-grave)
205	Í	Capital I, acute accent (I-acute)
206	Î	Capital I, circumflex accent (I-circ)
207	Ï	Capital I, dieresis or umlaut mark (I-uml)
208	Ð	Capital Eth, Icelandic (ETH)
209	Ñ	Capital N, tilde (N-tilde)
210	Ò	Capital O, grave accent (O-grave)
211	Ó	Capital O, acute accent (O-acute)
212	Ô	Capital O, circumflex accent (O-circ)
213	Õ	Capital O, tilde (O-tilde)
214	Ö	Capital O, dieresis or umlaut mark (O-uml)
215	×	Multiplication sign
216	Ø	Capital O, slash (O-slash)
217	Ù	Capital U, grave accent (U-grave)
218	Ú	Capital U, acute accent (U-acute)
219	Û	Capital U, circumflex accent (U-circ)
220	Ü	Capital U, dieresis or umlaut mark (U-uml)
221	Ý	Capital Y, acute accent (Y-acute)
222	Þ	Capital THORN, Icelandic (THORN)
223	ß	Small sharp s, German (sz ligature) (szlig)
224	à	Small a, grave accent (a-grave)
225	á	Small a, acute accent (a-acute)
226	â	Small a, circumflex accent (a-circ)
227	ã	Small a, tilde (a-tilde)
228	ä	Small a, dieresis or umlaut mark (a-uml)
229	å	Small a, ring (a-ring)
230	æ	Small ae dipthong (ligature) (ae-lig)
231	ç	Small c, cedilla (c-cedil)
232	è	Small e, grave accent (e-grave)

(Continued)

ISO Latin Character Set *(Concluded)*

Decimal Value	Character	Description	Decimal Value	Character	Description
233	é	Small e, acute accent (e-acute)	245	õ	Small o, tilde (o-tilde)
234	ê	Small e, circumflex accent (e-circ)	246	ö	Small o, dieresis or umlaut mark (o-uml)
235	ë	Small e, dieresis or umlaut mark (e-uml)	247	÷	Division sign
236	ì	Small i, grave accent (i-grave)	248	ø	Small o, slash (o-slash)
237	í	Small i, acute accent (i-acute)	249	ù	Small u, grave accent (u-grave)
238	î	Small i, circumflex accent (i-circ)	250	ú	Small u, acute accent (u-acute)
239	ï	Small i, dieresis or umlaut mark (i-uml)	251	û	Small u, circumflex accent (u-circ)
240	ð	Small eth, Icelandic (eth)	252	ü	Small u, dieresis or umlaut mark (u-uml)
241	ñ	Small n, tilde (n-tilde)	253	ý	Small y, acute accent (y-acute)
242	ò	Small o, grave accent (o-grave)	254	þ	Small thorn, Icelandic (thorn)
243	ó	Small o, acute accent (o-acute)	255	ÿ	Small y, dieresis or umlaut mark (y-uml)
244	ô	Small o, circumflex accent (o-circ)			

BIOS Beep Codes and Error Messages

While this information is provided in other sections throughout the book, I felt that it would be a good idea to collate it into a single place for quick acquisition. Please note that each version of BIOS by a given manufacturer will change from version to version. Settings described in the Award BIOS setup will also be available in most other brands of BIOS, although they may be located in different sections. Beep codes and error messages are based on information provided by the manufacturers and are subject to change.

BIOS Setup (Award)

Table D.1 Standard CMOS Setup

Setting	Options	Description
Date	Page Up/Page Down	Changes System Date
Time	Page Up/Page Down	Changes System Time
Hard Disks/Type	Auto/User/None	Settings for IDE HDD
Hard Disks/Mode	Normal/LBA/Large/Auto	HDD Translation Method
Drive A	Various Settings	Enables/Disables Floppy A
Drive B	Various Settings	Enables/Disables Floppy B
Video	EGA/VGA, CGA-40, CGA-80, Mono	Establishes type video used
Halt On	Various Options	Stops POST on selected errors

BIOS FEATURES SETUP

Setting	Options	Description
Boot Virus Detection	Enabled/Disabled	Warns of any attempt to write to the boot sector
CPU Level 1 Cache	Enabled/Disabled	Enables read/write operations to L1 cache built into CPU
CPU Level 2 Cache	Enabled/Disabled	Enables read/writer operations to L2 cache built into CPU
CPU Level 2 Cache ECC Check	Enabled/Disabled	Turns on/off ECC Mode
Quick Power On Self Test	Enabled/Disabled	Full Test/Tests only selected system components on cold boot
HDD Sequence	IDE/SCSI	Where to look for MBR
Boot Sequence	Options Vary	Determines the order of devices in which POST looks for the MBR
Boot Up Floppy Seek	Enabled/Disabled	Tests floppy drive to see if it has 40 or 80 tracks
Floppy Disk Access Control	R/W, Read Only	Security Access for floppy drive
HDD Block Mode Sectors	Options Vary	
HDD S.M.A.R.T capability	Enabled/Disabled	IDE SMART Capable?
PS2 Mouse Function Control	Enabled/Auto	Looks to PS2 for mouse
OS2 Onboard Memory	Enabled/Disabled	Use OS2 memory mapping

PCI/VGA Palette Snoop	Disabled/Enabled	Allows Video adapters to directly access RAM looking for video information
Video ROM/BIOS Shadowing	Enabled/Disabled	Allows copying of BIOS routines to upper memory for enhanced performance
C8000-DFFFF Shadowing (multiple entries)	Enabled/Disabled	Allows copying of Supplemental BIOS to specific addresses
Boot Up NumLock Status	On/Off	Determines whether number lock on keyboard is on or off after system boots
Typomatic Rate Setting	Disabled/Enabled	Disabled turns off *Typomatic Rate* and *Typomatic Delay*
Typomatic Rate	Options vary	Sets speed at which characters repeat when a key on the keyboard is held down
Typomatic Delay	Options vary	Sets time that elapses before keys begin to repeat when a key on the keyboard is held down
Security Option	System/Setup	Determines where security is controlled

CHIPSET FEATURES SETUP

EDO Autoconfiguration	Enabled/Disabled	Allows chipset to control EDO timing functions
EDO Read Burst Timing	Varies	Sets number of clock cycles for Burst Mode read operations
EDO Write Burst Timing	Varies	Sets number of clock cycles for Burst Mode write operations
EDO RAS Precharge	3T, 4T	Sets number of clock cycles for RAS Precharge
EDO RAS/CAS Delay	2T, 3T	Sets number of clock cycles for RAS/CAS Delay
SDRAM Configuration	Varies	Sets clock speed of SDRAM
SDRAM RAS Precharge	Auto, 3T, 4T	Sets number of clock cycles for RAS Precharge
SDRAM RAS/CAS Delay	Auto, 3T, 2T	Sets number of clock cycles for RAS/CAS Delay
SDRAM Banks Close Policy	Arbitration, Page-Miss	
Graphics Aperture Size	Varies	
Video Memory Cache Mode	UC, USWC	Determines how Video Memory addresses cache
PCI 2.1 Support	Enabled/Disabled	Disabled setting drops system back to PCI Version 1.0
Memory Hole at 15M-16M	Enabled/Disabled	Enables/disables use of these memory addresses
Onboard FDC Controller	Enabled/Disabled	Allows you to disable the floppy disk drive

(Continued)

Table D.1 Standard CMOS Setup (*Continued*)

Setting	Options	Description
	CHIPSET FEATURES SETUP	
Onboard Floppy Swap A/B	Enabled/Disabled	Switches drives A and B
Onboard Serial Port 1	Various settings/Disabled	Allows reconfiguring or disabling Serial Port 1
Onboard Serial Port 2	Various settings/Disabled	Allows reconfiguring or disabling Serial Port 2
Onboard Parallel Port	Various settings/Disabled	Allows reconfiguring or disabling Parallel Port
Parallel Port Mode	Normal, ECC, ECC/ECP	Sets up parallel communications
ECP DMA Select	Varies	Sets DMA channel used by ECP Parallel mode
UART2 Use Infrared	Enabled/Disabled	Sets infrared port to UART2
Onboard PCI/IDE Enable	Both, Primary, Secondary, Disabled	Enables/disables IDE ports
IDE DMA Mode	Auto/Disable	Disables, autoselects Direct Memory Access
IDE 0/1 – Master/Slave	Various	Sets PIO mode and DMA channel for specific device
	POWER MANAGEMENT SETUP	
Power Management	User Defined, Disabled, Min, Max	Determines PM Method
Video Off Option	Suspend ‡ Off, Always On	Determines how the monitor is managed
Video Off Method	Various Options	Determines method by which monitor is shut down
HDD Power Down	Various	How long before hard drive shuts down
Suspend Mode	Various	How long before hard drive goes into suspended mode
PWR Button	Soft-off, Suspend, No Function	Determines how the power button affects power supply
Power Up on Modem ACT	Enabled/Disabled	Modem wakes machine?
AC Power Loss Restart	Enabled/Disabled	Automatically restarts machine when AC power is restored
Wake on LAN	Enabled/Disabled	NIC wakes machine?

PNP AND PCI SETUP

PNP OS Installed?	Yes/No	Is the Operating System PnP Compliant?
Slot 1-? IRQ (several entries)	Auto, various settings	Manually assign an IRQ to a specific slot or let PnP handle allocations?
PCI Latency Timer	Various settings	Number of clock cycles for PCI latency
IRQ 3-15 Used by ISA (several entries)	Yes/No	Is this IRQ assigned to a legacy ISA device?
Force Update ESCD	Enabled/Disabled	Forces reallocation of resources on POST

LOAD BIOS DEFAULTS?	Reloads factory Settings. No internal settings.
SUPERVISOR PASSWORD	Allows entry of supervisor password
USER PASSWORD	Allows entry of User password
IDE HDD AUTODETECT	Automatically detects and configures devices on Primary and Secondary IDE ports

BIOS BEEP CODES

Beep codes are the distress calls your computer issues when it is unable to start up successfully. Each manufacturer has its own set of codes it uses to translate what's going on during the POST process into something the user can understand, if he or she knows how to translate the code.

Table D.2 Beep Codes for AMI BIOS Chips

AMI BIOS Codes		
1 short	DRAM refresh error	The programmable interrupt controller or programmable timer has probably failed. Could indicate chipset failure.
2 short	Base 64K Memory parity error	A memory parity error has occurred in the first 64K of RAM. Could be a bad RAM chip.
3 short	Base 64K System memory failure	A memory error has occurred in the first 64K of RAM. Could be a bad RAM chip.
4 short	System timer	The system clock/timer IC has failed. This can also indicate a failure in the first bank of memory.
5 short	Processor	The CPU itself failed.
6 short	Keyboard controller Gate A20 error	The keyboard controller IC has failed. This affects more than the keyboard, because Gate A20 is used to switch the processor to protected mode. Could indicate chipset failure.
7 short	Virtual mode processor error	Either the CPU or the chipset has generated an exception error.
8 short	Display memory R/W test	The system video adapter is either missing or has failed.
9 short	ROM BIOS checksum error	The contents of the system BIOS ROM does not match the value checksum expected. Most likely bad BIOS.
10 short	CMOS shutdown register read/write error	The shutdown for the CMOS has failed
11 short	Cache error	L2 cache is faulty
1 long, 3 short	Cache error	Memory failure above 64K
1 long, 8 short	Display test failure	The system video adapter is either missing or has failed.

The Award BIOS has its own set of beeps and uses the far less than most other brands. Since the Award is one of the most common brands of BIOS out there, if you're going to memorize any codes at all, these are the ones to memorize.

Table D.3 Award BIOS Codes

No Beep	Power Supply, System Board, Speaker	Check power supply for current
Continuous beep	Power Supply, System Board	Power supply is delivering current, but may be bad
Repeating short beeps	Memory Error	Possible bad memory, or poorly seated memory
1 long, 1 short	System Board	
1 long, 2 or 3 short	Display Adapter	Possibly defective video adapter, possibly poorly seated video adapter
1 short	System OK	
2 short	POST Error displayed on monitor	Turns error codes over to display

Phoenix is in the business of making custom BIOSs for different manufacturers. Therefore, its screens show more variance than any other brand. You won't always know that it is actually a Phoenix BIOS. If it doesn't identify itself on boot and resembles nothing in the first section on BIOS settings, it might (or might not) be safe to assume it is Phoenix. In any case, Phoenix uses beep codes more than any other brand. Therefore, its list of codes is much longer.

Table D.4 Phoenix BIOS Codes

1-1-2	CPU test failure	The CPU is faulty. Replace the CPU.
Low 1-1-2	System board select	The motherboard is having an undetermined fault. Replace the motherboard.
1-1-3	CMOS read/write	The real time clock/CMOS is faulty. Replace the CMOS if possible.
Low 1-1-3	Extended CMOS RAM	The extended portion of the CMOS RAM has failed. Replace the CMOS if possible.
1-1-4	BIOS ROM checksum error	The BIOS ROM has failed. Replace the BIOS or upgrade if possible.
1-2-1	PIT failure	The programmable interrupt timer has failed. Replace if possible. Likely chipset failure.
1-2-2	DMA failure	The DMA controller has failed. Likely chipset failure.
1-2-3	DMA read/write failure	The DMA controller has failed. Likely chipset failure.
1-3-1	RAM refresh failure	The RAM refresh controller has failed. Likely chipset failure.
1-3-2	64KB RAM failure	The test of the first 64KB RAM has failed to start.

(Continued)

Table D.4 Phoenix BIOS Codes *(Continued)*

1-3-3	First 64KB RAM failure	The first RAM IC has failed. Likely chipset failure.
1-3-4	First 64KB logic failure	The first RAM control logic has failed.
1-4-1	Address line failure	The address line to the first 64KB RAM has failed.
1-4-2	Parity RAM failure	The first RAM IC has failed. Replace if possible.
1-4-3	EISA failsafe timer test	Replace the motherboard.
1-4-4	EISA NMI port 462 test	Replace the motherboard.
2-1-1	64KB RAM failure	Bit 0; This data bit on the first RAM IC has failed. Likely chipset failure.
2-1-2	64KB RAM failure	Bit 1; This data bit on the first RAM IC has failed. Likely chipset failure.
2-1-3	64KB RAM failure	Bit 2; This data bit on the first RAM IC has failed. Likely chipset failure.
2-1-4	64KB RAM failure	Bit 3; This data bit on the first RAM IC has failed. Likely chipset failure.
2-2-1	64KB RAM failure	Bit 4; This data bit on the first RAM IC has failed. Likely chipset failure.
2-2-2	64KB RAM failure	Bit 5; This data bit on the first RAM IC has failed. Likely chipset failure.
2-2-3	64KB RAM failure	Bit 6; This data bit on the first RAM IC has failed. Likely chipset failure.
2-2-4	64KB RAM failure	Bit 7; This data bit on the first RAM IC has failed. Likely chipset failure.
2-3-1	64KB RAM failure	Bit 8; This data bit on the first RAM IC has failed. Likely chipset failure.
2-3-2	64KB RAM failure	Bit 9; This data bit on the first RAM IC has failed. Likely chipset failure.
2-3-3	64KB RAM failure	Bit 10; This data bit on the first RAM IC has failed. Likely chipset failure.
2-3-4	64KB RAM failure	Bit 11; This data bit on the first RAM IC has failed. Likely chipset failure.
2-4-1	64KB RAM failure	Bit 12; This data bit on the first RAM IC has failed. Likely chipset failure.
2-4-2	64KB RAM failure	Bit 13; This data bit on the first RAM IC has failed. Likely chipset failure.
2-4-3	64KB RAM failure	Bit 14; This data bit on the first RAM IC has failed. Likely chipset failure.
2-4-4	64KB RAM failure	Bit 15; This data bit on the first RAM IC has failed. Likely chipset failure.
3-1-1	Slave DMA register failure	The DMA controller has failed. Replace the controller if possible.

(Continued)

Table D.4   Phoenix BIOS Codes *(Continued)*

3-1-2	Master DMA register failure	The DMA controller has failed. Replace the controller if possible.
3-1-3	Master interrupt mask register failure	The interrupt controller IC has failed.
3-1-4	Slave interrupt mask register failure	The interrupt controller IC has failed.
3-2-2	Interrupt vector error	The BIOS was unable to load the interrupt vectors into memory. Replace the motherboard.
3-2-3	Reserved	
3-2-4	Keyboard controller failure	The keyboard controller has failed. Likely chipset failure.
3-3-1	CMOS RAM power bad	Replace the CMOS battery or CMOS RAM if possible.
3-3-2	CMOS configuration error	The CMOS configuration has failed. Restore the configuration or replace the battery if possible.
3-3-3	Reserved	
3-3-4	Video memory failure	There is a problem with the video memory. Replace the video adapter if possible.
3-4-1	Video initialization failure	There is a problem with the video adapter. Reseat the adapter or replace the adapter if possible.
4-2-1	Timer failure	The system's timer IC has failed. Likely chipset failure.
4-2-2	Shutdown failure	The CMOS has failed. Replace the CMOS IC if possible.
4-2-3	Gate A20 failure	The keyboard controller has failed. Likely chipset failure.
4-2-4	Unexpected interrupt in protected mode	This is a CPU problem. Replace the CPU and retest.
4-3-1	RAM test failure	System RAM addressing circuitry is faulty. Replace the motherboard.
4-3-3	Interval timer channel 2 failure	The system timer IC has failed. Likely chipset failure.
4-3-4	Time of day clock failure	The real time clock/CMOS has failed. Replace the CMOS if possible.
4-4-1	Serial port failure	A error has occurred in the serial port circuitry.
4-4-2	Parallel port failure	A error has occurred in the parallel port circuitry.
4-4-3	Math coprocessor failure	The math coprocessor has failed. If possible, replace the MPU. Most likely a new CPU is needed.

Common Chipsets

There have been several manufacturers of chipsets over the years, and it is neither my intention nor the publisher's to slight any manufacturer. However, time and space restraints prevent me from publishing every chipset ever seen by man. For the purposes of this section, I have taken the chipsets most commonly seen today and included them in this list.

Table D.5 Intel Chipsets

Chipset Name	Code Name	CPU Supported	Bus	Max RAM	RAM Types	AGP	IDE	USB	PCI	Error Checking	Dual Processors
430LX	Triton	P5	60, 66	192MB	FPM	No	BMIDE	No	2.0	Parity	No
430NX	Neptune	P54	50, 60, 66	512MB	FPM	No	BMIDE	No	2.0	Parity	Yes
430FX	Triton I	P54	60, 66	128MB	FPM/EDO	No	BMIDE	No	2.0	None	No
430HX	Triton II	P54/55	60, 66	512MB	FPM/EDO	No	BMIDE	Yes	2.1	Parity/ECC	Yes
430VX	Triton III	P54/55	50, 60, 66	128MB	EDO/SDRAM	No	BMIDE	Yes	2.1	None	No
430TX	Triton IV (unofficial)	P54/55	50, 60, 66	256MB	EDO/SDRAM	No	UDMA/33	Yes	2.1	None	No
440FX	Natoma	P6/PII	60, 66	1GB	FPM/EDO/BEDO	No	UDMA/33	No	2.1	Parity/ECC	Yes
450GX	Orion	P6	60, 66	4GB	FPM	No	BMIDE	No	2.1	Parity/ECC	QUAD
450KX	Mars	P6	60, 66	1GB	FPM	No	BMIDE	No	2.1	Parity/ECC	Yes
450NX	Deschutes	Xeon	100	8GB	EDO	No	UDMA/33	Yes	2.1	Parity/ECC	Yes
440LX	None	PII/Celeron	66	1GB	EDO/SDRAM	1x	UDMA/33	No	2.1	Parity/ECC	Yes
440EX	None	PII/Celeron	66	256MB	EDO/SDRAM	1x	UDMA/33	Yes	2.1	None	No
440BX	None	PII/PIII/Celeron	66, 100	1GB	EDO/SDRAM	1x, 2x	UDMA/33	Yes	2.1	Parity/ECC	Yes
440GX	None	PII/Xeon	133	1GB	SDRAM	2x	UDMA/33	Yes	2.1	Parity/ECC	No
440ZX	None	PII/Celeron	66, 100	256MB	EDO/SDRAM	1x, 2x	UDMA/33	Yes	2.1	None	No
440ZX66	None	Celeron	66	256	EDO/SDRAM	1x, 2x	UDMA/33	Yes	2.1	None	No
810	Whitney	Celeron	66, 100	512MB	SDRAM	1x, 2x	UDMA/66	Yes	2.2	None	No
810E	Whitney	PIII/Celeron	66, 100, 133	512MB	SDRAM	1x, 2x	UDMA/66	Yes	2.2	None	No
815	Solano	PIII/Celeron	66, 100, 133	512MB	SDRAM	1x, 2x, 4x	UDMA/66	Yes	2.2	None	No
820	Camino	PIII/Celeron	100, 133	1GB	RDRAM[1]	1x, 2x, 4x	UDMA/66	Yes	2.2	ECC	Yes
830	Almador	PIII	133	1.5GB	SDRAM	1x, 2x, 4x	UDMA/66	Yes	2.2	ECC	Yes
840	Carmel	PIII/Xeon	100, 133	4GB	RDRAM	1x, 2x, 4x	UDMA/66	Yes	2.2	ECC	DUAL PIII QUAD
XEON 850	Willamette	PIV	400	2GB	RDRAM	1x, 2x, 4x	UDMA/100	Yes	2.2	ECC	No

Listing of Intel chipsets since the release of the Pentium CPU

VIA chipsets have long been a standard of the industry. The ones listed here in no way, shape, or form represent every chipset it ever made. Instead I have chosen to provide information on those chipsets that support the most commonly seen CPUs.

Table D.6 VIA Chipsets

Chipset Name	CPU Supported	Bus	Max RAM	RAM Types	AGP	IDE	USB	PCI	Error Checking
VP*	P54	50, 60, 66	512MB	FPM, EDO, BEDO, SDRAM	No	UDMA/33	Yes	2.1	None
VP2*	P54, P55	50, 60, 66	512MB	FPM, EDO, SDRAM	No	UDMA/33	Yes	2.1	ECC
VP2/97*	P54, P55	50, 60, 66	512MB	FPM, EDO, SDRAM	No	UDMA/33	Yes	2.1	ECC
VPX*	P54, P55	66, 75	512MB	FPM, EDO, SDRAM	No	UDMA/33	Yes	2.1	No
VPX/97*	P54, P55	66, 75	512MB	FPM, EDO, SDRAM	No	UDMA/33	Yes	2.1	No
VP3*	P54, P55	50, 60, 66	1GB	FPM, EDO, SDRAM, DDRAM	1x, 2x	UDMA/33	Yes	2.1	ECC/Parity
MVP3*	P54, P55	66, 75, 83, 100	1GB	FPM, EDO, SDRAM	1x, 2x	UDMA/33	Yes	2.1	ECC/Parity
MVP4*	P54, P55	66, 75, 83, 100	768MB	FPM, EDO, SDRAM	1x, 2x	UDMA/66	Yes	2.2	ECC/Parity
Apollo†	P6	66	1GB	FPM, EDO	No	UDMA/33	Yes	2.1	ECC
Apollo PRO*	P6, PII	66, 100	1GB	FPM, EDO, SDRAM, DDRAM, ESDRAM. VC SDRAM	1x, 2x	UDMA/33	Yes	2.1	ECC/Parity
Apollo PRO+*	P6, PII	66, 100	1GB	FPM, EDO, SDRAM, VC SDRAM	1x, 2x	UDMA/33	Yes	2.1	ECC/Parity
Apollo PRO 133*	PIII, Celeron	66, 100, 133	1.5GB	FPM, EDO, SDRAM, VC SDRAM	1x , 2x	UDMA/66	Yes	2.2	ECC/Parity
Apollo PRO 133A†	PIII, Celeron	66, 100, 133	2GB	FPM, EDO, SDRAM, DDRAM, ESDRAM. VC SDRAM	1x, 2x, 4x	UDMA/66	Yes	2.2	ECC/Parity
PM-601*	PIII, Celeron	66, 100, 133	1GB	FPM, EDO, SDRAM, VC SDRAM	1x, 2x	UDMA/66	Yes	2.2	No
PM-133*	PIII, Celeron	66, 100, 133	2GB	FPM, EDO, SDRAM, ESDRAM, VC SDRAM	1x, 2x, 4x	UDMA/66	Yes	2.2	ECC/Parity
Apollo PRO 266†	PIII	66, 100, 133	4GB	SDRAM, VC SDRAM, DDRAM	1x, 2x, 4x	UDMA/66	Yes	2.2	ECC
KX-133*	AMD K7	200	2GB	EDO, SDRAM, VC SDRAM, DDRAM	1x, 2x, 4x	UDMA/66	Yes	2.2	ECC/Parity
KT-133*	AMD K7, Duron	200	2GB	SDRAM, VC SDRAM, DDRAM	1x, 2x, 4x	UDMA/66	Yes	2.2	No
KM-133*	AMD K7, Duron	200, 266	1.5GB	FPM, EDO, SDRAM, VC SDRAM	1x, 2x, 4x	UDMA/66	Yes	2.2	No

List of VIA Chipsets for the K7 and later

*No Dual Processor; † Dual Processor

The Opti chipsets were targeted at the mass-market, lower-priced computers that could be used in schools and corporations or by individuals on a budget. They tend to be problem-free for the most part, but will never win any awards for their blazing performance. Despite that, they still provide more than acceptable system performance, all else being equal.

Table D.7 Opti Chipsets

Chipset Name	CPU Supported	Bus	Max RAM	RAM Types	AGP	IDE	USB	PCI	Error Checking
Python	P5, P54	50, 60, 66	128MB	FPM	No	BMIDE	No	1.0/VLB	Parity
Cobra	P5, P54	50, 60, 66	128MB	FPM	No	BMIDE	No	1.0/VLB	Parity
Viper	P54, P55	50, 60, 66	512MB	FPM, EDO, SDRAM	No	BMIDE	No	2.0	Parity
Viper N	P54, P55	50, 60, 66	512MB	FPM, EDO	No	BMIDE	No	2.0	Parity
Viper N+	P54, P55	50, 60, 66	512MB	FPM, EDO	No	BMIDE	No	2.0	Parity
Viper MAX	P54, P55	50, 60, 66	512MB	FPM, EDO, BEDO, SDRAM	No	BMIDE	Yes	2.0	Parity
Viper Xpress	P54, P55	40, 50, 60, 66	512MB	FPM, EDO	No	BMIDE	Yes	2.1	Parity
Vendetta	P54	50, 60, 66	512MB	FPM, EDO, SDRAM	No	UDMA/33	No	2.1	ECC/Parity
Discovery	P6	60, 66	512MB	FPM, EDO, SDRAM	Yes	UDMA/33	Yes	2.1	ECC/Parity

List of Opti Chipsets

*No Dual Processor; †Dual Processor

Silicon Integrated Systems Corporation specializes in chipsets that support large numbers of onboard peripherals. In this respect, the company has made a very respectable niche for itself in the market. Its chipsets, for the most part, are solid and reliable and provide for reasonably good performance.

Table D.8 SiS Chipsets

Chipset Name	CPU Supported	Bus	Max RAM	RAM Types	AGP	IDE	USB	PCI	Error Checking
501–503*	P54	50, 60, 66	128MB	FPM, EDO	No	BMIDE	No	1.0	No
5511–5513†	P54	50, 60, 66	512MB	FPM, EDO	No	BMIDE	No	2.0	Parity
5571*	P54, P55	50, 60, 66, 75	384MB	FPM, EDO, SDRAM	No	BMIDE	No	2.0	No
5581*	P54, P55	50, 55, 60, 66, 75	384MB	FPM, EDO, SDRAM	No	UDMA/33	Yes	2.0	No
5582*	P54, P55	50, 55, 60, 66, 75	384MB	FPM, EDO, SDRAM	No	UDMA/33	Yes	2.0	No
5591*	P54, P55	50, 55, 60, 66, 75	768MB	FPM, EDO, SDRAM	1x, 2x	UDMA/33	Yes	2.1	No
5592*	P54, P55	50, 55, 60, 66, 75	768MB	FPM, EDO, SDRAM	1x, 2x	UDMA/33	Yes	2.1	No
5596*	P54	50, 60, 66	512MB	FPM, EDO	No	BMIDE	Yes	2.1	No
5597*	P54, P55	50, 55, 60, 66, 75	384	FPM, EDO, SDRAM	No	UDMA/33	Yes	2.1	No
5598*	P54, P55	50, 55, 60, 66, 75	384	FPM, EDO, SDRAM	No	UDMA/33	Yes	2.1	No
530*	P54, P55	66, 75, 83, 95, 100	1.5GB	SDRAM	1x, 2x	UDMA/66	Yes	2.2	No
540*	P54, P55	66, 75, 83, 95, 100	1.5GB	SDRAM, VC SDRAM	1x, 2x, 4x	UDMA/66	Yes	2.2	No
5600†	PII	60, 66, 100	1.5GB	FPM, EDO, SDRAM	1x, 2x	UDMA/33	Yes	2.1	ECC
600†	PII	60, 66, 100	1.5GB	FPM, EDO, SDRAM	1x, 2x	UDMA/33	Yes	2.1	ECC
620*	PII	60, 66, 75, 83, 100	1.5GB	SDRAM	1x, 2x	UDMA/66	Yes	2.2	No
630*	PIII, Celeron	66, 100, 133	3GB	SDRAM, VC SDRAM	1x, 2x, 4x	UDMA/66	Yes	2.2	No
630E*	PIII, Celeron	66, 100, 133	3GB	SDRAM	1x, 2x, 4x	UDMA/66	Yes	2.2	No
730S*	AMD K7, Duron	200	1.5GB	SDRAM	1x, 2x, 4x	UDMA/66	Yes	2.2	No

Listing of SiS Chipsets

* No Dual Processor; † Dual Processor

ANSWERS TO CHAPTER EXERCISES

CHAPTER 1

BRAIN DRAIN

1. List and explain each of the basic functions that define a computer.

    Answers should include the terms *calculate, copy,* and *compare.* They should also show an awareness that the basic CPU functions limit calculation abilities to addition, subtraction, multiplication, and division of whole numbers.

3. You have a hexadecimal address of 02FE:CCC0. Convert that address to binary.

    1011111111011001100110000000 is the correct answer.

5. Describe the five primary system busses and their functions.

    CPU Bus: Direct communication with the chipset and cache.

    Address Bus: Maintains, tracks and locates addresses of each individual device in the system.

    Local Bus: A direct path between the CPU and RAM or the CPU and L2 cache.

    The I/O Bus: The path that data uses to move from device to device as either input or output.

    The Power Bus: The wires that supply raw electricity to the various components on the motherboard.

THE 64K$ QUESTIONS

1. Which of the following is *not* a basic function of a computer?

    A: Provide user data for input

3. A byte that consists of the bits 0 1 1 1 0 0 1 0 has a decimal value of:

    B. 114

5. Which character set included control codes as part of the basic set?

    A. ASCII

7. Which of the primary system busses provides direct communications between the CPU and the chipset?

    A. The CPU Bus

9. Which of the primary system busses is responsible for locating data in the system?

    D. The Address Bus

Chapter 2

Brain Drain

1. List as many onboard components as you can that will be found on both AT-style and ATX-style motherboards.

    Typically, an AT-style motherboard will have only a large DIN connector for the keyboard. Some AT motherboards did feature serial and parallel ports as well, but they were the exception and not the rule.

3. Put together a list of as many expansion devices as you can think of that would require a slot on the expansion bus.

    Answers will vary here, but the list would include:

    SCSI adapters, modems, sound cards, video cards, specialized I/O controllers (including device controllers, USB, and Firewire), video capture cards, and add/on IDE controllers.

5. This task should be accomplished with a partner. Place a fully assembled computer on the table in front of you. Without looking at the back and using the sense of touch only, reach around to the back of the computer and identify as many connectors as you can.

    Sorry. I'm not your partner.

The 64K$ Questions

1. A key precautionary measure to take before working inside a computer system is to:

    D. Protect the CPU from EMI. Generally, there is little danger of electrical shock to the technician working inside of a computer, unless taking the power supply apart.

3. On an AT-style power supply the correct orientation of the P8 and P9 connectors was:
   a: Black wires to the inside, colored wires to the outside.

5. A DIMM socket is equipped with _____ pin connectors.
   B. 168 and D. 184 are both correct. SDRAM uses the 168-pin design, while DDR uses the 184-pin.

7. A 40-pin ribbon cable connector is the hookup for _____.
   D. The IDE port.

9. A 25-pin male connector with two rows of female pins is _____.
   C. A parallel port Or D. An external SCSI port.

CHAPTER 3

BRAIN DRAIN

1. Discuss the three primary measurements of electricity covered in this chapter and how they relate to one another.

   Voltage is the differential charge between two surfaces. Amperage is the number of electrons per second that flows from one surface to the other over a conductor. Resistance is the tendency for the conductor to prevent some of the electrons from passing. Together, the three of them dictate how many watts of electricity are produced, which is the measurement of how much work that current can do.

3. Discuss why those three components would be needed by a motherboard.

   Capacitors act to clean up current and eliminate fluctuations, resistors are used to "slow down" current for devices that need less juice, and coils eliminate any residual AC current as well as filter out low-frequency signals.

5. Talk about why a power supply can be such a problem to troubleshoot when it fails slowly.

   Many of the symptoms of a failing power supply mimic the symptoms of other devices, such as memory or hard drives. For example, if a power supply is too slow in achieving full output, a hard disk might try to initialize before there is sufficient current to power it. Extreme drop in voltage can flush CPU registers and memory even when the fluctuation didn't last long enough to cause a complete system shutdown. This can look like an application failure.

THE 64K$ QUESTIONS

1. Which of the following devices is used to reduce the amount of amperage on a circuit?
   C. A resistor

3. Which of the following devices would be measured in microfarads?

   A. A capacitor

5. What device will keep an individual computer running for a few minutes after a total power failure?

   D. An uninterrupted power supply

7. Power is provided to the motherboard from an AT power supply by way of _____.

   C. A pair of 6-pin connectors

9. Which of the following could be signs of a failing power supply?

   D. All of the above

Chapter 4

Brain Drain

1. Discuss why the computer enclosure might be the first decision a designer makes when putting together a new model of computer.

   A couple of things make this a critical decision to make first. For one, where is the system to be located? A full-tower design doesn't fit very well on a classroom desktop. Conversely, a micro desktop might not be the best thing to put on the floor. Also, consider how many devices the system must eventually support. That micro desktop won't go very far if you need a CD-RW, a DVD, a backup tape drive, and an internal Zip drive.

3. What are the pros and cons of using aluminum versus steel in designing a computer case?

   Aluminum is much lighter and it dissipates heat faster. But it's more expensive and more difficult to mill, making it a far more expensive choice. An advantage of steel over aluminum is that it blocks EMI much better than does aluminum.

5. List as many individual components that make up the enclosure as you can think of.

   The frame, the case cover, the drive bays, the front and back panels, and the wiring harness are all parts of the enclosure.

The 64K$ Questions

1. Which of the following is a low-profile form factor?

   C. LBX

3. An advantage of aluminum over steel in enclosure construction is _____. (Choose all that apply.)

    A. Light-weight and D. It dissipates heat better.

5. Failing to replace the backplane filler after removing an expansion card is not a good idea, because _____.

    D. All of the above.

7. Hot-swappable drives are designed to fit into a _____ bay.

    A. 5^1/$_4$″ half-height

9. Which of the following is not likely to be a part of a typical wiring harness found in an enclosure?

    B. RLL. RLL is an old hard disk encoding method that will be discussed later in the book.

CHAPTER 5

BRAIN DRAIN

1. Discuss as many differences between at AT-style motherboard and an ATX-style motherboard as you can think of.

    First and foremost, the basic components of the motherboard, relative to the backplane, are rotated 90 degrees to that of the AT board. ATX boards generally feature far more integrated peripherals soldered onto the board than did AT. Also, ATX motherboards, by default, are designed to support advanced power management. An offshoot of this is that on/off functions are controlled by the motherboard and not the power supply.

3. Give an overview of the functions of the system BIOS.

    The BIOS contains the POST program, which brings the system from a cold start, checks all system components to make sure they're working properly and then performs Plug 'n Play scans. It contains a Setup program that runs from the BIOS chip, which allows the user to input parameters that BIOS will use in later boots. Finally, it contains the Bootstrap Loader, which goes out and finds the master boot record and turns the boot process over to the OS.

5. Discuss why we need to have a separate expansion bus.

    Designers can't expect to build every computer they ever plan to sell with every device that's ever been invented for personal computing. For one thing, that would make computers prohibitively expensive for most people, and for another, different people have different needs. Also, we need a bus with a consistent speed for add-on peripherals. It wouldn't do to have to redesign a network card every time a faster CPU came out.

The 64K$ Questions

1. A typical motherboard consists of _____ layers of substrate.
   C. Four

3. How many IDE controllers typically reside on an ATX-style motherboard?
   D. Zero. The motherboard typically has two ports, each of which supports two drives. The controller, however, is on the device itself.

5. POST is a function of _____.
   C. The BIOS

7. CMOS stands for _____.
   C. Complimentary Metal-Oxide Semiconductor

9. The Plug 'n Play Recognition Scan is a part of _____.
   B. POST

Chapter 6

Brain Drain

1. Describe how a semiconductor works and explain why it is such a useful material in making CPUs.
   A semiconductor is a substance that either allows a current to pass, or blocks it completely, based on whether or not the current reaches or exceeds a certain threshold voltage. This unique characteristic allows designers to create a "switch" based on whether or not that voltage is reached.

3. Explain why the 8088 CPU was only capable of recognizing 1MB of memory.
   The 8088 possessed a 20-bit address bus. As such, its total memory map could be 2^{20} bits wide. That value is 1,048,576, or 1MB.

5. Describe in as much detail as you can how the system moves data into the CPU after you press a certain key on your keyboard.
   When a key is first pressed, it prompts a chip on the keyboard to do three things. First it issues an interrupt request to the CPU, notifying the CPU that there is

data on the way. Next it generates a make code that indicates the key has been pressed. And when the key is released, it generates a break code. The make and break code are combined to generate the actual data that will be sent to RAM. The keyboard controller chip will then move that data to a buffer in memory where it will stay until the CPU orders the prefetch to go retrieve it.

THE 64K$ QUESTIONS

1. The binary language is an offshoot of the work of _____.
   A. George Boole

3. The address bus of the 8088 was _____ bits wide.
   C. 20

5. In the example used in Question 4, what technology would allow the CPU to actually *process* those lines of code before the user made a selection, discarding any data generated by the wrong subroutine?
   D. Speculative Execution

7. It is not possible for a CPU to have more than one FPU.
   B. False

9. The following is a collection of very useful circuits that appears on all modern CPU, but was not a part of the original 8088.
   d. L2 Cache

CHAPTER 7

BRAIN DRAIN

1. Briefly describe the processor generations and how they differ in speed and bus width.
   Processor generations generally are defined by a key change in architectural design. Generation One processors consist of the 8088 and its clones. Generation Two included the 286s, Three the 386s, and so on. Pentiums are easier to differentiate because they are Pentium II, III, and IV. It's not so easy with aftermarket designs. With the exception of the move from the 386 to the 486, each generation doubled the external data bus until the release of the Pentium. It has since stabilized at 64 bits. The internal data bus stabilized at 32 bits. While clock speeds have gotten faster with each generation, there is no real formula you can use to correlate the advances to a specific generation.

3. Discuss why raw processor speed has far less impact on system performance than other factors, such as the amount of L1 cache or the amount of system memory installed.

> With the average application run by the average user, the CPU actually spends more time waiting for data that it does processing it. So by increasing the clock speed of the CPU by 200 percent, you are in effect increasing its idle time by 200 percent. If you speed up delivery of data to the CPU by that same margin, you increase performance by a substantially greater margin.

5. The fifth-generation CPUs showed a rather remarkable diversity of characteristics. Discuss some of the Generation-5 CPUs and how they differed.

> The basic 3.3V Pentium was really nothing more than an improvement on the original design. The MMX follows quickly on its bootheels, adding multimedia extensions. AMD offerings, such as the K6-2 added an instruction set for 3D graphics rendering.

THE 64K$ QUESTIONS

1. Which of the following saw no change in the migration from the 8086 to the 80286?
   d. The ALU

3. Which CPU was the first to support protected mode?
   c. The 80286

5. The 80286 microprocessor has a _____-bit address bus.
   C. 24

7. The address bus of the 80486 was twice that of the 80386.
   B. False

9. The AMD series of 80386 CPU suffered several compatibility issues when using Microsoft operating systems.
   B. False

CHAPTER 8

BRAIN DRAIN

1. In as much detail as you can recall, describe a typical memory I/O operation from beginning to end.

> Starting with the CPU, the control unit issues a request for data to the prefetch. First, the prefetch searches all cache locations. When it doesn't find it there, it turns the search over to the chipset, where the memory control circuit confirms

that the data the CPU has requested does indeed reside in memory and that the first bit resides at this specific address. That address represents the X-Y coordinates of a spreadsheet-like grid. First, the row access strobe locates the correct row in which the data reside and subsequently turns the search over to the column access strobe, which finds the correct column. Once the address has been located, data can be moved in bursts until the next cycle must be completed. Depending on the type of memory this may be anywhere from two to four cycles.

3. What were some key differences that made SDRAM so much faster than EDO?

SDRAM moves some of the MCC circuitry over to the memory module, in essence making it part of the chipset. As a result, data can be accessed on each and every cycle of the CPU's front-side bus.

5. Describe how ECC differs from parity and what makes it a superior error checking mechanism.

Parity was simply an error checking mechanism. It counted the number of 1s in a byte. If there was an even number of 1s, it set the parity bit to 1 to assure that there was an odd number. If there was as odd number of 1s parity was set to 0 to keep the number odd. On the receiving end all 1s were counted. If there was an even number in the byte, including the parity bit, then a nonmaskable interrupt was generated and the computer locked up. ECC performs a mathematical calculation on the bits in the data being sent. The same calculation is performed on the receiving end. If the numbers in the ECC field match, the data is accepted. A single-bit error can be detected and corrected. An error of two or more bits will result in a nonmaskable interrupt and the computer will lock up.

THE 64K$ QUESTIONS

1. Memory I/O operations are controlled by _____.
   C. The MCC

3. A SIMM differs from a DIMM in its design in that _____.
   B. The terminating tabs on either side of the base of a DIMM can be assigned a separate function.

5. A typical DRAM cell consists of a transistor paired with _____.
   D. A microscopic capacitor.

7. Once the MCC has determined that the data being sought actually resides in RAM and resolves the address, the next thing to happen is a _____.
   A. Prerefresh

9. DDRAM is so named because it _____.
   C. Moves two bits of data for each clock cycle.

CHAPTER 9

BRAIN DRAIN

1. Discuss how IRQs, I/O addresses and DMA channels are critical to configuring a device on the expansion bus and some of the problems you might encounter.

   IRQs are like the doorbell for the CPU. When any given device wants to send data to the CPU or the CPU wants to send data to that device, either the device or the CPU will send an electrical signal down the IRQ line, alerting it to be ready for incoming data. Since neither device responds on the very same clock cycle they need to know where they're sending that data when the CPU is ready. The I/O address is a buffer area where data can be stored. The base I/O identifies the device, while any given devices can have a number of buffer addresses. DMA channels are direct circuits from the device to memory. A device configured to use DMA can dump data directly to memory once the I/O operation has been negotiated by the CPU.

3. What is the purpose of an I/O address?

   An I/O address is like any other address. It's how you find a specific house, or in this case device. Only in the case of an I/O address, it is actually a virtual address rather than a physical one. It is where the data either generated or required by a device will be found when either the CPU or the device goes looking for that data.

5. List the different expansion busses used by computer systems over the years in the order that they appeared.

   The PC Bus, ISA, MCA, EISA and VLB (about the same time), PCI, PCMCIA, AGP and PCI-X.

THE 64K$ QUESTIONS

1. An I/O Address is _____.

   D. A specific memory location that the CPU uses to locate data from a specific device.

3. An IRQ is _____.

   A. An electrical channel that notifies the CPU (or allows the CPU to notify a device) that there is data ready to be moved.

5. Which of the following busses were backwardly compatible with ISA? (Choose all that apply.)

   B. VLB and C. EISA

7. At what speed does an AGP 8x video card run?

    C. 133Mhz

9. When two devices on two different busses that operate at completely different speeds need to communicate, the process that allows this is _____.

    D. Flow control

CHAPTER 10

BRAIN DRAIN

1. Briefly describe how pressing on the W key on a keyboard generates data and moves it to the CPU for processing.

    When you first press the key, the keyboard's controller chip generates an interrupt to notify the CPU that there is data coming its way. It then issues a make code to indicate when the key was first pressed, and when the key is released, it issues a break code. The combination of the make and break code generates the data that will be sent to memory. The keyboard controller circuitry in the chipset will translate that data into what will be sent to the CPU.

3. Describe how a mouse does its job.

    The mouse ball turns rollers attached to a perforated wheel. A light beam shines through the perforations, creating a flickering beam. A photosensitive receptor converts that beam to electrical impulses that the mouse driver uses to interpret relative position of the mouse cursor.

5. Describe a method by which computerization will assure that the person bagging your order does not give you onion rings instead of fries.

    Computerize the production line rather than use humans.

THE 64K$ QUESTIONS

1. When you press down on a key, data is generated by two signals. These are the _____ and the _____. (Select two.)

    B. Break and D. Make

3. The type of mouse that uses a perforated wheel that spins in front of an LED is called a _____ mouse.

    D. Optomechanical. You might see it described as a mechanical mouse in a lot of literature. But technically, that is not correct.

5. A CCD is a _____.

   D. Charge Coupled Device

7. The file format frequently used by video editors is _____.

   D. MJPEG

9. Which of the following is not a form of touchscreen monitor?

   Resistive interpolative

CHAPTER 11

BRAIN DRAIN

1. List as many forms of removable media as you can.

   Lists will vary, but should include at the minimum: floppy diskettes, super-floppies, Zip drives, and Jaz drives. Syquest cartridges could be included as well. There have been others in the past. CD-ROMs and removable hard disks are technically not considered removable media, even though they are.

3. If you have an application that consists of 245MB worth of files and you want to run it from removable media, what options would be best?

   A Syquest would be best, because it is faster. But a 750MB Zip or a Jazz drive would work quite nicely as well.

5. Discuss as many differences as you can between DAT and DLT tape drives.

   DAT drives use helical-scan read/write mechanisms, while, as the name implies, DLTs use a linear read/write mechanism. The tape differs as well. DAT is a metal oxide tape, while DLT is metal film. DAT can store larger amounts of data per square inch of medium and can read and write data to the tape more quickly. DAT is much less expensive.

THE 64K$ QUESTIONS

1. 5.25″ floppy disk drives were available in _____ and _____ sizes. (Choose two)

   A. 360KB and C. 1.2MB

3. Double density floppies featured _____ sectors per track.

   D. 40

5. How many bytes are there per sector on a floppy disk?

   C. 512

7. The "click of death" is a failure that appears on _____.
    A. Zip drives

9. Two tape drives that use linear recording technology are_____ and _____.
    A. QIC and C. DLT

CHAPTER 12

BRAIN DRAIN

1. Describe how CHS defines the capacity of a hard drive.

    CHS stands for cylinders, heads, and sectors-per-track. There are 512 bytes per sector. A hard drive can only have so many platter surfaces. This will determine the number of heads. Each surface will have so many tracks. Multiplying the number of cylinders times the number of heads times the number of tracks per sector times 512 is the total capacity of the drive.

3. Describe how data is stored to a hard disk and then subsequently read back?

    The hard disk controller converts incoming digital data into pulses of electricity, which charge a magnet on the write head. The write head uses magnetic fluxes to apply charges to the platter surface. On playback, these fluxes are read by the write head. A magnetized data unit indicates a 1, lack of magnetization indicates a 0. Since the platter is spinning by the R/W heads at very high rates of speed, a very accurate timing mechanism assures that the heads remain synchronized with each other.

5. In as much detail as you can, define how the FAT works.

    The hard drive is divided into file allocation units, which consist of 2 to 64 sectors, depending on the file system used and the size of the partition. For each FAU, there is an entry in FAT. This entry will have fields for file name, whether the FAU is available for use or not, if it is the last FAU of the file contained, and a pointer to the next FAU of that file, if it is not. More advanced file systems, such as NTFS use a database system, rather than file tables and can include much more information in each entry.

THE 64K$ QUESTIONS

1. The physical surface on which data is stored on a hard drive is known as a
    _____.

    D. Platter

3. Modern hard drives use a _____ to move the actuator arms.
    A. Voice coil

5. Of the following encoding systems, which is most likely to be used on a hard drive purchased today?

     A. EPRML

7. As a systems administrator, you want to enforce as much security in your organization as you possibly can. Therefore you have decided that all computers will run an OS that uses the _____ file system.

     C. NTFS

9. What part of the MBR is created and added during the OS installation?

     D. OS pointer

Chapter 13

Brain Drain

1. List as many hard disk interfaces as you can think of.

     At the very minimum, the list should include IDE, Serial ATA, and SCSI. Older interfaces include ST506/412, MFM, and ESDI.

3. Discuss as many improvements of the second generation of IDE compared to the first generation as you can think of.

     First generation IDE only supports hard drives and one IDE port per computer. Each port supported two devices, so first-generation IDE basically supported two hard disks. The second generation introduced ATA. We now have two ports of two channels each for a total of four devices and a number of different types of devices are supported.

5. Based on the discussion generated by Question 4, describe what is happening to the hard disk on each step along the way.

     The partitioning of the hard drive prepares the MBR, including the file system executable and the partition tables. The formatting procedure scans the surface of the hard disk for defects and writes out the first set of file allocation tables. The installation of the OS adds the OS point to the MBR.

The 64K$ Questions

1. The ST-506 hard disk drive offered a maximum capacity of _____ MB.

     B. 5

3. Which of the following was *not* a feature of the first generation of IDE?

     C. It supported devices other than hard drives.

5.   Most hard drives in use today use _____ addressing.
     D. LBA

7.   The Microsoft utility that re-creates the MBR is _____.
     A. FORMAT

9.   A CS cable differs from a standard IDE cable in that _____.
     D. The twenty-eighth conductor has been clipped between the center connector and the one on the end.

CHAPTER 14

BRAIN DRAIN

1.   You've just installed an older SCSI card you pulled from another machine. It was working fine in the other machine, but now the only device the system recognizes is the hard drive. The tape drive and CD-ROM are ignored. What are some of the things that may have caused this?

     For one thing, it might be a really old first-generation SCSI card that was designed specifically for hard drives. Other factors to look at are termination (including the host adapter) and the device IDs of the devices installed.

3.   What was the one thing lacking from the very first release of SCSI specifications that caused so much confusion. What was one of the problems caused and why did this omission cause the problem?

     There was no predefined command set. As a result, controller cards designed for one device wouldn't work with other devices. This was because manufacturers were only interested in supporting the device they were selling.

5.   Discuss why termination of a SCSI chain is necessary. What happens if you don't terminate the chain properly and why is it this happens?

     When an electrical signal travels down a wire, it doesn't simply stop or fly out into space when it reaches the end. Unless there is something there to absorb that current and dissipate it, it will turn around and travel down the wire in the opposite direction. It is not possible to encode data under these conditions. A terminating resistor coverts the current to heat and dissipates it into the air.

THE 64K$ QUESTIONS

1.   How many devices could a SCSI-I chain support?

     C. 8. But that number includes the host controller, which is considered to be a device on the chain. So only 7 additional devices can be hung off the controller.

3. What are two methods of terminating a SCSI chain?

    B. Installing a resistor into a specially designed socket. And D. Setting a jumper on the last device on the chain. In the case of D, it is still a resistor. It's simply a resistor that is already in place.

5. How many devices can be supported by a parallel SCSI-III chain?

    E. None of the Above. SPI supports fifteen devices, including the host adapter.

7. High-voltage differential devices cannot be on the same chain as a single-ended device.

    B. False. They can be installed on the same chain as long as a SCSI Expander was installed between the two devices. However, this was actually a more expensive alternative than simply installing a separate host adapter for each chain.

9. Which of the following is an example of Serial SCSI?

    C. FireWire

CHAPTER 15

BRAIN DRAIN

1. Describe in as much detail as possible how an image is generated on a typical CRT monitor.

    The graphics adapter sends out a burst of signals to each of three electron guns. The graphics adapter controls the strength of the stream of electrons generated by each gun. A deflection yoke sends the electrons across the back of the CRT, where a phosphorous coating has been applied. The stream of electrons causes the coating to emit a glow.

3. Why are TFT displays considered better than passive matrix displays?

    Speed. Plain and simple. Modern TFTs are also brighter and can be viewed from wider angles, but this is due more to improvements in design.

5. What are the factors that contribute to the overall speed of a graphics card?

    The speed of the RAMDAC, the type and speed of the memory used and the bus (AGP 2x, 4x, 8x or PCI-X).

THE 64K$ QUESTIONS

1. In a CRT Monitor, the phosphors are separated from one another by _____.

    B. A shadow mask

3. Smoother animation is made possible by a technique called _____.
    C. Frame Buffering

5. If a programmer wants her colors to appear more natural with smoother blending, she will take advantage of a technique called _____.
    D. Dithering

7. The LCD most likely used on a PDA is a _____.
    A. Common Plane

9. Programmers can add extra effects to graphics without changing the actual color by using _____.
    The alpha channel

CHAPTER 16

BRAIN DRAIN

1. Discuss in as much detail as possible how data is written to a conventional CD and subsequently read back. Include in your discussion as many components of the CD-ROM drive as you can recall.

    Data is applied to a thin aluminum surface by punching holes called pits into a spiral track. The optical stylus shines a laser beam into the track. Where there are no pits the beam is reflected back into a photoelectric cell that converts the light to electrical current. Where there are no pits, no light is reflected back. This results in a pulsating electrical current which is converted to digital data.

3. Describe how it is possible to have a double-sided, double-layered DVD.

    A double-sided disc actually consists of two DVDs bonded together back-to-back. Each of these discs consists of two layers of recorded medium, separated by a microscopically thin layer of gold. When the read laser is focused on one layer, it ignores the other, and vice versa.

5. In as much detail as you can muster, describe how each component of a computer system contributes to the overall multimedia process. Don't confine your thinking to just this chapter, but consider what you've learned from previous chapters as well.

    CPU speed is important because a decision has to be made as to what data sets are going to be sent to what devices. The amount of RAM is also important because the fewer trips to the hard drive we have to make the faster overall performance is going to be. As far as the video card is concerned, both speed and overall capabilities come into play. Speed dictates how fast frames can be processed and sent to the monitor, while other capabilities dictate image quality. And when an application is being run directly from the CD-ROM, then the speed of that device is a critical factor.

THE 64K$ QUESTIONS

1. The first CD-ROMs designed for use on a computer provided data throughput of _____.

   B. 150KB/s

3. The recording layer on a CDR consists of _____.
   A. Pthalocyanine dye

5. Which of the following media separates two separate recording layers with a microscopically thin layer of gold.
   D. DVD

7. The 15-pin connector on the back of a sound card is used for what device? Choose all that apply.
   A. Joystick and D. MIDI devices

9. The conversion of an analog wave form into a digital signal is known as _____.
   Pulse Code Modulation

CHAPTER 17

BRAIN DRAIN

1. Describe in as much detail as possible the differences between how a line printer and a dot matrix printer compile images.

   Older line printers generated only a single line of type at a time and delivered it to the printer. Later generations divided the page into zones, but either way, generating graphics was a process that ranged from impossible to primitive. Dot matrix printers treated the page as a single graphic and outputted the entire page at once. In this way, images could be created. Line printers are extremely fast and suitable for form generation, while dot matrix printers will be needed any time pictures must be drawn.

3. What are the key differences between thermal inkjet printers and piezoelectric inkjet printers?

   Both types begin with very tiny tubes that fill with ink. The thermal printer has a mechanism that keeps the ink in the print head heated to just below its boiling point. When a drop of ink is needed, a heating coil applies just enough heat to pass the boiling point and a bubble of ink pops out. The piezoelectric printer uses a crystal instead. An electrical charge causes the crystal to vibrate, forcing a drop of ink onto the page.

5. List as many different things as you can that define an IEEE-1284-compliant device and/or cable.

    It must support compatibility mode, nibble mode, byte mode, EPP, and ECP modes.

THE $64K QUESTIONS

1. Two different forms of impact printer include (pick two) _____.

    C. Dot matrix and D. Daisy wheel

3. During the laser printing process, the paper is charged by _____.

    D. The transfer roller

5. What component prevents the paper from adhering to the print drum after the toner is transferred?

    A. The separation pad

7. If you wished to hang a scanner, an external CD-ROM, and a printer all off the same parallel port, which mode would be most suitable?

    D. ECP

9. A printer capable of duplex printing does what?

    It prints on both sides of the page.

CHAPTER 18

BRAIN DRAIN

1. Should you desire to set up a small network in your home, what would be the bare necessities you would need to get up and running?

    You would need transceivers in each device to be networked, some form of media over which the data will travel, and network-aware operating systems installed on each computer to be networked.

3. In detail, discuss the difference between a collision domain and a broadcast domain.

    A collision domain consists of all devices that are competing for bandwidth on the same network segment. A broadcast domain consists of all devices on a network that will receive one another's broadcasts. Collision domains can be broken up using switches; broadcast domains are broken up using routers.

5. Discuss the differences between hardware protocols and networking protocols.

   A hardware protocol dictates how data will be broken down and prepared for broadcast over the medium. A networking protocol allows communications to occur between different types of devices on the network.

The 64K$ Questions

1. The maximum distance twisted-pair cable can be run without assistance is _____.

   B. 100 meters

3. The proper device for interconnecting a token ring network segment to an Ethernet segment is a _____.

   D. Bridge

5. In order to interconnect two autonomous networks into a singler larger network, you would need a _____.

   C. Router

7. Two hardware protocols that make use of a ring topology are _____ and _____. (Pick two.)

   C. FDDI and D. Token Ring

9. The protocol of choice for the Internet is

   C. TCP/IP

Chapter 19

Brain Drain

1. Describe in detail two main tricks a modem must perform to transmit data over a telephone wire.

   First, it must convert parallel data into serial format for transmission over the wire. Then it must take digital data and turn it into an analog electrical signal. On the receiving end, it must reverse both processes.

3. Describe in detail how asynchronous communication works and where it might be used.

   With asynchronous communications, the transmitting device simply throws data onto the wire and assumes it will get there. There is no error correction possible, although error detection in the form of parity is sometimes used. It is used for broadcasts, browsing the network, and transmissions of single packets of data.

5.   What are some limitations of DSL?

The user must be within 18,000 feet of the telecom's central office, and the signal can't pass over fiber, past bridge taps, or cross loading coils.

THE 64K$ QUESTIONS

1.   What device on a modem is responsible for serial/parallel conversions?

A. The UART

3.   A device that can only transmit data, but not receive it is working in _____ mode.

C. Simplex

Half-duplex

5.   When transferring large files, most modems manufactured today use _____ as their error correction method.

C. CRC

7.   Basic Rate ISDN provides _____.

C. 2 64K B channels and 1 16K D channel

9.   Cable modem users should ALWAYS install a

B. Firewall

CHAPTER 20

BRAIN DRAIN

1.   How many different components can you think of that are designed differently for laptops than they are desktops?

At a minimum the list should include the keyboard, pointing device, hard drive, memory, and all removable drives. The display is debatable because LCD displays are becoming more popular for desktop machines these days.

3.   Describe the three main forms of battery used by laptops over the years and how they differ.

NiCad batteries were the earliest. They suffered greatly from battery memory and had a very poor ration of charging time to operating time. Ni-MH batteries greatly improved on the charge ratio, but still suffered from battery memory. Today's Li-Ion batteries don't suffer from battery memory at all and have very favorable charge ratios.

5. You own a laptop computer and a docking station. Nearly every time you boot your machine it goes through the Plug 'n Play process. Why is this and how can you stop this from happening?

> The docking station has a completely different device configuration than the bare laptop. So the OS needs to reconfigure each time the machine boots. By configuring a different hardware profile for each configuration, during the boot process you will be prompted to select which way you want the OS to boot.

THE 64K$ QUESTIONS

1. The memory package typically used by notebook computers is the _____.
   B. SO-DIMM

3. However, many older laptops were equipped with _____ displays.
   A. Passive matrix

5. Two characteristics that might prevent two different AC adapters from being interchangeable are _____ and _____. (Pick two.)
   B. The type of connector used to interconnect the adapter to the laptop, and
   D. Output voltage

7. Which layer of a PC card driver notifies the computer when a device has been removed or inserted?
   D. Socket Services

9. What pointing device is most sensitive to the person's individual electrostatic charge?
   The trackpad

CHAPTER 21

BRAIN DRAIN

1. Discuss the differences between open-ended questions and closed-ended questions. Make up a list of open-ended questions.

> An open-ended question will result in a reply that leads to the possibility of further questioning. A closed-ended question results in an answer that goes nowhere. Make up your own darned list.

3. How many different places can you think of that might provide documentation and/
    or troubleshooting help for a problem you can't diagnose?

    A hard-copy manual; the CD of the OS driver or application causing the problem;
    and Web-based options, including the manufacturer's support site as well as
    independent sites such as http://basichardware.50megs.com.

5. Why is a slowly failing power supply such a problem?

    Because it can mimic the symptoms of just about every other device on the
    system, yet still power the computer.

THE $64K QUESTIONS

1. Which of the following issues is addressed by re-creating a problem before trying to
    fix it?

    D. User errors

3. Of the following list, which one will test a serial port without having either the device
    or the cable affect the test?

    A. A loopback adapter

5. Boot failure problems are rarely the result of _____ failure.

    C. Software. A corrupted OS can prevent a system from getting past POST. But
    the system itself has booted to the point of locating the hard disk. An argument
    could be made that a corrupted boot sector is a software problem. But I'm not
    getting involved in that argument. It's purely semantic.

7. The twenty-eighth wire on a floppy disk cable is the _____ wire.

    C. Master/slave indicator

9. What two drive size limitations appear as a result of older BIOS?

    B. 8GB and C. 32GB

INDEX